Object-Oriented Application Development Using Microsoft® Visual Basic® .NET

E. Reed Doke
John W. Satzinger
Susan Rebstock Williams
David E. Douglas

THOMSON
COURSE TECHNOLOGY™

Australia • Canada • Mexico • Singapore • Spain • United Kingdom • United States

THOMSON
COURSE TECHNOLOGY

Object-Oriented Application Development Using Microsoft® Visual Basic® .NET

by E. Reed Doke, John W. Satzinger, Susan Rebstock Williams, and David E. Douglas

Senior Vice President, Publisher:
Kristen Duerr

Senior Editor:
Jennifer Muroff

Executive Editor:
Jennifer Locke

Product Manager:
Tricia Boyle

Development Editor:
Lisa Ruffolo, The Software Resource

Associate Marketing Manager:
Angela Laughlin

Associate Product Manager:
Janet Aras

Editorial Assistant:
Christy Urban

Production Editor:
Christine Gatliffe

Cover Designer:
Abigail Scholz

Compositor:
GEX Publishing Services

Manufacturing Coordinator:
Laura Burns

Printed in Canada

1 2 3 4 5 6 7 8 9 WC 07 06 05 04 03

For more information, contact Course Technology, 25 Thomson Place, Boston, Massachusetts, 02210.

Or find us on the World Wide Web at: www.course.com

ISBN 0-619-15934-0

Object-Oriented Application Development Using Microsoft® Visual Basic® .NET

BRIEF

Contents

TABLE OF

Contents

Preface

This text covers three-tier object-oriented application development using Microsoft Visual Basic .NET and the Visual Studio .NET integrated development environment (IDE). The text emphasizes developing business information systems for CIS and MIS students and practitioners. We assume readers have some introductory computer programming experience, but experience with object-oriented programming and the Visual Basic (VB) programming language or VB .NET are not required. The text therefore takes readers who know a little about programming from introducing VB .NET syntax and object-oriented concepts all the way through designing and building a three-tier object-oriented VB .NET application using a graphical user interface (GUI) and relational database.

Interest in the object-oriented approach to information system development is skyrocketing, and Microsoft has released VB .NET as an OO language that can be used to implement true object-oriented applications. Although many VB .NET programming texts are available, most cover introductory and advanced programming techniques, but do not emphasize object-oriented solutions requiring an OO approach to systems analysis and design. This text presents OO application development by following an iterative approach to systems analysis, design, and implementation. Object-oriented models and techniques based on the Unified Modeling Language (UML) are used throughout, and all VB .NET programming examples and exercises are based on the three-tier design approach. After introducing a business case study, use cases are developed, a class diagram is drawn, problem domain classes are designed and implemented, GUI classes are designed and implemented, and data access classes that interact with a relational database are designed and implemented. Finally, a portion of the business application is ported to the Web using WebForms and ASP.NET. Along the way, readers become immersed in the OO approach to system development as they build their VB programming skills.

The Intended Audience

Most university degree programs offering CIS and MIS degrees have responded to OO development by covering object-oriented programming and object-oriented development in a variety of ways. We designed this text to be flexible enough to accommodate many situations. Students with a variety of programming and MIS courses can use this book in an introductory OO Development course. Appropriate candidates include students who have already taken an introductory programming concepts course (the programming language does not matter). A system development course using this text introduces the VB .NET programming language, OO concepts and terminology, three-tier design, UML, and iterative development. When students later take analysis and design and database management courses, they will have experience with the complete OO development process.

This text can also be used in an advanced development course where the students have had an introductory VB .NET programming course that did not emphasize OO development. The introductory VB .NET syntax and IDE material (Chapters 2, 3, and 4) can be skimmed. More time can then be spent on OO analysis and design and UML in Chapter 5. More advanced readers can move rapidly through the book and complete a more elaborate business system project.

Some readers have already studied UML and the object-oriented approach in an analysis and design course. The text is still appropriate for these readers as less time can be spent on the OO analysis and design and more on implementation. This text shows readers with UML experience how the OO models are actually implemented—something students and practitioners really appreciate. Therefore, this text can provide a capstone experience for many readers.

THE APPROACH

Many useful features are built into the text to provide a comprehensive learning experience. Some of the features are important to the OO analysis and design focus of the text. The text uses:

- **Business information system examples**: The analysis, design, and programming examples emphasize business problems of interest to CIS and MIS students.
- **Unified Modeling Language (UML)**: UML models are used extensively to describe system requirements for examples, including use case diagrams, class diagrams, and sequence diagrams. Then the models are used to guide the design and implementation of the system examples.
- **Iterative development**: A realistic iterative approach to development is emphasized throughout the text. The organization of the text is based on an iterative approach that leaves readers with a clear view of how analysis, design, and implementation flow during an iteration.
- **Three-tier design**: The OO design approach uses three-tier design, which divides the system into separate tiers for the GUI, the problem domain classes, and the data access classes. The organization of the text is based on the three-tier view, and each iteration addresses all three tiers.
- **Design for Windows applications and Web-based development**: The approach used for analysis and design is applicable to VB .NET applications and to Web-based ASP.NET development.
- **The Bradshaw Marina case study**: An integrated case study is used throughout the text. The case has moderate complexity to provide readers with the experience of seeing a system project conceived, modeled using UML, and constructed following an iterative, three-tier design approach.

Overview of This Book

The text organizes 16 chapters into five parts. A more complete overview of the text is provided in Chapter 1. The five parts include:

- Part 1: Object-Orientation and VB .NET Fundamentals
- Part 2: Developing Problem Domain Classes
- Part 3: Developing Graphical User Interface (GUI) Classes
- Part 4: Developing Data Access Classes
- Part 5: Deploying the Three-Tier Application

The major outcome for an OO programming course using this text is to provide a firm foundation for the entire OO development process. The three-tier design approach is emphasized throughout, so that user interface classes, problem domain classes, and data access classes will remain distinct from the beginning. UML is used to show a model of every example.

Chapter 1 provides an overview of key OO concepts and introduces VB .NET. The Bradshaw Marina case study described in Chapter 5 is used to illustrate the concepts and UML models. In keeping with iterative development and three-tier design, the text begins by modeling problem domain classes in Chapter 6. The problem domain classes are then implemented and tested. Next, the graphical user interface (GUI) classes are added as the front end that interacts with problem domain classes in Chapters 10 through 12. Data access classes are then added that allow data to be stored in a relational database in Chapters 13 and 14. Finally, the three tiers are combined into a complete system module in Chapter 15. Windows applications are emphasized in most of the text, but Chapter 16 shows how to port some of the Bradshaw Marina application to the Web using Web Forms and ASP.NET.

By the end of the text, students will have implemented key parts of a working system as shown in the examples, including Windows applications and Web-based applications. Hands-on Exercises and Projects provide opportunities for students to implement additional parts of the system in parallel with the examples.

Each chapter in *Object-Oriented Application Development Using Microsoft Visual Basic .NET* includes the following elements to enhance the learning experience:

- **Chapter Objectives**: Each chapter begins with a list of the important concepts to be mastered within the chapter. This list provides you with a quick reference to the contents of the chapter as well as a useful study aid.

Hands-on

Hands-on Exercises: As new concepts are presented in each chapter, step-by-step instructions allow you to actively apply the concepts you are learning. In each chapter, you pause to review important concepts, and can perform the exercises in class or as homework problems.

- **Chapter Examples**: Several related VB .NET examples are presented and fully explained in each chapter to demonstrate chapter concepts. All the code for chapter examples is provided on the Instructor's Resource CD.
- **Chapter Summaries**: Each chapter's text is followed by a summary of chapter concepts. These summaries provide a helpful way to recap and revisit the ideas covered in each chapter.
- **Review Questions**: End-of-chapter assessment begins with a set of approximately 15–20 review questions that reinforce the main ideas introduced in each chapter. These questions ensure that you have mastered the concepts and understand the information you have learned.
- **Discussion Questions**: Several discussion questions that can be used for class discussion or homework assignments are included for every chapter.
- **Projects**: End-of-chapter projects provide challenging development experiences related to the chapter concepts.

Teaching Tools

The following supplemental materials are available when this book is used in a classroom setting. All of the teaching tools available with this book are provided to the instructor on a single CD.

Electronic Instructor's Manual. The Instructor's Manual that accompanies this textbook includes:

- Additional instructional material to assist in class preparation, including suggestions for lecture topics.
- Solutions to all end-of-chapter materials, including the Review Questions, Discussion Questions, and Projects.

ExamView®. This textbook is accompanied by ExamView, a powerful testing software package that allows instructors to create and administer printed, computer (LAN-based), and Internet exams. ExamView includes hundreds of questions that correspond to the topics covered in this text, enabling students to generate detailed study guides that include page references for further review. The computer-based and Internet testing components allow students to take exams at their computers, and also save the instructor's time by grading each exam automatically.

PowerPoint Presentations. This book comes with Microsoft PowerPoint slides for each chapter. These are included as a teaching aid for classroom presentation, to make available to students on the network for chapter review, or to be printed for classroom distribution. Instructors can add their own slides for additional topics they introduce to the class.

Data Files. Data files, containing all of the data necessary for the Hands-on Exercises and Projects are provided through the Course Technology Web site at **www.course.com**, and are also available on the Teaching Tools CD-ROM.

Solution Files. Solutions to end-of chapter Review Questions, Hands-on Exercises, and Projects are provided on the Teaching Tools CD-ROM and may also be found on the Course Technology Web site at **www.course.com**. The solutions are password protected.

Distance Learning. Course Technology is proud to present online test banks in WebCT and Blackboard, as well as MyCourse 2.0, Course Technology's own course enhancement tool, to provide the most complete and dynamic learning experience possible. Instructors are encouraged to make the most of your course, both online and offline. For more information on how to access your online test bank, contact your local Course Technology sales representative.

About the Authors

E. Reed Doke is a clinical professor of information systems and associate director for the Information Technology Research Center in the Walton College of Business at the University of Arkansas, Fayetteville. He holds BS and MBA degrees from Drury University and received his Ph.D. in management and computer information systems from the University of Arkansas. Dr. Doke worked for several years as a software developer and information systems manager prior to joining academia and continues to assist firms with systems development problems. He has published six books and numerous articles on software design and object-oriented development.

John W. Satzinger holds a Ph.D. in MIS from the Claremont Graduate University and is a professor of CIS at Southwest Missouri State University. Dr. Satzinger was previously on the faculty of Cal Poly Pomona and the University of Georgia and has focused on object-oriented development for over a decade. He has written dozens of articles on user interface design, group work, and system development. His most recent books include *Systems Analysis and Design in a Changing World, Second edition* and *Object-Oriented Application Development Using Java*, both published by Course Technology.

Susan Rebstock Williams is an associate professor of information systems at Georgia Southern University. She received a BS in math and computer science as well as an MBA from Southwest Missouri State University, and earned a Ph.D. in information systems from Oklahoma State University. Dr. Williams has thirteen years of experience as a programmer, analyst, and information systems manager. She has conducted corporate training programs in Java and OO development, and currently leads a major grant-funded software development project. Dr. Williams has written several articles and one textbook dealing with software development and design.

David E. Douglas is a professor in the Information Systems Department of the Sam M. Walton College of Business at the University of Arkansas. He was department chair for thirteen years and was chair when the department designed and implemented a doctoral program in information systems. He has published four software application texts and written numerous articles. Additionally, he has developed and conducted many training programs for industry. He received his Ph.D. from the University of Arkansas.

THE COURSE TECHNOLOGY OBJECT-ORIENTED APPLICATION DEVELOPMENT SERIES

The original vision proposed to Course Technology by Reed Doke and John Satzinger led to a series of texts on OO development that each includes a different OO language. Each text is based on the same iterative, three-tier OO model and uses the same Bradshaw Marina case study. The series began with *Object-Oriented Application Development Using Java* in 2002, and this VB .NET text is the second in the series. A text featuring Visual C# .NET is also planned. Reed Doke and John Satzinger are the series editors for the Object-Oriented Application Development Series at Course Technology.

ACKNOWLEDGEMENTS

Completing a text like this requires the dedication and hard work of many people. The editorial staff at Course Technology was quite receptive to the idea for a series of books about the entire OO system development process. As usual at Course Technology, we were fortunate to find interested, excited, and future-oriented people to work with who quickly recognized what we wanted to accomplish with this text. The Senior Editor, Jennifer Muroff, provided a productive working environment for us. She assembled and coordinated a great editorial and production team headed by Product Manager Tricia Boyle. First and foremost on that team was Developmental Editor Lisa Ruffolo. Lisa really understood where we were going with this text, and her contributions have been substantial. Lisa understands both programming and writing, giving her the skills to both identify errors and to make valuable suggestions. If you like something specific about this text, it was probably Lisa's idea.

Production Editor Christine Gatliffe had to deal with everything from UML diagram standards, fairly elaborate chapter examples for quality assurance testing, and a schedule that included chapter submissions from four authors traveling on three continents. Many others were also involved in the production of this text, including copy editors, quality assurance testers, graphic artists, and proofreaders. We also want to thank Associate Product Manager Janet Aras for her support and hard work on the Instructors Resource Kit (IRK). We also thank student assistant Adam Ham (GSU) for his help in developing many of the solutions to hands-on exercises and projects.

We would also like to thank our families for being so understanding about all of the time we had to invest in this project.

Last but not least we want to acknowledge and thank the team of reviewers who stood by us from the beginning and helped to see this project through. Their contributions were always insightful and useful. It would be impossible to produce a book like this without interested and knowledgeable reviewers. We were very fortunate. The reviewers were: Louise Darcey, Texas A&M University; Bill Hardgrave, University of Arkansas; Frank Lilja, Pineland Technical College; Bill Sypawka, PITT Community College.

Dedications

To Emily Kay Doke — ERD

To JoAnn, Brian, and Kevin — JWS

To Lois and Alvin — SRW

To Stacey, Debbie, Jennifer, Jon David, Mom, and Dad — DED

Read This Before You Begin

To the User

Data Files

To complete the steps and projects in this book, you will need data files that have been created for this book. Your instructor will provide the data files to you. You also can obtain the files electronically from the Course Technology Web site by connecting to *www.course.com*, and then searching for this book title.

Each chapter in this book has its own set of data files that you use to review the examples and perform the Hands-on Exercises and end-of-chapter Projects. Data files for each chapter are stored in a separate folder within the chapter folder. The folder names identify when you need the files. For example, the data files for the first example in Chapter 9 are stored in the Chap09/Example1 folder. Throughout this book, you will be instructed to open files from or save files to these folders.

You can use a computer in your school lab or your own computer to complete the chapters, Hands-on Exercises, and Projects in this book.

Using Your Own Computer

To use your own computer to complete the chapters, Hands-on Exercises, and Projects in this book, you will need the following:

- **A computer that can run Microsoft Visual Studio .NET**. Pentium II-class processor, 450 megahertz (MHz) or higher personal computer running Windows 2000 Professional, Windows XP Professional Edition or Windows NT 4.0 with 160 MB RAM and 2.0 GB hard disk space available.
- **Windows 2000 Professional or Windows XP Professional**. For the Web applications in Chapters 12 and 16, you need Internet Information Services (IIS) installed and operational to run the sample applications on your own computer. IIS 5.0 ships with Windows 2000 Professional, and IIS 5.1 ships with Windows XP Professional. IIS 6.0 will ship with Windows .NET Server 2003. Patches for IIS can be downloaded from the Microsoft Web site, *www.microsoft.com*.
- **Microsoft Visual Basic .NET**. Install VB .NET according to the instructions that accompany Microsoft Visual Studio .NET.
- **A Zip-compatible utility program (such as WinZip)**. You will need a Zip-compatible utility program (such as WinZip) to install the data files.

- **Microsoft Internet Explorer or Netscape Navigator browser software**. You will need either Microsoft Internet Explorer or Netscape Navigator. If you do not have either program, you can download them for free from *www.netscape.com* or *www.microsoft.com*, respectively.
- **Microsoft Access**. The database applications in this text are based on Microsoft Access 2000 or higher.
- **Data files**. You will not be able to complete the chapters and projects in this book using your own computer unless you have the data files. You can get the data files from your instructor, or you can obtain the data files electronically from the Course Technology Web site by connecting to *www.course.com*, and then searching for this book title. After you copy the files to your system, you may need to change the file attributes from read only to archive so that you can edit them.

Visit Our World Wide Web Site

Additional materials designed especially for this book might be available for your course on the World Wide Web. Go to *www.course.com* and periodically search this site for more details.

To the Instructor

To complete the chapters in this book, your users must use a set of data files. These files are included in the Instructor's Resource Kit. They also may be obtained electronically through the Course Technology Web site at *www.course.com*. Follow the instructions in the Help file to copy the data files to your server or standalone computer. You can view the Help file using a text editor such as WordPad or Notepad.

Once the files are copied, you should instruct your users how to copy the files to their own computers or workstations, including which folder you want them to use.

Course Technology Data Files

You are granted a license to copy the data files to any computer or computer network used by individuals who have purchased this book.

PART 1

Object-Orientation and VB .NET Fundamentals

CHAPTER

1

Object-Oriented System Development with VB .NET

In this chapter you will:

- Learn about OO development and VB .NET
- Understand object-oriented concepts
- Recognize the benefits of OO development
- Preview the approach this book uses to teach you OO development

Object-oriented information system development involves analysis, design, and implementation of information systems using object-oriented programming languages, technologies, and techniques, and is usually referred to simply as "OO" (pronounced "oh oh") or as "the OO approach." Microsoft has recently released its .NET (pronounced "dot net") framework, which encourages object-oriented information system development, and many system developers see this release as evidence that the OO approach to system development is finally becoming mainstream. The thoroughly updated and redesigned Visual Basic .NET (VB .NET) will significantly affect the transition to OO development. VB .NET now provides a pure object-oriented programming language that can be used to develop information systems using all of the OO concepts and techniques that have previously been possible only with languages like C++ and Java.

Many system developers still have misconceptions about OO and OO development. OO often means something different to different information system developers depending upon their background or perspective. For example, to some developers OO means a graphical user interface (GUI) written with Visual Basic for an otherwise traditional application. To others OO means anything involved with client-server or Web-based systems. Still others say that OO means systems written with an OO programming language such as C++ or Java, regardless of the application.

When developing business systems, OO means using an object-oriented approach to system analysis (**OOA**), an object-oriented approach to system design (**OOD**), and an object-oriented approach to programming (**OOP**) for the entire system development project. OO is not only about a graphical user interface, or client-server relationships, or programming with C++, Java, or now VB .NET. Simply learning an OO programming language does not completely involve you in OO. Object-oriented development is a way of thinking, a complete approach to system analysis, system design, and programming.

This text presents an integrated and comprehensive overview of OO system development to introduce information systems students and practitioners to the OO approach. This text emphasizes OO programming using the VB .NET programming language, and it assumes you have some introductory programming background. But experience with OO programming in general, or Visual Basic programming in particular, is not required. Similarly, it is helpful if you have some experience with system analysis and design techniques and database management, but experience with OOA and OOD is not required.

With this book, you will learn how to develop complete business information systems using the OO approach from start to finish. Most business system developers, both students and practitioners, want to learn this approach because it is the direction most business organizations are heading. Therefore, this text provides a foundation in OOA, OOD, and OOP so you can get started with OO information system development using VB .NET.

UNDERSTANDING OO DEVELOPMENT AND VB .NET

Object-oriented development is often compared to traditional, procedural development. The **object-oriented approach** to information systems defines a system as a collection of objects that work together to accomplish tasks. The objects can carry out actions when asked, and each object maintains its own data. The procedural approach to information systems, on the other hand, defines a system as a set of procedures that interact with data. The data are maintained in files separate from the procedures. When the procedure executes, or runs, data files are created or updated. Figure 1-1 shows the difference between object-oriented and procedural development.

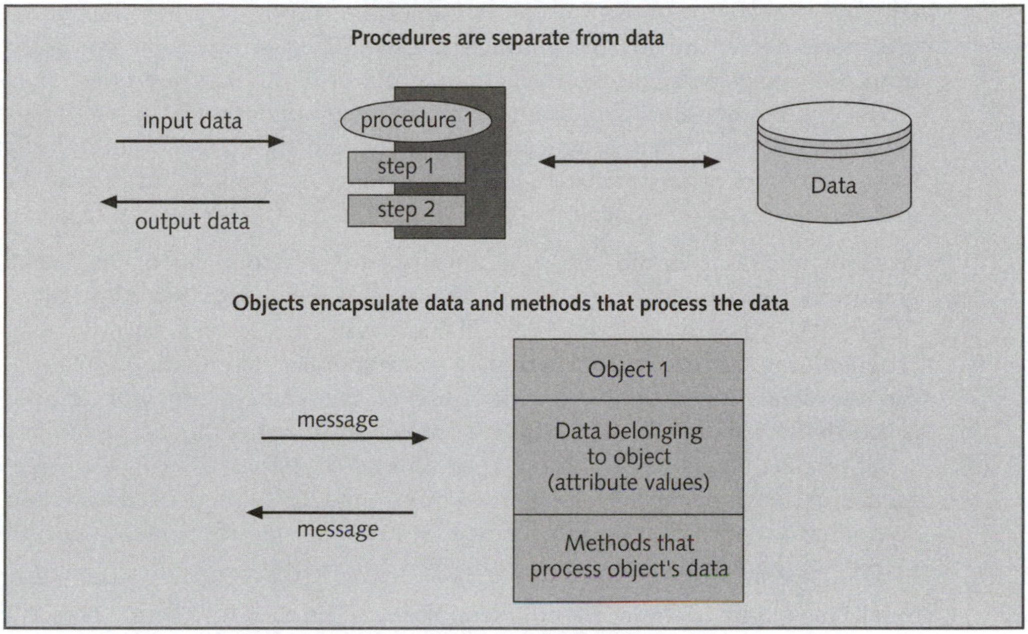

Figure 1-1 Procedural approach versus object-oriented approach

A procedure accepts an input, processes it, and then updates data in a separate data file. A specific object, however, receives a message and then updates its own internal data. The implications of what seems a simple distinction can actually be significant in terms of analysis, design, and programming, as you will see in the chapters ahead.

Object-Oriented Programming

Many people think object-oriented development is relatively new, but it dates back several decades. Object-oriented programming started in the 1960s in Norway with the development of the **Simula** programming language, the first language designed for running computer simulations. Programming problems that involve simulations require a different approach from procedural programming because simulations involve objects like ships and planes or customers in lines waiting for bank tellers. Therefore, defining types of objects that maintain their own data values and giving them the ability to behave independently is a useful way for a simulation program to work.

For example, in a bank simulation, one type of object is a customer, and all customers can enter the bank, get in a line, wait in line, and advance to the next position in line. A teller line might be another type of object, able to add customers and move customers through the line to the teller. Before running the simulation, probabilities are set for the expected number of customers that enter the bank per hour and the expected time it takes for a teller to serve each customer. When the simulation runs, customers enter the bank, get in the shortest line, and advance through the line based on numbers randomly generated from probability distributions. Because each object (customers and lines) can behave and interact with other objects, the simulation can be run under many different assumptions to determine the maximum length of a teller line and the longest wait a customer might have. Outcomes of the simulation are used to make decisions about the number of tellers to have on duty at different times of the day.

A major milestone in the history of OO was the development of the **SmallTalk** programming language by Alan Kay and associates at the Xerox Palo Alto Research Center (Xerox PARC) in the early 1970s. SmallTalk was the first general-purpose object-oriented programming language. Kay envisioned a revolutionary computing environment where the user would interact directly with objects on the screen of a notebook-sized computer called the Dynabook. In the late 1960s a notebook-sized computer seemed impossible—recall that Hal the computer in the 1968 film *2001: A Space Odyssey* was large enough to fill half of the spaceship. Because the electronics and hardware needed to build a notebook computer did not yet exist, Kay focused on the software programming environment that might run the machine.

SmallTalk was the software environment, and Kay designed it to define objects in an application that interact with the user and with other objects. SmallTalk was initially used for GUI applications, similar to those later popularized by the Apple Macintosh computer almost a decade later. SmallTalk has since been used for developing business information systems that include business application objects such as bank customers who make deposits and withdrawals.

Additional object-oriented programming languages have been developed, including Objective-C, Eiffel, and most notably **C++**. C++ is an object-oriented extension to the C procedural language, so when C++ was first introduced, many procedural programmers were already familiar with its syntax. This helped make C++ a leading object-oriented language, although it is not purely object-oriented because programmers can still use C++ to write procedural programs if they want. Microsoft has provided a version of C++ as part of Visual Studio for many years. Many special-purpose OO languages have also been developed by other vendors, such as an object-oriented version of COBOL designed to appeal to business programmers. Figure 1-2 lists some of the object-oriented programming languages in use today.

In 1995, Sun Microsystems introduced **Java** as a pure OO language with syntax similar to C++ and other features that make it appropriate for Internet applications, such as the ability to download programs (Applets) from the Internet that can run on any computer platform. Microsoft immediately released a version of Java called J++. Because Java is a pure OO language and can be used to develop applications on any platform, including Web-based applications, it has been an excellent choice for learning OO development and for developing OO systems.

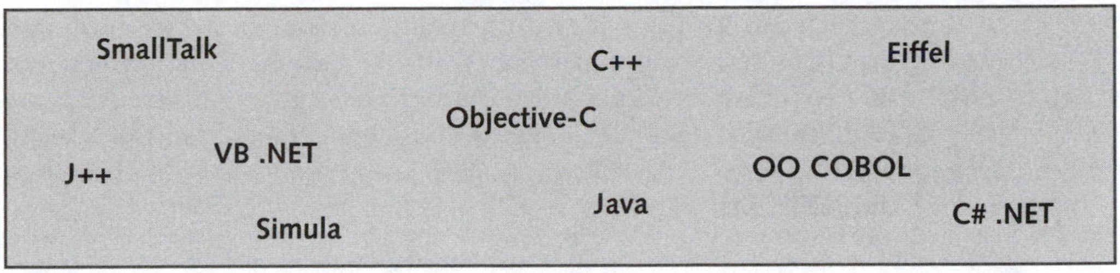

Figure 1-2 Some object-oriented programming languages

Microsoft recently released a more direct competitor to Java as part of the .NET framework, named **C#** (pronounced "C sharp"), and now with the release of VB .NET and its pure OO features, Microsoft hopes to dominate OO and Web-based development. VB .NET is now an excellent choice for learning OO development and for developing OO systems.

The Microsoft .NET Framework and VB .NET

The .NET framework is described by Microsoft as a new computing platform that simplifies development for distributed environments such as the Internet. It has two main components that provide the programmer unprecedented flexibility: the .NET common language runtime and the .NET framework class library. The **.NET Common Language Runtime** (**CLR**) manages code at execution, providing core services such as memory management, thread execution, code safety verification, data typing, compilation, and other services. These services save developer time and help to improve the quality of programs. Developers can use a variety of programming languages that the CLR environment can compile and execute. Therefore, programmers can use the language of their choice, including any of the .NET programming languages such as VB .NET, C++ .NET, C# .NET, or J++ .NET, and still take advantage of the features of the runtime. The goal of the CLR is to allow programmers to write different parts of an application with different programming languages, depending on the expertise of the programmer, and ensure that the parts can work together.

The CLR uses an intermediate code to achieve this goal. Each programming language compiles its source code into an intermediate code. The CLR then takes the intermediate code and compiles it into machine language at execution, using a feature called just-in-time compilation. The intermediate compile step allows the runtime to integrate different programming languages into one application. It also provides the benefit of allowing the application to run on different platforms (i.e., platform independence) without recompiling.

The **.NET framework class library** provides reusable classes of objects that work with the CLR. A programmer using any of the .NET programming languages can use these classes to include functionality needed in the application. Classes that provide useful support are included, such as string management, collections, database connectivity, and file management. When a programmer learns how to use the functionality provided by a .NET framework class, that knowledge can be applied to any other .NET programming language. Additionally, classes are included that support specialized needs, such as console applications, Windows GUI applications (Windows Forms), ASP .NET applications (Web Forms), and XML Web services.

The ambitious goals of the .NET framework were realized in the production release of Microsoft Visual Studio .NET in 2002. The common language runtime and .NET framework class library are integrated with the Visual Studio .NET integrated development environment (IDE) to provide system developers with a complete set of languages and tools for developing OO and Web-based applications.

Microsoft decided to include its popular visual development tool, Visual Basic, in the .NET framework and in Visual Studio .NET. But Visual Basic needed a major overhaul to fit in. Previously, Visual Basic had been a stand-alone product that evolved from interpreted BASIC and Microsoft Quick Basic beginning in 1991. Visual Basic made it easy for programmers to develop desktop Windows applications because it included Windows objects such as forms, buttons, labels, and text boxes that the programmer could drag and drop into the application. It also took an event-driven approach to handling Windows events such as mouse clicks. It retained the flexible and easy-to-learn syntax for writing procedural code that it inherited from Quick Basic. Over time, Visual Basic became the leading rapid application development tool used for Windows applications. But even in Version 6.0 (the latest version available until 2002), it was still not completely object-oriented. Visual Basic also continued to include many quirks and limitations that bothered programmers more formally trained using C and C++. Most VB programmers used some OO concepts and techniques for the user interface, but the rest of the application was developed using procedural programming.

With the introduction of VB .NET, however, Visual Basic has now become a full-blown OO programming language that shares the common language runtime and .NET framework class library with the other .NET languages. To accomplish this, Microsoft had to make many changes to Visual Basic that existing VB programmers might find unfamiliar. But these changes allow VB programmers to accomplish anything a Java or C++ programmer can accomplish when developing OO systems. As a result, the future of VB .NET appears very bright.

Object-Oriented Analysis and Design

You learned earlier that OO development is not only about OO programming. Figure 1-3 illustrates how object-oriented analysis, design, and programming are all required for OO system development.

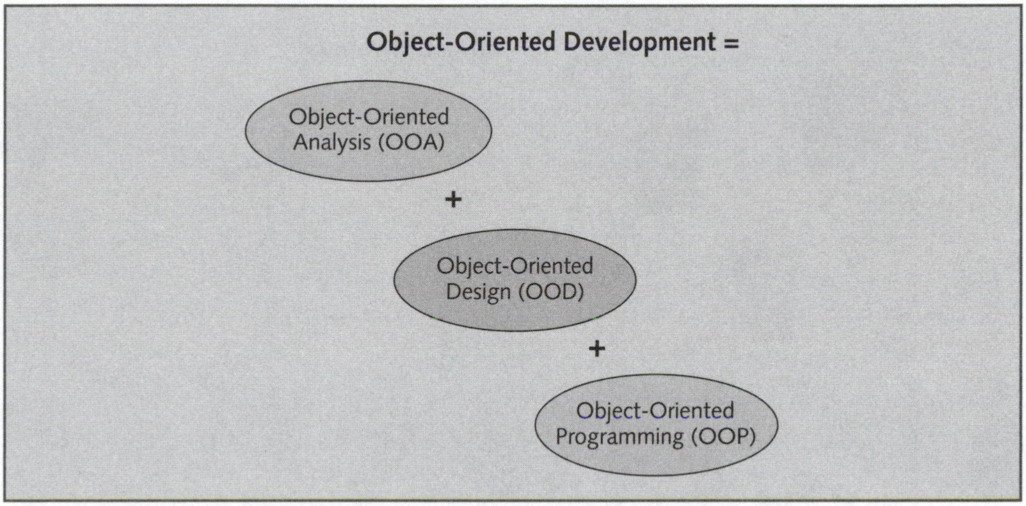

Figure 1-3 Object-oriented development

As interest in OO development grew in the early 1980s, system designers needed object-oriented analysis and object-oriented design techniques to help them develop systems. Early OOA and OOD techniques emerged in the late 1980s. Several key procedural system development methodologists turned their attention to OO analysis and design techniques. Ed Yourdon, for example, was instrumental in developing structured analysis and structured design techniques. James Martin is credited with creating the information engineering development techniques in an attempt to improve structured analysis and design. Both Yourdon and Martin went on to write books on OOA and OOD. Other people—including Grady Booch, James Rumbaugh, and Ivar Jacobson—proposed OOA and OOD techniques based on their work in industry. Booch, Rumbaugh, and Jacobson eventually joined forces to define what is now the standard object-oriented analysis and design modeling notation—the **Unified Modeling Language** (**UML**).

This text shows you how to interpret and create UML models as you learn about OO development. UML assumes a **model-driven approach** to analysis and design, meaning that as a developer, you create graphical models of the system requirements and the system design. Diagrams with symbols such as rectangles, lines, ovals, and squares show what the system is required to accomplish and how a system component should be built. Standard use of these symbols on UML diagrams makes it easier for system developers to communicate with each other during development. Traditional structured analysis and design and information engineering also use a model-driven approach. They create graphical models, such as data flow diagrams (DFDs), entity-relationship diagrams (ERDs), and structure charts during system development. However, in OO development with UML, you create different types of models. OOA and OOD use **class diagrams**, **use case diagrams**, **sequence diagrams**, **statecharts**, and others, as shown in Figure 1-4. Relying on these models to build and analyze systems defines the OO approach as model-driven.

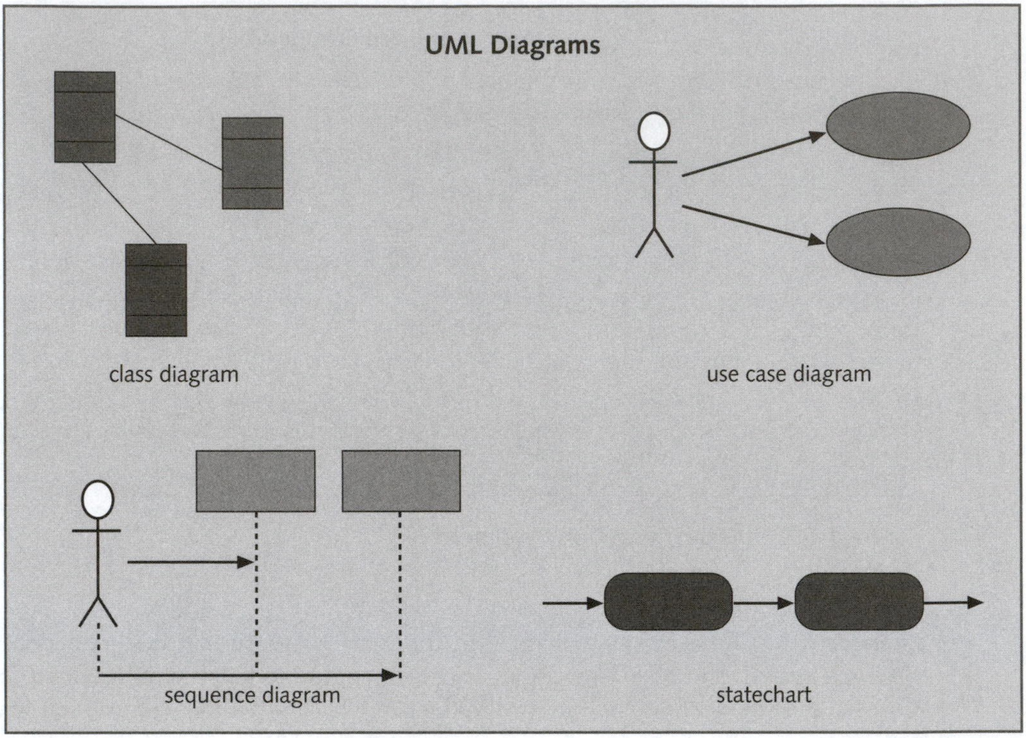

Figure 1-4 Class diagrams, use case diagrams, sequence diagrams, and statecharts

However, OOA and OOD require more than modeling notation. The system development life cycle (SDLC) is a project management framework that defines project phases and activities within phases that are completed when developing a system. The phases typically are named planning, analysis, design, implementation, and support. The SDLC was first created for traditional system development, but it also applies to OO development. In addition to building a system in these phases, OO developers usually follow an iterative approach to analysis, design, and implementation. Iteration means repeating a process or task, so an iterative approach to development means that you complete some analysis, some design, and some implementation, and then complete more analysis, more design, and more implementation.

Techniques such as prototyping and joint application development (JAD) are also usually part of OO development. Prototyping means creating a working model of one or more parts of a system to give users a chance to see and evaluate something concrete. During JAD sessions, key system stakeholders and decision makers work together to define system requirements and designs in a short period of time. Project management, interviewing and data collection, user interface design, testing, and conversion techniques, among others, are required when using OO development, as they are in traditional system development. So, even though the OO approach is different from procedural programming in terms of what a system is and how it works, using the SDLC approach and other project management techniques means that OOA and OOD have much in common with more traditional information system development.

UNDERSTANDING OBJECT-ORIENTED CONCEPTS

As discussed previously, object-oriented development assumes that a system is a collection of objects that interact to accomplish tasks. To understand and discuss this development method, you should be familiar with the key concepts that apply to objects and OO, shown in Figure 1-5. These concepts are briefly introduced in this section, and are explained and demonstrated more completely throughout the book.

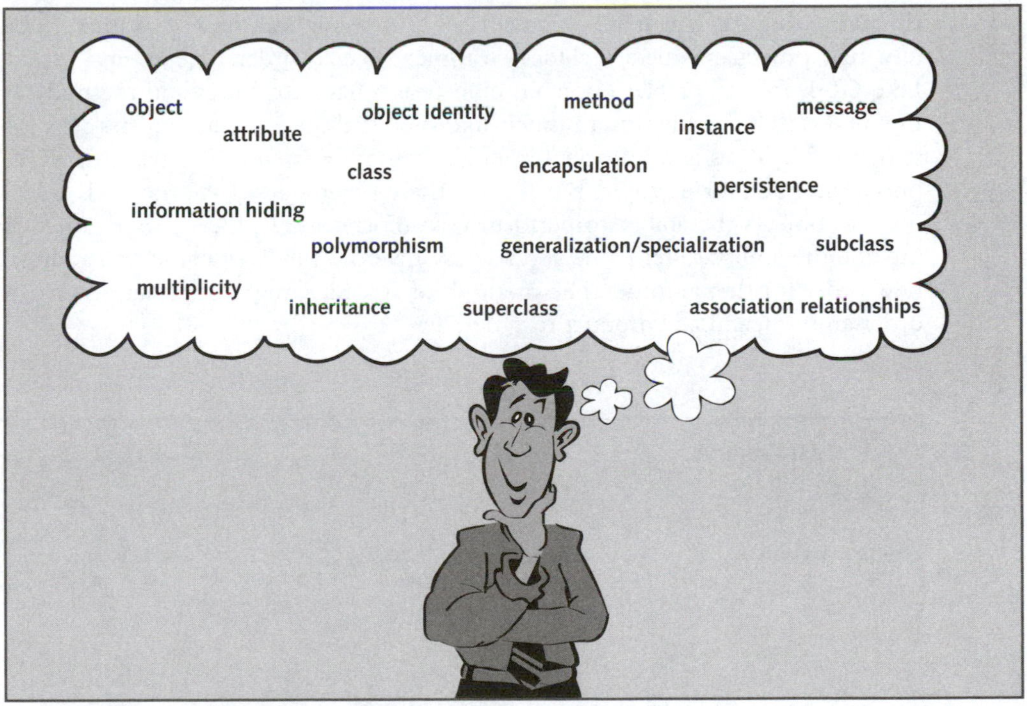

Figure 1-5 Key OO concepts

Objects, Attributes, and Methods

An **object** in a computer system is like an object in the real world—it is a thing that has attributes and behaviors. A computer system can have many types of objects, such as GUI objects that make up the user interface and the system and problem domain objects that are the focus of the application. A **GUI object** uses graphics, such as a button or label, to represent part of a system. A GUI object has **attributes**, which are characteristics that have values: the size, shape, color, location, and caption of a button or label, for example. A form or window has attributes, such as height and width, border style, and background color. These GUI objects also have behaviors or **methods**, which describe what an object can do. For example, a button can be clicked, a label can display text, and a form or window can change size and appear or disappear. Figure 1-6 lists some GUI objects with their attributes and methods.

GUI objects are the easiest to understand because users (and developers) can see them and interact with them directly. But OO systems contain other types of objects, called **problem domain objects**, which are specific to a business application. For example, a business system that processes orders includes customer objects, order objects, and product objects. Like GUI objects, problem domain objects also have attributes and methods, as shown in Figure 1-7. The attributes are much like the attributes of data entities in ERDs used in structured analysis and information engineering: Each customer has a name, address, and phone number, for example. But in OO, these objects also have methods, giving problem domain objects the ability to perform tasks. For example, the methods of each customer include the ability to set name and address, give the values of name and address, and add a new order for the customer. The methods of an order might be to set order date, calculate order amount, and add product to order.

GUI Objects	Attributes	Methods
Button	size, shape, color, location, caption	click, enable, disable, hide, show
Label	size, shape, color, location, text	set text, get text, hide, show
Form	width, height, border style, background color	change size, minimize, maximize, appear, disappear

Figure 1-6 Attributes and methods of GUI objects

Problem Domain Objects	Attributes	Methods
Customer	name, address, phone number	set name, set address, add new order for customer
Order	order number, date, amount	set order date, calculate order amount, add product to order, schedule order shipment
Product	product number, description, price	add to order, set description, get price

Figure 1-7 Attributes and methods in problem domain objects

Object Interactions and Messages

Objects interact by sending **messages** to each other, asking another object to invoke, or carry out, one of its methods. In other words, a customer object representing a customer named Bill gets a message to add a new order for itself. Order number 143, once added, then calculates the order amount and accomplishes other tasks. Objects interacting by sending messages to carry out tasks is the main concept of OOA and OOD.

Figure 1-8 shows an order-processing system (containing Customer Bill) as a collection of interacting objects. The user interacts with GUI objects, and the GUI objects interact with problem domain objects by sending messages.

The order-processing system works as follows:

1. The user types information about a product into a text box, and then clicks the button. The click results in a message to the button.
2. The button knows that when it is clicked, it should request that Customer Bill add a new order, so the button sends the message to Customer Bill, a problem domain object representing a customer.
3. Customer Bill knows how to add a new order because that is a method all customers have. To add an order, Customer Bill sends a message to create an order object.
4. The new order object assigns itself an order number (Order 143) and then asks the text box for its text, which the text box supplies. Order 143 uses the text to identify the products the user entered for the order.
5. Order 143 sends an add-to-order message to each product asking it to add itself to the order, in this case a message to Chair 213 and to Lamp 453.
6. Chair 213 and Lamp 453 add themselves to the order and supply information about their price and availability.

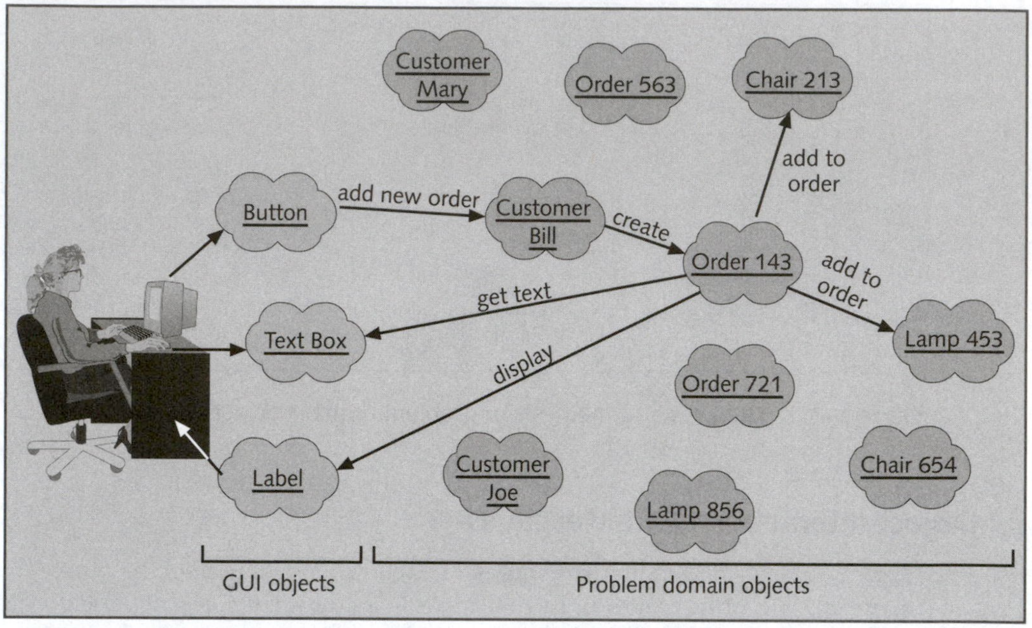

Figure 1-8 Order-processing system where objects interact by sending messages

7. Order 143 completes the task by calculating the order amount and sending a message to the label asking it to display information about the completed order to the user.

Encapsulation and Information Hiding

The objects Customer Bill and Order 143 each have attributes and methods, giving them the ability to respond to messages. **Encapsulation** means that an object has attributes and methods combined into one unit. By combining attributes and methods, you do not need to know the internal structure of the object to send messages to it. You only need to know what an object can do for you. Encapsulation hides the internal structure of objects, also protecting them from corruption. This is what is meant by **information hiding** in OO, another key concept.

Each object also has a unique **identity**, meaning you can find it, or refer to it, and send it a message. You need to know an object's identity before you can ask the object to do something for you, such as adding a chair to an order. The object's identity is usually stored as a memory address. The system uses a specific object like Customer Bill over a period of time, so it requires some mechanism for keeping it available. **Persistent objects** are those that are defined as available for use over time. If a system uses thousands of customer objects, each with their own orders, the system must be able to remember all of them.

Classes, Instances, and Associations

An order-processing system has many customer objects, one for each real-world customer (see Figure 1-9). All of the customer objects are *classified* as a type of thing—a customer—so in OO development, you refer to the Customer class when you are talking about all of the customer objects. The **class** defines what all objects of the class represent. When you are talking about computer programming and objects, you can refer to the objects as **instances** of the class. When an object is created for the class, it is common to say the class is *instantiated*. Therefore, the terms "instance" and "object" are often used interchangeably.

You have seen that objects interact by sending messages, but they also maintain **association relationships** among themselves. A customer object maintains associations with order objects that apply to the customer, for example, so the customer object can find and inquire about its orders—a customer places an order. Each order object is associated with products—an order includes a product (see Figure 1-10). Object associations are conceptually similar to relationships in an entity-relationship diagram, except each object is responsible for maintaining its relationships with other objects.

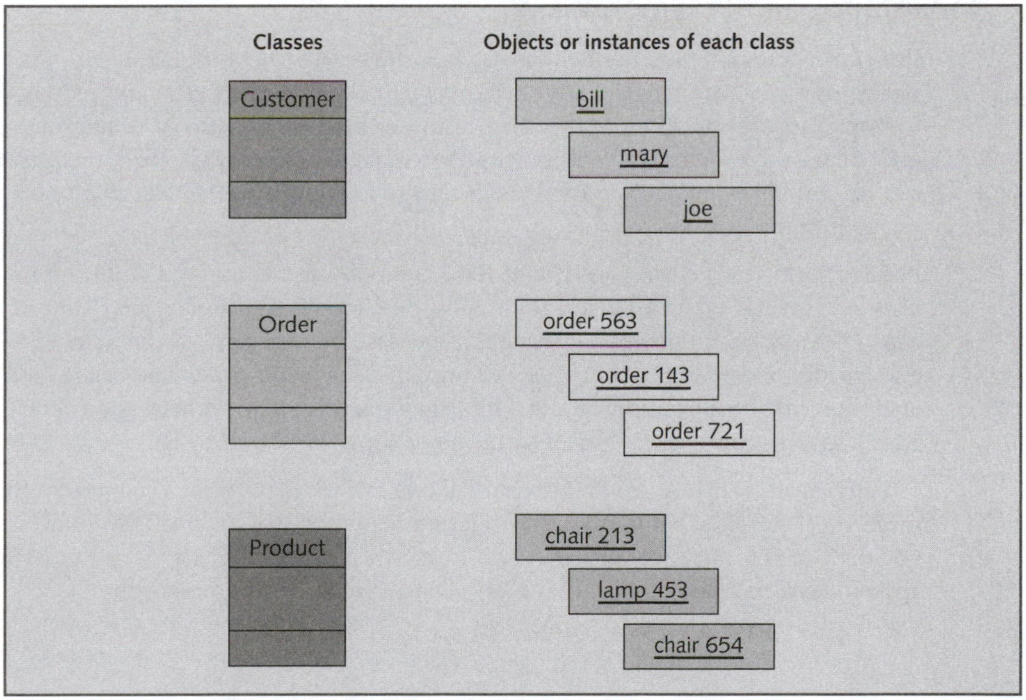

Figure 1-9 Class versus object or instances of the class

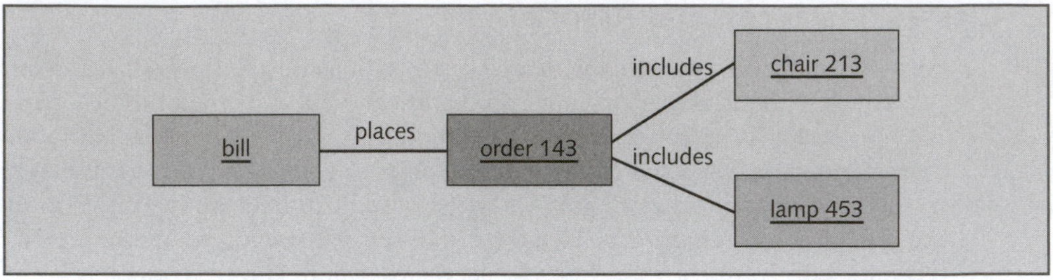

Figure 1-10 Associating objects with other objects

Some association relationships are one-to-one, such as when one order is associated with one customer, and some associations are one-to-many, such as when one customer places many orders. UML refers to the number of associations as the **multiplicity** of the association. Those familiar with entity-relationship diagrams use the term **cardinality** for the same concept.

Inheritance and Polymorphism

Probably the most often used concept when discussing OO is the concept of **inheritance**, where one class of objects takes on characteristics of another class and extends them. For example, an object belonging to the Customer class might also be something more general, such as a person. Therefore, if the Person class is already defined, the Customer class can be defined by extending the Person class to take on more specific attributes and methods required of a customer.

For example, the Person class might have attributes for name and address. The Customer class is a special type of person with additional attributes for shipping address and credit card information. Similarly, a sales clerk object is also a person, so the Sales Clerk class can also be defined by extending the Person class. For example, a sales clerk has additional attributes for job title and pay rate. The Person class is a **superclass,** and both Customer and Sales Clerk are **subclasses**. This relationship is shown in Figure 1-11.

Classifying objects helps to identify special types of problem domain objects, which provide more specific information about the requirements for the system. The result of extending general classes into more specific subclasses is referred to as a **generalization/specialization hierarchy**, sometimes called an **inheritance hierarchy**.

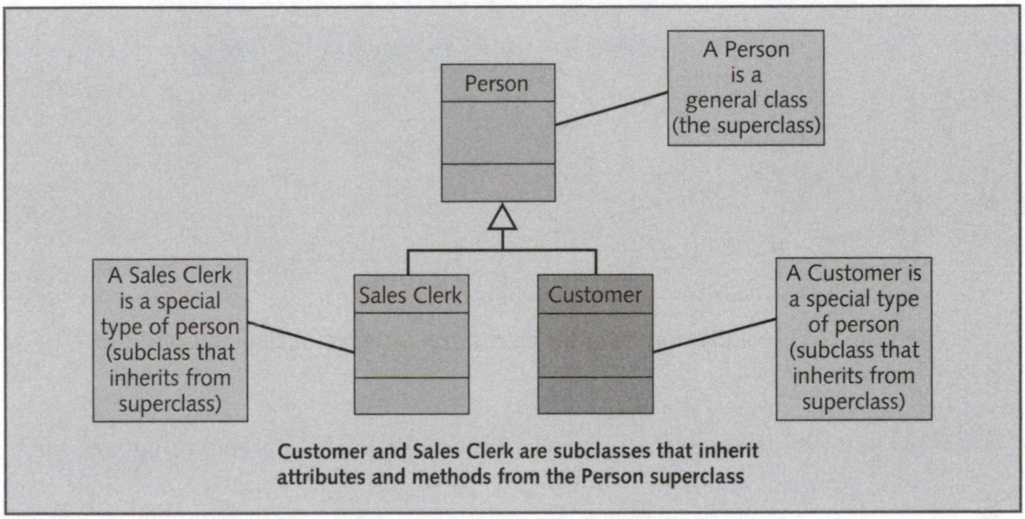

Figure 1-11 Superclass and subclasses

Attributes are not the only characteristics inherited from a superclass. Subclasses also inherit methods and association relationships. A final key concept that is related to generalization/specialization hierarchies and inheritance of methods is **polymorphism**, which means "many forms." In OO, polymorphism refers to the way different objects can respond in their own way to the same message. For example, a dialog box, a network connection, and a document might each receive a message to *close*. Each knows how to close and does so in its own way when asked. The sender of the message does not need to know what type of object it is or how it does it; the sender only needs to know that the object responds to the *close* message. Classes are polymorphic if their instances can respond to the same message.

For example, a bank has several types of bank accounts, including money market accounts and passbook accounts. Both types of accounts calculate interest, but they follow different rules for interest. The sender of the message *calculateInterest* does not need to know what type of account it is, only that it calculates interest when asked (see Figure 1-12). This greatly simplifies processing when all bank account objects can be sent the same message and the job is done correctly and completely by each object.

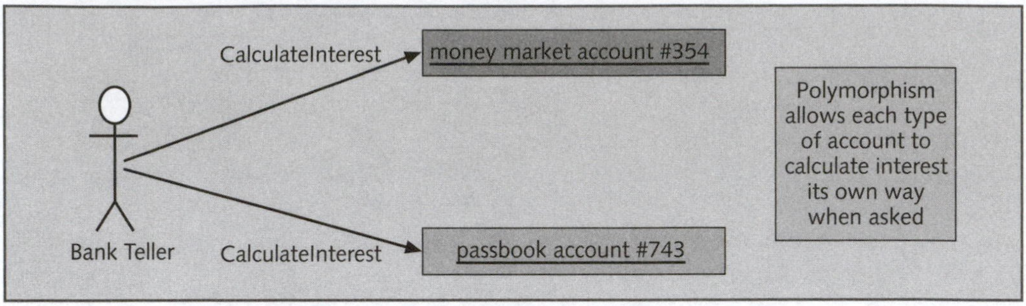

Figure 1-12 Polymorphism for two different types of bank accounts

As you read through this text and complete VB .NET programming assignments, you will master the subtleties of these OO concepts.

Recognizing the Benefits of OO Development

The object-oriented approach was originally found to be useful in computer simulations and for graphical user interfaces, but why is it being used in more conventional information system development? The two main reasons are the benefits of naturalness and reuse.

Objects Are More Natural

Naturalness refers to the fact that people usually think about their world in terms of objects, so when people talk about their work and discuss system requirements, it is natural to define the classes of objects involved. Additionally, OOA, OOD, and OOP all involve modeling classes of objects, so the focus remains on objects throughout the development process.

Some experienced system developers continue to avoid OO, arguing that OO is really not as natural as procedural programming. In fact, many experienced developers have had difficulty learning OO. Because procedural programming was the first approach to programming they learned, it might seem more natural to them now. But for most people, including those new to programming, procedural programming is very difficult. Few people can think through and write complex procedural code. For most new programmers learning about system development, OO does seem fairly natural. In addition, object-orientation is natural to system users. They can easily discuss the objects involved in their work. Classes, classification, and generalization/specialization hierarchies are the natural way people organize their knowledge.

Classes of Objects Can Be Reused

In addition to naturalness, the ability to reuse classes and objects is another benefit of object-oriented development. **Reuse** means that classes and objects can be invented once and used many times. Once a developer defines a class, such as the Customer class, it can be reused in many other systems that have customer objects. If the new system has a special type of customer, the existing Customer class can be extended to a new subclass by inheriting all that a customer is, and then adding the new characteristics. Classes can be reused in this manner during analysis, design, or programming.

When programming, you do not have to see the source code for the class that is being reused, even if you are defining a new class that inherits from it. This simplifies development. Object-oriented programming languages come with class libraries that contain predefined classes most programmers need. The .NET framework class library discussed previously is an example. GUI classes such as buttons, labels, text boxes, and check boxes come in .NET class libraries. As a programmer, you do not need to create these classes from scratch. Instead, you use the class to create objects you need for your GUI. Other useful classes are also included in class libraries, such as those to connect to databases or networks, and to hold collections of objects.

LEARNING OO DEVELOPMENT

This book provides a comprehensive guide to OO system development, including OOA, OOD, and OOP. You will use object-oriented programming to learn and practice the OO concepts, so it may look like a programming text to you. But you are only learning VB .NET as a means to understand object-oriented system development. The same OO concepts and techniques are used with any pure OO language. This section provides a roadmap for the organization of the text.

Introducing Three-Tier Design

As you will see, the book is organized according to an approach to OO development called **three-tier design**. Three-tier design requires that the collection of objects that interact in an OO system be separated into three categories of classes—problem domain classes, GUI classes, and data access classes. As discussed previously, problem domain classes are the classes of objects specific to the business application, such as the Customer class, Order class, and Product class. GUI classes define the objects that make up the user interface to the application, such as forms, buttons, labels, list boxes, and text boxes. The third category includes data access classes, which work with the database management system to store information about objects for later use, making the problem domain objects persistent.

Three-tier design requires that OO system developers define three categories of classes when designing and building the system. First, the developers identify and specify the problem domain classes. Once these are specified, the developers define how GUI classes will be used to allow the user to interact with the problem domain classes. Finally, they specify data access classes to allow problem domain classes to interact with the database. Once all three tiers are completed, they are ready to work together as a complete system.

The core of this book is organized according to the three tiers of OO development. To understand OO development using VB .NET, you first need to understand basic OO concepts and the basics of the VB .NET language syntax. Part 1 introduces OO development and VB .NET. Parts 2 through 5 follow the process of OO development based on the three-tier design approach: problem domain classes, GUI classes, and data access classes. Problem domain classes are covered first because they are the focus during OOA. OOD involves adding GUI classes that users interact with and adding data access classes to allow object persistence using a database. Adding GUI classes is covered in Part 3, adding data access classes is covered in Part 4, and the three tiers are combined in Part 5 into both a Windows application and a Web-based application. Each of the book's five parts is described in more detail below.

Part 1: Object-Orientation and VB .NET Fundamentals

Part 1 covers OO concepts and introduces the VB .NET programming language. This first chapter sets the stage for OO development and defines the key OO concepts and benefits. Chapters 2, 3, and 4 turn to VB .NET more specifically, introducing the Visual Studio IDE and VB .NET in Chapter 2. Chapter 3 introduces the VB .NET language syntax. As with any other programming language, you first need to learn the basic syntax and rules. VB .NET uses variables, computations, and structured programming constructs such as statements, decisions, loops, and arrays. If you have had an introductory course in VB, you might skim Chapter 3 to review the syntax and to learn about any changes required by VB .NET. If VB is new to you, Chapter 3 provides a concise overview of the key programming constructs.

Chapter 4 introduces VB .NET programming using classes supplied in the .NET framework class library. This approach provides an object-oriented view of VB, and begins to show the power of interacting with object instances and methods and the benefits of reuse. Using these classes demonstrates how inheritance and instantiation (making an instance of a class) actually work. The rest of the text focuses on business systems and more complete VB .NET applications.

Chapter 5 introduces OO analysis and OO design concepts and describes the business case study that is used throughout the text—Bradshaw Marina. Chapter 5 also covers the UML models used during OOA and OOD, including the use case diagram, class diagram, and sequence diagram. These diagrams are used throughout the text to show the value of taking a model-driven approach to development. The models show what the system is used for, what classes are involved, and what messages are sent from object to object. The VB .NET code written to implement the Bradshaw Marina system is based on the details in the models.

Part 2: Developing Problem Domain Classes

Part 2 shows how to use VB .NET to create new problem domain classes that are specific to the business system being developed. In Bradshaw Marina, these classes include boats, docks, and slips. Chapter 6 demonstrates how to create a problem domain class with a few attributes and methods. An approach to testing new classes is introduced where tester programs are written to send messages to instantiate classes and to invoke methods of instances. Chapter 7 continues the discussion of problem domain classes, adding data validation and introducing VB .NET's new approach to handling errors—throwing exceptions. Method overloading and more on custom methods are also covered.

Chapter 8 introduces generalization/specialization and inheritance for problem domain classes. In the Bradshaw system, Sailboat and Powerboat are subclasses of Boat. Adding subclasses and overriding superclass methods are two important concepts you will explore in this chapter. Interfaces, custom exceptions, and examples of polymorphism are also covered.

Chapter 9 shows how to implement association relationships among objects. You will investigate one-to-one associations. For example, a boat is kept in a slip (one-to-one association). You might ask a slip to tell you what boat is contained in it, requiring a slip to ask a boat for information. The chapter extends the example to one-to-many associations, where a dock has many slips. Now you can ask a dock for a list of all slips and information on the boat in each slip.

Part 3: Developing GUI Classes

Part 3 describes how to create graphical user interface classes with which the user can interact. The GUI classes in turn interact with problem domain classes. Chapter 10 surveys the VB .NET GUI components available for creating Windows Forms. In Chapter 11, you use multiple Windows Forms to create more complete dialogs that allow the user to interact with the Bradshaw Marina system. Chapter 12 shows you how to create Web Forms to facilitate Web development for Bradshaw Marina. HTML and ASP .NET are also introduced.

Part 4: Developing Data Access Classes

Part 4 covers the third tier—data access classes. Data access classes are used to manage database interactions and achieve object persistence. Chapter 13 shows examples of using files, relational databases, and object serialization to achieve object persistence. Object serialization and object-oriented database management systems might be the future of data access classes, but for now, most developers work with relational databases for this purpose. Therefore, Chapter 14 explores relational database management and the structured query language (SQL) for data access classes in more detail.

Part 5: Deploying the Three-Tier Application

Part 5 shows how GUI classes, problem domain classes, and data access classes function together as three tiers to create a complete client-server system. The emphasis in this text is on business systems, and you'll see how the complete OO development process comes together in the Bradshaw Marina examples in Chapter 15. Finally, Chapter 16 demonstrates Web-based technologies and shows you how to deploy the Bradshaw Marina examples on the Web using Web Forms, ASP .NET, and XML.

Once you have worked through this text, you will understand how all three tiers are designed and implemented using OO development and VB .NET to create a complete business system, from OOA to OOD to OOP, including deployment on the Web.

Chapter Summary

- Object-oriented information system development includes object-oriented analysis (OOA), object-oriented design (OOD), and object-oriented programming (OOP).
- Object-oriented (OO) systems are viewed as collections of interacting objects that accomplish tasks, and the first OO programming began in the 1960s with the Simula language. SmallTalk, C++, Java, and most recently C# and VB .NET are examples of OO languages. The Microsoft .NET framework is a new computing platform that simplifies development of OO applications.
- The OO development process includes much more than just programming. A model-driven approach using Unified Modeling Language (UML) diagrams defines requirements and designs prior to programming. Other system development principles and techniques are also used in OO development.
- Key object-oriented concepts include objects, classes, instances, messages, encapsulation and information hiding, association relationships, inheritance, and polymorphism.
- The benefits of OO development include naturalness and reuse. Classes and objects are a natural way for people to think about the world. Once classes are defined, they can be reused in other systems.
- This text is organized into five parts and explains the three-tier design approach to OO development. The three tiers include problem domain classes, graphical user interface (GUI) classes, and data access classes.
- Part 1 provides an introduction to OO and VB .NET. Part 2 emphasizes defining and programming problem domain classes. Part 3 emphasizes adding a graphical user interface to the system. Part 4 emphasizes adding data access classes to allow object persistence using a database management system, and Part 5 combines the three tiers—GUI classes, problem domain classes, and data access classes—into a finished system, and demonstrates how to deploy the application on the Web.

Key Terms

.NET Common Language Runtime (CLR)
.NET framework class library
association relationship
attribute
C#
C++
cardinality
class
class diagram
encapsulation
generalization/specialization hierarchy
GUI object
identity
information hiding
inheritance
inheritance hierarchy
instance
Java
message
method
model-driven approach
multiplicity
naturalness
object
object-oriented analysis (OOA)
object-oriented approach
object-oriented design (OOD)
object-oriented information system development
object-oriented programming (OOP)
persistent object
polymorphism
problem domain object
reuse
sequence diagram
Simula
SmallTalk
statechart
subclass
superclass
three-tier design
Unified Modeling Language (UML)
use case diagram
VB .NET

Review Questions

1. The analysis, design, and implementation of information systems using object-oriented programming languages, technologies, and techniques is called:
   a. object-oriented development
   b. procedural development
   c. inheritance
   d. information engineering
2. OO development includes which of the following?
   a. only OOA and OOP
   b. only OOD and OOP
   c. OOA, OOD, and OOP
   d. structured analysis and design

3. Which of the following is *not* an example of an OO programming language?
   a. SmallTalk
   b. Pascal
   c. C++
   d. Java

4. The first general-purpose pure OO language was:
   a. SmallTalk
   b. Pascal
   c. C++
   d. Java

5. Which of the following languages is not from Microsoft?
   a. C#
   b. J++
   c. VB .NET
   d. Java

6. Which are the two key components of the .NET framework?
   a. common language runtime and .NET framework class library
   b. Visual Basic and Quick Basic .NET
   c. Java virtual machine and JDK
   d. servlets and applets

7. UML is an acronym for:
   a. Uniform Model Limitations
   b. Unknown Meta Language
   c. Unified Modeling Language
   d. Untyped Machine Language

8. A model-driven approach to development is used for:
   a. traditional, procedural development only
   b. object-oriented development only
   c. small hobby systems
   d. both traditional and OO development

9. Which of the following is *not* a technique used in either traditional or OO development?
   a. project management
   b. interviewing
   c. program testing
   d. class diagramming
10. Which of the following is *not* a diagram defined by UML?
    a. entity-relationship diagram
    b. class diagram
    c. use case diagram
    d. sequence diagram
11. An object-oriented system is defined as:
    a. a collection of interacting objects that accomplish tasks
    b. classes and procedures that are separate from data
    c. data flow applications that process inputs into outputs
    d. any system designed for the Internet
12. A thing that has attributes and behaviors is called a(n):
    a. scenario
    b. use case
    c. object
    d. method
13. A characteristic of an object that takes on a value is called a(n):
    a. class
    b. use case
    c. method
    d. attribute
14. What an object is capable of doing in terms of behavior is called a(n):
    a. class
    b. use case
    c. attribute
    d. method

15. Objects that make up the user interface of the system are called:
   a. problem domain objects
   b. data access objects
   c. GUI objects
   d. visual objects

16. Objects that are specific to the business application are called:
   a. problem domain objects
   b. data access objects
   c. GUI objects
   d. visual objects

17. A request sent asking an object to invoke, or carry out, one of its methods is called a(n):
   a. command
   b. invocation
   c. attribution
   d. message

18. Encapsulation hides the internal structure of objects, protecting them from corruption. This is also referred to as:
   a. information hiding
   b. polymorphism
   c. inheritance
   d. generalization/specialization

19. Each object has a unique address, meaning you can find it, or refer to it, and send it a message. This is referred to as the:
   a. object key
   b. class identifier
   c. index value
   d. object identity

20. Persistent objects are those that:
   a. are available to use over time
   b. never give up when sending a message
   c. are usually important enough to be given priority
   d. make up the user interface

21. A class and an object are:

a. different because a class is an instance and an object is a category

b. the same

c. different because a class is like an instance and an object is like an association

d. different because a class is a type of thing and an object is a specific instance

22. Which of the following is an association relationship?

a. A customer is a special type of person.

b. A person has an attribute called name.

c. A customer enrolls in a credit program.

d. A credit program is a special type of account.

23. The number of associations possible between classes of objects is called:

a. polymorphism

b. multiplicity

c. relationships

d. methods

24. An example of a superclass of the class Car is:

a. Motor Vehicle

b. Sports Car

c. Sport Utility Vehicle

d. Truck

25. An example of a subclass of the class Truck is:

a. Motor Vehicle

b. Sports Car

c. Station Wagon

d. Dump Truck

26. According to the concept of polymorphism, a blender and a washing machine:

a. are both tangible objects

b. can both be told to spin

c. are types of household appliances

d. are problem domain objects for a retail store

27. Two benefits of OO development are:
    a. naturalness and reuse
    b. methods and messages
    c. association and generalization/specialization
    d. clients and servers

28. Three-tier design divides a system into the following categories of classes:
    a. GUI classes, database classes, and operating system classes
    b. problem domain classes, operating system objects, and GUI classes
    c. problem domain classes, GUI classes, and data access classes
    d. GUI classes, procedural classes, and data access classes

Discussion Questions

1. This chapter (and the whole book) argues that OO development is much more than programming. List and discuss at least four of the system development activities and tasks that do not directly involve programming. Is OO development any different in this regard than traditional development? Discuss.
2. OO is not new, but it has taken a while to catch on with business system development. Discuss some of the reasons for this. Are there still some factors holding back OO development? Will the Microsoft .NET framework and VB .NET make much of a difference? Discuss.

Projects

1. Talk with some of your colleagues and friends about procedural programming versus OO programming. Develop a list of at least five specific issues about both approaches that seem natural or unnatural.
2. Problem domain classes are a key part of OOA. What are some of the key problem domain classes that would apply to a system for scheduling courses at a university? Expand at least two of these classes into generalization/specialization hierarchies, with a superclass and subclasses.
3. In Project 2, you listed problem domain classes for a system for scheduling courses at a university. What are at least three association relationships between the problem domain classes?
4. Consider the GUI classes that make up one finished Windows Form in a system. The form contains many specific GUI objects. List as many of these GUI classes as you can. What are some generalization/specialization hierarchies of GUI classes? What are some association relationships among these classes found on a typical Windows Form?

CHAPTER

2

The Visual Studio .NET Development Environment

In this chapter you will:

- Explore the Visual Studio .NET development environment
- Create a project using Visual Basic .NET
- Compile and execute a VB .NET program
- Use the visual form designer
- Explore the debugging tool
- Explore the help facility

In Chapter 1 you were introduced to the fundamental characteristics of object-oriented system development. You learned about the benefits of the object-oriented approach and the tools (such as UML) used by information systems professionals to model system requirements. You examined fundamental object-oriented concepts, such as objects, methods, inheritance, and encapsulation.

You also learned that Visual Basic .NET is part of Microsoft's Visual Studio .NET, which is itself a part of the larger .NET technology. Visual Studio .NET supports the Windows 2000, Windows XP, and Windows NT 4.0 operating systems and includes several languages (such as C++ .NET, C# .NET, and of course, Visual Basic .NET). Recall that two important pieces of the .NET framework are the Common Language Runtime (CLR) and the .NET class library. The CLR and class library support common services that are used by all of the .NET languages.

In this chapter, you will learn how to use VB .NET to write and execute simple programs. You will begin by exploring the basic features of the .NET development environment. You will learn how to use various tools and windows to create simple applications. You will also be introduced to the features of the VB .NET debugging tool and help facilities. After completing this chapter you will have firsthand experience with VB .NET and understand how to use the development environment to create, modify, and execute programs.

Exploring the Visual Studio .NET Development Environment

In Chapter 1 you learned that VB .NET is one of several languages supported by Microsoft's Visual Studio .NET integrated development environment. An **integrated development environment (IDE)** is a set of software tools that helps you code, test, and document the programs you write. As you will see, Visual Studio .NET is a powerful tool designed to meet today's demand for rapid deployment of software systems and Web applications. In this book, you will develop applications using the Visual Basic .NET programming language. However, the knowledge you gain about the Visual Studio .NET development environment will apply to any of the other .NET languages.

Like most IDEs, Visual Studio .NET includes many tools that support software development tasks. These range from simple text editors, to intelligent editors that recognize patterns as you type and can complete code for you, to visual development tools that generate code based on pictures you draw. Visual Studio .NET makes it easy to organize, compile, and execute your programs, and provides facilities to help you test your programs and isolate errors that keep them from running as you intend. Visual Studio .NET also provides extensive help facilities to assist you in the process of writing programs. Together these tools simplify programming tasks, making your job as a programmer easier and reducing the time it takes to develop working programs.

Visual Studio .NET includes many features. In this chapter you will concentrate on understanding the concepts, tools, and windows that are essential for developing VB .NET programs.

Getting Started with VB .NET

In order to complete the exercises in this section, you must first install Visual Studio .NET on your computer. The DVD that accompanies this text includes a 60-day trial version of Visual Studio .NET. You can find instructions for installing the software in the preface of this text. If you have not already done so, please install this software now. Once the software is installed, starting VB .NET is a simple matter.

To start VB .NET in Windows XP Professional:

1. Click the **Start** button, point to **All Programs**, point to **Microsoft Visual Studio .NET**, and then click **Microsoft Visual Studio .NET**. See Figure 2-1.
2. A splash screen identifying the Visual Studio .NET languages installed on your computer momentarily appears, and then you see the Microsoft Development Environment (MDE) window. Verify that the MDE window resembles Figure 2-2. (Your screen may vary slightly depending on settings for your computer.)

NOTE: Note that the figures in this book use Windows XP in classic view, which looks similar to Windows 2000.

2

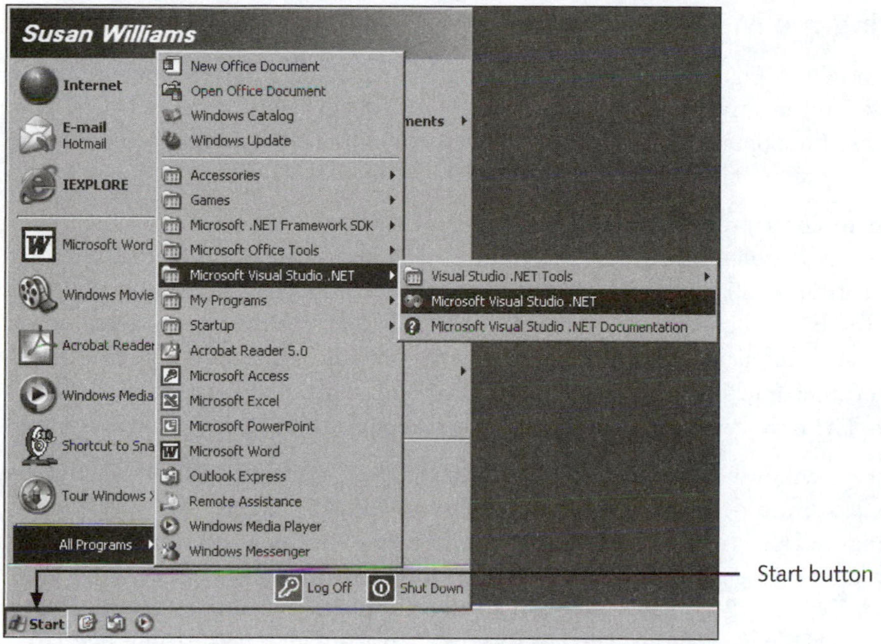

Figure 2-1 Launching Visual Studio .NET

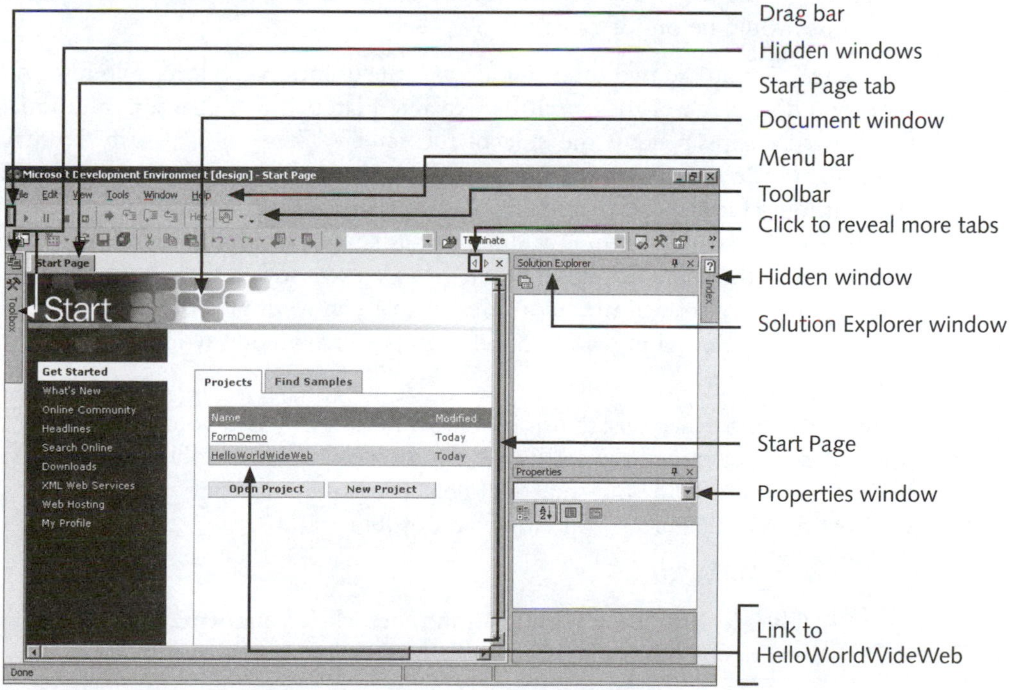

Figure 2-2 The Microsoft Development Environment

Exploring the MDE

As shown in Figure 2-2, the MDE includes a menu bar, various toolbars, and several windows. You use the menu bar to select commands that perform tasks such as opening and closing files; opening and closing projects; compiling, executing, and debugging programs; and accessing help facilities.

The toolbars provide buttons for many of the most common commands. To learn the names of these buttons, point to a button and wait for the ScreenTip. A number of different toolbars are available. You can reveal or hide toolbars by right-clicking any empty space on the toolbar and checking or unchecking a toolbar name. (An alternate way to reveal or hide toolbars is to click Tools on the menu bar, click Customize, and then click the Toolbars tab.) You can change the position of any toolbar by using the drag bar to move it to a new location. The drag bar is the set of short lines that appear on the left edge of the toolbar.

Various windows fill the remainder of the screen. The MDE includes a number of different windows, and depending on your configuration, you may not see all the windows shown in Figure 2-2. Notice, however, that the Start Page occupies most of the screen and appears as a tabbed page within a document window. Multiple documents may be open at one time. Figure 2-2 contains two tabbed document pages—the Start Page and a document named HelloWorldWideWeb.vb. To select a document, click its tab. The tab for the currently selected document appears in bold text. In Figure 2-2, the Start Page is the selected (or active) document. When working with a large number of documents, you can use the left and right arrows in the title bar of the document window to reveal tabbed pages that otherwise would be out of view.

In Figure 2-2, you see two other windows—the Solution Explorer window and the Properties window. Each of these will be explained later in this chapter. Additionally, observe the tabs that appear along the side of the screen. These tabs identify hidden windows. **Hidden windows** enable you to keep frequently needed tools and resources readily available without cluttering the screen. You can reveal a hidden window by moving the mouse over its tab. The hidden window slides out as shown in Figure 2-3. When you move the mouse out of the space occupied by the revealed window, it slides back to its hidden position. Figure 2-3 also identifies icons that enable you to display the Solution Explorer window, the Properties window, and another important window you will learn about shortly called the Toolbox.

If this is the first time you are using Visual Studio .NET and you accepted the default settings when you installed the software, your screen should resemble Figure 2-2 very closely. If it does not, the following steps will help you configure your system so that your MDE window matches Figure 2-2 as closely as possible.

To configure your system:

1. Click **Tools** on the menu bar, and then click **Customize**. The Customize dialog box opens. See Figure 2-4.
2. Click the **Toolbars** tab, if necessary, to select it.

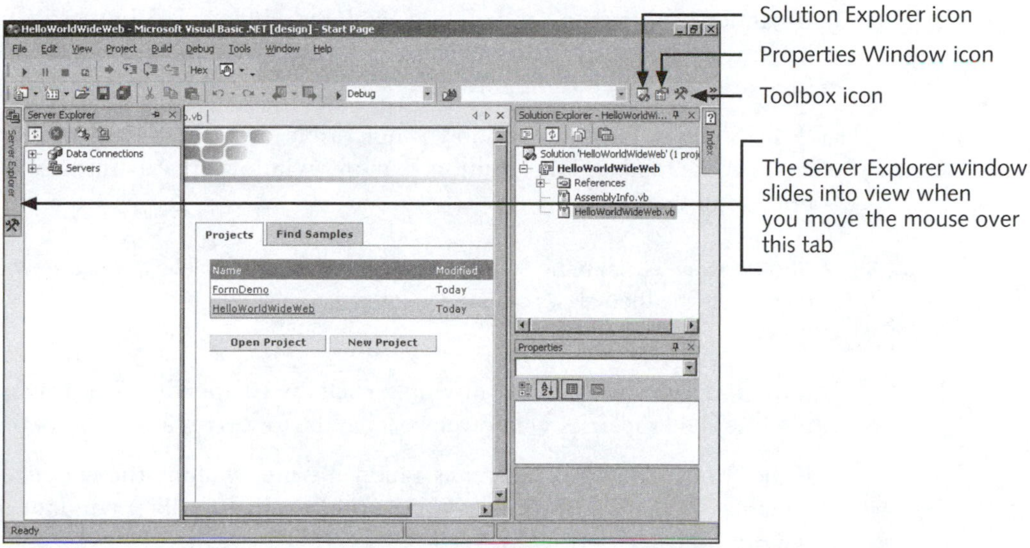

Figure 2-3 Revealing a hidden window

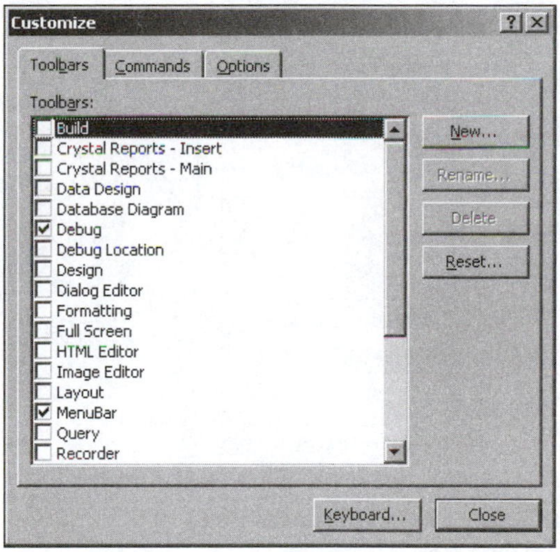

Figure 2-4 The Customize dialog box

3. Make sure that the only items checked are **Menu Bar**, **Standard**, and **Debug**. Later, you may want to customize your settings by adding additional toolbars to your configuration.
4. Click **Close** to close the dialog box and apply the changes.

5. If windows other than the Solution Explorer window and Properties window are visible, close them. You can close any window by clicking the **Close** button (the X in the upper-right corner).

6. If the Solution Explorer window is not visible, click the **Solution Explorer** icon on the toolbar. The Solution Explorer window appears in the upper-right portion of the MDE.

TIP

Another way to make the Solution Explorer window visible is to click View on the menu bar, and then click Solution Explorer.

7. If the Properties window is not visible, click the **Properties Window** icon on the toolbar. The Properties window appears in the lower-right portion of the MDE.

8. If the Toolbox does not appear as a hidden window along the left edge of the screen, click the **Toolbox** icon on the toolbar. The Toolbox window appears, as shown in Figure 2-5.

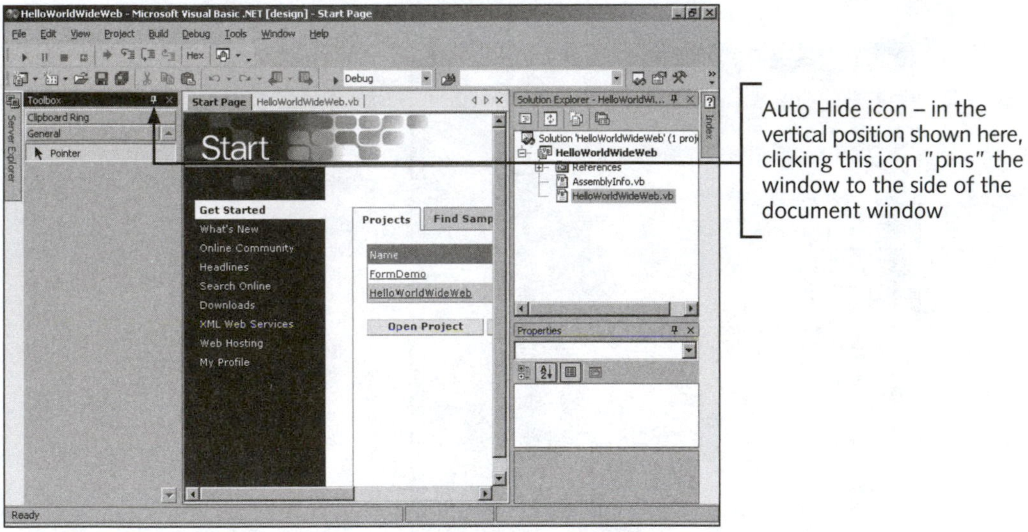

Figure 2-5 The Toolbox window

9. In the title bar of the Toolbox window, click the **Auto Hide** icon, and then move the mouse to the center of the screen. This attaches, or "pins," the Toolbox to the MDE as a hidden window.

Understanding the Start Page

The Start Page automatically loads in the document window when you start Visual Studio .NET. As shown in Figure 2-6, the Start Page contains links to a number of useful resources, many of which are online. In this chapter, you will explore the Get Started link. Clicking the Get Started link is one way to begin a new project or continue working on an existing project. When you click the Get Started link, you see a list of projects you have recently worked on. You also see two buttons, as shown in Figure 2-6.

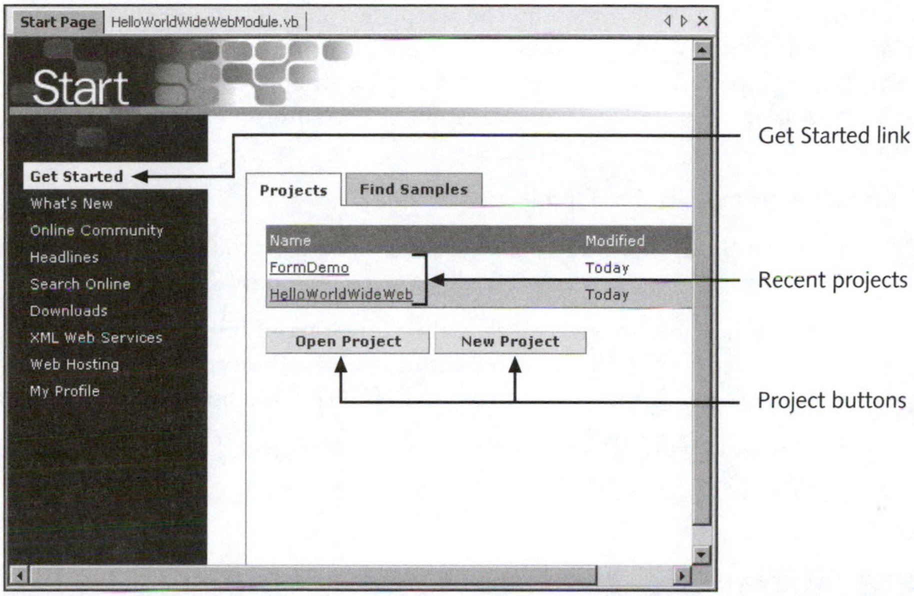

Figure 2-6 The Start Page

To open a project on the list, click the project name. If you want to work on a project that is not on the list, click the Open Project button to navigate to any project in any folder. Click the New Project button to create a project.

TIP

If you inadvertently close the Start Page, you can click Help on the menu bar, and then click Show Start Page to bring it back into view.

Creating a Project Using VB .NET

A programming tradition when learning a new language is to write a program that displays the message "Hello World." For your first VB .NET project, you will continue this tradition, but expand the message to "Hello World Wide Web."

When you create a VB .NET project, you must identify the type of project you want to create. Recall that Visual Studio .NET supports several different programming languages; therefore, when you create a Visual Basic project, you must identify the project type as Visual Basic. You must also identify the template you want to use, and specify the project name and location. VB .NET provides a number of different programming templates. A **template** is a pattern for creating a specific type of application. In this chapter you will work with two templates: the Console Application template and the Windows Application template.

To create your first VB .NET project:

1. If you have not already done so, launch Visual Studio .NET. The Start Page, Solution Explorer window, and Properties window appear.
2. If it is not already selected, click the **Get Started** link on the Start Page. You see a list of recent projects, together with the Open Project and New Project buttons. If this is the first time you have used VB .NET, the list of projects is empty.
3. Click the **New Project** button to create a project. The New Project dialog box opens, as shown in Figure 2-7.

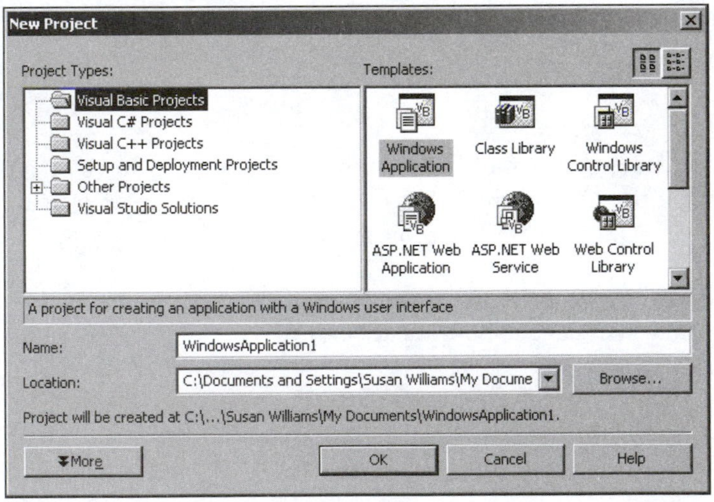

Figure 2-7 The New Project dialog box

4. If it is not already selected, click the **Visual Basic Projects** folder in the Project Types pane. In the Templates pane, you identify the type of application you want to create. For your first project, you will create a console application. A **console application** executes at the command line rather than within the Windows environment.

5. To select the console application template, move the scroll bar in the Templates pane down, and then click the **Console Application** icon.

6. In the Name text box of the New Project dialog box, you specify the name of your project. If this is your first console application, the Name text box contains the default project name ConsoleApplication1. Delete the default project name and type **HelloWorldWideWeb** in the Name text box.

7. In the Location text box, you specify the parent folder for your project. Your project will be saved as a subfolder within the folder you specify. If the folder or subfolders you specify do not already exist, VB .NET creates them for you. For this project, specify the Chap02 folder within your work folder as the location. You can find instructions for creating and naming your work folder in the preface of this text. See Figure 2-8.

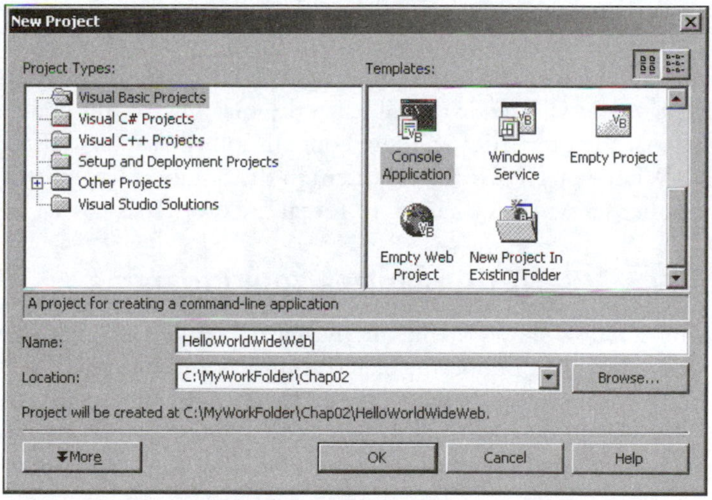

Figure 2-8 Specifying the new project type, template, name, and location

8. Click **OK**. As shown in Figure 2-9, a tabbed page named Module1.vb appears in the document window. The Solution Explorer window and Properties window contain information about your new project.

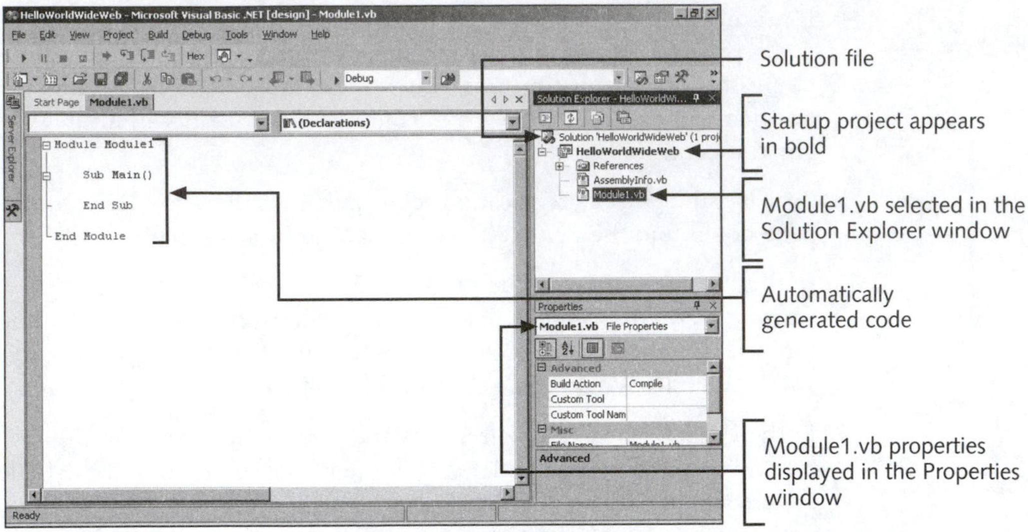

Figure 2-9 Module1.vb, the Solution Explorer window, and the Properties window for the HelloWorldWideWeb project

Take a moment to examine the contents of the Module1.vb document, the Solution Explorer window, and the Properties window. Notice in the Module1.vb document that VB .NET has automatically generated some code for you. This code is based on the Console Application template you selected. You will learn the meaning of this code in the next chapter. Observe also that the Properties window contains information about the file properties of Module1.vb. When you click a different item in the Solution Explorer window, the information in the Properties window changes to reveal the properties of that item.

Understanding the Way VB .NET Organizes Your Programs

The Solution Explorer window shows the hierarchical arrangement of items that comprise the solution you are building. It is important that you understand the way VB .NET organizes these items and the relationships between them. In VB .NET the programs you write are named with a .vb file extension. By default, VB .NET names programs as Module1.vb, Module2.vb, and so forth. You will soon learn how to assign more descriptive names to your programs.

Visual Studio .NET uses projects and solutions to organize and manage programs and other files needed in your application. A **project** is a mechanism for grouping related files. For instance, a project might contain several program files, image files, and other miscellaneous items. A **solution** is a container for one or more projects. The solution file appears at the top of the hierarchy in the Solution Explorer window. When a solution contains more than one project, you must designate the startup project. The **startup project** is the project that will execute first when you run your application. Most of the solutions you create in this text will contain only one project, and by default, VB .NET will designate that project as the startup project. In the Solution Explorer window, the project file designated as the startup project appears in bold text, as shown in Figure 2-9.

Notice in Figure 2-9 that in addition to Module1.vb, the HelloWorldWideWeb project contains a References folder and a program module named AssemblyInfo.vb. These items contain information needed by the system to complete your solution and execute your program. The plus and minus icons to the left of items in the hierarchy indicate that you may expand or collapse these items, respectively.

Using the Text Editor

For this example, you will use the text editor to alter the contents of Module1.vb so that it displays the message "Hello World Wide Web" when the program executes. The Visual Studio .NET text editor (also called the code editor) provides standard text editing capabilities, as well as color-coding, code indentation, and code completion features. By default, Visual Basic keywords appear in blue, comments appear in dark green, and other text appears in black. Notice in Figure 2-9 that blocks of code appear at different levels of indentation. Although indentation is not required for your program to work properly, it improves readability and is considered good programming practice. The text editor helps you adhere to this practice by automatically indenting blocks of code for you as you type.

The text editor includes a code completion feature called **IntelliSense** that helps you complete lines of code by matching words. As you type, the text editor recognizes partial class and method names and suggests possible matches for the name you are typing. To complete the class or method name, you select the appropriate item from a list.

As with most text editors, you can also use shortcut keys to perform standard editing functions such as positioning the insertion point, selecting text, performing cut/copy/paste operations, and searching text.

To modify the contents of the Module1.vb program module:

1. In the Module1.vb document window, position the insertion point at the end of the line that reads "Sub Main ( )" and press **Enter**. A new line opens. Notice that the insertion point automatically indents under the word "Main."
2. Type the following partial line of code: **`Console.`** (Be sure to type the period.)
3. When you type the period at the end of the word Console, a pop-up window appears. See Figure 2-10. This window lists the methods and properties of the Console class, which you will learn more about later. For now, you should recognize that these methods and properties represent choices for completing the partial line of code that you have begun. This code completion feature is called IntelliSense.

TIP You can also type Ctrl+J to list the members of a class for statement completion when editing code.

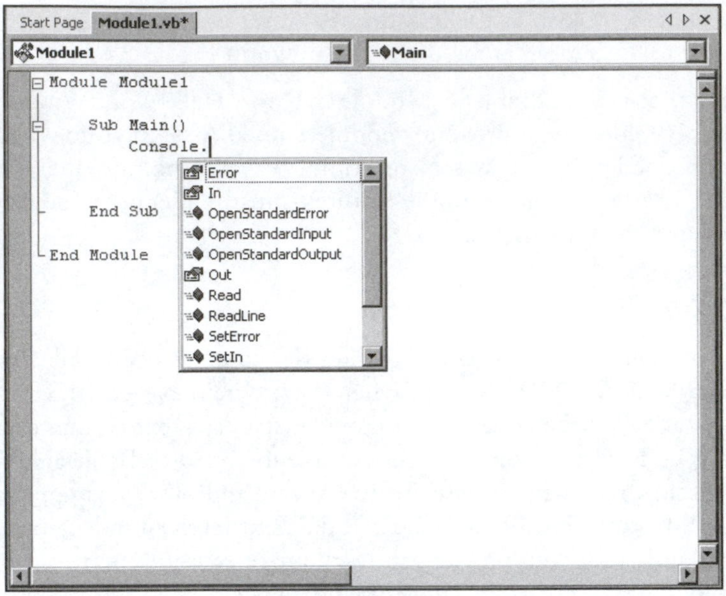

Figure 2-10 The IntelliSense feature

4. In the pop-up window, move the scroll bar down until you see the WriteLine option. Double-click **WriteLine**. Notice that WriteLine is appended to the code you previously typed.
5. Type **("Hello World Wide Web")** immediately after the word WriteLine. As you type, additional messages and windows appear and offer help and advice on completing the line of code, as shown in Figure 2-11. You will learn more about these messages and windows later in this text.
6. Save your work by clicking the **Save** icon on the toolbar.

Modifying the Text Editor Settings

When using the text editor, you may find it helpful to customize some of the settings. For example, you may want to change the font type, font size, or color of the text in the code editor window.

To change the font size of the text in the code editor window:

1. Click **Tools** on the menu bar, and then click **Options**. The Options dialog box appears.
2. If it is not already selected, click the **Environment** folder.
3. If necessary, click the **Environment** folder a second time to reveal its contents.
4. Click **Fonts and Colors**.

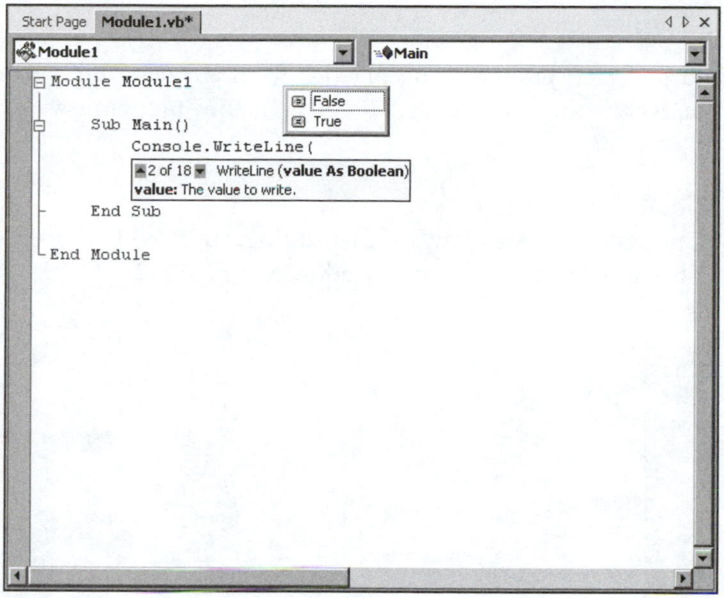

Figure 2-11 Additional IntelliSense messages

5. If necessary, select **Text Editor** in the Show settings for list box.
6. In the Size list box, select **12**, and then click **OK**. The text in the code editor window changes to a 12-point font.

It is often helpful to display line numbers in the text editor. This enables you to easily refer to specific lines of code.

To display line numbers within the source code:

1. Click **Tools** on the menu bar, and then click **Options**. The Options dialog box appears.
2. If it is not already selected, click the **Text Editor** folder.
3. If necessary, click the **Text Editor** folder a second time to reveal its contents, and then click the **Basic** subfolder that appears beneath it.
4. Click the **Line numbers** check box to turn this feature on, and then click **OK**. The source code in the text editor window now includes line numbers.

You can use a similar approach to customize many settings within the Microsoft Development Environment.

NOTE: The figures in this chapter show the default text editor settings (font size of 10 points and no line numbers).

Renaming Module1.vb

It is a common and preferred programming practice to assign descriptive names to the programs you write. Recall that by default, VB .NET names programs as Module1.vb, Module2.vb, and so on.

To rename Module1.vb:

1. In the Solution Explorer window, click **Module1.vb**. The file properties of Module1.vb appear in the Properties window. See Figure 2-12.

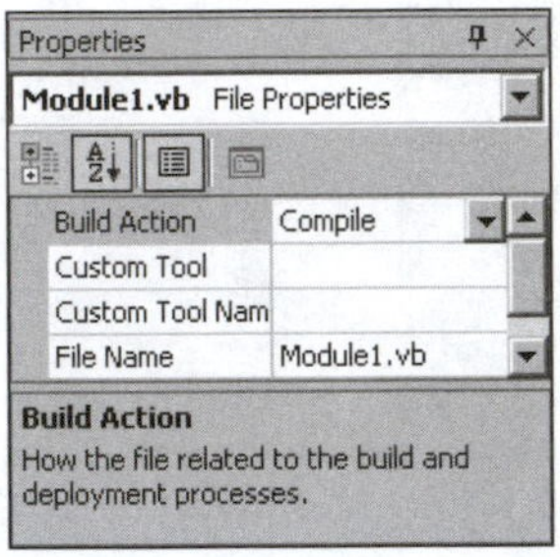

Figure 2-12 The file properties of Module1.vb

2. Use the scroll bar in the Properties window to locate the File Name property. Click the **File Name** property in the Properties window. In the text box to the right of the File Name property, delete the default file name Module1.vb, type **HelloWorldWideWeb.vb**, and press **Enter**. This renames the file. See Figure 2-13.

Figure 2-13 Renaming Module1.vb as HelloWorldWideWeb.vb

TIP: An alternate way to change the file name is to right-click the file name in the Solution Explorer window, and then use the Rename option to rename the file.

3. You see that the file name now reads HelloWorldWideWeb.vb in the File Name property box and in the Solution Explorer window. The tab name in the document window also changes to HelloWorldWideWeb.vb. See Figure 2-14.

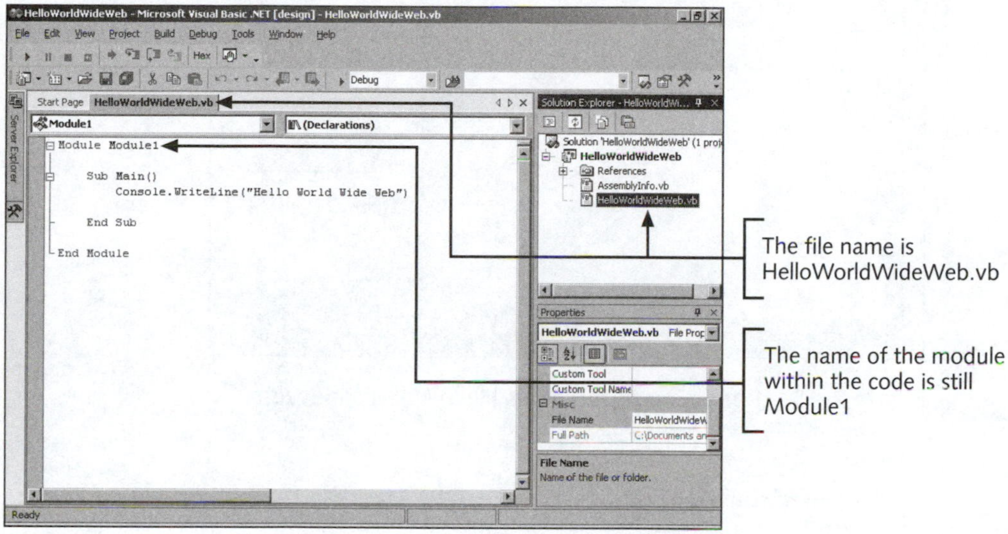

Figure 2-14 The MDE after renaming Module1.vb as HelloWorldWideWeb.vb

4. Notice that changing the file name had no effect on the code in the HelloWorldWideWeb.vb document. The first line of code still reads `Module Module1`, indicating that within the source code, this program is still identified as Module1. Although it is not required for your program to work properly, it is good programming practice to rename this module in the source code with an appropriate, descriptive name.
5. To change the module name in the source code, click in the document window. On the first line of code, delete the word **`Module1`** and type **`HelloWorldWideWeb`**, as shown in Figure 2-15.
6. On the toolbar, click the **Save** icon to save your changes to HelloWorldWideWeb.vb.

Setting the Startup Object

You are almost ready to compile and execute your console application. However, because you changed the module name within the source code, you must also change the project properties to identify HelloWorldWideWeb as the startup object. The **startup object** is the module where execution begins when VB .NET runs your application.

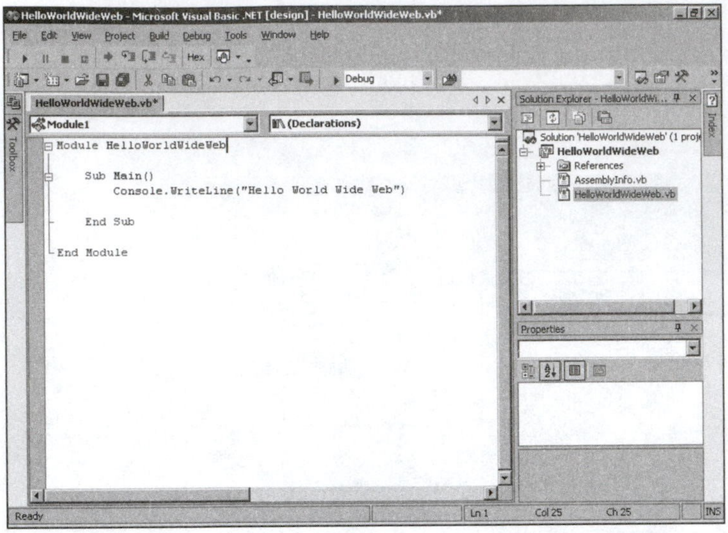

Figure 2-15 Renaming Module1 as HelloWorldWideWeb

To set the startup object:

1. In the Solution Explorer window, right-click the **HelloWorldWideWeb** project icon.
2. On the shortcut menu, click **Properties**. The HelloWorldWideWeb Property Pages dialog box opens, as shown in Figure 2-16.

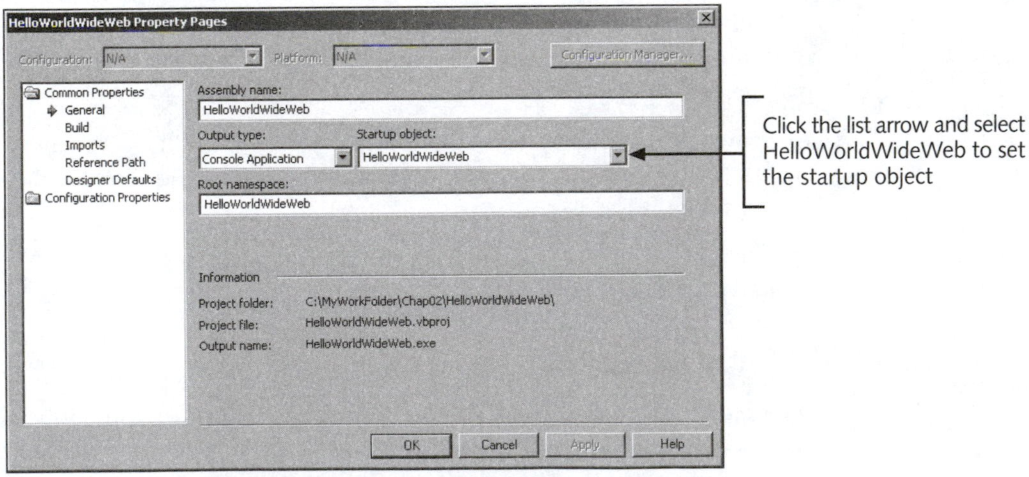

Figure 2-16 The HelloWorldWideWeb Property Pages dialog box

3. Click the **Startup object** list arrow, click **HelloWorldWideWeb**, and then click **OK**.

TIP

An alternate way to display the HelloWorldWideWeb Property Pages dialog box is to select the HelloWorldWideWeb project icon in the Solution Explorer window, and then click either the Properties icon in the Solution Explorer window or the Property Pages icon in the Properties window. See Figure 2-17.

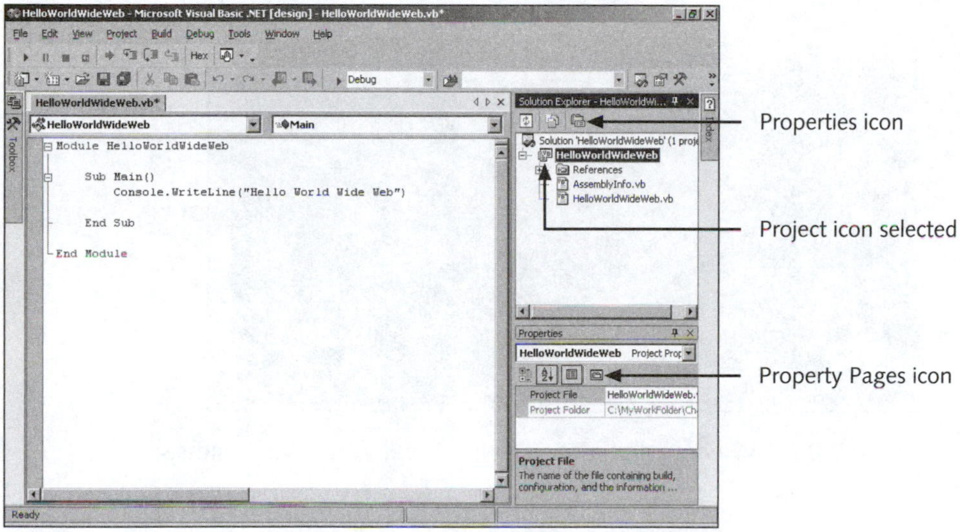

Figure 2-17 Alternate ways to display the Property Pages dialog box

You are now ready to compile and execute your program.

Compiling and Executing a VB .NET Program

You can compile and execute your program in several different ways. You can use options on the Build and Debug menus or toolbars, or use shortcut key combinations. The approach you use is simply a matter of preference. For now, you will use menu options.

To compile and execute your program:

1. Click **Debug** on the menu bar, and then click **Start Without Debugging**.
2. If you have not made an error, an Output window appears in the lower portion of the screen and informs you that VB .NET successfully built your application. See Figure 2-18. Then a window opens and displays the message "Hello World Wide Web," as shown in Figure 2-19.

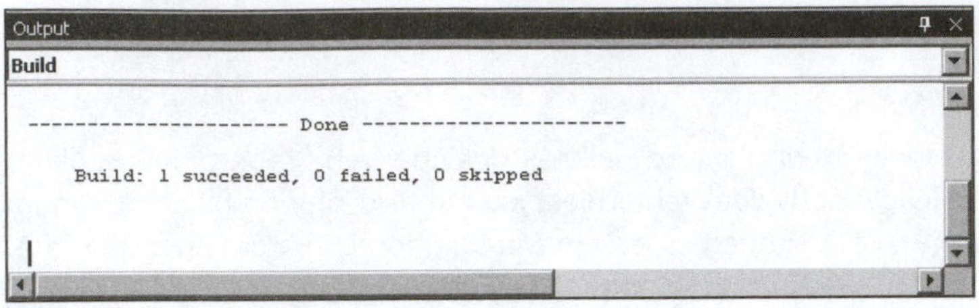

Figure 2-18 Output window

Figure 2-19 Window displaying "Hello World Wide Web" message

TIP If you made an error, you will see a message box informing you that there were build errors and asking you if you wish to continue, as shown in Figure 2-20. Click No to view information about the errors. Error messages appear in a Task List pane in the lower portion of the screen, as shown in Figure 2-21. You can jump directly from an error message to the line of code that caused the problem by double-clicking the error message.

Figure 2-20 Build error message box

3. Close the window displaying the "Hello World Wide Web" message by clicking its **Close** button.
4. Close the Output window.

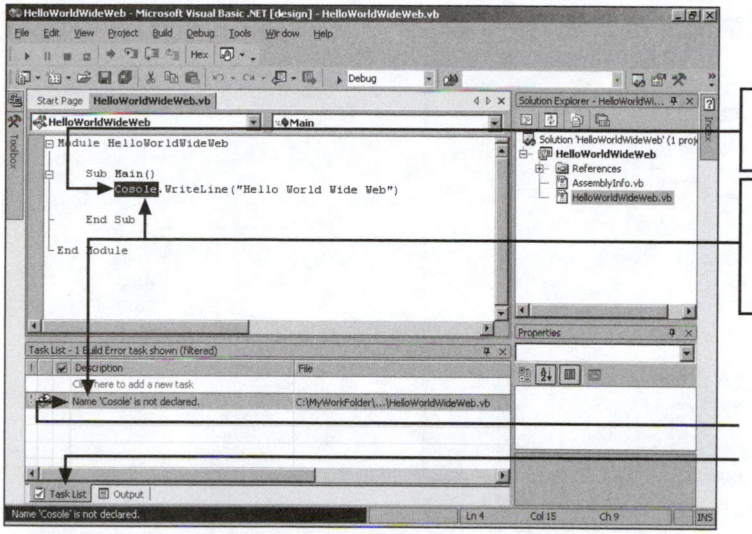
The word Console is misspelled
Double-clicking error message takes you to the line of code that caused the problem
Error message
Task List pane

Figure 2-21 An error message in the Task List pane

USING THE VISUAL FORM DESIGNER

Although you will create a number of console applications as you work through this text, you will also create many Windows applications. A **Windows application** is one that runs in the Windows environment. When you create Windows applications, you will use a visual form editor in addition to the text editor.

A visual editor allows you to select icons representing various components (such as buttons, text boxes, and lists), and then place and arrange them on the screen. As you manipulate these icons, VB .NET generates the programming statements required to build the form that you see. As you reposition icons or change their properties, the code is dynamically updated to reflect your changes. Using the visual editor, you can quickly create forms for Windows applications, such as the one shown in Figure 2-22.

The visual form editor in the MDE is known as the Windows Forms Designer. When the Windows Forms Designer is active, the Toolbox contains visual components such as text boxes, buttons, and labels. You select elements from the Toolbox to dynamically design input forms. You use the Properties window to adjust the properties of components on your form, such as changing the color of a button or the font within a text box. As you arrange and manipulate these items, VB .NET dynamically generates the source code that makes your form work. In this chapter you will learn how to create a simple Windows application using the Windows Forms Designer. You will learn much more about the Windows Forms Designer in Chapter 10.

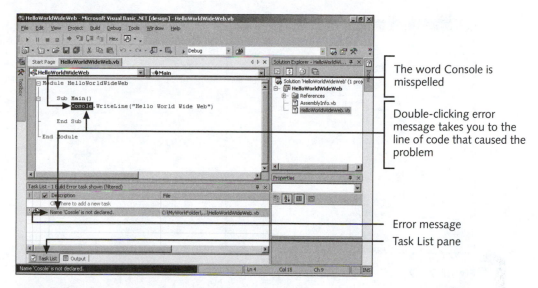

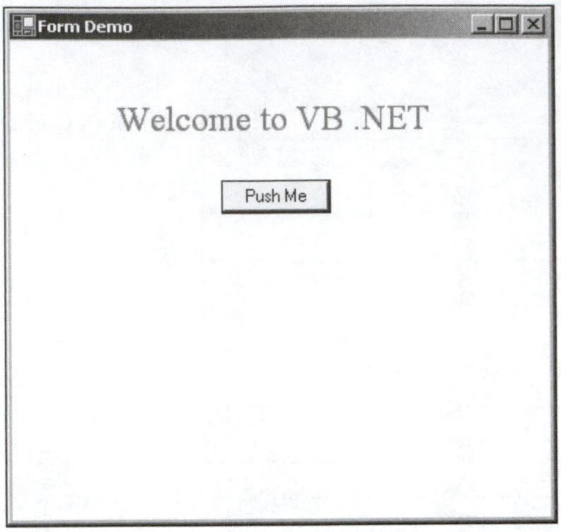

Figure 2-22 A Windows application form

Creating a Windows Application

You will now create a VB .NET project for a Windows application. You will use the Windows Forms Designer to create an input form for the application. Recall that when you create a project, you must identify the project type and template you want to use, and specify the project name and location.

To create a Windows application:

1. Click the **Start Page** tab in the document window.
2. If it is not already selected, click the **Get Started** link.
3. Click the **New Project** button. The New Project dialog box appears.
4. In the New Project dialog box, click the **Visual Basic Projects** folder in the Project Types pane, if necessary. Click the **Windows Application** icon in the Templates pane.
5. If this is your first Windows application, the Name text box will contain the default project name WindowsApplication1. Delete the default project name and type **FormDemo** in the Name text box.
6. In the Location text box, specify the parent folder for your project. You may accept the default location or use the Browse button to select an alternate location.
7. Click **OK**. As shown in Figure 2-23, the Windows Forms Designer appears as a tabbed document labeled Form1.vb [Design]. By default, the Windows Forms Designer names your forms Form1.vb, Form2.vb, and so on.

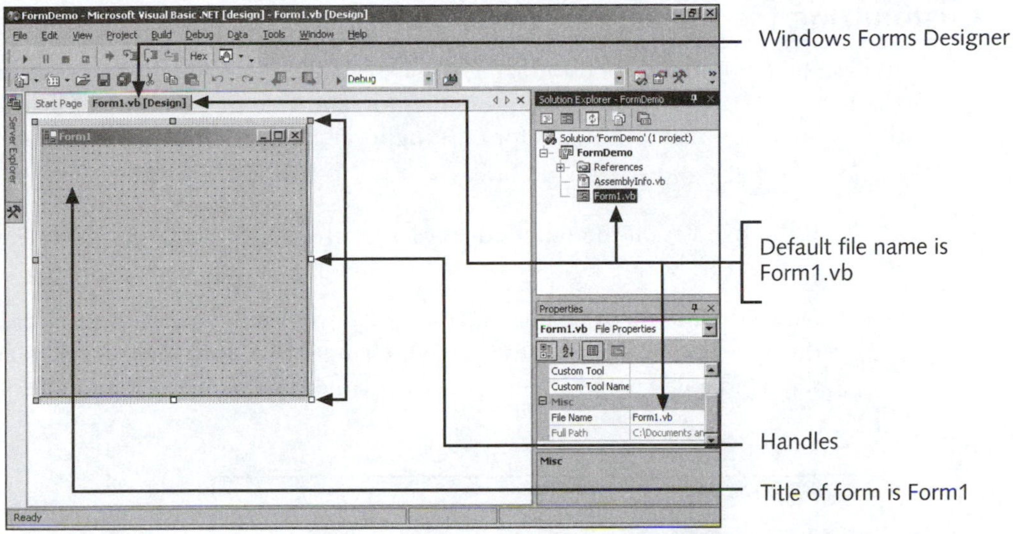

Figure 2-23 The Windows Forms Designer

Notice that the Solution Explorer window contains information about this project and its associated elements. The Properties window shows the properties of the Form1.vb file. The title of the form is Form1—the same as the .vb file name. Notice also the appearance of the form. The background contains tick marks arranged in a grid to help you align the components you place on the form. This grid is visible only while you are designing the form, and will not be seen when your application executes.

Along the outer edges of the form you see small, white boxes called handles. A **handle** is a special type of button that allows you to resize a form. When you move the mouse over one of the handles, the appearance of the mouse pointer changes to a double arrow. When you see the double arrow, you can resize the form by clicking and dragging the handle.

You will now complete steps to customize the form so that it appears as shown in Figure 2-22. First, you will change the size, background color, and title of the form. Then you will add a welcome message and button to the form. Finally, you will complete steps to ensure that when your program is running and you click the button, a thank-you message appears in a pop-up window, as shown in Figure 2-24.

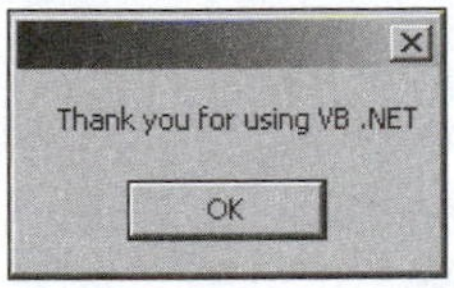

Figure 2-24 Thank-you message generated by the FormDemo program

Customizing the Appearance of a Form

You have many options for customizing the appearance of a form. In this chapter, you will learn how to change the size, background color, and title of a form. In Chapter 10, you will explore additional techniques for creating more complex forms.

To change the size of a form:

1. If the handles on the outer edges of a form are not visible, click inside the form to select it.
2. Move the mouse over the handle in the lower-right corner of the form. When the appearance of the mouse pointer changes to a double arrow, click and drag the handle down and to the right to enlarge the form. See Figure 2-25.

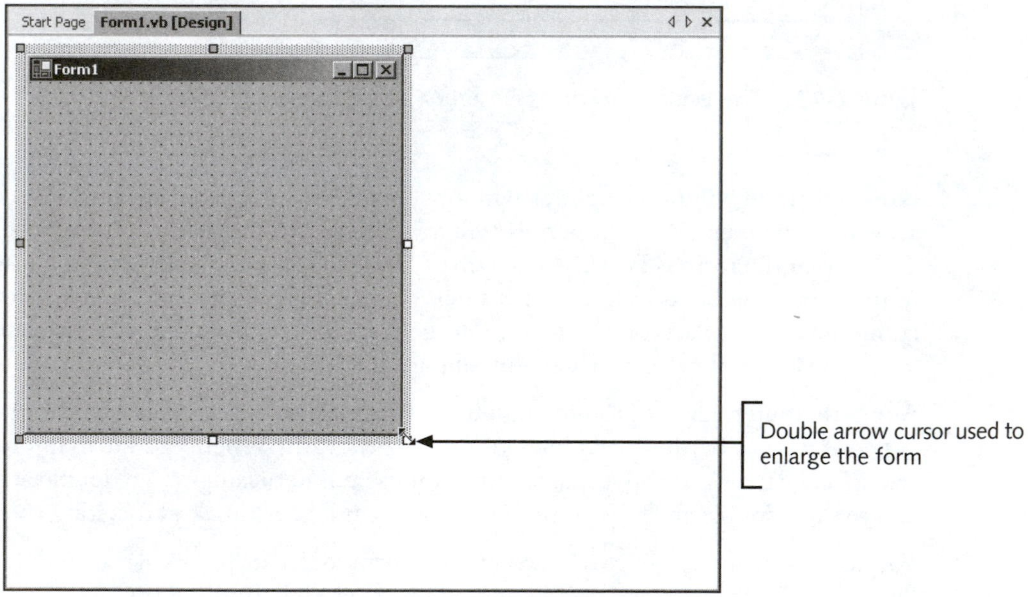

Figure 2-25 Enlarging the form

To change the title and background color of a form:

1. Make sure that the form is selected.

An item on a form, including the form itself, is selected when its handles are visible.

2. Scroll through the Properties window until you see the Text property. Click the **Text** property to select it. Delete the default value (Form1), type **Form Demo**, and press **Enter**, as shown in Figure 2-26. The title of the form changes to Form Demo.

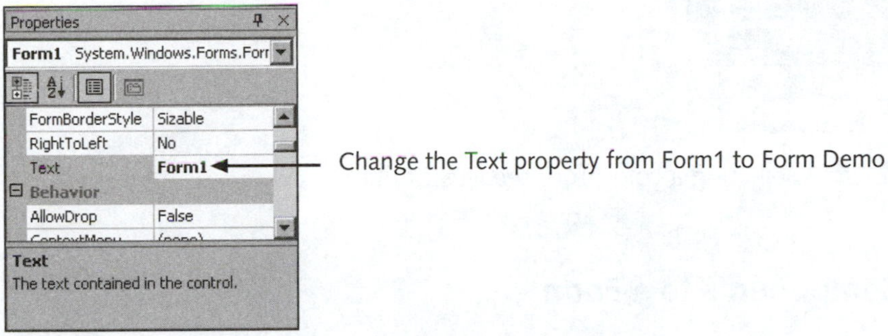

Figure 2-26 Changing the title of the form

3. Scroll up in the Properties window until you locate the BackColor property. Click the **BackColor** property to select it. A list arrow appears next to the current value of this property, as shown in Figure 2-27.

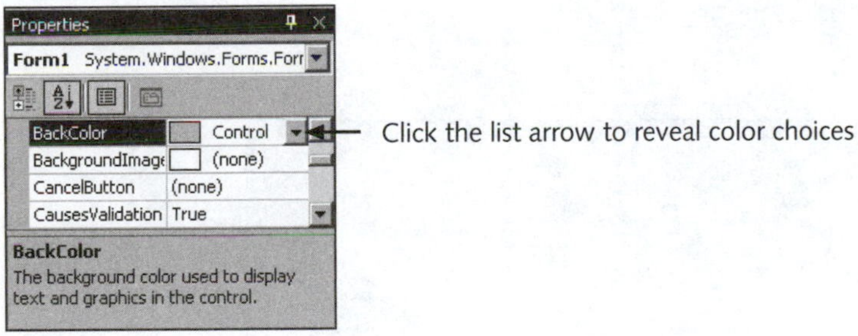

Figure 2-27 Changing the background color of the form

4. Click the **list arrow** to see the color choices, which are grouped into three different sets: Custom, Web, and System. Click the **Custom** tab, and then click the **white** color square. See Figure 2-28. The background of the form changes to white.

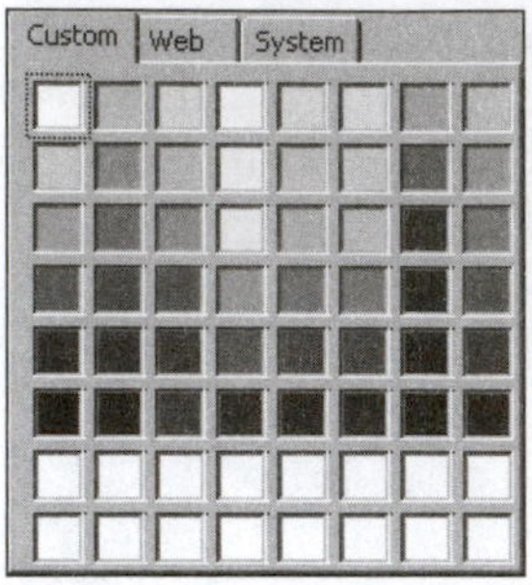

Figure 2-28 Selecting a color from the Custom tab

Adding Components to a Form

To add components to a form, you need the Toolbox. If you have followed the steps in this chapter, the Toolbox appears as a hidden window on the left side of your screen. If you do not see the hidden Toolbox window, click the Toolbox icon on the toolbar to open it.

TIP: An alternate way to open the Toolbox is to click View on the menu bar, and then click Toolbox.

You can now "pin" the Toolbox as a hidden window by clicking its Auto Hide icon. Your screen should resemble Figure 2-29.

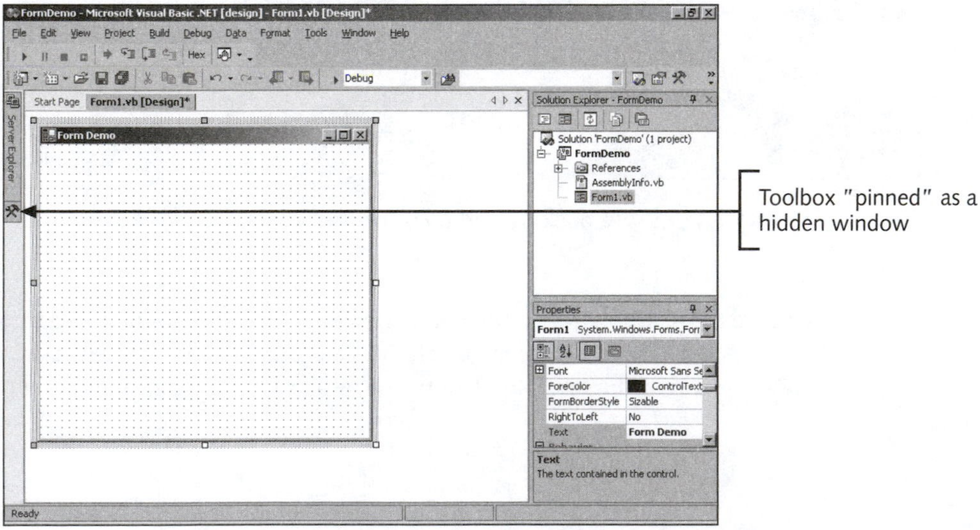

Figure 2-29 The MDE after making changes to the form and pinning the Toolbox

To add a welcome message to your form:

1. Position the mouse over the **Toolbox** tab to reveal its contents. You see a number of components, including labels, buttons, and text boxes, as shown in Figure 2-30.

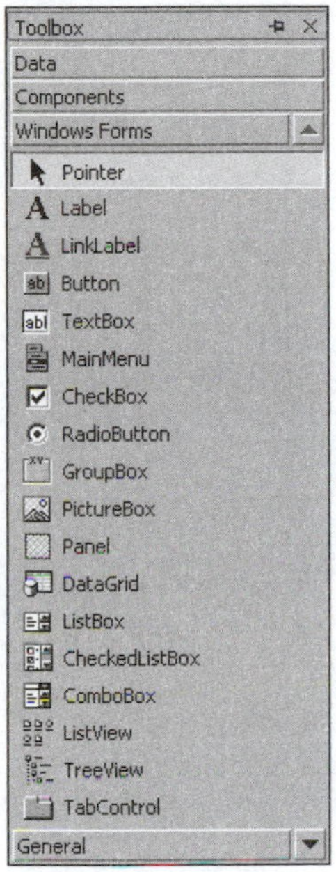

Figure 2-30 Contents of the Toolbox when the Windows Forms Designer is active

2. Double-click **Label** to add a label to the form, and then move the mouse toward the center of the screen so that the Toolbox slides back into its hidden position. You see a label on the form. By default, the label text is "Label1".
3. Drag the handle on the lower-right corner of the label down and to the right to enlarge the label, as shown in Figure 2-31.
4. Scroll through the Properties window until you locate the Text property. Select the **Text** property and delete the default value (Label1). Type **Welcome to VB .NET**, and then press **Enter**.
5. To change the color of the label text, select the **ForeColor** property in the Properties window. A list arrow appears next to the current value of this property. Click the **list arrow** to see the color choices. Click the **Custom** tab, and then click the **red** color square. The label text changes to red.
6. To change the label font, select the **Font** property in the Properties window. A button containing an ellipsis (...) appears to the right of the current value of the Font property. See Figure 2-32.

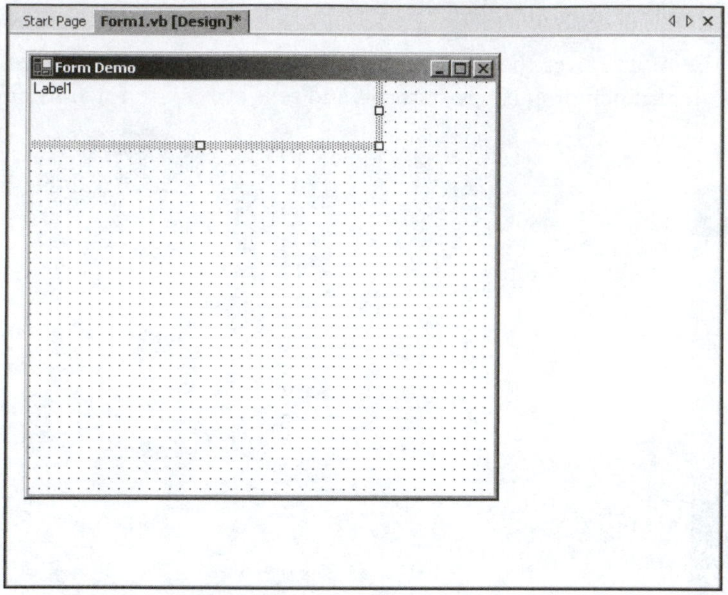

Figure 2-31 Enlarging the label

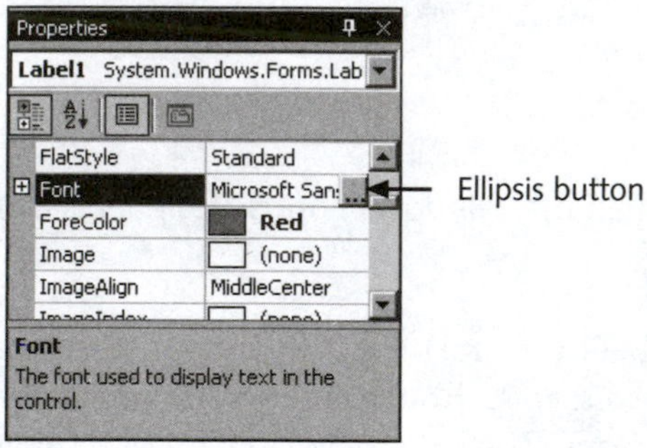

Figure 2-32 The Font property and ellipsis button

7. Click the **ellipsis (...)** button. You see a Font dialog box, as shown in Figure 2-33. In the Font pane click **Times New Roman**, and in the Size pane click **18**. Click **OK** to apply the changes and close the dialog box. The label font reflects your changes.

8. To center the label text within the area occupied by the label, select the **TextAlign** property in the Properties window. Click the **list arrow** in the text box to the right of this property. You see a box with nine rectangles, as shown in Figure 2-34. These rectangles represent the position of the text within the label component—upper left, upper center, upper right, and so on. Click the rectangle in the center of the box to indicate that you want the text centered in the label.

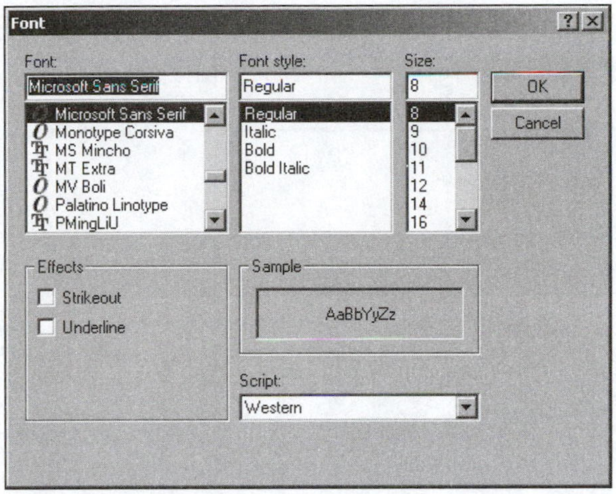

Figure 2-33 The Font dialog box

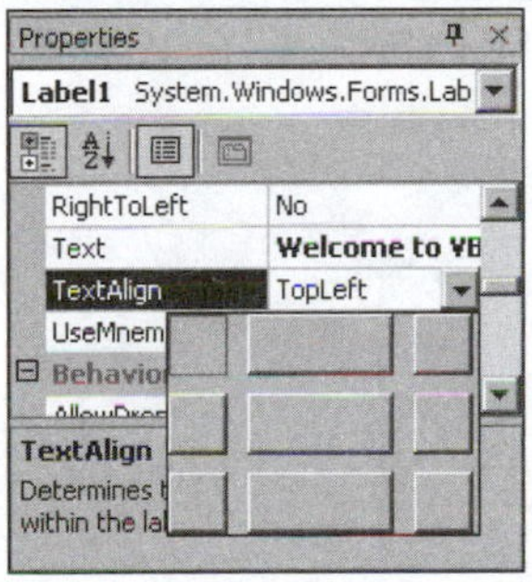

Figure 2-34 Setting the TextAlign property

9. Point to the label. The mouse pointer changes to a four-headed arrow, as shown in Figure 2-35. When this pointer (referred to as the move pointer) is visible, you can drag a component to a new position on the grid.
10. Drag the label to the position shown in Figure 2-36.

TIP

To center the label horizontally in the form, you can also select the label and then click Format on the menu bar. Point to Center in Form, and then click Horizontally.

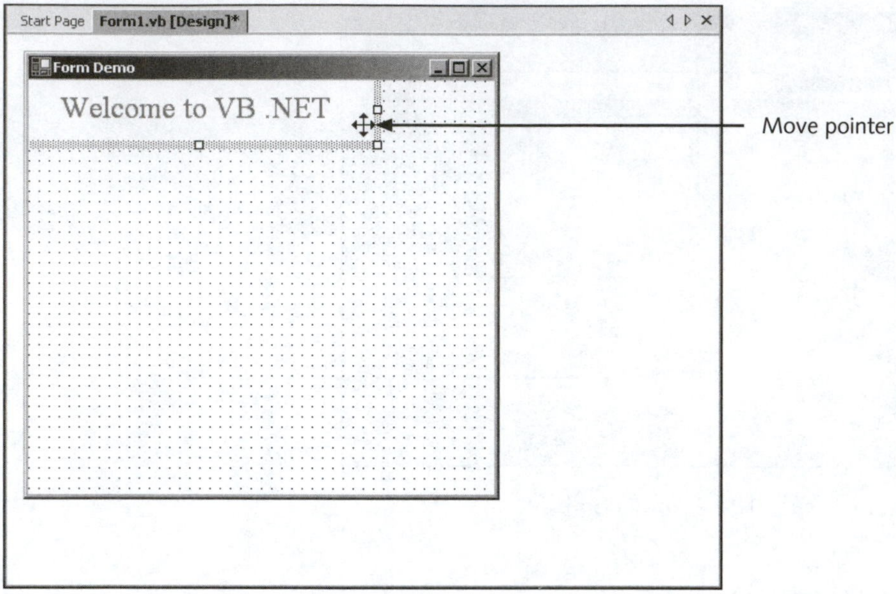

Figure 2-35 Dragging the label to a new position

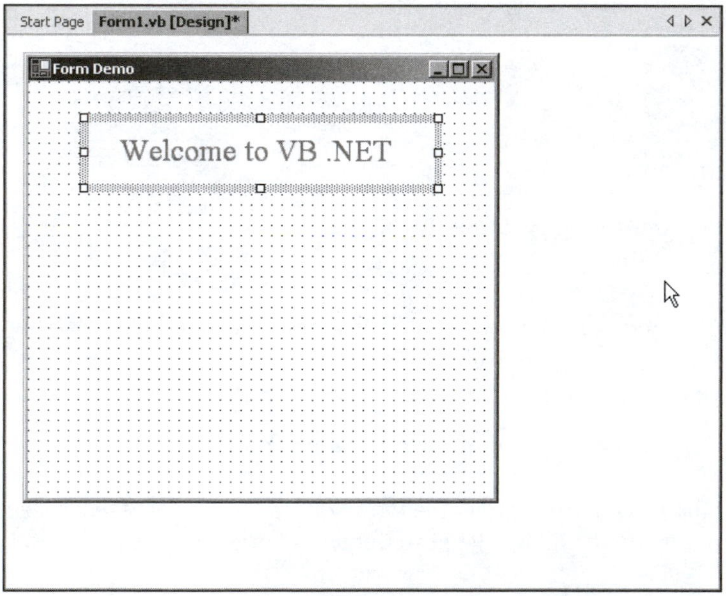

Figure 2-36 The form with the label in its new position

To add a button to the form:

1. Point to the **Toolbox** tab to reveal the Toolbox. Double-click **Button**, and then move the mouse toward the center of the screen so that the Toolbox returns to its hidden position.

TIP

To add a component to a form, you can also click that component in the Toolbox. When you move the mouse toward the center of the screen, a pointer appears that corresponds to the component type you selected. Drag to draw the component on the form.

2. Drag the button to center it on the form just below the welcome message. See Figure 2-37.

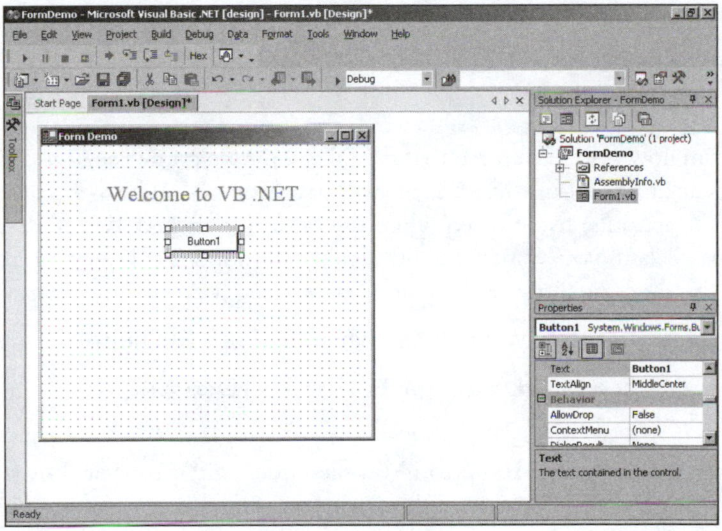

Figure 2-37 Adding the button to the form

Notice that the button is the currently selected component (its handles are visible), and thus its properties appear in the Properties window.

3. In the Properties window, select the **Text** property, change its value to **Push Me**, and press **Enter**.

4. Select the **BackColor** property and change it to yellow or another color of your choice. The initial design of your form is now complete, and appears in Figure 2-38.

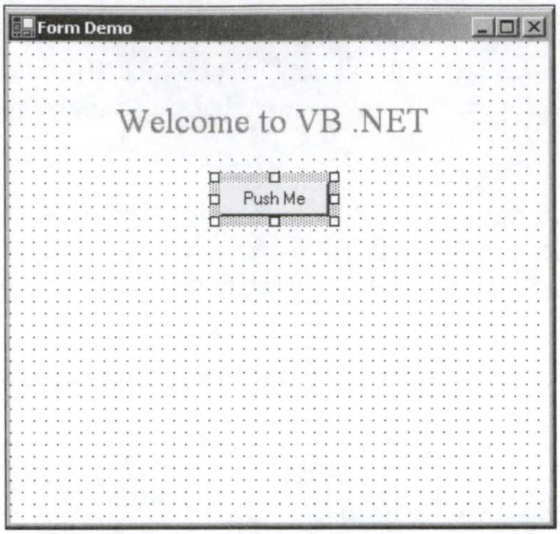

Figure 2-38 Completed design of Form1

If you run your form now, you see a form that contains your welcome message and Push Me button. However, clicking the Push Me button will have no effect. This is because you have not yet identified the action(s) to be taken when the button is clicked. Recall that when the Push Me button is clicked, you want your program to respond by displaying a thank-you message. To build this functionality, use the text editor to add code to your program.

To add code that displays a thank-you message when the Push Me button is clicked:

1. If it is not already selected, select the **Form1.vb [Design]** page in the document window.
2. Double-click the **Push Me** button. You see code similar to that shown in Figure 2-39. VB .NET generated this code for you based on the actions you completed in the Windows Forms Designer. The meaning of this code will be explained in later chapters of this text.

   Notice that the insertion point in the code window is located within a block of code that begins with the words `Private Sub Button1_Click`. This line of code is the beginning of the procedure that is responsible for responding to a click of the Push Me button.
3. At the insertion point, type **`MessageBox.Show("Thank you for using VB .NET")`**, as shown in Figure 2-40. Note the behavior of the IntelliSense feature as you type.

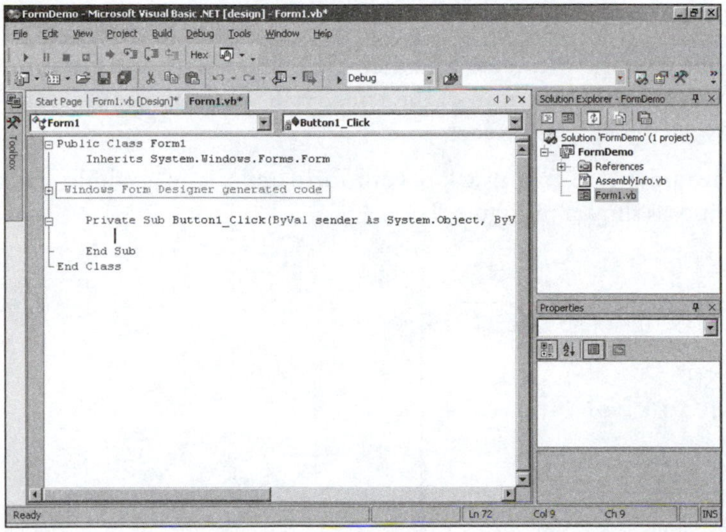

Figure 2-39 Code generated by the Windows Forms Designer

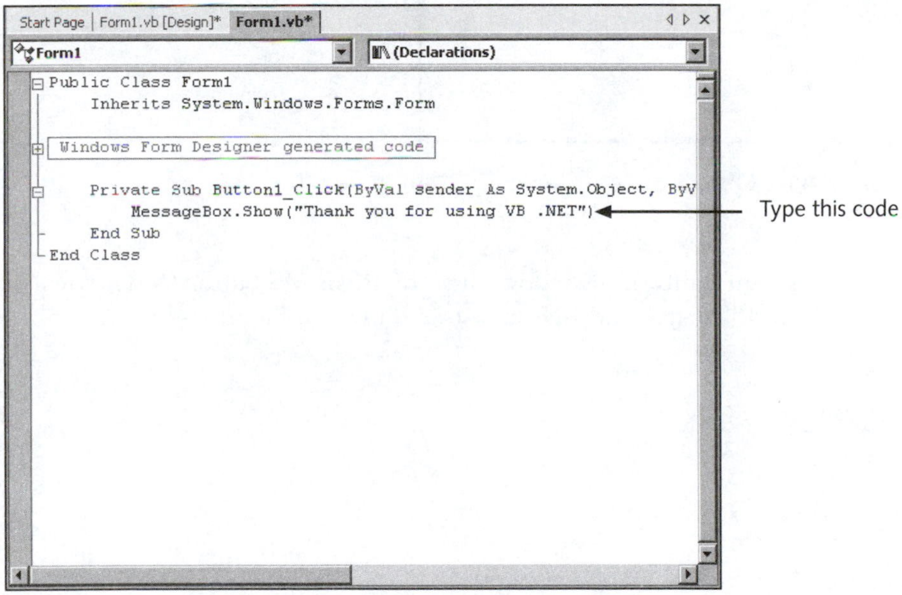

Figure 2-40 Adding the code to make the button work

4. Observe that the tabs for the code editor window and the Windows Forms Designer window both include an asterisk (*). The asterisk indicates that the contents of these windows have changed since they were last saved. To save the contents of both windows, click the **Save All** icon on the menu bar.

To compile and execute your program:

1. Click **Debug** on the menu bar, and then click **Start Without Debugging**. An Output window at the bottom of the screen tells you whether VB .NET was able to successfully build your project.
2. If you have not made any mistakes, your form appears in a window entitled FormDemo, as shown in Figure 2-41.

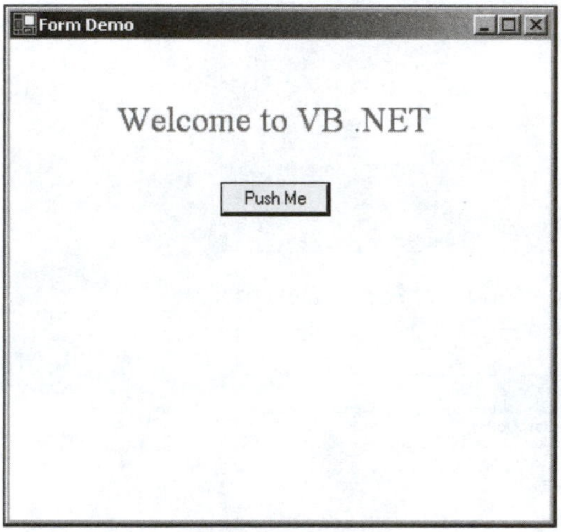

Figure 2-41 Output of FormDemo

3. In the FormDemo window, click the **Push Me** button. A window containing your thank-you message appears, as shown in Figure 2-42.

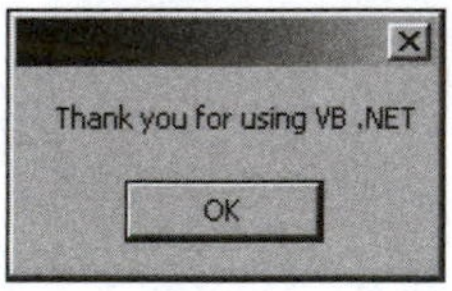

Figure 2-42 The thank-you message

4. Click **OK** to close the window, and then click the **Close** button in the FormDemo window to close your form. Also close the Output window.

You now have an idea of the power and flexibility of the VB .NET development environment. You have seen how the Toolbox and Properties window work together to help you create applications quickly and easily. Next you will learn about two other powerful features of the VB .NET development environment: the debugging tool and the help facility.

EXPLORING THE DEBUGGING TOOL

Visual Studio .NET includes a powerful tool commonly known as a debugger. A **debugger** helps you isolate errors that keep your program from running as intended. The debugger has many features, only one of which is introduced in this chapter. You will learn more about the debugger later in this text.

In this chapter, you will learn how to use the debugger to set breakpoints. A **breakpoint** is a flag that tells the debugger to temporarily suspend execution of your program at a particular point. While program execution is suspended, you can view information that may help you determine the source of a problem. In Chapter 4, you will learn techniques for troubleshooting a program after a breakpoint has been reached.

Getting Started with the Debugger

Before you begin exploring the VB .NET debugger, you should understand its role. A debugger is intended to help you identify errors in your program that occur while the program is running. The debugger cannot help you find coding errors that prevent your program from being built successfully. Stated another way, VB .NET must be able to successfully build your program before you can use the debugger.

Setting Breakpoints

Recall that a breakpoint is a flag in your program that tells the debugger to pause execution of the program. For this program, you will set a breakpoint at the line of code that displays the thank-you message.

To set a breakpoint:

1. In the code window, right-click the **MessageBox.Show** statement. A menu appears, as shown in Figure 2-43.
2. Click **Insert Breakpoint** on the shortcut menu. The code editor window appears, as shown in Figure 2-44. Notice that the MessageBox.Show statement is highlighted, indicating that the breakpoint has been set.

When you execute your program in debug mode, program execution will temporarily be suspended just before this line of code.

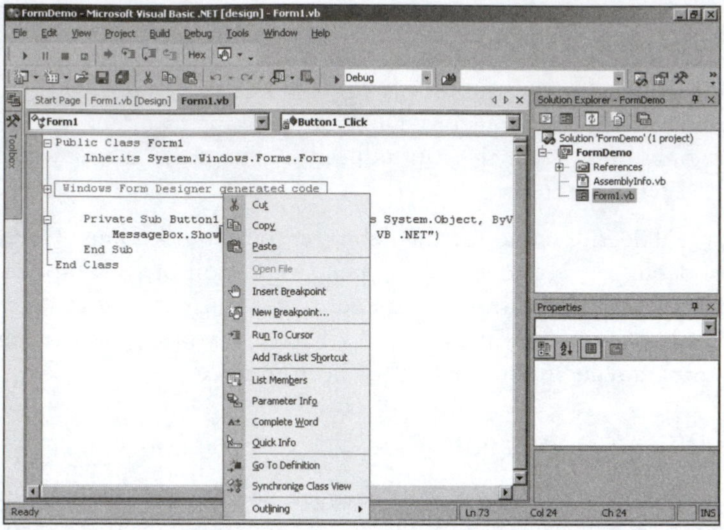

Figure 2-43 The menu for inserting a breakpoint

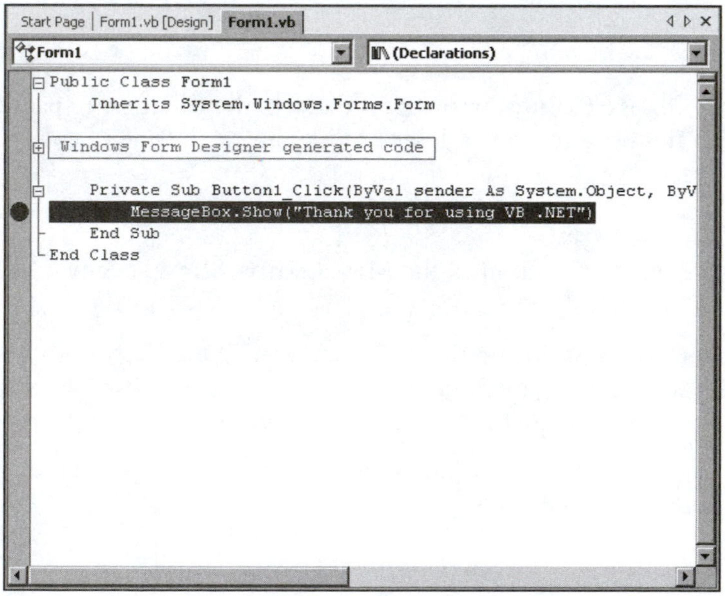

Figure 2-44 Setting a breakpoint in the code window

To execute your program in debug mode:

1. Click **Debug** on the menu bar, and then click **Start**. Several windows containing information used by the debugger open along the bottom of the screen, and then your form appears.
2. Click the **Push Me** button on your form. The code editor window opens. Notice that the MessageBox.Show statement is highlighted in yellow, indicating that the breakpoint has been reached. See Figure 2-45. At this point, execution of your program is suspended. Later in this text you will learn how to perform other steps to isolate program errors while execution is suspended.

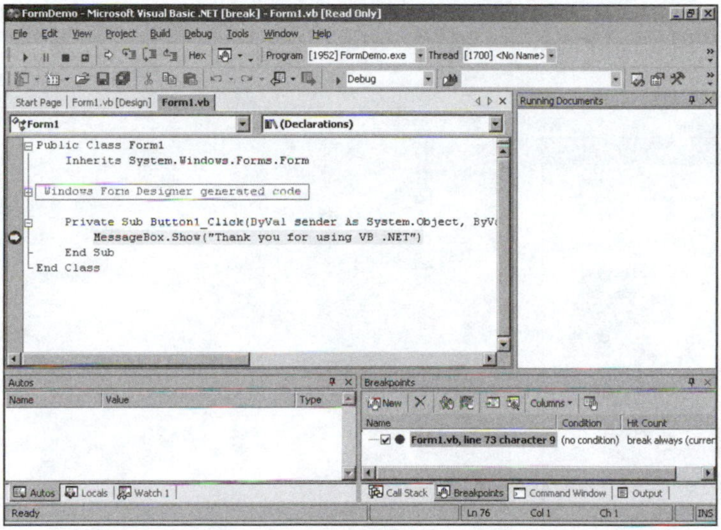

Figure 2-45 Program execution suspended at the breakpoint

3. To resume program execution, click **Debug** on the menu bar, and then click **Continue**. The MessageBox.Show statement executes, and the window containing your thank-you message appears.
4. Click **OK** to close the window, and then close the FormDemo program execution window by clicking its **Close** button.
5. Close the Output window by clicking its **Close** button.
6. On the File menu, click **Close Solution** to close the project.

EXPLORING THE HELP FACILITY

The VB .NET development environment includes extensive help facilities that enable you to access help in many different ways. As with most Windows applications, you can search for help on a specific item, browse a table of contents, or scroll through an alphabetized index of topics. In addition, VB .NET includes two other powerful help features—dynamic help and context-sensitive help—that may be new to you. In this section, you will explore the help facilities of the VB .NET development environment and learn how to use many of their features.

Accessing Help

You can access most of the help features of VB .NET through options on the Help menu. The Help menu is shown in Figure 2-46.

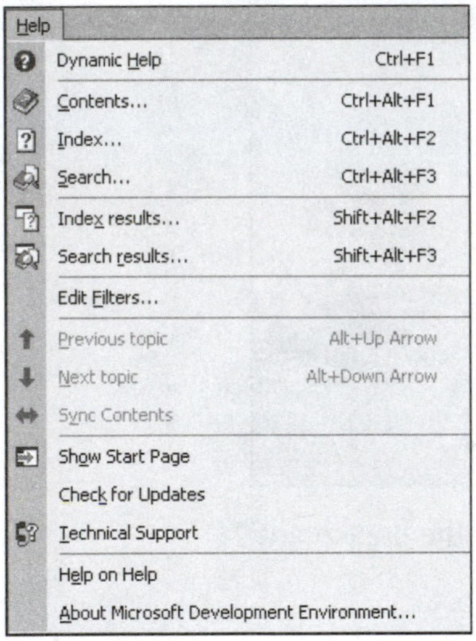

Figure 2-46 The Help menu

When you select an option from the Help menu, a corresponding window opens within the IDE.

To make sure the windows you see resemble the ones in this text as closely as possible:

1. In the document window, close all documents except the Start Page.
2. Close all tool windows, including the Solution Explorer and Properties windows. Your screen should resemble Figure 2-47.

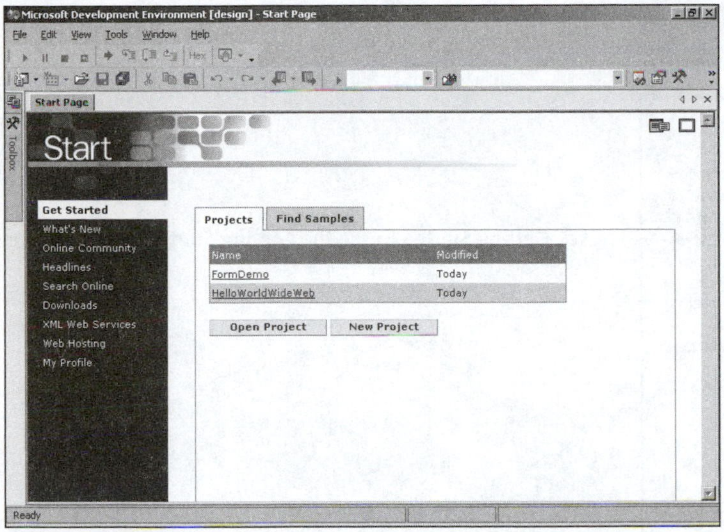

Figure 2-47 The MDE with only the Start Page document open

Exploring the Contents Option on the Help Menu

The Contents option on the Help menu displays a list of help topics in a format that resembles a table of contents.

To open the Contents window:

1. On the Help menu, click **Contents**. The Contents window appears.
2. If necessary, select **Visual Basic** from the Filtered by text box.

TIP Recall that Visual Studio .NET includes several languages other than Visual Basic. Setting the value in this text box to Visual Basic limits the scope of help topics to those associated with Visual Basic. If you change this value, you will see help topics associated with other Visual Studio .NET languages.

3. Notice that the Contents window organizes help topics in a hierarchical fashion. Plus and minus signs to the left of nodes in the hierarchy identify topics that you can expand or collapse, respectively. Expanding a node reveals a list of additional subtopics and documents that pertain to that item. Collapsing a node hides those details. Click the **plus sign** to the left of the Visual Studio .NET node to expand the node, and then click the **plus sign** to the left of the Visual Basic and Visual C# subnode to see a list of its subtopics. You see a hierarchy similar to the one shown in Figure 2-48. The nodes in the hierarchy you see may vary slightly from Figure 2-48 depending on the settings for your computer.
4. You can click any item in the hierarchy to display a page in the document window. For example, click **Getting Started**. Information about this topic appears in a tabbed page in the document window, as shown in Figure 2-49.

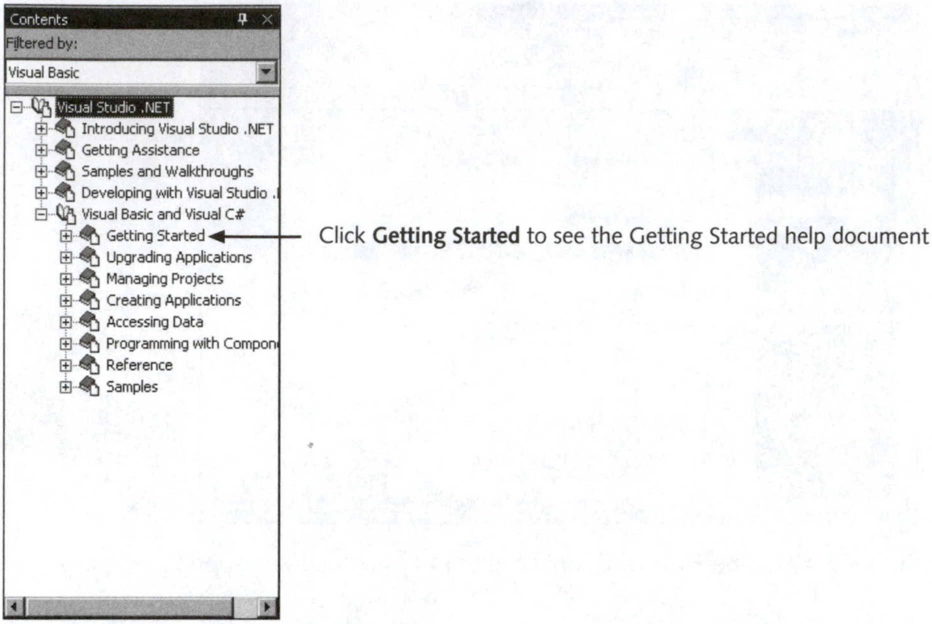

Figure 2-48 Expanding the hierarchy of topics in the Contents window

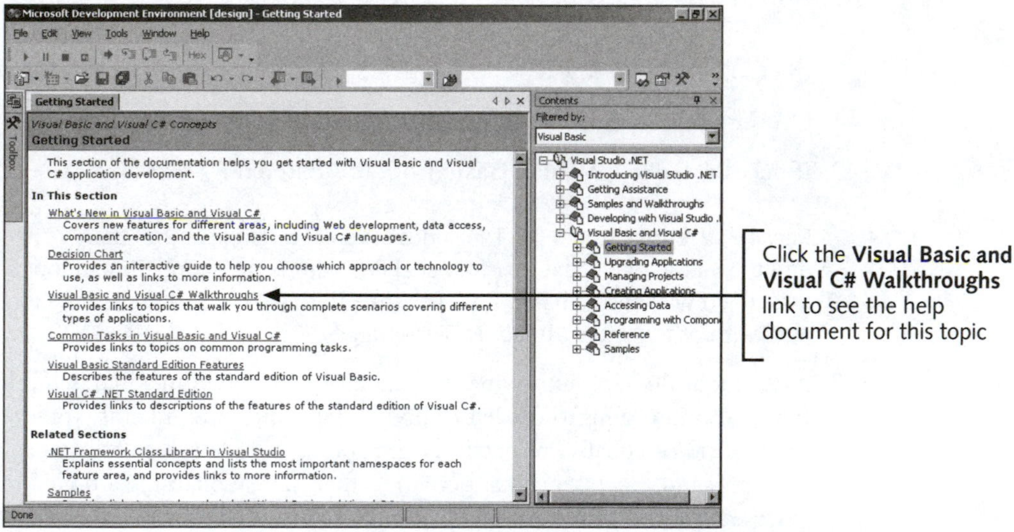

Figure 2-49 The Getting Started help document

5. You can click links within the document window to navigate to pages that contain more detailed information. For example, click the **Visual Basic and Visual C# Walkthroughs** link. The help page appears in the document window, as shown in Figure 2-50.

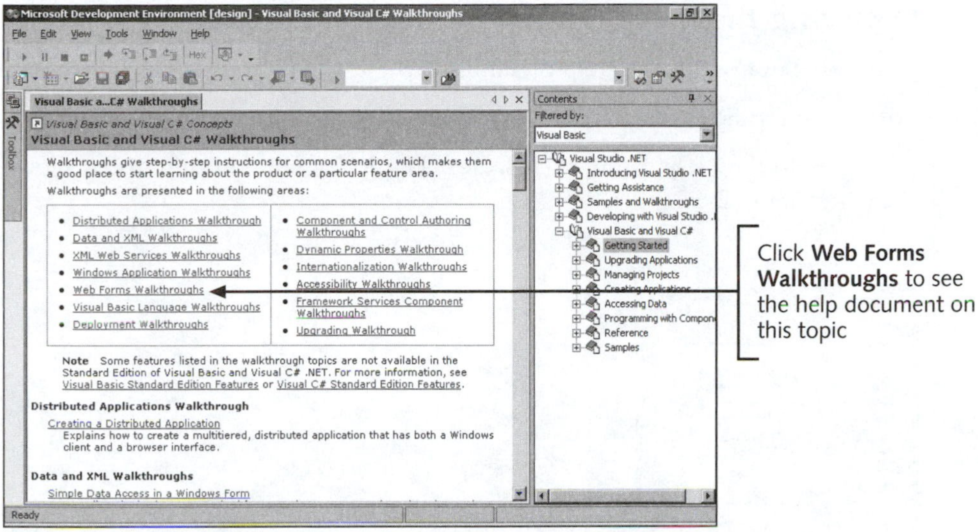

Figure 2-50 The Visual Basic and Visual C# Walkthroughs help document

6. Click the **Web Forms Walkthroughs** link, and then click the **Creating a Basic Web Forms Page** link to view help information on this topic. See Figure 2-51.

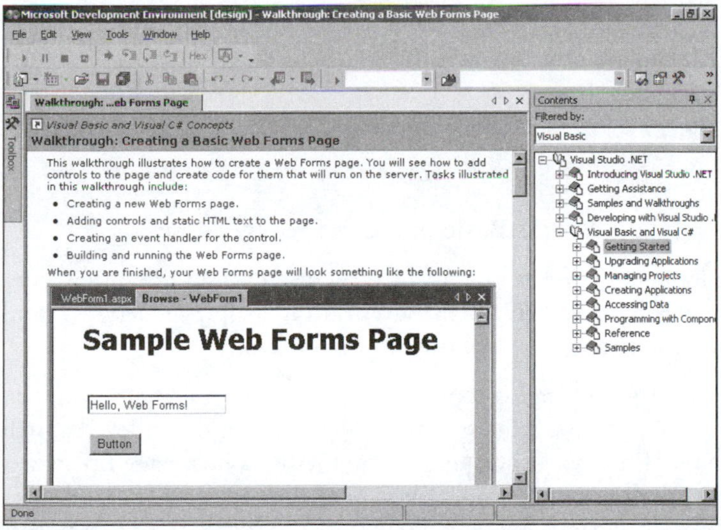

Figure 2-51 The Creating Basic Web Forms help document

7. Close the Contents window by clicking its **Close** button.

Exploring the Index Option on the Help Menu

The Index option on the Help menu displays a list of help topics in alphabetical order.

To open the Index window:

1. On the Help menu, click **Index**. The Index window appears, as shown in Figure 2-52.

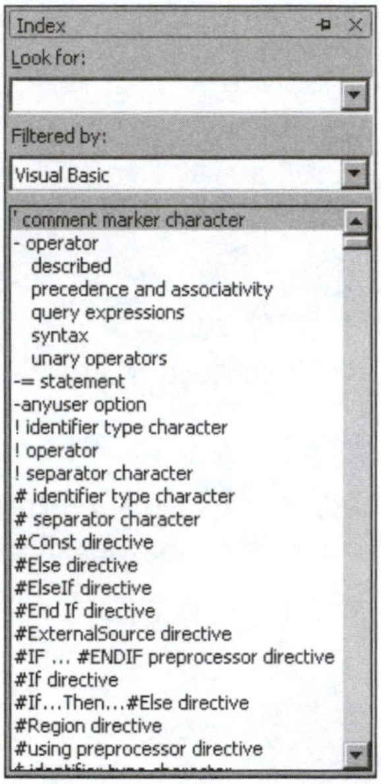

Figure 2-52 The Index window

2. If necessary, select **Visual Basic** in the Filtered by list box.
3. You can locate an item on the list by scrolling through the index. For example, scroll down and click **.NET Framework**. The help page for this item appears in the document window, as shown in Figure 2-53.
4. An alternate way to locate a topic in the index is to specify the topic in the Look for text box. As you type, the system locates items in the index that match your specification. When you click an item on the list, a help page opens within the document window. For example, click the **Look for** text box, and press the **Del** key to delete its current contents. Type **build** to locate this term in the index. As you type, notice how the system selects the item in the index that most closely matches your specification. Press **Enter** to display the currently selected help page. You see the information shown in Figure 2-54.

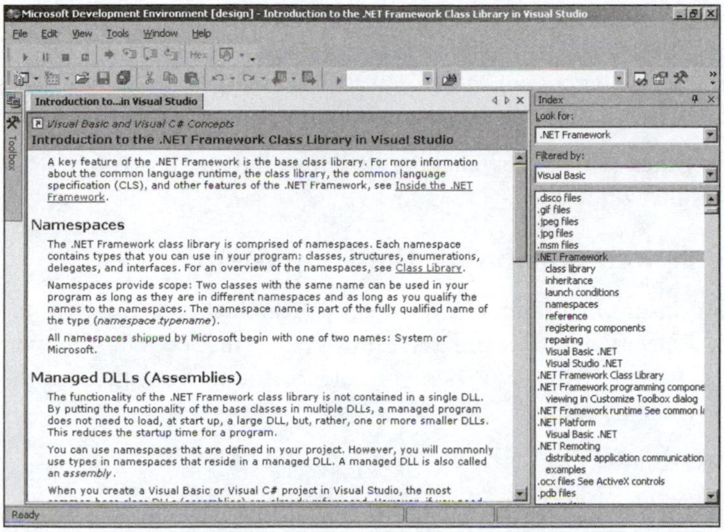

Figure 2-53 The .NET Framework help document

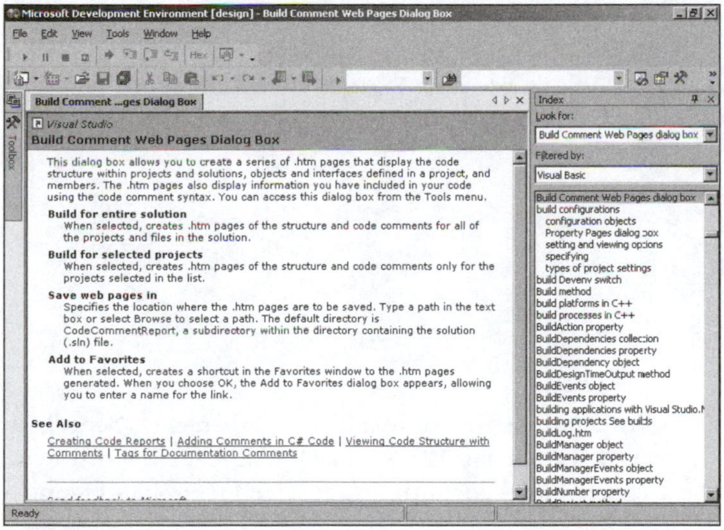

Figure 2-54 Using the Look for option of the Index window

TIP

Some items in the index have multiple help pages (or targets) associated with them. When you select one of these items, an Index Results window listing the targets appears within the IDE. Click an item on this list to open the desired help page.

Some items in the index serve only as a mechanism for identifying a group of related help pages. These items are referred to as parent entries and do not have help pages associated directly with them. When you click one of these items, you will see an Empty Index Entry page, which prompts you to select one of its child entries.

5. Close the Index window by clicking its **Close** button. If it is open, also close the Index Results window.

Exploring the Search Option on the Help Menu

The Search option on the Help menu allows you to search the database of help pages for those that contain a specific word or phrase. A list of pages that contain the word or phrase appears in a Search Results window. When you select an item from this list, the associated help page appears in the document window.

To open the Search window:

1. On the Help menu, click **Search**. The Search window appears, as shown in Figure 2-55.

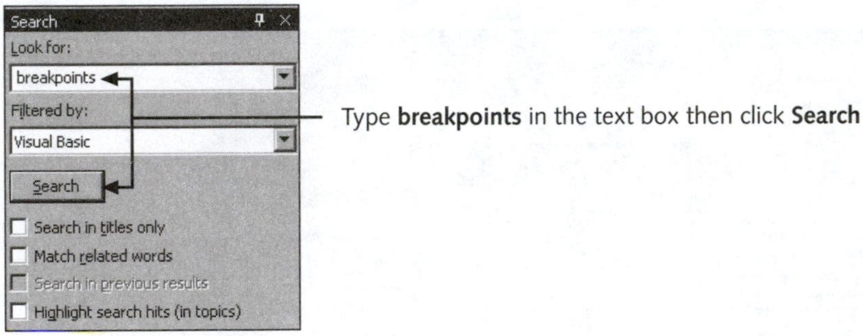

Figure 2-55 The Search window

2. Type **breakpoints** in the Look for text box, and then click **Search**. A Search Results window appears listing 123 topics. Double-click the first item on the list to open the associated help document. Your screen resembles Figure 2-56.

3. You can search for matches in titles only, match related keywords, search in previous results, as well as highlight hits. Revise your search by clicking the **Search in titles only** check box. This limits the search to pages that include the keyword in the title. Also, click the **Highlight search hits (in topics)** check box so that the keyword you are searching for will be highlighted in the resulting help pages. Click **Search**.

4. Notice that the Search Results window now includes only 12 entries. Double-click the first item in the list to open the associated help document. Observe that the word "breakpoints" is highlighted, as shown in Figure 2-57.

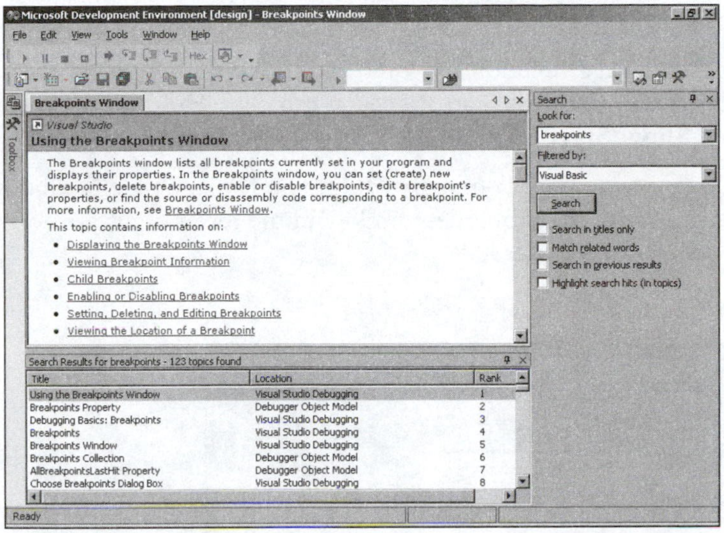

Figure 2-56 Using the Breakpoints Window help document

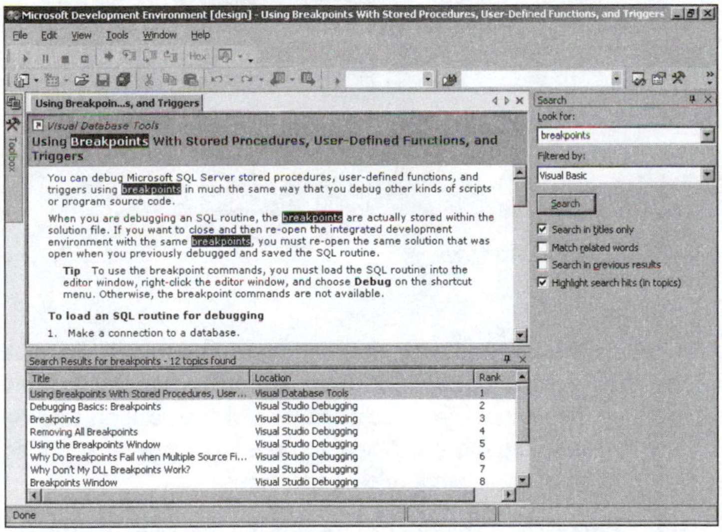

Figure 2-57 Revising the search

5. Close the Search, Search Results, and document windows.

Exploring the Dynamic Help Option on the Help Menu

The Dynamic Help option on the Help menu is a powerful feature that dynamically identifies help topics in response to actions you take.

To see how dynamic help works:

1. Open the Start Page, Solution Explorer, and Properties windows. Recall that if you inadvertently close the Start Page, you can click **Help** on the menu bar, and then click **Show Start Page** to bring it back into view.
2. On the Help menu, click **Dynamic Help**. The Dynamic Help window appears as a tab group with the Properties window in the lower-right portion of the screen, as shown in Figure 2-58.

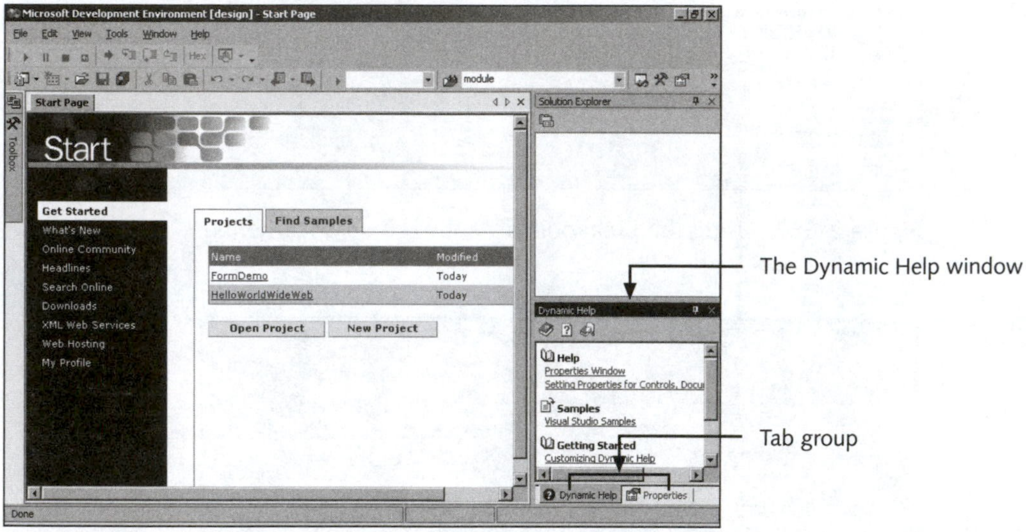

Figure 2-58 The Dynamic Help window

TIP

If the Dynamic Help window appears in a different location, right-click its title bar. Make sure that the Dockable option is checked, and then drag the window across the screen. As you drag the window, you see an outline of the position the window will occupy when you release the mouse. When you see an outline of a tabbed pane in the lower-right portion of the screen, release the mouse.

3. Click the **Start Page** tab in the document window to select it, if necessary. The Dynamic Help window shows links to pages that will help you get started, as shown in Figure 2-59.
4. Click the **Solution Explorer** title bar to select the Solution Explorer window. Notice that the contents of the Dynamic Help window change to provide links to help pages that deal with the Solution Explorer.
5. Open the FormDemo project. If necessary, click the **Form1.vb[Design]** tab to view the form in design view.

TIP

If you inadvertently close the Form1.vb[Design] tab, you can open it again by double-clicking Form1.vb in the Solution Explorer window. Alternately, you can select Form1.vb in the Solution Explorer window, and then click the View Designer icon. (See Figure 2-60.)

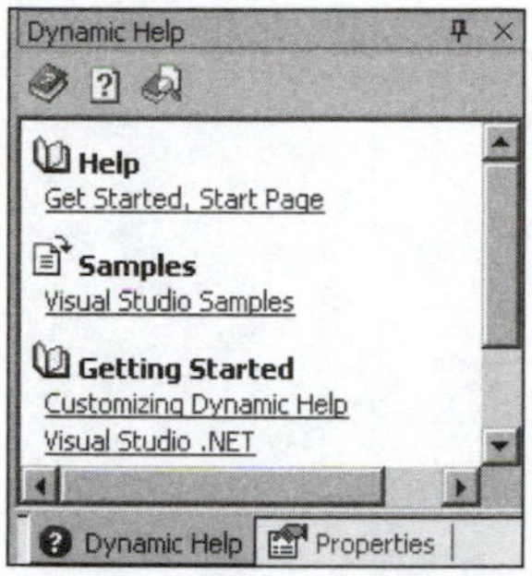

Figure 2-59 The Dynamic Help window with the Start Page selected

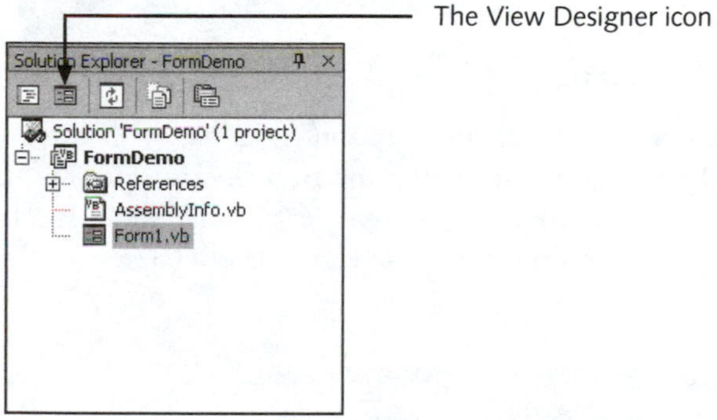

Figure 2-60 The View Designer icon in the Solution Explorer window

6. The input form you designed earlier in this chapter appears in the document window, and the contents of the Dynamic Help window change to reflect help topics associated with the Windows Forms Designer.
7. In the Form1.vb [Design] document window, click the **Push Me** button to select it. Notice that the contents of the Dynamic Help window change to reflect help topics that deal with buttons, as shown in Figure 2-61.

The Dynamic Help feature will respond in a similar fashion to actions you take as you work with various windows, tools, and elements of VB .NET.

Exploring Context-Sensitive Help

Another powerful help feature in VB .NET is context-sensitive help. This option does not appear on the Help menu, but you can invoke it by pressing the F1 key.

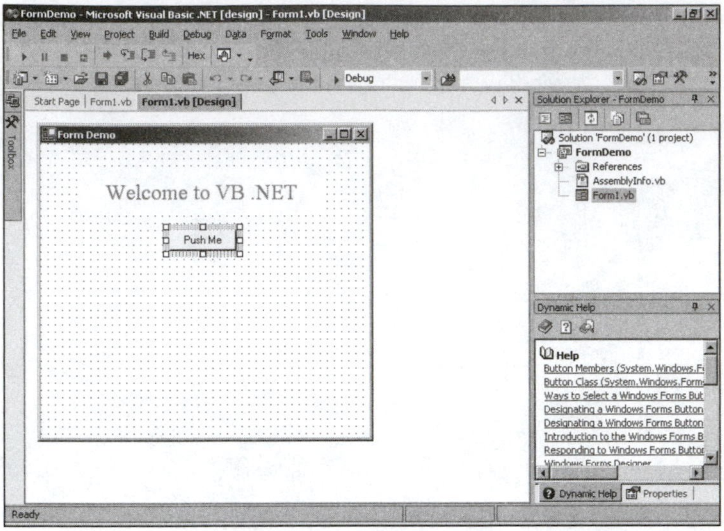

Figure 2-61 The Dynamic Help window with the Push Me button selected

To see how context-sensitive help works:

1. Continuing from the steps in the previous section (with the Push Me button selected), press the **F1** key. A page describing the Button class opens in the document window, as shown in Figure 2-62. You will learn more about the Button class and the information presented on this help screen in later chapters of this text.

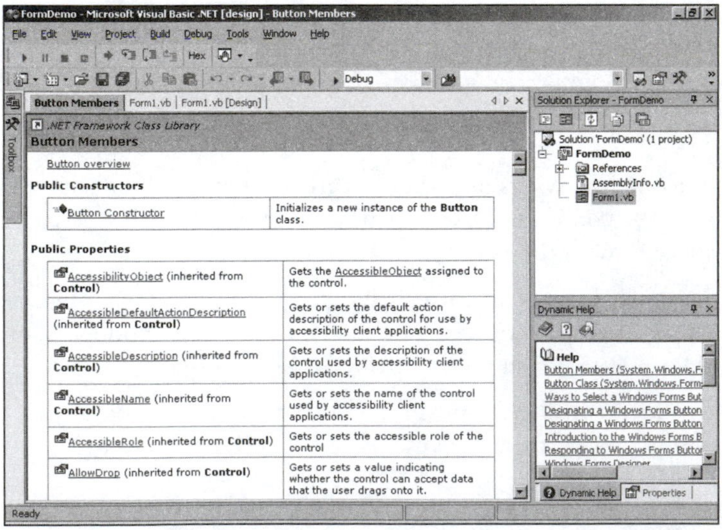

Figure 2-62 Context-sensitive help for the Push Me button

2. Click the **Form1.vb [Design]** tab to return to the Windows Forms Designer window. Double-click the **Push Me** button to open the code window. You see the code and the breakpoint you created earlier in the document window.
3. If necessary, position the insertion point at the beginning of the word **MessageBox** on the line of code where the breakpoint is set. Observe that the contents of the Dynamic Help window change to provide links to pages that provide MessageBox information.
4. Press the **F1** key. A page describing the MessageBox class opens in the document window.
5. Click the **Form1.vb** tab to return to the code window. Click on the word **Private**, and then press the **F1** key. Information about the Private keyword appears in a document window, as shown in Figure 2-63.
6. Close all open windows and exit VS .NET.

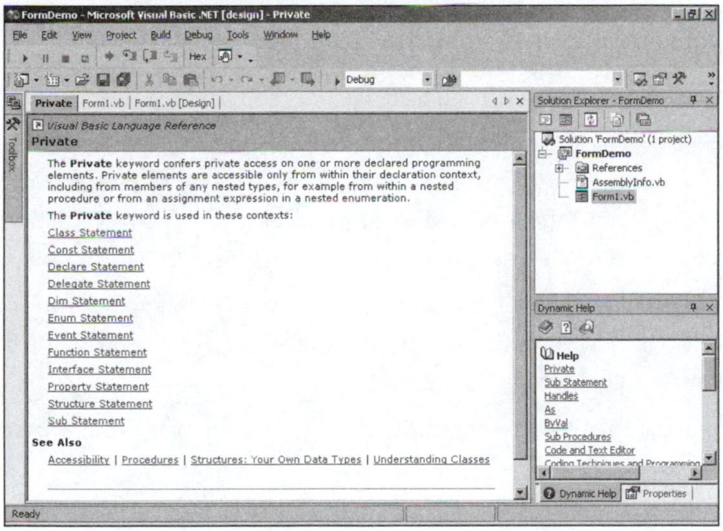

Figure 2-63 Context-sensitive help for the Private keyword

You can press the F1 key at any time to obtain help on virtually any keyword, component, window, or other element of VB .NET.

Chapter Summary

- Visual Studio .NET is an integrated development environment (IDE). An IDE is a set of software tools that helps you code, debug, and test a system as you develop it.
- Visual Basic .NET is one of the programming languages supported by the Visual Studio .NET IDE.
- Visual Studio .NET is part of Microsoft's .NET technology. Two important pieces of the .NET framework are the Common Language Runtime (CLR) and the class library. The CLR and the class library support common services used by all the Visual Studio .NET languages.
- The Visual Studio .NET IDE includes tools that assist you with text editing, visual form editing, program compilation and execution, debugging, and program organization and management.
- The VB .NET text editor supports color-coding, indentation, and code completion features.
- The VB .NET visual form editor, known as the Windows Forms Designer, is a visual development tool that generates code from pictures you draw.
- VB .NET uses a hierarchical arrangement of solutions and projects to organize the programs you write. Solutions and projects can be thought of as containers. A project contains the files that comprise an application. A solution contains one or more projects. Solutions with multiple projects are sometimes needed for large systems.
- VB .NET provides many options that allow you to customize the appearance of your screen and the tools that you use. This includes the ability to pin tools to the development environment as hidden windows.
- A debugger is a tool that helps you identify problems that prevent your program from running as intended.
- A breakpoint is a flag that instructs the debugger to temporarily suspend execution of your program. While execution is suspended, you can perform steps to locate the source of the error.
- The help facility of VB .NET provides many options for accessing help, including the Contents window, the Index window, the Search window, Dynamic Help, and context-sensitive help.

2

Key Terms

breakpoint
console application
debugger
handle
hidden window
integrated development environment (IDE)
IntelliSense
project
solution
startup object
startup project
template
Windows application

Review Questions

1. What is an IDE? Why is an IDE useful?
2. What are the major tools in the Visual Studio .NET IDE and what are the primary features of each?
3. What is the difference between a text editor and a visual form editor?
4. What is the purpose of the Solution Explorer?
5. What is the purpose of the Toolbox?
6. What is the purpose of the Properties window?
7. What is the purpose of the document window?
8. What does it mean to add a breakpoint to a program? How are breakpoints useful?
9. What primary kinds of help are available to you in VB .NET? Which do you think you will prefer? Why?
10. Explain the difference between dynamic help and context-sensitive help.
11. What is meant by the term "startup project?" How do you identify the startup project?
12. What is meant by the term "startup object?" When is it necessary to set the startup object? How do you set the startup object?
13. What is the purpose of the ForeColor property of a label?
14. What is the purpose of the Text property of a button?
15. How do you "pin" a tool window?
16. What is a hidden window? Why are hidden windows useful?

17. What is the difference between the Contents option and the Index option on the Help menu?
18. What is the purpose of a debugger? When can one be used?
19. What is the difference between Visual Studio .NET and Visual Basic .NET?
20. What is a console application? How does a console application differ from a Windows application?

Discussion Questions

1. What are the major benefits of using an IDE? What are the potential drawbacks?
2. Now that you have gained some experience using an IDE, describe in your own words how you believe an IDE can improve your productivity as a programmer.
3. Compare and contrast the following terms: project, solution, and program.
4. Do you think that IDE code generation tools, like the one you used in this chapter, will one day replace the need for programmers? Why or why not?
5. Explain the importance of the Toolbox and Properties windows for creating Windows applications. Discuss how these tools work together in the process of creating Windows forms.

Projects

1. Create a Windows application named MyFirstProgram, and save it in the Chap02\Projects folder in your work folder. Change the background color of the form to light green. Add the label "This is my first program" to the form. Change the label text to dark blue. Change the background color of the label to yellow. Change the font of the label to Comic Sans MS, bold, point size 20. If necessary, adjust the size of the label and the form so that the entire label is visible. Position the label at the bottom center of the form. Save your project and run your form.
2. Add a button to the form you began in Project 1. Change the button text to "What is my name?" Change the background and foreground colors as well as the font of the button text according to your preferences. Adjust the size of the button

if necessary. Position the button in the center of the form. Save your project and run your form.

3. Continue your work from Project 2 and add the code necessary to make the button work. When the button is pressed, display the message "My name is *your name*" (where *your name* is your actual name). When the message box is dismissed, display a second message: "VB .NET is fun!" Save your project and run your form.

4. Rename the module from Project 3 as MyFirstModule. Change the startup object accordingly. Save your project and run your form.

5. Continuing your work from the previous projects, add a breakpoint to MyFirst-Program that suspends execution before the second message box is shown. Save your project and run your form in debug mode. When the breakpoint is reached, resume program execution and verify that your program responds as it should.

CHAPTER

3

VB .NET Programming Fundamentals

In this chapter you will:

- Learn about the VB .NET programming language
- Write a VB .NET module definition
- Use VB .NET variables and data types
- Compute with VB .NET
- Write decision-making statements
- Write loops
- Declare and access arrays

Chapter 1 introduced you to object-oriented system development, basic OO concepts, and the OO vocabulary. You learned about OO and its brief history. Chapter 2 explored the VB .NET IDE and illustrated how to enter and run simple programs. In this chapter you will learn the fundamentals of the VB .NET programming language, including its syntax and structure.

This book assumes that you are familiar with the basics of a programming language. Although VB .NET requires that you learn a new syntax, many of the VB .NET statements will likely seem familiar to you. For example, the if-then-else syntax and the "while" and "do" looping statements are similar in many programming languages.

This chapter shows you how to write a module definition; declare variables; write computational statements, decision-making statements, and loops; and create and access arrays. After completing this chapter, you will have a basic understanding of the VB .NET syntax and be able to design and write simple VB .NET programs. This chapter focuses on presenting the fundamentals of programming in VB .NET, while Chapter 4 explores VB .NET in more detail as an object-oriented language.

Introducing VB .NET

VB .NET is a new language, released in early 2002, yet it has already achieved popularity and widespread acceptance. VB .NET was designed to be a powerful, full-featured, object-oriented development language that was easy to learn and use. More importantly, VB .NET, as the name suggests, was designed to support the development of applications for networked environments.

The power in VB .NET comes, in part, from its large, useful class library, which contains hundreds of prewritten classes. These classes provide methods to accomplish tasks ranging from simple number formatting to establishing network connections and accessing relational databases. Many of these supplied classes and their methods are illustrated in this and subsequent chapters.

VB .NET is object-oriented, which means it implements the OO concepts you learned about in Chapter 1: class, instance, method, attribute, encapsulation, inheritance, and polymorphism. By adopting the OO model, VB .NET encourages good software design that can dramatically reduce debugging and maintenance chores. Chapter 4 discusses the OO aspects of VB .NET in more detail.

Writing a VB .NET Module Definition

In Chapter 2 you explored the VB .NET IDE by writing simple module and form definitions named HelloWorldWideWebModule.vb and HelloWorldWideWebForm.vb, respectively. This section describes HelloWorldWideWebModule.vb in more detail. Figure 3-1 repeats the HelloWorldWideWebModule.vb listing, and Figure 3-2 shows the output.

```
' Chapter 2 Module definition HelloWorldWideWebModule
Module HelloWorldWideWebModule
   Sub Main()
      Console.WriteLine("Hello World Wide Web")
   End Sub
End Module
```

Figure 3-1 HelloWorldWideWebModule.vb listing

```
Hello World Wide Web
```

Figure 3-2 HelloWorldWideWebModule output

This VB .NET code is structured as a **module definition**, which begins with `Module` and ends with `End Module`. You can also write VB .NET statements in a **form definition** or a

class definition. A form definition is used to create a GUI and is described in Chapter 10. Class definitions are written to represent objects and are explained and illustrated in Chapter 6.

The VB .NET statements consist of **keywords** (**`Module, Sub, End Sub`**) and **identifiers** (**`HelloWorldWideWeb`**). Keywords have special meaning to VB .NET. The VB .NET keywords used in this book are listed in Table 3-1.

Table 3-1 Selected Keywords

`And`	`As`	`Boolean`	`ByRef`
`Byte`	`ByVal`	`Case`	`Catch`
`Char`	`Const`	`Decimal`	`Default`
`Delegate`	`Dim`	`Do`	`Double`
`Each`	`Else`	`ElseIf`	`End`
`False`	`Finally`	`For`	`Friend`
`Function`	`Handles`	`If`	`Implements`
`Imports`	`In`	`Inherits`	`Integer`
`Interface`	`Is`	`Long`	`Loop`
`Me`	`Mod`	`Module`	`MustInherit`
`MustOverride`	`MyBase`	`MyClass`	`Namespace`
`New`	`Next`	`Not`	`Nothing`
`NotInheritable`	`NotOverridable`	`Object`	`On`
`Option`	`Optional`	`Or`	`Overloads`
`Overridable`	`Overrides`	`Private`	`Property`
`Protected`	`Public`	`Return`	`Select`
`Set`	`Shadows`	`Shared`	`Short`
`Single`	`Static`	`Step`	`Structure`
`Sub`	`Then`	`Throw`	`To`
`True`	`Try`	`Until`	`When`
`While`	`With`	`WithEvents`	`Xor`

A VB .NET identifier is the name you assign to things such as modules, procedures, and variables. The VB .NET rules for identifiers are, like many things in VB .NET, quite simple.

- Identifiers can be any length you choose.
- They can include any letter or number, but no spaces.
- They must begin with a letter of the alphabet.

The code you write in VB .NET is not case sensitive. You can type **`Module`** or **`module`**. Also, although the VB .NET compiler does not require you to indent code, good programming practice encourages indentation, as shown in the examples in this text. You learned in Chapter 2 how to set the *Pretty Listing* option, which tells the VB .NET editor to capitalize keywords and insert appropriate indentation for you.

Notice that HelloWorldWideWebModule consists of only six lines. The first line is a **comment**. You use comment lines to add explanations to your code, which the compiler ignores. A VB .NET comment begins with a single quote (`'`) and can be on a line by itself or at the end of a line of code.

```
' Chapter 2 Module definition HelloWorldWideWebModule
```

The second line begins with a **module header** line, which contains the keyword **`Module`** followed by the module name, `HelloWorldWideWebModule`.

```
Module HelloWorldWideWebModule
```

Lines 3 through 5 represent a **procedure**. Procedures begin with a **procedure header**. A procedure header is written to identify the procedure and describe some of its characteristics, such as its name. This procedure header consists of a header beginning with another keyword, **`Sub`**, and then the procedure name, `Main`.

```
Sub Main()
```

You will learn more about VB .NET procedures later, but in general, a procedure contains statements that you write to do some processing. VB .NET has two types of procedures: Sub and Function. These two types of procedures are described in more detail later; however, the main difference between the two is that a Function procedure can return a value but a Sub procedure cannot.

Whenever a module has a procedure named Main, this procedure is automatically invoked when the module is loaded into memory; the Main procedure is what executes. This means that when the HelloWorldWideWebModule file is loaded into memory, the Main procedure begins running.

The following Main procedure contains a single statement that is executed to display your message:

```
Console.WriteLine("Hello World Wide Web")
```

This statement, like many you see in VB .NET, invokes a method to do the real work of displaying the message. `Console` is a class that provides methods to accomplish various tasks. One of these methods, `WriteLine`, displays text that is passed to it. In this example, the information that is contained in parentheses, called an **argument**, is sent to the `WriteLine` method, which then displays it.

Because the argument is included between quotation marks (`"Hello World Wide Web"`), VB .NET recognizes it as a character string **literal**. A literal is what you call a value defined within a statement.

Hands-on Exercise 1

1. All of the VB .NET examples, including HelloWorldWideWebModule.vb, are included as part of the data files that accompany this text. You should take a few minutes now to locate HelloWorldWideWebModule.vb in a folder named Chap03\Examples\Ex01.
2. Create a folder on your system named **Chap03\Exercises** and copy **HelloWorldWideWebModule.vb** to this folder.
3. Start Visual Studio .NET. Use the VB .NET IDE to create a project named **Exercise1** and add the module **HelloWorldWideWebModule.vb** to this project:
   a. Click **File** on the menu bar, point to **New**, and then click **Project**.
   b. In the New Project window, select **Visual Basic Projects** in the Project Types area, select the **Empty Project** template, enter **Exercise1** in the Name text box, and then select the **Chap03\Exercises** folder. Click **OK** to close the New Project window.
   c. Right-click the project name (**Exercise1**) in the Solution Explorer window, point to **Add** on the shortcut menu, and then click **Add Existing Item**. Locate and select **HelloWorldWideWebModule.vb**, and then click the **Open** button.
   d. When the HelloWorldWideWebModule.vb file appears in your Solution Explorer window, double-click it to view the code.
4. Set the startup object to HelloWorldWideWebModule. To do so, right-click the project name (**Exercise1**) in the Solution Explorer window, and then select **Properties** on the shortcut menu. In the Exercise1 Property Pages dialog box, select **General** under Common Properties, if necessary, click the **Startup object** list arrow in the Exercise1 Property Pages window, and then select **HelloWorldWideWebModule**. This tells VB .NET to begin execution with the Main procedure in HelloWorldWideWebModule.
5. Still in the Exercise1 Property Pages window, click the **Output type** list arrow and select **Console Application**. This tells the IDE to display your output in a console window. Click the **OK** button to close the Exercise1 Property Pages window.
6. Modify the HelloWorldWideWebModule.vb code to display your name on one line and your course name and section on a second line. Save the modified HelloWorldWideWebModule.vb file in your Chap03\Exercises folder.
7. Test your modifications. Click **Debug** on the menu bar, and then select **Start Without Debugging** to execute the code in HelloWorldWideWebModule. Press **Enter** to close the console. Then close the project.

USING VB .NET VARIABLES AND DATA TYPES

You declare a variable to contain data. A variable is the name of a place in memory that can contain data. For example, you can write the following statement to add two values together:

```
a = b + c
```

In this example `a`, `b`, and `c` are variables. They are the names of memory locations that contain data. For example, if variable `b` contains the number 2 and `c` contains the number 4, then after this statement is executed, `a` contains the number 6. Figure 3-3 shows these three variables after the statement is executed.

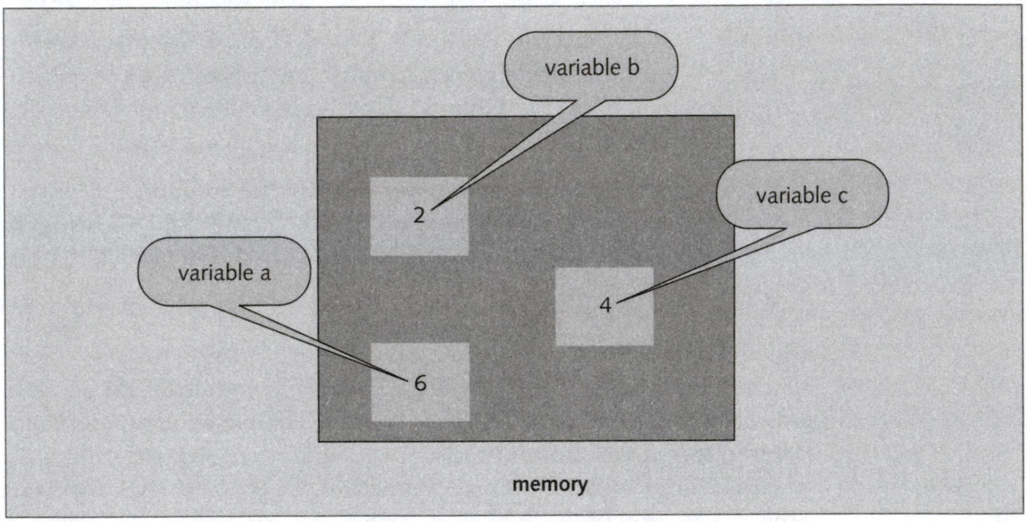

Figure 3-3 Variables containing data

All variables have a data type, name, and value. Each of these characteristics is defined in the following list:

- *Data type* –The data type specifies the kind of data the variable can contain. VB .NET is particular about data types. For example, you cannot store a number containing a decimal point into a variable that is expecting only integer values. The specific data types are described in the next section.
- *Name* –A variable name is an identifier you create to refer to the variable.
- *Value* –Every variable refers to a memory location that contains data. You can specify this value. If you do not assign the variable a value, then VB .NET assigns a default value. Numeric variables are initialized to zero, the character variable is initialized to **Nothing**, and the Boolean variable is initialized to false. **`Nothing`** is a keyword representing the value of nothing.

Declaring and Initializing Variables

Before you can declare a variable, you must specify the data type the variable will use. VB .NET has nine **primitive data types**, shown in Table 3-2. They are called primitive data types to distinguish them from more complex data types, such as class names, which are discussed in Chapter 4.

Table 3-2 VB .NET Primitive Data Types

	Type	Range of Values	Size
Numeric with no decimals	1. Byte 2. Short 3. Integer 4. Long	0 to 255 –32,768 to 32,767 –2,147,483,648 to 2,147,483,647 ±9,223,372,036,854,775,807	8 bits 16 bits 32 bits 64 bits
Numeric with decimals	5. Single 6. Double 7. Decimal	±1.5E–45 to ±3.4E+38 ±5.0E–324 to ±1.7E+308 1.0E–28 to 7.9E+28	32 bits 64 bits 128 bits
Other	8. Boolean 9. Char	True or False any Unicode character	16 bits 16 bits

You use the first four data types to contain numeric data without decimals (`Byte`, `Short`, `Integer`, and `Long`). You use the next three data types to contain numeric data with decimals (`Single`, `Double`, and `Decimal`). The primitive data type `Boolean` contains only one of two possible values: `True` or `False`.

You use the primitive data type `Char` for variables that contain a single character of text. To show text of more than one character, you use the String class, explored in a later section and more thoroughly in Chapter 4. The following examples focus on `Integer`, `Double`, and `Boolean` and their use.

To declare a VB .NET variable, you write the keyword **`Dim`** followed by the name (identifier) you want to use, the keyword **`As`**, and then the data type.

```
' declare variables
Dim i As Integer
Dim d As Double
Dim b As Boolean
```

Next, you can add code to populate the variables by assigning each a value. The following statements assign the integer value 1 to `i`, the value 2.5 to `d`, and the value `True` to `b`. The equal sign in these statements is called the **assignment operator**. This operator assigns the value on the right side of the equal sign to the variable named on the left side.

```
' populate the variables
i = 1
d = 2.5
b = True
```

You also can write code to both declare and initialize the variable in one statement. For example, the following statements declare the variables as before, and then assign them to the values indicated.

```
' declare variables
Dim i As Integer = 1
Dim d As Double = 2.5
Dim b As Boolean = True
```

You can declare several variables of the same data type in one statement. For example, if `x`, `y`, and `z` will be data type `Integer`, you can declare them as in the following code:

```
Dim x, y, z As Integer
```

In general, you use variables to hold data. You can initialize a variable either when it is declared or later using an assignment statement.

Changing Data Types

Note that the seven numeric data types in Table 3-2 have different capacities. For example, a variable with data type `Byte` can have a maximum value of only 255, yet data type `Integer` has maximum value of 2.1 billion. Similarly, data type `Single` has a capacity of 3.4E+38, but `Double` has a capacity of 1.7E+308, significantly more.

For example, assume you have defined and populated variables `i` and `d` as follows:

```
Dim i As Integer = 123
Dim d As Double
d = i
```

The first statement defines variable `i` as data type `Integer` and populates it with 123. The second statement defines variable `d` as data type `Double`. The last statement assigns the contents of `i` to `d`. Following the execution of this statement, variable `d` will contain the value 123.

However, consider the result if you write the following statements:

```
Dim i As Integer
Dim d As Double = 456.789
i = d
```

The first statement defines variable `i` as data type `Integer`. The second defines variable `d` as data type `Double` and populates it with 456.789. The third statement assigns the contents of variable `d` to `i`. Variable `i`, however, is data type `Integer`, which means that it cannot hold decimal positions. When the value 456.789 is assigned to `i`, the decimal positions are truncated, resulting in a loss of precision. When you assign the value from one variable to another, if the first variable's data type has a smaller capacity than the data type of the second variable, loss of precision can occur.

VB .NET provides you with an option called **Option Strict**, which helps prevent the unintentional loss of precision when assigning values to variables. Option Strict is a compiler option that you can set to either **On** or **Off**. There are two ways to set this option. First, you can write **Option Strict On** or **Option Strict Off** at the beginning of your module. Or, you can right-click the project name in the Solution Explorer window to open the Property Pages window, and then select Build under Common Properties and select On or Off in the Option Strict list box.

If you have set Option Strict to On, then whenever you write an assignment statement that may result in a loss of precision, the VB .NET compiler displays an error message. You can override the compiler's objection by invoking a method in the Convert class. You can modify the previous example as follows:

```
Dim i As Integer
Dim d As Double = 456.789
i = Convert.ToInt32(d)
```

The last line of code invokes the method ToInt32 in the Convert class. This method receives variable d as an argument, rounds it to the nearest integer value, and the result, 457, is assigned to variable i. Note that you are assuming responsibility for any loss of precision in this operation. The compiler has warned you of the potential error, and by using the Convert methods you have accepted this potential error.

VB .NET has another option called **Option Explicit**, which is generally set to On. With Option Explicit On, you must define a variable before you can use it in a statement. However, if you have set Option Explicit Off, then the VB .NET compiler automatically defines a variable if you use it in a statement without first defining it. On the surface this may appear to be an attractive choice; however, if you misspell a variable name in a statement after you have defined it, VB .NET defines a new variable with the misspelled name without notifying you. For example, assume you have defined an Integer variable named examScore. Later in your code, however, you misspell it as exmScore. VB .NET creates a new variable for you named exmScore.

Using Constants

It is often useful to declare a **constant**, a variable with a value that does not change. You use constants to contain values—such as a company name, tax identification number, or phone number—that do not change, or change rarely.

The code to declare a constant is identical to what you use to declare a variable, but with the keyword **Const** instead of **Dim**, as in the following code. However, constants must be initialized in the same statement that declares them. By convention, you capitalize constant names. If the name consists of more than one word, you also separate the words with the underscore character. For example, to declare a constant for a sales tax rate of 7.5 percent, you write:

```
Const SALES_TAX_RATE As Double = 7.5;
```

This code declares a variable named SALES_TAX_RATE as data type Double, initializes it to 7.5, and the value cannot be changed.

Using Reference Variables

You have seen that variables hold data. Actually, there are two kinds of variables: **primitive variables** and **reference variables**. Until now, you have studied primitive variables. A primitive variable is declared with one of the nine primitive data types and actually contains the data you put there.

In contrast, a reference variable uses a class name as a data type and refers to or points to an instance of that class. A reference variable does not actually contain the data; instead, it refers to an instance of a class that contains the data. For example, you may have noticed that string data, a collection of characters, is not one of the primitive data types. Instead, string data is contained in an instance of the String class, one of the classes supplied with VB .NET.

In the last section of this chapter, you will learn about arrays. Arrays contain data, and are also accessed using a reference variable.

You declare a String reference variable, just as you declared primitive variables, by first specifying the variable name you want to use, followed by the data type, which is the class name String. You can declare reference variable `s` with data type `String` by writing the following code:

```
Dim s As String
```

This code creates a variable named `s`, but does not initialize it to a value. It does not yet point to a String instance. In fact, it doesn't point anywhere and has a null value. You can assign a value to a String variable just as you assign a value to a primitive variable. The following code assigns the characters `"Hello Again"` to the String variable named `s`:

```
s = "Hello Again"
```

You also can declare a String reference variable and assign a value to it in one step, as you did with primitive variables:

```
Dim s As String = "Hello Again"
```

Earlier you defined an `Integer` variable named `i` and populated it with 123. Variable `i` is a primitive variable *containing* the value 123, while String variable `s` is a reference *pointing to* or *referencing* an instance of the String class that contains `"Hello Again"`. Figure 3-4 shows this distinction graphically.

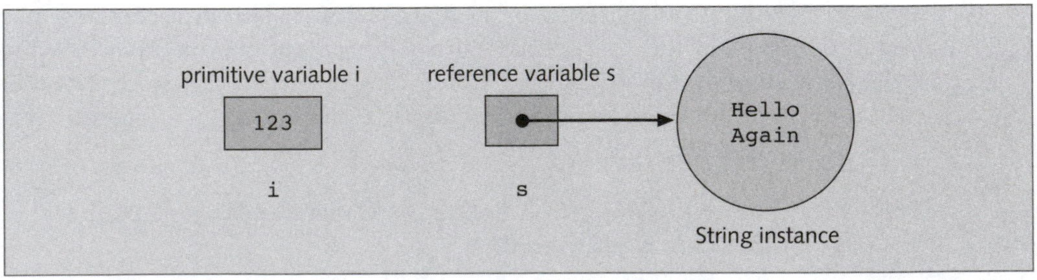

Figure 3-4 Contrasting primitive and reference variables

Figure 3-4 shows that variable `i` actually contains 123, but that variable `s` points or refers to an instance of the String class that contains `"Hello Again"`.

The distinction between primitive and reference variables becomes especially important when you want to work with instances and invoke their methods. Chapter 4 explores these ideas in greater detail and illustrates how to invoke methods in the String class.

Creating a VB .NET Module to Demonstrate Variables

A VB .NET module that demonstrates declaring variables and constants called VariableDemo.vb is listed in Figure 3-5.

```
' Chapter 3 VariableDemo Example 2
Option Strict On
Module VariableDemo
   Sub Main()
      ' declare variables
      Dim i As Integer = 123
      Dim d As Double = 456.789
      Dim b As Boolean = True
      Dim s As String = "Hello Again"
      ' a constant must be populated when it is declared
      Const SALES_TAX_RATE As Double = 7.5
      ' display variable contents
      Console.WriteLine("i, an Integer datatype contains " & i)
      Console.WriteLine("d, a Double datatype contains " & d)
      Console.WriteLine("b, a Boolean datatype contains " & b)
      Console.WriteLine("s, a String contains " & s)
      Console.WriteLine("SALES_TAX_RATE, a constant datatype Double
        contains " & SALES_TAX_RATE)

      ' illustrate ToInt32 convert method
      i = Convert.ToInt32(d)
      Console.WriteLine("After invoking Convert.ToInt32(d), i
        contains " & i)
   End Sub
End Module
```

Figure 3-5 VariableDemo.vb listing

This module begins with a comment, followed by `Option Strict On`. As in HelloWorldWideWebModule, VariableDemo begins with a module header, followed by the Main procedure. The Main procedure begins with code that declares and populates three primitive variables, a String reference variable, and a constant.

```
' declare variables
Dim i As Integer = 123
Dim d As Double = 456.789
Dim b As Boolean = True
```

```
Dim s As String = "Hello Again"
' a constant must be populated when it is declared
Const SALES_TAX_RATE As Double = 7.5
```

Once the variables are declared and values are assigned, you add statements to display their values.

```
' display variable contents
Console.WriteLine("i, an Integer datatype contains " & i)
Console.WriteLine("d, a Double datatype contains " & d)
Console.WriteLine("b, a Boolean datatype contains " & b)
Console.WriteLine("s, a String contains " & s)
Console.WriteLine("SALES_TAX_RATE, a constant datatype Double
contains " & SALES_TAX_RATE)
```

These statements invoke the method `WriteLine` in the `Console` class. Invoking a method means that you send it a message asking it to execute. To write a statement that invokes a method, you write a reference to the class or object (`Console`) followed by a period or dot, and then add the method name you want to use (`WriteLine`).

Often when you invoke a method, you send it one or more values, called arguments, enclosed in parentheses. For example, the first statement above sends the following argument:

```
("i, an Integer datatype contains " & i)
```

The value `"i, an Integer datatype contains "` is simply a String literal and `&` is the **concatenation operator**, which joins the literal with the contents of the variable `i` for display. The concatenation operator automatically converts numeric or Boolean values to string values before the `WriteLine` method is invoked.

The output from VariableDemo.vb is shown in Figure 3-6.

```
i, an Integer datatype contains 123
d, a Double datatype contains 456.789
b, a Boolean datatype contains True
s, a String contains Hello Again
SALES_TAX_RATE, a constant datatype Double contains 7.5
After invoking Convert.ToInt32(d), i contains 457
```

Figure 3-6 VariableDemo output

Hands-on Exercise 2

1. Locate **VariableDemo.vb** in the folder named Chap03\Examples\Ex02 in the book's data files, and then copy it to your Chap03\Exercises folder.
2. Use the VB .NET IDE to create a project named **Exercise2**, add the module **VariableDemo.vb**, and then set the startup object to **VariableDemo** and the

output type to **Console Application**. Refer to the instructions for Hands-on Exercise 1 to review how to create a project and add a module.

3. Click **Debug** on the menu bar, and then select **Start Without Debugging** to execute the code in VariableDemo.vb. Your output should match Figure 3-6. Press **Enter** to close the console window.
4. Add code to VariableDemo.vb to declare and populate primitive variables for data types `Integer` and `Double`. Store 245 in the `Integer` variable and 123456.789 in the `Double` variable. Then add code to display the contents of these new variables.
5. Add code at the end of the module to attempt to assign the contents of the `Double` variable to the `Integer` variable, and then display your new result. What error do you get? Remember that `Option Strict On` is set. Set `Option Strict Off` and execute the code again.
6. Close the project.

Computing with VB .NET

VB .NET uses the familiar **arithmetic operators** for addition, subtraction, multiplication, and division (+, –, *, /) that are used in other programming languages. Similarly, VB .NET employs parentheses to group parts of an expression and establish precedence according to standard algebraic rules. In addition, VB .NET uses a **remainder operator** (Mod), also called the **modulus operator**, to produce a remainder resulting from the division of two integers. VB .NET also uses the **integer division operator** (\) to produce an integer result. Finally, the caret (^) is used for exponentiation. These arithmetic operators are listed in Table 3-3.

Table 3-3 VB .NET Arithmetic Operators

Operator	Description	Example	Result
+	addition	11 + 2	13
–	subtraction	11 – 2	9
*	multiplication	11 * 2	22
/	division	11 / 2	6
\	integer division	11 \ 2	5
Mod	remainder	11 Mod 2	1
^	exponentiation	4 ^ 2	16

Note that the data types conversion must be correct for the division operator to work correctly.

In addition to these arithmetic operators, VB .NET includes the Math class, which contains methods to accomplish exponentiation, rounding, and numerous other tasks. Table 3-4 lists some of the Math class methods.

Table 3-4 Selected Math Class Methods

Method	Description
`Pow(x,y)`	Returns the value of `x` raised to the power of `y`
`Round(x, n)`	Returns `x` rounded to `n` decimals
`Sqrt(x)`	Returns the square root of `x`

To invoke one of these methods, you write the name of the class (Math), a period, the name of the method, and then any arguments required. The Math class returns the resulting value after doing the computation. For example, the following statement computes the square root of 16.

```
Dim answer As Double = Math.Sqrt(16)
```

When this statement is executed, four things happen:

1. A variable named **`answer`** with data type **`Double`** is created.
2. The **`Sqrt`** method in the Math class is invoked and the argument 16 is passed to it.
3. The **`Sqrt`** method computes the square root of the argument and returns it.
4. The value returned, 4, is assigned to the variable **`answer`**.

The module listed in Figure 3-7, ComputationDemo.vb, demonstrates the use of the arithmetic operators and two of the methods in the Math class.

```
' Chapter 3 ComputationDemo Example 3

Option Strict On

Module ComputationDemo

   Sub Main()

      ' declare variables
      Dim a, b, c As Integer
      Dim d As Double

      ' populate variables
      a = 11
      b = 2
      c = 4

      ' add, subtract, multiply and display result
      Console.WriteLine("a + b = " & (a + b))
      Console.WriteLine("a - b = " & (a - b))
      Console.WriteLine("a * b = " & (a * b))

      ' Integer division
      Console.WriteLine("Remainder a Mod b = " & (a Mod b))
      c = Convert.ToInt32(a / b) ' decimal results require
          Convert.ToInt32
```

```
        Console.WriteLine("Division a / b = " & c)
        c = a \ b
        Console.WriteLine("Integer division a \ b = " & c)
        c = 4   ' repopulate c

        ' Double division
        d = a / b
        Console.WriteLine("Double division a / b = " & d)
        d = 456.789     ' repopulate d

        ' illustrate some Math class methods
        Console.WriteLine("c to b power = " & Math.Pow(c, b))
        Console.WriteLine("square root of c = " & Math.Sqrt(c))
        Console.WriteLine("d rounded is = " & Math.Round(d, 2))

    End Sub

End Module
```

Figure 3-7 ComputationDemo.vb listing

3

Similar to previous examples, this module has a single procedure (method) named Main that begins executing when the module is loaded into memory. The Main procedure begins with code that declares three primitive `Integer` variables named `a`, `b`, and `c`, a `Double` primitive named `d`, and then populates `a`, `b`, and `c`.

Next comes three statements invoking the `WriteLine` method to display the result of computational expressions involving variables `a` and `b`.

```
Console.WriteLine("a + b = " & (a + b))
Console.WriteLine("a - b = " & (a - b))
Console.WriteLine("a * b = " & (a * b))
```

The argument format in these statements is slightly different from what you have seen in previous examples because these arguments actually contain arithmetic expressions that compute values. For example, the argument in the first statement is `("a + b = " & (a + b))`. First VB .NET computes the sum `(a + b)`, concatenates this result with the string literal `"a + b = "`, and then passes the concatenated string to the `WriteLine` method, which then displays it.

Next is a statement illustrating division using the Mod (remainder) operator.

```
Console.WriteLine("Remainder a Mod b = " & (a Mod b))
```

This statement divides the contents of `a` (11) by the contents of `b` (2) and produces the remainder (11 divided by 2 is 5 with a remainder of 1).

Next is a statement that divides `Integer` variable `a` (containing 11) by `Integer` variable `b` (containing 2). Because the result contains a decimal position (5.5), you must invoke the `Convert.ToInt32` method to convert the result to `Integer` before assigning it to the `Integer` variable `c`. Note that the result is rounded to 6.

```
' decimal results require Convert.ToInt32
c = Convert.ToInt32(a / b)
Console.WriteLine("Integer division a / b = " & c)
```

Next is a statement that illustrates the integer division operator. Dividing `a` by `b` using integer division produces a result of 5.

```
c = a \ b
Console.WriteLine("Integer division a \ b = " & c)
```

Double division is illustrated in the next statement. Variable `a` is again divided by variable `b`; however, this example assigns the result (5.5) to variable `d`, which was defined as data type `Double`. This means that no loss of precision occurs and you do not need to invoke a `Convert` method.

```
' Double division
d = a / b
Console.WriteLine("Double division a / b = " & d)
```

The final three statements in ComputationDemo.vb demonstrate using methods in the Math class.

```
' illustrate some Math class methods
Console.WriteLine("c to b power = " & Math.Pow(c, b))
Console.WriteLine("square root of c = _
   " & Math.Sqrt(c))
Console.WriteLine("d rounded is = _
   " & Math.Round(d, 2))
```

The first of these invokes the `Pow` method, which will raise the contents of variable `c` (containing 4) to the power of the contents of variable `b` (containing 2). The second statement invokes the `Sqrt` method, which will compute and return the square root of variable `c`. The final statement invokes the `Round` method, which will round the contents of variable `d` (456.789) to two decimal positions (456.79).

The output of this code is shown in Figure 3-8.

```
a + b = 13
a – b = 9
a * b = 22
Remainder a Mod b = 1
Division a / b = 6
Integer division a \ b = 5
Double division a / b = 5.5
c to b power = 16
square root of c = 2
d rounded is = 456.79
```

Figure 3-8 ComputationDemo output

Hands-on Exercise 3

1. Locate **ComputationDemo.vb** in the folder named Chap03\Examples\Ex03 in the book's data files, and then copy it to your Chap03\Exercises folder on your hard disk.
2. Use the VB .NET IDE to create a project named **Exercise3**, add the module **ComputationDemo.vb**, and then set the startup object to **ComputationDemo** and the output type to **Console Application**. Refer to the instructions for Hands-on Exercise 1 to review how to create a project and add a module.
3. Click **Debug** on the menu bar, and then select **Start Without Debugging** to execute the code in ComputationDemo.vb. Your output should match Figure 3-8. Press **Enter** to close the console window.
4. The formula to compute the present value of a future value is:
   presentValue = futureValue / (1 + annualInterestRate) raised to the yearsInFuture power
   a. Declare and populate the following variables (choose your data types carefully):
      presentValue = 0
      futureAmount = 1000
      annualInterestRate = .085
      yearsInFuture = 10
   b. Add statements to ComputationDemo.vb to compute and display your presentValue. You will need to invoke the `Pow` method in the Math class to perform exponentiation. Try rounding your answer to two decimal positions using the `Round` method.
5. Close the project.

VB .NET also supports the use of the assignment operator (=) together with the arithmetic operators (+, -, *, /) to create assignment operators. For example, if you want to add 5 to a variable named `total`, you could write either one of the following statements:

```
total = total + 5
total += 5
```

Writing Decision-Making Statements

Often when you are writing business applications, you want to determine whether a condition is true, and then take some action based on that determination. For example, in a credit card processing application, you may want to see if the card's credit limit has been reached or exceeded, and if so, reject the charge. You write decision-making statements to evaluate conditions and execute statements based on that evaluation.

VB .NET provides two ways to write decision-making statements: the If statement and the Select Case statement. The VB .NET If statement, similar to if statements used in other programming languages, evaluates an expression and then executes one or more statements if the expression is true and can then execute another statement or group of statements if the expression is false. The Select Case statement, similar to the Select statement used in some other languages, is like a multiple-path if statement. It evaluates a variable for multiple values, and then executes a statement or group of statements, depending on the contents of the variable being evaluated.

Writing If Statements

The VB .NET If statement interrogates a logical expression that evaluates to true or false. An expression often compares two values using **logical operators** to see whether they are equal or whether one is less than the other. In the credit card processing example mentioned earlier, to see if the credit card balance is greater than the credit limit, the expression is: `creditCardBalance >= creditLimit`. Additional examples of expressions are `examScore > passingScore`, `studentAge < 21`, and `studentId = scholarshipId`. A logical expression can be replaced by a Boolean variable. Table 3-5 lists the logical operators.

Table 3-5 VB .NET Logical Operators

Operator	Description
=	equal to
>	greater than
>=	greater than or equal to
<	less than
<=	less than or equal to
<>	not equal to

The VB .NET If statement has two forms. The first, sometimes called a simple If, evaluates an expression and then executes one or more statements if the expression is true. The second form, the If-Else, evaluates an expression, then executes one or more statements if the expression is true or executes a second statement or set of statements if it is false. The logic of these two forms is shown in Figures 3-9 and 3-10.

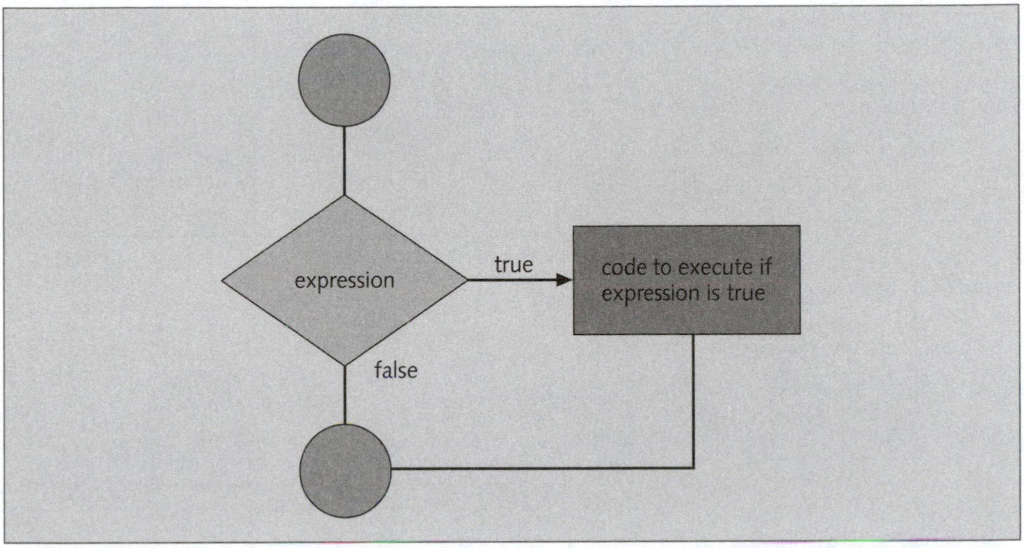

Figure 3-9 Simple If statement logic

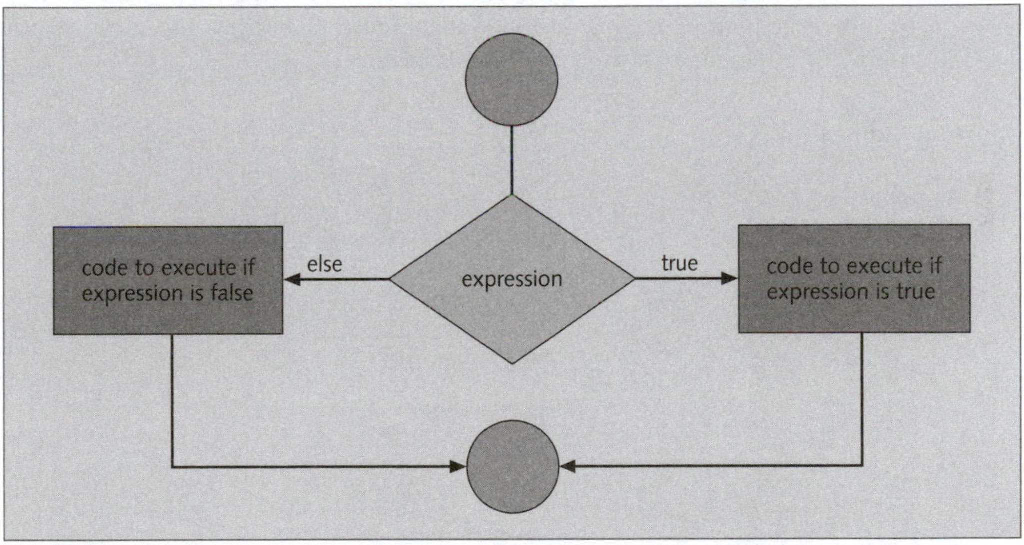

Figure 3-10 If-Else statement logic

The simple If statement format is shown in Figure 3-11. Note that there are two forms of the simple If. When you want to execute a single statement if the expression evaluates to true, you put the statement on the same line as the If-Then and omit the keywords **`End If`**. However, when you want to execute multiple statements, you use the second form by writing the statements on separate lines following the If-Then and write **`End If`** as the last line.

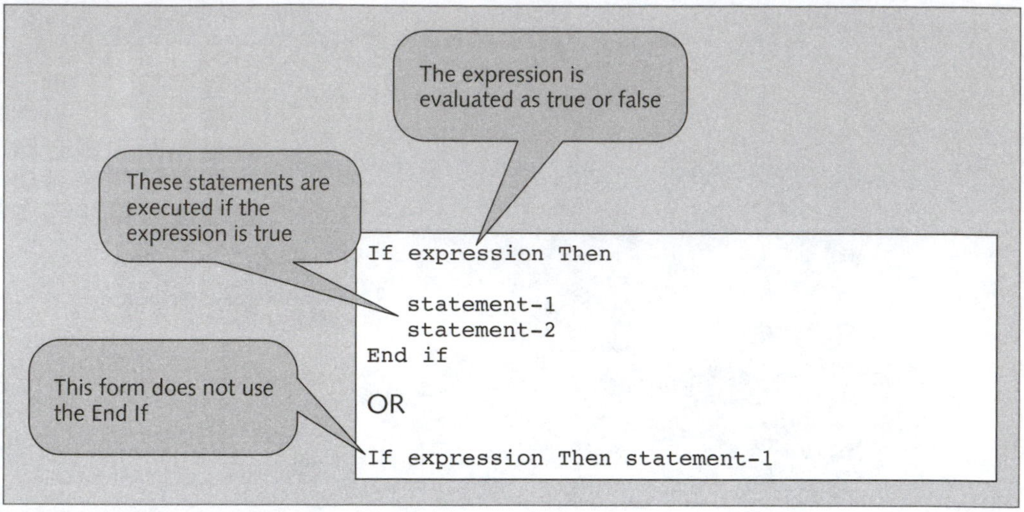

Figure 3-11 Simple If statement format

The If-Else format is shown in Figure 3-12. You use If-Else when you want to execute one or more statements if the expression evaluates to true, but you also want to execute one or more other statements if the expression is false.

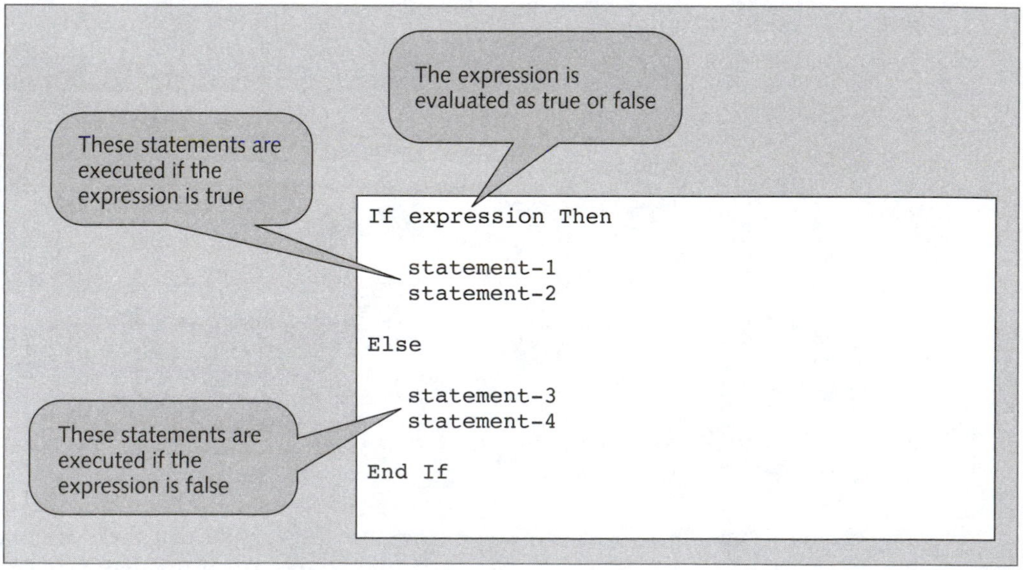

Figure 3-12 If-Else statement format

The module listed in Figure 3-13, IfDemo.vb, demonstrates both forms of the If statement.


```
' Chapter 3 IfDemo Example 4
Option Strict On
Module IfDemo
   Sub Main()
      Dim i As Integer = 1
      ' simple If
      If i < 10 Then Console.WriteLine("Simple If without End If:
         i < 10")
      ' use End If
      If i > 0 Then
         Console.WriteLine("Simple If with End If: i > 0")
      End If

      ' If that executes multiple statements
      If i = 1 Then
         Console.WriteLine("i equals 1")
         Console.WriteLine("You can write an If statement")
         Console.WriteLine("that executes multiple statements")
      End If

      ' If - Else
      If i = 2 Then
         Console.WriteLine("i equals 2")
      Else
         Console.WriteLine("If-Else: i does not equal 2")
      End If

      ' compound logical expressions
      If i = 1 Or i = 2 Then
         Console.WriteLine("Compound expression using Or:
           i equals 1 or 2")
      End If
      If i > 0 And i < 3 Then
         Console.WriteLine("Compound expression using And:
           i is > 0 and < 3")
      End If

      ' nested if to replace compound expression
      If i > 0 Then
         If i < 3 Then
            Console.WriteLine("Nested If: i is > 0 and < 3")
         End If
      End If

      ' ElseIf
      If i = 2 Then
         Console.WriteLine("i equals 2")
      ElseIf i <> 2 Then
         Console.WriteLine("Use ElseIf: i does not equal 2")
      End If

      ' Xor: only one expresison is true
      If i = 1 Xor i = 2 Xor i = 3 Then
```

```
            Console.WriteLine("Use Xor: i = 1 Xor i = 2 Xor
              i = 3 True")
         End If
         ' Xor: two expresisons are true
         If i = 1 Xor i = 2 Xor i < 3 Then
            Console.WriteLine("Use Xor: i = 1 Xor i = 2 Xor
              i < 3 True")
         Else
            Console.WriteLine("Use Xor: i = 1 Xor i = 2 Xor
              i < 3 False")
         End If

      End Sub
   End Module
```

Figure 3-13 IfDemo.vb listing

This module, similar to the previous examples, has a Main procedure that begins executing when the module is loaded into memory. The Main procedure begins with a statement declaring an `Integer` variable named `i`, initializing its value to 1.

```
Dim i As Integer = 1
```

Next is a simple If statement that evaluates the expression (`i < 10`) without an **`End If`**. If the expression is true, the **`WriteLine`** method is invoked to display the literal `"i < 10"`.

```
' simple If
If i < 10 Then Console.WriteLine("Simple If without End If: i < 10")
```

You use this form of the If when you want to execute a single statement when the expression is true. However, if you want to execute more than one statement, you use the second form with **`End If`**, as in the following example:

```
' use End If
If i > 0 Then
   Console.WriteLine("Simple If with End If: i > 0")
End If
```

The next example illustrates an If-Else statement. Here the expression being evaluated is `i = 2`. Because this expression evaluates to false, the statement following the **`Else`** is executed.

```
' If - Else
If i = 2 Then
   Console.WriteLine("i equals 2")
Else
   Console.WriteLine("If-Else: i does not equal 2")
End If
```

A **compound expression** consists of two or more expressions joined using the logical operators `Or` or `And`. The compound expression in the next example, `(i = 1 Or i = 2)`, reads "does variable `i` contain the value 1 or the value 2?" Because `i` does contain 1, this compound expression evaluates to true. The second statement contains the expression `(i > 0 And i < 3)`, which is interpreted as: "does the variable `i` contain a value that is greater than 0 *and* less than 3?" Again, because `i` contains 1, this compound expression is also true.

```
' compound logical expressions
If i = 1 Or i = 2 Then
   Console.WriteLine("Compound expression using Or: i equals 1 or 2")
End If
If i > 0 And i < 3 Then
   Console.WriteLine("Compound expression using And: i is > 0 and < 3")
End If
```


A **nested If** is an If statement written inside another If statement. Often you can replace a compound expression with a nested If. The following nested If example produces the same result as the preceding example using a compound expression. Notice that the second and third lines are indented to improve readability.

```
' nested if to replace compound expression
If i > 0 Then
   If i < 2 Then
      Console.WriteLine("Nested If: i is > 0 and < 2")
   End If
End If
```

VB .NET provides a statement called **`ElseIf`** which, as the name suggests, combines the keywords **`Else`** and **`If`**. The following statement first evaluates the expression `i = 2`. Because `i = 2` is false, **`ElseIf`** evaluates the expression `i <> 2` (`i` not equal to 2), which is indeed true.

```
' ElseIf
If i = 2 Then
   Console.WriteLine("i equals 2")
ElseIf i <> 2 Then
   Console.WriteLine("Use ElseIf: i does not equal 2")
End If
```

Figure 3-14 shows the output from IfDemo.

```
Simple If without End If: i < 10
Simple If with End If: i > 0
i equals 1
You can write an If statement
that executes multiple statements
If-Else: i does not equal 2
Compound expression using Or: i equals 1 or 2
Compound expression using And: i is > 0 and < 3
Nested If: i is > 0 and < 3
Use ElseIf: i does not equal 2
Use Xor: i = 1 Xor i = 2 Xor i = 3 True
Use Xor: i = 1 Xor i = 2 Xor i < 3 False
```

Figure 3-14 IfDemo output

Hands-on Exercise 4

1. Locate **IfDemo.vb** in the folder named Chap03\Examples\Ex04 in the book's data files, and then copy it to the Chap03\Exercises folder on your hard disk.
2. In VB .NET, create a project named **Exercise4**, add the module **IfDemo.vb**, and then set the startup object to **IfDemo** and the output type to **Console Application**. Refer to the instructions for Hands-on Exercise 1 to review how to create a project and add a module.
3. Click **Debug** on the menu bar, and then select **Start Without Debugging** to execute the code in IfDemo.vb. Verify that your output is the same as that shown in Figure 3-14. Then press **Enter** to close the console window.
4. Add code to IfDemo.vb to assign and display a letter grade based on an exam score using the following list. Write the code using If-Else statements. Test your statements using a score from each category to ensure your logic is correct.
5. Close the project.

Exam Score	Letter Grade
>=90	A
>=80 and < 90	B
>=70 and < 80	C
>=60 and < 70	D
< 60	F

Writing Select Case Statements

VB .NET implements the case structure with a statement called Select Case. This statement acts like a multiple-way If statement by transferring control to one of several statements or group of statements, depending on the value of a variable. Use a Select Case statement when you want to make a decision and there are more than two values you want to evaluate.

For Hands-on Exercise 4, you might have created a variable named `examScore` so you could display a letter grade based on the `examScore` contents. You wrote a solution to this problem using If statements in the Hands-on Exercise. However, you can also use the Select Case statement:

```
Select Case examScore
Case Is >= 90
   Console.WriteLine("The Grade is A")
Case 80 To 89
   Console.WriteLine("The Grade is B")
Case 70 To 79
   Console.WriteLine("The Grade is C")
```

```
Case 60 To 69
   Console.WriteLine("The Grade is D")
Case Else
   Console.WriteLine("The Grade is F")
End Select
```


The basic structure of the Select Case statement begins with the keyword **`Select Case`** followed by a variable name, and then by one or more Case statements, which are then followed by one or more statements to be executed if the variable contains the value or values specified. In this example, the variable is being evaluated. Each Case statement evaluates the contents of variable **`examScore`** for the value specified.

Each case can specify a relational operator (`Case Is >= 90`), a range of values (`Case 80 To 99`), or a list of values (`Case 10, 15, 20`). Note the use of the keywords **`Is`** and **`To`**. Also, note that the statement following **`Case Else`** is executed if none of the previous Case statements has been executed.

The Select Case statement is a powerful tool that can sometimes help you write simpler code by replacing lengthy nested If statements.

Writing Loops

Assume that you want to display the numbers 1 through 3. One technique is to write three statements displaying these values:

```
Console.WriteLine(1);
Console.WriteLine(2);
Console.WriteLine(3);
```

However, this method is time-consuming if you want to display the numbers 1 through 100, for example. An alternative technique is to write a loop. Loops are powerful programming tools that provide for the repeated execution of one or more statements until a terminating condition occurs. You can write loops to sum values, count things, and as you will see later in this chapter, access arrays. You write VB .NET loops using one of three sets of keywords: **`Do While`**, **`Do Until`**, or **`For Next`**, which are discussed in detail in the following sections.

Writing Do While Loops

The following code shows a loop to display the numbers 1 through 3:

```
' do while loop
' declare and initialize loop counter variable
Dim i As Integer = 1
Do While i <= 3
   Console.WriteLine("do while loop: i = " & i)
   i += 1
Loop
```

This loop, called a Do While loop, begins with a statement declaring an integer variable named `i` and initializing it to 1. Variable `i` is called a **loop counter** because it counts the number of times the loop is executed. Next come the keywords **`Do While`** followed by a logical expression `(i <= 3)`. The body of the loop contains two statements. The Do While loop continues executing these statements as long as the expression evaluates to true. When the expression becomes false, the loop terminates.

In this example, the loop body consists of two statements. The first displays the string literal `"do while loop: i = "` concatenated with the contents of variable `i`. The second statement increments `i`. Note the use of the shortcut add statement. You could have written `i = i + 1` instead of `i += 1`.

The first time this loop executes, `i` contains 1, which is displayed, and then `i` is incremented. The second time the loop executes, `i` contains 2, which is displayed, and then `i` is again incremented. The loop continues to the third iteration. At the beginning of the third iteration, `i` contains 3, which is displayed, and then `i` is incremented to 4. Next, the Do While expression evaluates to false and the loop terminates.

Note how easy it is to modify this loop to display the integer values between 1 and 1000. You simply change the expression to `(i <= 1000)`.

Incidentally, you can easily write an infinite loop. An infinite loop is a loop that never terminates, at least not without outside intervention. If you omit the statement to increment the loop counter, it will remain at its initial value and the expression will never be false. The following code creates an infinite loop:

```
' infinite do while loop
' declare and initialize loop counter variable
Dim i As Integer = 1
Do While i <= 3
   Console.WriteLine("do while loop: i = " & i)
Loop
```

Because `i` is not incremented, its value remains 1 and the Do While expression remains true.

VB .NET provides a variation of the Do While loop in the form of a While loop, which functions identically to the Do While loop. The following code displays the values 1, 2, and 3, the same as the previous example.

```
' while loop
i = 1  ' re-initialize loop counter variable
While i <= 3
   Console.WriteLine("While loop: i = " & i)
   i += 1
End While
```

Writing Do Until Loops

In the previous section, you saw how to write a Do While loop to display the integers 1 through 3. You can do the same thing using a Do Until loop. The following code displays 1, 2, and 3 just as the Do While loop did in the previous example.

```
' do until loop
i = 1  ' re-initialize loop counter variable
Do Until i > 3
   Console.WriteLine("do until loop: i = " & i)
   i += 1
Loop
```

Note the similarities between this Do Until code and the earlier Do While loop. The first statement here initializes a loop counter named `i`. Next, you write the keywords **`Do Until`** and the expression that, when true, will end the loop, followed by the statements you want to execute each time the loop repeats. These statements are identical to those in the Do While loop. At the end of the loop, you write the keyword **`Loop`**.

The difference between a Do While and Do Until loop is that the Do While loop executes *while* the expression is true. The Do Until loop executes *until* the expression is false.

Writing Post-Test Loops

In general, programming languages provide two kinds of loops: the **pre-test loop** and the **post-test loop**. The pre-test loop tests the terminating condition at the *beginning* of the loop, and the post-test loop checks at the *end*. Figure 3-15 maps the logic of these two loop structures. The post-test loop always executes the statements in the body of the loop at least once. In contrast, if the loop-terminating condition in a pre-test Do While loop is initially false, the loop exits without executing the statements in the loop body. Similarly, if the loop-terminating condition in a pre-test Do Until loop is initially true, the loop exits and the statements in the loop body are not executed. You will use a post-test loop when you want the statements in the loop to execute at least once, regardless of the state of the terminating condition. Use a pre-test loop when you want to exit the loop without executing any of the loop statements, if conditions warrant. The Do While and Do Until loops can be written as either pre-test or post-test loops. The For Next and While loops are always pre-test.

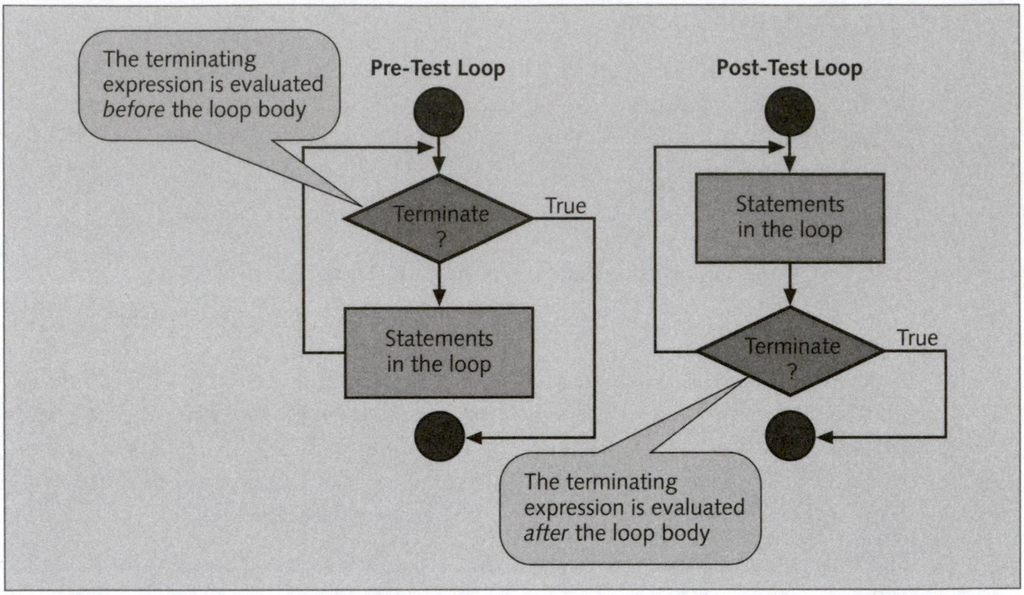

Figure 3-15 Loop structures

You can change a Do While loop from pre-test to post-test by moving the While clause to follow the loop statement, as in the following code:

```
' post-test do while loop
i = 1  ' re-initialize loop counter variable
Do
   Console.WriteLine("post-test do while loop: i = " & i)
   i += 1
Loop While (i <= 3)

' post-test do until loop
i = 1  ' re-initialize loop counter variable
Do
   Console.WriteLine("post-test do until loop: i = " & i)
   i += 1
Loop Until (i > 3)
```

Each of these loops displays the values 1, 2, and 3.

The following code illustrates the distinction between pre-test and post-test loop logic:

```
' pre-test & post-test loop compared
i = 1  ' re-initialize loop counter variable
' pre-test evaluates the expression at start of loop
Do While i > 3  ' expression initially false
   Console.WriteLine("pre-test executed")
Loop
```

```
' post-test evaluates the expression at end of loop
Do
   Console.WriteLine("post-test executed")
Loop While i > 3  ' expression initially false
```

3

The first statement initializes variable `i` to 1. Next comes a Do While loop with the expression `(i > 3)`, which is initially false. Because this is a pre-test Do While loop, it evaluates the expression at the beginning of the loop. The expression is false, and the statement within the loop is never executed.

The second loop is a post-test Do While loop. This means that the expression `(i > 3)` is evaluated at the end of the loop. Even though the expression is initially false, the statement in the loop executes once before the loop terminates. In this example, the pre-test and post-test versions of the Do While loop behave differently. Figure 3-16 contrasts a Do While loop with a Do Until loop.

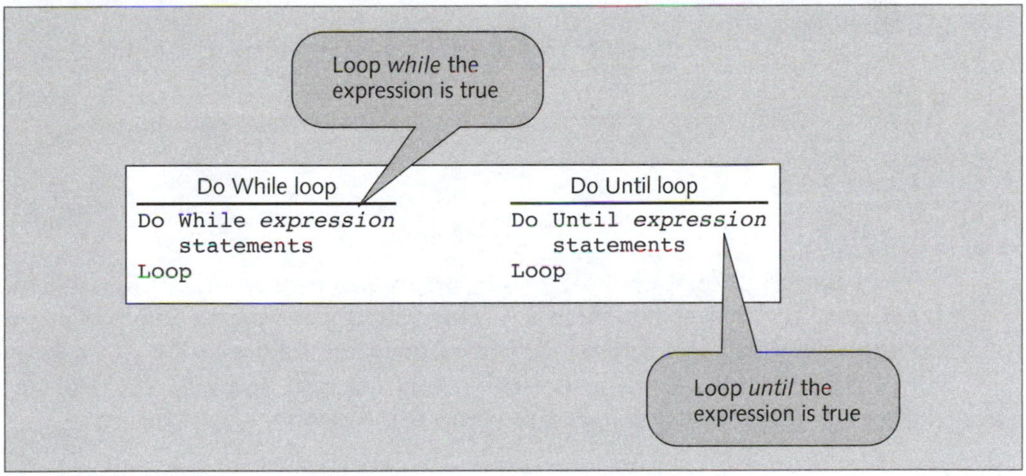

Figure 3-16 Contrasting Do While and Do Until loops

In summary, use a post-test loop when you want to force the execution of the statements in the loop body at least once, regardless of the expression's evaluation. Use a pre-test loop when you do not want to force this execution.

Writing For Next Loops

The VB .NET For Next loop allows you to include loop counter initialization and incrementing code as a part of the For statement, which simplifies and shortens your code. In addition, it always uses pre-test logic; it evaluates the terminating expression at the beginning of the loop. To illustrate, the following For Next loop displays the numbers 1, 2, and 3, similar to the previous Do loop examples.

```
' for next loop
For i = 1 To 3 Step 1
   Console.WriteLine("for next loop: i = " & i)
Next
```

As you can see, the For Next loop requires less code than Do loops because you can include the code to initialize, test, and increment the loop counter in a single line.

Figure 3-17 shows what each part of the statement does.

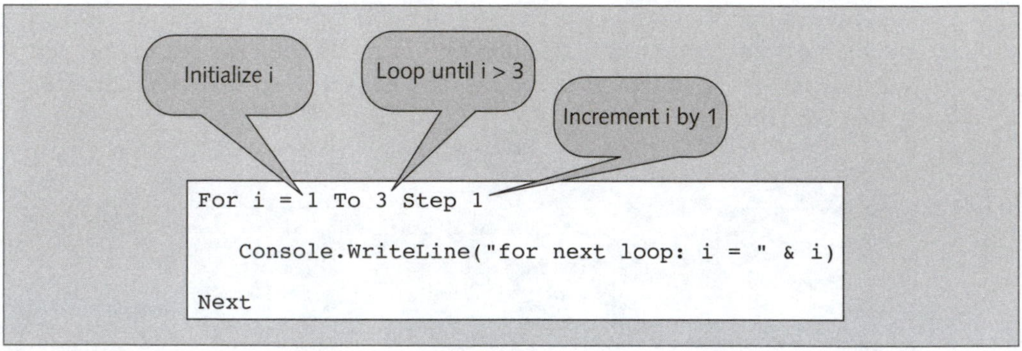

Figure 3-17 For Next loop

The keyword **`Step`** is optional if you want to increment your loop variable by 1 for each iteration. The default step value is 1. However, if you want to add a different value, you must specify that in a Step value. For example, the following For Next loop has a Step value of 2; it adds 2 to the loop variable `i` during each iteration. Note that the loop continues until `i` is greater than 3. This means that this loop will display 1 and 3.

```
' for next loop
For i = 1 To 3 Step 2
   Console.WriteLine("for next loop: i = " & i)
Next
```

Writing Nested Loops

Sometimes you may want to write a loop within a loop, which is called a **nested loop**. Nested loops are particularly useful when processing data arranged in rows and columns. You can use an outer loop to move across columns and an inner loop to access each row.

You can construct nested loops using any combination of Do While, Do Until, or For Next loops, although For Next loops generally reduce the number of lines of code. The following illustrates a For Next loop within another For Next loop. The outer loop uses a loop counter named `m` and the inner loop uses a counter named `n`.

```
' nested loop
Dim m, n As Integer
For m = 1 To 2
   For n = 1 To 3
      Console.WriteLine("nested loop: m = " & m & ",
        n = " & n)
   Next
Next
```


In this example, the outer loop executes twice, and each time it executes, the inner loop executes three times. In other words, while variable `m` contains 1, variable `n` will be incremented from 1 to 2 and then 3. For each iteration of the inner loop, the contents of both variables are displayed. The `WriteLine` method is invoked a total of six times. Note that this example omits the Step clause because the increment for each iteration is the default, 1.

All of the previous examples are contained in LoopDemo.vb, listed in Figure 3-18. The output from this code is shown in Figure 3-19.

```
' Chapter 3 LoopDemo Example 5
Option Strict On
Module LoopDemo
   Sub Main()
   ' do while loop
      ' declare and initialize loop counter variable
   Dim i As Integer = 1
   Do While i <= 3
      Console.WriteLine("do while loop: i = " & i)
      i += 1
   Loop

   ' while loop
   i = 1  ' re-initialize loop counter variable
   While i <= 3
      Console.WriteLine("While loop: i = " & i)
      i += 1
   End While

   ' do until loop
   i = 1  ' re-initialize loop counter variable
   Do Until i > 3
      Console.WriteLine("do until loop: i = " & i)
      i += 1
   Loop

   ' pre-test & post-test loop compared
   i = 1  ' re-initialize loop counter variable
   ' pre-test evaluates the expression at start  of loop
   Do While i > 3  ' expression initially false
      Console.WriteLine("pre-test executed")
   Loop

   ' post-test evaluates the expression at end of loop
```

```
   Do
      Console.WriteLine("post-test executed")
   Loop While i > 3  ' expression initially false

   ' for next loop
   For i = 1 To 3 Step 1
      Console.WriteLine("for next loop: i = " & i)
   Next

   ' nested loop
   Dim m, n As Integer
   For m = 1 To 2
      For n = 1 To 3
         Console.WriteLine("nested loop: m = " & m & ", n = " & n)
      Next
   Next

   End Sub
End Module
```

Figure 3-18 LoopDemo.vb listing

```
do while loop: i = 1
do while loop: i = 2
do while loop: i = 3
While loop: i = 1
While loop: i = 2
While loop: i = 3
do until loop: i = 1
do until loop: i = 2
do until loop: i = 3
post-test executed
for next loop: i = 1
for next loop: i = 2
for next loop: i = 3
nested loop: m = 1, n = 1
nested loop: m = 1, n = 2
nested loop: m = 1, n = 3
nested loop: m = 2, n = 1
nested loop: m = 2, n = 2
nested loop: m = 2, n = 3
```

Figure 3-19 LoopDemo output

Hands-on Exercise 5

1. Locate **LoopDemo.vb** in the Chap03\Examples\Ex05 folder in the book's data files, and then copy it to the Chap03\Exercises folder on your hard disk.
2. Use the VB .NET IDE to create a project named **Exercise5**, add the module **LoopDemo.vb**, and then set the startup object to **LoopDemo.vb** and the output type to **Console Application**. Refer to the instructions for Hands-on Exercise 1 to review how to create a project and add a module. Execute the code without debugging. Verify that your output is the same as that shown in Figure 3-19. Press **Enter** to close the output window.
3. Add statements to LoopDemo.vb that use a For Next loop to display the even integers 10, 8, 6, 4, and 2. *Hint*: The Step value can be negative.
4. Close the project.

Declaring and Accessing Arrays

Like most other languages, VB .NET lets you declare arrays to create a group of several variables *with the same data type*. Arrays consist of elements, and each element behaves like a variable, except that all of the array elements must have the same data type.

Array elements, like all variables, either can contain primitive data or can be reference variables. Recall that reference variables point to instances of a class, such as String, or as you will shortly see, to an array. The next chapter describes reference variables in more detail and includes several examples.

Arrays can be either one-dimensional or multidimensional. A **one-dimensional array** consists of elements arranged in a single row. Conceptually, a **two-dimensional array** has *both* rows and columns, and a **three-dimensional array** is like a cube, with rows, columns, and pages. However, VB .NET implements multidimensional arrays as arrays of arrays; therefore, you are not restricted by rectangles and cubes. Both one- and two-dimensional arrays are illustrated in the following sections.

Using One-Dimensional Arrays

If you need to have five integer values, such as test scores from an exam, you could declare and use five integer variables, as in the following code:

```
Dim testScore1 As Integer = 75
Dim testScore2 As Integer = 80
Dim testScore3 As Integer = 70
Dim testScore4 As Integer = 85
Dim testScore5 As Integer = 90
```

An alternative is to use a one-dimensional array. To declare a five-element array with integer elements, you could write the following lines of code:

```
' declare an integer array with 5 elements
Dim testScores(4) As Integer
```

This code declares an array reference variable `testScores`, and then creates an array instance containing five elements, each with data type `Integer`. Note that you write the number 4 in parentheses to define five elements. This is because VB .NET numbers the array elements beginning with zero. When you write the number 4 in an array definition, you are specifying that the last element number is 4, which really means that your array has *five elements*.

You can access the individual elements of the array by writing the array reference variable, `testScores`, followed by the index value of the element enclosed in parentheses. In the five-element array example above, the first element can be accessed by writing `testScores(0)`, the second element by writing `testScores(1)`, and so forth. Note that index values begin with 0, instead of 1. This is why you specify 4 when you define the array; 4 is the index of the last element, which is actually the *fifth* element.

The code to initialize the array elements is similar to that code used previously to initialize the variables. The following code assigns the value 75 to the first array element (index value 0), 80 to the second, and so on.

```
testScores(0) = 75
testScores(1) = 80
testScores(2) = 70
testScores(3) = 85
testScores(4) = 90
```

If you wish, you can declare and populate the array using a single statement, as shown in the next code sample. This code is noticeably shorter and works well with smaller arrays.

```
Dim testScores() As Integer = {75, 80, 70, 85, 90}
```

Note that `testScores` is a reference variable. It points or refers to an array instance with five integer elements containing the values shown in Figure 3-20. The array instance has an attribute named `Length` that contains the number of elements in the array, which in this example is five. You will see how this attribute is used in an upcoming example.

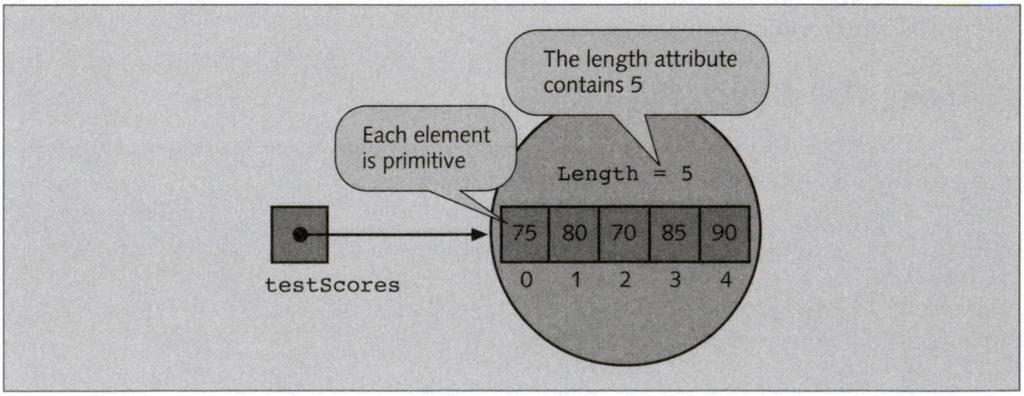

Figure 3-20 A five-element `Integer` array

You write statements to display the contents of each array element similar to the way you display the contents of individual variables. The following statements display the contents of each element of the `testScores` array. Notice that these statements are similar to each other; the only difference is the descriptive literal and the index value.

```
Console.WriteLine("test score 1 = " & testScores(0))
Console.WriteLine("test score 2 = " & testScores(1))
Console.WriteLine("test score 3 = " & testScores(2))
Console.WriteLine("test score 4 = " & testScores(3))
Console.WriteLine("test score 5 = " & testScores(4))
```


Assume that you want to compute the average of the values stored in `testScores`. Logically, you first compute the sum of the elements, and then divide by 5. One technique is to write five addition statements, and then divide, as in the following code.

```
Dim average As Double
average = average + testScores(0)
average = average + testScores(1)
average = average + testScores(2)
average = average + testScores(3)
average = average + testScores(4)
average = average / 5
Console.WriteLine ("average score is " & average)
```

Notice that the five addition statements are identical *except for the index value*. The first index value is 0, the second is 1, and so forth. This suggests that you can write a loop to do the computation instead of writing numerous addition statements. A loop is especially appropriate when working with larger arrays. You can certainly write five statements to compute the sum of an array with five elements; however, it is impractical to write 100 statements to compute the sum of an array having 100 elements.

To illustrate, you can write a For Next loop to compute the sum of the array contents, as in the following code.

```
Dim average As Single
Dim i As Integer
For i = 0 To 4
   average += testScores(i)
Next
```

Here the addition statement, which now uses the `+=` assignment operator, is executed five times. The first time it is executed, the index variable `i` contains 0 and therefore points to the first element of `testScores`. On the second iteration, `i` contains 1, pointing to the second element, and so forth. Note that you can easily change this loop to compute the sum of an array with 100 elements by changing the terminating expression from `0 To 4` to `0 To 99`. After the loop, you can write a statement to divide by 5 to compute the average.

Figure 3-20 showed you that an array is an instance with the attribute `Length` containing the number of array elements. The array `testScores` has five elements; therefore, `Length` contains 5 and you can substitute the expression `Length - 1` for 4 in the loop. Using the

`Length` attribute eliminates the need to change the loop code if the number of array elements is changed. The following code will work for an array of any size:

```
Dim average As Single
Dim i As Integer
For i = 0 To testScores.Length - 1
   average += testScores(i)
Next
```

A module named ArrayDemo.vb showing these array examples is listed in Figure 3-21, and the output is shown in Figure 3-22.

```
' Chapter 3 ArrayDemo Example 6
Option Strict On
Module ArrayDemo
   Sub Main()
   ' declare an integer array with 5 elements
   Dim testScores(4) As Integer
   ' populate the array
   testScores(0) = 75
   testScores(1) = 80
   testScores(2) = 70
   testScores(3) = 85
   testScores(4) = 90

   'display the element contents
   Console.WriteLine("test score 1 = " & testScores(0))
   Console.WriteLine("test score 2 = " & testScores(1))
   Console.WriteLine("test score 3 = " & testScores(2))
   Console.WriteLine("test score 4 = " & testScores(3))
   Console.WriteLine("test score 5 = " & testScores(4))

   ' compute the average score using length attribute
   Dim average As Single
   Dim i As Integer
   For i = 0 To testScores.Length - 1
      average += testScores(i)
   Next
   average = average / testScores.Length
   Console.WriteLine("the average test score is " & _
      average)
   End Sub
End Module
```

Figure 3-21 ArrayDemo.vb listing

```
test score 1 = 75
test score 2 = 80
test score 3 = 70
test score 4 = 85
test score 5 = 90
the average test score is 80
```

Figure 3-22 ArrayDemo output

Hands-on Exercise 6

1. Locate **ArrayDemo.vb** in the folder named Chap03\Examples\Ex06 in the book's data files, and then copy it to the Chap03\Exercises folder on your hard disk.
2. Use the VB .NET IDE to create a project named **Exercise6**, add the module **ArrayDemo.vb**, and then set the startup object to **ArrayDemo** and the output type to **Console Application**. Refer to the instructions for Hands-on Exercise 1 to review how to create a project and add a module. Execute the code without debugging. Verify that your output is the same as that shown in Figure 3-22. Press **Enter** to close the console window.
3. Add code to ArrayDemo.vb to iterate the `testScores` array using a For Next loop to determine and display the letter grade for each exam, using the following list. Write the code using nested if statements.
4. Close the project.

Exam Score	Letter Grade
>=90	A
>=80 and < 90	B
>=70 and < 80	C
>=60 and < 70	D
< 60	F

Using Multidimensional Arrays

In addition to one-dimensional arrays, VB .NET supports multidimensional arrays. Recall that conceptually, a two-dimensional array is like a table with rows and columns, and a three-dimensional array is like a cube, with rows, columns, and pages. Each dimension has its own index. Generally you work with either one- or two-dimensional arrays.

You can expand the previous test scores example to use a two-dimensional array with five rows and two columns. The two columns represent the two tests and the five rows represent the five students, as shown in Table 3-6. The first column contains the same values as the previous one-dimensional array, `testScores`.

Table 3-6 Test Scores

	Test 1	Test 2
Student 1	75	80
Student 2	80	90
Student 3	70	60
Student 4	85	95
Student 5	90	100

You declare a two-dimensional array similar to the way you declare a one-dimensional array, but you specify both the number of rows and columns. The following code declares an `Integer` array named `testScoreTable` with five rows and two columns. Note that you specify the index of the last row (4) and the last column (1).

```
Dim testScoreTable(4, 1) As Integer
```

Populate this array using the same technique used with the one-dimensional array earlier.

```
' populate the elements in column 1
testScoreTable(0, 0) = 75
testScoreTable(1, 0) = 80
testScoreTable(2, 0) = 70
testScoreTable(3, 0) = 85
testScoreTable(4, 0) = 90

' populate the elements in column 2
testScoreTable(0, 1) = 80
testScoreTable(1, 1) = 90
testScoreTable(2, 1) = 60
testScoreTable(3, 1) = 95
testScoreTable(4, 1) = 100
```

VB .NET implements multidimensional arrays by creating an array of arrays. The two-dimensional array structure for the `testScoreTable` example is shown graphically in Figure 3-23.

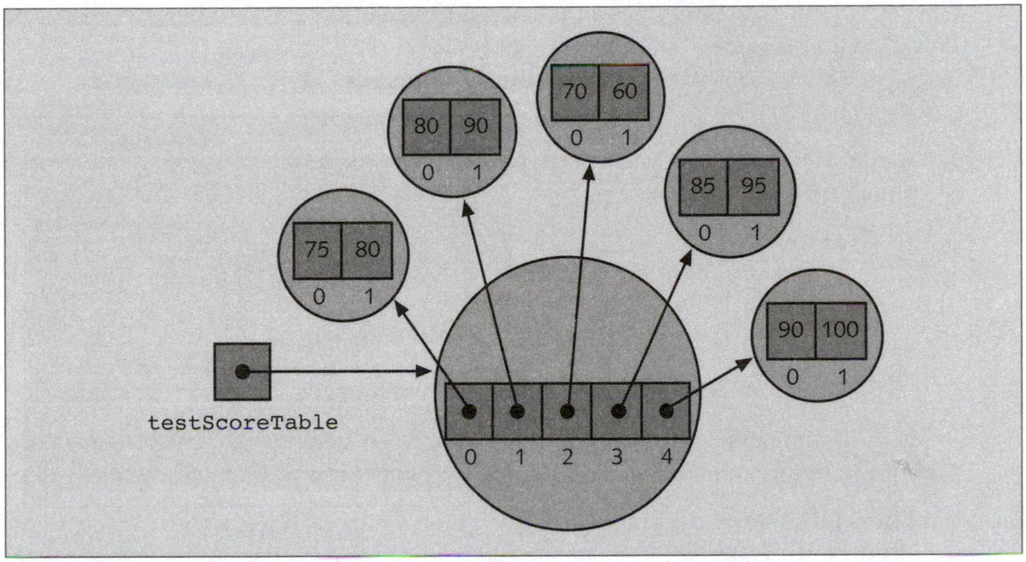

Figure 3-23 An array of arrays

The reference variable **`testScoreTable`** points to the array instance containing five elements, one for each row. Each of these elements, in turn, is a reference to a second array instance containing two elements, one for each column. You should note that there are actually six array instances shown. Each of them contains elements and has a length attribute. Because each row of a two-dimensional array is actually a separate array object, each row does not have to be the same length. In other words, you can create a two-dimensional array where the first row has two elements, the second row five elements, and so forth. Although you usually work with two-dimensional arrays having rows of the same length, you have the option of having rows with different lengths.

In this example, each column represents a separate test. Column 1 contains the scores for test 1, and column 2 contains the scores for test 2. There are three distinct approaches you may take to compute the average for each test. First, you can write individual statements to compute the sum of each column, and then compute its average. Second, you can write two loops to compute the average for each column. Or you can write a nested loop, a loop within a loop to add the two columns and compute their average.

The following code illustrates the first approach by computing the sum of column 1, and then its average. Notice that these computation statements use the assignment operator **+=**, which sums **`average`** and the **`testScoreTable`** element, and then assigns the result to **`average`**. Also, notice that the column index remains 0, but that the row index goes from 0 to 4. You would need to write similar code to compute the average for the second column.

```
average = 0
average += testScoreTable(0, 0)
average += testScoreTable(1, 0)
average += testScoreTable(2, 0)
```

```
average += testScoreTable(3, 0)
average += testScoreTable(4, 0)
Console.WriteLine("test  1 average is " & average/5)
```

The second approach is to write two loops, one for each column, to compute the sum and average. The following code illustrates a loop for the first column. You would need to write a similar loop for column 2.

```
average = 0
' sum column 1
For row = 0 To 4
   average += testScoreTable(row, 0)
Next
Console.WriteLine("test  1 average is " & average/5)
```

In this example the row index is named **row**. Again, note that the column index remains a constant 0 throughout the execution of this loop, but that **row** is incremented for each iteration.

The third solution to compute the average score for each test is to write a nested loop. In this example, the outer loop will iterate twice, once for each column. The inner loop will iterate five times *for each iteration* of the outer loop.

```
' compute the average test score using nested for next loop
Dim row, col As Integer
Dim average As Single
For col = 0 To 1
   average = 0
   For row = 0 To 4
      average += testScoreTable(row, col)
Next  ' end of inner loop
   ' compute the column average
   average = average / 5
   Console.WriteLine("test " & (col + 1) & _
      " average score is " & average)
Next              ' end of outer loop
```

This example begins by declaring two counter variables and the variable **average**, which will contain the computation results. Next is the code for the outer loop, which will execute twice, once for each column. The outer loop counter here is named **col** and is used as the column index. The first time the loop executes, **col** will contain 0, and the second time it will contain 1.

The first statement within the outer loop initializes **average** to zero. The outer loop executes twice, once for each column. After its first iteration, **average** will contain the average of the first column. It must be reset to zero before the computation for the second column begins.

The inner loop comes next and uses a loop counter named **row**, which is used as the row index. The inner loop executes five times, once for each row. The single statement within the inner loop simply adds the contents of the array element indexed by **row** and **col** to the variable **average**.

```
average += testScoreTable(row, col)
```

After the inner loop iterates five times, **average** contains the column total. Next comes a statement to divide the total by 5 to compute the average. Following that, the last statement in the outer loop displays the average.

```
average = average / 5
Console.WriteLine("test " & (col + 1) & _
   " average score is " & average)
```

Figure 3-24 lists TwoDimArrayDemo.vb, and its output is shown in Figure 3-25.

```
' Chapter 3 TwoDimArrayDemo Example 7
Option Strict On
Module TwoDimArrayDemo
   Sub Main()
   ' declare an integer array with 5 rows and 2 columns
   Dim testScoreTable(4, 1) As Integer
   ' populate the elements in column 1
   testScoreTable(0, 0) = 75
   testScoreTable(1, 0) = 80
   testScoreTable(2, 0) = 70
   testScoreTable(3, 0) = 85
   testScoreTable(4, 0) = 90
   ' populate the elements in column 1
   testScoreTable(0, 1) = 80
   testScoreTable(1, 1) = 90
   testScoreTable(2, 1) = 60
   testScoreTable(3, 1) = 95
   testScoreTable(4, 1) = 100

   ' compute the average test score using nested loop
   Dim row, col As Integer
   Dim average As Single
   For col = 0 To 1
      average = 0
      For row = 0 To 4
         average += testScoreTable(row, col)
   Next  ' end of inner loop

      ' compute the column average
      average = average / 5
      Console.WriteLine("test " & (col + 1) & _
         " average score is " & average)
   Next  ' end of outer loop
   End Sub
End Module
```

Figure 3-24 TwoDimArrayDemo.vb listing

```
test 1 average score is 80
test 2 average score is 85
```

Figure 3-25 TwoDimArrayDemo output

Hands-on Exercise 7

1. Locate **TwoDimArrayDemo.vb** in the folder named Chap03\Examples\Ex07 in the book's data files, and then copy it to the Chap03\Exercises folder on your hard disk.
2. Use the VB .NET IDE to create a project named **Exercise7**, add the module **TwoDimArrayDemo.vb**, and then set the startup object to **TwoDimArrayDemo** and the output type to **Console Application**. Refer to the instructions for Hands-on Exercise 1 to review how to create a project and add a module. Execute the code without debugging. Verify that your output is the same as that shown in Figure 3-25. Close the console window.
3. Add code to display a letter grade for each student for each exam using the grade-assignment logic from Hands-on Exercise 6. In addition to the letter grade, display the exam number (column number + 1) and the student number (row number + 1).
4. Close the project, and exit Visual Studio .NET.

Chapter Summary

- VB .NET is a new language developed by Microsoft and released in early 2002. It is designed to be a powerful, full-featured, object-oriented development language and has achieved enormous popularity and widespread acceptance.
- VB .NET comes with a large class library containing hundreds of prewritten classes with methods to accomplish various tasks, ranging from establishing network connections to accessing relational databases.
- An identifier is the name of a class, method, or variable.
- A comment begins with a single quote (`'`) and can be on a line by itself or at the end of a line of code.
- If a module has a procedure or method named Main, it is automatically invoked when the module is loaded into memory; the Main procedure is what executes.
- You declare a variable to name a place in memory that can contain data. All variables have a data type, name, and value.
- VB .NET has nine primitive data types. These are called primitive data types to distinguish them from more complex data types, such as class names, which are discussed in Chapter 4.

- To declare a variable, you write the keyword **`Dim`**, the name you want to use, and the keyword **`As`**, followed by the data type you wish to use. You can declare several variables of the same data type in one statement.
- The equal sign (=) is called the assignment operator. This operator assigns the value on the right side of the equal sign to the variable named on the left side.
- If Option Explicit On is set, you must invoke a method in the Convert class when assigning the contents of one variable to a variable with a data type with less capacity than the first variable.
- The code to declare a constant is identical to the one you use to declare a variable, but with the keyword **`Const`** instead of **`Dim`**.
- Constants must be initialized in the same statement that declares them.
- VB .NET has two kinds of variables: primitive variables and reference variables. A primitive variable is a variable declared with one of the nine primitive data types and actually contains the data you put there. In contrast, a reference variable uses a class name as a data type and refers to or points to an instance of that class. A reference variable does not actually contain the data; instead, it refers to an instance of a class that contains the data.
- The concatenation operator (`&`) joins two string values.
- VB .NET uses the familiar arithmetic operators for addition, subtraction, multiplication, and division (`+`, `-`, `*`, `/`).
- VB .NET uses a remainder operator (`Mod`), sometimes called the modulus operator, to produce a remainder resulting from the division of two integers.
- The Math class, one of the supplied classes in VB .NET, has methods to accomplish exponentiation, rounding, and numerous other tasks.
- VB .NET supports the use of the assignment operator (=) together with the arithmetic operators (`+`, `-`, `*`, `/`) to create assignment operators (`+=`, `-=`, `*=`, `/=`).
- VB .NET provides two ways to write decision-making statements: the If statement and the Select Case statement.
- The If statement interrogates a logical expression that evaluates to true or false. An expression often compares two values using logical operators to see if they are equal or if one is less than the other.
- The If statement has two forms. The first form evaluates an expression and then executes one or more statements if the expression is true. The second form, called an If Else, evaluates an expression, executes one set of statements if the expression is true or executes a second set of statements if it is false.

- A nested If is an If statement written inside another If statement.
- A compound expression consists of two expressions joined using the logical operators `Or` or `And`.
- The *equal to* operator is the equal sign (=), and the *not equal to* operator is <>, or `Not =`.
- VB .NET implements the case structure with a statement called Select Case, which acts like a multiple-way If statement by transferring control to one of several statements or sets of statements, depending on the value of an expression.
- You write VB .NET loops using one of three keywords: **`Do While`**, **`Do Until`**, or **`For Next`**. You can replace the **`Do While`** with **`While`**.
- There are two kinds of loops: the pre-test loop and the post-test loop. The pre-test loop tests the terminating condition at the beginning of the loop, and the post-test loop checks at the end. Do While and Do Until loops can be either pre-test or post-test, but For Next loops are always pre-test.
- A nested loop is a loop within a loop.
- A one-dimensional array consists of elements arranged in a single row. A two-dimensional array has both rows and columns, and a three-dimensional array is like a cube, with rows, columns, and pages.
- You access the individual elements of an array by writing the array reference variable followed by the index value of the element enclosed in parentheses.
- The array instance has an attribute named `Length` that contains the number of elements in the array.

Key Terms

argument
arithmetic operator
assignment operator
class definition
comment
compound expression
concatenation operator
constant
form definition
identifier
integer division operator
keyword
literal
logical operator
loop counter
module definition
module header
modulus operator
nested If
nested loop
Nothing
one-dimensional array
Option Explicit
Option Strict
post-test loop
pre-test loop
primitive data type

primitive variable
procedure
procedure header
reference variable
remainder operator
three-dimensional array
two-dimensional array

Review Questions

1. What is an IDE?
2. What is a VB .NET identifier? What are the rules for creating one?
3. What is a keyword?
4. What is a primitive variable?
5. How can you tell if an identifier is a constant?
6. What does the keyword `Nothing` mean?
7. What is an argument?
8. What is the Main procedure?
9. Explain the difference between the divide and the remainder operators.
10. What is the purpose of the Select Case statement?
11. What are the two types of loops? How does VB .NET implement each of these?
12. What is an index?
13. How do you declare a one-dimensional array?
14. How can you tell that an array is actually an instance?
15. What is the Length attribute of a one-dimensional array?

Discussion Questions

1. Discuss the advantages of using methods instead of built-in functions.
2. What impact does using methods have on the number of keywords a language requires?
3. Why do you think VB .NET has three separate statements to write loops? Is it not simpler to use just one, such as the For Next loop?

4. Can you think of any benefit to having Option Explicit and Option Strict set to on? Would it be simpler and easier to allow you to assign values from one data type to another without forcing you to worry about data types?

Projects

1. Assume a bank account begins with a balance of $100 and earns interest at an annual rate of 5 percent. The interest is computed at the end of each year using the following formula:

```
newBalance = previousBalance * (1 + interestRate)
```

   Write a module named ComputeInterest to compute and display this account balance at the end of each year for a five-year period. Do not use loops for Project 1.

2. Repeat Project 1 using a Do While loop, a Do Until loop, and then a For Next loop. Which loop do you believe is most appropriate for this problem?

3. The following table contains quarterly sales figures for five departments:

	Quarter 1	Quarter 2	Quarter 3	Quarter 4	Total
Department 1	750	660	910	800	
Department 2	800	700	950	900	
Department 3	700	600	750	600	
Department 4	850	800	1000	950	
Department 5	900	800	960	980	
Total					

   Design and write a module named SalesAnalysis that will:

   a. Declare a two-dimensional integer array named Sales. Populate the first four columns using the above data.

   b. Write a loop to compute and populate the Total column. Within the loop, display each department total as it is computed.

   c. Write a loop to compute and populate the Total row. Within the loop, display each quarter's total as it is computed.

4. Continue working with Project 3 by writing a nested loop that will compute and display:

   a. the percentage of total sales made by each department for each quarter and overall

   b. the percentage of total sales made each quarter

CHAPTER

4

VB .NET Programming with Supplied Classes

In this chapter you will:

- Use the namespaces and classes supplied with VB .NET
- Use the `String` class
- Create a String array
- Use the `ArrayList` class
- Work with dates
- Format numeric output
- Use the `MessageBox` class
- Display a `Form`

The previous chapter presented VB .NET fundamentals, including an overview of the VB language and its syntax. You saw how to declare and initialize variables and how to write computational statements. In addition, you learned about writing loops, coding decision-making statements, and working with arrays.

You saw that the VB .NET syntax is simple and straightforward. Much of this simplicity is accomplished by using methods in predefined classes that are supplied as part of VB .NET. This chapter focuses on working with some of these supplied classes. You begin by learning more about the `String` class and seeing how to create and access a String array.

The chapter then introduces the `ArrayList` class and illustrates how you can use it like a dynamically resizable array. Next you will explore how to format data, both string and numeric, to create more attractive and readable output.

You will learn how to work with dates using the `Date` class and then discover the power of the `MessageBox` class, which you will use to display messages in various formats, and then determine the user's response to the message.

After completing this chapter, you will understand the importance of the supplied classes and be able to use methods in several of them. In the next part of the book, you begin developing your own classes, which are the building blocks of object-oriented applications.

USING THE NAMESPACES AND CLASSES SUPPLIED WITH VB .NET

VB .NET is part of Microsoft's Visual Studio .NET, which is itself a part of the larger .NET technology. Included in Visual Studio .NET are several languages such as C++ .NET, C# .NET, and VB .NET. Two important pieces of the .NET framework are the **Common Language Runtime (CLR)** and the .NET class library. The CLR supports common services such as data types that are used by all of the Visual Studio .NET languages, providing standardization and reducing duplication. In addition, the class library can be used by any of the CLR languages.

The .NET class library consists of hundreds of predefined classes and their methods, organized into **namespaces**. A namespace is a group of related classes, similar to a library. You use the keyword **`Imports`** to give the compiler access to classes contained in specific namespaces. You can also assign classes to a namespace that you define. Table 4-1 lists selected namespaces and shows a few of the classes within each namespace.

Table 4-1 Selected Namespaces and Classes

Namespace	Selected Classes	Discussed in Chapter(s)

`System`	`Array`
	`Console`
	`Convert`
	`DateTime`
	`Exception`
	`TimeSpan`
	`String`
	`Math`
		2, 3, 4

`System.Collections`	`ArrayList`	4
`System.IO`	`StreamReader` `StreamWriter`	13

`System.Data`	`DataRow`
	`DataTable`
	`DataSet`
		13, 14, 15

`System.Data.OleDb`	`OleDbCommand`
	`OleDbConnection`
	`OleDbDataAdapter`
	`OleDbParameter`
		13, 14, 15

`System.Windows.Forms`	`Button`
	`CheckBox`
	`Form`
	`Label`
	`Menu`
	`MenuItem`
	`RadioButton`
	`TextBox`
		10, 11, 15

Table 4-1 Selected Namespaces and Classes (continued)

Namespace	Selected Classes	Discussed in Chapter(s)
System.Web	System.data System.data.oledb System.Collections System.Web System.Web.UI System.Web.UI.WebControls System.Web.Services	16

4

The first two of these namespaces, `System` and `System.Collections`, are used in this chapter. `System` is automatically imported by the compiler; however, if you want to access the methods or attributes of classes in any of the other namespaces, you must write the keyword **`Imports`** followed by the namespace you need. If you omit the **`Imports`** statement, the compiler will be unable to locate the class, and error messages will result.

Classes in `System.Windows.Forms` are used in Chapters 10 and 11, which deal with developing GUI classes. The classes in `System.Data`, `System.IO`, and `System.Data.OleDb` are used in Chapters 13 and 14 to access data in relational databases. Chapter 16, which deals with Web deployment, employs classes in `System.Web`.

USING THE `String` CLASS

As in many other languages, a string is a collection of characters. VB .NET, however, stores string data in instances of the `String` class, a member of the `System` namespace. You saw in the previous chapter that you can declare a string using code similar to that used to declare a primitive value:

```
Dim s1 As String = "Hello Again"
```

This code actually creates an instance of the `String` class. This is called **instantiating** a class and means you are creating an instance of the class. The statement performs three functions: It first tells VB .NET to create a variable named `s1` whose data type is `String`; it then creates an instance of the `String` class and populates the instance with the string value "Hello Again"; and finally it assigns the location of the new instance to the variable `s1`. Using the data type `String` means that `s1` will point to, or reference, a `String` instance; it is a *reference* variable. Object-oriented programming involves instantiating numerous classes, as you will see throughout this text. Figure 4-1 shows the `String` instance you just created.

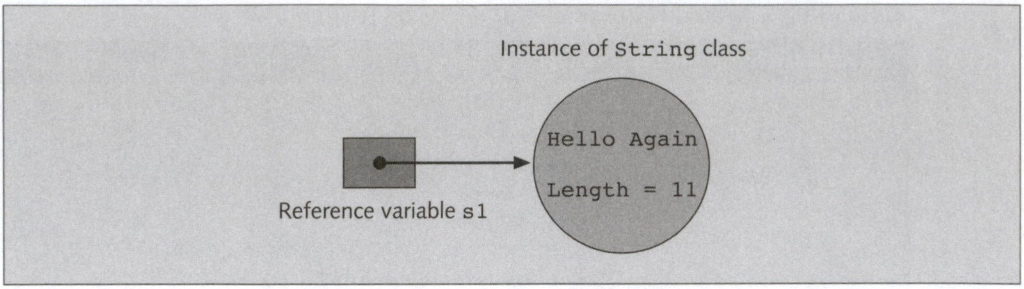

Figure 4-1 A `String` instance

As a class, `String` has several useful methods and properties. A property is a special kind of VB .NET method that appears like an attribute that you can access, such as a public variable. Chapter 6 describes properties in more detail and shows you how to write them. Table 4-2 lists selected methods and properties in the `String` class. Notice that most of the methods are invoked using a reference variable (`s` in these examples), but that the `Copy` method is invoked by specifying the class name, `String`.

Table 4-2 Selected `String` Methods and Properties

Method/Property Name	Description
`s.Chars(i)`	Method gets the character in the `String` instance `s` at index `i` (relative to zero)
`String.Copy(s)`	Method returns a new `String` instance, which is a copy of `s`
`s.EndsWith("a")`	Method returns Boolean True if the `String` instance `s` ends with the string value "a"; otherwise returns `False`
`s.Equals(s1)`	Method compares values character-by-character in `String` instances `s` and `s1` and returns either `True` or `False`
`s.IndexOf("a")`	Method returns the index (relative to zero) of the first occurrence of the character "a" in `String` instance `s`. A return of –1 means not found. A value of 0 means `s` contains nothing.
`s.Insert(i, "a")`	Method inserts the string value "a" into `s` beginning at index `i` (relative to zero) and returns the new `String` instance
`s.Length`	Property gets the number of characters in the string, its length
`s.Replace("a","b")`	Method searches `s` for the string value "a", replaces it with the string "b", and returns the new `String` instance
`s.Split("a")`	Method returns a String array containing substrings separated by "a"
`s.StartsWith("a")`	Method returns Boolean `True` if `String` instance `s` begins with the string value "a"; otherwise returns `False`

Table 4-2 Selected `String` Methods and Properties (continued)

Method/Property Name	Description
`s.Substring(i,j)`	Method returns a new `String` instance containing the string of characters in instance `s` beginning at index `i` and ending at `j` (relative to zero)
`s.ToUpper()`	Method returns a new `String` instance containing the contents of instance `s` converted to uppercase
`s.ToLower()`	Method returns a new `String` instance containing the contents of instance `s` converted to lowercase

The following discussion and examples illustrate the use of the `String` methods listed in Table 4-2. There are two important characteristics of `String` instances. First, string values in VB .NET are **immutable**: They cannot be changed. Methods that appear to change a string value, such as `Insert`, `Replace`, and `ToUpper`, actually create and return a new `String` instance.

Second, each character in a `String` instance has an index that indicates its position. However, as you saw with arrays in Chapter 3, index values in VB .NET begin with zero. This means that the first character's index is 0, the second's is 1, and so on. Earlier you defined a new string variable named `s1`, created a `String` instance containing "Hello Again," and populated `s1` by writing the single statement:

```
Dim s1 As String = "Hello Again"
```

Figure 4-2 illustrates the index values for each character in this string.

H	e	l	l	o		A	g	a	i	n
0	1	2	3	4	5	6	7	8	9	10

Figure 4-2 String s1 index values

Note that in Figure 4-1 the `String` property named `Length` contains the number of characters in the string, which is 11 in this example. You can access the Length property by writing the reference variable and `Length`.

```
' Length property contains the number of characters
Console.WriteLine("length of s1 is " & s1.Length)
```

Using String Methods

Assume for a moment that you want to create a duplicate of the **String** instance **s1** and reference this copy with a reference variable named **s2**. The following statement invokes the **Copy** method, which returns a second **String** that is a copy of the **String** sent as an argument to the method.

```
' create a copy of s1
Dim s2 As String = String.Copy(s1)
Console.WriteLine("s2, a copy of s1, contains " & s2)
```

If you were to write the following statement, you would simply create a reference variable that references the same instance as the first. In other words, both **s1** and **s2** point to, or reference, the same **String** instance that contains "Hello Again."

```
Dim s2 As String = s1    ' assign the contents of s1 to s2
```

When you invoke the **Copy** method, you create a *second* instance, which is referenced by **s2**.

Incidentally, a common error for VB .NET programmers is to attempt to invoke an instance method using a reference variable that has not yet been initialized. In other words, the variable contains nothing and *does not point to an instance*, so VB .NET cannot possibly invoke the method you request. When you make this error, VB .NET terminates the execution of your code and displays a message stating that you have a NullReferenceException. When you get this message, look for the statement containing the reference variable that caused the error and then add the code needed to initialize the reference variable.

The **Chars** method returns the character at a specified index. The following statement invokes **Chars** for the **String** instance referenced by **s1**, and passes an argument of 6. The method returns the character at index 6, which is "A."

```
Console.WriteLine("char at index 6 of s1 is " & s1.Chars(6))
```

You saw in Chapter 3 that you use the equal sign (=) in an expression to see whether two values are equal. You can use this same approach to compare two string values. In this example the instance referenced by **s2** is a copy of the **s1** instance, so they contain equal values.

```
If s1 = s2 Then Console.WriteLine("s1 = s2")
```

You can also invoke the **String** method **Equals** to see whether two string values are the same. In fact, when you use the equal sign as above, the VB .NET compiler actually generates code to invoke **Equals**. Note that VB .NET is case sensitive when comparing string values.

```
Console.WriteLine("s1.Equals(s2) returns " & s1.Equals(s2))
```

The purpose of the **SubString** method is to extract one or more characters from a **String** instance, then return a new **String** instance containing the extracted characters. The first argument is the index of the first character to extract, and the second argument is the number of characters to extract. The following example will begin at index 0 and extract five characters (Hello).

```
Console.WriteLine("s1.Substring(0, 5) returns " & s1.Substring(0, 5))
```

As its name suggests, you invoke the **Replace** method when you want to replace one or more characters in a string with one or more other characters. You send two arguments to **Replace**. The first is a string containing the characters to be replaced, and the second is a string containing the replacement characters. This example replaces the **String** "Hello" with the **String** "Hi" in **s1**. Remember that **String** instances are immutable: They cannot be changed. Methods such as **Replace** actually create and return a new **String** instance. In these examples you are passing the **String** instances that are being returned to the **WriteLine** method.


```
Console.WriteLine("s1.Replace(Hello, Hi) returns " & _
    s1.Replace("Hello", "Hi"))
Console.WriteLine("After Replace s1 contains " & s1)
```

You use the **Insert** method to insert one or more characters into an existing string beginning at a specified index. The following statement inserts the word "There" beginning at index 6, which follows the space after "Hello."

```
Console.WriteLine("s1.Insert(6, There ) returns " & _
   s1.Insert(6, "There "))
```

The **StartsWith** method compares the string argument with the beginning characters of the **String** instance, then returns **True** or **False** depending on whether there is a match. **EndsWith** is similar, except it compares the ending characters with the argument. The first example in the following code invokes **StartsWith**, passing the argument "Hi." Because the instance referenced by **s1** contains "Hello Again" and does not begin with "Hi," the method returns **False**. The second example invokes **EndsWith** and returns **True** because the **s1** instance does end with "Again."

```
Console.WriteLine("s1.StartsWith(Hi) returns " & s1.StartsWith("Hi"))
Console.WriteLine("s1.EndsWith(Again) returns " & s1.EndsWith("Again"))
```

If you want to change the case of a string value to uppercase or lowercase, you can invoke methods named **ToUpper** or **ToLower**. **ToUpper** returns a string containing the original string converted to uppercase. Similarly, **ToLower** converts a string to lowercase.

```
Console.WriteLine("s1 uppercase is " & s1.ToUpper())
```

You invoke the **IndexOf** method to search a **String** instance for a specific value. This method will return the index of the beginning of the value or –1 if no matching value was found. The following example searches the **s1** instance for the value "Again," which begins at index 6.

```
Console.WriteLine("s1.indexof(Again) returns " & s1.IndexOf("Again"))
```

Sometimes you will want to convert numeric values to a string. For example, if you have an **Integer** value named **i** that has been populated with 5, you can convert this value to a string by invoking the **ToString** method.

```
    ' convert an integer to String
   Dim i As Integer = 5
   Console.WriteLine("value of Convert.ToString(i) is " & _
      Convert.ToString(i))
```

You can also convert string values containing numeric data to primitive data types such as `Integer` or `Single` by invoking methods in the `Convert` class. The following example converts the contents of the `String` instance `s3`, which contains the number 5, to an `Integer` value by invoking the `Convert` class method `ToInt32`.

```
   Dim s3 As String = "5"
   Console.WriteLine("value of Convert.ToInt32(s3) is " & _
      Convert.ToInt32(s3))
```

StringDemo.vb contains the examples described in the previous section. Figure 4-3 lists the code in StringDemo.vb, and Figure 4-4 shows its output.

```
' Chapter 4 StringDemo Example 1
Option Strict On
Module StringDemo
   Sub Main()

      Dim i As Integer
      ' create a String instance
      Dim s1 As String = "Hello Again"
      Console.WriteLine("s1 contains " & s1)

       ' Length property contains the number of characters
      Console.WriteLine("length of s1 is " & s1.Length)
      ' create a copy of s1
      Dim s2 As String = String.Copy(s1)
      Console.WriteLine("s2, a copy of s1, contains " & s2)
      Console.WriteLine("char at index 6 of s1 is " & s1.Chars(6))
      If s1 = s2 Then Console.WriteLine("s1 = s2")
      Console.WriteLine("s1.Equals(s2) returns " & s1.Equals(s2))
      Console.WriteLine("s1.Substring(0, 5) returns " & _
         s1.Substring(0, 5))
      Console.WriteLine("s1.Replace(Hello, Hi) returns " & _
         s1.Replace("Hello", "Hi"))
      Console.WriteLine("After Replace s1 contains " & s1)
      Console.WriteLine("s1.Insert(6, There ) returns " & _
         s1.Insert(6, "There "))
      Console.WriteLine("s1.StartsWith(Hi) returns " & _
         s1.StartsWith("Hi"))
      Console.WriteLine("s1.EndsWith(Again) returns " & _
         s1.EndsWith("Again"))
      Console.WriteLine("s1 uppercase is " & s1.ToUpper())
      Console.WriteLine("s1.indexof(Again) returns " & _
         s1.IndexOf("Again"))
      ' convert an integer to String
      i = 5
      Console.WriteLine("value of Convert.ToString(i) is " & _
         Convert.ToString(i))
```

```
      Dim s3 As String = "5"
      Console.WriteLine("value of Convert.ToInt32(s3) is " & _
         Convert.ToInt32(s3))
   End Sub
End Module
```

Figure 4-3 StringDemo.vb listing

```
s1 contains Hello Again
length of s1 is 11
s2, a copy of s1, contains Hello Again
char at index 6 of s1 is A
s1 = s2
s1.Equals(s2) returns True
s1.Substring(0, 5) returns Hello
s1.Replace(Hello, Hi) returns Hi Again
After Replace s1 contains Hello Again
s1.Insert(6, There ) returns Hello There Again
s1.StartsWith(Hi) returns False
s1.EndsWith(Again) returns True
s1 uppercase is HELLO AGAIN
s1.indexof(Again) returns 6
value of Convert.ToString(i) is 5
value of Convert.ToInt32(s3) is 5
```

Figure 4-4 StringDemo output

Hands-on Exercise 1

1. All of the VB .NET examples are included as part of the data files that accompany this text. Take a few minutes to locate a folder named Chap04\Examples\Ex01.
2. If necessary, create a folder named Ex01 in the Chap04\Exercises folder in your work folder, and copy **StringDemo.vb** from Chap04\ Examples\Ex01 to the Ex01 folder on your hard disk.
3. Open the VB .NET IDE.
4. Click **File** on the menu bar, point to **New**, and then click **Project**.
5. In the New Project dialog box, select **Visual Basic Projects** as the project type, if necessary, select the **Empty Project** template, enter **Exercise1** in the Name box, and select the Chap04\Exercises\Ex01 folder in your work folder. Click **OK** to close the New Project dialog box.

6. Right-click the project name (**Exercise1**) in the Solution Explorer window, point to **Add**, select **Add Existing Item**, locate **StringDemo.vb** in your work folder, and click the **Open** button.
7. The StringDemo.vb file should appear in your Solution Explorer window. Double-click the file to view the code.
8. Right-click the project name (**Exercise1**) in the Solution Explorer window, select **Properties** from the shortcut menu, select **General** under Common Properties, if necessary, click the **Startup object** list box in the Exercise1 Property Pages dialog box, and select **StringDemo**. This tells VB .NET to begin execution with the Main procedure in StringDemo.
9. Still in the Exercise1 Property Pages dialog box, click the **Output type** list box and select **Console Application**. This tells the IDE to display your output in a console window. Click **OK** to close the Property Pages dialog box.
10. Click **Debug** on the menu bar, and then click **Start Without Debugging** to execute the code in StringDemo. Your output should match that shown in Figure 4-4. Press **Enter** to close the console window.
11. Insert the following statements in the beginning of the Main method:

```
Dim myinfo As String
Console.WriteLine(myinfo.ToUpper())
```

12. Click **Debug** on the menu bar, and then click **Start Without Debugging** to execute the modified code in StringDemo. You will encounter the NullReferenceException message described earlier because the reference variable was defined but not initialized. It does not refer to a specific `String` instance, and therefore its `ToUpper` method cannot be invoked.
13. Correct the following statement:

```
Dim myinfo As String
```

to:

```
Dim myinfo As String = "****"
```

Type your name and course number in place of `****`.

14. To test your modifications, click **Debug** on the menu bar, and then click **Start Without Debugging** to execute the modified code in StringDemo. Press **Enter** to close the console window.
15. Save the project, and leave VB .NET open for the next Hands-on Exercise.

CREATING A STRING ARRAY

In Chapter 3 you created an array of integer elements with the statement:

```
' declare an integer array with 5 elements
Dim testScores(4) As Integer
```

This code declares the array reference variable **testScores**, creates an array instance consisting of five elements, each of data type `Integer`, and then points **testScores** to the array. You then can access a specific element using an index. Recall that 0 is the index of the first element, 1 the second, and so forth.

The code to create a String array is similar:

```
' declare a String array with 4 elements
Dim stringArray(3) As String
```

This statement declares an array reference variable **stringArray**, creates an array instance containing four elements, each of which is a reference variable whose data type is `String`, and then points **stringArray** to the array instance. Note that the elements of the **testScores** array are primitive variables of data type `Integer`. However, the elements of **stringArray** are reference variables of data type `String`. Remember that when you define an array, you specify the index of the last element, not the number of elements.

Next you write statements to create four `String` instances and populate the array elements with references to these instances. Figure 4-5 shows the array and `String` instances.

```
stringArray(0) = "Hello"
stringArray(1) = "World"
stringArray(2) = "Wide"
stringArray(3) = "Web"
```

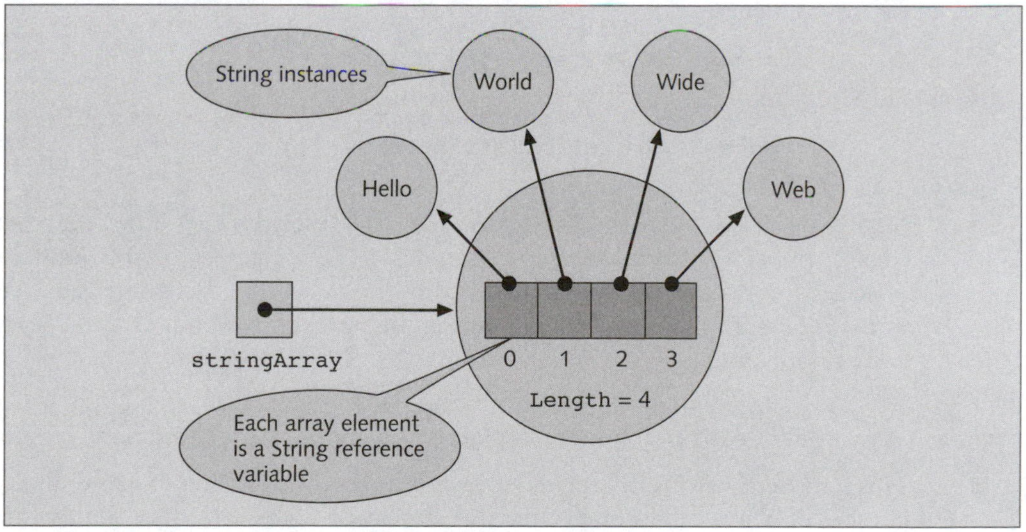

Figure 4-5 Array of `String` reference variables

The variable **stringArray** is a reference variable that points to the array instance. The array instance contains four elements, each of which is a reference variable pointing to a specific `String` instance. The four `String` instances contain the values shown. The array attribute named `Length` contains the number of array elements.

You can also populate a String array by invoking the `Split` method. The following code first creates a `String` instance containing "Hello World Wide Web." Notice that the individual words are separated by spaces. You then invoke the `Split` method for the `String` instance by passing an argument of space. The method returns a String array containing the words that were separated by spaces. The space is called a delimiter, and it can be any character, such as a comma or a period.

```
' declare a String
 Dim s As String = "Hello World Wide Web"
' extract words delimited by space to populate a String array
Dim stringArray() As String = s.Split(" ")
```

Just like an array of primitives, you can access a specific element using the index of that element. For example, if you want to display each of the `String` values in this example, you write the following code:

```
// display each String value
Console.WriteLine(stringArray(0))
Console.WriteLine(stringArray(1))
Console.WriteLine(stringArray(2))
Console.WriteLine(stringArray(3))
```

Of course, instead of writing a separate statement for each element, you can write a loop to display the values:

```
' display the values using a loop
 Dim i As Integer
 For i = 0 To stringArray.Length - 1
    Console.WriteLine(stringArray(i))
Next
```

Note that this code uses the `Length` *property* to test for the end of the array. `Length` contains 4; therefore, `stringArray.Length - 1` evaluates to 3. You should distinguish between the `Length` property of an array instance and the `Length` property of the `String` class. To illustrate, you can display the number of elements in the array using the `Length` attribute:

```
' display the number of elements
Console.WriteLine(stringArray.Length & " elements")
```

This statement will display the number of elements, 4. However, if you want to display the number of characters in one of the `String` instances, you retrieve the `Length` attribute for that instance. Here you display the length of the fourth `String` instance (index 3), which contains "Web." The value displayed by this code is 3.

```
' display the number of characters in the last element
Console.WriteLine("length of Web is " & stringArray(3).Length)
```

You can invoke additional String methods for the String instances referenced by the array elements just like you did in the previous section for individual String instances. For example, to invoke ToUpper for the String instance referenced by the first array element, you write:

```
' invoke ToUpper method for the first element
Console.WriteLine(stringArray(0).ToUpper())
```


You can also search for a specific value in an array. For example, suppose you want to search stringArray for the value "Web." You begin by creating a String instance referenced by the variable searchValue containing the value you want to find, as in the following code:

```
' search for the value "Web"
Dim searchValue As String = "Web"
```

You next declare an index i and initialize it to 0. You also declare a Boolean variable named found and initialize it to False. The found variable will later be set to True when you find the value you are seeking.

```
Dim found As Boolean = False
Dim i As Integer = 0
```

You then write a Do While loop that iterates as long as the index is less than the number of array elements (i < stringArray.Length) and the Boolean variable found remains False. Within the loop, you write a single If statement that invokes the Equals method for the searchValue instance to see whether its contents match the instance referenced by the array element indexed by i. If the instance contents match, found is set to True to terminate the loop. However, if the contents do not match, the index is incremented, and as long as the index remains less than the number of array elements, the loop continues.

```
Do While i < stringArray.Length And Not found
   If stringArray(i).Equals(searchValue) Then
      found = True
   Else
      i += 1
   End If
Loop

If found Then Console.WriteLine("found " & searchValue)
```

Note that in the If statement you use the String instance method Equals, instead of the equal operator (=). Following the loop, you can interrogate found to see whether a matching value was detected, and display an appropriate message.

The Array class provides you with a method named Sort that sorts the elements. The following statement invokes the Sort method for the String array. When you display the contents now, the string values appear in ascending order.

```
' sort the string array into ascending sequence and then display
Array.Sort(stringArray)
```

The complete code for StringArrayDemo.vb is shown in Figure 4-6, with the output in Figure 4-7.

```
' Chapter 4 StringArrayDemo Example 2
Module StringArrayDemo
   Sub Main()
   ' declare a String
   Dim s As String = "Hello World Wide Web"
   ' extract words delimited by space to populate a String array
   Dim stringArray() As String = s.Split(" ")

   ' display the values using a loop
   Dim i As Integer
   For i = 0 To stringArray.Length - 1
      Console.WriteLine(stringArray(i))
   Next

   ' display the number of elements
   Console.WriteLine(stringArray.Length & " elements")
   ' display the number of characters in the last element
   Console.WriteLine("length of Web is " & stringArray(3).Length)
   ' invoke ToUpper method for the first element
   Console.WriteLine(stringArray(0).ToUpper())

   ' search for the value "Web"
   Dim searchValue As String = "Web"
   Dim found As Boolean = False
   i = 0
   Do While i < stringArray.Length And Not found
      If stringArray(i).Equals(searchValue) Then
         found = True
      Else
         i += 1
      End If
   Loop
   If found Then Console.WriteLine("found " & searchValue)

   Console.WriteLine() ' blank line
   ' sort the string array into ascending sequence and then display
   Array.Sort(stringArray)
   For i = 0 To stringArray.Length - 1
      Console.WriteLine(stringArray(i))
   Next
   End Sub
End Module
```

Figure 4-6 StringArrayDemo.vb listing

```
Hello
World
Wide
Web
4 elements
length of Web is 3
HELLO
found Web

Hello
Web
Wide
World
```

Figure 4-7 StringArrayDemo output

Hands-on Exercise 2

1. Locate **StringArrayDemo.vb** in the folder named Chap04\Examples\Ex02 in this book's data files, and then copy it to your work folder.
2. Use the VB .NET IDE to create a project named **Exercise2**, add the module **StringArrayDemo.vb**, set the startup object to **StringArrayDemo**, and set the output type to **Console Application**. Refer to the instructions for Hands-on Exercise 1 to review how to create a project and add a module.
3. Click **Debug** on the menu bar, and then click **Start Without Debugging** to execute the code in StringArrayDemo. Your output should match Figure 4-7.
4. Add a loop to the end of the Main method (before the `Sort` statement) in StringArrayDemo.vb to display the array elements in reverse order. Your output should read Web, Wide, World, and Hello. (*Hint*: Use a For Next loop with a negative step value.)

USING THE `ArrayList` CLASS

As you have seen, array elements are actually variables. As such, they may be either primitive or reference variables, depending on how you declare the array. In Chapter 3 you created an array of primitive elements, and in the previous section you saw how to create an array of `String` reference elements. As powerful as they are, however, arrays have a significant limitation: They are fixed in size. It is extremely difficult to change the number of array elements as your code is executing.

You use the `ArrayList` class, a member of the `System.Collections` namespace, to create an array that is dynamically resizable. This means that you can change the number of elements of an `ArrayList` *while your code is executing*. The `ArrayList` class also provides several useful methods, some of which are illustrated in this section. Table 4-3 lists several commonly used `ArrayList` methods, and the remainder of this section illustrates their use.

Table 4-3 Selected `ArrayList` Methods and Properties

Method/Property Name	Description
`Add(o)`	Method places a reference to the object instance o into the next available element
`Contains(o)`	Method determines whether object o is in the `ArrayList`, returns `True` or `False`
`Capacity`	Property sets or gets the number of elements
`Count`	Property gets the number of populated elements
`Item(i)`	Property sets or gets the object referenced by the element at index `i`
`IndexOf(o)`	Method returns the index of the element referencing object instance o if it exists; returns –1 if object is not found
`Remove(o)`	Method removes the first occurrence of object o
`Reverse()`	Method reverses the element sequence

In order to use an `ArrayList`, you first create an instance of the `ArrayList` class. The following code declares the reference variable `anArrayList`, creates an `ArrayList` instance containing three elements, and assigns its reference to `anArrayList`. As you will see shortly, when you add more than three elements, the `ArrayList` will automatically increase its size. Note that the following code uses the keyword **`New`**, which invokes a special method in `ArrayList` called the **constructor**. You will work more with constructor methods in Chapter 6. For now, you should know that the constructor is invoked when you instantiate a class. The value in parentheses, 3, is an argument that is sent to the constructor method, indicating the number of elements you wish to create. Note that unlike an array, where you specify the index of the last element, when instantiating the `ArrayList` class you specify the actual number of elements.

```
' create an ArrayList instance with 3 elements
Dim anArrayList As ArrayList = New ArrayList(3)
```

Next you write code to create four instances of the `String` class, just like before.

```
' create String instances
Dim s1 As String = New String("Hello")
Dim s2 As String = New String("World")
Dim s3 As String = New String("Wide")
Dim s4 As String = New String("Web")
```

You then invoke the **ArrayList** method **Add** to populate the first two elements.

```
' populate the first two elements
anArrayList.Add(s1)
anArrayList.Add(s2)
```

Note that you can create the **String** instance and populate an **ArrayList** element using a single statement. The following statement creates the **String** instance and passes its reference to the **Add** method, which stores the reference in the next available element of the **ArrayList**. This approach eliminates the need for the additional **String** reference variable.


```
anArrayList.Add("Hello")
```

Next you access the **Capacity** property to get and display the total number of elements, and then you access the **Count** property to get and display the number of *populated* elements. In this example, **anArrayList** now has three elements, two of which are populated. Therefore, the first statement displays 3 and the second displays 2.

```
Console.WriteLine("number of elements = " & anArrayList.Capacity)
Console.WriteLine(anArrayList.Count & " are populated")
```

ArrayList has a built-in search method, **Contains**. This method iterates the **ArrayList** instance, searching for an element that references the object instance specified. In this example, the method looks for an element referencing the string value "Hello." The following code will display **True**, because the first element of **anArrayList** does, in fact, reference the **String** literal "Hello."

```
' search for "Hello"
Console.WriteLine("the ArrayList contains Hello: " & _
   anArrayList.Contains("Hello"))
```

Next, you add the last two **String** instances from the previous code to the **ArrayList**. Although the original **ArrayList** instance has only three elements, when the fourth element is added, the number of elements increases automatically.

```
' populate two more elements
anArrayList.Add(s3)
anArrayList.Add(s4)
Console.WriteLine("number of elements = " & anArrayList.Capacity)
Console.WriteLine(anArrayList.Count & " are populated")
```

You invoke the **IndexOf** method to obtain the index of a value stored in an **ArrayList**. The following example displays the index of the String literal "Wide," which is in the third element with an index of 2.

```
' get the index of "Wide"
Console.WriteLine("the index of Wide is " & _
   anArrayList.IndexOf("Wide"))
```

Finally, you invoke the **Reverse** method to reverse the order of the elements in an **ArrayList**. You can also write a loop to display the contents of the **String** instances referenced by the elements. This code is similar to the code in the previous section that displayed the `String` instances referenced by the array. The previous array code was:

```
' display the values using a loop
 Dim i As Integer
 For i = 0 To stringArray.Length - 1
    Console.WriteLine(stringArray(i))
Next
```

The code to reverse the elements, iterate the `ArrayList`, and display the `String` instances is:

```
' reverse the elements, then loop to display the contents
anArrayList.Reverse()
Dim i As Integer
For i = 0 To anArrayList.Count - 1
   Console.WriteLine(anArrayList.Item(i))
Next
```

There are two differences between the array and `ArrayList` code. First, the array loop executes while `i < stringArray.Length` and the `ArrayList` loop continues while `i < anArrayList.Count`. The second difference is in the code to retrieve the string data. The array code simply retrieves `stringArray(i)`, but the `ArrayList` loop uses the `Item` method to get the string reference at index `i`. The listing for ArrayListDemo.vb is shown in Figure 4-8, and the output is shown in Figure 4-9. Notice that the class includes a statement to import `System.Collections`, which makes the `ArrayList` class available to the compiler.

```
' Chapter 4 ArrayListDemo Example 3
Imports System.Collections
Module ArrayListDemo
   Sub Main()
      ' create an ArrayList instance with 3 elements
      Dim anArrayList As ArrayList = New ArrayList(3)
      ' create String instances
      Dim s1 As String = New String("Hello")
      Dim s2 As String = New String("World")
      Dim s3 As String = New String("Wide")
      Dim s4 As String = New String("Web")

      ' populate the first two elements
      anArrayList.Add(s1)
      anArrayList.Add(s2)
      Console.WriteLine("number of elements = " & anArrayList.Capacity)
      Console.WriteLine(anArrayList.Count & " are populated")

      ' search for "Hello"
      Console.WriteLine("the ArrayList contains Hello: " & _
         anArrayList.Contains("Hello"))

      ' populate two more elements
      anArrayList.Add(s3)
      anArrayList.Add(s4)
```

```
      Console.WriteLine("number of elements = " & anArrayList.Capacity)
      Console.WriteLine(anArrayList.Count & " are populated")
      ' get the index of "Wide"
      Console.WriteLine("the index of Wide is " & _
         anArrayList.IndexOf("Wide"))
      ' reverse the elements, then loop to display the contents
      anArrayList.Reverse()
      Dim i As Integer
      For i = 0 To anArrayList.Count - 1
         Console.WriteLine(anArrayList.Item(i))
      Next
   End Sub
End Module
```

Figure 4-8 ArrayListDemo.vb listing

```
number of elements = 3
2 are populated
the ArrayList contains Hello: True
number of elements = 6
4 are populated
the index of Wide is 2
Web
Wide
World
Hello
```

Figure 4-9 ArrayListDemo output

Hands-on Exercise 3

1. Locate **ArrayListDemo.vb** in the folder named Chap04\Examples\Ex03 in this book's data files, and then copy it to your work folder.
2. Use the VB .NET IDE to create a project named **Exercise3**, add the module **ArrayListDemo.vb**, set the startup object to **ArrayListDemo**, and set the output type to **Console Application**. Refer to the instructions for Hands-on Exercise 1 to review how to create a project and add a module.
3. Click **Debug** on the menu bar, and then click **Start Without Debugging** to execute the code in ArrayListDemo. Your output should match Figure 4-9.
4. Add a loop to the end of the Main method (before the `Reverse` statement) in ArrayListDemo.vb to display the array elements in reverse order. Your output should read Web, Wide, World, and Hello. (*Hint*: Use a For Next loop with a negative step value.)

WORKING WITH DATES

While developing systems, you often need to work with dates. For example, many systems deal with today's date, due dates, order dates, employment dates, dates of birth, expiration dates, and so forth. VB .NET provides classes with methods that let you retrieve the current system date, format date values, perform arithmetic on date fields, and compare date values. These methods are illustrated in this section.

In the following example you use two classes: `DateTime` and `TimeSpan`. A `DateTime` instance contains an actual date value and a `TimeSpan` instance contains the difference between two dates. These classes are in the `System` namespace, which is automatically imported by the compiler; therefore, you do not need to add an **`Imports`** statement. You begin by defining a reference variable named `today` with data type `DateTime` and populating it with a reference to a `DateTime` instance that contains the current date and time. `Today` is a property of `DateTime` that gets the system date and returns a `DateTime` instance. If you also want to capture the current time, then you should access the `Now` property, as in the following example:

```
' create an instance of DateTime populated with the system date & time
Dim today As DateTime = DateTime.Now
Console.WriteLine("Today is " & today)
```

Sometimes you might need to perform arithmetic on a date value. For example, you might need to determine the date for a month from today or a year from today. The `DateTime` class has methods that will add a value to the month, day, or year. These are appropriately named `AddMonths`, `AddDays`, and `AddYears`, respectively. You pass these methods an argument that is the value you want added. To add one month, you invoke `AddMonths(1)`. The following code invokes `AddMonths` to add one to the current month, creating a DateTime instance named `aMonthFromToday` that contains the new date value. Then `AddYears` is invoked to add one to the current year, creating an instance named `aYearFromToday`.

```
' add 1 to today's month
Dim aMonthFromToday As DateTime = today.AddMonths(1)
Console.WriteLine("One Month From Today is " & aMonthFromToday)
' add 1 to today's year
Dim aYearFromToday As DateTime = today.AddYears(1)
Console.WriteLine("One Year From Today is " & aYearFromToday)
```

The `WriteLine` methods above display the date in "mm/dd/yyyy" format. If the date instance `today` contains February 15, 2003, then the previous statements will display it as 02/15/2003. You can format the way a date is displayed by invoking its `ToString` method and passing arguments that describe the desired format. For example, if you want the date displayed as February 15, 2003, then you write the following statement:

```
Console.WriteLine("(MMMM dd, yyyy) is " & today.ToString("MMMM dd,yyyy"))
```

Table 4-4 lists selected **ToString** format characters that you combine to produce the output you want. Notice the difference between uppercase and lowercase "M." Lowercase indicates minute, and uppercase represents month. You can insert commas, spaces, colons, and other characters into the format string.

Table 4-4 Selected ToString Format Characters

Format Characters	Description
d	Day as a number (1–7)
dd	Day as a number with leading zero (01–07)
ddd	Three-character day name (Sun)
dddd	Full day name (Sunday)
M	Month as a number (1–12)
MM	Month as a number with leading zero for single digit (01–12)
MMM	Three-character month name (Feb)
MMMM	Full month name (February)
m	Minute without leading zeros
mm	Minute with leading zeros
s	Second without leading zeros
ss	Second with leading zeros
t	Displays "A" for AM and "P" for PM
tt	Displays "AM" or "PM"
y	Single-digit year number without leading zeros (3)
yy	Two-digit year number (03)
yyyy	Four-digit year number (2003)

The following statements illustrate the use of these format characters:

```
' illustrate various date formats
Console.WriteLine("MMMM dd, yyyy " & today.ToString("MMMM dd, yyyy"))
Console.WriteLine("MM/dd/yy hh:mm:ss tt " & _
   today.ToString("MM/dd/yy hh:mm:ss tt"))
Console.WriteLine("dddd, MMMM dd, yyyy " & _
   today.ToString("dddd, MMMM dd, yyyy"))
Console.WriteLine("MMMM yy " & today.ToString("MMMM yy"))
```

You can create a **DateTime** instance containing a specific date. The following example creates two date instances. The first, named **eleanorsBirthday**, contains December 15, 1998, and the second, named **emilysBirthday**, contains April 6, 2002. The last two statements display these dates in "monthname day, year" format.

```
' create specific dates
Dim eleanorsBirthday As DateTime = New DateTime(1998, 12, 15)
Dim emilysBirthday As DateTime = New DateTime(2002, 4, 6)
Console.WriteLine("Eleanor's Birthday is " & _
   eleanorsBirthday.ToString("MMMM dd, yyyy"))
Console.WriteLine("Emily's Birthday is " & _
   emilysBirthday.ToString("MMMM dd, yyyy"))
```

You can invoke the `DateTime Subtract` method to compute the number of days between two `DateTime` instances. This method returns an instance of the `TimeSpan` class that you use to hold a span of time, whether measured in hours, minutes, seconds, or days. First you declare a variable named `ageDifference`, whose data type is `TimeSpan`, and then you invoke the `Subtract` method for the `DateTime` instance referenced by `emilysBirthday`, passing `eleanorsBirthday` as an argument. The `Subtract` method computes the difference between the two `DateTime` instances and returns a `TimeSpan` instance assigning its reference to `ageDifference`. You can then invoke the `TotalDays` method to obtain the number of days that was computed.

```
' compute the difference between two dates
Dim ageDifference As TimeSpan
ageDifference = emilysBirthday.Subtract(eleanorsBirthday)
Console.WriteLine("The age difference is " & _
   ageDifference.TotalDays() & " days")
```

The `DateTime` class also has a method named `Compare` that will compare two `DateTime` instances and return –1, 0, or +1, depending on whether the first `DateTime` instance is less than, equal to, or greater than the second. In the following example, `emilysBirthday` contains April 6, 2002 and `eleanorsBirthday` contains December 15, 1998. When you compare these two, `emilysBirthday` is greater than `eleanorsBirthday`, so the method returns +1.

```
' compare two dates - Compare returns -1, 0, or +1 for <, =, >
If DateTime.Compare(emilysBirthday, eleanorsBirthday) < 0 Then
   Console.WriteLine("Emily is older than Eleanor")
Else
   Console.WriteLine("Emily is younger than Eleanor")
End If
```

Figure 4-10 shows the complete listing of DateDemo.vb, and Figure 4-11 shows its output.

```
' Chapter 4 DateDemo Example 4
Module DateDemo
  Sub Main()
      ' create a DateTime instance populated with the system date & time
      Dim today As DateTime = DateTime.Now
      Console.WriteLine("Today is " & today)
      ' add 1 to today's month
      Dim aMonthFromToday As DateTime = today.AddMonths(1)
      Console.WriteLine("One Month From Today is " & aMonthFromToday)
      ' add 1 to today's year
      Dim aYearFromToday As DateTime = today.AddYears(1)
      Console.WriteLine("One Year From Today is " & aYearFromToday)
      ' illustrate various date formats
      Console.WriteLine("MMMM dd, yyyy " & _
         today.ToString("MMMM dd, yyyy"))
      Console.WriteLine("MM/dd/yy hh:mm:ss tt " & _
         today.ToString("MM/dd/yy hh:mm:ss tt"))
      Console.WriteLine("dddd, MMMM dd, yyyy " & _
         today.ToString("dddd, MMMM dd, yyyy"))
```

```
      Console.WriteLine("MMMM yy " & today.ToString("MMMM yy"))
      ' create specific dates
      Dim eleanorsBirthday As DateTime = New DateTime(1998, 12, 15)
      Dim emilysBirthday As DateTime = New DateTime(2002, 4, 6)
      Console.WriteLine("Eleanor's Birthday is " & _
         eleanorsBirthday.ToString("MMMM dd, yyyy"))
      Console.WriteLine("Emily's Birthday is " & _
         emilysBirthday.ToString("MMMM dd, yyyy"))

      ' compute the difference between two dates
      Dim ageDifference As TimeSpan
      ageDifference = emilysBirthday.Subtract(eleanorsBirthday)
      Console.WriteLine("The age difference is " & _
         ageDifference.TotalDays() & " days")
      ' compare two dates - Compare returns -1, 0, or +1 for <, =, >
      If DateTime.Compare(emilysBirthday, eleanorsBirthday) < 0 Then
         Console.WriteLine("Emily is older than Eleanor")
      Else
         Console.WriteLine("Emily is younger than Eleanor")
      End If
   End Sub
End Module
```

Figure 4-10 DateDemo.vb listing

```
Today is 2/15/2003 4:35:47 PM
One Month From Today is 3/15/2003 4:35:47 PM
One Year From Today is 2/15/2004 4:35:47 PM
MMMM dd, yyyy February 15, 2003
MM/dd/yy hh:mm:ss tt 02/15/03 04:35:47 PM
dddd, MMMM dd, yyyy Saturday, February 15, 2003
MMMM yy February 03
Eleanor's Birthday is December 15, 1998
Emily's Birthday is April 06, 2002
The age difference is 1208 days
Emily is younger than Eleanor
```

Figure 4-11 DateDemo output

Hands-on Exercise 4

1. Locate **DateDemo.vb** in the folder named Chap04\Examples\Ex04 in this book's data files, and then copy it to your work folder.

2. Use the VB .NET IDE to create a project named **Exercise4**, add the module **DateDemo.vb**, set the startup object to **DateDemo**, and set the output type to **Console Application**. Refer to the instructions for Hands-on Exercise 1 to review how to create a project and add a module.
3. Click **Debug** on the menu bar, and then click **Start Without Debugging** to execute the code in DateDemo. Your output should be similar to Figure 4-11; the dates will differ.
4. Add statements to the beginning of the Main method in DateDemo.vb to
   - Create a date instance named `myBirthday populated with your date of birth.`
   - Display your birth date as mm/dd/yy, mm/dd/yyyy, dd/mm/yy, and monthname dd, yyyy.

Formatting Numeric Output

You will frequently want to format your output to make it more attractive and easier to read. Formatting means inserting commas, decimal places, dollar signs, percent symbols, parentheses, hyphens, and so forth. In the previous section you saw how to format dates. In this section you will learn how to format numeric data.

In Chapter 3 you learned about data types and saw that VB .NET has two kinds of variables: primitive and reference. Primitive variables contain one of the primitive data types (`Integer`, `Single`, `Boolean`, etc.), and reference variables point to, or reference, instances of a class, such as `String`. Each of the VB .NET primitive data types is represented by a **structure**. A structure is similar to a class in that it has methods, but the data is primitive and stored in a variable instead of an instance. This means that when you declare a primitive variable, you can invoke certain methods associated with that variable, even though it is primitive. One of these methods, `ToString`, is used to format numeric data. In fact, the `ToString` method is frequently used to convert numeric data to string data.

To illustrate, if you have an integer value that you want to display in currency format with dollar signs, commas, and two decimal positions, you can invoke the `ToString` method with an argument of "C." The following code will display the integer value 1234 as $1,234.00. Notice that this code invokes the `ToString` method for the primitive variable `i`.

```
' illustrate two ways to format integer as currency
Dim i As Integer = 1234
Dim s As String = i.ToString("C")
Console.WriteLine("Integer 1234 with C format is " & s)
```

You can also pass a **format mask** to the `ToString` method. A format mask is a series of characters that describes the format you want to use. In this example you specify where you want to place the dollar sign, comma, and decimal point. In addition, you indicate whether you want to have leading zeros suppressed by using the # character.

```
s = i.ToString("$#,##0.00")
Console.WriteLine("Integer 1234 with $#,##0.00 format is " & s)
```

You can format any number as currency. If you have a `Double` value—say, 12345.67 contained in the variable `d`—you can format the value as currency by invoking `ToString` using variable `d`.

```
' illustrate two ways to format Double as currency
Dim d As Double = 12345.67
s = d.ToString("C")
Console.WriteLine("Double 12345.67 with C format is " & s)
s = d.ToString("$##,##0.00")
Console.WriteLine("Double 12345.67 with $##,##0.00 format is " & s)
```

If you have more than two decimal positions in a value that you are formatting as currency, VB .NET will round your value to two decimal positions. In the following example, the `Double` value 12345.678 is rounded to $12,345.68:

```
' show that rounding occurs
d = 12345.678
s = d.ToString("C")
Console.WriteLine("Double 12345.678 with C format is " & s)
s = d.ToString("$##,##0.00")
Console.WriteLine("Double 12345.678 with $##,##0.00 format is "& s)
```

You can format a number with or without a dollar sign, with or without commas, or as a percentage, as in the following examples:

```
' illustrate percent, numeric with comma, numeric without comma
Console.WriteLine("Double 12345.67 as percentage is " & _
   d.ToString("P"))
Console.WriteLine("Double 12345.67 as numeric with commas is " & _
   d.ToString("N"))
Console.WriteLine("Double 12345.67 as numeric no commas is " & _
   d.ToString("F"))
```

Sometimes you will want to format values such as a telephone number or Social Security number. You can invoke the `ToString` method with a format mask, as in the following example:

```
' format ss no & phone no
Dim phoneNo As Double = 1234567890
s = phoneNo.ToString("(###) ###-####")
Console.WriteLine("phone number format example " & s)
Dim ssNo As Double = 123456789
s = ssNo.ToString("###-##-####")
Console.WriteLine("Social Security number format example " & s)
```

Figure 4-12 shows the FormatDemo.vb listing, and Figure 4-13 contains the output.

```
' Chapter 4 FormatDemo Example 5
Module FormatDemo
   Sub Main()
      ' illustrate two ways to format integer as currency
      Dim i As Integer = 1234
      Dim s As String = i.ToString("C")
      Console.WriteLine("Integer 1234 with C format is " & s)
      s = i.ToString("$#,##0.00")
      Console.WriteLine("Integer 1234 with $#,##0.00 format is " & s)

      ' illustrate two ways to format Double as currency
      Dim d As Double = 12345.67
      s = d.ToString("C")
      Console.WriteLine("Double 12345.67 with C format is " & s)
      s = d.ToString("$##,##0.00")
      Console.WriteLine("Double 12345.67 with $##,##0.00 format " & s)
      ' show that rounding occurs
      d = 12345.678
      s = d.ToString("C")
      Console.WriteLine("Double 12345.678 with C format is " & s)
      s = d.ToString("$##,##0.00")
      Console.WriteLine("Double 12345.678 with $##,##0.00 format " & s)

      ' illustrate percent, numeric with comma, numeric without comma
      Console.WriteLine("Double 12345.67 as percentage is " & _
         d.ToString("P"))
      Console.WriteLine("Double 12345.67 as numeric with commas " & _
         d.ToString("N"))
      Console.WriteLine("Double 12345.67 as numeric no commas " & _
         d.ToString("F"))

      ' format ss no & phone no
      Dim phoneNo As Double = 1234567890
      s = phoneNo.ToString("(###) ###-####")
      Console.WriteLine("phone number format example " & s)
      Dim ssNo As Double = 123456789
      s = ssNo.ToString("###-##-####")
      Console.WriteLine("Social Security number format example " & s)
   End Sub
End Module
```

Figure 4-12 FormatDemo.vb listing

```
Integer 1234 with C format is $1,234.00
Integer 1234 with $#,##0.00 format is $1,234.00
Double 12345.67 with C format is $12,345.67
Double 12345.67 with $##,##0.00 format is $12,345.67
Double 12345.678 with C format is $12,345.68
Double 12345.678 with $##,##0.00 format is $12,345.68
Double 12345.67 as percentage is 1,234,567.80 %
Double 12345.67 as numeric with commas is 12,345.68
Double 12345.67 as numeric no commas is 12345.68
phone number format example (123) 456-7890
Social Security number format example 123-45-6789
```

Figure 4-13 FormatDemo output

Hands-on Exercise 5

1. Locate **FormatDemo.vb** in the folder named Chap04\Examples\Ex05 in this book's data files, and then copy it to your work folder.
2. Use the VB .NET IDE to create a project named **Exercise5**, add the module **FormatDemo.vb**, set the startup object to **FormatDemo**, and set the output type to **Console Application**. Refer to the instructions for Hands-on Exercise 1 to review how to create a project and add a module.
3. Click **Debug** on the menu bar, and then click **Start Without Debugging** to execute the code in FormatDemo. Your output should match Figure 4-13.

USING THE `MessageBox` CLASS

You use a message box to display a message and, if you want, to get a response. The `MessageBox` class is a member of the `System.Windows.Forms` namespace, which contains numerous other GUI classes such as `Form`, `Button`, `Label`, and `TextBox`. You must import `System.Windows.Forms` to make the `MessageBox` class available to the compiler. You will work with the other GUI classes in Chapters 10 and 11.

`MessageBox` has a single method named `Show` that creates an instance of the `MessageBox` class and makes a message box appear. The `Show` method can receive up to four arguments. The first argument is the message you want to display, which can be in the form of a string literal or variable. The second argument is the caption you want to display in the message box. The third argument specifies the buttons you want displayed, and the last argument indicates the type of icon you want to see.

In its simplest form, you send a single argument containing the message you want to display. For example, you can display the message "Hello Again" by writing the following code. Note that this form automatically displays an OK button. Figure 4-14 shows the results of this code.

```
' display a message
MessageBox.Show("Hello Again")
```

Figure 4-14 `MessageBox` with a message

You can display a message, along with a caption, by passing two arguments to the `Show` method, as in the following example. The output is shown in Figure 4-15.

```
'display a message and a caption
MessageBox.Show("Hello Again", "MessageBox Demo")
```

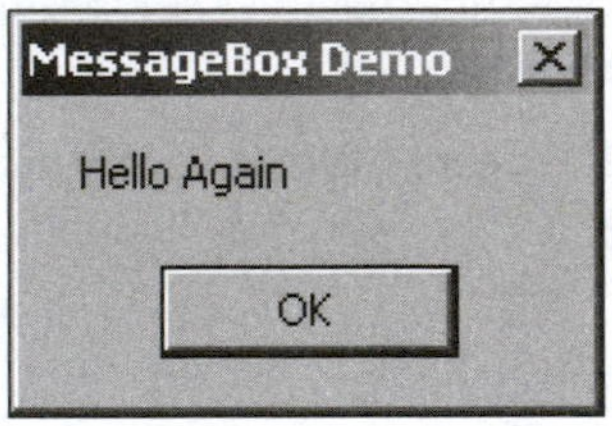

Figure 4-15 `MessageBox` with a message and caption

You can display various combinations of buttons. When you type `MessageBoxButtons` as the third argument for the `Show` method, the IntelliSense feature displays a list of your choices, as shown in Figure 4-16.

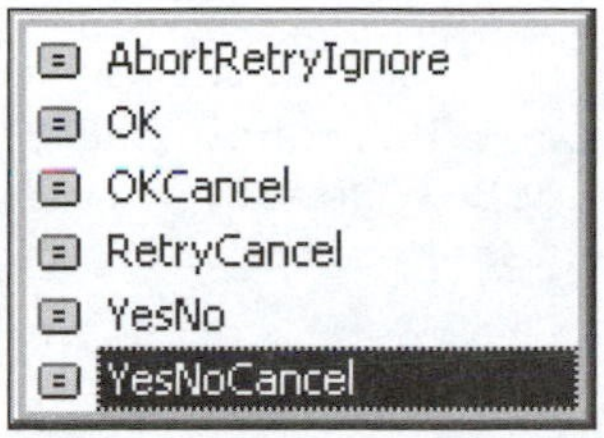

Figure 4-16 `MessageBox` button options

If you select `MessageBoxButtons.YesNoCancel` as your third argument, the message box shown in Figure 4-17 appears.

```
'display a message, caption, Yes/No/Cancel buttons
MessageBox.Show("Hello Again", "MessageBox Demo", _
   MessageBoxButtons.YesNoCancel)
```

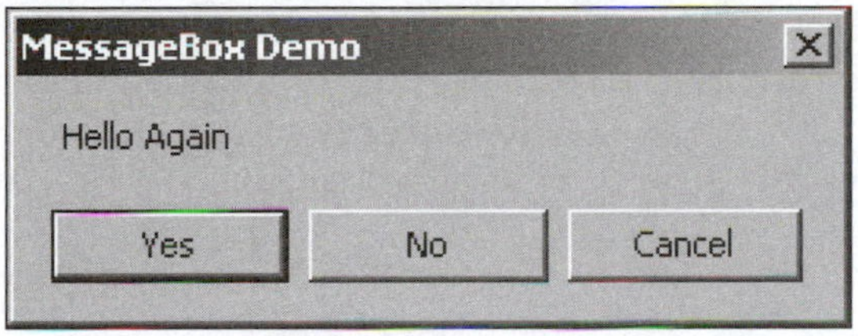

Figure 4-17 `MessageBox` with Yes, No, and Cancel buttons

You can also specify that an icon be displayed in the message box. When you type `MessageBoxIcon` as the fourth argument for the `Show` method, IntelliSense displays a list of your choices, as shown in Figure 4-18.

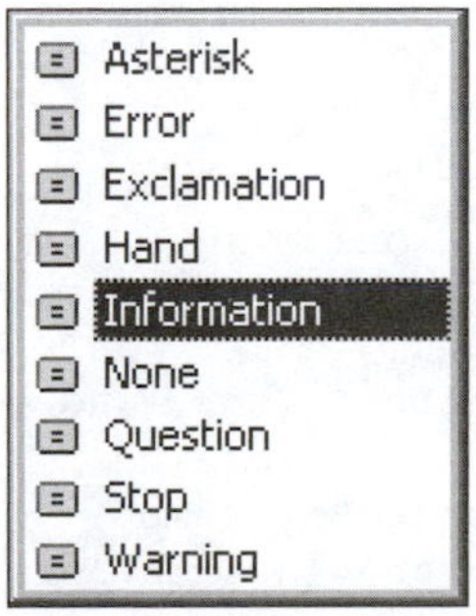

Figure 4-18 `MessageBox` icon options

If you select the information icon, the message box shown in Figure 4-19 is displayed.

```
'display message, caption, Yes/No/Cancel buttons, and Icon
MessageBox.Show("Hello Again", "MessageBox Demo", _
   MessageBoxButtons.YesNoCancel, MessageBoxIcon.Information)
```

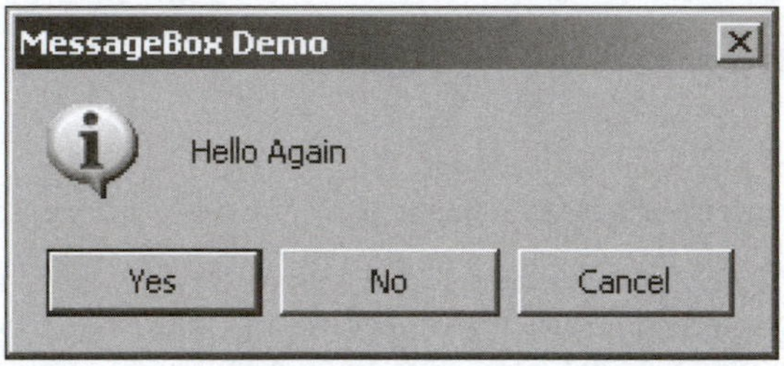

Figure 4-19 `MessageBox` with buttons and icon

Finally, you can obtain a return value from the **`Show`** method that indicates which button was clicked. The returned value is data type `DialogResult`, and you can compare it to specific values using an If statement. When you type `DialogResult`, IntelliSense lists your choices, as shown in Figure 4-20.

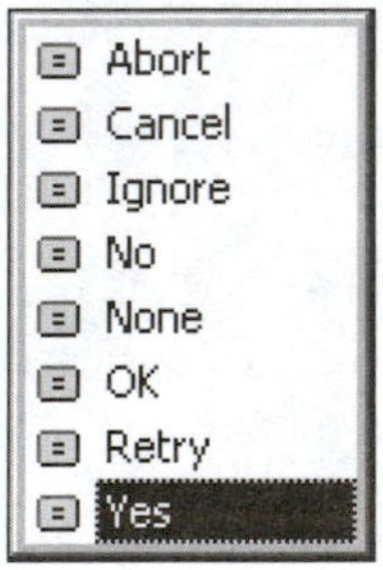

Figure 4-20 `DialogResult` values

The following example displays the Yes, No, and Cancel buttons in the message box, then determines which button was clicked and displays a message.

```
'display message, caption, Yes/No/Cancel buttons, Icon, and get result
Dim result As DialogResult
result = MessageBox.Show("Hello Again", "MessageBox Demo", _
   MessageBoxButtons.YesNoCancel, MessageBoxIcon.Information)
If result = DialogResult.Yes Then
   Console.WriteLine("The Yes button was clicked")
```

```
    End If
    If result = DialogResult.No Then
        Console.WriteLine("The No button was clicked")
    End If
    If result = DialogResult.Cancel Then
        Console.WriteLine("The Cancel button was clicked")
    End If
```

Figure 4-21 shows the complete MessageBoxDemo.vb listing.


```
' Chapter 4 MessageBoxDemo Example 6
Option Strict On
Imports System.Windows.Forms
Module MessageBoxDemo
   Sub Main()
      ' display a message
      MessageBox.Show("Hello Again")
      'display a message and a caption
      MessageBox.Show("Hello Again", "MessageBox Demo")
      'display a message, caption, Yes/No/Cancel buttons
      MessageBox.Show("Hello Again", "MessageBox Demo", _
         MessageBoxButtons.YesNoCancel)
      'display message, caption, Yes/No/Cancel buttons, and Icon
      MessageBox.Show("Hello Again", "MessageBox Demo", _
         MessageBoxButtons.YesNoCancel, MessageBoxIcon.Information)
      'display message, caption, Yes/No/Cancel buttons, Icon, and get
result
      Dim result As DialogResult
      result = MessageBox.Show("Hello Again", "MessageBox Demo", _
         MessageBoxButtons.YesNoCancel, MessageBoxIcon.Information)
      If result = DialogResult.Yes Then
         Console.WriteLine("The Yes button was clicked")
      End If
      If result = DialogResult.No Then
         Console.WriteLine("The No button was clicked")
      End If
      If result = DialogResult.Cancel Then
         Console.WriteLine("The Cancel button was clicked")
      End If
   End Sub
End Module
```

Figure 4-21 MessageBoxDemo.vb listing

Hands-on Exercise 6

1. Locate **MessageBoxDemo.vb** in the folder named Chap04\Examples\Ex06 in this book's data files, and then copy it to your work folder.

2. Use the VB .NET IDE to create a Windows Application named **Exercise6**, add the module **MessageBoxDemo.vb**, set the startup object to **MessageBoxDemo**, and set the output type to **Console Application**. Refer to the instructions for Hands-on Exercise 1 to review how to create a project and add a module.

3. Click **Debug** on the menu bar, and then click **Start Without Debugging** to execute the code in MessageBoxDemo.

4. In the last message box in the code, change the buttons being displayed to **AbortRetryIgnore** and the icon to **Warning**, and then rerun MessageBoxDemo to verify that your changes are correct.

DISPLAYING A `Form`

`Form` is another class in the `System.Windows.Forms` namespace. In this section you will create a form instance, give it a title, make it visible and invisible, and then invoke its `Dispose` method. The following example uses a module named GuiModule.vb and a `Form` named GuiForm.vb. The module contains instructions to instantiate GuiForm.vb, then make it visible and invisible. GuiForm.vb is a subclass of `Form`, so it inherits `Form` attributes and methods.

GuiModule imports `System.Windows.Forms` to make the `Form` class available to the compiler. You begin by defining a variable named `myForm` with data type `GuiForm` and creating a new instance of a `GuiForm`.

```
Dim myForm As GuiForm
myForm = New GuiForm()
```

Next you set the new form's text property to `"My GUI Form Demo"` and its background color to `System.Drawing.Color.Brown`.

```
myForm.Text = "My GUI Form Demo"
myForm.BackColor = System.Drawing.Color.Brown
```

You use a message box to determine when to make the form visible and not visible and when to dispose of it. This code is placed inside a Do Until loop. The message box button clicked is stored in a variable named `result`. The loop terminates when the variable indicates that the Cancel button has been clicked. The message box that is displayed is shown in Figure 4-22, and the form that is displayed is shown in Figure 4-23. GuiModule.vb is listed in Figure 4-24.

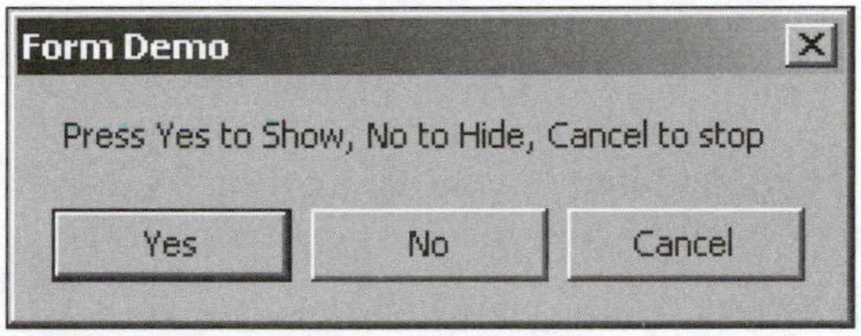

Figure 4-22 MessageBox displayed by FormDemo

Figure 4-23 Form displayed by FormDemo

```
' Chapter 4 GuiModule Example 7
Option Strict On
Imports System.Windows.Forms
Module GuiModule
   Sub Main()
      Dim myForm As GuiForm = New GuiForm()
      myForm.Text = "My GUI Form Demo"
      myForm.BackColor = System.Drawing.Color.Brown
      ' use MessageBox to determine what to do
      Dim result As DialogResult
      Do Until result = DialogResult.Cancel
         result = MessageBox.Show("Press Yes to Show, No to Hide, _
           Cancel to stop", "Form Demo", MessageBoxButtons.YesNoCancel)
         If result = DialogResult.Yes Then myForm.Visible = True
         If result = DialogResult.No Then myForm.Visible = False
      Loop
      myForm.Dispose()
   End Sub
End Module
```

Figure 4-24 GuiModule.vb listing

Hands-on Exercise 7

1. Locate **GuiForm.vb** and **GuiModule.vb** in the folder named Chap04\Examples\Ex07 in this book's data files, and then copy them to your work folder.
2. Use the VB .NET IDE to create a project named **Exercise7**, open a Windows Application for the Templates list, add the module **GuiModule.vb** and the form **GuiForm.vb**, set the startup object to **GuiModule**, and set the output type to **Console Application**. Refer to the instructions for Hands-on Exercise 1 to review how to create a project and add a module.
3. Click **Debug** on the menu bar, and then click **Start Without Debugging** to execute the code in GuiModule. You should see the message box in Figure 4-22. When you click the **Yes** button, you should see the form in Figure 4-23.
4. Experiment with background colors. Use IntelliSense to determine which colors are available to you. Rerun GuiModule to verify that your changes are correct.

Chapter Summary

- A VB .NET namespace is a library of related classes. Use the `Imports` statement to make classes in the various packages available to the compiler. The .NET library consists of hundreds of namespaces containing numerous predefined classes and their methods. The `System` namespace is automatically imported by the compiler, but if you work with other supplied classes, you must write an `Imports` statement.
- VB .NET string data is contained in an instance of the `String` class. This class contains several useful methods to manipulate string data. String values are immutable: They cannot be changed.
- The `Length` property of an array instance indicates the number of array elements. The `Length` property of the `String` class contains the number of characters in the string.
- The `ArrayList` class is like a dynamically resizable array, and it has methods to accomplish various tasks. You use the `ArrayList` class, a member of the `System.Collections` namespace, to create an array that is dynamically resizable.
- A `DateTime` instance contains the actual date value, and a `TimeSpan` instance contains the difference between two dates. These classes are in the `System` namespace, which is automatically imported by the compiler; therefore, you do not need to add an `Imports` statement.

- Formatting means inserting commas, decimal places, dollar signs, percent symbols, parentheses, hyphens, and so forth. Each of the VB .NET primitive data types is represented by a structure. A structure is similar to a class in that it has methods, but the data is primitive and stored in a variable instead of an instance. This means that when you declare a primitive variable, you can invoke certain methods associated with that variable, even though it is primitive. One of these methods, `ToString`, is used to format numeric data. You can also pass a format mask to the `ToString` method. A format mask is a series of characters that describes the format you want to use.
- You use a message box to display a message and, if you want, to get a response. The `MessageBox` class is a member of the `System.Windows.Forms` namespace, which you must import to make it available to the compiler. `MessageBox` has a single method named `Show` that creates an instance of `MessageBox` and makes it visible. The `Show` method can receive up to four arguments.
- `Form` is also a class in the `System.Windows.Forms` namespace. You can create a form instance, give it a title, make it visible and invisible, and then invoke its `Dispose` method. You can set various form properties, including background color.

Key Terms

Common Language Runtime (CLR)
constructor
format mask
immutable
instantiate
namespace
structure

Review Questions

1. The term "namespace" refers to:
   a. assigning a name to a module
   b. assigning a name to a class
   c. a library of classes
   d. an instance method of a class

2. To instantiate a class means to:

a. erase variables within a class

b. create variables within a class

c. create an instance of a class

d. invoke an instance method of a class

3. The correct statement to invoke the String `ToUpper` method for a `String` instance `aString` is:

a. `aString.ToUpper()`

b. `String.ToUpper(aString)`

c. `ToUpper.String()`

d. `aString.String(ToUpper)`

4. The index of the first character of a string value is:

a. 1

b. 0

c. the value you specify when you declare the string

d. 2

5. The String `SubString` method:

a. returns an index

b. returns a string

c. returns a primitive

d. returns a character

6. The index of the first element of an array is:

a. 1

b. 0

c. the value you specify when you declare the string

d. 2

7. Each element in a String array is:

a. a primitive variable

b. null

c. a reference variable

d. It depends on the data type you specify.

8. To obtain the number of elements in a String array named `sArray`, you would write:

a. `sArray.Length`

b. `sArray.LengthOf`

c. `String.Length`

d. `StringArray.Length`

9. String values in VB .NET:

a. cannot be changed

b. are a primitive data type

c. can be either primitive or reference

d. cannot be placed into an array

10. The elements of an `ArrayList`:

a. begin with an index value of 0

b. can contain only primitive values

c. begin with an index value of 1

d. must be data type `array`

11. The `ArrayList` method that returns the number of elements is:

a. `Size`

b. `numberOfElements`

c. `Capacity`

d. There is no such method.

12. An instance of the `DateTime` class contains:

a. a calendar instance

b. a date and time value

c. only a date value

d. only a time value

13. An instance of the `TimeSpan` class contains:

a. the difference between two dates

b. a date and time value

c. only a date value

d. only a time value

14. What is `Color.red?`

a. a method

b. an attribute

c. a constant

d. a property

15. The `MessageBox` class:

a. has a single method named `View`

b. has a single method named `Show`

c. has no methods

d. is part of a form

Discussion Questions

1. List several benefits of using methods instead of built-in functions.
2. `String` instances are immutable. What implications does this have for methods such as `SubString` and `ToUpper` that return a `String` instance?
3. It appears that you could always use an `ArrayList` instead of an array. Why should you ever use an array?
4. The `DateTime` class does not have an `Equals` method. How can you use the `Compare` method to determine whether two date values are the same?

Projects

1. Rewrite ArrayDemo.vb from Chapter 3 using an `ArrayList`.
2. Create a four-row, three-column String array containing the following data. Then write code to display the contents of each row with appropriate labels.

Table 4-5 Airline Departure Information

Flight	Gate	Destination
AA 7401	C33	St. Louis
AA 431	D8	Dallas
Delta 94	A12	Atlanta
United 155	B4	Chicago

3. Redesign and rewrite Project 2 using an `ArrayList` with four elements, one for each row. Each element will contain a reference for a three-element array with one element for each column (flight, gate, and destination).

4. Figure 4-5 illustrates a String array graphically. Draw an illustration of the two-dimensional String array in Project 2.

CHAPTER

5

Object-Oriented Analysis and Design

In this chapter you will:

- Explore OOA and OOD
- Understand the Unified Modeling Language (UML)
- Use three-tier design in OO development
- Learn about the Bradshaw Marina case study

VB .NET provides a comprehensive and easy-to-use programming environment for exploring object-oriented concepts and object-oriented programming. You explored some of its functionality in Chapters 2, 3, and 4. However, as discussed in Chapter 1, object-oriented application development is much broader than OO programming. As with any system development project, OO development requires a thorough understanding of the problem the system is supposed to solve. Additionally, even a simple project requires a blueprint defining how the components created by VB .NET fit together to solve the problem. Therefore, before you start programming and testing, you must identify what functions the system must perform and carefully design the architecture of the new system. In short, you must complete system analysis and system design activities for the system development project.

This chapter briefly reviews analysis and design concepts and activities for OO development using VB .NET. It begins by discussing object-oriented analysis and object-oriented design, including iterative and incremental approaches to development. This chapter introduces the Unified Modeling Language (UML) to illustrate model-driven development, emphasizing the use case diagram, class diagram, and sequence diagram. It also examines the three-tier design approach to illustrate the transition from OO analysis to OO design. Finally, it introduces the Bradshaw Marina case study, which is used for examples throughout this text.

The VB .NET programming concepts and techniques that are presented in the remaining sections of the text all follow from the three-tier design approach, and most programming examples are based on the Bradshaw Marina case study and the models described in this chapter.

Exploring OOA and OOD

As in any approach to development, **system analysis** means to study, understand, and define the requirements for the system. **System requirements** define what the system needs to accomplish for the users in business terms. These requirements are usually described using diagrams, or models. A **model** depicts some aspect of the real world, in this case some aspect of the required system. You need a collection of models to describe all aspects of the system requirements because any given model usually highlights only a part. The models created during system analysis are often called **logical models** because they show what is required in the system independent of the technology used to implement it. **System design** means to create models showing how the various system components will be implemented using specific technology. Models created during system design are often called **physical models**.

Creating logical models of the system requirements during analysis and then physical models during design is referred to as **model-driven development**. As discussed in Chapter 1, traditional procedural development creates requirements models such as the data flow diagram (DFD) to show inputs, outputs, and processes, and the entity-relationship diagram (ERD) to show the details about stored data. Design models include structure charts and relational database schemas.

Models created using OO development are different from traditional models, however, because OO needs to depict, or model, different constructs. Rather than modeling data and processes separately, for example, OO development requires models that define classes of objects and depict object interactions. OO models and notation are based on UML, which is discussed in detail in the following section. These models include the use case diagram, class diagram, and sequence diagram, among others.

Because OO development focuses on classes of objects beginning with analysis, and then continuing through design and programming, it works very well with an iterative approach to development, discussed in Chapter 1. Iterative development means that you analyze first, design, and then program to address some of the system requirements. Then you repeat the analyze-design-program cycle to address additional requirements. In other words, you only complete some analysis before beginning design, and only complete some design before programming. See Figure 5-1.

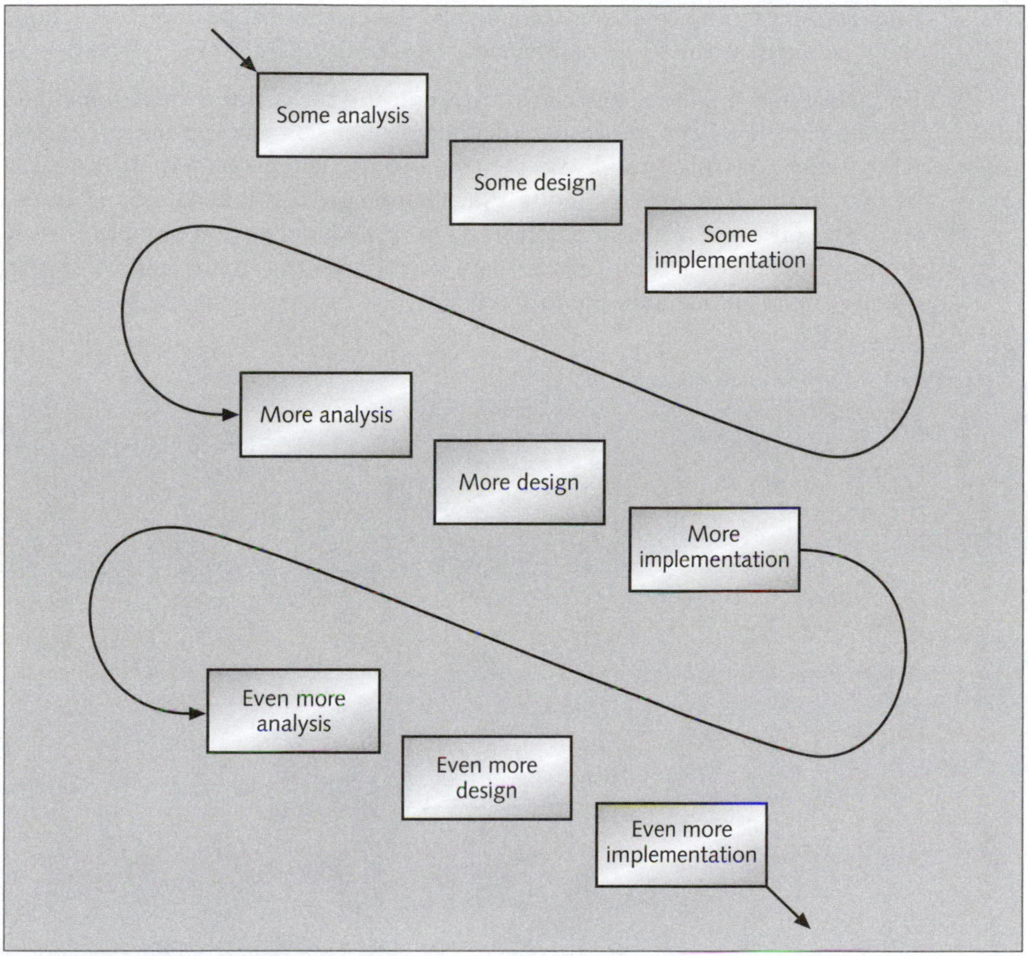

Figure 5-1 Iterative development

Iterative development contrasts with an earlier approach referred to as the **waterfall method**, where all of analysis was completed before design could start and all of design was completed before programming could start. As with the OO approach, the traditional approach now also uses iterative development extensively. But iterative development works more smoothly and seamlessly with OO because each iteration involves refining and adding classes.

Incremental development means some of the system is completed and put into operation before the entire system is finished. Important subsystems might be completed first, for example. Later, additional subsystems are added as they are completed. Incremental development is also used extensively with OO development. Iterative development and incremental development work together well. Several iterations might be required to finish the first subsystem that is released into production, for example, and then additional iterations are required to finish and then integrate the second subsystem.

An increasingly popular approach to development is the **spiral model**, shown in Figure 5-2. To emphasize the iterative nature of development, the project appears in Figure 5-2 as a spiral starting in the middle and working its way out. Each project has its own set of problems, or risks, so the developers should first identify the greatest risks to the success of the project and focus on them in the first iteration. The development team completes analysis, design, prototyping, and evaluation tasks for each iteration, starting in the middle of the spiral. Then the next iteration builds on the first iteration.

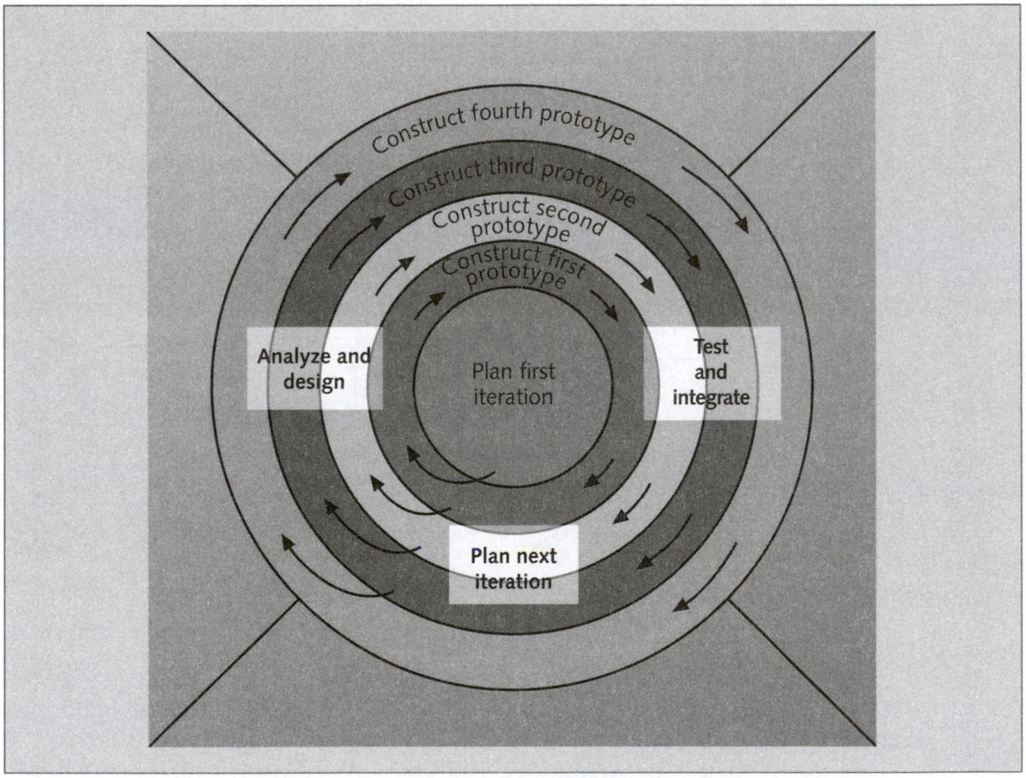

Figure 5-2 Spiral model of system development

Object-oriented development also requires other traditional system development tools and techniques, as discussed in Chapter 1: project planning, project management, feasibility assessment, management reviews, user involvement, joint application development, prototyping, unit and system testing, and conversion. In other words, most of the key concepts, tools, and techniques covered in any analysis and design course still apply to OO development.

UNDERSTANDING THE UNIFIED MODELING LANGUAGE

Object-oriented development requires a collection of models that depict system requirements and designs. UML defines a standard set of constructs and diagrams that you can use to model OO systems. Prior to 1997, developers used a variety of OO modeling notations, which made it difficult for project teams to communicate with each other. A standard modeling approach was clearly needed. Of the many people involved in developing OO modeling notations, three key developers joined forces to define and set the standard: Grady Booch, James Rumbaugh, and Ivar Jacobson, all of Rational Software (*www.rational.com*). Their set of diagrams and diagramming notation became the Unified Modeling Language, which is now accepted as the standard by the Object Management Group (OMG), an industry association dedicated to improving OO development practices. The use case diagram, class diagram, and sequence diagram are three of the diagrams they developed to model OO systems.

You can find complete information on UML and all of the diagrams and constructs at *www.rational.com*. Also explore the many books that summarize UML and explain its subtleties and specific details, including *The Unified Modeling Language User Guide* (1999) by Booch, Rumbaugh, and Jacobson.

Creating and Interpreting the Use Case Diagram

The first step in system modeling is to define the main system functions—what the system must allow the user to do. Each system function is called a **use case**. For example, in a system that processes orders, *record a sale* is a required system function and therefore a use case. Breaking down the system into a list of use cases allows developers to divide the work and focus on specific system functions. Typically, each iteration of the analysis-design-programming cycle addresses a few use cases at a time. This approach is similar to the one used in traditional system development because structured analysis also begins with functional decomposition.

The use case diagram shows two key concepts: the use case and the actor. The **actor** is the person or entity using the system. An example of a use case diagram is shown in Figure 5-3.

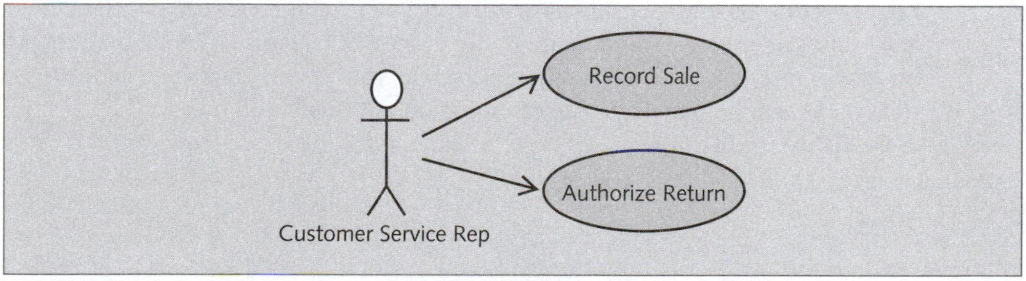

Figure 5-3 Example of a UML use case diagram

Here one actor, a customer service representative, needs the system for two use cases, *record sale* and *authorize return*. The actor is shown as a stick figure. A line with an arrow connects the actor to each use case. The use case is shown as an oval. An actor does not have to be a person. An actor can also represent a subsystem or a device that provides inputs or receives outputs.

How does the developer identify use cases? One approach is to identify *events* the system must respond to, as in the traditional structured approach to development. Three types of events can affect a system: external events, temporal events, and state events. An **external event** is something that happens outside the system and requires the system to respond, as when a customer buys a product or returns a product. When a customer buys a product, the system use case is *record sale*. When the customer wants to return a product, the use case is *authorize return*.

Each use case can be documented as a series of steps users follow when they interact with the system to complete the task. The steps users follow can be listed to document the use case. Sometimes the main steps have several variations, called **scenarios**. For example, the steps followed when a sale is recorded for a new customer might be different from the steps followed when a sale is recorded for an existing customer. Examples of external events, use cases, and scenarios are shown in Figure 5-4.

A **temporal event** occurs at a specific point in time, such as at the end of each day or at the end of the month. For example, monthly bills or statements, late notices, paychecks, and daily or monthly reports are produced according to a schedule. These events should also lead to use cases and perhaps multiple scenarios. Less user interaction is required to implement use cases based on temporal events, but they produce important system outputs. A **state event** occurs when the properties of an object change so as to require system processing. For example, inventory levels dropping below the reorder point would require a reorder use case, or a student's GPA falling below a specified level would require a GPA warning notification use case.

The process of identifying and documenting use cases involves extensive interaction with users. Users typically find external events to be a useful way to think about the system they use. Some users might name or describe a use case when they are thinking about the reasons they use the system. If so, you should be sure to document the event that triggers it. The user might focus on many specific scenarios. If so, you should be sure to combine them appropriately into one use case and document the event that triggers it. Try to keep the users focused on events first, however, because temporal and state events might not be obvious, and some external events might trigger use cases that do not involve all users.

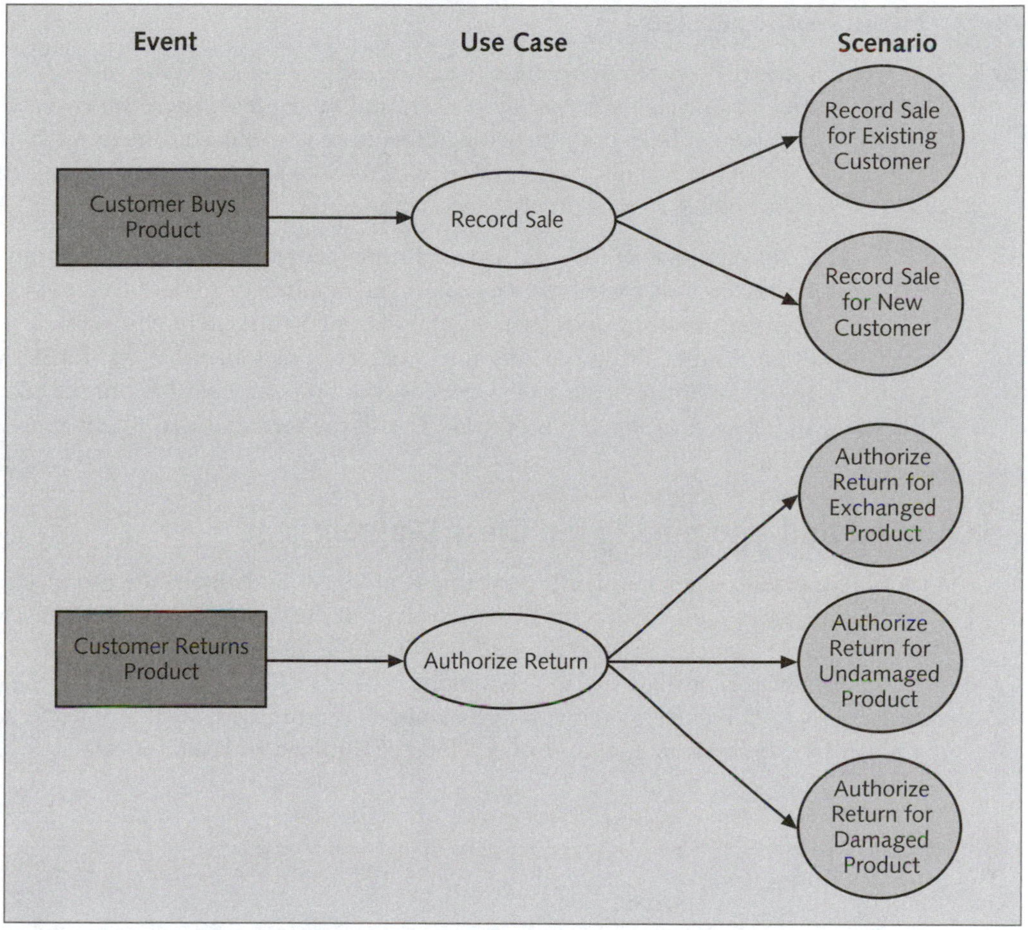

Figure 5-4 Events, use cases, and scenarios

As you and your development team identify use cases, you draw use case diagrams. One use case diagram might show all of the use cases and all of the actors for the system. If the system is large, you might draw one use case diagram for each subsystem. Other use case diagrams might focus on particular actors, showing only use cases involving the actors. These are useful when reviewing use cases with users.

Each use case needs to be documented and described in detail. As mentioned earlier, one way to document a use case is to list the steps followed by the actor to use the system. The steps involve interactions between the actor and the system, much like a dialog or script. UML defines an additional diagram that can be used to document use cases—an **activity diagram**. Sometimes a dialog or activity diagram is created for each scenario for a use case. The amount of detail and the number of diagrams depends upon the complexity of the use case.

Hands-on Exercise 1

1. Consider a system with these use cases: *add new course*, *schedule course section*, *register student*, *assign instructor*, *produce class list*, and *record grades*. There are two actors: department head and instructor. Students do not interact directly with this system. Draw a use case diagram showing the use cases and the actors, making assumptions about which actor is the user for each use case.

2. Consider a system for a video rental store that responds to the following external events: customer wants to become a member, member wants to rent videos, and member returns videos. Name the use case for the system corresponding to each event. Assume that processing might differ if a new member was formerly a member, if a member wants to rent videos when the member has unreturned videos, and if a returned video is overdue. List all the scenarios that might apply to each use case.

Creating and Interpreting the Class Diagram

In object-oriented development, everything is an object, and objects are grouped into classes. Therefore, a key model shows the classes involved in the system, called the class diagram. The class symbol is a rectangle with three sections (see Figure 5-5). Include the name of the class in the top section, attributes of the class in the middle section, and methods of the class in the bottom section. Figure 5-5 shows a class named Customer with attributes name, address, and phone. The methods are AddCustomer, UpdateCustomer, and AddToOrder.

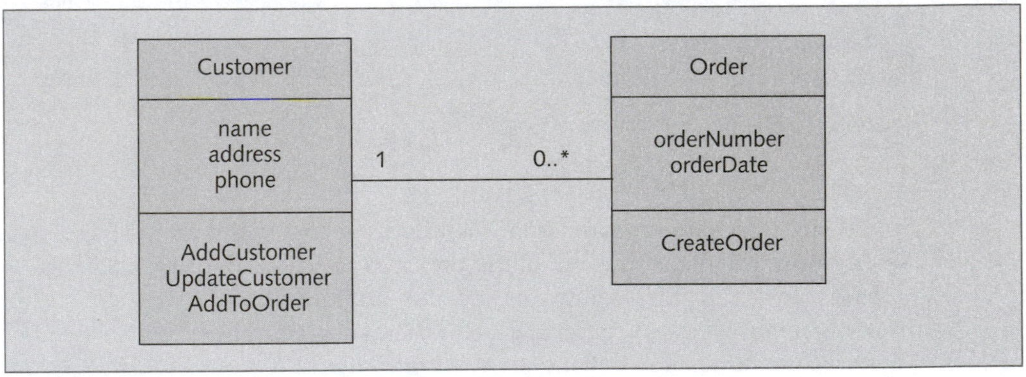

Figure 5-5 Class diagram example (Customer and Order)

Another class on the diagram is named Order. The association relationship between the Customer class and the Order class is shown with a line connecting the two classes. A customer places many orders, and an order is placed by only one customer. The number of associations between classes is written on each end of the line. UML refers to the number of associations as multiplicity (the same concept as cardinality on ERDs). Here the asterisk means many, so 0..* means that a customer places zero to many orders. Sometimes only the asterisk is shown to indicate zero or more. A mandatory relationship would be shown as 1..*, meaning one to many. This implies that a customer is not added to the system until he or she places an order. Be sure to read association relationships in both directions, from left to right and right to left.

The class diagram also shows generalization/specialization hierarchies (inheritance). Figure 5-6 expands the class diagram to include two subclasses of Order: MailOrder and PhoneOrder. The triangle symbol on the line below the Order box indicates it has subclasses. PhoneOrder inherits all of the attributes and methods of Order, but also includes additional attributes for the name of the phone representative and the duration of the phone call. MailOrder does not include the same additional attributes, but it does include the postmark date. A MailOrder instance, then, has values for three attributes (order number, order date, and postmark date). A PhoneOrder instance, however, has values for four attributes (order number, order date, phone order clerk, and call duration).

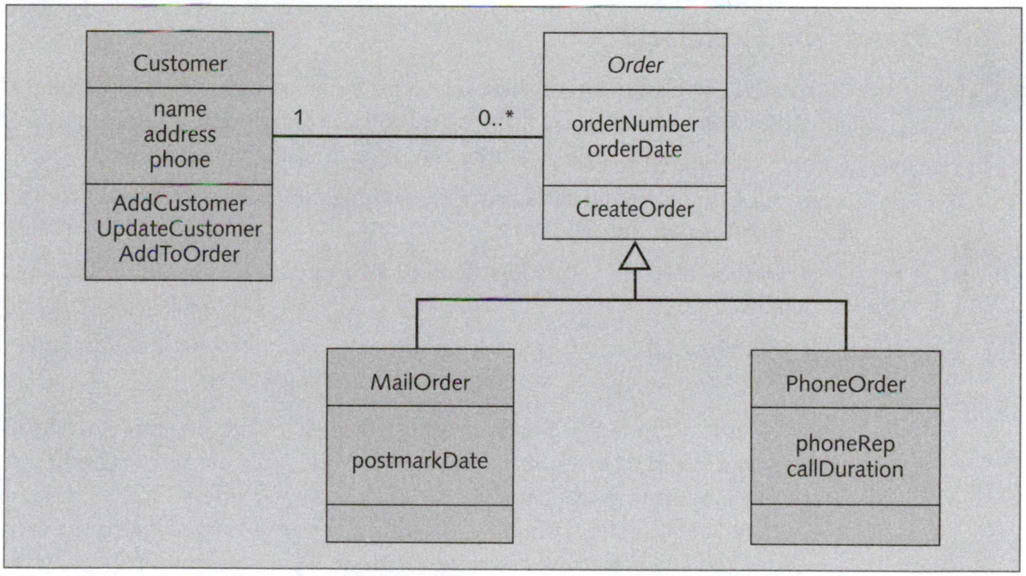

Figure 5-6 Class diagram extended to show generalization/specialization (inheritance)

Note that the name of the Order class is in italics, which indicates it is an **abstract class**. You do not create objects for an abstract class; it only serves to allow subclasses to inherit from it. Therefore, any order must be either a mail order or a phone order in this example. Note also that all orders must be associated with a customer. Both mail orders and phone orders inherit the requirement for an association as well as the attributes and methods.

You will see many examples of class diagrams in this text. Class diagrams are usually created as use cases are identified. Use case descriptions often mention specific classes with which the actor interacts, for example, revealing classes to add to the class diagram. Sometimes you identify more classes when talking with users, revealing additional use cases that need to be documented. Remember that the process followed is iterative.

Class diagrams also evolve during analysis and design to become more detailed. Initial class diagrams might only show key attributes and custom methods. As the model evolves, more attributes are added, more methods are added, and more details about each attribute and method are included. You learned earlier that OO development works very well with iterative development. One reason is the use of the class diagram in both analysis and design, adding to it as the project progresses. Then, OO programming means writing statements to define the classes. Classes remain the focus throughout.

Many additional diagram symbols and conventions for class diagrams are not discussed here. UML provides details to handle any interaction or object that might ever appear in a model. The examples in this text address the basic class diagram constructs—classes, association relationships, and inheritance—that are important to business systems.

Hands-on

Hands-on Exercise 2

1. Extend the class diagram shown in Figure 5-6 to show the following additional classes and association relationships. Be sure to include important attributes and show multiplicity for both directions of each association:
   - All Orders contain one or more Order Lines with an attribute for quantity of the item on the order line.
   - Each Order Line is associated with a Product with a product ID, description, and price.
   - A Phone Order, but not a Mail Order, is associated with a Customer Service Representative with an employee ID and name.
2. In Chapter 1, Projects 2 and 3, you listed some of the key problem domain classes and association relationships that would apply to a system for scheduling courses at a university. Your answer included classes such as Student, Professor, Course, Course Section, Department, and College. Draw a class diagram showing these classes and association relationships. Include some attributes for each class and indicate multiplicity for all association relationships.

Creating and Interpreting a Sequence Diagram

A sequence diagram shows interactions between objects in a system, usually for one use case or scenario. Therefore, the sequence diagram is another way to describe each use case. Because an OO system is a collection of interacting objects, the sequence diagram highlights this interactivity and is often referred to as a **dynamic model**. The class diagram does not highlight object interactions, so it is often referred to as a **static model**.

The actor can be shown as a stick figure or as a rectangle. Objects are shown as rectangles. The vertical lines below the actor and the objects are called **lifelines** and represent a sequence of time. The lifeline is shown as either a dashed line or a narrow box. The narrow box represents a period of time when it is an **active object**—that is, when it is executing or controlling part of the interaction. The horizontal arrows represent messages sent or received in sequence. Data returned in response to a message is shown as a dashed line.

Figure 5-7 shows an example of a sequence diagram for the scenario discussed earlier: *record sale for existing customer.*

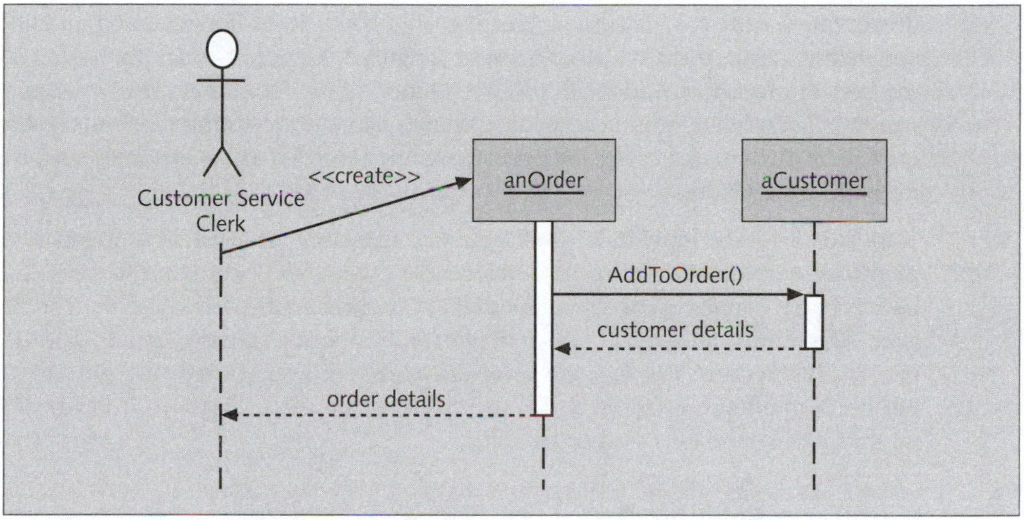

Figure 5-7 Sequence diagram for scenario *record sale for existing customer*

The actor, a customer service representative, sends a message asking the Order class to create a new order object, named anOrder. The <<create>> message points directly to the rectangle representing the new order. The new order object is immediately active (the lifeline below it is a narrow box), and it sends a message to the existing customer object named aCustomer asking it to add itself to the new order. The message from anOrder to aCustomer goes to the lifeline because it is an existing customer that has been created previously. When the message is received, aCustomer becomes active. The customer object returns information about the customer that the order object needs to finish its processing and then becomes inactive. Finally, the new order object returns information about the new order to the customer service representative and then becomes inactive.

There are several ways to name objects in a sequence diagram. Object names are always underlined and begin with a lowercase letter, and class names are always capitalized. Figure 5-7 uses generic object names to clarify the class. For example, anOrder is a name for a generic order object. It begins with a lowercase letter and includes the name of the class for clarity. Similarly, aCustomer is the name used for a generic customer object. Another approach is to include the name of the class after the name of the object, separated by a colon. Using this approach, Figure 5-7 objects would be named anOrder:Order or aCustomer:Customer (all underlined, as they are in the diagram). This approach is much clearer when the name of the object is very specific, for example, apollo13:Spacecraft, lisa:Editor, or susan:Professor.

If only a class name is used on a sequence diagram (not underlined), it means a class, rather than an object, is involved in the interaction. Classes can have shared methods and shared attributes that might be used in a use case or scenario.

Message names are written above the message line. The <<create>> message to anOrder is a stereotype action that results in creating an object. It is implemented in different ways depending upon the OO development language. Other messages are calls to invoke a method. For example, AddToOrder() is a method of the Customer class, invoked by the message AddToOrder() from the object anOrder. A name representing the return value is written on the dashed message line—customer details returned by aCustomer and order details returned by anOrder.

Standards vary for how and when sequence diagrams are used. Sometimes sequence diagrams are developed early in the development process to document use cases and scenarios. As with class diagrams, you can draw them at first with little detail, and then add more detail later. Sometimes developers prefer to create sequence diagrams later in the development process. Remember also that the actor can represent a subsystem or a device rather than a person. Sometimes an actor is not shown on a sequence diagram. Instead, all interaction might be triggered by a class or an object.

Hands-on Exercise 3

Draw a sequence diagram based on the following interactions between a video store clerk and objects in a video rental system. The scenario is named *rent video to existing member*.

1. Actor sends a <<create>> message to create a new Rental object named aRental; the message includes arguments for memberID and videoID.
2. aRental sends an AddMemberToRental message to a Member object based on memberID named aMember, which returns member details.
3. aRental sends a RentVideo message to a Video object based on the video named aVideo, which returns video details.
4. aRental returns all rental details to the actor.

USING THREE-TIER DESIGN IN OO DEVELOPMENT

The UML diagrams discussed in the previous section are used in both OO analysis and OO design. This is different from the traditional structured approach, in which structured analysis uses DFDs and ERDs, and structured design uses structure charts. This is one of the benefits of OO development—the same modeling constructs are used throughout the system development life cycle.

A useful way to look at the distinction between OOA and OOD is based on the *three-tier design* approach, introduced in Chapter 1. The three tiers include graphical user interface (GUI) classes, problem domain classes, and data access classes. Three-tier design requires that OO system developers separate three categories of classes when designing and building a system. First, you identify and specify the problem domain classes, the classes of objects that involve the users' work. Once these are specified, you define how GUI classes will be used to allow the user to interact with the problem domain classes. Finally, you specify data access classes that allow problem domain classes to interact with the database. Once all three tiers are completed, they are ready to work together as a complete system.

Figure 5-8 shows the three tiers in a simple order processing system, similar to an example in Chapter 1. The user interacts with a graphical user interface, usually made up of windows that contain GUI objects such as menus, buttons, text boxes, and labels. The user clicks a mouse and presses keys to get the system to respond. The user does not directly interact with problem domain objects; rather, the GUI objects interact with problem domain objects based on the actions of the user. By separating the user interface classes from the problem domain classes, you can focus on the problem domain classes independent of the user interface.

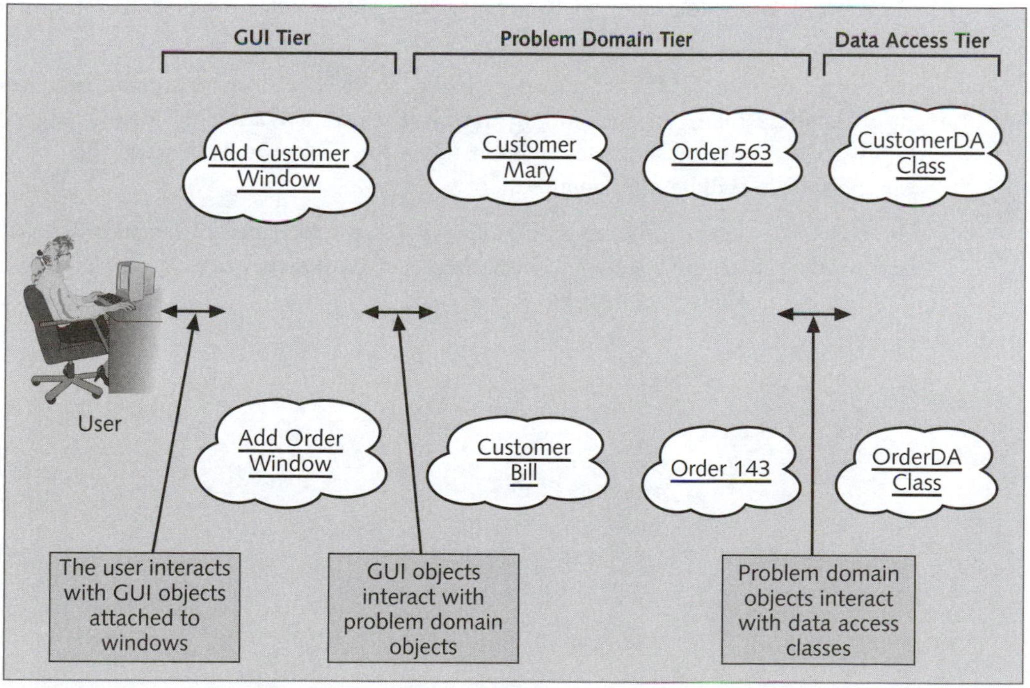

Figure 5-8 The three tiers in three-tier design

When a new problem domain object is created, some database management function is required to make the object persistent, that is, able to be used over time. The processing required to store information about objects to make them persistent is also kept separate from the problem domain classes by defining a separate data access class for each problem domain class to handle the data storage details. There are many ways to store data about objects (as you will see in Chapters 13 and 14), and by separating the data storage details from the problem domain classes, you can focus on problem domain classes independent of the database.

Separating GUI classes, problem domain classes, and data access classes supports the objective of creating loosely coupled system components. Loosely coupled components are beneficial because you can modify a component with minimal effects on other components. For example, changing the database management system used for the system would only require changing the data access classes, not the GUI classes or the problem domain classes. Similarly, changing the user interface would not require changing the data access classes. The three-tier design approach, therefore, makes it easier to maintain and enhance the system. Additionally, independent components are easier to reuse, a major objective of OO development.

Three-tier design also provides a framework for defining OOA and OOD. The previous class diagram examples show problem domain classes Customer and Order. OOA involves identifying and modeling the problem domain classes. The previous sequence diagram example shows only problem domain objects instantiated from the classes—anOrder and aCustomer. As you identify and model the problem domain classes and the object interactions, you are creating logical models of the system requirements, the main objective of system analysis. These models are logical models because they show what processing is required without showing *how* the system will be implemented.

As you move into OOD, you need to make design decisions about the user interface and about database management. Adding the GUI classes and then the data access classes turns the class diagrams and sequence diagrams into physical models because they begin to show *how* the system will be implemented.

The sequence diagram shown in Figure 5-9 is a physical model because it shows how the user interacts with the system and how the system interacts with a database.

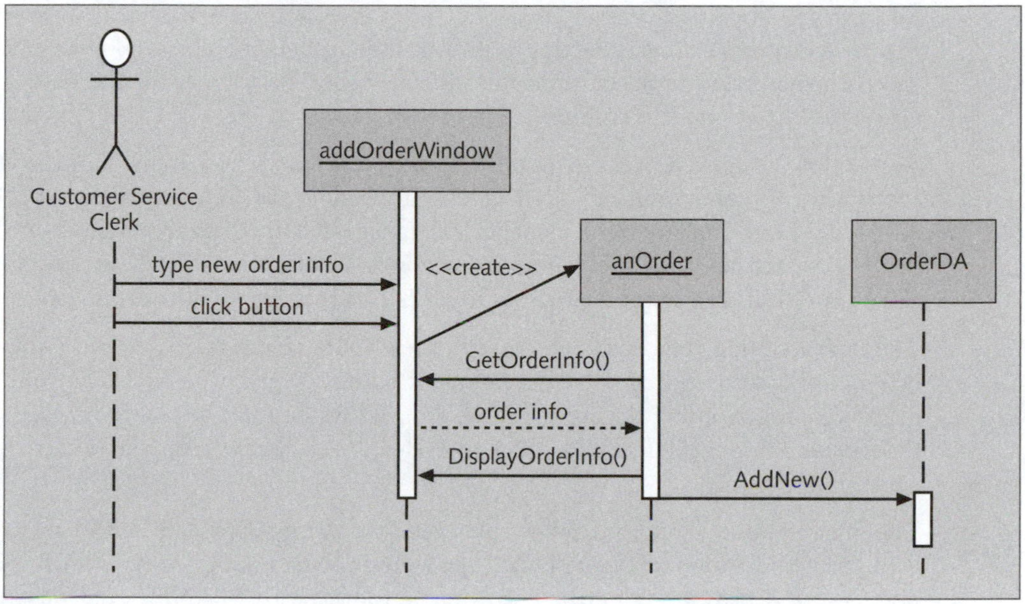

Figure 5-9 Sequence diagram adding GUI object and data access class

1. The user types information about a new order using a GUI named addOrderWindow, which contains text boxes, labels, and buttons.
2. Then the user clicks a button on the addOrderWindow GUI to ask the system to add the order.
3. The addOrderWindow GUI sends a <<create>> message to the Order class to create a new order object, named anOrder.
4. The new order object asks the GUI object for the order information, invoking the GetOrderInfo method defined for the GUI, and the GUI returns the information previously typed by the user.
5. The order object completes its processing and sends a message to the GUI asking it to display the new order details for the user to review, invoking the GUI's method DisplayOrderInfo.
6. Finally, the order object sends a message to the Order data access class (OrderDA) asking it to add the new order to the database. The OrderDA class takes care of all database interaction required to store the new order.

Three-tier design works well with iterative and incremental development. Each iteration might address a few of the system use cases. First, you define and model problem domain classes important to the use cases. Then you create a sequence diagram for each use case or scenario, showing only problem domain objects. You might begin to write OO code to define the problem domain classes and begin to conduct problem domain class testing.

You can also begin to define required GUI classes for each use case or scenario. Each sequence diagram can be expanded to include the GUI classes. The GUI classes can be tested and then integrated with the problem domain classes. Prototypes for the first iteration are now available for users to evaluate.

As you develop the OO code to implement the GUI classes, you might begin to write a data access class for each problem domain class to handle database management. Data access classes also can be added to the sequence diagrams. Next, the data access classes are tested and then integrated with the problem domain classes. Finally, the GUI classes, problem domain classes, and data access classes are ready to work together for the first iteration.

The next iteration repeats the process for a few more of the use cases. Note that three-tier design works well with iterative development because you can move easily from analysis to design to programming during each iteration, always building upon the models as you go. Prototypes are available early for users to evaluate, and system components remain as independent as possible.

The organization of this book follows the three-tier design approach. Part 2, starting with the next chapter, discusses problem domain classes and programming them with VB .NET. Part 3 discusses GUI classes—Windows Forms programmed with VB .NET and Web Forms programmed with ASP .NET—and making them interact with users and problem domain classes. Part 4 discusses data access classes and making them interact with problem domain classes. Then all three tiers are tied together into one application with GUI, problem domain, and data access classes functioning together in Part 5, including a Windows desktop application and a Web-based application. That is how object-oriented business systems are typically developed.

Hands-on Exercise 4

You completed a sequence diagram for a scenario named *rent video to existing member* in Hands-on Exercise 3. Expand your sequence diagram to include a GUI object named rentVideoWindow and a data access class named RentalDA. RentalDA can store information about the rental in the database when asked by a Rental problem domain object using the message AddNewRental.

INTRODUCING THE BRADSHAW MARINA CASE STUDY

The Bradshaw Marina case study is used throughout this text to demonstrate OO development principles and practices. The examples used for VB .NET programming are based on this case. This section describes Bradshaw Marina and its need for a computer system. Some UML diagrams are presented to explain the system requirements. Additional diagrams are presented in later chapters that cover specific OO development issues using VB .NET.

When a business determines it needs a computer system, it works with a team of developers to design and develop the system. One of the first tasks for the development team is to analyze the business and identify the functions the system will perform. The following section describes Bradshaw Marina and defines the system it wants to automate. Next, the development team begins object-oriented analysis to identify the use cases and scenarios required, creating use case diagrams. Then the development team identifies required problem domain classes and creates the class diagram. Finally, the team develops sequence diagrams to model object interactions. In the Bradshaw Marina case study, you are a member of the development team.

Exploring the Background of Bradshaw Marina

Bradshaw Marina is a privately owned corporation that rents boat slips and provides boat services on Clinton Lake, a large inland lake located in the midwestern United States. The lake was constructed in the 1970s primarily to provide flood control and to generate limited amounts of electrical power. The U.S. Army Corps of Engineers manages the lake and restricts construction near its shores, creating an ideal natural wildlife habitat in addition to providing a beautiful parklike setting for boaters. Bradshaw is the largest of the three marinas on the lake. The three marinas accommodate approximately 600 boats in slips: 450 sailboats and 150 powerboats. Bradshaw's boat population is around 350 sailboats and 75 powerboats, although it plans to expand these capacities.

Bradshaw Marina would like to have an automated system to track their customers, the slips they lease, and the boats in the slips. Initially, the system will simply maintain basic information for customers, slips, and boats, and perform day-to-day business tasks. These tasks include creating a lease, computing the lease amount for a slip, and assigning a boat to a slip. The marina also wants to use the system to search for information, such as vacant slips and slips leased to a specific customer.

Bradshaw eventually wants to enhance the system so they can add boat service records, which will help them track tasks such as hauling a boat, painting the bottom of a boat, or working on the engine of a boat. Later, they want to add billing features to the system. They want to be able to use the system to generate bills for both slip leases and boat services, record payments, send late notices, and produce accounts receivable and other accounting reports. For now, it will help to include information on customers, slips, and boats.

Identifying Bradshaw Use Cases and Scenarios

The first step in the OOA process is identifying use cases that fall within the scope of the system. The main events of interest involve customers—when a customer leases a slip, when a customer buys a new boat, and so on. Because these events involve customers, boats, and slips, the use cases also focus on customers, boats, and slips. Your development team initially spends a lot of time talking with Bradshaw staff about the events involving customers that result in use cases.

For example, use cases involving customers might include *add new customer* and *maintain customer information*. A new customer is added when he or she leases a slip, and customer information is maintained whenever a customer changes address or phone number. Similarly, use cases involving leases include *lease slip*, *renew slip lease*, and *transfer lease*. Use cases involving boats include *add new boat* and *maintain boat information*. In addition, the system should maintain information about slips and the docks that contain slips. Finally, the system needs to process queries and process reports. You work with other members of the development team to create the use case diagram indicating these use cases, which is shown in Figure 5-10.

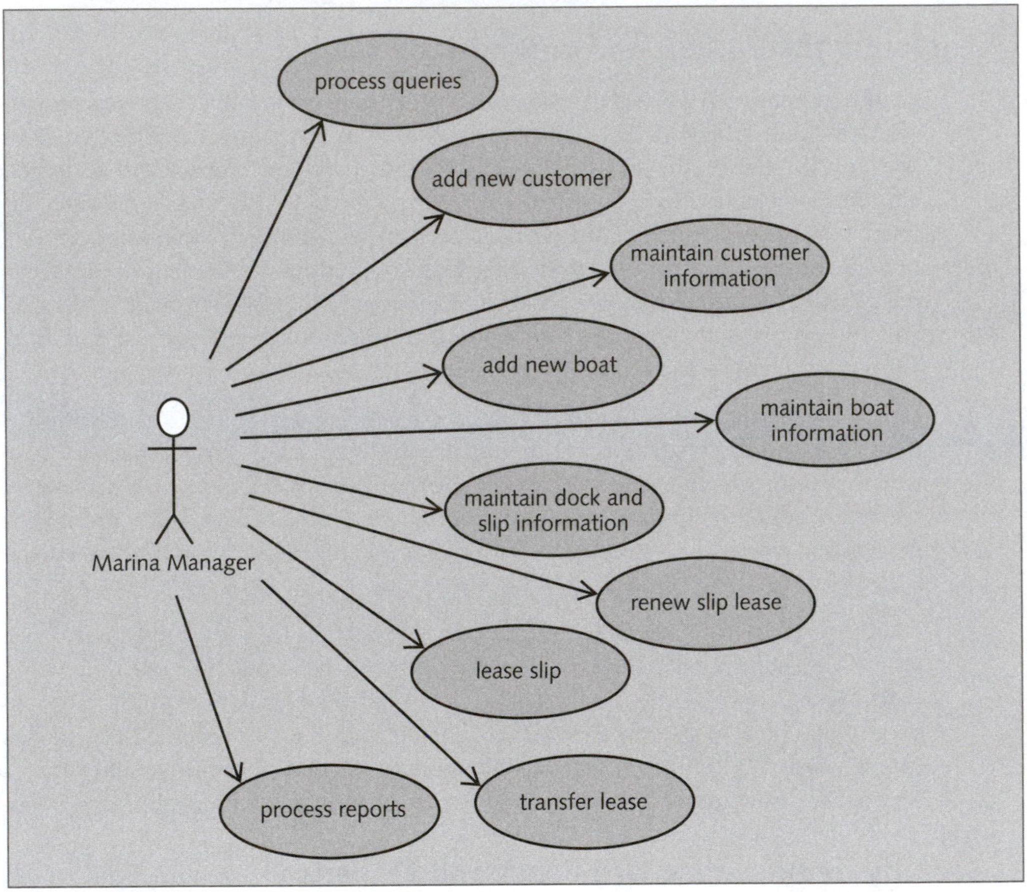

Figure 5-10 Bradshaw Marina use case diagram

Several scenarios could be associated with each use case, so you and your team might decide to divide up the list of use cases and work separately on scenarios. For example, the *lease slip* use case might have many scenarios you should discuss further with Bradshaw. One scenario might be *lease slip to existing customer* and another scenario *lease slip to new customer*. Further, another scenario might be *lease annual slip to customer* and another *lease daily slip to customer*.

Scenarios can become very specific. It might take several attempts to create a comprehensive and mutually exclusive list of scenarios for the more important use cases. For example, given the situations involving existing customers, new customers, annual slip leases, and daily slip leases, the scenarios for one use case might be finalized as follows:

- *Lease annual slip to existing customer*
- *Lease annual slip to new customer*
- *Lease daily slip to existing customer*
- *Lease daily slip to new customer*

Identifying Bradshaw Problem Domain Classes

Once you identify the use cases and scenarios, you explore the problem domain classes involved in the use cases. You and the team meet with Bradshaw Marina again to ask about the things that are involved in the work of the marina, in this case the customers, boats, leases, slips, and docks. The first step is to begin an initial class diagram that includes these potential classes, as shown in Figure 5-11.

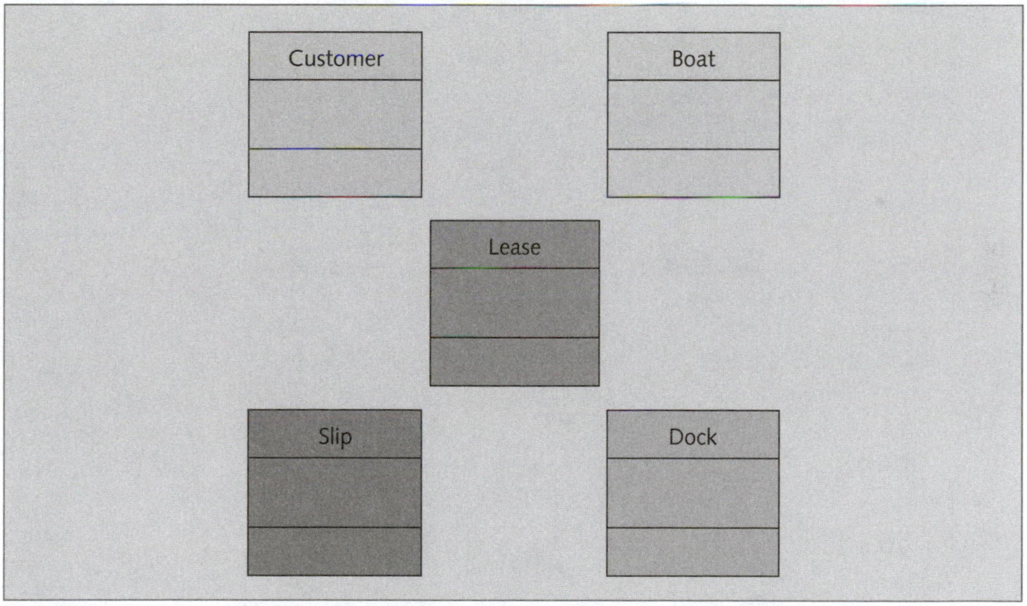

Figure 5-11 Bradshaw Marina initial class diagram

One of the first questions your team asks is about docks and slips. Sometimes the users talk about docks and sometimes they talk about slips. What exactly is a dock? What exactly is a slip? Sometimes you find that users might be using two terms for the same concept. Other times you find that user terms take on very specific meanings that you will need to understand. Remember, the problem domain classes reflect detailed user knowledge about their work. Your task is learning as much about the users' knowledge as possible. Is a slip a special type of dock (generalization/specialization hierarchy)? Or is it something else?

It turns out (after quite a few explanations and sketches) that Bradshaw Marina defines a dock as an entire floating structure that boat owners walk out on to get to their boats (see Figure 5-12). A slip, on the other hand, is defined as one space on a dock where a boat can be tied up. That is what a customer leases. Therefore, a slip is not a special kind of dock; it is something separate that is associated with a dock. This is just one example of the importance of learning about the users and their work.

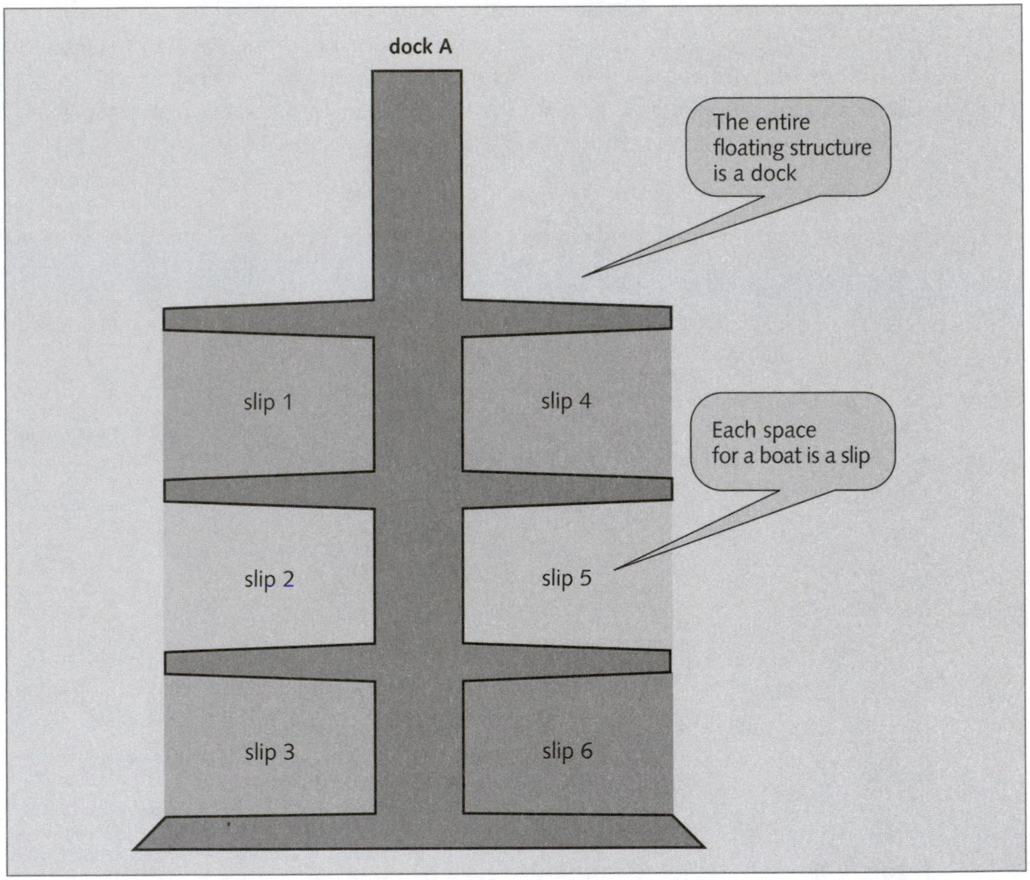

Figure 5-12 A dock contains slips

As you continue to look more closely at the initial classes, you see that you need more specialized information about boats, slips, and leases in the system. For example, Bradshaw has two types of boats: sailboats and powerboats. Bradshaw also has two types of slips: regular and covered. Finally, Bradshaw provides two types of leases: an annual lease and a daily lease. You refine the classes to show the generalization/specialization hierarchies that require inheritance, as in Figure 5-13.

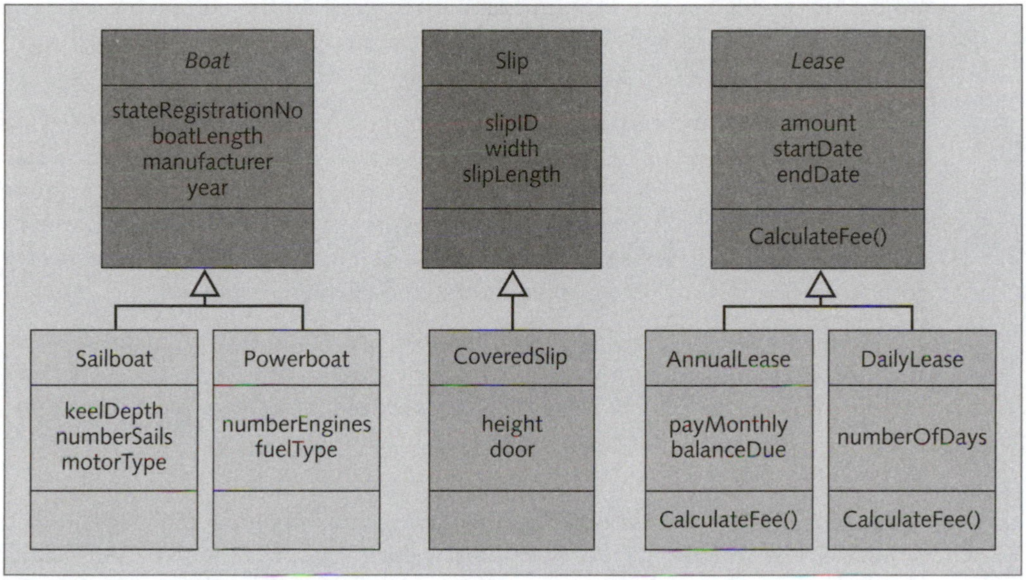

Figure 5-13 Refined classes showing generalization/specialization hierarchies (inheritance)

Because a boat must be either a sailboat or a powerboat, the Boat class is an abstract class (shown in italics), meaning it is only used for inheritance. The Lease class is also an abstract class because any lease must be a daily lease or an annual lease. A slip, on the other hand, might be a regular slip or a covered slip. A covered slip is a special type of regular slip; therefore, the Slip class is a concrete class (not abstract).

As you continue modeling problem domain classes, you begin to list the more specific pieces of information about each class—the attributes. You determine that all boats have a state registration number, length, manufacturer, and model year. Sailboats have additional attributes: a keel depth, number of sails, and motor type. Powerboats have different additional attributes: number of engines and fuel type. The reason the Sailboat and Powerboat subclasses are included is because of the different mix of attributes.

You find that slips are identified with a slip number. Bradshaw has slips in various widths and lengths. Some slips are covered, and the cover height is needed. Some covered slips have a door that can be closed to protect the boat. Sailboats cannot use the covered slips because of their mast height.

All leases are required to store a dollar amount for the lease, a start date, and an end date, so these are attributes of the Lease class. Annual leases can be paid for monthly, and the balance due needs to be tracked. Daily leases must be paid in advance, so there is no need to store a balance due. The number of days of the daily lease is required, however. The dollar amount of an annual lease and a daily lease are calculated differently. The annual lease amount is based on the slip width, but the daily lease amount is based on the number of days. Therefore, the CalculateFee method is different for each lease, and CalculateFee is shown as a method of each subclass to highlight this difference.

Once these details are finalized for boats, slips, and leases, the other classes—Customer and Dock—are considered. The complete class diagram showing all problem domain classes is shown in Figure 5-14. Docks are identified by a letter (A, B, C, etc.) and by location (North Cove, South Shore, etc.). Some docks have electrical service and some have water. Customers are boat owners who lease slips from the marina. The system should maintain standard customer information, including name, address, and telephone number.

Additional methods are included for Slip, Boat, and Dock. Not all methods are included on the class diagram, particularly during the early stages of OOA, but important methods are often included. The Slip class is responsible for leasing itself, so it has a method named LeaseSlip. A boat is assigned to a slip or removed from a slip, so Boat has two methods listed. A dock contains slips, so Dock has a method named AddSlipToDock.

You complete the class diagram by identifying and modeling the association relationship among classes. You already recognized that a dock contains slips and a slip is contained on a dock, for example. The line between Slip and Dock represents the association. Multiplicity is recorded on both ends of the line—a dock contains one or more (1..*) slips. A slip is contained on one and only one (1) dock.

There are other association relationships. A boat is optionally assigned to a slip and each slip optionally contains one boat (multiplicity is represented on both ends as an optional association, written as 0..1). It is therefore possible for Bradshaw to have information about a boat even if it is not assigned to a slip. A customer optionally owns one boat, but a boat must be owned by one and only one customer. Therefore, a customer can lease a slip even if a boat is not yet owned, but there is no reason for Bradshaw to maintain information for a boat without an owner. The multiplicity constraints define information about these business policies of users.

A final association relationship is between Slip and Customer. A customer optionally leases a slip, and a slip is optionally leased by a customer. But this association is really more complex. In fact, the Lease class defined previously exists as a byproduct of the association between Customer and Slip, so Lease is called an **association class** and is attached to the association line with a dashed line. Association classes are much like associative data entities on ERDs. They are very common in business systems, and association classes are implemented much like any other class. The notation helps to show that the association class exists only because of the association.

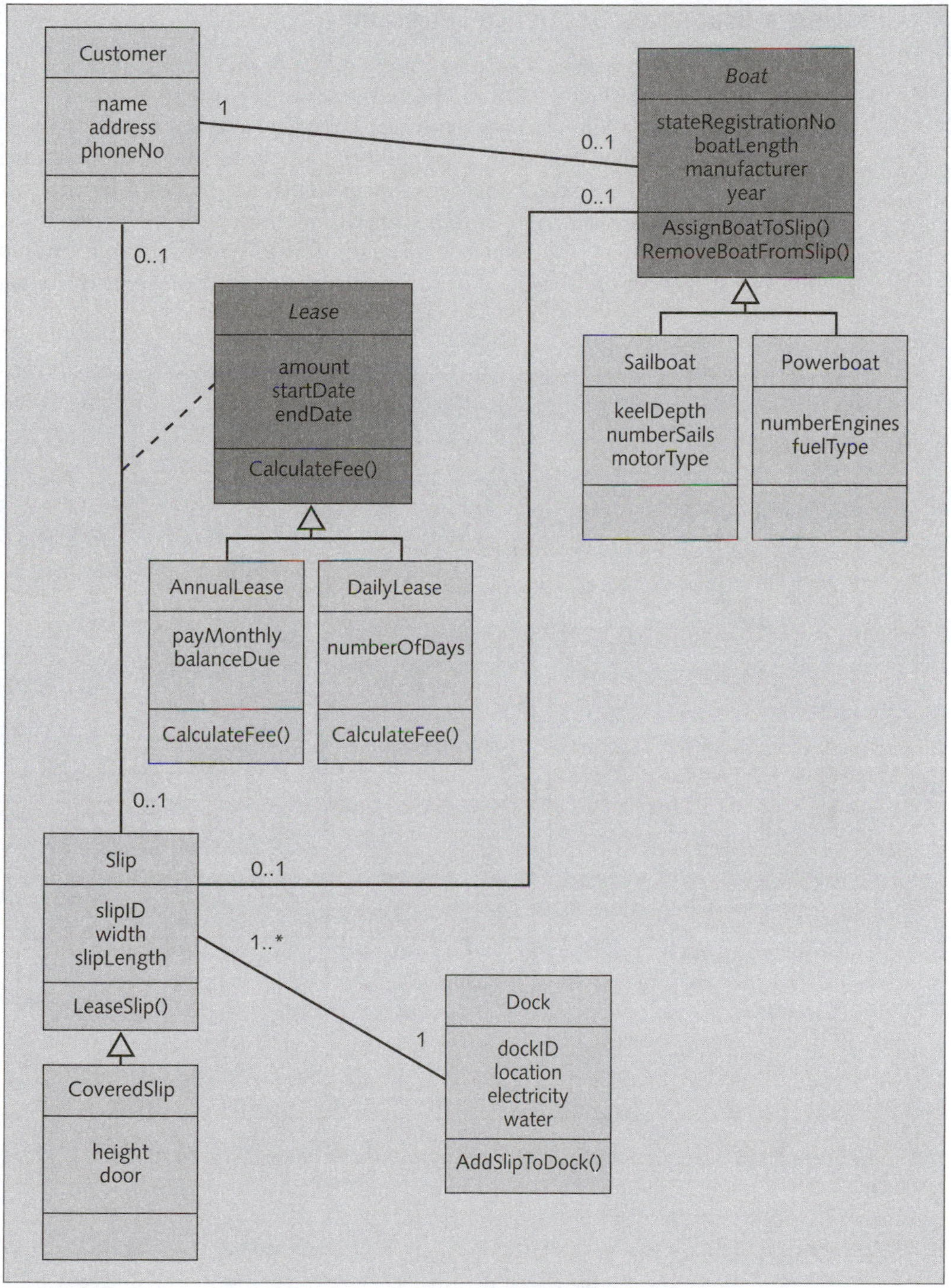

Figure 5-14 Bradshaw Marina refined class diagram

Creating a Bradshaw Sequence Diagram

The development team already indicated some methods on the class diagram for Bradshaw Marina, as shown earlier in Figure 5-14. For example, the Boat class has a method AssignBoatToSlip, the Slip class has a method LeaseSlip, and the Lease class has a method CalculateFee. These methods result from exploring scenarios and documenting them with sequence diagrams. These three methods, for example, are required by the scenario *lease annual slip to existing customer*, one of four scenarios identified for the previous use case *lease slip*. Figure 5-15 shows the sequence diagram for this scenario. You should create a sequence diagram for each scenario of each use case, but only one example is shown here.

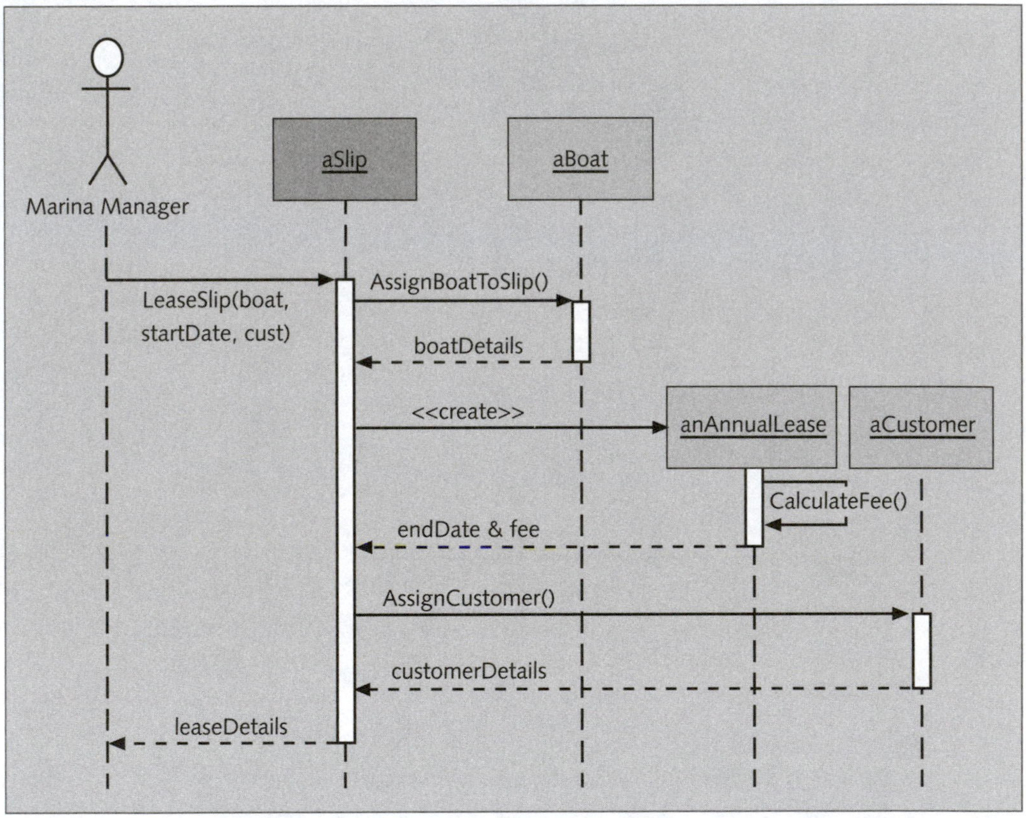

Figure 5-15 Sequence diagram for scenario *lease annual slip to existing customer*

In this scenario, the actor is the marina manager. To lease a slip, the actor sends the LeaseSlip message to the specific slip object (aSlip), supplying information about the boat, the start date, and the customer. The LeaseSlip method of aSlip interacts with other objects to complete the scenario.

The slip sends the AssignBoatToSlip message to the boat, for example, which returns boat details. Next, the slip asks the AnnualLease class to create a new lease object, supplying the start date. The new lease object (anAnnualLease) invokes its own method, CalculateFee, shown as a message to itself on the activated lifeline, and then it returns the end date and fee to the slip. Next, aSlip sends a message to the customer object asking it to assign itself to the lease, and the customer object returns customer details. Finally, the slip returns all of the lease information to the actor—boat details, lease details, and customer details.

This sequence diagram is a logical model showing only problem domain objects. As you move from OOA to OOD, you will expand the diagram to show the GUI objects the actor interacts with and the data access classes that handle interaction with the database. You will see many sequence diagrams in this text that illustrate VB .NET code examples.

But now that you have documented the use cases, the scenarios, the problem domain classes, and some of the object interactions, you are ready to begin writing some OO program code to define the problem domain classes for Bradshaw Marina. And that is what you will learn how to do beginning with the next chapter.

As you continue with this text, you will learn how to implement generalization/specialization hierarchies, association relationships, GUI classes, and data access classes so you can complete the Bradshaw Marina system, including porting the application to the Web.

Chapter Summary

- System analysis means to study, understand, and define the requirements for the system. System requirements define what a system needs to accomplish for the users in business terms using a collection of models.
- Model-driven development means creating logical and physical models during analysis and design to show what is required and how it will be implemented.
- Iterative development, in contrast to the waterfall method, means that analysis, design, and programming are performed in parallel, with the process repeated several times until the project is done. Incremental development means part of the system is put to use first before the rest is finished. The spiral model is a newer approach to showing iteration on a system project.
- The Unified Modeling Language (UML) defines a standard set of models and constructs that can be used to model OO systems. Three UML diagrams are emphasized in this text.
- The use case diagram shows all of the system functions, called use cases, carried out by a user, called an actor. Use cases are defined by looking for events to which the

system is required to respond—external events, temporal events, or state events. Each use case might be described by several more specific scenarios.

- The class diagram shows the classes of objects that interact in the system, including generalization/specialization hierarchies and association relationships.
- The sequence diagram shows the messages that the actor sends to objects and that objects send to each other during a use case or a more specific scenario.
- The three-tier design approach divides classes of objects into GUI classes used for the user interface, problem domain classes used in the users' work, and data access classes used to interact with the database management system. Three-tier design helps separate concerns of OOA and OOD, but more importantly it results in a client-server architecture that is easier to deploy and maintain.
- Bradshaw Marina is a case study used throughout this text. Bradshaw rents boat slips to customers on Clinton Lake, and they need a system to track customers, boats, slips, and leases. The use case diagram, class diagram, and one of the many sequence diagrams that form the basis for the design and programming examples in this text are introduced in this chapter.

Key Terms

abstract class
active object
activity diagram
actor
association class
dynamic model
external event
incremental development
lifeline
logical model
model
model-driven development
physical model
scenario
spiral model
state event
static model
system analysis
system design
system requirements
temporal event
use case
waterfall method

Review Questions

1. A model is:
   a. always a physical object shown in three dimensions
   b. a representation of some aspect of the real world
   c. only created for simple "toy" systems
   d. only useful for classroom examples

2. In OO development, a model is:
   a. something created only during OOD
   b. something created during both OOA and OOD
   c. rarely used to depict system requirements
   d. always a physical model
3. System analysis means to:
   a. define what the system needs to accomplish for users in business terms
   b. create programs using OO technology that users will like
   c. create models showing how the various system components will be implemented with specific technology
   d. develop systems using only OO development techniques
4. System design means to:
   a. define what the system needs to accomplish for users in business terms
   b. create programs using OO technology that users will like
   c. create models showing how the various system components will be implemented with specific technology
   d. develop systems using OO development techniques
5. Creating logical models of the system requirements during analysis and then physical models during design is the idea behind:
   a. iterative development
   b. model-driven development
   c. incremental development
   d. spiral development

6. Some of the system is completed and put into operation before the entire system is finished when using:
   a. iterative development
   b. model-driven development
   c. incremental development
   d. spiral development
7. To emphasize the iterative nature of development, the project is shown as a spiral starting in the middle and working its way out when using:
   a. iterative development
   b. model-driven development
   c. incremental development
   d. spiral development
8. Grady Booch, James Rumbaugh, and Ivar Jacobson are the individuals responsible for defining and standardizing:
   a. structured analysis and design
   b. the Unified Modeling Language (UML)
   c. the spiral model
   d. OOA and OOD
9. The UML diagram that shows the system users and system functions is called the:
   a. use case diagram
   b. class diagram
   c. sequence diagram
   d. activity diagram
10. The UML diagram that shows the classes of objects involved in the system is called the:
    a. use case diagram
    b. class diagram
    c. sequence diagram
    d. activity diagram
11. The UML diagram that shows how objects interact is called the:
    a. use case diagram
    b. class diagram
    c. sequence diagram
    d. activity diagram

12. There are many other UML diagrams that are not shown in this chapter, including the:
    a. use case diagram
    b. class diagram
    c. sequence diagram
    d. activity diagram
13. The class diagram is an example of a:
    a. narrative model
    b. dynamic model
    c. traditional development model
    d. static model
14. The sequence diagram is an example of a:
    a. narrative model
    b. dynamic model
    c. traditional development model
    d. static model
15. On a class diagram, the lines that are drawn to connect two classes represent a(n)
    a. attribute
    b. method
    c. association relationship
    d. lifeline
16. Which of the following shows that as few as zero but as many as one object may be involved in an association?
    a. 0..*
    b. 1..*
    c. 0..1
    d. 1
17. Which of the following shows that as few as one but possibly many objects may be involved in an association?
    a. 0..**
    b. 1..*
    c. 0..1
    d. 1

18. On a class diagram, the symbol representing a generalization/specialization hierarchy is:

a. a dashed line

b. a triangle pointing to the superclass

c. a diamond on one end of the association line

d. indicated by the attributes listed in the class symbol

19. On a sequence diagram, an activated object is represented as:

a. a dashed lifeline

b. a stick figure

c. a rectangle with the name capitalized and not underlined

d. a narrow box on the lifeline

20. On a sequence diagram, an actor is represented as:

a. a dashed lifeline

b. a stick figure

c. a rectangle with the name capitalized and not underlined

d. a narrow box on the lifeline

21. The three tiers in three-tier design include all of the following *except* the:

a. operating system tier

b. GUI tier

c. problem domain tier

d. data access tier

22. In three-tier design, the first tier considered is the:

a. operating system tier

b. GUI tier

c. problem domain tier

d. data access tier

Discussion Questions

1. What is the difference between a logical model and a physical model? Describe how a sequence diagram can be either a logical or a physical model. Can a class diagram also be either? What would make a class diagram more physical?

2. OO development works well with iteration and incremental development. Discuss some of the reasons why this is true.
3. Without UML, it would be difficult for system developers to communicate about their work on a system project. Discuss why this is so.
4. The Bradshaw Marina case study describes initial system requirements, some additional functions they want to add in the near future, and even more functions they want to include further down the line. Discuss how you might use incremental development to approach all of Bradshaw's needs.

Projects

1. Given a system with six use cases, list the specific steps to be followed based on the three-tier design approach for developing the system, assuming you plan to have three iterations addressing two use cases each. Be as specific as possible in terms of diagrams drawn and programming completed.
2. The Bradshaw Marina case study describes (1) initial system requirements, (2) some additional functions they want to add in the near future, and (3) even more functions they want to include further down the line (see discussion question 4 above). List at least three use cases for the functions desired in the second phase of the project. List at least four use cases desired for the third phase of the project.
3. Consider the additional Bradshaw Marina requirements for recording boat services for customers. What additional problem domain class would you add to the class diagram? What are the association relationships between this class and other classes? Might this class be expanded to a generalization/specialization hierarchy? If so, what are some potential subclasses. Are there any other problem domain classes you might add? Draw the complete class diagram for Bradshaw that includes all existing classes plus one or more new classes.
4. Figure 5-15 shows a sequence diagram for the Bradshaw scenario *lease slip to existing customer*. Draw a similar sequence diagram for the scenario *lease annual slip to new customer*.

PART 2

Developing Problem Domain Classes

CHAPTER

6

Writing a Problem Domain Class Definition

In this chapter you will:

- Learn VB .NET naming conventions
- Develop a problem domain (PD) class definition
- Define attributes
- Write methods and properties
- Test a PD class
- Create an instance
- Write a constructor method
- Write a TellAboutSelf method
- Write a Tester class as a Form

In Part 1 you learned that OO systems employ the three-tier design model, consisting of three different categories of classes: graphical user interface (GUI) classes, which provide the user interface for data input and display; problem domain (PD) classes, which model the essential business entities; and data access (DA) classes, which provide data storage and retrieval services. Here in Part 2 you will learn how to write class definitions for the PD classes using VB .NET. In Part 3 you will work with the GUI classes, and in Part 4 you will work with the DA classes. In Part 5 you will develop a complete application by connecting the GUI, PD, and DA classes.

You read about Bradshaw Marina in the previous chapter. You will use this case to illustrate the development of an OO system throughout the remainder of the book. This case involves only a few PD classes, yet it provides examples of all the OO concepts you read about in Part 1.

In this chapter you will see how to design and write a class definition for Customer. This definition will include attributes and methods to store and retrieve the attribute values. To test your Customer class definition, you will write a second class, named TesterOne, to create instances of Customer and test the methods that access the attribute values. You will then write a third class, named TesterTwo, that duplicates the tasks in TesterOne but uses a GUI form instead of a module.

VB .NET Naming Conventions

Recall from Chapters 3 and 4 that VB .NET programmers have adopted a style for writing identifiers, which are the names you assign to classes, class definitions, attributes, and methods:

- Class names start with a capital letter. Examples of class names are Customer and Boat.
- Attribute names begin with a lowercase character, but subsequent words comprising the name are capitalized. Examples of attribute names are address and phoneNo.
- Method names begin with an uppercase character, and subsequent words are capitalized. Method names usually contain an imperative verb describing what the method does, followed by a noun. Examples of method names are GetPhoneNo, SetAddress, and ComputeLease.

Developing a PD Class Definition

Recall that the Bradshaw Marina system has several PD classes, such as Customer, Boat, Slip, and Dock, and that there are interactions and relationships among many of these: a Customer *owns* a Boat, a Boat *is assigned to* a Slip, and a Customer *leases* a Slip, for example. Some of the classes have inheritance relationships. Both Sailboat and Powerboat are *subclasses* of Boat; Sailboat *is* a Boat and Powerboat *is* a Boat.

You begin developing the marina's system by writing a class definition for each of the PD classes. These class definitions are based on *some* of the features of their real-world counterparts. You saw earlier that you model an object's characteristics by defining attributes and you model the behavior by writing methods. In other words, each class definition will contain the attributes and methods that make the objects behave as required by the system.

The VB .NET code you write to represent a class is called a **class definition**. You begin developing the Bradshaw Marina system by first writing a definition for the Customer class. This class, representing all of the marina's customers, is shown in Figure 6-1. You will design and write class definitions for some of the marina's additional PD classes in subsequent chapters.

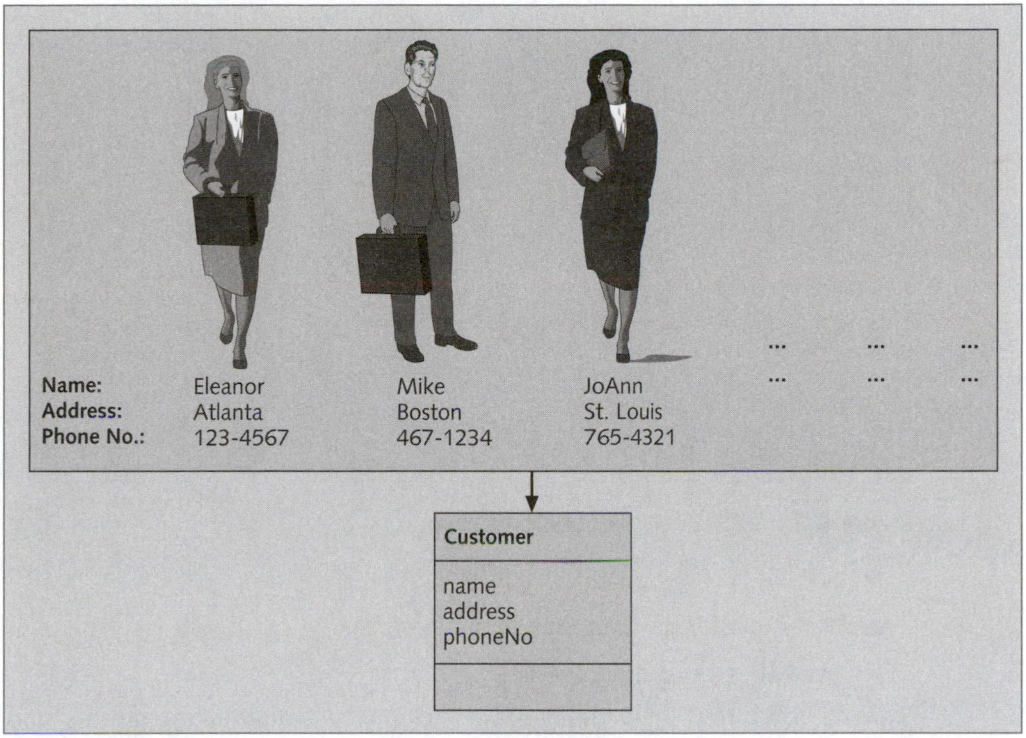

Figure 6-1 The Customer class represents customers

The Customer class has attributes for the customer's name, address, and telephone number as outlined in the case description. (Refer to the Bradshaw Marina case study in Chapter 5.) You will declare these attributes in the class definition you write. In addition, you will write methods to create a customer instance, assign values to the attributes, and then retrieve attribute values from the customer instance.

Class Definition Structure

The structure of a class definition consists of a **class header** followed by attribute definitions and then method code. The class header is a line of code that identifies the class and some of its characteristics. The end of the class is indicated by an end class statement. Figure 6-2 illustrates the structure of a VB .NET class definition.

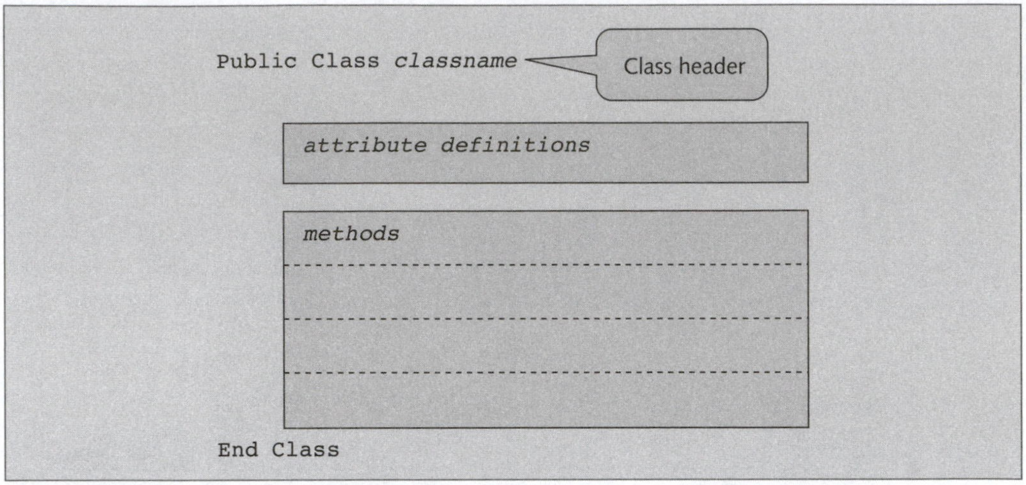

Figure 6-2 VB.NET class definition structure

The class header for the Customer definition is:

```
Public Class Customer
```

The VB .NET IDE editor shows keywords in blue; within the text of this book, VB .NET keywords are in bold Courier font. The keyword **`Public`** indicates that this class has public accessibility, meaning anyone can use it. The keyword **`Class`** indicates that this line of code is a class header, and `Customer` establishes the class name.

Defining Attributes

The Customer class diagram shows three attributes: name, address, and phone number. You define attributes by declaring variables for each one. You recall from Chapter 3 that you declared a variable by writing the keyword **`Dim`**, the variable name, the keyword **`As`**, and then its data type. You write an attribute definition the same way, except you replace the keyword **`Dim`** with **`Private`**. You use the `String` data type to define the Customer attributes as:

```
'attributes
Private name As String
Private address As String
Private phoneNo As String
```

When defining attributes, you can specify the **accessibility** of a variable as **`Public`**, **`Private`**, **`Protected`**, or **`Friend`**. The keyword **`Public`** allows any class to access the variable directly, while **`Private`** prohibits direct access, and the variable is accessible only within the class where it is defined. The keyword **`Protected`** allows subclasses to have direct access, while **Friend** permits classes within the same **assembly** access. An assembly is a collection of one or more projects deployed as an application. You can assign your project and all of its classes to a specific assembly.

You choose the accessibility depending on the type of variable being declared. **Public** is generally used for constants that need access by other classes. In Chapter 1 you read about encapsulation, which hides the internal structure of attributes from other objects. When defining attributes in class definitions, you use **Private** to restrict access by other classes. This restriction implements the notion of encapsulation and data hiding by preventing others from accessing the data directly. You will, however, provide **accessor methods** that can be invoked to access the attribute values.

WRITING METHODS AND PROPERTIES

Problem domain classes do not function alone. Instead, their methods provide services to other objects in a system. You saw earlier that in OO systems objects interact in much the same way as real-world objects. This interaction is simulated when one object sends a message to another object to invoke a method. One way of viewing this interaction between objects is to apply the basic client-server model. The object sending the message becomes the **client object**, while the object receiving the message is the **server object**. Figure 6-3 shows the relationship between a client object and a server object in a client/server model.

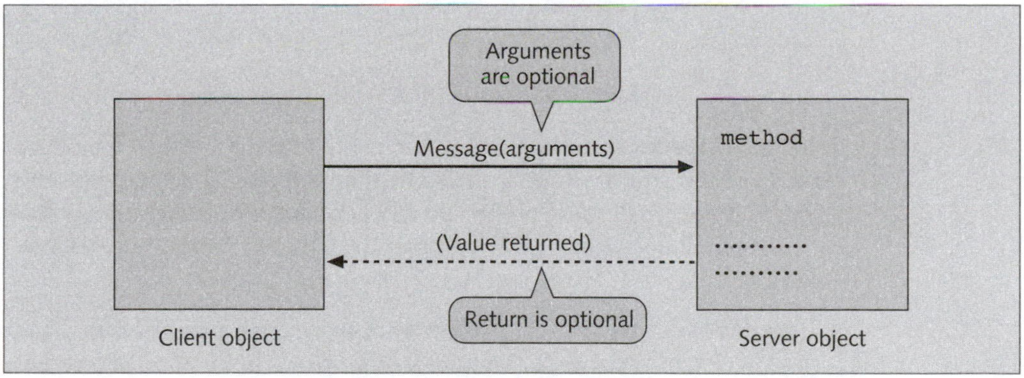

Figure 6-3 Client-server interaction

The client sends a message invoking a server method, perhaps sending along values in the form of arguments. The server method performs the requested task, and may return a value to the client. In Chapter 4, for example, you wrote statements invoking methods in several of the supplied classes such as Math and String. Applying this client-server model to those examples, your statements were client code invoking server methods in the supplied classes.

Methods are written using **procedures**. VB .NET has two types of procedures: **Sub procedures** and **Function procedures**. The difference between a Sub procedure and a Function procedure is that a Sub procedure does not return a value and a Function procedure does.

A Sub procedure definition begins with a **procedure header** followed by one or more statements. This structure is shown in Figure 6-4.

```
accessibility Sub procedurename(parameter list)

    method statements

End Sub
```

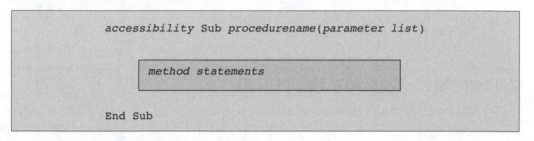

Figure 6-4 VB .NET Sub procedure structure

The method header shown in Figure 6-4 contains four parts:

1. *accessibility*–The accessibility (**Public, Private**, **Protected**, or **Friend**) for a method is the same as that described earlier for variables. Generally, you assign **Public** accessibility to methods because you want other objects to invoke them.

2. **Sub**–This keyword indicates that this is a Sub procedure.

3. *procedurename*–This indicates the name of the procedure. You learned previously that method names begin with an uppercase character, with subsequent words capitalized, and that they usually contain an imperative verb describing what the method does, followed by a noun. Examples of method names are ComputeServiceCharge and RecordPayment.

4. (*parameter list*)–**Arguments** are passed into **parameters**. The parameter list consists of variable declarations you write so the method can receive arguments being sent from client objects. If values are sent to the method, VB .NET insists that the data types of the argument variables be compatible with the parameter variables. For example, you cannot pass an argument with data type `Integer` into a parameter variable with data type `String`. If no argument is being passed to the method, then the parameter list is an empty set of parentheses.

Similar to a Sub procedure, a Function procedure definition begins with a procedure header followed by one or more statements. This structure is shown in Figure 6-5.

```
accessibility Function procedurename(parameter list) As datatype

    method statements

End Function
```

Figure 6-5 VB .NET Function procedure structure

The method header shown in Figure 6-5 contains five parts:

1. `accessibility`–The accessibility (**`Public`**, **`Private`**, **`Protected`**, or **`Friend`**) is described earlier in this section.
2. **`Function`**–This keyword indicates that this is a Function procedure.
3. `procedurename`–This indicates the name of the procedure.
4. `(parameter list)`–The parameter list consists of variable declarations you write so the method can receive arguments being sent from client objects.
5. **`As`** `datatype`–Function procedures return a single variable. You write its data type here (`Integer`, `Double`, `String`, etc.).

The class definition for Customer has three attributes, each with private accessibility, which prevents client objects from accessing them directly. Instead, you write accessor methods that clients can invoke to store and retrieve attribute values.

Accessor methods are often called **standard methods** and are typically not shown on class diagrams because developers assume they are included. In contrast, methods that you write to perform other functions are called **custom methods** and are shown on class diagrams. The next chapter shows you how to design and write custom methods.

There are two types of accessor methods: those that *get* attribute values and those that *set* attribute values. Accessors that retrieve values are called get accessor methods, or simply **getters**, and are named with the prefix "Get" followed by the attribute name; you will write three getter methods, named GetName, GetAddress, and GetPhoneNo, for the Customer class definition. Similarly, accessor methods that change attribute values are called set accessor methods, or **setters**, and are named with the prefix "Set" followed by the attribute name. You will also write a setter method for each attribute: SetName, SetAddress, and SetPhoneNo. You write Sub procedures for setters and Function procedures for getters because they return a value. The general format for getters and setters is:

```
// getter format
Public Function GetAttributeName() As attributeDataType
   Return attributeName
End Function
// setter format
Public Sub SetAttributeName(ByVal attributeDataType parameterName)
   attributeName = parameterName
End Sub
```

The getter method header specifies the data type of the attribute it will return and has an empty parameter list. The getter method has a single statement using the keyword **Return** to send the contents of the attribute variable to the invoking client object. Methods can return only a single variable value, although it can be a reference variable pointing to an instance that can contain numerous values. Figure 6-6 lists the three getter methods for the Customer class definition.

```
'get accessor methods
Public Function GetName() As String
   Return name
End Function

Public Function GetAddress() As String
   Return address
End Function

Public Function GetPhoneNo() As String
   Return phoneNo
End Function
```

Figure 6-6 Getter methods for Customer

Client objects send setter method arguments that are used to populate attributes. Therefore, you must declare a parameter variable to receive this argument. Setter methods sometimes have statements to verify that the values they receive are valid. Chapter 7 illustrates setter methods that validate data. The setters in this chapter will have a single statement that assigns the value received to the attribute variable. Figure 6-7 lists the three set accessor methods for Customer.

```
'set accessor methods
Public Sub SetName(ByVal aName As String)
   name = aName
End Sub

Public Sub SetAddress(ByVal anAddress As String)
   address = anAddress
End Sub

Public Sub SetPhoneNo(ByVal aPhoneNo As String)
   phoneNo = aPhoneNo
End Sub
```

Figure 6-7 Setter methods for Customer

You can also write a **property** to set and get attribute values. A property is similar to a method, but to a client it appears as an attribute. A property begins with a header indicating that you are writing a property definition and ends with **`End Property`**. Because the property contains code to both set and get an attribute value, as shown in Figure 6-8, the header also specifies the data type of the attribute being returned. The get section returns the name attribute, and the set section populates the name attribute with the value received.

```
' property named CustomerName
   Public Property CustomerName() As String
      Get
         Return name
      End Get
      Set(ByVal aName As String)
         name = aName
      End Set
   End Property
```

Figure 6-8 Property for CustomerName

You have now completed the class definition for Customer, which is listed in Figure 6-9. This code defines the three attributes and includes getter and setter methods for each of them. The code also defines a property.

```
' Chapter 6 Customer class Example 1
Public Class Customer

     'attributes
     Private name As String
     Private address As String
     Private phoneNo As String

     'get accessor methods
     Public Function GetName() As String
           Return name
     End Function
     Public Function GetAddress() As String
           Return address
     End Function
     Public Function GetPhoneNo() As String
           Return phoneNo
     End Function

     'set accessor methods
     Public Sub SetName(ByVal aName As String)
           name = aName
     End Sub
     Public Sub SetAddress(ByVal anAddress As String)
           address = anAddress
     End Sub
     Public Sub SetPhoneNo(ByVal aPhoneNo As String)
           phoneNo = aPhoneNo
     End Sub

     ' property named CustomerName
     Public Property CustomerName() As String
        Get
           Return name
        End Get
        Set(ByVal aName As String)
           name = aName
        End Set
     End Property

End Class
```

Figure 6-9 Customer class definition listing

TESTING A PD CLASS

To simulate the way a client might send messages, you can write a small tester class named TesterOne to invoke methods in the Customer class definition you just completed. TesterOne, listed in Figure 6-10, is similar to the classes you developed in Chapters 3 and 4.

```
Chapter 6 TesterOne class Example 1

Module TesterOne

  Sub Main()
    Dim firstCustomer As Customer = New Customer() ' create instance

    ' use property to populate name
    firstCustomer.CustomerName = "Eleanor"

    ' invoke set accessors to populate attributes
    firstCustomer.SetName("Eleanor")
    firstCustomer.SetAddress("Atlanta")
    firstCustomer.SetPhoneNo("123-4567")

    ' define variables to contain attribute values retrieved
    Dim customerName, customerAddress, customerPhoneNo As String

    ' use property to retrieve name
    customerName = firstCustomer.CustomerName

    ' invoke get accessors to retrieve attributes
    customerName = firstCustomer.GetName()
    customerAddress = firstCustomer.GetAddress()
    customerPhoneNo = firstCustomer.GetPhoneNo()

    ' display the retrieved attribute values
    Console.WriteLine("The name is " + customerName)
    Console.WriteLine("The address is " + customerAddress)
    Console.WriteLine("The phone is " + customerPhoneNo)

  End Sub

End Module
```

Figure 6-10 TesterOne.vb listing

In this example, TesterOne is a client and Customer is the server. TesterOne has a single method named Main, just like the classes you developed in Chapters 3 and 4. TesterOne is the startup object for the project and its Main method begins execution when it is loaded. The statements in Main then create a customer instance, use the CustomerName property and invoke setter methods to initialize the attributes values for the instance, and then retrieve and display the attribute values by using the CustomerName property and invoking getter methods. The following section takes you step by step through the Main method in TesterOne.

CREATING AN INSTANCE

You learned in Chapter 3 that VB .NET has two categories of variables: primitive and reference. Primitive variables use one of the primitive data types and actually contain data. Reference variables, on the other hand, use a class name as a data type and contain a memory address that points to or references an instance of a class. In Chapter 4 you learned that an instance resides in an area of memory and can contain data; you also created instances of the `String` and `DateTime` classes. In the TesterOne example, you create an instance of the Customer class you just completed and use a variable with data type Customer to reference this instance. You also invoke setter methods to assign the customer's name, address, and phone number.

In this example there are two steps in creating an instance of a class. First you declare a reference variable named `firstCustomer` using data type Customer, and then you use the **`New`** keyword to create the instance. These two steps are combined into a single statement in the following example:

```
Dim firstCustomer As Customer = New Customer() ' create instance
```

After the class is instantiated, the variable `firstCustomer` points to the newly created Customer instance shown in Figure 6-11.

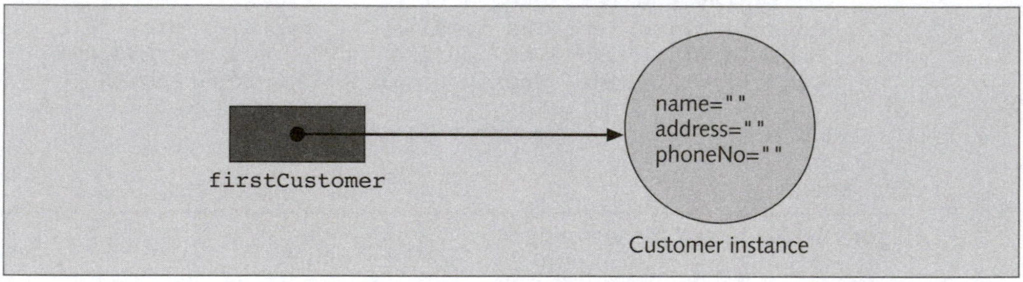

Figure 6-11 Customer instance

Notice that the attributes for the instance in Figure 6-11 have no values. You next write statements to populate the instance attributes, either by invoking setter methods or properties. In this example you can use the CustomerName property to populate the name attribute. Recall that a property can have both a getter and setter capability; in this example you invoke its setter capability by writing the following code:

```
' use property to populate name
firstCustomer.CustomerName = "Eleanor"
```

Earlier you saw that a property appears to a client as an attribute instead of a method. In the previous code it *appears* that you assigned the name value ("Eleanor") to a variable named

CustomerName in the firstCustomer instance. However, this statement actually invokes the setter code contained within the property definition.

You can also invoke the setter methods to populate the customer's attributes. You pass arguments to these methods, which then assign values to the attributes. Notice that you invoke these methods by specifying the reference variable `firstCustomer`, not the class name Customer. You do this because accessor methods are associated with individual instances (customers) instead of the Customer class. Each customer has an individual name, address, and telephone number.

```
' invoke set accessors to populate attributes
firstCustomer.SetName("Eleanor")
firstCustomer.SetAddress("Atlanta")
firstCustomer.SetPhoneNo("123-4567")
```


You studied sequence diagrams in the previous chapter and saw how they were used to show interactions between objects in a system. Figure 6-12 contains a sequence diagram showing the communication between TesterOne and Customer to create and populate a customer instance. Recall that a horizontal line represents a message from one object to another, which means that a client object (TesterOne) is invoking methods in a server object (Customer).

As you can see from Figure 6-12, a customer instance is created first, and then the three setter methods are invoked to populate the attributes. A little later you will learn how to write a special method, called a **constructor**, to populate instance attributes, which eliminates the statements you write to invoke the setters.

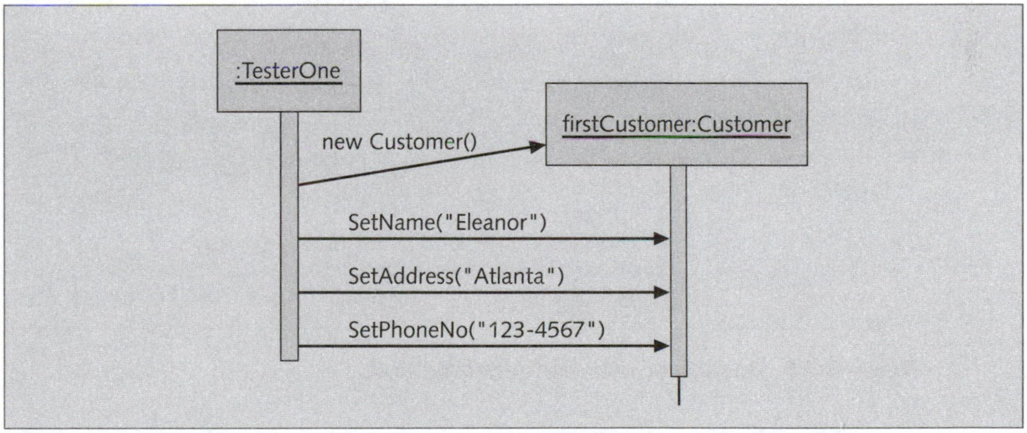

Figure 6-12 Sequence diagram to create and populate a customer instance

The customer instance now has values for its attributes and reflects the structure shown in Figure 6-13.

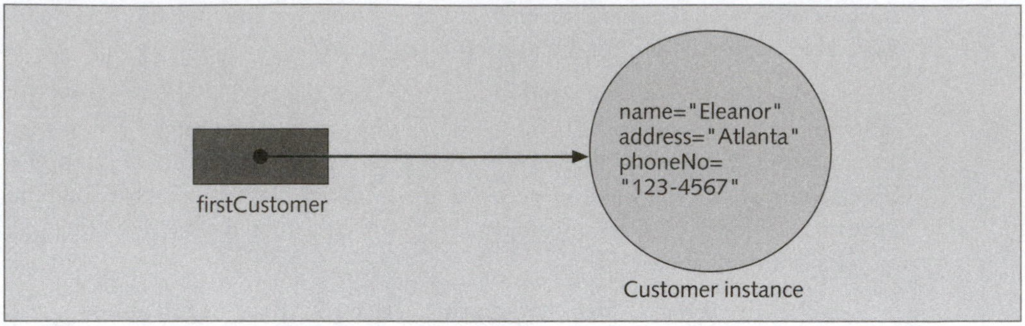

Figure 6-13 Customer instance with attribute values

To verify that the setter methods worked correctly, you next write code to retrieve the attribute values from the customer instance and display them. First, you define three string variables to receive the values to be retrieved.

```
' define variables to contain attribute values retrieved
Dim customerName, customerAddress, customerPhoneNo As String
```

Next, you write statements to invoke the getter methods to retrieve the values stored in the name, address, and phoneNo attributes for this customer instance and assign the values returned to the variables you previously defined. These statements are shown with explanations in Figure 6-14.

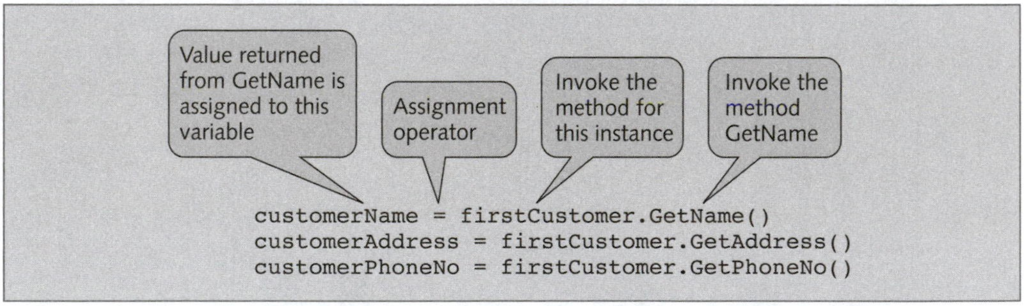

Figure 6-14 Invoking Customer getter methods

Note that you could have written a statement to invoke the getter part of the CustomerName property to retrieve the customer's name. This code would appear as:

```
' use property to retrieve name
customerName = firstCustomer.CustomerName
```

The final task for TesterOne is to display the attribute values you just retrieved. Here you invoke the `WriteLine` method, just as you did in Chapters 3 and 4, to display values. Recall that this method is being invoked for the Console class. You pass the arguments contained in parentheses to the `WriteLine` method in Console. The arguments consist of a literal concatenated with the attribute values previously retrieved.

```
' display the retrieved attribute values
Console.WriteLine("The name is " + customerName)
Console.WriteLine("The address is " + customerAddress)
Console.WriteLine("The phone is " + customerPhoneNo)
```

Figure 6-15 contains a sequence diagram showing all of the interactions between TesterOne and Customer and between TesterOne and Console to display the values retrieved. Notice that the diagram shows the values being returned from the getter methods as dashed horizontal lines. In this example, TesterOne remains the client and both Customer and Console play the role of servers.

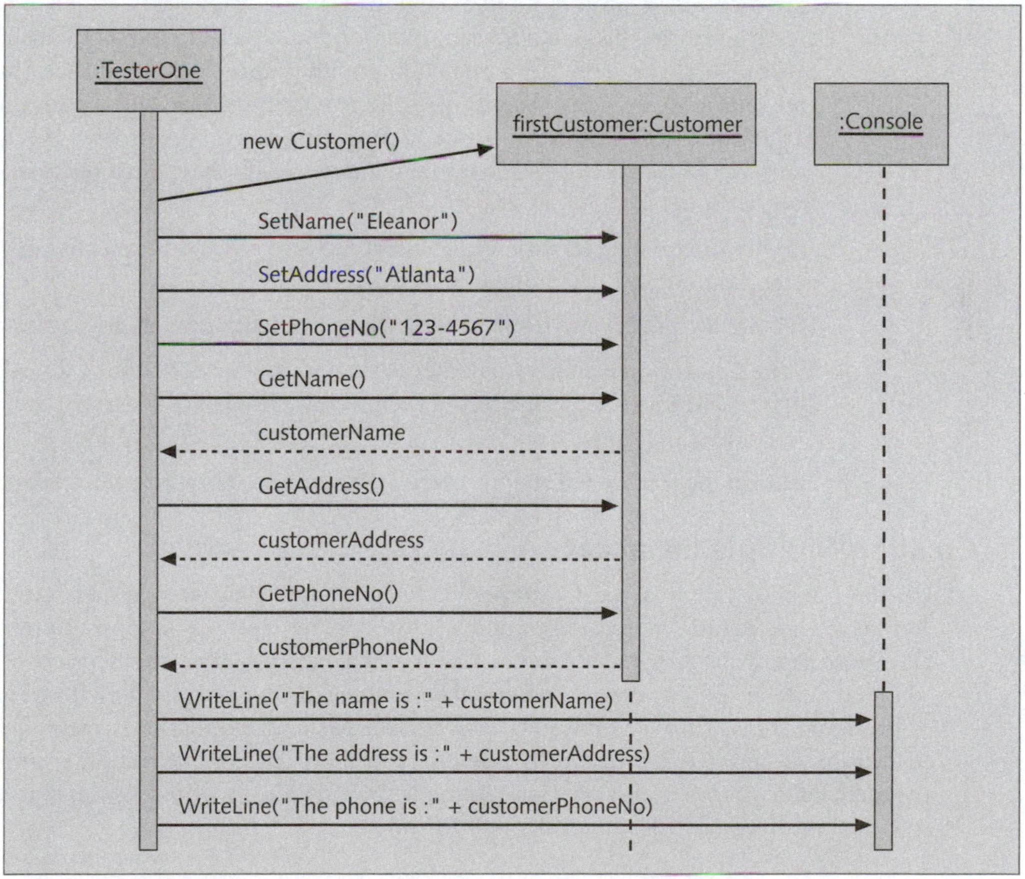

Figure 6-15 Sequence diagram for TesterOne

The output displayed by TesterOne is shown in Figure 6-16. A line is displayed each time the `WriteLine` method is invoked.

```
The name is Eleanor
The address is Atlanta
The phone is 123-4567
```

Figure 6-16 TesterOne output

Hands-on Exercise 1

1. Locate Example1 in the Chap06\Examples\Ex01 folder in the book's data files. Create a folder named **Chap06\Exercises\Ex01** in the work folder on your system, and then copy the **Example1** folder to this folder. Note that this folder contains a complete project. Unlike previous Hands-on Exercises, which asked you to create a project, this one has been done for you. Open the project with VB .NET by double-clicking the file name ending with .vbproj. You should see Customer.vb and TesterOne.vb in the Solution Explorer window. Click **Debug** on the menu bar, and then click **Start Without Debugging** to run the project. Recall that you can press **Enter** to close the console window. Verify that your output matches the output shown in Figure 6-16.
2. Modify the existing statements in TesterOne to create a customer using your own name, address, and telephone number.
3. Rebuild the project and run it to verify that your modifications are working correctly.
4. Write a new property for Customer named CustomerAddress for the address attribute. Modify TesterOne to use the property instead of the SetAddress and GetAddress methods.
5. Rebuild the project and run it to verify that your modifications are working correctly.

Creating Multiple Instances

In the previous example, the Customer class represented Bradshaw Marina customers. You wrote a class definition for Customer and used it to create a single customer instance, Eleanor. Bradshaw Marina obviously has many customers, and the Customer class you defined will be used to create and populate numerous instances, as shown in Figure 6-17. This figure shows that the Customer class represents all of the marina's customers. The class definition is derived from the class diagram, and then the class definition is instantiated as needed. Each customer instance thus represents an individual marina customer. In this example the customers are Eleanor, Mike, and JoAnn.

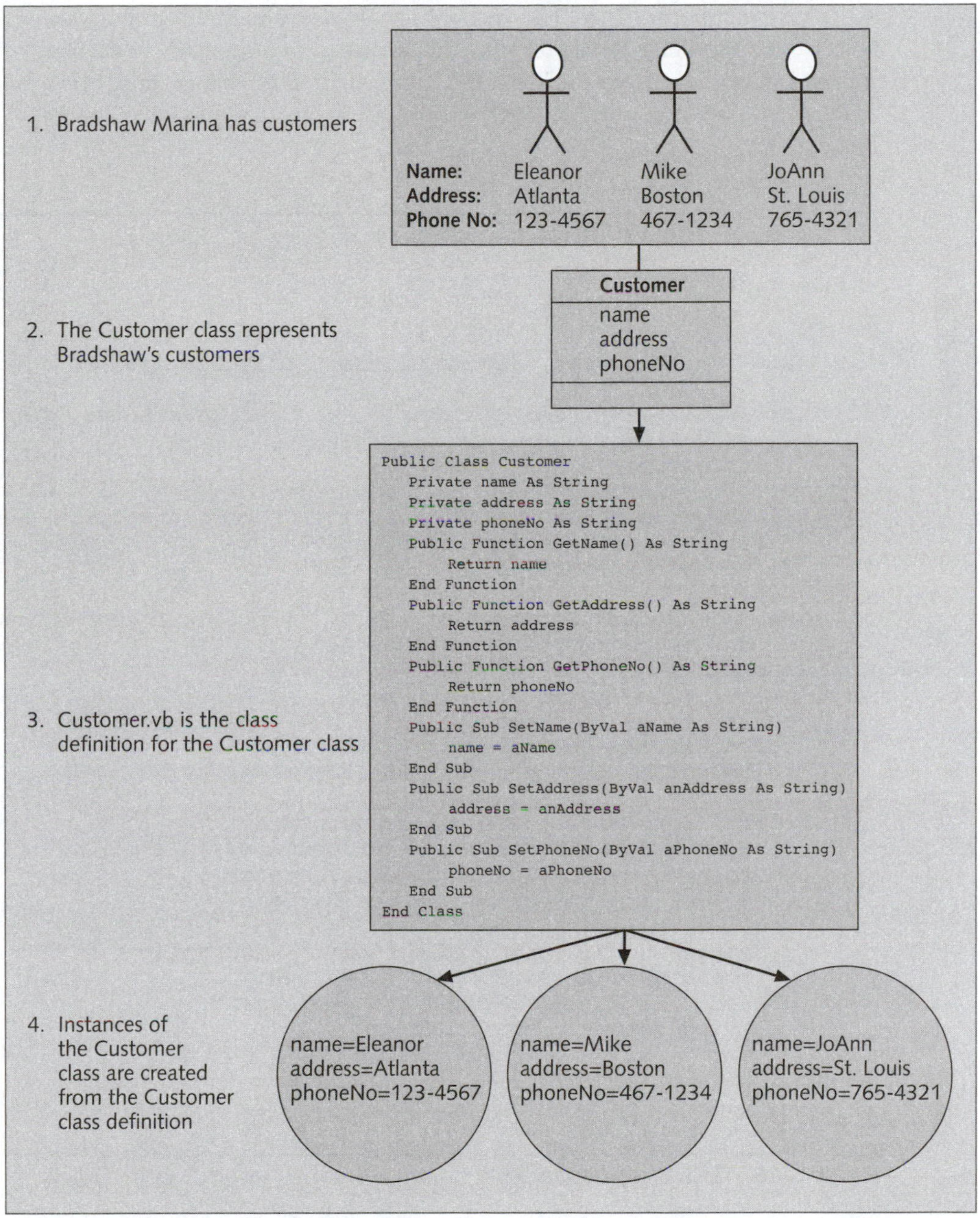

Figure 6-17 Instances of Bradshaw Marina's customers

Next, you will write a second tester class, named TesterTwo, that will create the three instances shown in Figure 6-17 using the Customer class definition you previously developed. You will then add statements to TesterTwo that will invoke setter methods to populate the attributes for all three customer instances, and then invoke getter methods to retrieve some of the attribute values. Finally, you will invoke a setter method to change an attribute value for one of the three instances, and then retrieve and display the changed value. TesterTwo is listed in Figure 6-18.

```
' Chapter 6 TesterTwo class Example 2

Module TesterTwo

   Sub Main()
      Dim firstCustomer, secondCustomer, thirdCustomer As Customer

      firstCustomer = New Customer()      ' create three customers
      secondCustomer = New Customer()
      thirdCustomer = New Customer()

      firstCustomer.SetName("Eleanor")    ' populate first instance
      firstCustomer.SetAddress("Atlanta")
      firstCustomer.SetPhoneNo("123-4567")

      secondCustomer.SetName("Mike")     ' populate second instance
      secondCustomer.SetAddress("Boston")
      secondCustomer.SetPhoneNo("467-1234")

      thirdCustomer.SetName("JoAnn")      ' populate third instance
      thirdCustomer.SetAddress("St. Louis")
      thirdCustomer.SetPhoneNo("765-4321")

      ' display names of all three customers
      Console.WriteLine(firstCustomer.GetName())
      Console.WriteLine(secondCustomer.GetName())
      Console.WriteLine(thirdCustomer.GetName())

      ' change phone no for 3rd customer & redisplay
         thirdCustomer.SetPhoneNo("818-1000")
      Console.WriteLine("changed 3rd phone is " +
         thirdCustomer.GetPhoneNo())

   End Sub

End Module
```

Figure 6-18 TesterTwo.vb listing

TesterOne used a single reference variable named **firstCustomer** with a data type of Customer to reference the single instance you created. In TesterTwo you create three instances; therefore, you need to define two additional reference variables. You can name these **secondCustomer** and **thirdCustomer**, as shown in the following code:

```
Dim firstCustomer, secondCustomer, thirdCustomer As Customer
```

You wrote one statement in TesterOne to create the customer instance:

```
firstCustomer = New Customer()
```

To create the two additional instances in this example, you can write similar statements:

```
secondCustomer = New Customer()
thirdCustomer = New Customer()
```


In the previous example you wrote three statements to invoke setters to populate the attributes for the first customer:

```
firstCustomer.SetName("Eleanor")      ' populate first instance
firstCustomer.SetAddress("Atlanta")
firstCustomer.SetPhoneNo("123-4567")
```

In TesterTwo, you can add similar statements to populate the additional two instances, as shown in the following code:

```
secondCustomer.SetName("Mike")       ' populate second instance
secondCustomer.SetAddress("Boston")
secondCustomer.SetPhoneNo("467-1234")

thirdCustomer.SetName("JoAnn")        ' populate third instance
thirdCustomer.SetAddress("St. Louis")
thirdCustomer.SetPhoneNo("765-4321")

' display names of all three customers
Console.WriteLine(firstCustomer.GetName())
Console.WriteLine(secondCustomer.GetName())
Console.WriteLine(thirdCustomer.GetName())
```

Note that TesterTwo creates three separate customer instances, each with its own identity, its own attribute values, and the ability to respond to messages. For example, when you ask **secondCustomer** to set its name to "Mike," its SetName method is invoked and the **name** attribute for the second customer instance is assigned the value "Mike."

Next, you can write statements to retrieve and display each customer's name. In this example, you combine code to invoke **GetName** with code that invokes **WriteLine**, passing along the value returned by **GetName**. Again, note that the following code uses the reference variable **firstCustomer** to invoke **GetName** for the first instance, and uses **secondCustomer** and **thirdCustomer** to invoke **GetName** for the second and third instances, respectively.

```
' display names of all three customers
Console.WriteLine(firstCustomer.GetName())
Console.WriteLine(secondCustomer.GetName())
Console.WriteLine(thirdCustomer.GetName())
```

You have learned how to invoke setter methods to populate an instance. You can also use setter methods to change attribute values. You can write the following code to change the third customer's phone number to 818-1000, and then retrieve and display the number again to verify that it was changed:

```
' change phone no for 3rd customer & redisplay
thirdCustomer.SetPhoneNo("818-1000")
Console.WriteLine("changed 3rd phone is " + thirdCustomer.GetPhoneNo())
```

The output from TesterTwo is shown in Figure 6-19. The first three lines display the three customer names; the last line displays the updated phone number.

```
Eleanor
Mike
JoAnn
changed 3rd phone is 818-1000
```

Figure 6-19 TesterTwo output

Hands-on Exercise 2

1. Locate Example2 in the Chap06\Examples\Ex02 folder in the book's data files. Create a folder named **Chap06\Exercises\Ex02** in the work folder on your system, and then copy the **Example2** folder to this folder. Open the project with VB .NET by double-clicking the filename ending with .vbproj. You should see Customer.vb and TesterTwo.vb in the Solution Explorer window. Click **Debug** on the menu bar, and then click **Start Without Debugging** to run the project. Verify that your output matches the output shown in Figure 6-19.
2. Add statements to TesterTwo that:
   - Create a customer instance using your own name, address, and phone number.
   - Retrieve and display the name, address, and phone number attributes.
   - Change your phone number to 123-4567, and then retrieve and display it.
3. Rebuild the project and run it to verify that your modifications are working correctly.

WRITING A CONSTRUCTOR METHOD

In the previous sections, you saw how to create customer instances and invoke the setter methods to populate the attributes. Although this approach works, you can simplify it by adding a constructor method to your Customer class definition. A constructor is a special method that is automatically invoked whenever you create an instance of a class using the keyword **New**. The constructor is unique in that it is named **New** and is written as a Sub procedure because it cannot return a value. Actually, even if you do not write a constructor, VB .NET creates a **default constructor** that doesn't do anything. The default constructor consists of only a header and an End Sub statement. The default constructor for Customer would look like the following code:

```
Public Sub New()
End Sub
```


You can write your own constructor, called a **parameterized constructor** because it can contain a parameter list to receive arguments that are used to populate the instance attributes. You want the constructor method for Customer to receive arguments for the three attributes: name, address, and phone number. The constructor will then invoke the setter methods to populate the attributes. This saves you code by eliminating the need for you to invoke each setter method to populate the three attributes. The parameterized constructor for Customer is:

```
'constructor (3 parameters)
Public Sub New(ByVal aName As String, ByVal anAddress As String, ByVal
   aPhoneNo As String)
   SetName(aName)
   SetAddress(anAddress)
   SetPhoneNo(aPhoneNo)
End Sub
```

You give this constructor method `Public` access and name it **New**. The parameter list consists of variable declarations named `aName`, `anAddress`, and `aPhoneNo`—each with data type `String`—that will receive attribute values for the three Customer attributes. The body of the constructor method invokes the three set accessor methods, passing the parameter variables containing the attribute values that were received.

An alternative design is to have the constructor assign the values directly to the attribute variables instead of invoking the setter methods, as in the following example:

```
Public Sub New(ByVal aName As String, ByVal anAddress As String, ByVal
   aPhoneNo As String)
   name = aName
   address = anAddress
   phoneNo = aPhoneNo
End Sub
```

In the next chapter you will learn how to add data validation code to the setter methods to ensure that only valid data is stored. When the setters have data validation statements, the constructor must invoke the setters to populate attributes so that the data validation will be performed.

Next, you write TesterThree to test the constructor method you added to your Customer class definition. Having the parameterized constructor simplifies the code you write for TesterThree because you do not have to write statements to invoke the three setter methods. You can begin as you did in TesterTwo by declaring reference variables for the three customer instances you will create:

```
Dim firstCustomer, secondCustomer, thirdCustomer As Customer
```

Next, you can write the statements to create the three instances; however, this time you pass the attribute values as arguments to the constructor method that is invoked as part of the instance creation process. You do not have to invoke the individual setter methods from TesterThree because the constructor in Customer now does this for you.

```
' create three customers
firstCustomer = New Customer("Eleanor", "Atlanta", "123-4567")
secondCustomer = New Customer("Mike", "Boston", "467-1234")
thirdCustomer = New Customer("JoAnn", " St. Louis ", "765-4321")
```

Finally, as before, you invoke the get accessor methods to retrieve the attribute values, and then display them. In this example, you retrieve and display the values without using variables to store the retrieved values. You invoke the getters within the `WriteLine` argument list, and then pass the values returned by the get accessor methods directly to the `WriteLine` method.

```
' display names of all three customers
Console.WriteLine(firstCustomer.GetName())
Console.WriteLine(secondCustomer.GetName())
Console.WriteLine(thirdCustomer.GetName())
```

The complete listing of TesterThree is shown in Figure 6-20, and the output is shown in Figure 6-21.

```
' Chapter 6 TesterThree class Example 3

Module TesterThree

   Sub Main()
      Dim firstCustomer, secondCustomer, thirdCustomer As Customer

      ' create three customers
      firstCustomer = New Customer("Eleanor", "Atlanta", "123-4567")
      secondCustomer = New Customer("Mike", "Boston", "467-1234")
      thirdCustomer = New Customer("JoAnn", "St. Louis", "765-4321")

      ' display names of all three customers
      Console.WriteLine(firstCustomer.GetName())
      Console.WriteLine(secondCustomer.GetName())
      Console.WriteLine(thirdCustomer.GetName())

   End Sub

End Module
```

Figure 6-20 TesterThree.vb listing


```
Eleanor
Mike
JoAnn
```

Figure 6-21 TesterThree output

Hands-on Exercise 3

1. Locate Example3 in the Chap06\Examples\Ex03 folder in the book's data files. Create a folder named **Chap06\Exercises\Ex03** in the work folder on your system, and then copy the **Example3** folder to this folder. Open the project with VB .NET by double-clicking the file name ending with .vbproj. You should see Customer.vb and TesterThree.vb in the Solution Explorer window. Click **Debug** on the menu bar, and then click **Start Without Debugging** to run the project. Verify that your output matches the output shown in Figure 6-21.

2. Add statements to TesterThree that:
   - Create a customer instance using your own name, address, and phone number. Remember that Customer now has a parameterized constructor, which means that you pass your name, address, and phone number as arguments to the constructor instead of invoking setter methods.
   - Retrieve and display the name, address, and phone number attributes.
   - Change your phone number to 123-4567, and then retrieve and display it.

3. Rebuild the project and run it to verify that your modifications are working correctly.

To summarize, you use a class definition to create instances. You write a class definition by first declaring private variables to represent the attributes. Then you write getter and setter methods for each attribute. You invoke getters to retrieve attribute values, and you invoke setters to store attribute values.

Constructor methods are automatically invoked when you instantiate a class. They are always named New and are written as Sub procedures because they do not return a value. You write a parameterized constructor to receive arguments used to populate attributes.

WRITING A TELLABOUTSELF METHOD

In previous examples the tester classes invoked the individual customer getter methods to retrieve attribute values. Although this approach works, it can require you to write lengthy client code, especially when the problem domain class has many attributes. More importantly, if attributes in the PD class are added, removed, or have their data type changed, client statements that invoke the getter methods may also require changes. In a functioning system, numerous clients request attribute values, and making changes to the PD attributes could force you to make changes in several other classes. Good design suggests that you insulate changes in one class from outside classes to reduce maintenance requirements.

An alternative to invoking individual getter methods is to write a single PD method that you invoke to retrieve all of the attribute values for an instance. An appropriate name for this method is TellAboutSelf; it will retrieve all of the attribute values, place them in a String instance, and then return the String instance to the invoking client. You want TellAboutSelf to have public accessibility, and because this method will return a value, you write it as a Function procedure.

```
'TellAboutSelf method
 Public Function TellAboutSelf() As String
   Dim info As String
   info = "Name = " & GetName() & _
          ", Address = " & GetAddress() & _
          ", Phone No = " & GetPhoneNo()
   Return info
End Function
```

This method for the Customer class has only three statements. The first statement declares a string variable named `info` to contain the attribute values. The second statement invokes the three getter statements, concatenating the values returned with descriptive literals and assigning the result to the string instance referenced by `info`. This statement uses the line continuation symbol (_) to continue the statement over three lines and make it more readable. The last statement returns the `info` variable to the invoking client method using the keyword **`Return`**.

Notice that to invoke the getter methods in this example you do not use an instance reference variable such as `aCustomer.GetName()`. This is because the TellAboutSelf method will be invoked for a specific customer instance by a client. Therefore, the code you write within the TellAboutSelf method is already being executed for a customer instance.

Next, you can write TesterFour, listed in Figure 6-22, to create three Customer instances as before. Unlike the previous examples, you will invoke TellAboutSelf for each customer instance to obtain attribute values instead of invoking the individual getter methods. Similar to TesterThree, you invoke TellAboutSelf within the argument for `WriteLine`. The output from TesterFour is shown in Figure 6-23.


```
' Chapter 6 TesterFour class Example 4

Module TesterFour

   Sub Main()
      Dim firstCustomer, secondCustomer, thirdCustomer As Customer

      ' create three customers
      firstCustomer = New Customer("Eleanor", "Atlanta", "123-4567")
      secondCustomer = New Customer("Mike", "Boston", "467-1234")
      thirdCustomer = New Customer("JoAnn", "St. Louis", "765-4321")

      ' display all info for all three customers
      Console.WriteLine(firstCustomer.TellAboutSelf())
      Console.WriteLine(secondCustomer.TellAboutSelf())
      Console.WriteLine(thirdCustomer.TellAboutSelf())

   End Sub

End Module
```

Figure 6-22 TesterFour.vb listing

```
Name = Eleanor, Address = Atlanta, Phone No = 123-4567
Name = Mike, Address = Boston, Phone No = 467-1234
Name = JoAnn, Address = St. Louis, Phone No = 765-4321
```

Figure 6-23 TesterFour output

Hands-on Exercise 4

1. Locate Example4 in the Chap06\Examples\Ex04 folder in the book's data files. Create a folder named **Chap06\Exercises\Ex04** in the work folder on your system, and then copy the **Example4** folder to this folder. Open the project with VB .NET by double-clicking the filename ending with .vbproj. You should see

Customer.vb and TesterFour.vb in the Solution Explorer window. Click **Debug** on the menu bar, and then click **Start Without Debugging** to run the project. Verify that your output matches the output shown in Figure 6-23.

2. Add statements to TesterFour that:
   - Create a customer instance using your own name, address, and phone number.
   - Retrieve and display the name, address, and phone number attributes using the TellAboutSelf method instead of the getter methods.
3. Rebuild the project and run it to verify that your modifications are working correctly.
4. Modify TellAboutSelf in Customer to use a single statement by eliminating the string variable named `info` and the statement that populates it. (*Hint*: Instead of invoking getters to populate `info`, simply invoke the getters within the return statement.)
5. Rebuild the project and run it to verify that your modifications are working correctly.

WRITING A TESTER CLASS AS A FORM

In previous examples the tester classes were written as modules and you created a console application to run them. Recall from Chapter 2 that when you create a project you can make it either a console application or a Windows application. You use a Windows application when you want to use a graphical user interface (GUI) form. You saw in Chapter 2 that a form is a visible GUI object that can have push buttons and other GUI objects.

In this section you will develop a Windows application with a form named TesterFive that will accomplish the same thing as the TesterFour module in the previous example. Before you continue, however, you may want to review the "Creating a Windows Application" section in Chapter 2. (Note that you will learn how to create GUI classes in Chapters 10 and 11.) The purpose of this section is to introduce another approach to writing tester classes: making them GUIs. Here you will not be asked to create a GUI, only to write statements within predefined event procedures. This example uses the Customer class from the previous example *without changes*.

The form you will use in this example is shown in Figure 6-24. This form has three buttons, with their text properties set to "Create," "Display," and "Close." These buttons are named btnCreate, btnDisplay, and btnClose, respectively. The "btn" prefix is a VB .NET naming convention that helps you identify the objects as buttons. When you click a button, you create what is called an **event** and you write a Sub procedure called an **event procedure**, or **event handler**, to be executed when the event occurs. In this example the Create button click event procedure will create three customer instances, and the Display button click event procedure will display information from the three customer instances. When you click the Close button, you will dispose of the form.

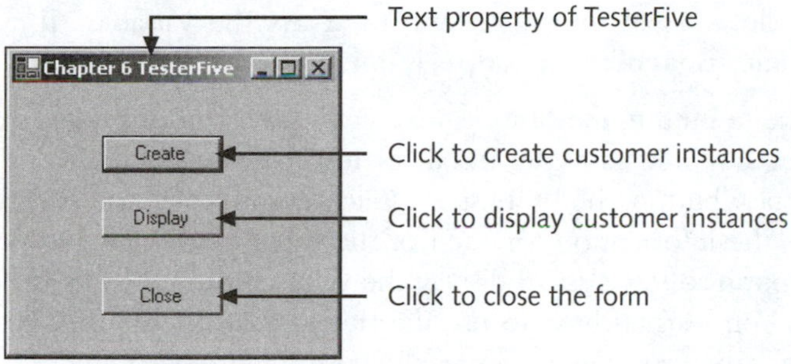

Figure 6-24 TesterFive Form

The code for the TesterFive class is shown in Figure 6-25.

```
Public Class TesterFive
   Dim firstCustomer, secondCustomer, thirdCustomer As Customer

   Private Sub btnCreate_Click(ByVal sender As System.Object, ByVal e
     As System.EventArgs) Handles btnCreate.Click
      ' create three customers
      firstCustomer = New Customer("Eleanor", "Atlanta", "123-4567")
      secondCustomer = New Customer("Mike", "Boston", "467-1234")
      thirdCustomer = New Customer("JoAnn", "St. Louis", "765-4321")
End Sub

   Private Sub btnDisplay_Click(ByVal sender As System.Object, ByVal e
     As System.EventArgs) Handles btnDisplay.Click
      ' display all info for all three customers
      MessageBox.Show(firstCustomer.TellAboutSelf())
      MessageBox.Show(secondCustomer.TellAboutSelf())
      MessageBox.Show(thirdCustomer.TellAboutSelf())
   End Sub

   Private Sub btnClose_Click(ByVal sender As System.Object, ByVal e As
     System.EventArgs) Handles btnClose.Click
      Me.Dispose()
   End Sub
End Class
```

Figure 6-25 TesterFive.vb listing

As you will learn in Chapter 10, when you create a Windows project with a form, VB .NET generates some code for you. Figure 6-25 does not show all of this generated code. The code shown here is for the three event procedures. Note that the three Customer reference variables (`firstCustomer`, `secondCustomer`, and `thirdCustomer`) are defined outside these procedures. This allows all of the procedures to access the variables. If a variable is defined within a procedure, its visibility, or **scope**, is limited to that procedure.

When you click the Create button, the btnCreate_Click event procedure is executed. This procedure simply creates the three customer instances, just like you did in TesterFour. Then, when you click the Display button, the btnDisplay_Click event procedure is executed. This procedure then displays the information for each of the three customers. However, in this example, you use the `MessageBox` class to display the values returned by TellAboutSelf for each customer instance. You learned how to use the `MessageBox` class in Chapter 4. The output from TesterFive for the first message box is shown in Figure 6-26.

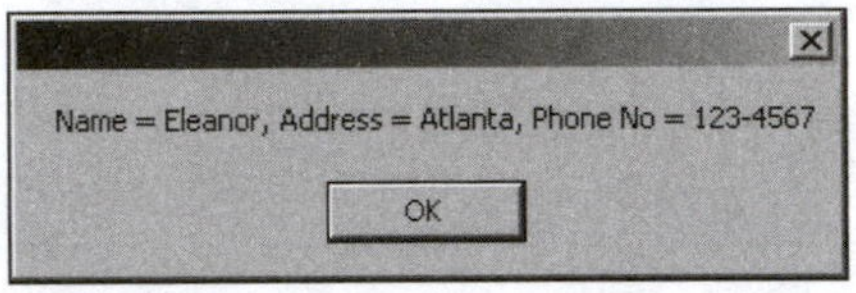

Figure 6-26 TesterFive output

Hands-on Exercise 5

1. Locate Example5 in the Chap06\Examples\Ex05 folder in the book's data files. Create a folder named **Chap06\Exercises\Ex05** in the work folder on your system, and then copy the **Example5** folder to this folder. Open the project with VB .NET by double-clicking the file name ending with .vbproj. You should see Customer.vb and TesterFive.vb in the Solution Explorer window. Click **Debug** on the menu bar, and then click **Start Without Debugging** to run the project. Verify that your output matches the output shown in Figure 6-26.
2. Add statements to TesterFive that:
   - Create a customer instance using your own name, address, and phone number.
   - Retrieve and display the name, address, and phone number attributes using a message box.
3. Rebuild the project and run it to verify that your modifications are working correctly.

Chapter Summary

- VB .NET programmers have adopted naming conventions for classes, methods, and variables. Class names and method names are capitalized, while variable names begin with a lowercase letter. When a name consists of more than one word, subsequent words are capitalized. Method names generally contain a verb describing what the method does.
- Problem domain classes represent real-world objects you want to represent in a system. Problem domain class definitions are written for each PD class.
- The VB .NET code you write to represent a class is called a class definition. A class definition consists of a class header, followed by variable definitions for attributes, followed by methods. The attribute definitions are variables that are created and populated for each instance created for the class.
- Accessor methods are written to provide access to the attribute values. Set accessors, also called setters, store values, while get accessors, also known as getters, retrieve them. Accessor methods are often called standard methods and are not generally shown on class diagrams.
- You can also use a property to provide access to attributes. A property contains both getter and setter code, but to a client it appears as an attribute.
- Applying the client-server model, methods function as servers by providing services to client objects. Client objects invoke server methods to perform tasks. Clients can send data to a method in the form of arguments. The invoked method receives arguments into parameter variables, which are declared in the method header. Methods can return a single variable to the client object.
- A special method, called a constructor, is automatically invoked whenever you instantiate a class. The constructor is written as a Sub procedure with the name New. You can write a parameterized constructor to receive values to populate the instance attributes.
- You can write a custom method named TellAboutSelf to retrieve all instance attribute values and return them in a string.

Key Terms

accessibility
accessor method
argument
assembly
class definition
class header
client object
constructor
custom method
default constructor
event
event handler
event procedure
Function procedure
getter
parameterized constructor
parameter
procedure header
procedure
property
scope
server object
setter
standard method
Sub procedure

Review Questions

1. What is a class definition?
2. What is an attribute?
3. What are the conventions for naming an attribute?
4. What is a primitive variable?
5. What is a reference variable?
6. What does a getter do?
7. What does a setter do?
8. Explain attribute accessibility.
9. Explain method accessibility.
10. Distinguish between an argument and a parameter.
11. What is a standard method?
12. Why do getters generally have an empty parameter list?
13. Why do you write setters as Sub procedures but getters as Function procedures?
14. What causes a constructor method to be invoked?
15. How are constructor methods named?
16. What is the default constructor?
17. What is a parameterized constructor?

Discussion Questions

1. Why would you not need accessor methods if the attributes were given public access?
2. How is a property different from an attribute? How is it different from a getter or setter method?
3. Explain how a method can return multiple values, even though only a single variable may be returned.
4. What is the benefit of having the constructor invoke setters to populate attributes instead of assigning the attribute values directly?
5. List the ways that using a TellAboutSelf method may reduce maintenance.
6. Assume that you have two customer instances. The first is referenced by a variable named `cashCustomer` and the second by a variable named `anotherCustomer`. What will be the result of executing the following statement?

```
Customer anotherCustomer = cashCustomer;
```


Projects

1. Assume that you are developing a system with a problem domain class named Employee that represents all of a firm's employees. Attributes you want to include are employeeName (data type `String`), dateEmployed (data type `DateTime`), and annualSalary (data type `Double`). You may want to review the `DateTime` class discussed in Chapter 4.
   a. Create a folder named **Chap06\Projects\Proj01** in your work folder, and then create a VB .NET project as a console application in this folder named Project1.
   b. Write a class definition for Employee. Include standard methods, a parameterized constructor, and a TellAboutSelf method.
   c. Write statements in TellAboutSelf to format dateEmployed in the "monthname day, year" format and annualSalary in currency format.
   d. Write a tester class named Project1Tester that creates three employees and then invokes TellAboutSelf for all three instances displaying the result.
   e. Build and test your classes to verify that they are working correctly.

2. Create a folder named **Chap06\Projects\Proj02** in your work folder and then create a VB .NET project as a console application in this folder named Project2.
    a. Using TesterFour from this chapter as a guide, design and write a tester class named Project2Tester that creates three customer instances; however, the references are to be placed in a three-element array.
    b. Assign the name "customers" to your array reference variable.
    c. Use data type Customer for the array elements.
    d. Use Customer.vb from Example4, which has the TellAboutSelf method.
    e. Write a loop in Project2Tester that iterates the array to display information for all three customer instances using TellAboutSelf.

CHAPTER

7

Adding Responsibilities to Problem Domain Classes

In this chapter you will:

- Write a new problem domain class definition
- Create custom methods
- Write class variables and methods
- Write overloaded methods
- Work with exceptions

In the previous chapter you learned how to write a definition for the Customer problem domain class. You defined Customer attributes and wrote standard methods to store and retrieve the attribute values. In this chapter you continue working with problem domain classes by writing a class definition for another Bradshaw Marina class called Slip. Instead of using standard methods exclusively, you will develop a custom method named LeaseSlip, which will calculate the lease fee for a slip.

In previous chapters you defined attributes and developed methods that were associated with individual instances. In this chapter you will declare variables and write methods for the Slip class that are *shared* among all instances.

The technique of overloading methods is explained and illustrated using the Slip constructor and the custom method LeaseSlip. Finally, you will add data validation logic for two of Slip's setter methods to verify that the arguments passed to the method are valid. You will learn how to define constants and how to create and throw an exception to signal to the client that invalid data has been detected and rejected.

WRITING A NEW PROBLEM DOMAIN CLASS DEFINITION

The system you are developing for Bradshaw Marina was introduced in Chapter 5, along with various problem domain classes, including Customer and Slip. In Chapter 6 you developed the class definition for Customer. In this chapter you will write a definition for the Slip class to extend your understanding of problem domain classes. Recall that the Slip class has three attributes—`slipId`, `slipWidth`, and `slipLength`—plus the custom method `LeaseSlip`, as shown in the class diagram in Figure 7-1.

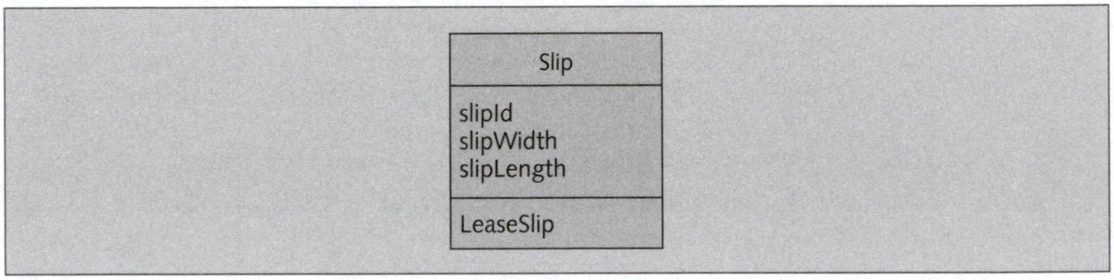

Figure 7-1 Class diagram for the Slip class

The class definition for Slip follows the same basic structure you used for writing the Customer class definition in Chapter 6. You begin with the class header, which specifies the name of the class.

```
Public Class Slip
```

Next you write the attribute definition statements. Here you assign all three attributes the data type **`Integer`**. Note that you want these definitions to have **`Private`** accessibility to encapsulate the attribute values. This keeps other objects from retrieving or changing the attribute values, except through accessor methods.

```
Private slipId As Integer
Private slipWidth As Integer
Private slipLength As Integer
```

Next you write a parameterized constructor because you want to automatically populate the three attributes whenever an instance of the Slip class is created. Remember that when you use the keyword **`New`** to instantiate a class, the class constructor is automatically invoked. When you instantiate the Slip class, you will pass the constructor arguments for the attributes `slipId`, `slipWidth`, and `slipLength`. Therefore, in the constructor header you declare three parameter variables to receive these arguments:

```
Public Sub New(ByVal aSlipId As Integer, ByVal aSlipWidth As Integer, _
    ByVal aSlipLength As Integer)
```

Note that the data types for these parameter variables match the data types for the attributes. In general, argument data types must be **assignment compatible** with parameter data types. This means that the argument variable must be able to be assigned to the parameter variable. For example, you cannot assign an argument with a `Double` data type to a parameter with an `Integer` data type, but you could assign an `Integer` data type to a `Double` data type.

Next you write statements to populate the Slip attributes. Like the parameterized constructor you wrote for the Customer class in Chapter 6, these statements invoke the setter methods to populate the attributes. To avoid redundant code, you have the constructor invoke setter methods to populate the attributes instead of directly assigning the values. Later in this chapter you will add data validation statements to two of your setter methods. If the constructor does not invoke these setters, it must also contain the data validation statements, which results in duplicate code and makes maintenance more difficult. A better design is to always have the constructor invoke setters. This means the setter is the only method that directly assigns values to attribute variables.


```
'invoke setter methods to populate attributes
SetSlipId(aSlipId)
SetSlipWidth(aSlipWidth)
SetSlipLength(aSlipLength)
```

Next you write a TellAboutSelf method. Recall that in Chapter 6 you wrote a TellAboutSelf method for Customer. That method invoked the getter methods `GetName`, `GetAddress`, and `GetPhoneNo`, concatenated the values returned with descriptive literals, and then returned a string containing the concatenated result.

Similarly, TellAboutSelf for the Slip class will invoke its three getters, concatenate the returned values with descriptive literals, and then return the result.

```
Public Function TellAboutSelf() As String
   Dim info As String
   info = "Slip: Id = " & GetSlipId() & ", Width = " & GetSlipWidth() _
       & ", Length = " & GetSlipLength()
   Return info
End Function
```

These TellAboutSelf methods are excellent examples of polymorphism. You have two methods with the same name, residing in different classes, that behave differently. When you invoke TellAboutSelf for Customer, you get the customer's name, address, and telephone number. However, when you invoke TellAboutSelf for Slip, you obtain the slip's ID, width, and length. These are called **polymorphic methods**.

The final step in writing the Slip class definition is to write the standard setter and getter methods.

```
'get accessor methods
Public Function GetSlipId() As Integer
   Return slipId
End Function

Public Function GetSlipWidth() As Integer
   Return slipWidth
End Function

Public Function GetSlipLength() As Integer
   Return slipLength
End Function

'set accessor methods
Public Sub SetSlipId(ByVal aSlipId As Integer)
   slipId = aSlipId
End Sub

Public Sub SetSlipWidth(ByVal aSlipWidth As Integer)
   slipWidth = aSlipWidth
End Sub

Public Sub SetSlipLength(ByVal aSlipLength As Integer)
   slipLength = aSlipLength
End Sub
```

The complete Slip class definition is listed in Figure 7-2.

```
' Chapter 7 Slip class Example 1

Public Class Slip

   'attributes
   Private slipId As Integer
   Private slipWidth As Integer
   Private slipLength As Integer

   'constructor (three parameters)
   Public Sub New(ByVal aSlipId As Integer, ByVal aSlipWidth As
Integer, ByVal aSlipLength As Integer)
      'invoke setter methods to populate attributes
      SetSlipId(aSlipId)
      SetSlipWidth(aSlipWidth)
      SetSlipLength(aSlipLength)
   End Sub
```

```
      'custom method TellAboutSelf
   Public Function TellAboutSelf() As String
      Dim info As String
      info = "Slip: Id = " & GetSlipId() & ", Width = " & _
         GetSlipWidth() & ", Length = " & GetSlipLength()
      Return info
   End Function

   'get accessor methods
   Public Function GetSlipId() As Integer
      Return slipId
   End Function
   Public Function GetSlipWidth() As Integer
      Return slipWidth
   End Function
   Public Function GetSlipLength() As Integer
      Return slipLength
   End Function

   'set accessor methods
   Public Sub SetSlipId(ByVal aSlipId As Integer)
      slipId = aSlipId
   End Sub
   Public Sub SetSlipWidth(ByVal aSlipWidth As Integer)
      slipWidth = aSlipWidth
   End Sub
   Public Sub SetSlipLength(ByVal aSlipLength As Integer)
      slipLength = aSlipLength
   End Sub

End Class
```

Figure 7-2 Slip class definition

7

In Chapter 6 you wrote several tester classes that invoked methods in your Customer class definition to ensure that the code was correct. Here you also write a tester class named TesterOne, but this time you will invoke methods in the Slip class definition. In addition, similar to the final example in Chapter 6, you will use a form instead of a module to contain your statements. You may want to review the section in Chapter 2 that describes how to create a form and use buttons.

The form for TesterOne is shown in Figure 7-3. The form contains three buttons, which are labeled "Test Slip," "Test Slip with Array," and "Close." These buttons are named `btnTestSlip`, `btnTestSlipArray`, and `btnClose`. Chapter 2 explained that when you click a button, you trigger an event. You write an event procedure for each button on your form, and these procedures are invoked when the corresponding button is clicked.

In the following example, you will write three event procedures for the three buttons. You name event procedures by combining the button name, an underscore character (_), and the word "Click."

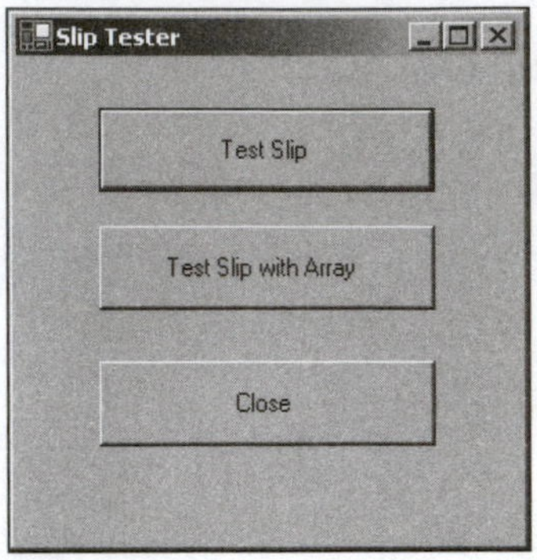

Figure 7-3 TesterOne form

The event procedure for the Test Slip button is shown in Figure 7-4. You write statements to create three Slip instances and then invoke TellAboutSelf for each instance to retrieve and display the attribute values. The output from this event procedure is shown in Figure 7-5.

```
Private Sub btnTestSlip_Click(ByVal sender As System.Object, ByVal e As
System.EventArgs) Handles btnTestSlip.Click
      'create three instances of Slip
      Dim slip1 As Slip = New Slip(1, 10, 20)
      Dim slip2 As Slip = New Slip(2, 12, 25)
      Dim slip3 As Slip = New Slip(3, 14, 30)

      Console.WriteLine("Begin Slip Test")
      Console.WriteLine(slip1.TellAboutSelf())
      Console.WriteLine(slip2.TellAboutSelf())
      Console.WriteLine(slip3.TellAboutSelf())
   End Sub
```

Figure 7-4 Event procedure for Test Slip button

```
Begin Slip Test
Slip: Id = 1, Width = 10, Length = 20
Slip: Id = 2, Width = 12, Length = 25
Slip: Id = 3, Width = 14, Length = 30
```

Figure 7-5 Output from `btnTestSlip_Click`

Chapter 5 introduced the UML sequence diagram and illustrated how it depicts the interaction between objects in a system. The statements in the `btnTestSlip_Click` event procedure cause TesterOne to interact with the three slip instances and the Console object. Figure 7-6 shows a sequence diagram for this interaction.

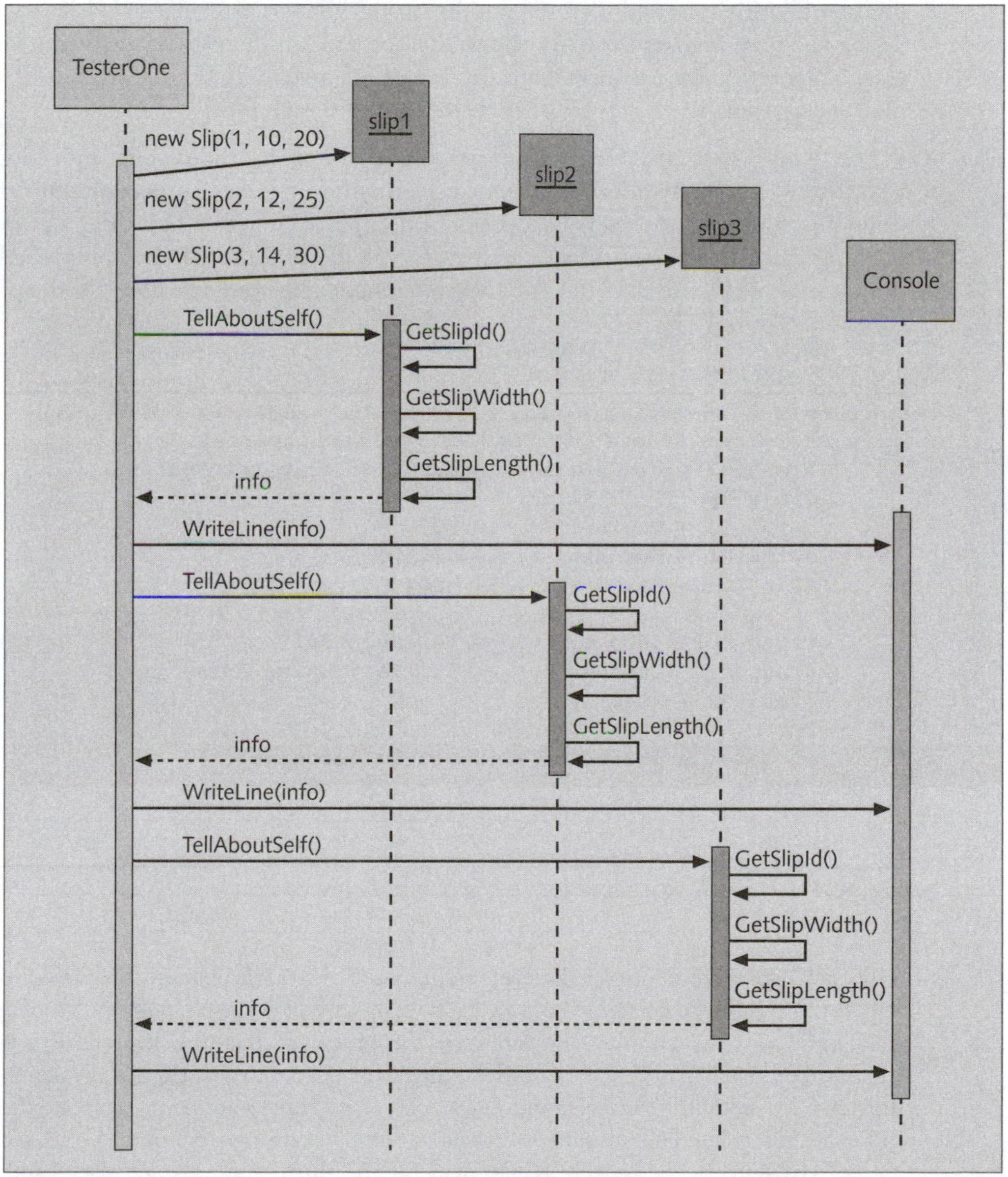

Figure 7-6 Sequence diagram for TesterOne and Slip

The five rectangles at the top of the diagram represent the objects in TesterOne, the instances of the Slip class—referenced by `slip1`, `slip2`, and `slip3`—and the Console object. First, TesterOne creates the three Slip instances populating the variables `slip1`, `slip2`, and `slip3` with references to the three Slip instances. Thus, `slip1` points to the first Slip instance, `slip2` to the second instance, and `slip3` to the third. TesterOne then invokes TellAboutSelf for the Slip instance referenced by `slip1`. Next TellAboutSelf invokes the three getter methods for the first Slip instance and then returns the String instance referenced by info to TesterOne. TesterOne then invokes the `WriteLine` method in Console, passing the String instance referenced by info as an argument. Similarly, TesterOne invokes TellAboutSelf for the second and third slips, passing the results returned to `WriteLine` each time.

When you click the Test Slip with Array button, the event procedure named `btnTestSlipArray_Click` is invoked. Like the first event procedure, this one creates three slip instances, invokes TellAboutSelf, and displays the result. This time, however, instead of using three separate reference variables for the three slip instances, the procedure uses a three-element array to hold the three Slip references. The complete code for the procedure is shown in Figure 7-7.

```
Private Sub btnTestSlipArray_Click(ByVal sender As System.Object, ByVal
   e As System.EventArgs) Handles btnTestSlipArray.Click
      'test Slip class using an array of Slip references
      Dim slips(2) As Slip
      slips(0) = New Slip(1, 10, 20)
      slips(1) = New Slip(2, 12, 25)
      slips(2) = New Slip(3, 14, 30)

      ' For-Next loop to invoke TellAboutSelf
      Console.WriteLine("Begin Slip Test using Array")
      Dim i As Integer
      For i = 0 To 2
         Console.WriteLine(slips(i).TellAboutSelf())
      Next i

   End Sub
```

Figure 7-7 Event procedure for Test Slip with Array button

The first statement defines a three-element array with each element identified as data type Slip. You use Slip as a data type because each element will contain a reference to an instance of the Slip class. You specify 2 in parentheses to indicate that the last element index is 2. Remember that VB .NET array index values always begin with 0, so an element with an index of 2 is really the third element. Next, you write three statements to create the three Slip instances, using literals as arguments passed to the Slip constructor for `slipId`, `slipWidth`, and `slipLength`, respectively. References for the three instances are placed into the three array elements indexed by 0, 1, and 2.

The last part of this procedure contains a For-Next loop to iterate the array, invoke TellAboutSelf for each Slip instance, and display the information returned. This loop executes three times using a loop variable named `i`. Recall that a For-Next loop initializes and increments your loop variable. In this example, `i` is initialized to 0 and then incremented by 1 at the end of each iteration. The single statement inside the loop is executed three times. The first time it is executed, `i` contains 0, the second time 1, and the last time 2. This means that the argument being passed to the **`WriteLine`** method, **`slips(i).TellAboutSelf()`**, will invoke TellAboutSelf for the Slip instance referenced by **`slips(0)`**, then **`slips(1)`**, and finally **`slips(2)`**. Note that this code uses a hard-coded value of 2 in the For-Next loop. A better design is to use the array **`Length`** attribute, which will work without modification for an array of any size.

The output from the **`btnTestSlipArray_Click`** procedure is shown in Figure 7-8.


```
Begin Slip Test using Array
Slip: Id = 1, Width = 10, Length = 20
Slip: Id = 2, Width = 12, Length = 25
Slip: Id = 3, Width = 14, Length = 30
```

Figure 7-8 Output from `btnTestSlipArray_Click`

The third button on the TesterOne form is labeled "Close," and its purpose is to terminate the application. This button is named **`btnClose`**; its event procedure is shown in the following code. This procedure contains a single statement that invokes the inherited method **`Dispose`**. This method terminates processing and removes the form from memory when you click the Close button. The keyword **`Me`** indicates that the method is to be invoked for the instance containing the code, which in this example is the form. You will work more extensively with forms in Chapters 10 and 11.

```
Private Sub btnClose_Click(ByVal sender As System.Object, ByVal
   e As System.EventArgs) Handles btnClose.Click
      Me.Dispose()
End Sub
```

Hands-on Exercise 1

1. Locate the Ex01 folder in the Chap07\Examples folder in the book's data files. Create a folder named **Chap07\Exercises\Ex01** in the work folder on your system, and then copy the contents of the **Ex01** folder to this folder. Open the Example1Slip project with VB .NET. You should see Slip.vb and TesterOne.vb in the Solution Explorer window. Note that this folder contains a complete project.

Unlike some previous Hands-on Exercises, which asked you to create a project, this one has been done for you. Build the project and then run and test it to verify that it matches the output shown in Figures 7-5 and 7-8.

2. Modify the For-Next loop in `btnTestSlipArray_Click` to use the array `Length` attribute instead of the hard-coded value 2. Remember that `Length` contains the number of elements (3), but that the last element's index is 2.
3. Add statements to expand the slip's array to five elements and then create two additional slip instances, adding their references to the new elements of the array:

ID	Width	Length
4	15	30
5	20	35

4. Rebuild the project and run it to verify that your modifications are working correctly.
5. Add a new button to the form named `btnTestSlipArrayList` with a text value of "Test Slip with ArrayList." Write an event procedure for this new button. Follow the technique used in `btnTestSlipArray_Click`, but use an ArrayList instead of an array to contain the Slip references.
6. Rebuild the project and run it to verify that your modifications are working correctly.

CREATING CUSTOM METHODS

So far, you have seen examples of accessor methods such as `GetSlipId`, `SetSlipWidth`, and so forth. These are called standard methods because most problem domain classes have them. This section introduces you to **custom methods**. Custom methods are methods you write to process data. In contrast, **accessor methods** are written to store and retrieve attribute values.

The custom method you will write here is named LeaseSlip, and in this chapter it computes the lease fee for a slip. This method is expanded in later chapters to link the slip to a customer and lease instance to implement association.

Bradshaw Marina computes a slip lease fee based on the width of a slip, as shown in Table 7-1. Fees range from $800 to $1,500 depending on the slip's width. Slip length is not considered when determining the fee because the length of a slip is usually proportional to its width. In other words, the wider a slip, the greater its length.

Table 7-1 Lease Fee Computation

Slip Width	Annual Lease Fee
10	$800
12	$900
14	$1,100
16	$1,500

This method is written as a Function procedure because it will return a value: the lease fee amount. Remember that Function procedures return values but Sub procedures do not. You use a Sub for methods that do not return values. Like all methods, this one begins with a method header. It will have **`Public`** accessibility because it can be invoked by any object. Because it will compute and return the lease fee, which is a dollar amount, you use **`Single`** for the `Return` data type.


```
Public Function LeaseSlip() As Single
```

To compute the lease fee, you could use either a series of If statements or a Select statement. The following code uses a Select statement because it is easier to write for this example. The first statement declares a **`Single`** variable named `fee`, which will contain the computed lease fee amount. Next, the **`Select Case`** statement tests the contents of the `slipWidth` attribute and then assigns a value to `fee` based on the contents.

```
Dim fee As Single
Select Case slipWidth
      Case 10
            fee = 800
      Case 12
            fee = 900
      Case 14
            fee = 1100
      Case 16
            fee = 1500
      Case Else
            fee = 0
End Select
Return fee
```

The **`Select Case`** statement terminates with `End Select`. Notice that the preceding code includes **`Case Else`**, which assigns a value of 0 to `fee` if the width of the slip is not 10, 12, 14, or 16. The last statement in the method returns the computed value to the invoking method. Remember that this method will play the role of a server method residing in the Slip class. Clients will invoke this method to determine the lease fee amount for the slip. Figure 7-9 lists the revised Slip class definition containing the LeaseSlip method.

```
' Chapter 7 Slip class Example 2
' Illustrate custom method LeaseSlip

Public Class Slip

      'attributes
      Private slipId As Integer
      Private slipWidth As Integer
      Private slipLength As Integer

      'constructor (three parameters)
      Public Sub New(ByVal aSlipId As Integer, ByVal aSlipWidth As _
         Integer, ByVal aSlipLength As Integer)
            'invoke setter methods to populate attributes
            SetSlipId(aSlipId)
            SetSlipWidth(aSlipWidth)
            SetSlipLength(aSlipLength)
      End Sub

      'custom method LeaseSlip calculates and returns fee
      Public Function LeaseSlip() As Single
            Dim fee As Single
            Select Case slipWidth
                  Case 10
                        fee = 800
                  Case 12
                        fee = 900
                  Case 14
                        fee = 1100
                  Case 16
                        fee = 1500
                  Case Else
                        fee = 0
            End Select
            Return fee
      End Function

      'custom method TellAboutSelf
   Public Function TellAboutSelf() As String
      Dim info As String
      info = "Slip: Id = " & GetSlipId() & ", Width = " _
        & GetSlipWidth() & ", Length = " & GetSlipLength()
      Return info
   End Function

   'get accessor methods
   Public Function GetSlipId() As Integer
      Return slipId
   End Function
   Public Function GetSlipWidth() As Integer
      Return slipWidth
   End Function
```

```
    Public Function GetSlipLength() As Integer
       Return slipLength
    End Function

    'set accessor methods
    Public Sub SetSlipId(ByVal aSlipId As Integer)
       slipId = aSlipId
    End Sub
    Public Sub SetSlipWidth(ByVal aSlipWidth As Integer)
       slipWidth = aSlipWidth
    End Sub
    Public Sub SetSlipLength(ByVal aSlipLength As Integer)
       slipLength = aSlipLength
    End Sub

End Class
```

Figure 7-9 Slip class definition with LeaseSlip method

Next, you will write a new tester class named TesterTwo. Instead of a form, however, you will write TesterTwo as a module. Like TesterOne, you begin by writing statements to declare a three-element array using data type Slip and then create three Slip instances.

```
' define an array of Slip references
Dim slips(2) As Slip
slips(0) = New Slip(1, 10, 20)
slips(1) = New Slip(2, 12, 25)
slips(2) = New Slip(3, 14, 30)
```

Next, you write a loop like the one you wrote in TesterOne, but here you invoke the LeaseSlip method for each slip instance and then display the fee that the method computes and returns. This loop executes three times: The first time `i` contains 0, the second 1, and the last 2. The single statement inside the loop performs the following tasks:

1. Invokes LeaseSlip for the Slip instance referenced by the array element indexed by the loop variable `i`, which will contain 0 for the first iteration, 1 for the second, and so forth

2. Invokes GetSlipId for the Slip instance referenced by the array element indexed by the loop variable `i`

3. Concatenates the literal `"Fee is "` with the fee returned by the LeaseSlip method and concatenates the literal `" for Slip "` with the ID returned by the GetSlipId method

4. Invokes the `WriteLine` method in the `Console` class, passing the concatenated String from Step 3 as an argument

Notice that this example uses `slips.Length - 1` as a terminating value instead of hard-coding 2. This reduces maintenance by permitting the loop to work with any size array.

```
'compute & display lease fee for all three slips
Console.WriteLine("Computing lease for all three slips:")
Dim i As Integer
For i = 0 To slips.Length - 1
   Console.WriteLine("Fee is " & slips(i).LeaseSlip() _
   & " for Slip " & slips(i).GetSlipId())
Next i
```

TesterTwo is listed in Figure 7-10, and the output is shown in Figure 7-11.

```
' Chapter 7 TesterTwo Example 2
Module TesterTwo
   Sub Main()

      ' define an array of Slip references
      Dim slips(2) As Slip
      slips(0) = New Slip(1, 10, 20)
      slips(1) = New Slip(2, 12, 25)
      slips(2) = New Slip(3, 14, 30)

      'compute & display lease fee for all three slips
      Console.WriteLine("Computing lease for all three slips:")
      Dim i As Integer
      For i = 0 To slips.Length - 1
         Console.WriteLine("Fee is " & slips(i).LeaseSlip() _
         & " for Slip " & slips(i).GetSlipId())
      Next i
   End Sub
End Module
```

Figure 7-10 TesterTwo.vb listing

```
Computing lease for all three slips:
Fee is 800 for Slip 1
Fee is 900 for Slip 2
Fee is 1100 for Slip 3
```

Figure 7-11 TesterTwo output

Hands-on Exercise 2

1. Locate the Ex02 folder in the Chap07\Examples folder in the book's data files. Create a folder named **Chap07\Exercises\Ex02** in the work folder on your system, and then copy the contents of the **Ex02** folder to this folder. Open the Example2-CustomMethod project with VB .NET. You should see Slip.vb and TesterTwo.vb in the Solution Explorer window. Like Hands-on Exercise 1, this folder contains a complete project. Build the project and then run it to verify that it matches the output shown in Figure 7-11.
2. Rewrite the fee computation in the LeaseSlip method using If statements.
3. Rebuild the project and run it to verify that your modifications are working correctly.

Writing Class Variables and Methods

In Chapter 6 you saw how to declare and use **instance variables** and **instance methods**. When you instantiate a class, the new instance receives a copy of all instance variables and methods. For example, each Slip instance created in the previous section had its own copy of the attribute variables `slipId`, `slipWidth`, and `slipLength`. Different slips have different ID numbers, and may have different widths and lengths. Similarly, the accessor methods and custom methods such as LeaseSlip are used for each instance. To avoid redundancy, VB .NET does not actually create separate copies of these instance methods; however, it appears that instance methods "belong" to each instance.

In this section you will learn about **class variables** and **class methods**. Class variables and methods are *shared* by all instances of the class—each instance does not have its own copy; there is a single copy for the class and each instance has access to it. The keyword **`Shared`** is used to declare class variables and class methods. If you omit **`Shared`**, then VB .NET uses nonshared variables and methods by default. When you instantiate a class, the instance gets copies of all nonshared variables and access to the nonshared methods, but *does not* get a copy of **`Shared`** variables and methods.

To illustrate the use of class variables and methods, assume that the Bradshaw Marina system needs to keep track of the total number of slips. You can track this number by declaring a **`Shared`** variable in the Slip class. The following statement declares a variable named `numberOfSlips` and initializes it to 0. Use **`Private`** accessibility here because `numberOfSlips` will be accessed only by methods within the Slip class.

```
Private Shared numberOfSlips As Integer = 0
```

Because new slips can be built at the marina to accommodate additional boat customers, add the following statement to the Slip constructor to increment `numberOfSlips` each time a slip instance is created:

```
'increment shared attribute
numberOfSlips += 1
```

Next, write a getter method to return the contents of **numberOfSlips**. You will write this method as a Function procedure because it returns a value; in this example the value is an integer. You make the method shared because it is not associated with any individual instance. Because the method is shared, you will invoke it using the class name, Slip. If it were non-shared, you would invoke it using a reference variable that pointed to an instance of the Slip class. You give this method **Public** accessibility because it will be invoked by other classes.

```
'shared (class) method
Public Shared Function GetNumberOfSlips() As Integer
   Return numberOfSlips
End Function
```

The revised Slip class definition is listed in Figure 7-12.

```
' Chapter 7 Slip class Example 3
' Illustrate shared (class) attributes and methods

Public Class Slip

      'attributes
      Private slipId As Integer
      Private slipWidth As Integer
      Private slipLength As Integer

      'shared (class) attribute
      Private Shared numberOfSlips As Integer = 0

   Public Sub New(ByVal aSlipId As Integer, ByVal aSlipWidth _
     As Integer, ByVal aSlipLength As Integer)
      'invoke setter methods to populate attributes
      SetSlipId(aSlipId)
      SetSlipWidth(aSlipWidth)
      SetSlipLength(aSlipLength)
      'increment shared attribute
      numberOfSlips += 1
   End Sub

   'custom method LeaseSlip calculates and returns fee
   Public Function LeaseSlip() As Single
      Dim fee As Single
      Select Case slipWidth
         Case 10
            fee = 800
         Case 12
            fee = 900
         Case 14
            fee = 1100
         Case 16
            fee = 1500
         Case Else
            fee = 0
```

```
      End Select
      Return fee
   End Function

   'custom method TellAboutSelf
   Public Function TellAboutSelf() As String
      Dim info As String
      info = "Slip: Id = " & GetSlipId() & ", Width = " _
        & GetSlipWidth() & ", Length = " & GetSlipLength()
      Return info
   End Function

   'shared (class) method
   Public Shared Function GetNumberOfSlips() As Integer
      Return numberOfSlips
   End Function

   'get accessor methods
   Public Function GetSlipId() As Integer
      Return slipId
   End Function
   Public Function GetSlipWidth() As Integer
      Return slipWidth
   End Function
   Public Function GetSlipLength() As Integer
      Return slipLength
   End Function

   'set accessor methods
   Public Sub SetSlipId(ByVal aSlipId As Integer)
      slipId = aSlipId
   End Sub
   Public Sub SetSlipWidth(ByVal aSlipWidth As Integer)
      slipWidth = aSlipWidth
   End Sub
   Public Sub SetSlipLength(ByVal aSlipLength As Integer)
      slipLength = aSlipLength
   End Sub

End Class
```

Figure 7-12 Slip class definition with shared variable and method

Begin TesterThree with a statement that declares three variables with data type Slip.

```
' define 3 Slip reference variables
Dim slip1, slip2, slip3 As Slip
```

Next, create the first Slip instance, and then retrieve and display the `numberOfSlips` attribute. You invoke the shared method GetNumberOfSlips by writing the class name, a period, and the method name.

```
' create slip instances & display numberOfSlips for each
slip1 = New Slip(1, 10, 20)
Console.WriteLine("Number of slips: " & Slip.GetNumberOfSlips())
```

This statement invokes GetNumberOfSlips for the Slip class, concatenates the value returned with the descriptive literal, and then passes this result to the `WriteLine` method in the `Console` class.

You also can substitute an instance reference variable for the class name, because VB .NET knows which class an instance belongs to and simply interprets the instance reference variable as the appropriate class name.

```
'retrieve and display number of slips using slip1 instead of Slip
Console.WriteLine("Number of slips using slip1: " & _
  slip1.GetNumberOfSlips())
```

This statement produces the same results as the previous one, even though you use the reference variable `slip1`. In fact, you also could have used `slip2` or `slip3`. VB .NET knows that the instance referenced by `slip1` is a member of the Slip class and therefore invokes the class method GetNumberOfSlips.

The complete listing of TesterThree.vb is shown in Figure 7-13, and its output is shown in Figure 7-14.

```
' Chapter 7 TesterThree Example 3

Module TesterThree
   Sub Main()

      ' define 3 Slip reference variables
      Dim slip1, slip2, slip3 As Slip
      ' create slip instances & display numberOfSlips for each
      slip1 = New Slip(1, 10, 20)
      Console.WriteLine("Number of slips: " & Slip.GetNumberOfSlips())
      slip2 = New Slip(2, 12, 25)
      Console.WriteLine("Number of slips: " & Slip.GetNumberOfSlips())
      slip3 = New Slip(3, 14, 30)
      Console.WriteLine("Number of slips: " & Slip.GetNumberOfSlips())

      'retrieve and display number of slips using slip1 instead of Slip
      Console.WriteLine("Number of slips using slip1: " & _
        slip1.GetNumberOfSlips())
   End Sub
End Module
```

Figure 7-13 TesterThree.vb listing

```
Number of slips: 1
Number of slips: 2
Number of slips: 3
Number of slips using slip1: 3
```

Figure 7-14 TesterThree output

Writing Overloaded Methods

In Part 1 of this book you learned about method signatures. A **method signature** consists of the method name and its parameter list. VB .NET identifies a method by its signature, *not only by its name.* Therefore, within a class definition you can write several methods with the same name, but as long as their parameter lists differ, VB .NET sees them as unique methods. A method that has the same name as another method in the same class, but a different parameter list, is called an **overloaded method**.

7

Do not confuse overloaded methods with **overridden methods** or polymorphism. You override a method by writing a method *with the same signature* as an *inherited* method. When you override a method, you are essentially replacing the inherited method. Chapter 8 illustrates how to override methods.

A polymorphic method exists when you have a method in one class with the same signature as a method *in a second class.* As you saw previously, polymorphism permits different objects to respond in their own way to the same message. The TellAboutSelf method is an example of a polymorphic method. You write a TellAboutSelf method for both the Customer class and the Slip class, and even though the methods have the same name, they do different things: They respond differently when invoked. The TellAboutSelf method in Customer returns customer information (name, address, and phone number), but TellAboutSelf in Slip returns slip information (ID, width, and length).

In contrast, an overloaded method has the same name as another method in the *same class*, but it has a different parameter list. In the next two sections, you will develop an overloaded constructor and then overload a custom method. Overridden and polymorphic methods are illustrated in subsequent chapters.

Overloading a Constructor

You may frequently need to use multiple constructors, each with a different parameter list. For example, assume that most slips at Bradshaw Marina are 12 feet wide and 25 feet long, but that a few have different widths and lengths. However, the current Slip constructor requires three arguments: `slipId`, `slipWidth`, and `slipLength`.

You can simplify the code required to create a slip by writing a second Slip constructor that has only the single parameter for `slipId`, and then include statements to assign the default values of 12 and 25 to `slipWidth` and `slipLength`, respectively. Using these default values eliminates the need to pass them when creating slips that are 12 feet wide and 25 feet long.

To further simplify the Slip class definition, you can use constants for the default width and length values, as shown in the following code. To define a constant in VB .NET, you write the keyword **`Const`**, and then you must assign a value. Note that these constants have **`Private`** accessibility: They will be accessed only by statements within the Slip class. Constants are shared by all Slip instances, even though you do not write the keyword **`Shared`**. They are **Const** because their value should not be changed, and they are **`Private`** because they will be accessed only by methods within the Slip class. Notice that you follow the VB .NET style by using uppercase identifiers and underscores to separate words within the identifier.

```
'constants
Private Const DEFAULT_SLIP_WIDTH As Integer = 12
Private Const DEFAULT_SLIP_LENGTH As Integer = 25
```

The second constructor method header appears to be the same as the original, except that it has only a single parameter to receive the `slipId` value. This constructor method has a single statement that invokes the original constructor, passing the ID plus the default width and length values as arguments. You use the keyword **`Me`** and specify **`New`** as a method name to invoke the three-parameter constructor for this class.

```
'1-parameter constructor
'Overloads keyword not used with constructors
Public Sub New(ByVal aSlipId As Integer)
    'invoke 3-parameter constructor, passing default values
    Me.New(aSlipId, DEFAULT_SLIP_WIDTH, DEFAULT_SLIP_LENGTH)
End Sub
```

TesterFour illustrates the creation of Slip instances that invoke both constructors. Recall that VB .NET determines which constructor to invoke by the argument list. If the argument consists of three values, the original constructor with three parameters is executed. If the argument consists of a single value, the new constructor with one parameter is invoked. In other words, the number of arguments determines which constructor is executed: VB .NET identifies a method by its signature, not only by its name.

The first statement in TesterFour creates a Slip instance by passing three arguments, which invokes the original constructor with three parameters.

```
'create slip using 3-parameter constructor
slip1 = New Slip(1, 10, 20)
```

The next statement passes the single argument for **slipId**, which invokes the second constructor. The second slip instance is then created using the default values of 12 and 25 for width and length, respectively.

```
'create slip using 1-parameter constructor
slip2 = New Slip(2)
```

The next two statements invoke TellAboutSelf for each Slip instance and display the result.

```
' retrieve & display info for both slips
Console.WriteLine(slip1.TellAboutSelf())
Console.WriteLine(slip2.TellAboutSelf())
```

The output displayed is:

```
Slip: Id = 1, Width = 10, Length = 20
Slip: Id = 2, Width = 12, Length = 25
```

Note that the second slip has the default values for width (12) and length (25).

Overloading a Custom Method

In addition to the constructor, you can actually overload any method. Assume that Bradshaw Marina permits a discounted lease fee under certain conditions. You can include the discounted fee feature by simply writing a second version of the LeaseSlip method that accepts a value for the percentage discount. This new method will overload the original LeaseSlip method you developed earlier in the chapter. Slip will now have two LeaseSlip methods, but they will have different signatures. The original LeaseSlip has an empty parameter list, but the second has a parameter variable named **aDiscountPercent**, which will receive the discount to be applied.

The header for this new method must contain the keyword **Overloads**. In addition, the method being overloaded must also contain **Overloads**. This means that you must insert **Overloads** in both headers. The new header appears as:

```
Public Overloads Function LeaseSlip(ByVal aDiscountPercent As Single) _
        As Single
```

This new method consists of three statements to compute and return the discounted lease fee. The first invokes the original LeaseSlip method, which computes and returns the lease fee, but without the desired discount. The second statement computes the discounted lease fee, and the third statement returns the fee to the invoking method. Note that you use the keyword **Me** to invoke LeaseSlip for "this" slip instance. You could have omitted **Me** because it is the default; however, writing it helps make your code clear.

```
'overloaded custom method LeaseSlip if discount requested
Public Overloads Function LeaseSlip(ByVal aDiscountPercent As Single) _
      As Single
      'invoke LeaseSlip() to get fee
      Dim fee As Single = Me.LeaseSlip()
      'calculate and return discount fee
      Dim discountFee As Single = fee * (100 - aDiscountPercent) / 100
      Return discountFee
End Function
```

Next, you can add statements to TesterFour to invoke both the original and the new LeaseSlip methods. VB .NET executes the appropriate method, depending on the argument list. If no argument is passed, then the original LeaseSlip method is invoked. However, if an argument is coded, then the overridden method is executed.

```
'compute lease for slip1 without a discount, then with a 10% discount
Console.WriteLine("slip1 fee is " & slip1.LeaseSlip())
Console.WriteLine("With a 10% discount it's " & slip1.LeaseSlip(10))

'lease slip2 without a discount, then with a 20% discount
Console.WriteLine("slip2 fee is " & slip2.LeaseSlip())
Console.WriteLine("With a 20% discount it's " & slip2.LeaseSlip(20))
```

The updated Slip class definition, with the overloaded constructor and LeaseSlip methods, is listed in Figure 7-15. TesterFour is listed in Figure 7-16, and its output is shown in Figure 7-17.

```
' Chapter 7 Slip class Example 4
' Illustrate overloading methods

Public Class Slip

   'attributes
   Private slipId As Integer
   Private slipWidth As Integer
   Private slipLength As Integer

   'shared (class) attribute
   Private Shared numberOfSlips As Integer = 0

   'constants
   Private Const DEFAULT_SLIP_WIDTH As Integer = 12
   Private Const DEFAULT_SLIP_LENGTH As Integer = 25

   '1-parameter constructor
   'Overloads keyword not used with constructors
   Public Sub New(ByVal aSlipId As Integer)
      'invoke 3-parameter constructor, passing default values
      Me.New(aSlipId, DEFAULT_SLIP_WIDTH, DEFAULT_SLIP_LENGTH)
   End Sub
```

```
'3-parameter constructor
Public Sub New(ByVal aSlipId As Integer, ByVal aSlipWidth As _
  Integer, ByVal aSlipLength As Integer)
   'invoke setter methods to populate attributes
   SetSlipId(aSlipId)
   SetSlipWidth(aSlipWidth)
   SetSlipLength(aSlipLength)
   'increment shared attribute
   numberOfSlips += 1

End Sub

'custom method LeaseSlip calculates and returns fee
Public Overloads Function LeaseSlip() As Single
   Dim fee As Single
   Select Case slipWidth
         Case 10
               fee = 800
         Case 12
               fee = 900
         Case 14
               fee = 1100
         Case 16
               fee = 1500
         Case Else
               fee = 0
   End Select
   Return fee
End Function

'overloaded custom method LeaseSlip if discount requested
Public Overloads Function LeaseSlip(ByVal aDiscountPercent As _
   Single) As Single
   'invoke LeaseSlip() to get fee
   Dim fee As Single = Me.LeaseSlip()
   'calculate and return discount fee
   Dim discountFee As Single = fee * (100 - aDiscountPercent) / 100
   Return discountFee
End Function

'custom method TellAboutSelf
Public Function TellAboutSelf() As String
   Dim info As String
   info = "Slip: Id = " & GetSlipId() & ", Width = " & _
      GetSlipWidth() & ", Length = " & GetSlipLength()
   Return info
End Function

'shared (class) accessor method
Public Shared Function GetNumberOfSlips() As Integer
   Return numberOfSlips
End Function

'get accessor methods
```

```
   Public Function GetSlipId() As Integer
      Return slipId
   End Function
   Public Function GetSlipWidth() As Integer
      Return slipWidth
   End Function
   Public Function GetSlipLength() As Integer
      Return slipLength
   End Function

   'set accessor methods
   Public Sub SetSlipId(ByVal aSlipId As Integer)
      slipId = aSlipId
   End Sub
   Public Sub SetSlipWidth(ByVal aSlipWidth As Integer)
      slipWidth = aSlipWidth
   End Sub
   Public Sub SetSlipLength(ByVal aSlipLength As Integer)
      slipLength = aSlipLength
   End Sub

End Class
```

Figure 7-15 Slip class definition with overloaded methods

```
' Chapter 7 TesterFour Example 4

Module TesterFour
   Sub Main()
      Dim slip1, slip2 As Slip

      'create slip using 3-parameter constructor
      slip1 = New Slip(1, 10, 20)

      'create slip using 1-parameter constructor
      slip2 = New Slip(2)

      ' retrieve & display info for both slips
      Console.WriteLine(slip1.TellAboutSelf())
      Console.WriteLine(slip2.TellAboutSelf())

      'compute lease for slip1 without discount, then with a 10% discount
      Console.WriteLine("slip1 fee is " & slip1.LeaseSlip())
      Console.WriteLine("With a 10% discount it's " & _
         slip1.LeaseSlip(10))
      'lease slip2 without a discount, then with a 20% discount
      Console.WriteLine("slip2 fee is " & slip2.LeaseSlip())
      Console.WriteLine("With a 20% discount it's " & -
        slip2.LeaseSlip(20))

   End Sub
End Module
```

Figure 7-16 TesterFour.vb listing

```
Slip: Id = 1, Width = 10, Length = 20
Slip: Id = 2, Width = 12, Length = 25
slip1 fee is 800
With a 10% discount it's 720
slip2 fee is 900
With a 20% discount it's 720
```

Figure 7-17 TesterFour output

Hands-on Exercise 3

1. Locate the Ex04 folder in the Chap07\Examples folder in the book's data files. Create a folder named **Chap07\Exercises\Ex03** in the work folder on your system, and then copy the **Ex04** folder to this folder. Open the Example4-OverloadedMethods project with VB .NET. You should see Slip.vb and TesterFour.vb in the Solution Explorer window. This folder contains a complete project. Build the project and then run it to verify that it matches the output shown in Figure 7-17.
2. Rewrite the overloaded LeaseSlip method to use a single statement by omitting the variable discount Fee.
3. Add a third constructor to Slip to accept arguments for `slipId` and `slipWidth`, but use the default `slipLength` of 25.
4. Add statements to TesterFour to invoke the constructor you added in Step 3.
5. Rebuild the project and run it to verify that your modifications are working correctly.

Working with Exceptions

VB .NET uses exceptions to notify you of errors, problems, and other unusual conditions that may occur while your system is running. An **exception**, like many other things in VB .NET, is an object instance. More specifically, it is an instance of the Exception class or one of its subclasses.

In Part 1 you saw that OO processing often uses the client-server model. A client invokes a method in a server, perhaps passing along arguments. The server performs its assigned task and may return a value to the invoking client. The server uses exceptions to inform the client of a problem. Perhaps the client sent an inappropriate or invalid argument, or perhaps the server cannot complete its normal processing because of some other condition.

When such unusual situations arise, the server can create an exception instance that contains information about the situation. The server then sends the exception instance to the invoking client. Of course, the client must be prepared to receive the exception and take appropriate action.

VB .NET uses five keywords to deal with exceptions: **`Try`**, **`Catch`**, **`Finally`**, **`End Try`**, and **`Throw`**. The first four are used by the client, while the last, **`Throw`**, is used by the server. This section illustrates the use of these keywords by adding data validation logic to the Slip class. Figure 7-18 illustrates the interaction between client and server methods dealing with exceptions.

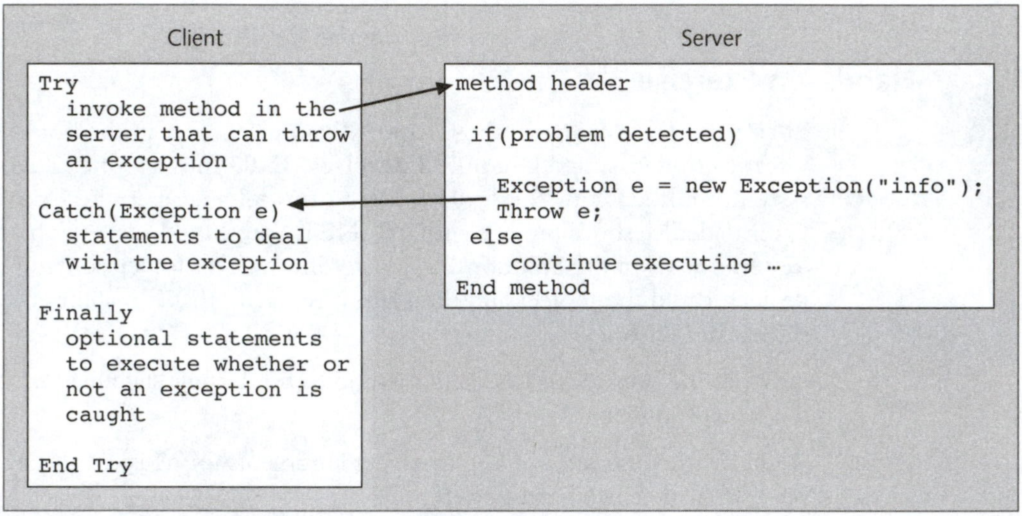
Client
Server
Try
invoke method in the
server that can throw
an exception
Catch(Exception e)
statements to deal
with the exception
Finally
optional statements
to execute whether or
not an exception is
caught
End Try
method header
if(problem detected)
Exception e = new Exception("info");
Throw e;
else
continue executing …
End method

Figure 7-18 Client-server exception handling

Whenever a client invokes a method that may create and throw an exception, the invoking code is placed in a **Try block**. A Try block begins with the keyword **`Try`** and ends with the keyword **`End Try`**. The client invokes the server method within the Try block. Then, if a situation warranting an exception is detected, the server method creates an exception instance and sends it to the invoking client using the keyword **`Throw`**. The client *catches* the exception instance in a **Catch block** and executes statements to deal with the exception. The **Finally block** is optional but, if included, will execute regardless of whether an exception is caught.

Data Validation for `slipId`

In the marina, slips are attached to a dock. Bradshaw Marina will never have more than 50 slips connected to a dock, so the `slipId` value should be within the range of 1 through 50. Therefore, you should add data validation logic to the `SetSlipId` method to verify that values passed to it are in the acceptable range of 1 through 50. You can add code in this method to create and throw an exception instance if a value outside the valid range is detected. The keyword **Throw** sends the exception instance to the invoking client method. The following example uses an existing VB .NET class named Exception; however, you can write and throw the exception classes that you write. In subsequent chapters you will learn how to write your own custom exception classes.

First, you add the constant `MAXIMUM_NUMBER_OF_SLIPS` to the Slip class. This approach simplifies future maintenance should Bradshaw Marina decide to have docks with more than 50 slips.

```
Private Const MAXIMUM_NUMBER_OF_SLIPS As Integer = 50
```

Next you write an If statement to see if the parameter value received (`aSlipId`) is within the valid range. If the value is outside the acceptable range, you instantiate the Exception class and then throw the instance to the invoking method. The code to instantiate the Exception class uses the familiar keyword **New**. Here you can pass a string literal describing the error to the Exception constructor. Notice that instead of writing the number 50 in the If statement, you write the constant `MAXIMUM_NUMBER_OF_SLIPS`. Similarly, you concatenate `MAXIMUM_NUMBER_OF_SLIPS` with the descriptive literal that becomes a part of the error message contained in the Exception instance. If the parameter value is within the acceptable range, the `Else` clause populates the `slipId` attribute.

```
Public Sub SetSlipId(ByVal aSlipId As Integer)
   'reject slipId if < 0 or > maximum
   If aSlipId < 1 Or aSlipId > MAXIMUM_NUMBER_OF_SLIPS Then
      Throw New Exception("Slip Id not between 1 and " _
         & MAXIMUM_NUMBER_OF_SLIPS)
   Else
      slipId = aSlipId
   End If
End Sub
```

Data Validation for `slipWidth`

Next, add code to the `SetSlipWidth` method to verify that the width parameter is one of the valid width values: 10, 12, 14, or 16. Recall that these values are used in computing the lease fee and therefore must be correct. First, store the valid width values in an integer array named `VALID_SLIP_WIDTHS` by adding the following code to the Slip class definition. Instead of writing the keyword **Const**, here you write **Shared** and **ReadOnly**. **Shared** means that all Slip instances share the variable, and **ReadOnly** means that the variable cannot be changed: It is a constant.

```
Private Shared ReadOnly VALID_SLIP_WIDTHS As Integer() = _
    {10, 12, 14, 16}
```

The validation logic will iterate the array, seeking a match between the parameter value received (`aSlipWidth`) and an array value. If a matching value is found, the parameter is valid. However, if the end of the array is reached without finding a matching value, then the parameter contains an invalid value, and you will create and throw an exception.

Like the array iteration loops you studied in Chapters 3 and 4, you first declare a Boolean variable named `validWidth` and initialize it to **`False`**. You then code a For-Next loop that will continue until it finds a matching width value or reaches the end of the array. Within the loop body is a single If statement that tests for a match between the parameter value (`aSlipWidth`) and the array element (`VALID_SLIP_WIDTHS(i)`). If a match is found, `validWidth` is set to **`True`**, which terminates the loop. Note that this loop uses `VALID_SLIP_WIDTHS.Length - 1` as an upper limit.

```
Dim validWidth As Boolean = False
'search for a valid width
Dim i As Integer
For i = 0 To VALID_SLIP_WIDTHS.Length - 1
   If aSlipWidth = VALID_SLIP_WIDTHS(i) Then validWidth = True
Next i
```

Following the loop is another If statement to test `validWidth`. If it is true, you populate the width attribute with the parameter value. If `validWidth` is not true, however, you create and throw an instance of Exception that contains a message describing the problem.

```
'if a valid width found, set value
If validWidth Then
   slipWidth = aSlipWidth
Else 'else throw exception
   Throw New Exception("Invalid Slip Width")
End If
```

In this example the setter methods are actually invoked by the constructor. This means that if a setter throws an exception to the constructor, the constructor will automatically throw it to the invoking client method. Of course, you could instead add Try blocks to the constructors and have them explicitly throw the exception if it is caught, but this would add needless code and complexity to your Slip class.

Figure 7-19 shows the revised Slip class definition, including the setter methods with data validation.

```
' Chapter 7 Slip class Example 5
' Illustrate Validation and Exceptions

Public Class Slip

      'attributes
      Private slipId As Integer
      Private slipWidth As Integer
      Private slipLength As Integer

      'shared attribute ("static" or "class variable")
      Private Shared numberOfSlips As Integer = 0
```

```
'constants
Private Const DEFAULT_SLIP_WIDTH As Integer = 12
Private Const DEFAULT_SLIP_LENGTH As Integer = 25

'constants for validation
Private Const MAXIMUM_NUMBER_OF_SLIPS As Integer = 50
Private Shared ReadOnly VALID_SLIP_WIDTHS As
Integer() = {10, 12, 14, 16}

    'first constructor (one parameter)
    'Overloads keyword not used with constructors
    Public Sub New(ByVal aSlipId As Integer)
           'invoke other constructor, passing default values
           Me.New(aSlipId, DEFAULT_SLIP_WIDTH, DEFAULT_SLIP_LENGTH)
    End Sub

    'second constructor (three parameters)
    Public Sub New(ByVal aSlipId As Integer, ByVal aSlipWidth As
    Integer, _
    ByVal aSlipLength As Integer)
          'invoke setter methods to populate attributes
          SetSlipId(aSlipId)
          SetSlipWidth(aSlipWidth)
          SetSlipLength(aSlipLength)
          'increment shared attribute
   numberOfSlips += 1
    End Sub

    'custom method LeaseSlip calculates and returns fee
    Public Overloads Function LeaseSlip() As Single
          Dim fee As Single
          Select Case slipWidth
                Case 10
                       fee = 800
                Case 12
                       fee = 900
                Case 14
                       fee = 1100
                Case 16
                       fee = 1500
                Case Else
                       fee = 0
          End Select
          Return fee
    End Function

    'overloaded custom method LeaseSlip if discount requested
    Public Overloads Function LeaseSlip(ByVal aDiscountPercent As
       Single) _
     As Single
           'invoke LeaseSlip() to get fee
           Dim fee As Single = Me.LeaseSlip()
           'calculate and return discount fee
           Dim discountFee As Single = fee *(100 - aDiscountPercent)
             / 100
```

```
    Return discountFee
End Function

'custom method TellAboutSelf
Public Function TellAboutSelf() As String
    Dim info As String
    info = "Slip: Id = " & GetSlipId() & ", Width = " &
    GetSlipWidth() _
     & ", Length = " & GetSlipLength()
    Return info
End Function

'shared accessor method (static method)
Public Shared Function GetNumberOfSlips() As Integer
    Return numberOfSlips
End Function

'get accessor methods
Public Function GetSlipId() As Integer
    Return slipId
End Function
Public Function GetSlipWidth() As Integer
    Return slipWidth
End Function
Public Function GetSlipLength() As Integer
    Return slipLength
End Function

'set accessor methods with validation
Public Sub SetSlipId(ByVal aSlipId As Integer)
    'reject slipId if < 0 or > maximum
    If aSlipId < 1 Or aSlipId > MAXIMUM_NUMBER_OF_SLIPS Then
        Throw New Exception("Slip Id not between 1 and " _
        & MAXIMUM_NUMBER_OF_SLIPS)
    Else
        slipId = aSlipId
    End If
End Sub
Public Sub SetSlipWidth(ByVal aSlipWidth As Integer)
    'reject slipWidth if not in list of valid values
    Dim validWidth As Boolean = False
    'search for a valid width
    Dim i As Integer
    For i = 0 To VALID_SLIP_WIDTHS.Length - 1
        If aSlipWidth = VALID_SLIP_WIDTHS(i) Then validWidth = True
    Next i

    'if  a validwidth found, set value
    If validWidth Then
        slipWidth = aSlipWidth
    Else 'else throw exception
        Throw New Exception("Invalid Slip Width")
    End If
End Sub
```

```
    Public Sub SetSlipLength(ByVal aSlipLength As Integer)
        'write validation for length as exercise
        slipLength = aSlipLength
    End Sub

End Class
```

Figure 7-19 Slip class definition with data validation

Catching Exceptions

Exceptions are thrown by server methods that are invoked by clients. Exceptions are used by the server to inform the client of a condition. In this example, Slip is the server; it has methods that will create and throw an exception if either an invalid slip ID or width is detected. In this example, TesterFive is the client that will test the data validation code in Slip.

Whenever your code invokes a method that might throw an exception, the invoking code must be prepared to catch the exception; otherwise, the .NET CLR will terminate processing if an exception is thrown and not caught. The first step in catching an exception is to place the invoking statement in a Try block, as shown in the following code and in Figure 7-20. A Try block begins with the keyword **Try** and is followed by code containing the invoking statement or statements, and ends with **End Try**. The following code first declares a slip reference variable named `aSlip`, followed by a Try block containing the statement that instantiates Slip.

```
Dim aSlip As Slip

Try 'force an exception with invalid slipID (150)
   aSlip = New Slip(150, 10, 25)
   Console.WriteLine(aSlip.TellAboutSelf())
Catch theException As Exception
   Console.WriteLine("An exception was caught: " & _
      theException.ToString())
End Try
```

Note that the Try block contains two statements. If the first statement causes an exception to be thrown, the second statement invoking TellAboutSelf is not executed because the exception is thrown. Instead, execution begins at the code following the keyword **Catch**.

The statement that instantiates Slip invokes its constructor and passes arguments for `slipId`, `slipWidth`, and `slipLength`. Recall that the constructor invokes the setter methods to populate the attributes. Therefore, when you instantiate the class and the constructor is invoked, it invokes `SetSlipId`, which contains code to throw an exception if an invalid `SlipId` is detected. The previous example deliberately passes an invalid value (150), which causes the setter to create and throw an exception.

Notice that the Slip constructor calls `SetSlipId`, which throws an exception, but that the constructor *does not* catch the exception. In this example, the constructor is not required to deal with the exception because it automatically rethrows an exception that was originally thrown by a method it invokes. If necessary, you could include code in the constructor to catch the exception, then simply throw it again, and it would be caught by the method that invoked the constructor.

Following the Try block in TesterFive, you can write a Catch block to receive and deal with the exception thrown by `SetSlipId`. Like a method header, the Catch block must specify a parameter variable to receive a reference to the exception instance. The parameter variable must indicate the data type, which in this example is the class name Exception. Within the Catch block is a statement invoking `WriteLine` to display the message contained in the exception instance. Note that the `ToString` method for the Exception instance is invoked and the value returned is then passed to the `WriteLine` method. In this example, `ToString` simply retrieves the descriptive text contained in the instance.

```
Catch theException As Exception
   Console.WriteLine("An exception was caught: " & _
      theException.ToString())
```

Next, add statements to TesterFive to test the validation code that was added to `SetSlipWidth`. Again, attempt to create a Slip instance within a Try block. Pass the first constructor a width value of 15, which is invalid.

```
Try 'force an exception with invalid width (15)
   aSlip = New Slip(1, 15, 25)
   Console.WriteLine(aSlip.TellAboutSelf())
```

Next, write a Catch block to catch the exception that will be thrown.

```
Catch theException As Exception
   Console.WriteLine("An exception was caught: " & _
      theException.ToString())
```

The keyword **`Finally`** is used to add statements that you want executed *whether or not an exception was caught*. TesterFive includes **`Finally`** statements to illustrate their use.

```
Finally
   Console.WriteLine("Finally block always executes")
```

Figure 7-20 shows the code for TesterFive. Its output is shown in Figure 7-21. Your output will be more detailed.

```
' Chapter 7 TesterFive Example 5
Module TesterFive
   Sub Main()
      Dim aSlip As Slip
      Try 'force an exception with invalid slipID (150)
         aSlip = New Slip(150, 10, 25)
         Console.WriteLine(aSlip.TellAboutSelf())
      Catch theException As Exception
         Console.WriteLine("An exception was caught: " & _
            theException.ToString())
      End Try
```

```
      Try 'force an exception with invalid width (15)
         aSlip = New Slip(1, 15, 25)
         Console.WriteLine(aSlip.TellAboutSelf())
      Catch theException As Exception
         Console.WriteLine("An exception was caught: " & _
           theException.ToString())
      Finally
         Console.WriteLine("Finally block always executes")
      End Try

      'create a Slip instance using valid id & width
      Try
         aSlip = New Slip(2, 10, 25)
         Console.WriteLine(aSlip.TellAboutSelf())
      Catch theException As Exception
         Console.WriteLine("An exception was caught: " & _
           theException.ToString())
      Finally
         Console.WriteLine("Finally block always executes")
      End Try

   End Sub
End Module
```


Figure 7-20 TesterFive.vb listing

```
An exception was caught: System.Exception: Slip Id not between 1 and 50
An exception was caught: System.Exception: Invalid Slip Width
Finally block always executes
Slip: Id = 2, Width = 10, Length = 25
Finally block always executes
```

Figure 7-21 TesterFive output

Hands-on Exercise 4

1. Locate the Ex05 folder in the Chap07\Examples folder in the book's data files. Create a folder named **Chap07\Exercises\Ex04** in the work folder on your system, and then copy the contents of the **Ex05** folder to this folder. Open the Example5-Exceptions project with VB .NET. You should see Slip.vb and TesterFive.vb in the Solution Explorer window. This folder contains a complete project. Build the project and then run it to verify that it matches the output shown in Figure 7-21.
2. Rewrite the data validation logic in `SetSlipWidth` to use If statements with literal values instead of the array.
3. Rebuild the project and run it to verify that your modifications are working correctly.

Hands-on Exercise 5

1. Locate the Ex05 folder in the Chap07\Examples folder in the book's data files. Create a folder named **Chap07\Exercises\Ex05** in the work folder on your system, and then copy the **Ex05** folder to this folder. Open the Example5-Exceptions project with VB .NET. You should see Slip.vb and TesterFive.vb in the Solution Explorer window. This folder contains a complete project. Build the project and then run it to verify that it matches the output shown in Figure 7-21.
2. Add statements to the `SetSlipLength` method in Slip to verify that the length value received is between 20 and 40, inclusive. Use appropriately named constants for these minimum and maximum values. Add try-catch statements to TesterFive to test your new data validation code.
3. Rebuild the project and run it to verify that your modifications are working correctly.

Chapter Summary

- Accessor methods are called standard methods because most problem domain classes have them, but they are generally not shown on class diagrams. Custom methods are methods you write to process data; these methods are included in class diagrams.
- The keyword **`Shared`** is used to declare class variables and methods. Class variables and methods are associated with the class instead of individual instances. When you instantiate a class, the new instance is given a copy of all instance variables and access to instance methods, but the new instance *does not* get a copy of static variables and methods.
- You invoke class methods by writing the class name, a period, and the method name. Instance methods are invoked by writing an instance reference variable, a period, and the method name. You can also invoke class methods using an instance reference variable.
- A method signature consists of the method name and its parameter list. VB .NET identifies a method by its entire signature, not only by its name. A method that has the same name as another method in the same class, but a different parameter list (a different signature), is called an overloaded method.
- VB .NET uses exceptions to notify you of errors, problems, and other unusual conditions that may occur while your system is running. An exception is an instance of the Exception class or one of its subclasses.

- VB .NET uses five keywords to deal with exceptions: **`Try`**, **`Catch`**, **`Finally`**, **`End Try`**, and **`Throw`**. The first four are used by the client, while the last, **`Throw`**, is used by the server.
- Whenever your code invokes a method that may throw an exception, you must be prepared to catch and deal with the exception; otherwise, the CLR will terminate processing if an exception is thrown and not caught.

Key Terms

accessor methods
assignment compatible
Catch block
class method
class variable
custom method
exception
Finally block
instance method
instance variable
method signature
overloaded method
overridden method
polymorphic method
Try block

Review Questions

1. Concatenating means ________________.
   a. separating items in a string
   b. subtracting numeric items
   c. joining items together
   d. displaying items
2. Shared variables ________________.
   a. are never populated
   b. are seldom replicated
   c. have only one copy
   d. are also called instance variables
3. A shared method ________________.
   a. may be invoked by referencing the class name
   b. may be invoked by referencing the instance name
   c. both a and b
   d. neither a nor b

4. Shared read-only variables are also called ________________.
   a. constants
   b. instance constants
   c. free variables
   d. none of the above
5. The keyword `Me` ________________.
   a. is invalid
   b. refers to the class and all of its static values
   c. refers to the instance attributes
   d. refers to the instance whose method is executing
6. A method's signature is ________________.
   a. its name
   b. its header
   c. its name and parameter list
   d. its arguments
7. An overloaded method ________________.
   a. cannot be invoked
   b. is a method with too many statements
   c. has the same parameter list as another method, but a different name
   d. has the same name as another method, but a different parameter list
8. Which of the following is NOT true about overloaded methods?
   a. A constructor may be overloaded.
   b. Accessor methods may not be overloaded.
   c. Custom methods may be overloaded.
   d. Accessor methods may be overloaded.
9. An exception is ________________.
   a. an instance
   b. an attribute
   c. a method
   d. none of the above

10. The keyword **Throw** ________________.
    a. sends an exception to the invoking method
    b. must be in the header of a method sending an exception
    c. is used together with the keyword **Return**
    d. is invalid

11. A method that can receive an exception ________________.
    a. will generally terminate
    b. must catch the exception
    c. both a and b
    d. neither a nor b

12. The keyword **Finally** ________________.
    a. is part of a Select Case statement
    b. will always be executed
    c. will be executed only if an exception is detected
    d. is invalid

13. An array's length attribute ________________.
    a. contains the number of populated elements
    b. contains the number of elements
    c. can only be used in a For-Next loop
    d. is invalid

14. When overloading a method you must ________________.
    a. change the method name
    b. specify Overloads in the method header unless it is a constructor
    c. specify Overloads in all of the method headers with the overloaded method name unless it is a constructor
    d. You cannot overload a method; the term is *override*.

15. Assignment compatible means that ________________.
    a. a variable may be assigned to another variable with a different data type
    b. a variable may be assigned to another variable with the same data type
    c. a variable can only be used with the data type Single
    d. you must convert the value to a String, then make the assignment

Discussion Questions

1. In this chapter, the Slip constructor methods invoke setter methods to populate the attributes. What problems are created if you instead write assignment statements in the constructors to populate the attributes?
2. In the Slip constructor methods, what are the benefits of having the one-parameter constructor invoke the three-parameter constructor? What changes would you need to make to the one-parameter constructor if it did not invoke the three-parameter constructor?
3. What problems would be created if you accidentally made the three Slip attributes shared?

Projects

1. Assume that Bradshaw Marina has added a dock containing 30 slips that are all the same size: 12 feet wide and 30 feet long. The ID for the first slip is 1, the second 2, and so forth through 30.
   a. Locate the Ex04 folder in the Chap07\Examples folder in the book's data files. Create a folder named **Chap07\Projects\Proj01\Project1** in the work folder on your system, and then copy the contents of the Ex04 folder to the Project1 folder.
   b. Add statements to TesterFour.vb that will create the 30 Slip instances described above. Place the slip references into an array.
   c. Add a loop to TesterFour to invoke TellAboutSelf for all 30 of these new slip instances.
2. Continue using the Example4-OverloadedMethods code as a guide to the following projects:
   a. Locate the Ex04 folder in the Chap07\Examples folder in the book's data files. Create a folder named **Chap07\Projects\Proj02\Project2** in the work folder on your system, and then copy the contents of the Ex04 folder to the Project2 folder.
   b. Add a method named GetFormattedFee to Slip. This method will receive no argument, invoke LeaseSlip to compute the fee, format the fee as currency, and return a string containing the formatted fee.

c. Add a second method to overload the method you added in Step b. This second method will receive a discount percentage as an argument, invoke the second LeaseSlip that receives a discount percentage argument, format the fee as currency, and return a string containing the formatted fee.

d. Add statements to TesterFour.vb that will verify that both of your new methods are working properly.

3. Continue using the Example4-OverloadedMethods code as a guide to the following projects:

a. Locate the Ex04 folder in the Chap07\Examples folder in the book's data files. Create a folder named **Chap07\Projects\Proj03\Project3** in the work folder on your system, and then copy the contents of the Ex04 folder to the Project3 folder.

b. Add a shared method named FormatFee to Slip. This method will receive a fee as an argument, format the fee as currency, and return a string containing the formatted fee.

c. Add statements to TesterFour that will verify that your new methods are working properly.

CHAPTER

8

Understanding Inheritance and Interfaces

In this chapter you will:

- Implement the Boat generalization/specialization class hierarchy
- Understand abstract and final classes and the `MustInherit` and `NotInheritable` keywords
- Override a superclass method
- Understand private versus protected access
- Explore the Lease subclasses and abstract methods
- Understand and use interfaces
- Use custom exceptions
- Understand the `Object` class and inheritance

In Chapters 6 and 7, you learned how to create and test VB .NET problem domain classes, and you created two PD classes for Bradshaw Marina: Customer and Slip. Recall that the Bradshaw Marina case, presented in Chapter 5, showed a generalization/specialization hierarchy for types of boats and types of leases. This chapter shows how to create the superclass Boat and then create and test two subclasses that inherit attributes and methods of Boat—Sailboat and Powerboat. Additional examples use the Lease class with its subclasses—AnnualLease and DailyLease.

Inheritance is a powerful mechanism in object-oriented programming because it lets you easily extend an existing class to simplify development and testing and to facilitate reuse. One of the most significant improvements to VB .NET over VB 6.0 is the ability to use inheritance. When you use inheritance, you work with the VB .NET keyword **`Inherits`** to extend a superclass into a subclass. In this chapter inheritance is used with problem domain classes and the VB .NET **`Exception`** class.

Once you implement the superclass Boat and the subclasses Sailboat and Powerboat, you can demonstrate polymorphism by having sailboat instances and powerboat instances respond to the TellAboutSelf method in their own ways. You can accomplish this by overriding superclass methods with new methods in subclasses that have the same signature as the methods in the superclass.

Other VB .NET programming techniques that apply to inheritance—abstract methods, interfaces, and custom exceptions—are also demonstrated in this chapter using the Lease subclasses. You can use several techniques to require classes to include methods to ensure that all instances can respond to the same message. First, you will learn how to use an abstract method in a superclass to require that a subclass implement a method. Second, you will explore interfaces as a VB .NET construct that can also require classes to implement methods.

Next, you will see how to use inheritance to extend classes other than problem domain classes. For example, you can create custom exceptions by extending the built-in VB .NET `Exception` class. Finally, the `Object` class is discussed as the superclass of all classes. The problem domain classes you create for Bradshaw Marina all implicitly extend `Object`, and `Object` methods are inherited by all of the classes.

Implementing the Boat Generalization/Specialization Hierarchy

In Chapter 5, you included the Boat class on the class diagram for Bradshaw Marina because Bradshaw needs to store information about all boats in the marina, including values for attributes such as a boat's state registration number, length, manufacturer, and model year. Figure 8-1 shows the Boat class from the Bradshaw class diagram. The VB .NET source code for the Boat class is shown in Figure 8-2.

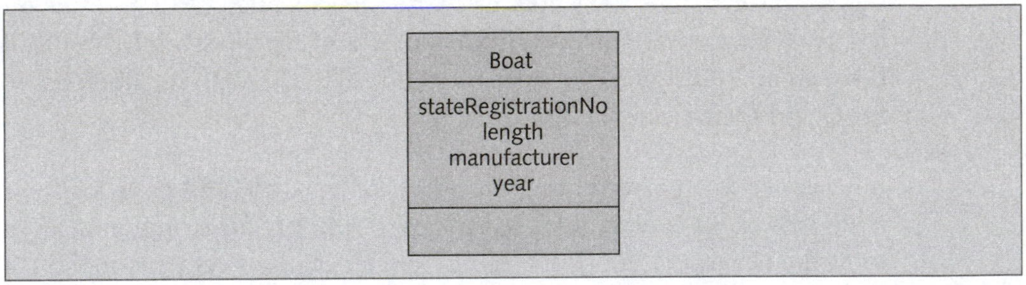

Figure 8-1 The Boat class

```
' Boat -- an initial Boat Class
' make abstract by inserting MustInherit keyword

Public Class Boat

   'attributes
   Private stateRegistrationNo As String
   Private length As Single
   Private manufacturer As String
   Private year As Integer

   'constructor (four parameters)
   Public Sub New(ByVal aStateRegistrationNo As String, _
      ByVal aLength As Single, _
      ByVal aManufacturer As String, ByVal aYear As Integer)
      'set values of attributes using accessor methods
      SetStateRegistrationNo(aStateRegistrationNo)
      SetLength(aLength)
      SetManufacturer(aManufacturer)
      SetYear(aYear)
   End Sub

   'TellAboutSelf method
   Public Overridable Function TellAboutSelf() As String
      Return (stateRegistrationNo & ", " & length & ", " & _
        manufacturer & ", " & year)
   End Function

   'Get accessor methods
   Public Function GetStateRegistrationNo() As String
      Return stateRegistrationNo
   End Function
   Public Function GetLength() As Single
      Return length
   End Function
   Public Function GetManufacturer() As String
      Return manufacturer
   End Function
   Public Function GetYear() As Integer
      Return year
   End Function

   'Set accessor methods
   Public Sub SetStateRegistrationNo(ByVal aStateRegNo As String)
      stateRegistrationNo = aStateRegNo
   End Sub
   Public Sub SetLength(ByVal aLength As Double)
      length = aLength
   End Sub
   Public Sub SetManufacturer(ByVal aManufacturer As String)
      manufacturer = aManufacturer
   End Sub
   Public Sub SetYear(ByVal aYear As Integer)
      year = aYear
   End Sub

End Class
```

Figure 8-2 Boat class definition

8

You write the Boat class header and the four Boat attributes as you did with Customer and Slip previously. The parameterized constructor accepts values for all four attributes. The Boat class includes eight standard accessor methods: four setter methods and four getter methods. Recall that you can also use properties to define `Get` and `Set` for each attribute, as discussed in Chapter 6. In this chapter, you will continue to write getter and setter methods instead of using properties. The constructor invokes the four set accessor methods as in previous examples. Note that the accessor methods do not include validation in this example to keep it brief (you will add validation in a Hands-on Exercise). The Boat class also includes a `TellAboutSelf` method that you will use later in this chapter.

Testing the Boat Superclass with a Windows Form

In most previous problem domain class examples, you created a console application and used a class module with a `Main` method to test your problem domain classes. A few examples in Chapter 6 and Chapter 7 used Windows forms as testers. In this chapter, you will use a Windows application and use a Windows form with buttons to test all problem domain classes. Using Windows form testers accomplishes the same important objective as using a class module: to systematically test each problem domain class to demonstrate that all functionality works as intended. You learned how to create a Windows form with buttons in Chapter 2.

Figure 8-3 shows a Windows form with four buttons. The first button, labeled "Test Boat Superclass," is named `btnBoat` and includes a `btnBoat_Click` event procedure. The code used to test the Boat class is included in the `btnBoat_Click` event procedure, as shown in Figure 8-4. The output is shown in Figure 8-5.

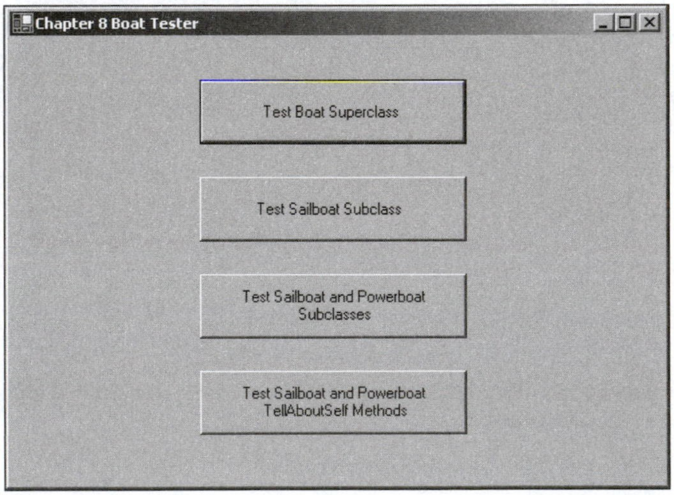

Figure 8-3 Boat Tester Windows Form

```
Private Sub btnBoat_Click(ByVal sender As System.Object, _
ByVal e As System.EventArgs) Handles btnBoat.Click

   Console.WriteLine("Begin Boat Test:")

   'declare 2 boat references
   Dim boat1 As Boat
   Dim boat2 As Boat

   'instantiate 2 boats
   boat1 = New Boat("MO1234", 28, "Tartan", 2001)
   boat2 = New Boat("CA9876", 32, "Catalina", 2003)

   'invoke getter methods for boat1
   Console.WriteLine("Boat No: " & boat1.GetStateRegistrationNo())
   Console.WriteLine("Length: " & boat1.GetLength())
   Console.WriteLine("Manufacturer: " & boat1.GetManufacturer())
   Console.WriteLine("Year: " & boat1.GetYear())

   'invoke getter methods for boat2
   Console.WriteLine("Boat No: " & boat2.GetStateRegistrationNo())
   Console.WriteLine("Length: " & boat2.GetLength())
   Console.WriteLine("Manufacturer: " & boat2.GetManufacturer())
   Console.WriteLine("Year: " & boat2.GetYear())

End Sub
```

Figure 8-4 Event procedure code to test initial Boat class

```
Begin Boat Test:
Boat No: MO1234
Length: 28
Manufacturer: Tartan
Year: 2001
Boat No: CA9876
Length: 32
Manufacturer: Catalina
Year: 2003
```

Figure 8-5 Boat test code output

The test code creates two Boat instances and then retrieves information about each boat using the getter methods. Output is displayed using the `Console.Writeline` method, as in previous chapters.

The sequence diagram that demonstrates how the test code interacts with Boat is shown in Figure 8-6. Note that the sequence diagram shows only one instance created by the test code. Boat is now ready to be used as a superclass.

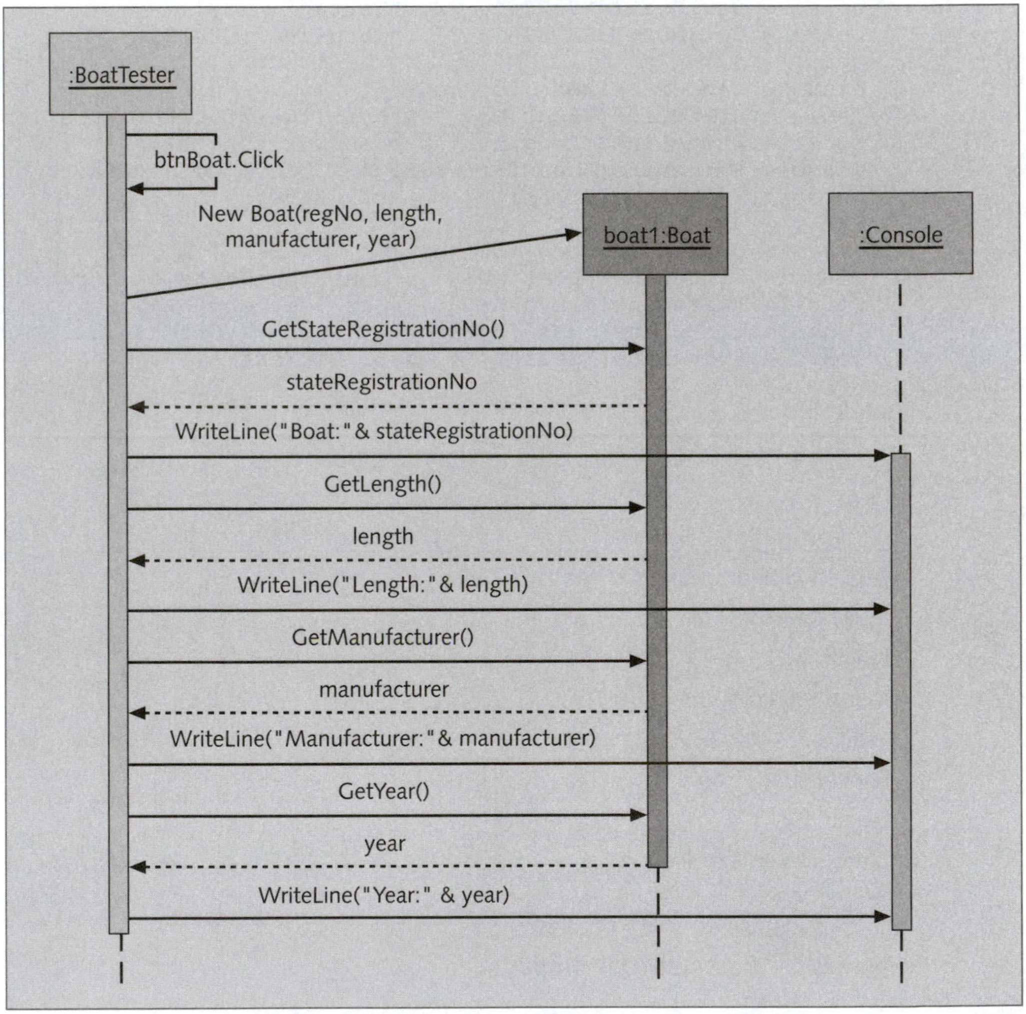

Figure 8-6 Sequence diagram for Boat test code

Hands-on Exercise 1

1. Locate the Example 1 Windows application in the folder Chap08\Examples\Ex01 in the book's data files. Create a folder named **Chap08\Exercises** in the work folder on your system, and then copy the **Ex01** folder to the Chap08\Exercises folder in your work folder. Open the project with VB .NET. You should see files such as Boat.vb, Sailboat.vb, and Powerboat.vb in the Solution Explorer window. Note that this is a Windows application containing a form with buttons. Build the proj-ect and run it. Click the **Test Boat Superclass** button and review the output to verify that it matches the output shown in Figure 8-5. The output will appear in the Output window. Close the Boat Tester form and console window.

2. Examine the Boat.vb source code file. Note that it does not include validation for the setter methods. Add reasonable validation statements to each setter method. For example, the registration number should be at least seven characters, manufacturer should be at least two characters, year should be between 1950 and 2004, and length should be between 10 and 100. If the value is not valid, set the value to a default value. You do not need to throw an exception.

3. Add a new button to the Boat Tester form labeled Test Boat Validation and named `btnTestBoatValidation`. Write test code in the event procedure that creates at least four boats with invalid values to test that the validation sets values to defaults as planned. Rebuild and run the application. Click your new button and verify that the validation works. Click the original **Test Boat Superclass** button and verify that the valid boat data still results in the same output as before.

4. Leave the Windows application open in VB .NET for the next Hands-on Exercise.

Using the `Inherits` Keyword to Create the Sailboat Subclass

The class diagram for the Bradshaw Marina system shows that there are special types of boats, and each special type of boat has attributes that all boats share plus additional attributes. For example, a sailboat has a keel depth (sometimes called draft), a number of sails, and a motor type (none, inboard, or outboard). A powerboat does not have sails and its keel depth is unimportant. However, a powerboat might have several engines, and you should know the number of engines and their fuel type (gas or diesel). The generalization/specialization hierarchy from the Bradshaw class diagram that shows special types of boats is reproduced in Figure 8-7.

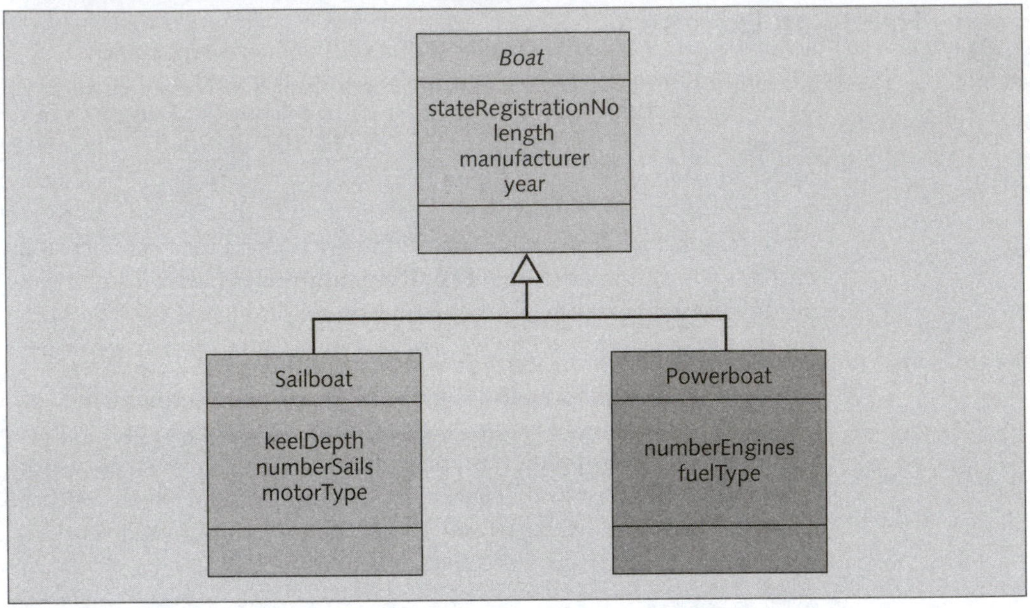

Figure 8-7 Generalization/specialization hierarchy for Boat classes

Recall that a generalization/specialization hierarchy means that a general superclass includes attributes and methods that are common to specialized subclasses. Instances of the subclasses inherit the attributes and methods of the superclass, and they include additional attributes and methods. The Boat class, with four attributes and eight accessor methods, is the superclass. Sailboat, with three additional attributes, and Powerboat, with two additional attributes, are two subclasses. Recall that the triangle symbol pointing to the Boat class in Figure 8-7 means Boat is the superclass on the class diagram.

To implement a subclass with VB .NET, use the **Inherits** keyword in the second line of the class header to indicate which class the new class is extending. For example, to define the Sailboat class as a subclass of Boat, the header would be:

```
Public Class Sailboat
   Inherits Boat
```

The rest of the class definition would include any attributes and any methods *in addition to* those inherited from the superclass. You do not have to list or define the inherited attributes or methods in the subclass.

The Sailboat class includes six accessor methods, two for each additional attribute. The VB .NET source code for the Sailboat class is shown in Figure 8-8. In the examples in this book, each PD class is defined in its own source code file, although VB .NET allows you to include more than one public class in a source code file.

```
' Sailboat -- a subclass of Boat

Public Class Sailboat
   Inherits Boat

   'attributes in addition to the four
   'inherited from Boat
   Private keelDepth As Double
   Private numberSails As Integer
   Private motorType As String

   'constructor (all seven attribute values as parameters)
   Public Sub New(ByVal aStateRegistrationNo As String, _
      ByVal aLength As Double, _
      ByVal aManufacturer As String, ByVal aYear As Integer, _
      ByVal aKeelDepth As Double, ByVal aNumberSails As Integer, _
      ByVal aMotorType As String)
      'invoke superclass constructor passing 4 values
      MyBase.New(aStateRegistrationNo, aLength, aManufacturer, aYear)
      'set additional attribute values
      SetKeelDepth(aKeelDepth)
      SetNumberSails(aNumberSails)
      SetMotorType(aMotorType)
   End Sub

   'TellAboutSelf overrides but does not invoke superclass method
   Public Overrides Function TellAboutSelf() As String
      Return (GetStateRegistrationNo() & ", " & GetLength() & _
         ", " & _
      GetManufacturer() & ", " & GetYear() & ", " _
      & keelDepth & ", " & numberSails & ", " & motorType)
   End Function

   'Get accessor methods
   Public Function GetKeelDepth() As Double
      Return keelDepth
   End Function
   Public Function GetNumberSails() As Integer
      Return numberSails
   End Function
   Public Function GetMotorType() As String
      Return motorType
   End Function

   'Set accessor methods
   Public Sub SetKeelDepth(ByVal aKeelDepth As Double)
      keelDepth = aKeelDepth
   End Sub
   Public Sub SetNumberSails(ByVal aNumberSails As Integer)
      numberSails = aNumberSails
   End Sub
   Public Sub SetMotorType(ByVal aMotorType As String)
      motorType = aMotorType
   End Sub

End Class
```

Figure 8-8 Sailboat class definition

8

You can write one or more constructors for the subclass. The Sailboat constructor shown in Figure 8-8 accepts seven parameters, four for the attributes defined in the Boat superclass and three additional attributes for those defined in the Sailboat subclass:

```
'constructor (all seven attribute values as parameters)
Public Sub New(ByVal aStateRegistrationNo As String, _
 ByVal aLength As Double, _
 ByVal aManufacturer As String, ByVal aYear As Integer, _
 ByVal aKeelDepth As Double, ByVal aNumberSails As Integer, _
 ByVal aMotorType As String)
```

The Sailboat constructor uses the **MyBase** keyword and the **New** method to invoke the constructor of the Boat superclass, passing it the four arguments the Boat class expects: registration number, length, manufacturer, and year. This way, the Boat constructor can complete any processing it provides to populate its private attributes (including any validation, such as that added in Hands-on Exercise 1):

```
'invoke superclass constructor passing 4 values
MyBase.New(aStateRegistrationNo, aLength, aManufacturer, aYear)
```

The `MyBase.New` call must be the first statement in the constructor, and it is required unless the superclass includes a default constructor without parameters. In that case, the superclass default constructor is automatically invoked.

When the Boat constructor is finished executing, control returns to the Sailboat constructor where the three remaining attribute values are set using the Sailboat set accessor methods:

```
'set additional attribute values
SetKeelDepth(aKeelDepth)
SetNumberSails(aNumberSails)
SetMotorType(aMotorType)
```

When the Sailboat constructor executes, it creates a Sailboat instance that has 14 standard accessor methods (plus the TellAboutSelf method, to be discussed later) and values for seven attributes. A test program can create one or more Sailboat instances and invoke any of the 14 methods, and the test program does not need to worry about whether inheritance is involved. Each Sailboat instance behaves as one unit that encapsulates attribute values and methods. The test program does not need to know the structure of the original generalization/specialization hierarchy to use the Sailboat class.

Inheritance is a powerful technique because you as programmer do not need to know how the Boat class is written to extend it. You do not need access to the source code. (In fact, you can extend a compiled class written with C# or J# when creating a new class with VB .NET.) As with any class in VB .NET, you only need the constructor signature and any required method signatures. Then you can extend the class as required.

Testing the Sailboat Subclass

Code that tests the Sailboat class is shown in Figure 8-9, with the output in Figure 8-10. This code is included in the event procedure for the button labeled "Test Sailboat Subclass" on the Boat Tester form. Two Sailboat instances are created using seven arguments each: the registration number, length, manufacturer, model year, keel depth, number of sails, and motor type. The getter methods are used to verify that the values are set correctly. Note that each Sailboat instance inherits the ability to get and set the four attribute values defined by the Boat class. When you look at the test code, you cannot tell that Sailboat is a subclass. The tester instantiates Sailboat and gets values back for seven attributes. The sequence diagram for the Sailboat test is shown in Figure 8-11.


```
Private Sub btnSailboat_Click(ByVal sender As System.Object, _
ByVal e As System.EventArgs) Handles btnSailboat.Click

   Console.WriteLine("Begin Sailboat Test:")

   'declare 2 Sailboat references
   Dim boat1 As Sailboat
   Dim boat2 As Sailboat

   'instantiate 2 Sailboats
   boat1 = New Sailboat("MO1234", 28, "Tartan", 2001, 4, 2, "outboard")
   boat2 = New Sailboat("CA9876", 32, "Catalina", 2003, 5, 3, "inboard")

   'invoke getter methods for boat1
   Console.WriteLine("Boat No: " & boat1.GetStateRegistrationNo())
   Console.WriteLine("Length: " & boat1.GetLength())
   Console.WriteLine("Manufacturer: " & boat1.GetManufacturer())
   Console.WriteLine("Year: " & boat1.GetYear())
   Console.WriteLine("Keel depth: " & boat1.GetKeelDepth())
   Console.WriteLine("Number of sails: " & boat1.GetNumberSails())
   Console.WriteLine("Motor type: " & boat1.GetMotorType())

   'invoke getter methods for boat2
   Console.WriteLine("Boat No: " & boat2.GetStateRegistrationNo())
   Console.WriteLine("Length: " & boat2.GetLength())
   Console.WriteLine("Manufacturer: " & boat2.GetManufacturer())
   Console.WriteLine("Year: " & boat2.GetYear())
   Console.WriteLine("Keel depth: " & boat2.GetKeelDepth())
   Console.WriteLine("Number of sails: " & boat2.GetNumberSails())
   Console.WriteLine("Motor type: " & boat2.GetMotorType())

End Sub
```

Figure 8-9 Event procedure code to test Sailboat class

```
Begin Sailboat Test:
Boat No: MO1234
Length: 28
Manufacturer: Tartan
Year: 2001
Keel depth: 4
Number of sails: 2
Motor type: outboard
Boat No: CA9876
Length: 32
Manufacturer: Catalina
Year: 2003
Keel depth: 5
Number of sails: 3
Motor type: inboard
```

Figure 8-10 Sailboat test code output

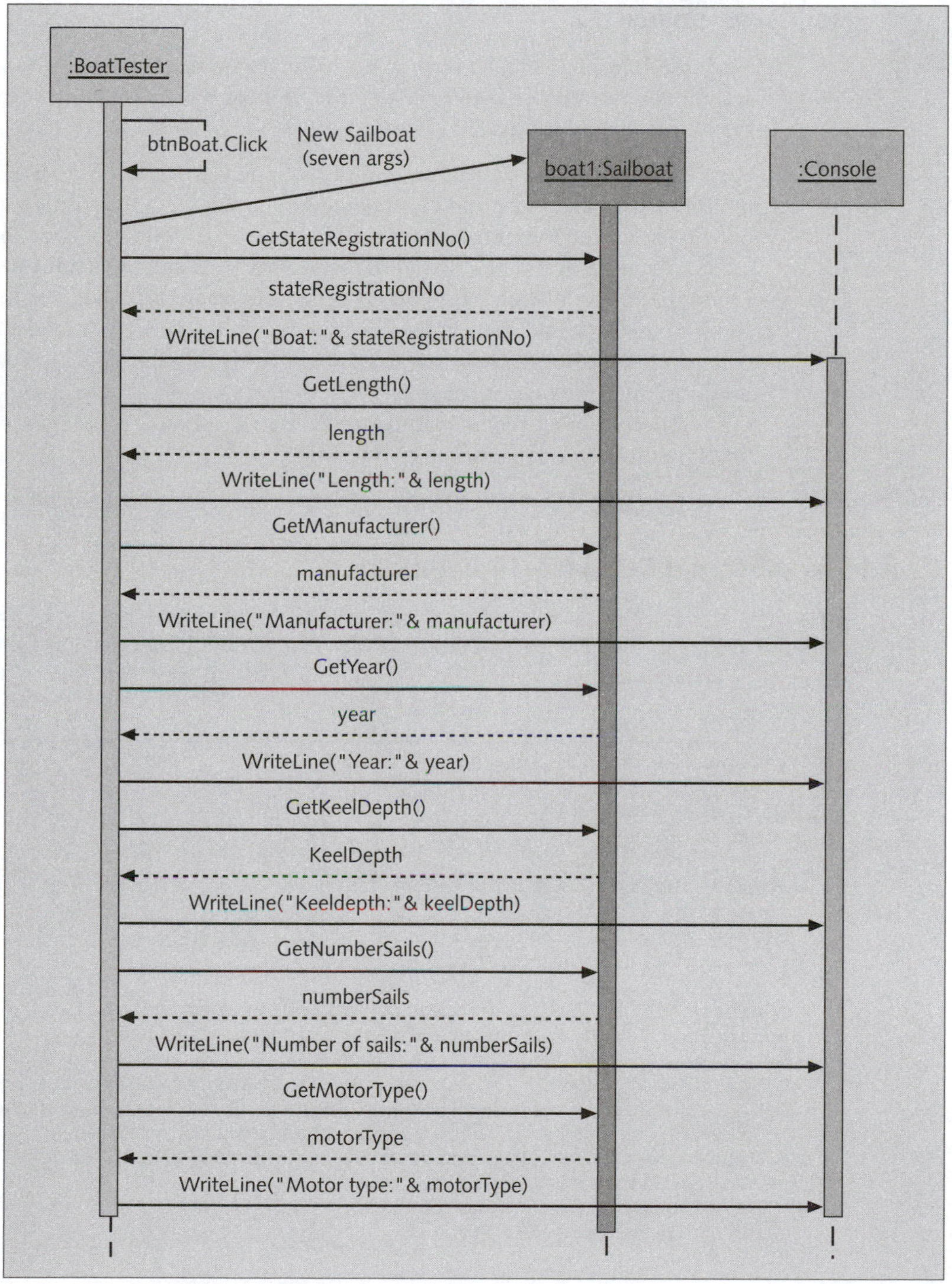

Figure 8-11 Sequence diagram for Sailboat test code

Hands-on Exercise 2

1. With the Example1 project open in VB .NET, examine the code for Sailboat.vb and for the event procedure for testing the Sailboat subclass. Run the example and verify that the output matches Figure 8-10.
2. Recall that you added validation to the Boat superclass, which is now inherited by Sailboat. Add a button and event procedure to the form to test the validation of Sailboat for the four attributes inherited from Boat. Write test code that creates sailboats with invalid values similar to the tester you wrote in Hands-on Exercise 1 to test that the validation sets values to defaults as planned. Rebuild and run the application. Click your new button and verify that the validation works. Click the original **Test Sailboat Subclass** button and verify that the valid boat data still results in the same output as before. Note that you would have to add validation to the additional three Sailboat methods to validate those values. For now, only the first four attributes of Sailboat have validation.
3. Leave the example open in VB .NET for the next Hands-on Exercise.

Adding a Second Subclass—Powerboat

Powerboat is the second subclass of Boat. The VB .NET source code for the Powerboat class is shown in Figure 8-12. Note that Powerboat also extends the Boat class, and the Powerboat class can be added without affecting the Sailboat class or the Boat class.

```
' Powerboat -- a subclass of Boat

Public Class Powerboat
   Inherits Boat

   'attributes in addition to the four
   'inherited from Boat
   Private numberEngines As Integer
   Private fuelType As String

   'constructor (all six attribute values as parameters)
   Public Sub New(ByVal aStateRegistrationNo As String, _
    ByVal aLength As Double, _
    ByVal aManufacturer As String, ByVal aYear As Integer, _
    ByVal aNumberEngines As Integer, ByVal aFuelType As String)
      'invoke superclass constructor passing four values
      MyBase.New(aStateRegistrationNo, aLength, aManufacturer, aYear)
      'set additional attribute values
      SetNumberEngines(aNumberEngines)
      SetFuelType(aFuelType)
   End Sub
```

```
    'TellAboutSelf method overrides then invokes superclass method
    'then concatenates two additional attribute values
    Public Overrides Function TellAboutSelf() As String
       Return (MyBase.TellAboutSelf() & ", " _
       & numberEngines & ", " _
       & fuelType)
    End Function

    'Get accessor methods
    Public Function GetNumberEngines() As Integer
       Return numberEngines
    End Function
    Public Function GetFuelType() As String
       Return fuelType
    End Function

    'Set accessor methods
    Public Sub SetNumberEngines(ByVal aNumberEngines As Integer)
       numberEngines = aNumberEngines
    End Sub
    Public Sub SetFuelType(ByVal aFuelType As String)
       fuelType = aFuelType
    End Sub

End Class
```

Figure 8-12 Powerboat class definition

The Powerboat class declares two attributes: `numberEngines` and `fuelType`. The constructor for Powerboat expects six parameters, four required by Boat plus two additional attributes for Powerboat. Similar to the Sailboat constructor, the Powerboat constructor also invokes the superclass constructor, using `MyBase.New` and passing the four arguments expected by the Boat class. Then the two remaining attributes are assigned using the setter methods of Powerboat:

```
'constructor (all six attribute values as parameters)
Public Sub New(ByVal aStateRegistrationNo As String, _
 ByVal aLength As Double, _
 ByVal aManufacturer As String, ByVal aYear As Integer, _
 ByVal aNumberEngines As Integer, ByVal aFuelType As String)
   'invoke superclass constructor passing four values
   MyBase.New(aStateRegistrationNo, aLength, aManufacturer, aYear)
   'set additional attribute values
   SetNumberEngines(aNumberEngines)
   SetFuelType(aFuelType)
End Sub
```

Now that you have created two subclasses of Boat, you can use both classes as needed. For example, a test program can create a few sailboats and a few powerboats, and get back information from any of the boats. Figure 8-13 shows the test code that creates both types of boats in the `btnSailAndPower_Click` event procedure. The output for the test program is shown in Figure 8-14, and the partial sequence diagram is shown in Figure 8-15. Note that the getter methods are used to test these subclasses. The TellAboutSelf method will be discussed later in this chapter.

```
Private Sub btnSailAndPower_Click(ByVal sender As System.Object, _
ByVal e As System.EventArgs) Handles btnSailAndPower.Click

   Console.WriteLine("Begin Sail and Powerboat Test:")

   'declare 2 Sailboat and 2 Powerboat references
   Dim boat1 As Sailboat
   Dim boat2 As Sailboat
   Dim boat3 As Powerboat
   Dim boat4 As Powerboat

   'instantiate 2 Sailboats and 2 Powerboats
   boat1 = New Sailboat("MO1234", 28, "Tartan", 2001, 4, 2, "outboard")
   boat2 = New Sailboat("CA9876", 32, "Catalina", 2003, 5, 3, "inboard")
   boat3 = New Powerboat("GA4567", 34, "Bayliner", 2002, 2, "gas")
   boat4 = New Powerboat("MO5678", 24, "Searay", 2003, 2, "gas")

   'invoke getter methods for Sailboat boat1 (7 attributes)
   Console.WriteLine("Boat No: " & boat1.GetStateRegistrationNo())
   Console.WriteLine("Length: " & boat1.GetLength())
   Console.WriteLine("Manufacturer: " & boat1.GetManufacturer())
   Console.WriteLine("Year: " & boat1.GetYear())
   Console.WriteLine("Keel depth: " & boat1.GetKeelDepth())
   Console.WriteLine("Number of sails: " & boat1.GetNumberSails())
   Console.WriteLine("Motor type: " & boat1.GetMotorType())

   'invoke getter methods for Sailboat boat2 (7 attributes)
   Console.WriteLine("Boat No: " & boat2.GetStateRegistrationNo())
   Console.WriteLine("Length: " & boat2.GetLength())
   Console.WriteLine("Manufacturer: " & boat2.GetManufacturer())
   Console.WriteLine("Year: " & boat2.GetYear())
   Console.WriteLine("Keel depth: " & boat2.GetKeelDepth())
   Console.WriteLine("Number of sails: " & boat2.GetNumberSails())
   Console.WriteLine("Motor type: " & boat2.GetMotorType())

   'invoke getter methods for Powerboat boat3 (6 attributes)
   Console.WriteLine("Boat No: " & boat3.GetStateRegistrationNo())
   Console.WriteLine("Length: " & boat3.GetLength())
   Console.WriteLine("Manufacturer: " & boat3.GetManufacturer())
   Console.WriteLine("Year: " & boat3.GetYear())
   Console.WriteLine("Number engines: " & boat3.GetNumberEngines())
   Console.WriteLine("Fuel type: " & boat3.GetFuelType())

   'invoke getter methods for Powerboat boat4 (6 attributes)
   Console.WriteLine("Boat No: " & boat4.GetStateRegistrationNo())
   Console.WriteLine("Length: " & boat4.GetLength())
   Console.WriteLine("Manufacturer: " & boat4.GetManufacturer())
```

```
    Console.WriteLine("Year: " & boat4.GetYear())
    Console.WriteLine("Number engines: " & boat4.GetNumberEngines())
    Console.WriteLine("Fuel type: " & boat4.GetFuelType())

End Sub
```

Figure 8-13 Event procedure code to test both Sailboat and Powerboat

```
Begin Sail and Powerboat Test:
Boat No: MO1234
Length: 28
Manufacturer: Tartan
Year: 2001
Keel depth: 4
Number of sails: 2
Motor type: outboard
Boat No: CA9876
Length: 32
Manufacturer: Catalina
Year: 2003
Keel depth: 5
Number of sails: 3
Motor type: inboard
Boat No: GA4567
Length: 34
Manufacturer: Bayliner
Year: 2002
Number engines: 2
Fuel type: gas
Boat No: MO5678
Length: 24
Manufacturer: Searay
Year: 2003
Number engines: 2
Fuel type: gas
```

Figure 8-14 Sailboat and Powerboat test output

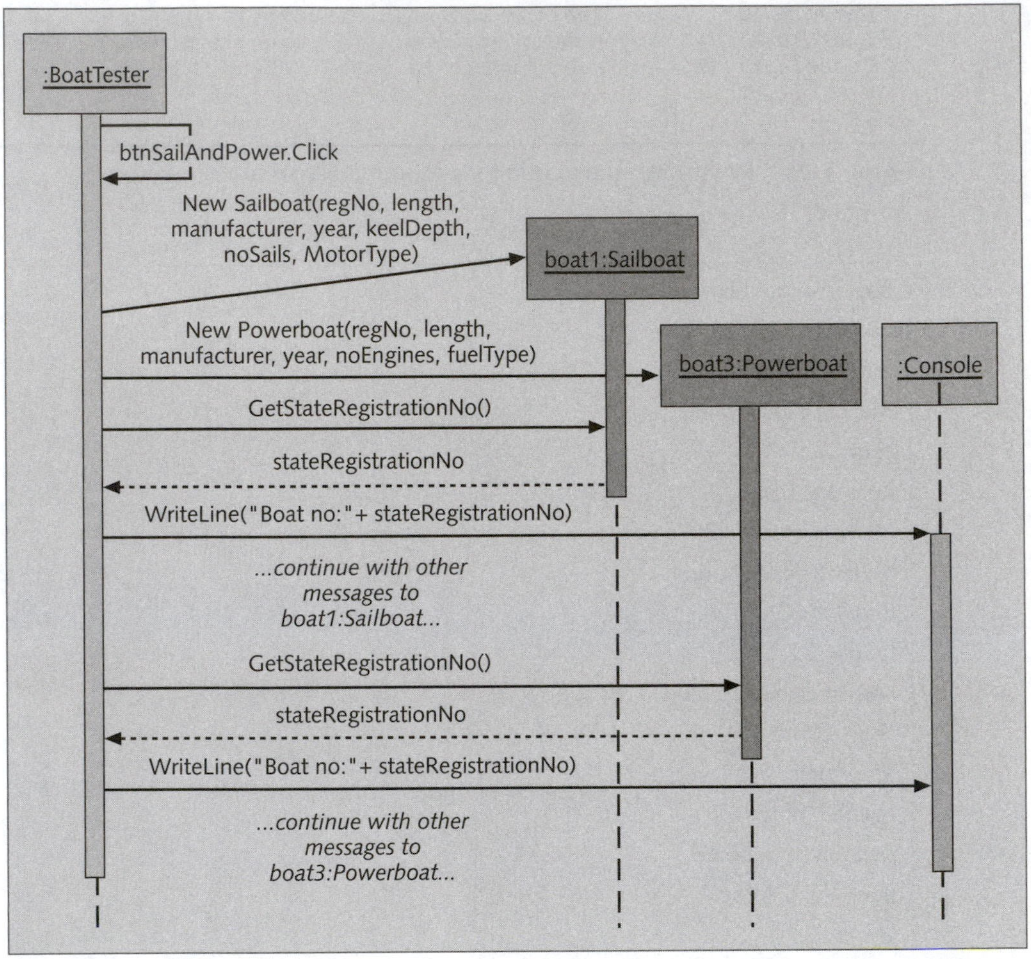

Figure 8-15 Partial sequence diagram for Sailboat and Powerboat test code

Once the boats are created, you can invoke the four getter methods inherited from the Boat class for either the sailboats or the powerboats. However, the sailboats have three additional getter methods that powerboats do not have. Powerboats have two additional getter methods that sailboats do not have. You cannot ask a powerboat for its number of sails. You cannot ask a sailboat for its number of engines.

Hands-on Exercise 3

1. With the Example1 project open in VB .NET, examine the Powerboat class definition in the Powerboat.vb source code file. Run the application and verify that the Test Sail and Powerboat test code produces the output shown in Figure 8-14.

2. Add a button and event procedure to the form to test the validation of Powerboat for the four attributes inherited from Boat. Write test code that creates powerboats with invalid values similar to the test code you wrote for Sailboat in Hands-on Exercise 2 to test that the validation sets values to defaults as planned. Rebuild and run the application. Click your new button and verify that the validation works. Click the original **Test Sailboat and Powerboat** button and verify that the valid boat data still results in the same output as before.

3. The ToString method returns the type of object the reference variable points to. You can use ToString to get a string representation of the name of the class. For example, the statement `Console.WriteLine("Boat type is: " & boat1.ToString())` would display `Example1.Sailboat` to represent the namespace plus class name represented by `boat1`. Modify the test code that tests both Sailboat and Powerboat so each boat displays whether it is a sailboat or a powerboat using the ToString method.

4. Leave the example open in VB .NET for the next Hands-on Exercise.

Understanding Abstract and Final Classes

The Boat and Sailboat examples earlier demonstrated the Boat class, the Sailboat class, and the Powerboat class. First, Boat instances were created, and then Sailboat and Powerboat instances were created. These are all examples of **concrete classes**—classes that can be instantiated. Notice that a concrete class can have subclasses, as shown in the initial example.

Using the `MustInherit` Keyword

You can create a class that is not intended to be instantiated. Instead, the class is only used to extend into subclasses. This is called an *abstract class*, as discussed in Chapter 5. For example, Bradshaw Marina only leases slips for sailboats and powerboats, and a boat must be one type or the other. Boat instances alone will never be created (except to be tested, as in Hands-on Exercise 1). On the class diagram, an abstract class is shown with its class name in italics.

The **`MustInherit`** keyword is used in the class header to declare an abstract class with VB .NET. To make the Boat class abstract, the header would read:

```
Public MustInherit Class Boat
```

The Sailboat and Powerboat classes can extend Boat exactly as before. But if the Boat class is abstract, the program that tests the Boat class results in a compile error saying that the **`New`** keyword cannot be used with a class declared with **`MustInherit`**. Therefore, never try to instantiate an abstract class; always extend it and then instantiate the subclass. The benefit of having the Boat superclass is that different types of boats can extend it; you do not have to rewrite code common to all boats. Use abstract classes to facilitate reuse. But remember, superclasses do not have to be abstract. The Slip class, for example, is a concrete class with a subclass named CoveredSlip. Bradshaw does want to instantiate Slip as well as CoveredSlip.

Using the `NotInheritable` Keyword

The previous examples show that classes are easy to extend, and that you do not need to have the source code for a class to extend it. Sometimes a class is created that should *not* be extended. For example, consider a class in a payroll program named Paycheck. The Paycheck class might have a method for calculating the pay amount. If the Paycheck class could be extended, you could add a method that changes the amount of a paycheck, bypassing validation and other controls that have been designed into the payroll system. Therefore, it might be desirable for security purposes to restrict the ability to extend a class.

The **`NotInheritable`** keyword is used to declare that a class cannot be extended. For example, if Bradshaw did not want the Powerboat class to be extended, the class header would be:

```
Public NotInheritable Class Powerboat
    Inherits Boat
```

Hands-on Exercise 4

1. Return to the original Boat.vb source code file in Example 1 and change the Boat class so it is abstract by inserting the **`MustInherit`** keyword. Rebuild the project. What happens?
2. Comment out (using the single quote character at the beginning of each line) all code in the `btnBoat_Click` event procedure that tests the Boat superclass and rebuild the project. (If you are using the project you modified with validation, you will have to comment out the `btnTestBoatValidation` event procedure also.) What happens now? When you click the buttons to test Sailboat and both Sailboat and Powerboat, the event procedures should still run correctly even though Boat is now abstract.
3. Change the Boat class to **`NotInheritable`** and rebuild the project. What happens?
4. You can change Boat back to abstract by leaving the **`MustInherit`** keyword for the rest of the chapter examples if you have commented out the event procedures that instantiate Boat. Otherwise, you can leave Boat as a concrete class for the next exercises.
5. Leave Example 1 open in VB .NET for the next Hands-on Exercise.

OVERRIDING A SUPERCLASS METHOD

A powerful capability of a subclass is to override a method contained in its superclass. **Method overriding** occurs when the method in the subclass will be invoked instead of the method in the superclass if both methods have the same signature. Recall that a method's signature consists of its name, return type, and parameter list. For example, the signature of the Sailboat method **SetNumberSails** with one **Integer** parameter is:

```
Public Sub SetNumberSails(ByVal aNumberSails As Integer)
```

Overriding a method allows the subclass not only to extend the superclass but also to modify the behavior of the superclass. Method overriding is different from method overloading, discussed in Chapter 7. Overloading means that two or more methods in the same class have the same name but a different return type or parameter list. Overriding means methods in both the superclass and the subclass have the same signature (the same name, return type, and parameter list).

Overriding the Boat TellAboutSelf Method

Method overriding is demonstrated by the TellAboutSelf method in Boat, Sailboat, and Powerboat. The TellAboutSelf method was shown as a custom method added to the Slip class in Chapter 7. You can add a TellAboutSelf method to classes to make it easier to get information about an instance of the class, including the Boat class. If you want the method to be overridable, include the **Overridable** keyword in the method header. You can then override the Boat TellAboutSelf method in the Sailboat class to allow the Sailboat class to tell about itself in its own way. The TellAboutSelf method for Boat is coded as follows, shown previously in Figure 8-2:

```
'TellAboutSelf method
Public Overridable Function TellAboutSelf() As String
   Return (stateRegistrationNo & ", " & length & ", " & _
     manufacturer & ", " & year)
End Function
```

When you test the Boat class as a concrete class, the TellAboutSelf method would return information about the registration number, length, manufacturer, and model year of the boat. If Boat has a Sailboat subclass without a TellAboutSelf method, the TellAboutSelf method inherited from Boat would return the first four attributes of the sailboat. But how can you find the other sailboat details?

Overriding the method is accomplished by using the same TellAboutSelf method signature in the subclass Sailboat but with the **Overrides** keyword in place of the **Overridable** keyword. The statements in the subclass method control what the system does when a sailboat instance is asked to tell about itself. The superclass method in Boat is ignored (overridden). The TellAboutSelf method written for Sailboat, shown previously in Figure 8-8, is written as follows:

```
'TellAboutSelf overrides but does not invoke superclass method
Public Overrides Function TellAboutSelf() As String
   Return (GetStateRegistrationNo() & ", " & GetLength() & ", " & _
   GetManufacturer() & ", " & GetYear() & ", " _
   & keelDepth & ", " & numberSails & ", " & motorType)
End Function
```

The Sailboat class TellAboutSelf method invokes the getter methods of the Boat class to get values for those attributes and then concatenates the values of the additional three sailboat attributes.

Overriding and Invoking a Superclass Method

Sometimes you might want to override a method by extending what the method does. For example, the Boat TellAboutSelf method already includes statements that return values for the four attributes that all boats have. The preceding Sailboat method replicates this code when it overrides the method.

The TellAboutSelf method demonstrated in the Powerboat class shows another approach. When the Powerboat TellAboutSelf method is invoked, it invokes the superclass method using the **`MyBase`** keyword along with the superclass method name. For example, in the statement `MyBase.TellAboutSelf()`, **`MyBase`** refers to the superclass and TellAboutSelf is the superclass method invoked. That way the statements in the superclass method are executed first, returning information to the subclass method. Then the subclass method continues executing statements specific to the powerboat. The returned string will contain information about all six of the powerboat attributes. The Powerboat TellAboutSelf method shown previously in Figure 8-12 is as follows:

```
'TellAboutSelf method overrides then invokes superclass method
'then concatenates two additional attribute values
Public Overrides Function TellAboutSelf() As String
   Return (MyBase.TellAboutSelf() & ", " _
   & numberEngines & ", " _
   & fuelType)
End Function
```

Testing Two Method-Overriding Approaches

The last event procedure on the Boat Tester form demonstrates method overriding in both Sailboat and Powerboat, shown in Figure 8-16. First, four boats are created. Next, the TellAboutSelf method is invoked for each boat.

```
Private Sub btnTellAboutSelf_Click(ByVal sender As System.Object, _
ByVal e As System.EventArgs) Handles btnTellAboutSelf.Click

   Console.WriteLine("Begin Sail and Powerboat TellAboutSelf Test:")

   'declare 2 Sailboat and 2 Powerboat references
   Dim boat1 As Sailboat
   Dim boat2 As Sailboat
   Dim boat3 As Powerboat
   Dim boat4 As Powerboat
```

```
    'instantiate 2 Sailboats and 2 Powerboats
    boat1 = New Sailboat("MO1234", 28, "Tartan", 2001, 4, 2, "outboard")
    boat2 = New Sailboat("CA9876", 32, "Catalina", 2003, 5, 3, "inboard")
    boat3 = New Powerboat("GA4567", 34, "Bayliner", 2002, 2, "gas")
    boat4 = New Powerboat("MO5678", 24, "Searay", 2003, 2, "gas")

    'invoke TellAboutSelf methods for Sailboats and Powerboats
    Console.WriteLine("Sailboat: " & boat1.TellAboutSelf())
    Console.WriteLine("Sailboat: " & boat2.TellAboutSelf())
    Console.WriteLine("Powerboat: " & boat3.TellAboutSelf())
    Console.WriteLine("Powerboat: " & boat4.TellAboutSelf())

End Sub
```

Figure 8-16 Event procedure for testing Sailboat and Powerboat TellAboutSelf method (polymorphism)

The output produced is shown in Figure 8-17, with all seven attributes listed for the sailboats and all six attributes listed for the powerboats. The partial sequence diagram for the test code is shown in Figure 8-18. Note how simple the interaction is now that each boat takes responsibility for telling about itself.

```
Begin Sail and Powerboat TellAboutSelf Test:
Sailboat: MO1234, 28, Tartan, 2001, 4, 2, outboard
Sailboat: CA9876, 32, Catalina, 2003, 5, 3, inboard
Powerboat: GA4567, 34, Bayliner, 2002, 2, gas
Powerboat: MO5678, 24, Searay, 2003, 2, gas
```

Figure 8-17 Sailboat and Powerboat TellAboutSelf output

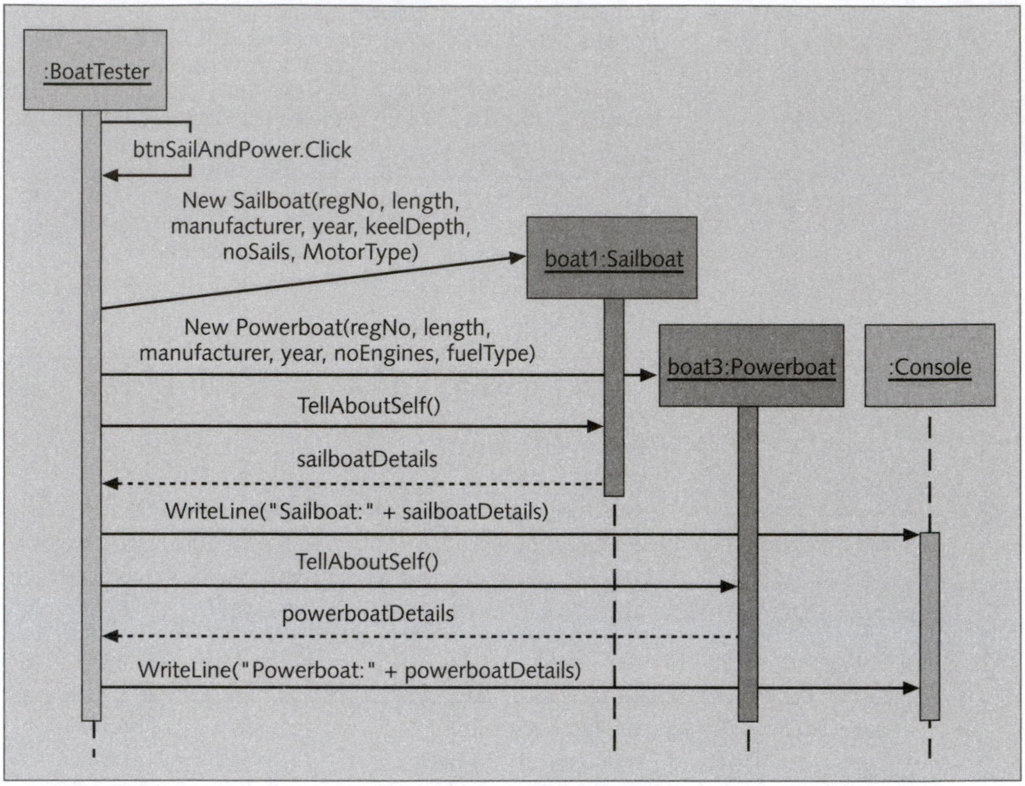

Figure 8-18 Sequence diagram for Sailboat and Powerboat TellAboutSelf test code

Hands-on Exercise 5

1. With the Example1 project open in VB .NET, examine and then run the Sailboat and Powerboat event procedure code that uses the TellAboutSelf methods. Verify that the output matches the output shown in Figure 8-17.
2. Modify Sailboat so its TellAboutSelf method invokes the superclass method, then extends it as done in Powerboat. Run the test code to verify that the output remains the same.
3. Add a new subclass of Sailboat named CruisingSailboat with a constructor and accessor methods. One additional attribute of CruisingSailboat stores the name of the life-raft manufacturer. Include a TellAboutSelf method that overrides and then invokes the Sailboat method and provides information on all attributes of a cruising sailboat.
4. Add another button to the form with an event procedure that creates two instances of three types of boats—sailboats, powerboats, and cruising sailboats—and displays information about each boat using TellAboutSelf. Build and run the project.
5. You can close this example, but leave VB .NET open for the next Hands-on Exercise.

Overriding, Polymorphism, and Dynamic Binding

The previous method-overriding example demonstrates one form of polymorphism and shows a clear benefit of polymorphism. Recall that polymorphism means objects of different classes can respond to the same message in their own way. Each subclass has its own way of telling about itself. As long as you know that the superclass has a TellAboutSelf method, you do not need to keep track of the specific subclass involved. You can send a message to the instance asking it to tell about itself. The instance will always respond, either by invoking the superclass method or by overriding it. Processing is simplified when it is not necessary to test to see what type of instance it is before sending the message. Instead, the responsibility for responding appropriately is left to the instance.

Consider an example where a payroll system produces paychecks for all employees in a company. The system uses different methods to calculate the pay amount for each type of employee. If the Employee class has a method named CalculatePay, subclasses such as HourlyEmployee, SalaryEmployee, and ManagementEmployee might override the CalculatePay method and calculate pay differently. The payroll system needs to go through all employee instances and ask each to calculate the pay without having to know what type of employee each instance represents. The responsibility for handling the calculation is delegated to the instance, simplifying the processing required by the system. System maintenance is also simplified, because as new types of employees are added, or as pay calculations are changed for one type of employee, the change does not necessarily affect the rest of the system.

VB .NET uses **dynamic binding** to resolve which method to invoke when the system runs and finds more than one method with the same name in a generalization/specialization hierarchy for a class. Making the decision at runtime provides flexibility when adding new subclasses that override superclass methods. For example, if a new type of powerboat is added (perhaps a personal watercraft) with its own TellAboutSelf method, any applications that interact with boats can invoke the new TellAboutSelf method as long as the object reference used was a personal watercraft.

Understanding Private Versus Protected Access

The previous Boat examples include attributes that are all declared as private, as described in Chapter 6. Declaring an attribute as private using the `Private` keyword means no other object can directly read or modify the value of the attribute. Instead, other objects must use the methods of the class to get or set values. This is what encapsulation and information hiding mean. By making the attributes private, you protect the integrity of the values of the attributes. No values can be changed without following validation procedures included in the set accessor methods. Similarly, no values can be retrieved unless a public getter method has been included for the attribute.

Private access also limits the ability of an instance of the subclass to directly access attributes defined by the superclass. This is ordinarily appropriate because any method of the subclass that needs the value of an attribute defined in the superclass can invoke the get accessor method to get the value. Notice that in the TellAboutSelf method for Sailboat the values of the attributes declared in Boat are accessed using the Boat get accessor methods, as shown again in the following code:

```
'TellAboutSelf overrides but does not invoke superclass method
'invokes getter methods of Boat
Public Overrides Function TellAboutSelf() As String
   Return (GetStateRegistrationNo() & ", " & GetLength() & ", " & _
   GetManufacturer() & ", " & GetYear() & ", " _
   & keelDepth & ", " & numberSails & ", " & motorType)
End Function
```

You can declare the attributes of a superclass so they can be accessed directly by methods in the subclass. **Protected access** means that attribute values can be directly accessed by subclasses. For example, boat attributes can be changed to protected access using the **`Protected`** keyword:

```
Public Class Boat

   'attributes
   Protected stateRegistrationNo As String
   Protected length As Single
   Protected manufacturer As String
   Protected year As Integer
```

The Sailboat TellAboutSelf method can then be changed to directly access the values of the attributes as follows:

```
'TellAboutSelf overrides but does not invoke superclass method
'directly accesses Boat protected attribute values
Public Overrides Function TellAboutSelf() As String
   Return (stateRegistrationNo & ", " & length & ", " & _
   manufacturer & ", " & year & ", " _
   & keelDepth & ", " & numberSails & ", " & motorType)
End Function
```

Note that the first four attribute values are defined in the Boat class. The last three are defined in the Sailboat class (and remain private rather than protected). A tester program that creates a sailboat using the revised Boat and Sailboat classes and invokes its TellAboutSelf method will work as expected.

Although you can declare attributes as public using the **`Public`** keyword, meaning that any object can directly access the value, avoid this technique because it violates encapsulation and information hiding. Similarly, you can restrict access to attributes in the same application using the **`Friend`** keyword or the **`Protected Friend`** keyword, but you should also avoid this technique for attributes.

As discussed in Chapter 3, a *local variable* is accessible only to statements within a method where it is declared, and it exists only as long as the method is executing. Local variables do not need to be declared as private, protected, friend, or public.

You also can declare methods using keywords **`Friend`**, **`Protected`**, or **`Private`**. Private methods can only be invoked from a method within the class. Not even subclass methods can invoke a private method of its superclass. Protected methods, however, can be invoked by a method in a subclass.

INTRODUCING THE LEASE SUBCLASSES AND ABSTRACT METHODS

For the Bradshaw Marina case, described in Chapter 5, the class diagram includes three generalization/specialization hierarchies that require inheritance: Boat, Slip, and Lease. Now that you have learned to use basic inheritance concepts with the Boat subclasses, this chapter continues to demonstrate some additional inheritance-related concepts using the Lease subclasses. The Lease class generalization/specialization hierarchy is also the first example where problem domain classes contain attributes that hold references to other objects rather than to primitive variables or strings. The problem domain classes for the Lease hierarchy have attributes that are references to DateTime instances. Business systems use dates extensively, so you also must understand how to use them. DateTime methods were introduced in Chapter 4.

The Lease generalization/specialization hierarchy is shown in the class diagram in Figure 8-19. Lease has two subclasses: AnnualLease and DailyLease.

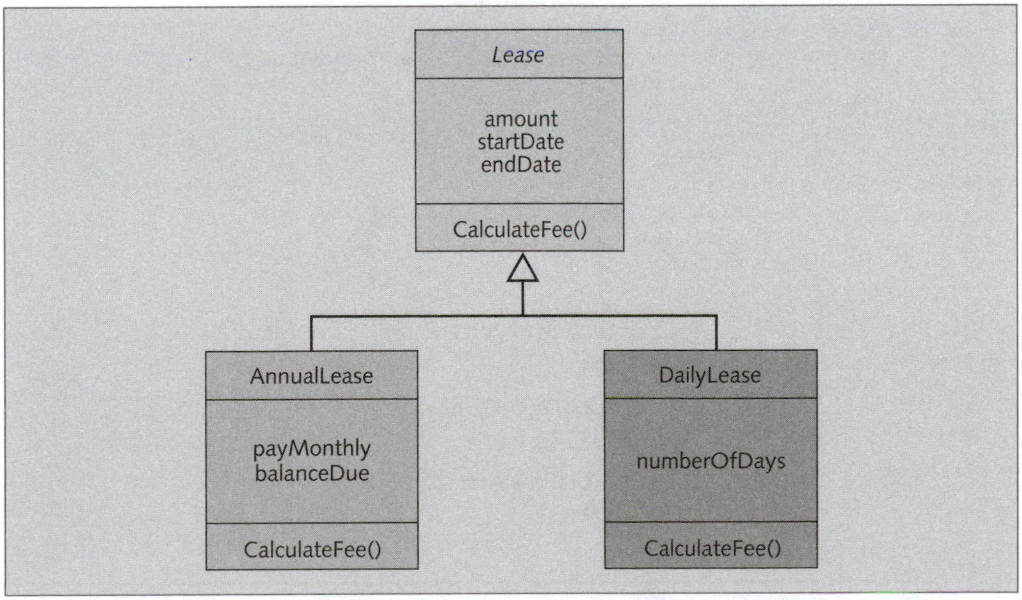

Figure 8-19 Lease generalization/specialization hierarchy

The Lease class is the superclass, and the class definition is shown in Figure 8-20. Lease has attributes for amount, start date, and end date. The Lease class is defined as abstract and includes the **MustInherit** keyword in the header. You can assume it has been tested previously before making it abstract.

```
' Lease -- an initial abstract Lease Class
' with an abstract method

Public MustInherit Class Lease

   'attributes
   Private amount As Double
   Private startDate As DateTime
   Private endDate As DateTime

   'constructor (1 parameter)
   Public Sub New(ByVal aStartDate As DateTime)
      SetStartDate(aStartDate)
      SetEndDate(Nothing)       ' endDate set by subclass
      SetAmount(0)
   End Sub

   'TellAboutSelf method
   Public Overridable Function TellAboutSelf() As String
      Return (startDate & ", " & endDate & ", " & amount)
   End Function

   'custom method CalculateFee based on slip width
   'abstract method all subclasses must implement
   Public MustOverride Function CalculateFee(ByVal aWidth As Integer) _
   As Single

   'Get accessor methods
   Public Function GetStartDate() As DateTime
      Return startDate
   End Function
   Public Function GetEndDate() As DateTime
      Return endDate
   End Function
   Public Function GetAmount() As Double
      Return amount
   End Function

   'Set accessor methods
   Public Sub SetStartDate(ByVal aStartDate As DateTime)
      startDate = aStartDate
   End Sub
   Public Sub SetEndDate(ByVal anEndDate As DateTime)
      endDate = anEndDate
   End Sub
   Public Sub SetAmount(ByVal anAmount As Double)
      amount = anAmount
   End Sub
End Class
```

Figure 8-20 Lease class definition

The three attributes declared in Lease include two reference variables for dates and one numeric value for the amount of the lease. The constructor accepts one parameter—a reference to a DateTime instance for the start date of the lease. The constructor sets the end date to **`Nothing`** and the amount of the lease to zero using standard setter methods. Subclasses set the end date and calculate the amount depending on the type of lease.

Adding an Abstract Method to Lease

Sometimes it is desirable to require that all subclasses include a method. For example, all Lease subclasses need a CalculateFee method because the subclasses are responsible for determining what the lease amount will be. Requiring all subclasses to have a method is also necessary for polymorphism. If a Lease subclass does not have a CalculateFee method, an error could occur if a lease instance without the method is asked to calculate a fee.

One way you can require that a subclass include, or implement, a method is to include an abstract method in the superclass. An **abstract method** is a method without any statements that must be overridden by all subclasses. If a class has an abstract method, the class must also be abstract. VB .NET uses the **`MustOverride`** keyword in the method header to declare an abstract method. Note that the Lease class has a method named CalculateFee that includes the **`MustOverride`** keyword. It accepts an `Integer` value representing the width of the slip and returns a `Single` value representing the fee for leasing the slip. But there is no method body. Because all types of leases must calculate the fee based on slip width, but each has its own way of doing it, an abstract method is used:

```
'custom method CalculateFee based on slip width
'an abstract method all subclasses must implement
Public MustOverride Function CalculateFee(ByVal aWidth As Integer) _
As Single
```

Implementing the AnnualLease Subclass

The class diagram in Figure 8-19 shows two Lease subclasses: AnnualLease and DailyLease. AnnualLease includes attributes `balanceDue` and `payMonthly`. The `balanceDue` attribute refers to the amount of the annual lease that remains unpaid. The `payMonthly` attribute is a `Boolean` that indicates whether monthly payments will be made for the annual lease. If the annual lease is paid monthly, `balanceDue` is initially set to eleven-twelfths of the lease amount, which assumes the first month is paid up front. If `payMonthly` is false, `balanceDue` will be zero.

The class definition for the AnnualLease class is shown in Figure 8-21. Although the class adds only two attributes, the constructor and some of the methods are more complex than previous examples.

```
' AnnualLease -- a subclass of Lease

Public Class AnnualLease
   Inherits Lease

   'attributes in addition to those inherited from Lease
   Private balanceDue As Single
   Private payMonthly As Boolean

   'constructor (three values as parameters)
   Public Sub New(ByVal aStartDate As DateTime, _
      ByVal aSlipWidth As Integer, _
      ByVal isPayMonthly As Boolean)
      'invoke superclass constructor
      MyBase.New(aStartDate)
      'calculate end date
      Dim yearLater as DateTime = aStartDate.AddYears(1)
      'invoke superclass method to set end date
      SetEndDate(yearLater)
      'invoke superclass SetAmount method after getting
      'fee amount from CalculateFee method
      SetAmount(CalculateFee(aSlipWidth))
      'set payMonthly
      SetPayMonthly(isPayMonthly)
      'set balance due if applicable
      If payMonthly Then
         setBalanceDue(GetAmount() - GetAmount()/12)
      Else
         SetBalanceDue(0)
      End If
   End Sub

   'custom method CalculateFee based on slip width
   Public Overrides Function CalculateFee(ByVal aWidth As Integer) _
   As Single
      Dim fee As Single
      Select Case aWidth
         Case 10
            fee = 800
         Case 12
            fee = 900
         Case 14
            fee = 1100
         Case 16
            fee = 1500
         Case Else
            fee = 0
```

```
      End Select
      Return fee
   End Function

   'TellAboutSelf overrides then invokes superclass method
   Public Overrides Function TellAboutSelf() As String
      Return MyBase.TellAboutSelf() & ", " _
      & balanceDue & ", " & payMonthly
   End Function

   'Get accessor methods
   Public Function GetBalanceDue() As Single
      Return balanceDue
   End Function
   Public Function GetPayMonthly() As Boolean
      Return payMonthly
   End Function

   'Set accessor methods
   Public Sub SetBalanceDue(ByVal aBalanceDue As Single)
      balanceDue = aBalanceDue
   End Sub
   Public Sub SetPayMonthly(ByVal isPayMonthly As Boolean)
      payMonthly = isPayMonthly
   End Sub

End Class
```

Figure 8-21 AnnualLease class definition with CalculateFee method

Be sure to include the **Inherits Lease** statement in the second line of the class header. Also be sure only to declare the additional attributes needed for an annual lease—**balanceDue** and **payMonthly**. The constructor accepts three parameters: the start date, the slip width, and the **Boolean payMonthly** value. The slip width value is needed to calculate the amount of the annual lease when the AnnualLease class is instantiated, although the slip width is not retained by the instance. This is the first example in this text that includes a parameter for the constructor that is not set as an attribute value. The **payMonthly** value is needed to calculate the balance due and is retained as an attribute value. The header for the AnnualLease constructor is:

```
'constructor (three values as parameters)
Public Sub New(ByVal aStartDate As DateTime, _
   ByVal aSlipWidth As Integer, _
   ByVal isPayMonthly As Boolean)
```

The constructor is more complex than previous examples. The first statement invokes the superclass constructor using the start date as an argument. The Lease constructor assigns the start date, sets the end date to **Nothing**, and sets the amount to zero, as discussed earlier.

Control then returns to the AnnualLease constructor, and the end date is calculated by adding one to the year of the start date using the **DateTime AddYears** method with an argument of 1. Then the SetEndDate method of the superclass is invoked to set the end date:

```
'calculate end date
Dim yearLater as DateTime = aStartDate.AddYears(1)
'invoke superclass method to set end date
SetEndDate(yearLater)
```

The next statement of the constructor also invokes a superclass method, this time the SetAmount method. But the amount is calculated first by invoking the CalculateFee method of AnnualLease, and the amount returned is immediately passed as an argument to SetAmount. The following example shows that method calls can be nested, and that they execute from the inside out (the CalculateFee method will be discussed in more detail later):

```
'invoke superclass SetAmount method after getting
'fee amount from CalculateFee method
SetAmount(CalculateFee(aSlipWidth))
```

The final statements set the **payMonthly** attribute value and then set the **balanceDue** attribute value. The **balanceDue** value is determined by the **Boolean payMonthly** value using an **If** block. If the lease is paid monthly, the balance due is eleven-twelfths of the lease amount; otherwise, the amount due is zero:

```
'set payMonthly
SetPayMonthly(isPayMonthly)
'set balance due if applicable
If payMonthly Then
   setBalanceDue(GetAmount() - GetAmount()/12)
Else
   SetBalanceDue(0)
End If
```

The Slip class demonstrated in Chapter 7 includes a method named LeaseSlip. This method calculated the fee for a lease based on the width of the slip to simplify the example. In the complete Bradshaw system, the Lease subclasses calculate the lease amount. Therefore, the CalculateFee method is now required in all Lease subclasses, and this is why the abstract method was added to the Lease superclass. The lease amount is calculated the same way as in the Slip example, using the width in a **Select Case** block and returning the fee. This method is invoked by the constructor before setting the amount of the annual lease, and it includes the **Overrides** keyword in the method header because it overrides the abstract method in Lease:

```
'custom method CalculateFee based on slip width
Public Overrides Function CalculateFee(ByVal aWidth As Integer) _
```

```
      As Single
         Dim fee As Single
         Select Case aWidth
            Case 10
               fee = 800
            Case 12
               fee = 900
            Case 14
               fee = 1100
            Case 16
               fee = 1500
            Case Else
               fee = 0
         End Select
         Return fee
      End Function
```

Implementing the DailyLease Subclass

The other Lease subclass is DailyLease, where a customer leases a slip for a short time, anywhere from a few days to several months. The DailyLease class definition is shown in Figure 8-22. A daily lease has one additional attribute—the number of days of the lease. This value is calculated based on the start date and end date. There are no monthly payments and no balance due for a daily lease.

```
' DailyLease -- a subclass of Lease

Public Class DailyLease
   Inherits Lease

   'attribute in addition to those inherited from Lease
   Private numberOfDays As Integer

   'constructor (three values as parameters)
   Public Sub New(ByVal aStartDate As DateTime, _
      ByVal anEndDate As DateTime, _
      ByVal aSlipWidth As Integer)
      'invoke superclass constructor
      MyBase.New(aStartDate)
      'calculate number of days
      Dim diff As System.TimeSpan
      diff = anEndDate.Subtract(aStartDate)
      Dim days as Integer = diff.Days()
      SetNumberOfDays(days)
      'invoke superclass method to set end date
      SetEndDate(anEndDate)
      'invoke superclass SetAmount method after getting
      'fee amount from CalculateFee method
      SetAmount(CalculateFee(aSlipWidth))
   End Sub
```

```
    'custom method CalculateFee based on slip width and number of days
    Public Overrides Function CalculateFee(ByVal aWidth As Integer) _
    As Single
       Dim fee As Single
       Select Case aWidth
          Case 10
             fee = 20 * numberOfDays
          Case 12
             fee = 25 * numberOfDays
          Case 14
             fee = 30 * numberOfDays
          Case 16
             fee = 35 * numberOfDays
          Case Else
             fee = 0
       End Select
       Return fee
    End Function

    'TellAboutSelf overrides then invokes superclass method
    Public Overrides Function TellAboutSelf() As String
       Return MyBase.TellAboutSelf() & ", " _
       & numberOfDays
    End Function

    'Get accessor method
    Public Function GetNumberOfDays() As Integer
       Return numberOfDays
    End Function

    'Set accessor method
    Public Sub SetNumberOfDays(ByVal aNumberOfDays As Integer)
       numberOfDays = aNumberOfDays
    End Sub

End Class
```

Figure 8-22 DailyLease class definition with CalculateFee method

The DailyLease constructor expects three parameters: the start date, end date, and slip width. AnnualLease calculates the end date based on the start date. DailyLease calculates the number of days based on the start date and the end date.

The constructor first invokes the superclass constructor passing the start date as an argument. Then the Subtract method of `DateTime` is used to return a TimeSpan instance (start date is subtracted from end date). The `Days` function of TimeSpan returns the number of days for the daily lease:

```
'calculate number of days
Dim diff As System.TimeSpan
diff = anEndDate.Subtract(aStartDate)
Dim days as Integer = diff.Days()
SetNumberOfDays(days)
```

The final statements of the DailyLease constructor invoke superclass methods to set the end date and the lease amount.

The CalculateFee method overrides the superclass abstract method, and the amount is calculated based on the slip width and the number of days of the lease. Slip width is passed as an argument from the constructor but is not retained. The number of days is calculated and set by the constructor. Note that even though the number of days is used in the calculation, it is not passed as an argument because the value is an attribute of the DailyLease class.

Testing the AnnualLease and DailyLease Classes

Now that you have two Lease subclasses, you can test them using the test code in the event procedures of the Chapter 8 Lease Tester form shown in Figure 8-23. One event procedure tests the AnnualLease subclass, shown in Figure 8-24.

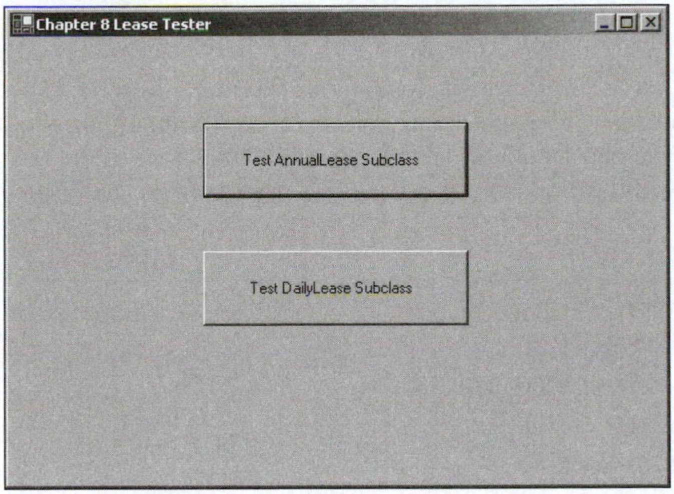

Figure 8-23 Lease Tester Windows form

```
Private Sub btnAnnualLease_Click(ByVal sender As System.Object, _
ByVal e As System.EventArgs) Handles btnAnnualLease.Click

   'instantiate some test dates
   Dim newDate As New DateTime(2004, 3, 15)
   Dim anotherDate As New DateTime(2004, 4, 10)

   'instantiate two annual leases
   Dim lease1 As New AnnualLease(newDate, 14, True)
   Dim lease2 As New AnnualLease(anotherDate, 16, False)
```

```
    'retrieve information about the annual lease
    Console.WriteLine("AnnualLease 1 information")
    Console.WriteLine("Dates: " & lease1.GetStartDate() & " " _
     & lease1.GetEndDate())
    Console.WriteLine("Amount/Balance/PayMonthly: " _
     & lease1.GetAmount() & " " & lease1.GetBalanceDue() & " " _
     & lease1.GetPayMonthly())

    'retrieve information about second annual lease
    Console.WriteLine("AnnualLease 2 information")
    Console.WriteLine("Dates: " & lease2.GetStartDate() & " " _
     & lease2.GetEndDate())
    Console.WriteLine("Amount/Balance/PayMonthly: " _
     & lease2.GetAmount() & " " & lease2.GetBalanceDue() & " " _
     & lease2.GetPayMonthly())

End Sub
```

Figure 8-24 Event procedure to test the AnnualLease class

To test the AnnualLease class, the test code first creates two dates to use for start dates for the leases. Next, it instantiates two annual leases, one with **`payMonthly`** true and one with **`payMonthly`** false. Different slip widths are used as well. The output to the console, shown in Figure 8-25, displays information about each annual lease using the getter methods.

```
AnnualLease 1 information
Dates: 3/15/2004 3/15/2005
Amount/Balance/PayMonthly: 1100 1008.333 True
AnnualLease 2 information
Dates: 4/10/2004 4/10/2005
Amount/Balance/PayMonthly: 1500 0 False
```

Figure 8-25 AnnualLease test code output

To test the DailyLease class, the test code creates three dates and instantiates two daily leases using pairs of dates for start date and end date. Two different slip widths are used. The output displayed to the console shows information about each daily lease using the getter methods. The code for testing DailyLease is shown in Figure 8-26, and the output is shown in Figure 8-27.

```
Private Sub btnDailyLease_Click(ByVal sender As System.Object, _
ByVal e As System.EventArgs) Handles btnDailyLease.Click

   'instantiate some test dates
   Dim newDate As New DateTime(2004, 3, 15)
   Dim anotherDate As New DateTime(2004, 4, 10)
   Dim thirdDate As New DateTime(2004, 4, 21)

   'instantiate two daily leases
   Dim lease1 As New DailyLease(newDate, anotherDate, 14)
   Dim lease2 As New DailyLease(anotherDate, thirdDate, 16)

   'retrieve information about first daily lease
   Console.WriteLine("DailyLease 1 information")
   Console.WriteLine("Dates: " & lease1.GetStartDate() _
    & " " & lease1.GetEndDate())
   Console.WriteLine("Amount/Number of Days: " & lease1.GetAmount() _
    & " " & lease1.GetNumberOfDays())

   'retrieve information about second daily lease
   Console.WriteLine("DailyLease 2 information")
   Console.WriteLine("Dates: " & lease2.GetStartDate() _
    & " " & lease2.GetEndDate())
   Console.WriteLine("Amount/Number of Days: " & lease2.GetAmount() _
    & " " & lease2.GetNumberOfDays())

End Sub
```


Figure 8-26 Event procedure to test DailyLease class

```
DailyLease 1 information
Dates: 3/15/2004 4/10/2004
Amount/Number of Days: 780 26
DailyLease 2 information
Dates: 4/10/2004 4/21/2004
Amount/Number of Days: 385 11
```

Figure 8-27 DailyLease test code output

Hands-on Exercise 6

1. Locate Example 2 in the folder Chap08\Examples\Ex02 in the book's data files. Copy the **Ex02** folder to the Chap08\Exercises folder in your work folder. Then open the project with VB .NET. Lease.vb, AnnualLease.vb, DailyLease.vb, and FormLeaseTester.vb should be included in the project. Build and run the example,

verifying that the Test AnnualLease Subclass and Test DailyLease Subclass buttons produce the output shown in Figures 8-25 and 8-27.

2. Temporarily remove the CalculateFee method from the AnnualLease class by inserting the comment character in front of each line of the method. Try to rebuild the project now that AnnualLease does not include the method. What happens? Remove the comment characters so AnnualLease compiles correctly.
3. Note that the Lease classes all include TellAboutSelf methods. Add a button to the Lease Tester form for testing both subclasses and their TellAboutSelf methods. Create at least two of each type of lease, and use an assortment of additional dates and slip widths. Build and run the example.
4. Think about the TellAboutSelf method in Lease. Lease is an abstract class, and CalculateFee is an abstract method. Why is TellAboutSelf not abstract? What would be gained and what would be lost if it were abstract?
5. Close this project, but leave VB .NET open for the next Hands-on Exercise.

Understanding and Using Interfaces

Adding an abstract method to the Lease superclass is one way to require that subclasses override the method, as shown for the CalculateFee method. Requiring a method in a class is often desirable when you want to assure all users of the class (mainly programmers developing systems that use the class) that all instances can invoke the method. Otherwise, sending a message invoking a method that is not included in the instance will result in an error.

Another approach to requiring methods in classes is to define an interface. An **interface** is a VB .NET component that defines abstract methods and constants that must be implemented by classes that use the interface. The concept is simple: Knowing how to use something means *knowing how to interface with it.* You interface with a car using a steering wheel, gas pedal, and brake pedal. You expect all cars to have these controls. It is desirable to standardize how to interface with something. If you were asked whether you know how to drive a Mars Rover, you might respond by saying, "Yes, if it has the usual car interface—a steering wheel and pedals."

In OO systems, you use or control object instances by sending them messages based on method signatures. The methods an instance can respond to can be defined as the *interface* to the instance. If you want to assure a programmer that an instance has a defined set of methods, you can define an interface and declare that the class *implements* the methods required by the interface. Now the programmer knows what the instances of the class are capable of doing.

Component-based development refers to the fact that components interact in a system using a well-defined interface but might be built using a variety of technologies. As long as you know how to interface with the component, it can be used in the system. It is not necessary to know the technology used or the internal structure of the component. Interfaces are an approach to defining how components can be used, and therefore play an important role in developing component-based systems.

VB .NET interfaces are also often explained in the context of inheritance, where classes that implement an interface are said to "inherit" the methods. Because a VB .NET class can inherit from only one superclass, but can also implement one or more interfaces, it is often said that interfaces allow VB .NET subclasses a form of **multiple inheritance**, the ability to inherit from more than one class.

Multiple inheritance means that a subclass is part of two or more generalization/specialization hierarchies. Consider the Mars Rover mentioned earlier. It is a special type of motor vehicle, inheriting all of the characteristics of a motor vehicle. But it might also be considered a special type of spacecraft, or a special type of robot. It often becomes difficult to decide what to use as the superclass and what should and should not be inherited. When a programming environment must deal with multiple inheritance, it is difficult for the compiler to reconcile issues such as which attributes to inherit and which methods to override.

Some OO programming languages—C++, for example—allow you to implement multiple inheritance. The designers of VB .NET deliberately decided *not* to allow multiple inheritance because of the complexity it can introduce. Similarly, C# .NET and Sun Microsystems' Java programming language do not allow multiple inheritance. Interfaces are therefore described as an alternate way to implement multiple inheritance with VB .NET and other OO languages. But you might find it more useful to think of interfaces as a way of defining how components can interact with each other.

Creating a VB .NET Interface

You create a VB .NET interface much like a class—using a header and including abstract methods that must be included in any class that implements the interface. In the Lease example, all subclasses are expected to include a method named CalculateFee. Therefore, you can create an interface requiring the inclusion of the CalculateFee method, named ILeaseInterface, instead of including the abstract method in Lease. An interface name begins with a capital letter "I" by convention, and using the word "interface" in the name helps to reinforce that it is an interface rather than a class.

An interface is written in a source code file and then compiled just like a class. The header for ILeaseInterface uses the **`Interface`** keyword in place of class, followed by the interface name. The complete ILeaseInterface definition is shown in Figure 8-28. One method header is included in this interface. Note that the **`Public`** keyword and the **`MustOverride`** keyword are not allowed in the method header. There is no code included for the method. All functionality must be defined by the class that implements the interface.

```
Public Interface ILeaseInterface
   'All lease classes must include CalculateFee method
   Function CalculateFee(ByVal aWidth As Integer) As Single
End Interface
```

Figure 8-28 ILeaseInterface definition

Once the interface is written and compiled, any class can implement it. Note that this interface only has one abstract method. Often interfaces have a long list of methods. Additionally, many interfaces are included with VB .NET.

The AnnualLease class can implement ILeaseInterface by using the **Implements** keyword in the class header along with the interface name. AnnualLease still extends Lease. The complete class header would be rewritten as:

```
Public Class AnnualLease
   Inherits Lease
   Implements ILeaseInterface
```

You could now remove the abstract method named CalculateFee from the Lease class as the interface requires that the CalculateFee method be included in AnnualLease. The CalculateFee method header must also be modified to show that it implements the method named CalculateFee in ILeaseInterface:

```
'custom method CalculateFee based on slip width
'required by ILeaseInterface
Public Function CalculateFee(ByVal aWidth As Integer) As Single _
Implements ILeaseInterface.CalculateFee
```

Implementing More Than One Interface

VB .NET classes can implement more than one interface. Assume Bradshaw Marina decided that all problem domain classes should implement an interface that requires the TellAboutSelf method. This way, the programmers can always be sure all instances can respond to the TellAboutSelf message. The source code for the interface definition named ICompanyInterface is shown in Figure 8-29.

```
Public Interface ICompanyInterface
   'all company classes must include a TellAboutSelf method
   Function TellAboutSelf() As String
End Interface
```

Figure 8-29 ICompanyInterface definition

You can use the DailyLease class to see how to use two interfaces with one subclass. Multiple interface names are separated by commas following the **Implements** keyword in the class header:

```
' DailyLease -- a subclass of Lease
' Implements two interfaces

Public Class DailyLease
   Inherits Lease
   Implements ILeaseInterface, ICompanyInterface
```

The CalculateFee method is now required by ILeaseInterface and the TellAboutSelf method is now required by ICompanyInterface. The CalculateFee method must be modified as in the AnnualLease example. The TellAboutSelf method header must be modified to indicate it implements the ICompanyInterface.TellAboutSelf method:

```
'TellAboutSelf overrides then invokes superclass method
'required by ICompanyInterface
Public Overrides Function TellAboutSelf() As String _
Implements ICompanyInterface.TellAboutSelf
```

The complete revised class definition for DailyLease is shown in Figure 8-30. In Hands-on Exercise 7, you will copy and run Example3 from the book's data files. That example includes the Lease classes and interfaces discussed here.


```
' DailyLease -- a subclass of Lease
' Implements two interfaces

Public Class DailyLease
   Inherits Lease
   Implements ILeaseInterface, ICompanyInterface

   'attribute in addition to those inherited from Lease
   Private numberOfDays As Integer

   'constructor (three values as parameters)
   Public Sub New(ByVal aStartDate As DateTime, _
      ByVal anEndDate As DateTime, _
      ByVal aSlipWidth As Integer)
      'invoke superclass constructor
      MyBase.New(aStartDate)
      'calculate number of days
      Dim diff As System.TimeSpan
      diff = anEndDate.Subtract(aStartDate)
      Dim days as Integer = diff.Days()
      SetNumberOfDays(days)
      'invoke superclass method to set end date
      SetEndDate(anEndDate)
      'invoke superclass SetAmount method after getting
      'fee amount from CalculateFee method
      SetAmount(CalculateFee(aSlipWidth))
   End Sub

   'custom method CalculateFee based on slip width and number of days
   'required by ILeaseInterface
   Public Function CalculateFee(ByVal aWidth As Integer) As Single _
```

```
    Implements ILeaseInterface.CalculateFee
       Dim fee as Single
       Select Case aWidth
          Case 10
             fee = 20 * numberOfDays
          Case 12
             fee = 25 * numberOfDays
          Case 14
             fee = 30 * numberOfDays
          Case 16
             fee = 35 * numberOfDays
          Case Else
             fee = 0
       End Select
       Return fee
    End Function

    'TellAboutSelf overrides then invokes superclass method
    'required by ICompanyInterface
    Public Overrides Function TellAboutSelf() As String _
    Implements ICompanyInterface.TellAboutSelf
       Return MyBase.TellAboutSelf() & ", " _
       & numberOfDays
    End Function

    'get accessor method
    Public Function GetNumberOfDays() As Integer
       Return numberOfDays
    End Function

    'set accessor method
    Public Sub SetNumberOfDays(ByVal aNumberOfDays As Integer)
       numberOfDays = aNumberOfDays
    End Sub

End Class
```

Figure 8-30 DailyLease class definition that implements two interfaces

USING CUSTOM EXCEPTIONS

Problem domain classes are not the only VB .NET classes that can be extended using inheritance. Any VB .NET class that is not declared **`NotInheritable`** can be extended. One example where extending a built-in class is desirable is to create a **custom exception**, an exception that is written specifically for an application.

You learned how to use VB .NET exceptions in Chapter 7. The Slip instance throws an exception if data values are not valid. It is often helpful to include more specific information about an error when throwing an exception. You can define a custom exception to provide information about why the error occurred. To do so, you define a new class that extends the

Exception class. Add attributes you want to remember for the custom exception. Add or override methods that you want the custom exception to invoke.

Defining LeasePaymentException

Consider the AnnualLease class. Annual leases allow customers to make monthly payments after providing an initial payment. To record the monthly payments, you must add another method to AnnualLease, and the method must validate the payment amount. If the payment is invalid, an exception must be thrown to ensure that the sender corrects any error. Therefore, you can define a custom exception that can be thrown by the method.

For the Bradshaw Marina system, create an exception named LeasePaymentException by defining a class that extends the Exception class. The class definition is shown in Figure 8-31.

```
'custom exception example

Public Class LeasePaymentException
   Inherits Exception

   'attributes of the custom exception
   Dim theLease As AnnualLease
   Dim paymentAmount As Single
   Dim exceptionMessage As String

   'constructor (2 parameters)
   Public Sub New(ByVal anAmount As Single, _
   ByVal aLease As AnnualLease)
      'invoke superclass constructor
      MyBase.New("Lease Payment Exception")
      theLease = aLease
      paymentAmount = anAmount
      exceptionMessage = "LeasePaymentException for lease " & _
         theLease.GetStartDate() & _
         " with amount due " & _
         theLease.GetBalanceDue() & _
         " but payment made of " & paymentAmount
   End Sub

   'override ToString method of Exception
   'to provide more specific information about this exception
   Public Overrides Function ToString() As String
      Return exceptionMessage
   End Function

   'accessor methods can also be included to return
   'specific exception information that might be needed

End Class
```

Figure 8-31 LeasePaymentException class definition

8

The class definition includes three attributes that will hold values for the amount of the invalid payment, a reference to the lease receiving the payment, and a message containing more specific information about what occurred.

Note that when LeasePaymentException is instantiated, it will hold a reference to the lease that threw the exception. The lease reference variable included as an attribute illustrates an important OO programming concept. Attributes of instances can contain references to other instances, as with the DateTime instances used with the Lease classes. This time the reference is to a problem domain class defined for the Bradshaw Marina system. In examples in the next chapter, you will learn more about the benefits of including reference variables as attributes when you implement association relationships among instances. Here, an instance of LeasePaymentException is associated with an instance of AnnualLease.

The LeasePaymentException class has a parameterized constructor that accepts values for the amount of the invalid payment and the reference to the AnnualLease instance. The constructor first invokes the superclass constructor (of the `Exception` class), passing a string that the constructor expects. Then values are assigned for all attributes, including the `exceptionMessage` string that includes specific values obtained directly from the AnnualLease instance. In other words, the LeasePaymentException instance asks the annual lease for its start date and amount due. This is an example of one instance sending a message to another instance and getting information back.

Recall that the `Exception` class includes the ToString method, which returns information about the exception. The ToString method is a method all classes have (see the section on the `Object` class later in this chapter) and `Exception` has its own version of ToString that returns any message passed to its constructor. You saw this in the `Exception` examples in Chapter 7. The LeasePaymentException class overrides the Exception ToString method to provide more specific information.

The partial sequence diagram in Figure 8-32 shows the interaction between LeasePaymentException and AnnualLease. Note that the new LeasePaymentException instance identifies which annual lease is involved and asks it for information that is then stored in the `exceptionMessage` string. This string is later returned to the method that catches the exception.

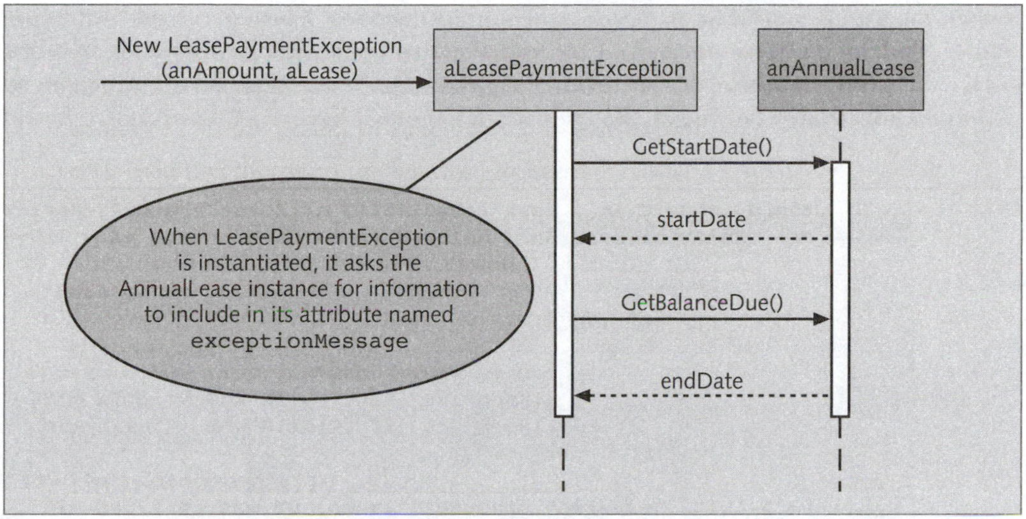

Figure 8-32 Partial sequence diagram showing LeasePaymentException and AnnualLease interacting in the constructor

Throwing a Custom Exception

The LeasePaymentException class was designed for use by the AnnualLease class. A custom method for AnnualLease can be added to the class to record a payment, named RecordLeasePayment, which expects to receive the amount of the payment. The RecordLeasePayment method throws a LeasePaymentException instance if the payment amount is not valid. This simplified example defines an invalid value as a payment that is greater than the amount due. Arguments passed to the constructor of the LeasePaymentException include the amount of the attempted payment and a reference to the annual lease held by the keyword **Me**. Otherwise, the payment amount is subtracted from the balance due:

```
'custom method RecordLeasePayment to demonstrate
'LeasePaymentException (custom exception)
Public Sub RecordLeasePayment(ByVal anAmount As Single)
   If anAmount > balanceDue Then
      Throw New LeasePaymentException(anAmount, Me)
   Else
      balanceDue -= anAmount
   End If
End Sub
```

Testing the LeasePaymentException

Figure 8-33 shows a Windows form labeled "Chapter 8 Interface and Customer Exception Tester," which you can use to test the modified Lease classes. An event procedure that tests AnnualLease with the RecordLeasePayment method and LeasePaymentException is shown in Figure 8-34. The output is shown in Figure 8-35. The **Try**, **Catch**, and **Finally** blocks are used because the RecordLeasePayment method throws an exception. Note the additional information about the exception included in the string returned in the **Catch** block. Recall that a **Finally** block is always executed.

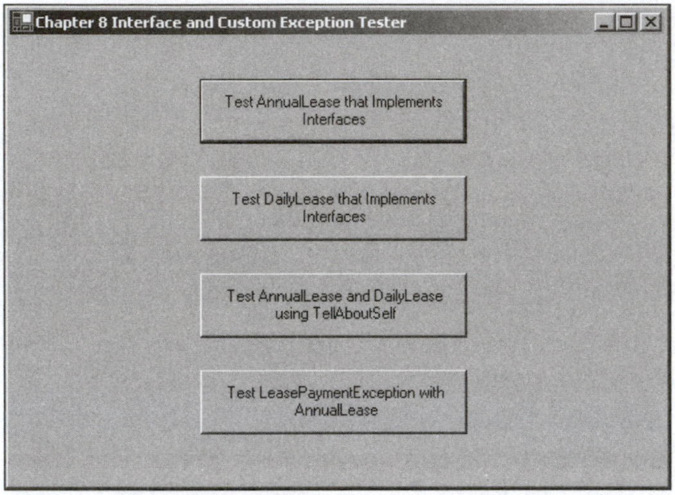

Figure 8-33 Interface and Custom Exception Windows form

```
Private Sub btnTestPaymentException_Click(ByVal sender _
As System.Object, ByVal e As System.EventArgs) _
Handles btnTestPaymentException.Click

   'create an annual lease amount 1100, balance due 1008.33
   Dim newDate as New DateTime(2004, 3, 15)
   Dim anotherDate as New DateTime(2004, 4, 10)
   Dim lease1 as New AnnualLease(newDate, 14, True)
   Console.WriteLine("Beginning balance is " & lease1.GetBalanceDue())

   'make a valid payment, balance will be 200.33
   Try
      lease1.RecordLeasePayment(800)
      Console.WriteLine("First payment successful. Balance is " _
      & lease1.GetBalanceDue())
   Catch theException As LeasePaymentException
      Console.WriteLine(theException.ToString())
   End Try

   'make an invalid payment, exception will be thrown by lease1
```

```
    Try
       lease1.RecordLeasePayment(800)
       Console.WriteLine("Second payment successful. Balance is " _
       & lease1.GetBalanceDue())
    Catch theException As LeasePaymentException
       Console.WriteLine(theException.ToString())
    Finally
       Console.WriteLine("End of second try catch block")
    End Try

End Sub
```

Figure 8-34 Event procedure to test the AnnualLease and LeasePaymentException classes

```
Beginning balance is 1008.333
First payment successful. Balance is 208.3333
LeasePaymentException for lease 3/15/2004 with amount due 208.3333 but payment made of
800
End of second try catch block
```

Figure 8-35 LeasePaymentException test code output

The annual lease costs $1,200.00 based on a slip width of 14 feet. Because `payMonthly` is true, the balance due is $1,008.33. A payment of $800 is attempted and is successful. An additional payment of $800 is attempted but fails because the balance due is only $208.33. A partial sequence diagram of the interaction for the test code is shown in Figure 8-36.

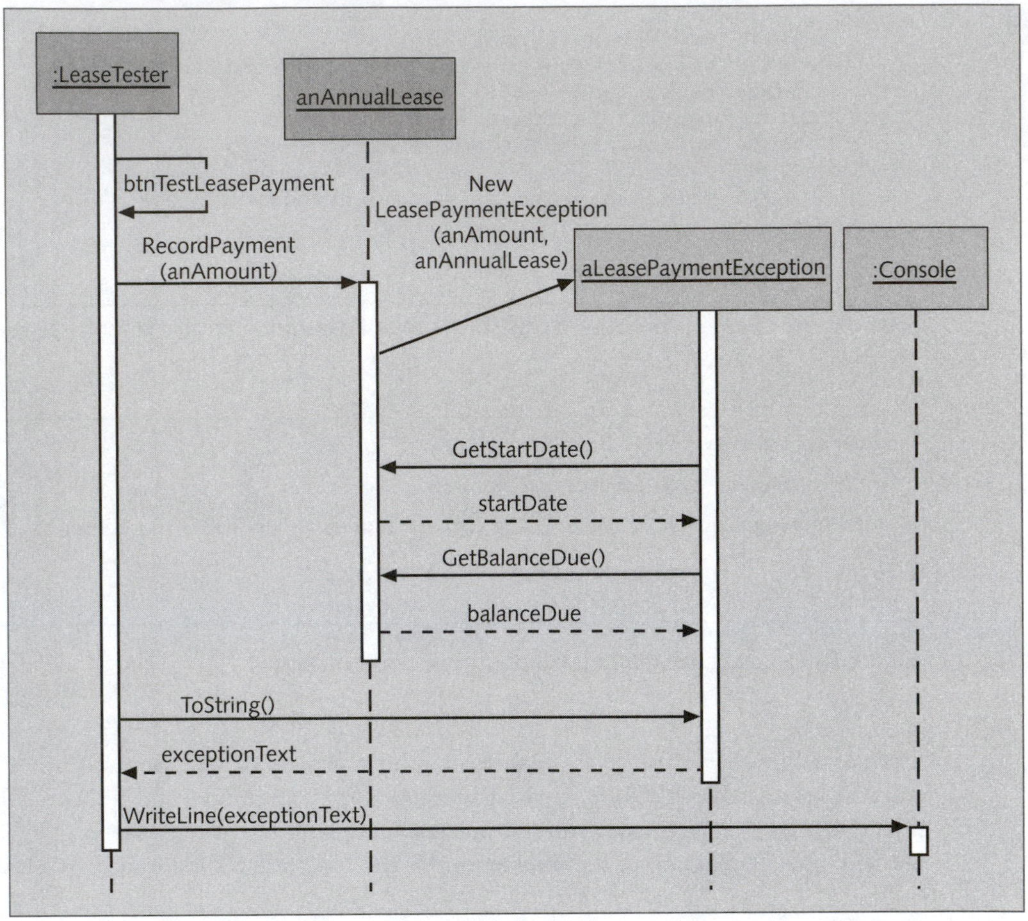

Figure 8-36 Partial sequence diagram showing test code interaction with

Hands-on Exercise 7

1. Locate Example3 in the folder Chap08\Examples\Ex03 in the book's data files. Copy the **Ex03** folder to the Chap08\Exercises folder in your work folder. Then open the project with VB .NET and build the project. Example3 includes the interface examples discussed earlier plus the custom exception example. New versions of Lease.vb, AnnualLease.vb, DailyLease.vb, and FormLeaseTester.vb are included. Additionally, ILeaseInterface.vb, ICompanyInterface.vb, and LeasePaymentException.vb are included in the project.

2. Run the Test AnnualLease, Test DailyLease, and Test Annual and Daily Lease event procedures to demonstrate the use of the interfaces. Temporarily remove the TellAboutSelf method required by ICompanyInterface from DailyLease using the comment character. Rebuild the project. What happens? Remove the comment

characters and rebuild. Now temporarily remove the CalculateFee method by inserting comment characters. Rebuild the project. What happens? Remove the comment characters and rebuild.

3. Examine the LeasePaymentException class definition and the event procedure for testing it. Run the example and verify that the output matches Figure 8-35. To test any software thoroughly, you should create a variety of test cases and list the expected output of each test case. Then when you run the test, you can verify that the output matches the expected output. Create a list of test cases for at least four annual leases with and without a balance due and with one or more payments. Record the expected output after each payment. Write test code that runs the test cases and verify that the expected output matches the actual output.
4. Close the project, and then close VB .NET.

UNDERSTANDING THE `Object` CLASS AND INHERITANCE

You have created a number of problem domain classes for Bradshaw Marina, and implemented subclasses by using the **`Inherits`** keyword. Subclasses inherit the functionality you included in the superclass. But how did the problem domain superclass gain the functionality it has? The answer is that all classes in VB .NET extend one common superclass named `Object`.

The `Object` class defines the basic functionality that any other class of objects needs in VB .NET. All built-in VB .NET class hierarchies have `Object` as the common ancestor. But any problem domain class you define also extends `Object`, although it is done implicitly for you. Therefore, it is useful to understand the `Object` class and its methods.

One method you have worked with already is the ToString method. All classes inherit ToString from the `Object` class. By default, ToString returns a string representation of the name of the class. Many classes override the ToString method to provide more specific information. The `Exception` class ToString method is one example you have used. Many developers override ToString in problem domain classes so it functions much like the TellAboutSelf method you have used for Bradshaw Marina.

Additional methods of the `Object` class are Equals, GetHashCode, GetType, ReferenceEquals, and the default `New` constructor. Problem domain classes you create can include the code that explicitly inherits from `Object` in the class header:

```
Public Class Lease
   Inherits Object
```

AnnualLease and DailyLease extend Lease, so they could not directly extend `Object`, but they both inherit `Object` methods as well as Lease methods. An AnnualLease instance referenced by the variable `lease1` could invoke the ToString method, which would return the name of the class:

```
Dim myLeaseInfo As String = lease1.ToString()
```

Chapter Summary

- Generalization/specialization hierarchies show superclasses and subclasses, and subclasses inherit characteristics of the superclass. Inheritance in VB .NET allows you to easily create subclasses by extending the capabilities of another class using the **`Inherits`** keyword. The subclass inherits the attributes and the methods of the superclass.
- The subclass constructor invokes the superclass constructor using the `MyBase.New` method as the first statement in the constructor, passing values as arguments.
- You can add a subclass to a superclass without affecting other subclasses. A subclass can also have its own subclasses.
- An abstract class is a class that is not instantiated and is declared using the **`MustInherit`** keyword in the class header. It exists only to serve as a superclass for one or more concrete subclasses that can be instantiated.
- A final class is a class that cannot be extended, either for security reasons or for efficiency, and is declared using the **`NotInheritable`** keyword in the class header.
- Method overriding means that a method in a subclass with the same name and signature as a method in the superclass will be invoked in place of the superclass method. A method can override and then invoke the superclass method to extend rather than completely replace the method using the **`MyBase`** keyword as a reference much like an object reference: `MyBase.MethodName()`.
- Method overriding in VB .NET allows a form of polymorphism where instances can respond to messages in their own way, without the requester needing to know the subclass of the instance. Dynamic binding allows this flexibility where at runtime the decision about what method to invoke is made.
- Private access for attributes means not even subclass methods can directly access the values of the attributes, but protected access allows direct access by subclass methods.
- The Lease generalization/specialization hierarchy is another example of inheritance in the Bradshaw Marina case study. AnnualLease and DailyLease both have their own ways of calculating the lease fee, and there are several ways to require that a method be included in a class to assure that all instances will respond to the same message.
- If you want to require that all subclasses include a method, you can include an abstract method in a superclass. Only an abstract class can include an abstract method.
- An interface is a VB .NET component that you can use to require that classes contain specific methods. An interface defines how to interact, or *interface*, with an

instance by defining methods that can be invoked. In component-based development, you create system components with well-defined interfaces to allow components to interact.

- The `Interface` keyword is used in the interface header to define an interface, which is created in a source code file and compiled like a class. The `Implements` keyword is used in the class header to define the interfaces for a class and in the header of methods required by the interface.
- Because an interface defines methods to include, it can also be thought of as a way to implement multiple inheritance, where a class inherits from more than one parent. But interfaces do not include methods to inherit; they only define abstract methods that must be included in a class that implements the interface.
- You can use the `Inherits` keyword to define classes that inherit from built-in VB .NET classes, such as to extend the `Exception` class into a custom exception. Any class that is not final can be extended. Custom exceptions are helpful when you need to provide detailed information following an exception.
- In VB .NET, the `Object` class is the superclass of all classes, and problem domain classes such as Boat and Lease implicitly extend the `Object` class. `Object` class methods are inherited by all classes.

Key Terms

In the following list, the key terms printed in Courier font are VB .NET keywords.

abstract method
component-based development
concrete class
custom exception
dynamic binding
`Implements`
`Inherits`
`Interface`
method overriding
multiple inheritance
`MustInherit`
`MyBase`
`NotInheritable`
`Private`
`Protected`
protected access
`Public`

Review Questions

1. Consider the terms superclass and subclass. In a generalization/specialization hierarchy, which is general and which is special?
2. Explain how inheritance applies in generalization/specialization? What is inherited by the subclass?
3. Sketch an example of how a generalization/specialization hierarchy is shown on a class diagram for a superclass named Car and a subclass named SportsCar.
4. What VB .NET keyword is used to allow one class to inherit from another class?
5. Write a class header for the SportsCar class, which inherits from Car.
6. Write a class header for an abstract class named Car.
7. What would happen if your tester program included the statement `Dim aCar as New Car(aMake, aModel)` if Car is an abstract class?
8. Where is the statement `MyBase.New(someValue)` written in a subclass?
9. What is the difference between method overloading and method overriding?
10. Explain how method overriding allows polymorphism. Give an example.
11. Write a statement that would invoke the superclass method after overriding it for a method named CalculateFee.
12. What are two reasons for declaring a class final using the **`NotInheritable`** keyword?
13. Write a class header for an abstract class named Paycheck.
14. Write a class header for a class named HourlyPaycheck, which extends Paycheck and is final.
15. What is the effect of assigning protected rather than private access to attributes in a superclass?
16. What keyword defines a method in a superclass that must be included in a subclass?
17. If a class includes an abstract method, can the class itself be instantiated? Explain.
18. Write an interface header for an interface named IBoatInterface.
19. Write a class header for a class named Sailboat, which implements IBoatInterface.
20. Explain what classes can be extended other than problem domain classes you create.
21. Explain why custom exceptions are important for business systems.

22. Write a class header for a custom exception named LeaseCreationException.
23. Assume LeaseCreationException is caught by a Try-Catch block in a tester program that instantiates DailyLease. Write the complete Try-Catch block that catches the exception and displays the message.
24. Write a class header for the Boat class that extends the `Object` class and implements IboatInterface and the ICompanyInterface.

Discussion Questions

1. Much is said about the importance of inheritance in object-oriented programming. Discuss several specific ways that inheritance makes OO development easier from the standpoint of the programmer.
2. Why would it be desirable to require that specific methods be included in any subclass that extends a class? In other words, why include abstract methods or implement interfaces?
3. In what ways is an interface important for component-based development? In what ways is an interface like inheritance?
4. In the Lease classes, must CalculateFee be public rather than private? Note that the method does not assign an amount; it just calculates and returns it based on the width. Discuss when public versus private access for methods is advisable.

Projects

1. Write an additional subclass for Boat named Rowboat and add it to your Boat class Example 1 project. A few specific attributes might apply to a rowboat, specifically type of material (wood, fiberglass, or inflatable) and oar type (paddles, wood oars, or metal oars). Include accessor methods for the new class, a TellAboutSelf method that overrides and then invokes the superclass method, and a program that tests the class. Draw a sequence diagram for the tester program.

2. Assume PersonalWatercraft is a subclass of Powerboat. What additional attributes might be applicable to a personal watercraft? Create the VB .NET class using at least two additional attributes and add accessor methods. Include a parameterized constructor that accepts values for all PersonalWatercraft attributes. Write a program to test the new class by instantiating a few personal watercraft and a few powerboats. Explain why Powerboat does not have to be, and should not be, changed to an abstract class.
3. Considering the PersonalWatercraft class in Project 2, explain what happens when the PersonalWatercraft constructor invokes the superclass constructor. Trace all statements that are executed from beginning to end by listing them. Add a TellAboutSelf method to the PersonalWatercraft class that overrides and then invokes the Powerboat class TellAboutSelf method. Explain what happens when the PersonalWatercraft TellAboutSelf method is invoked. Trace all statements that are executed.
4. Consider an additional lease type named OneDayLease that can be added to your Example3 Lease project. This lease has the same end date as start date and the lease fee is a flat fee rather than based on slip width. There are no attributes in addition to the Lease class attributes. Create OneDayLease as a subclass of Lease, implementing ILeaseInterface and ICompanyInterface. Write a program to test the class.
5. Recall the validation added to the Boat class in Hands-on Exercise 1. Take your solution and create a custom exception named BoatException to throw if any of the values are invalid. Write a program to test valid and invalid values.

CHAPTER

9

Implementing Association Relationships

In this chapter you will:

- Identify association relationships on Bradshaw Marina's class diagram
- Associate VB .NET classes in a one-to-one relationship
- Add functionality to the Boat class
- Associate Dock and Slips in a one-to-many relationship
- Add the Boat and Customer classes to the Slip example
- Create and use an association class—Lease

In Chapter 8 you learned how to implement generalization/specialization hierarchies that provide inheritance relationships from a superclass to a subclass. The class diagram shows these hierarchies. But a class diagram also shows *association relationships* between classes, and these relationships are important to business information systems. Lines between classes on a class diagram that can be described by verb phrases are association relationships. For example, the Bradshaw Marina system requires several association relationships between classes: A customer *owns* a boat, and a boat *is assigned to* a slip. For the Bradshaw Marina managers, knowing this information is as important as knowing the name and address of a customer and the manufacturer and length of a boat, so association relationships model key requirements for a business information system.

This chapter shows how to use VB .NET to implement association relationships between classes. Once you have implemented a one-to-one association relationship, you will learn how to navigate from one instance to another. For example, you can navigate instances to find information about the customer who owns a boat. You will also explore one-to-many association relationships to find information about each slip that is part of a dock. Finally, you will learn how to create and use an association class—the Lease class that was introduced in Chapter 8.

Identifying Association Relationships on Bradshaw Marina's Class Diagram

In Chapter 5 you learned about the information system requirements for Bradshaw Marina. The Bradshaw Marina class diagram shows the problem domain classes the system needs. This class diagram is shown again in Figure 9-1. The classes introduced so far include Customer, Slip, Boat (including subclasses), and Lease (including subclasses). The class diagram also shows how instances of the classes are associated, or connected, to each other. It is important to know, for example, which boat is assigned to a slip and which customer owns the boat. Association relationships on the class diagram indicate that the system requires information about these associations.

Association relationships are shown on the class diagram as lines connecting classes. These associations connect instances of a class with instances of another class. The numbers written at both ends of the line indicate the multiplicity of the association (recall that 1..1 means one and only one, and 1..* means one or more). Using association relationships in a class diagram, you can navigate from instance to instance following the association. For example, if you have a Customer instance, you can find the Boat instance associated with the customer. Once you have the Boat instance, you can find the Slip instance for the boat.

Business information systems usually have many association relationships. These relationships are important in business systems because they indicate requirements that must be remembered or stored by the system. The Bradshaw class diagram shows the following association relationships, all of which define information the Bradshaw Marina system needs to track:

- A customer owns a boat.
- A boat is owned by a customer.
- A boat is assigned to a slip.
- A slip contains a boat.
- A dock contains many slips.
- A slip is attached to a dock.
- A slip is leased to a customer (Lease is an association class).
- A customer leases a slip (Lease is an association class).

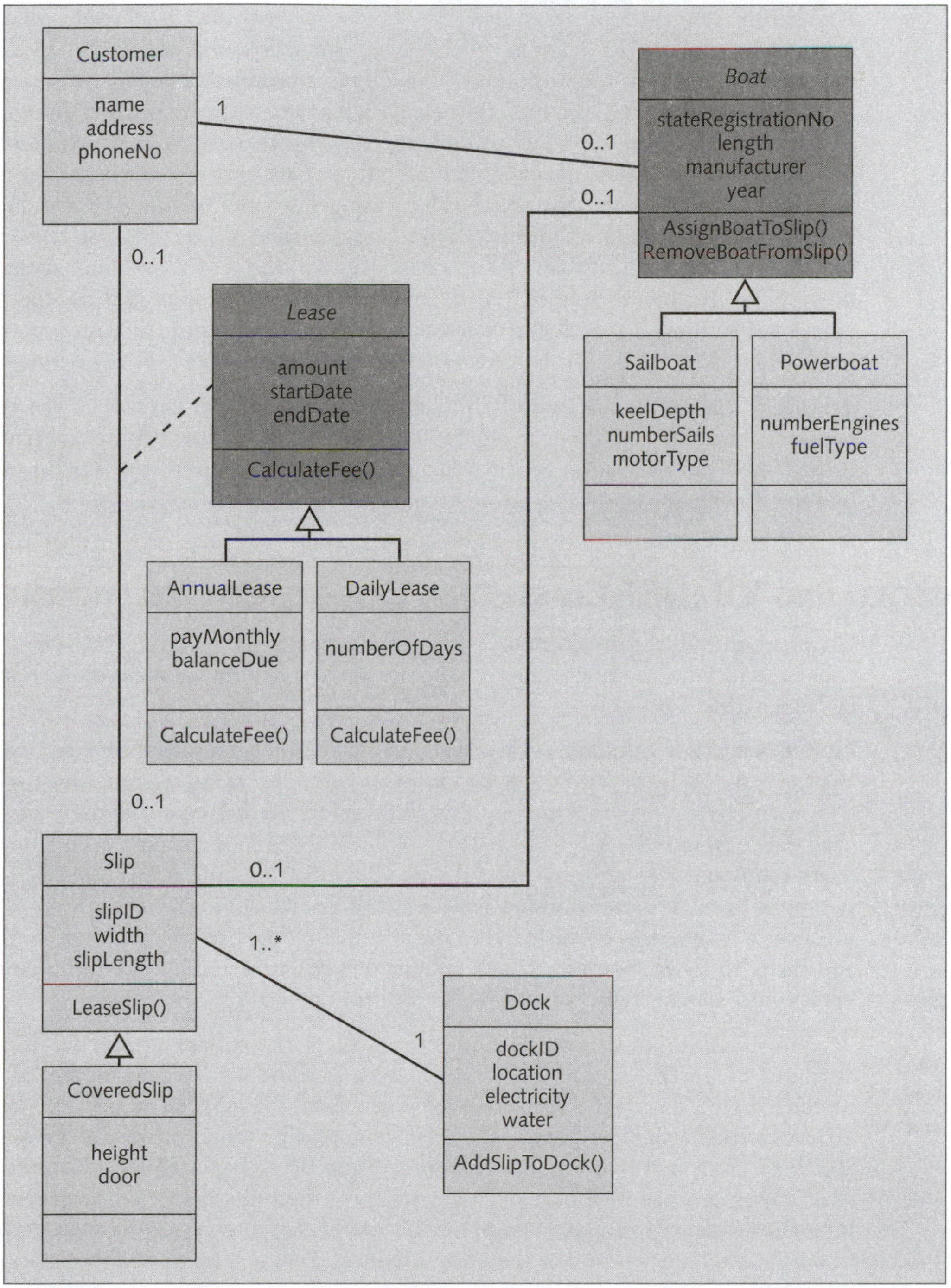

Figure 9-1 Bradshaw Marina class diagram

Association relationships are sometimes shown as *aggregation relationships* or *composition relationships* on the class diagram. (A diamond symbol on one end of the association line indicates aggregation or composition.) An aggregation relationship is a strong association in which one instance "contains" the other, such as a town that contains shopping centers or schools. A composition relationship is also a strong association in which one instance is composed of or "part of" another, such as walls that are part of a building. You implement aggregation and composition relationships using the same techniques as the association relationships demonstrated in this chapter. Some analysts do not include them at all during analysis, and the Bradshaw Marina class diagram does not show them. Other analysts, however, might use a composition relationship between a dock and its slips (a dock is composed of slips) if they feel it helps convey more information about the nature of the association.

The Lease class is an example of an *association class* that exists because of the relationship between a slip and a customer, as discussed in Chapter 5. It is shown as a class connected by a dashed line to an association between Slip and Customer. You implement an association class like any other class with VB .NET and then associate it with other classes.

ASSOCIATING VB .NET CLASSES IN A ONE-TO-ONE RELATIONSHIP

Chapter 6 introduced the Customer class and Chapter 8 introduced the Boat class, including Sailboat and Powerboat subclasses. Customer and Boat have an association relationship: A customer owns a boat.

Note that the line on the class diagram represents *two* relationships between Customer and Boat, one for each "direction." First, a customer *owns* a boat, and second, a boat *is owned by* a customer. The system developer must carefully define each direction of the relationship, and each direction must be handled separately with VB .NET. For example, each direction of the relationship might differ on whether it is mandatory or optional. A boat must be owned by a customer (mandatory relationship between Boat and Customer), but a customer who does not own a boat might be included in the system (optional relationship between Customer and Boat). In other associations, the multiplicity is different in each direction. For example, a dock contains many slips, but a slip is part of only one dock.

To implement an association relationship in VB .NET, you use a reference variable as an attribute of a class. Figure 9-2 reviews how a reference variable points to an actual instance; in this example, a Customer reference variable points to a Customer instance and a Boat reference variable points to a Boat instance. Therefore, if you add a reference variable for a Customer instance as an attribute in the Boat class, each Boat instance can point to a Customer instance and invoke the customer's methods. If you add a reference variable for a Boat instance as an attribute in the Customer class, each Customer instance can point to a Boat instance and invoke the boat's methods. That is how association relationships are implemented with VB .NET.

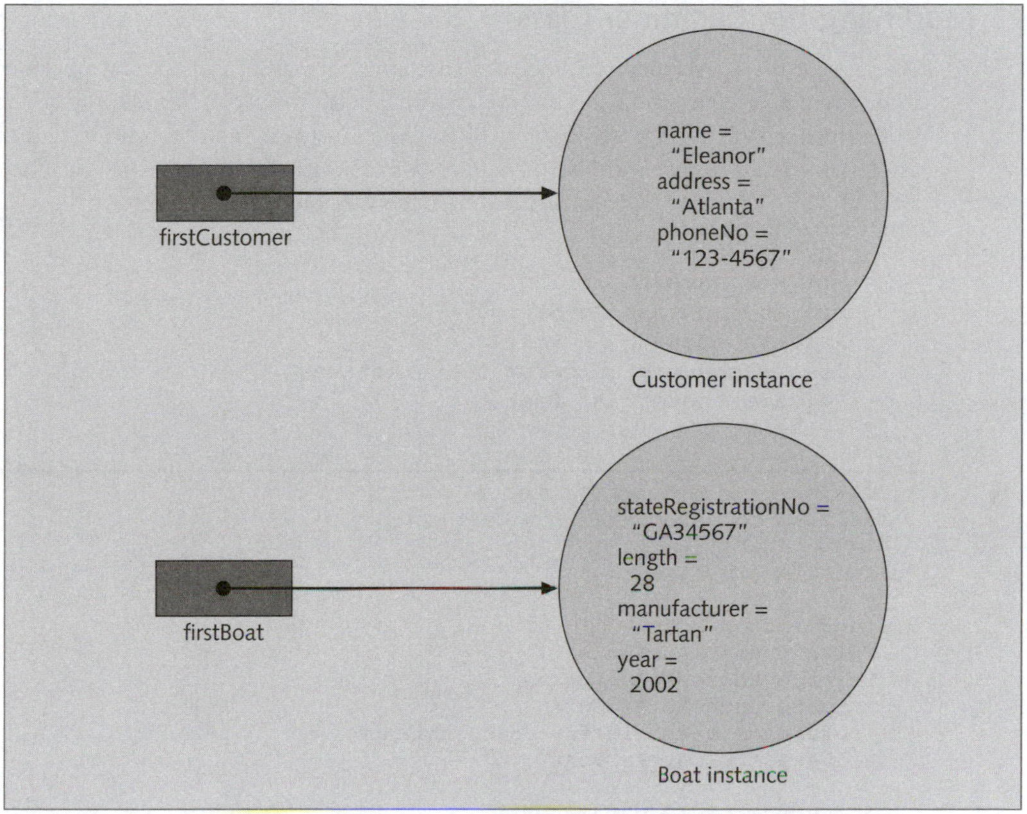

Figure 9-2 Reference variables (firstCustomer and firstBoat) point to actual instances (customer named Eleanor and boat number GA34567)

The tester programs you have written up to this point include reference variables that are used to point to instances and invoke their methods. You have also seen `String` and `DateTime` reference variables used as attributes of classes for Bradshaw Marina examples in this text. A string, such as the name of a boat manufacturer, is an instance of the `String` class to which the manufacturer attribute of Boat points. A `DateTime` instance, such as the start date of a lease, is an instance of the `DateTime` class to which the `startDate` attribute of Lease points.

This chapter introduces nothing new about the concept of reference variables as attributes. What is new is the use of reference variables to implement association relationships among problem domain classes. The examples in this chapter will be easy for you to follow if you understand the difference between a reference variable and an instance.

Modifying the Customer Class

Recall that the Customer class includes attributes for name, address, and phone number. To implement a one-to-one association relationship with the Boat class, simply add an attribute to Customer that holds a reference to a boat. The Customer class definition that includes the association relationship is shown in Figure 9-3. The list of attributes to the Customer class now includes three strings plus a Boat reference variable named `theBoat`:

```
'attributes
Private name As String
Private address As String
Private phoneNo As String
'reference variable for Boat instance
Private theBoat As Boat
```

```
' Customer class from Chapter 6
' Modified to Associate with Boat

Public Class Customer

   'attributes
   Private name As String
   Private address As String
   Private phoneNo As String
   'reference variable for Boat instance
   Private theBoat As Boat

   'constructor (3 parameters)
   Public Sub New(ByVal aName As String, ByVal anAddress As String, _
     ByVal aPhoneNo As String)
      SetName(aName)
      SetAddress(anAddress)
      SetPhoneNo(aPhoneNo)
      SetBoat(Nothing)
   End Sub

   'TellAboutSelf method
   Public Function TellAboutSelf() As String
      Return name & ", " & address & ", " & phoneNo
   End Function

   'get accessor methods (including GetBoat)
   Public Function GetName() As String
      Return name
   End Function
   Public Function GetAddress() As String
      Return address
   End Function
   Public Function GetPhoneNo() As String
      Return phoneNo
   End Function
```

```
   Public Function GetBoat() As Boat
      Return theBoat
   End Function

   'set accessor methods (including SetBoat)
   Public Sub SetName(ByVal aName As String)
      name = aName
   End Sub
   Public Sub SetAddress(ByVal anAddress As String)
      address = anAddress
   End Sub
   Public Sub SetPhoneNo(ByVal aPhoneNo As String)
      phoneNo = aPhoneNo
   End Sub
   Public Sub SetBoat(ByVal aBoat As Boat)
      theBoat = aBoat
   End Sub

End Class
```

Figure 9-3 Modified Customer class definition

Note that the Boat reference variable points to a Boat instance; it is not a value representing the boat ID number or some other value used as a key or identifier to a boat. Key values or identifiers are used to implement relationships in relational databases, as when a foreign key is included in a table so it can be joined to another table. The reference variable, on the other hand, points directly to the Boat instance.

Accessor methods are also added to the Customer class—one to set the Boat reference variable and one to get the Boat reference variable. The setter method accepts a Boat reference as a parameter and assigns the reference to the attribute:

```
Public Sub SetBoat(ByVal aBoat As Boat)
   theBoat = aBoat
End Sub
```

The getter method returns the reference. Note that the return type is Boat.

```
Public Function GetBoat() As Boat
   Return theBoat
End Function
```

The constructor now sets the Boat reference variable to **`Nothing`** using the `SetBoat` method. After the Customer instance is created, the Boat reference variable can be set to an actual Boat reference.

Figure 9-4 shows a Windows form labeled Chapter 9 Customer Boat Tester with two buttons. The event procedure for the first button tests the revised Customer class, establishing an association between a customer and a boat. Note that the Boat class has not been changed; Boat is not being asked to associate with Customer. Only one direction of the association is implemented and tested. The test code is shown in Figure 9-5.

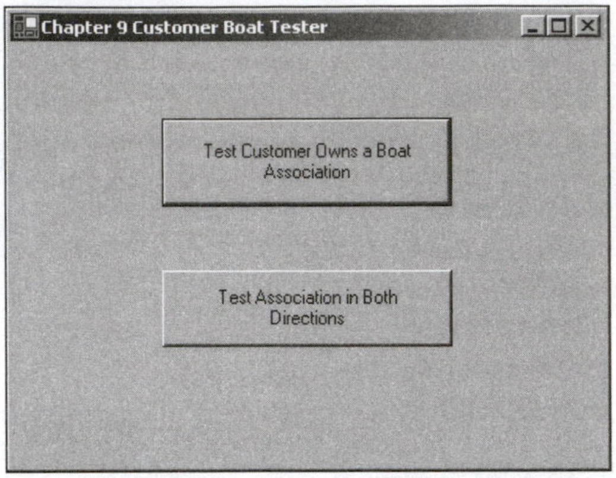

Figure 9-4 Customer Boat Tester Windows form

```
Private Sub btnTestCustomerToBoat_Click(ByVal sender As _
System.Object, ByVal e As System.EventArgs) Handles _
btnTestCustomerToBoat.Click

    'create customer instance
    Dim customer1 As New Customer("Eleanor", "Atlanta", "123-4567")
    'create boat instance
    Dim boat1 As New Boat("GA34567", 28, "Tartan", 2002)
    'ask customer1 to set its boat reference to boat1
    customer1.SetBoat(boat1)
    'get customer information
    Console.WriteLine("Customer is " & customer1.TellAboutSelf())
    'get boat reference from customer
    Dim returnedBoat As Boat = customer1.GetBoat()
    'get the information on the boat
    Console.WriteLine("Boat info is " _
     & returnedBoat.TellAboutSelf())
    'navigate directly from customer to boat
    Console.WriteLine("Again boat info is " _
     & customer1.GetBoat().TellAboutSelf())
```

Figure 9-5 Event procedure code to test Customer owns a Boat association

Figure 9-6 shows the sequence diagram that illustrates the interaction in the event procedure, and Figure 9-7 shows the output produced.

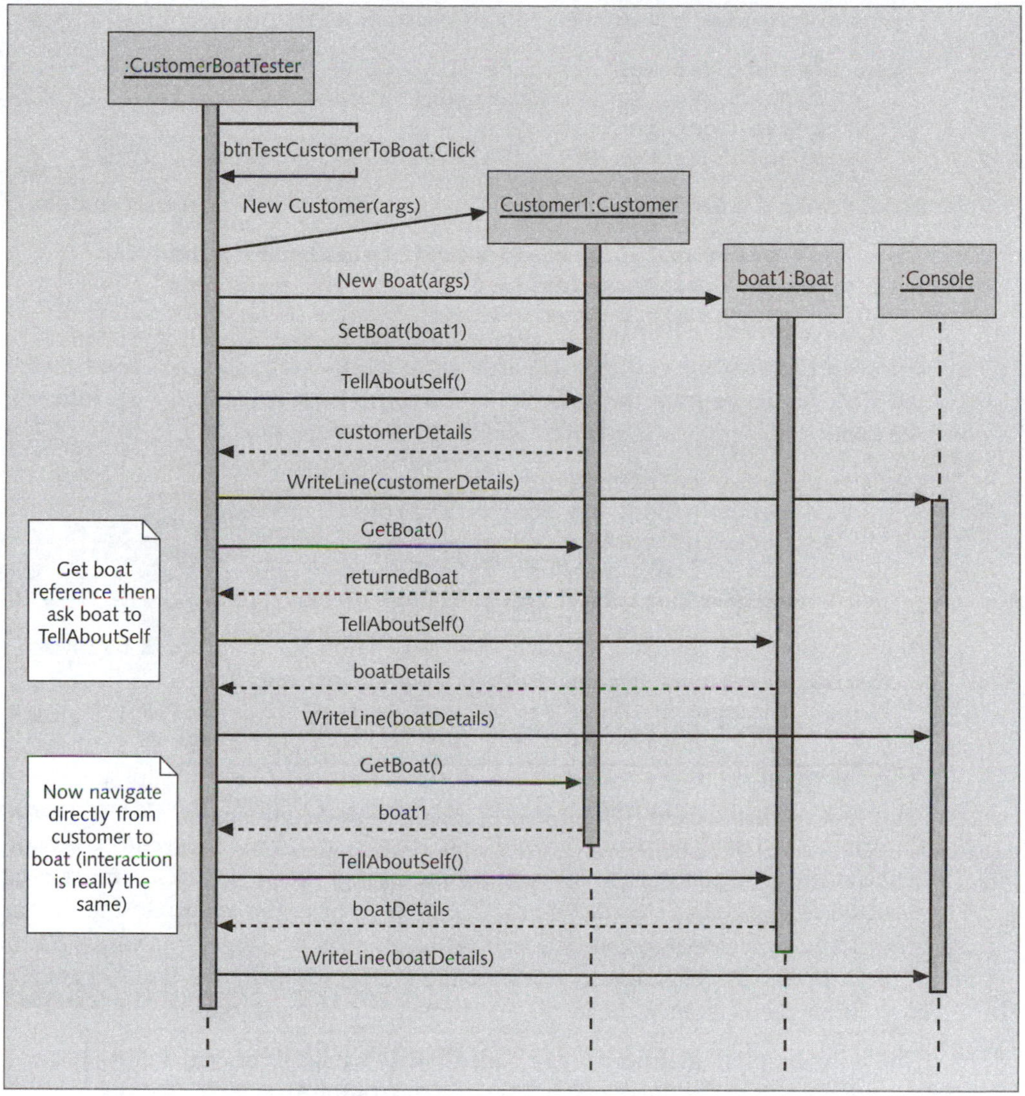

Figure 9-6 Sequence diagram showing Customer and Boat interaction


```
Customer is Eleanor, Atlanta, 123-4567
Boat info is GA34567, 28, Tartan, 2002
Again boat info is GA34567, 28, Tartan, 2002
```

Figure 9-7 Customer owns Boat test code output

First, you instantiate a customer and a boat using the following code:

```
'create customer instance
Dim customer1 As New Customer("Eleanor", "Atlanta", "123-4567")
'create boat instance
Dim boat1 As New Boat("GA34567", 28, "Tartan", 2002)
```

Next, invoke the **SetBoat** method of Customer using the Boat reference **boat1**:

```
'ask customer1 to set its boat reference to boat1
customer1.SetBoat(boat1)
```

Next, the customer's TellAboutSelf method is invoked to verify that customer information is correct. Now that the customer has a value for its Boat reference, the tester program can get the Boat reference from the customer and use the Boat reference to get information about the boat:

```
'get boat reference from customer
Dim returnedBoat As Boat = customer1.GetBoat()
'get the information on the boat
Console.WriteLine("Boat info is " _
 & returnedBoat.TellAboutSelf())
```

A more powerful approach to navigating association relationships is to invoke a series of methods in one statement. Consider the following statement:

```
customer1.GetBoat().GetStateRegistrationNo()
```

The statement should be read from left to right. First, the Customer instance assigned to the reference variable **customer1** receives a message to invoke its **GetBoat** method. The Customer instance returns a reference to the boat. Next, the returned Boat reference replaces the first part of the statement, so the Boat instance receives a message to invoke its **GetStateRegistrationNo** method, which returns the state registration number as a string. Any public method of Boat can be accessed in this way by navigating from the customer to the boat. Therefore, if you have the Customer reference, you can get any information about the customer's boat.

The following statement in the test code directly navigates from the customer to the boat to ask the boat to return information using the boat's TellAboutSelf method:

```
'navigate directly from customer to boat
Console.WriteLine("Again boat info is " _
 & customer1.GetBoat().TellAboutSelf())
```

Modifying the Boat Class

Up to this point, the Boat class has not been modified, but the Customer class now implements the one-to-one association relationship with Boat. A Boat instance, however, has no way of knowing about the customer. In other words, only one direction of the relationship has been implemented, from Customer to Boat. The Boat class can also be modified by adding a Customer reference variable as an attribute along with two accessor methods. That way, the other direction of the relationship can be implemented: A boat *is owned by* a customer. The modified Boat class definition is shown in Figure 9-8.

```
' Boat class from Chapter 8 used as concrete class
' Modified to associate with Customer

Public Class Boat

   'attributes
   Private stateRegistrationNo As String
   Private length As Single
   Private manufacturer As String
   Private year As Integer
   'reference variable for Customer instance
   Private theCustomer As Customer

   'constructor (four parameters)
   Public Sub New(ByVal aStateRegistrationNo As String, _
      ByVal aLength As Single, _
      ByVal aManufacturer As String, ByVal aYear As Integer)
      'set values of attributes using accessor methods
      SetStateRegistrationNo(aStateRegistrationNo)
      SetLength(aLength)
      SetManufacturer(aManufacturer)
      SetYear(aYear)
      SetCustomer(Nothing)
   End Sub

   'TellAboutSelf method
   Public Overridable Function TellAboutSelf() As String
      Return (stateRegistrationNo & ", " & length & ", " & _
        manufacturer & ", " & year)
   End Function

   'Get accessor methods (including GetCustomer)
   Public Function GetStateRegistrationNo() As String
      Return stateRegistrationNo
   End Function
   Public Function GetLength() As Single
      Return length
   End Function
   Public Function GetManufacturer() As String
      Return manufacturer
   End Function
   Public Function GetYear() As Integer
      Return year
   End Function
   Public Function GetCustomer() As Customer
      Return theCustomer
   End Function
```

```
   'Set accessor methods (including SetCustomer)
   Public Sub SetStateRegistrationNo(ByVal aStateRegistrationNo _
      As String)
      stateRegistrationNo = aStateRegistrationNo
   End Sub
   Public Sub SetLength(ByVal aLength As Single)
      length = aLength
   End Sub
   Public Sub SetManufacturer(ByVal aManufacturer As String)
      manufacturer = aManufacturer
   End Sub
   Public Sub SetYear(ByVal aYear As Integer)
      year = aYear
   End Sub
   Public Sub SetCustomer(ByVal aCustomer As Customer)
      theCustomer = aCustomer
   End Sub

End Class
```

Figure 9-8 Modified Boat class definition

The code for the event procedure that tests the association in both directions is shown in Figure 9-9, and the output produced is shown in Figure 9-10.

```
Private Sub btnTestBothDirections_Click(ByVal sender As _
   System.Object, ByVal e As System.EventArgs) Handles _
   btnTestBothDirections.Click

      'create two customer instances
      Dim customer1 As New Customer("Eleanor", "Atlanta", "123-4567")
      Dim customer2 As New Customer("JoAnn", "St Louis", "987-6543")
      'create two boat instances
      Dim boat1 As New Boat("GA34567", 28, "Tartan", 2002)
      Dim boat2 As New Boat("MO12345", 32, "Catalina", 2003)
      'establish association for first customer and boat
      customer1.SetBoat(boat1)
      boat1.SetCustomer(customer1)
      'establish association for second customer and boat
      customer2.SetBoat(boat2)
      boat2.SetCustomer(customer2)

      'navigate directly from customer1 to boat1
      Console.WriteLine("Boat info is " _
      & customer1.GetBoat().TellAboutSelf())
      'navigate directly from boat1 to customer1
      Console.WriteLine("Customer info is " _
      & boat1.GetCustomer().TellAboutSelf())

      'do the same for second customer
      Console.WriteLine("Boat info is " _
```

```
        & customer2.GetBoat().TellAboutSelf())
        'navigate directly from boat2 to customer2
        Console.WriteLine("Customer info is " _
        & boat2.GetCustomer().TellAboutSelf())
End Sub
```

Figure 9-9 Event procedure code to test association in both directions

```
Boat info is GA34567, 28, Tartan, 2002
Customer info is Eleanor, Atlanta, 123-4567
Boat info is MO12345, 32, Catalina, 2003
Customer info is JoAnn, St Louis, 987-6543
```

Figure 9-10 Test code output for Customer and Boat association in both directions

In the test code, two customers and two boats are instantiated. Then the customers are associated with their boats, and the boats are associated with their customers:

```
'establish association for first customer and boat
customer1.SetBoat(boat1)
boat1.SetCustomer(customer1)
'establish association for second customer and boat
customer2.SetBoat(boat2)
boat2.SetCustomer(customer2)
```

To complete the test, each customer is asked about its boat, navigating directly. Plus, each boat is asked about its customer, again navigating directly. For `customer1` and `boat1` the code is as follows:

```
'navigate directly from customer1 to boat1
Console.WriteLine("Boat info is " _
& customer1.GetBoat().TellAboutSelf())
'navigate directly from boat1 to customer1
Console.WriteLine("Customer info is " _
& boat1.GetCustomer().TellAboutSelf())
```

Hands-on Exercise 1

1. Locate **Example1** in the Chap09\Examples\Ex01 folder in the book's data files. Create a folder named **Chap09\Exercises** in the work folder on your system, and then copy the **Ex01** folder to the Chap09\Exercises folder in your work folder. Then open the project with VB .NET. You should see files such as Customer.vb and Boat.vb along with a Windows form file. Build the project and run it. Click the **Test Customer Owns a Boat** button and review the output to verify that it matches the output shown in Figure 9-7.

2. Examine the Customer.vb source code file to note the modifications allowing a customer to be associated with a boat. Examine the event procedure test code. Modify the event procedure to instantiate some additional customers and boats, associate customers with boats, and then verify that the associations work correctly.
3. Examine the modified Boat.vb source code file and note that even though a boat can be associated with a customer, it was not necessary to use that capability when testing the customer-to-boat association shown previously (the original Boat class from Chapter 8 could be used). Now run the application and click the **Test Association in Both Directions** button to verify that the output matches the output shown in Figure 9-10. Examine the event procedure test code. Modify the event procedure to instantiate some additional customers and boats, associate customers with boats, and then verify that the associations work correctly.
4. Close the Example1 project.

ADDING FUNCTIONALITY TO THE BOAT CLASS

The Customer and Boat example in the previous section implements both directions of the association relationship. You can use additional techniques to increase the functionality of classes that have association relationships. For example, you can include a custom method in Boat that establishes the association between Boat and Customer in both directions in one step. Additionally, because Bradshaw Marina does not want to keep information about a boat if its owner is not a customer, you can make the association between Boat and Customer mandatory rather than optional by adding a Customer reference parameter to the Boat constructor. Finally, because a boat must be associated with a customer, the Boat TellAboutSelf method can be modified to return information about the boat and the customer. These enhancements are described in this section using the project named Example2. The Boat class definition with these additional capabilities is shown in Figure 9-11.

```
' Boat class with additional capabilities

Public Class Boat

   'attributes
   Private stateRegistrationNo As String
   Private length As Single
   Private manufacturer As String
   Private year As Integer

   'reference variable for Customer instance
   Private theCustomer As Customer

   'constructor (four parameters plus customer reference)
   Public Sub New(ByVal aStateRegistrationNo As String, _
      ByVal aLength As Single, _
      ByVal aManufacturer As String, ByVal aYear As Integer, _
      ByVal aCustomer As Customer)
```

```
      'set values of attributes using accessor methods
      SetStateRegistrationNo(aStateRegistrationNo)
      SetLength(aLength)
      SetManufacturer(aManufacturer)
      SetYear(aYear)
      'because boat must have a customer, assign it in constructor
      AssignBoatToCustomer(aCustomer)
   End Sub

   'custom method to establish associations in both directions
   Public Sub AssignBoatToCustomer(ByVal aCustomer As Customer)
      SetCustomer(aCustomer)      'set customer reference for boat
      aCustomer.SetBoat(Me)       'ask customer to set its boat
   End Sub

   'TellAboutSelf method that gets customer info also
   Public Overridable Function TellAboutSelf() As String
      Return "boat number " & stateRegistrationNo & ", " _
      & length & ", " & manufacturer & ", " & year _
      & " customer for boat is " & theCustomer.TellAboutSelf()
   End Function

   (Continue with Get and Set accessor methods)
   . . .
   . . .

End Class
```

Figure 9-11 Boat class definition (partial) with additional capabilities

9

The method named `AssignBoatToCustomer` is a custom method added to Boat that accomplishes more than the setter method `SetCustomer`. It does invoke the `SetCustomer` method, but it also asks the customer to set its boat attribute to **`Me`**, meaning to this boat. In other words, the Boat instance sends a message to the Customer instance. Therefore, the `AssignBoatToCustomer` method establishes the association relationship in both directions when invoked:

```
'custom method to establish associations in both directions
Public Sub AssignBoatToCustomer(ByVal aCustomer As Customer)
   SetCustomer(aCustomer)  'set customer reference for boat
   aCustomer.SetBoat(Me)   'ask customer to set its boat
End Sub
```

This method can be invoked from a tester program using a statement such as the following:

```
boat1.AssignBoatToCustomer(customer1)
```

When the `AssignBoatToCustomer` method is invoked, the Boat instance invokes its `SetCustomer` method, passing the Customer reference. The Boat instance then invokes the customer's `SetBoat` method, passing a reference to the boat assigned to the keyword **`Me`**.

Note that the `AssignBoatToCustomer` method can be used to update the customer who owns a boat, replacing the prior customer. Both the customer and the boat are updated in one step.

Another enhancement to Boat occurs because Bradshaw Marina does not want to keep information about a boat if its owner is not a customer. Therefore, when a boat is instantiated, it could require a Customer reference as a parameter in the constructor. That way, the relationship between Boat and Customer becomes mandatory instead of optional. You cannot instantiate Boat without supplying a valid Customer reference. The header for the constructor for Boat becomes:

```
'constructor (four parameters plus Customer reference)
Public Sub New(ByVal aStateRegistrationNo As String, _
   ByVal aLength As Single, _
   ByVal aManufacturer As String, ByVal aYear As Integer, _
   ByVal aCustomer As Customer)
```

The code in the constructor sets values for all attributes and then invokes the `AssignBoatToCustomer` method discussed previously, which sets the customer attribute of the boat and asks the customer to set its boat attribute. Now when a boat is instantiated, the associations between the customer and the boat and between the boat and the customer are established automatically.

```
'set values of attributes using accessor methods
SetStateRegistrationNo(aStateRegistrationNo)
SetLength(aLength)
SetManufacturer(aManufacturer)
SetYear(aYear)
'because a boat must have a customer, assign it in constructor
AssignBoatToCustomer(aCustomer)
```

An additional modification to Boat is an enhanced TellAboutSelf method. Because the association between Boat and Customer is mandatory, the TellAboutSelf method can return information about the boat (as shown previously), and it can also get information about the customer who owns the boat and return that information, too. The string returned by the method includes information that the Boat instance gets directly from the Customer instance:

```
'TellAboutSelf method that gets customer info also
Public Overridable Function TellAboutSelf() As String
   Return "boat number " & stateRegistrationNo & ", " _
   & length & ", " & manufacturer & ", " & year _
   & " customer for boat is " & theCustomer.TellAboutSelf()
End Function
```

Figure 9-12 shows a sequence diagram that illustrates how the TellAboutSelf method works. As in the `AssignBoatToCustomer` method, a message is sent from one instance to another (objects interacting) to complete a task.

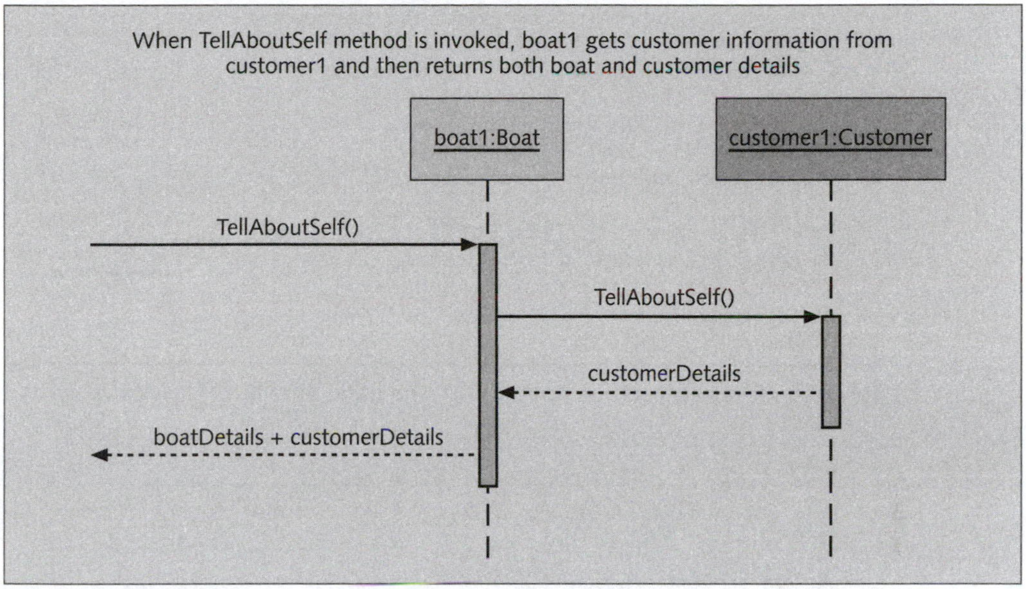
When TellAboutSelf method is invoked, boat1 gets customer information from customer1 and then returns both boat and customer details
boat1:Boat
customer1:Customer
TellAboutSelf()
TellAboutSelf()
customerDetails
boatDetails + customerDetails

Figure 9-12 Partial sequence diagram showing Boat TellAboutSelf method

An event procedure to test the new Boat class capabilities is shown in Figure 9-13, and the output is shown in Figure 9-14. The test code is simplified because the Boat constructor requires a Customer reference variable, the `AssignBoatToCustomer` method is invoked by the constructor, and the TellAboutSelf method returns information about the boat and the customer. A sequence diagram for this interaction is shown in Figure 9-15. Note that in this example, the association is tested in both directions, but when you invoke TellAboutSelf for the customer, boat information is not returned.

```
Private Sub btnTestBothDirections_Click(ByVal sender _
As System.Object, ByVal e As System.EventArgs) _
Handles btnTestBothDirections.Click

      'create two customer instances
      Dim customer1 As New Customer("Eleanor", "Atlanta", "123-4567")
      Dim customer2 As New Customer("JoAnn", "St Louis", "987-6543")

      'create two boat instances passing customer references
      Dim boat1 As New Boat("GA34567", 28, "Tartan", 2002, customer1)
      Dim boat2 As New Boat("MO12345", 32, "Catalina", 2003, customer2)

      'navigate directly from customer1 to boat1
      Console.WriteLine("Boat info is " _
      & customer1.GetBoat().TellAboutSelf())
```

```
        'navigate directly from boat1 to customer1
        Console.WriteLine("Customer info is " _
        & boat1.GetCustomer().TellAboutSelf())

        'do the same for second customer
        Console.WriteLine("Boat info is " _
        & customer2.GetBoat().TellAboutSelf())

        'navigate directly from boat2 to customer2
        Console.WriteLine("Customer info is " _
        & boat2.GetCustomer().TellAboutSelf())

    End Sub
```

Figure 9-13 Event procedure code to test the additional Boat class capabilities

```
Boat info is boat number GA34567, 28, Tartan, 2002 customer for boat is Eleanor, Atlanta,
123-4567
Customer info is Eleanor, Atlanta, 123-4567
Boat info is boat number MO12345, 32, Catalina, 2003 customer for boat is JoAnn, St Louis,
987-6543
Customer info is JoAnn, St Louis, 987-6543
```

Figure 9-14 Customer and enhanced Boat test code output

Hands-on Exercise 2

1. Locate the **Example2** project in the Chap09\Examples\Ex02 folder in the book's data files. Copy the **Ex02** folder to the Chap09\Exercises folder in your work folder, and then open the project with VB .NET. You should see files such as Customer.vb and Boat.vb along with a Windows form file. Note that this project includes the new version of Boat and the new version of the Boat Customer Tester form with the test code shown above. Build the project and run it. Click the **Test Association in Both Directions – Modified Boat** button and review the output to verify that it matches the output shown in Figure 9-14.

2. Modify Customer.vb by enhancing its TellAboutSelf method so it returns information about the customer's boat. Remember that a customer is not required to have a boat, so include an **`If`** statement and the **`Is`** operator to test whether the boat attribute is **`Nothing`** before attempting to get boat information. Also, do not invoke the Boat TellAboutSelf method to get boat information because that method invokes the Customer TellAboutSelf method. Instead, invoke the getter methods.

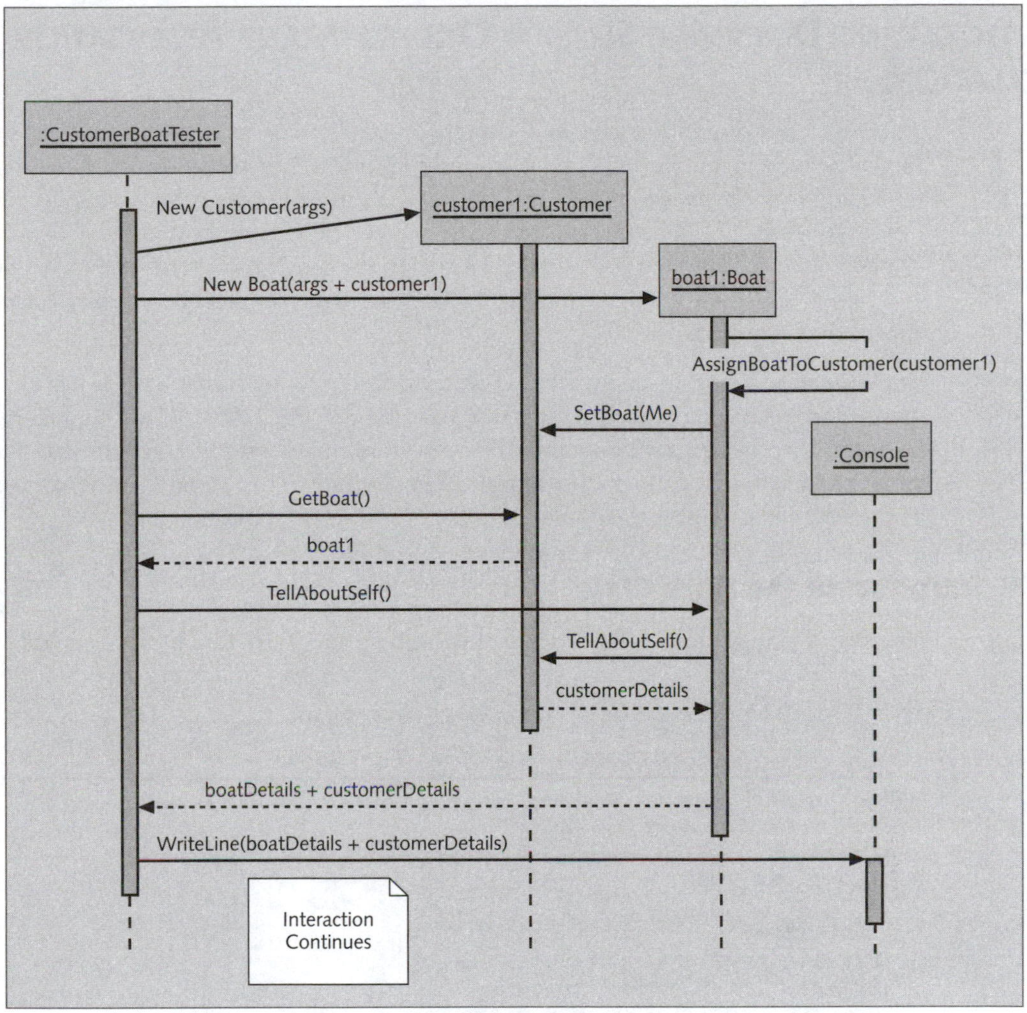

Figure 9-15 Partial sequence diagram for Customer and Boat test code

3. Add an additional button and test code that tests your new Customer TellAboutSelf method with a customer who has a boat and with a customer who does not have a boat.
4. Close the Example2 project.

Associating Dock and Slips: A One-to-Many Association Relationship

The Slip class was introduced in Chapter 7, and Slip has an association relationship with Dock, as seen in Figure 9-1. The relationship goes in two directions: A slip is *attached to* a dock, and a dock *contains* many slips. The association relationship between Slip and Dock is one-to-one, so it is implemented the same way as the Customer and Boat associations you worked with in the previous section. However, the association relationship between Dock and Slip is one-to-many, indicated by the 1..* notation on the association line, so a different approach is required.

Implementing a one-to-many association relationship requires that a dock instance have reference variables for more than one slip. You can use the `ArrayList` class (introduced in Chapter 4) to instantiate a container that can hold many reference variables, so you can use an `ArrayList` in the Dock class to hold many Slip reference variables. You can use methods of the `ArrayList` class to add Slip references and retrieve Slip references.

Introducing the Dock Class

The initial class definition for Dock is shown in Figure 9-16. The Dock class has four attributes: an ID number, a location, and two Boolean variables indicating whether the dock has electricity and water.

```
' Dock class (new to Chapter 9)
' each dock has many slips

Public Class Dock

   'attributes
   Private dockId As String
   Private location As String
   Private electricity As Boolean
   Private water As Boolean

   'references to slips associated with dock (1 to many)
   Private slips As ArrayList

   'constructor (four parameters)
   Public Sub New(ByVal aDockID As String, _
   ByVal aLocation As String, _
   ByVal anElectricity As Boolean, ByVal aWater As Boolean)
      'invoke setter methods to populate attributes
      SetDockId(aDockID)
      SetLocation(aLocation)
      SetElectricity(anElectricity)
      SetWater(aWater)
      slips = New ArrayList()
   End Sub
```

```
    'add the slip reference to the ArrayList instance
    Public Sub AddSlip(ByVal aSlip As Slip)
       slips.Add(aSlip)
    End Sub

    'return the ArrayList containing slip references
    Public Function GetSlips() As ArrayList
       Return slips
    End Function

    'TellAboutSelf method
    Public Function TellAboutSelf() As String
       Dim dockDetails As String
       dockDetails = "Dock " & dockId _
        & " location " & location & " has electricity " _
        & electricity & " has water " & water
       Return dockDetails
    End Function

    'get accessor methods
    Public Function GetDockId() As String
       Return dockId
    End Function
    Public Function GetLocation() As String
       Return location
    End Function
    Public Function GetElectricity() As Boolean
       Return electricity
    End Function
    Public Function GetWater() As Boolean
       Return water
    End Function

    'set accessor methods
    Public Sub SetDockId(ByVal aDockId As String)
       dockId = aDockId
    End Sub
    Public Sub SetLocation(ByVal aLocation As String)
       location = aLocation
    End Sub
    Public Sub SetElectricity(ByVal anElectricity As Boolean)
       electricity = anElectricity
    End Sub
    Public Sub SetWater(ByVal aWater As Boolean)
       water = aWater
    End Sub

End Class
```

Figure 9-16 Dock class definition

A fifth attribute that implements the one-to-many association relationship is an **ArrayList** named **slips**.

```
'references to slips associated with dock (1 to many)
Private slips As ArrayList
```

The constructor for Dock sets values for the four attributes. Then it instantiates the new **ArrayList** and assigns it to the **slips** attribute:

```
slips = New ArrayList()
```

A method is added to Dock that returns the **slips** reference variable much like any other getter method. Note that the type returned is an **ArrayList**.

```
'return the ArrayList containing slip references
Public Function GetSlips() As ArrayList
   Return slips
End Function
```

To add a slip to the dock, a custom method is included named **AddSlip**. The **AddSlip** method is invoked by the Slip **AddSlipToDock** method, as shown in the Slip class definition in the following section. The **slips.Add(aSlip)** statement is used to add a Slip reference to the **ArrayList** referenced by the variable **slips**. This allows a dock to have more than one slip.

```
'add the slip reference to the ArrayList instance
Public Sub AddSlip(ByVal aSlip As Slip)
   slips.Add(aSlip)
End Sub
```

Associating the Slip Class with Dock

The Slip class was introduced in Chapter 7, and many features were added to it, including constants and exceptions for validation. A simplified version of the Slip class is used in this example. The initial Slip class definition that associates with Dock is shown in Figure 9-17.

```
' Slip class -
' Modified from Chapter 7 to associate with Dock

Public Class Slip

   'attributes
   Private slipId As Integer
   Private slipWidth As Integer
   Private slipLength As Integer

   'reference variable points to one dock
   Private theDock As Dock

   'constructor (three parameters plus a Dock reference)
   Public Sub New(ByVal aSlipId As Integer, _
```

```
    ByVal aSlipWidth As Integer, ByVal aSlipLength As Integer, _
    ByVal aDock As Dock)
       'invoke setter methods to populate attributes
       SetSlipId(aSlipId)
       SetSlipWidth(aSlipWidth)
       SetSlipLength(aSlipLength)
       'invoke custom method for Dock association
       AddSlipToDock(aDock)
    End Sub

    'assign slip to dock (both directions of association)
    Public Sub AddSlipToDock(ByVal aDock As Dock)
       theDock = aDock          ' assign dock reference to attribute
       aDock.AddSlip(Me)        ' ask dock to add Me as slip
    End Sub

    'custom TellAboutSelf gets slip and dock information
    Public Function TellAboutSelf() As String
       Dim slipDetails As String
       slipDetails = "Slip " & slipId _
        & " width " & slipWidth & " length " & slipLength _
        & " attached to " & theDock.TellAboutSelf()
       Return slipDetails
    End Function

    'get accessor methods
    Public Function GetSlipId() As Integer
       Return slipId
    End Function
    Public Function GetSlipWidth() As Integer
       Return slipWidth
    End Function
    Public Function GetSlipLength() As Integer
       Return slipLength
    End Function
    Public Function GetDock() As Dock
       Return theDock
    End Function

    'set accessor methods
    Public Sub SetSlipId(ByVal aSlipId As Integer)
       slipId = aSlipId
    End Sub
    Public Sub SetSlipWidth(ByVal aSlipWidth As Integer)
       slipWidth = aSlipWidth
    End Sub
    Public Sub SetSlipLength(ByVal aSlipLength As Integer)
       slipLength = aSlipLength
    End Sub

End Class
```

Figure 9-17 Initial Slip class definition

9

Slip is modified much like Boat to implement a mandatory one-to-one association relationship. First, a Dock reference variable is added as an attribute of Slip. Standard accessor methods for the Dock reference attribute are also added. Next, the constructor is modified to expect a Dock reference parameter. Therefore, when a slip is instantiated, it must be associated with a dock. A statement in the constructor also invokes the slip's `AddSlipToDock` method, which establishes the association in both directions by invoking the dock's `AddSlip` method passing the **`Me`** keyword. The `AddSlipToDock` method is as follows:

```
'assign slip to dock (both directions of association)
Public Sub AddSlipToDock(ByVal aDock As Dock)
   theDock = aDock    ' assign dock reference to attribute
   aDock.AddSlip(Me) ' ask dock to add Me as slip
End Sub
```

Slip also includes a TellAboutSelf method that returns information about the slip and its dock.

```
'custom TellAboutSelf gets slip and dock information
Public Function TellAboutSelf() As String
   Dim slipDetails As String
   slipDetails = "Slip " & slipId _
    & " width " & slipWidth & " length " & slipLength _
    & " attached to " & theDock.TellAboutSelf()
   Return slipDetails
End Function
```

Testing the Dock and Slip Association Relationship

An event procedure that tests the Dock and Slip association relationship is shown in Figure 9-18, and the output produced is shown in Figure 9-19.

```
Private Sub btnDockHasSlips_Click(ByVal sender As System.Object, _
ByVal e As System.EventArgs) Handles btnDockHasSlips.Click

   'declare dock and slip references
   Dim dock1 As Dock
   Dim slip1 As Slip
   Dim slip2 As Slip
   Dim slip3 As Slip

   'create the dock
   dock1 = New Dock(1, "Main Cove", True, False)

   'create three slip instances for the dock
   slip1 = New Slip(1, 10, 20, dock1)
   slip2 = New Slip(2, 12, 25, dock1)
   slip3 = New Slip(3, 14, 25, dock1)
```

```
        'verify Dock to Slip association (1 to many)
        'first get ArrayList of slips from dock
        Dim slips As ArrayList = dock1.GetSlips()
        'get dock information and count of slips
        Console.WriteLine("Dock " & dock1.GetDockId() & " has " _
         & slips.Count() & " slips")
        'get information about each slip from slip's ArrayList
        Console.WriteLine("Slips for Dock " & dock1.GetDockId())
        Dim i As Integer
        For i = 0 To slips.Count() - 1
           Console.WriteLine("  " & slips.Item(i).TellAboutSelf())
        Next

        'get dock information from a slip navigating directly (1 to 1)
        Console.WriteLine("The Dock for Slip " & slip1.GetSlipId())
        Console.WriteLine("  " & slip1.GetDock().TellAboutSelf())

        'get dock information from a slip using TellAboutSelf (1 to 1)
        Console.WriteLine("Slip information (including dock) for Slip " _
         & slip1.GetSlipId())
        Console.WriteLine("  " & slip1.TellAboutSelf())

    End Sub

End Class
```

Figure 9-18 Event procedure to test the Dock and Slip association relationship

```
Dock 1 has 3 slips
Slips for Dock 1
 Slip 1 width 10 length 20 attached to Dock 1 location Main Cove has electricity True has water False
 Slip 2 width 12 length 25 attached to Dock 1 location Main Cove has electricity True has water False
 Slip 3 width 14 length 25 attached to Dock 1 location Main Cove has electricity True has water False
The Dock for Slip 1
  Dock 1 location Main Cove has electricity True has water False
Slip information (including dock) for Slip 1
 Slip 1 width 10 length 20 attached to Dock 1 location Main Cove has electricity True has water False
```

Figure 9-19 Output for test of Dock and Slip association relationship

9

First, one Dock and three Slip reference variables are declared. Then one dock and three slips are instantiated. Each slip is passed the same Dock reference, so all three slips are associated with the dock and the dock is associated with each slip automatically.

Now the tester program can test the associations in both directions. First, the one-to-many association is tested by asking the dock for its `ArrayList` using the `GetSlips` method. The number of slips can be verified by using the `Count` method of `ArrayList`:

```
'first get ArrayList of slips from dock
Dim slips As ArrayList = dock1.GetSlips()
'get dock information and count of slips
Console.WriteLine("Dock " & dock1.GetDockId() & " has " _
 & slips.Count() & " slips")
```

Once the tester program has the `slips ArrayList`, each slip can be accessed using a **`For`** loop that repeats based on the count of slips. The `Item` property of `ArrayList` is used to retrieve each Slip reference, and the Slip TellAboutSelf method is invoked for each slip.

```
'get information about each slip from slip's ArrayList
Console.WriteLine("Slips for Dock " & dock1.GetDockId())
Dim i As Integer
For i = 0 To slips.Count() - 1
   Console.WriteLine("   " & slips.Item(i).TellAboutSelf())
Next
```

The final section of the code tests the association between Slip and Dock, a one-to-one association. The direct navigation approach is used to get the dock reference from the slip and then to get the dock information. Next the slip's TellAboutSelf method is used to get slip and dock information.

```
'get dock information from a slip navigating directly (1 to 1)
Console.WriteLine("The Dock for Slip " & slip1.GetSlipId())
Console.WriteLine("   " & slip1.GetDock().TellAboutSelf())

'get dock information from a slip using TellAboutSelf (1 to 1)
Console.WriteLine("Slip information (including dock) for Slip " _
 & slip1.GetSlipId())
Console.WriteLine("   " & slip1.TellAboutSelf())
```

Hands-on Exercise 3

1. Locate **Example3** in the Chap09\Examples\Ex03 folder in the book's data files. Copy the **Ex03** folder to the Chap09\Exercises folder in your work folder, and then open the project with VB .NET. You should see files such as Dock.vb and Slip.vb along with a Windows form file. Build the project and run it. Click the **Test Dock and Slip Association** button and review the output to verify that it matches the output shown in Figure 9-19.

2. Add a second dock and two slips to the event procedure. Add code that verifies that all association relationships work correctly so the tester shows information about both docks.

3. Close the Example3 project.

ADDING THE BOAT AND CUSTOMER CLASSES TO THE SLIP EXAMPLE

The Slip class definition can be modified to include a Boat reference attribute and accessor methods because there is an association between Slip and Boat. The modifications to Slip include first adding a Boat reference attribute to Slip, and then adding **GetBoat** and **SetBoat** methods. Because the association between Slip and Boat is optional, do not modify the constructor to require a Boat reference. Example4 in the book's data files includes the modified version of Slip.

The Boat class also needs to be modified to associate with Slip. First, add a Slip reference attribute and accessor methods to Boat. Then add a method to Boat named **AssignBoatToSlip**. A boat does not have to be assigned to a slip initially, so the Slip reference attribute defaults to **Nothing** and the constructor does not invoke the method. (See the partial Boat class definition in Figure 9-20.)


```
' Boat class associates with Customer and Slip

Public Class Boat

   'attributes
   Private stateRegistrationNo As String
   Private length As Single
   Private manufacturer As String
   Private year As Integer

   'reference variables for Customer and Slip instances
   Private theCustomer As Customer
   Private theSlip As Slip

   'constructor (four parameters plus customer reference)
   Public Sub New(ByVal aStateRegistrationNo As String, _
      ByVal aLength As Single, _
      ByVal aManufacturer As String, ByVal aYear As Integer, _
      ByVal aCustomer As Customer)
      'set values of attributes using accessor methods
      SetStateRegistrationNo(aStateRegistrationNo)
      SetLength(aLength)
      SetManufacturer(aManufacturer)
      SetYear(aYear)
      'because boat must have a customer, assign it here
      AssignBoatToCustomer(aCustomer)
   End Sub
```

```
   'custom method to associate with customer in both directions
   Public Sub AssignBoatToCustomer(ByVal aCustomer As Customer)
      SetCustomer(aCustomer)   'set customer reference for boat
      aCustomer.SetBoat(Me)    'ask customer to set its boat to Me
   End Sub

   'custom method to associate with slip in both directions
   Public Sub AssignBoatToSlip(ByVal aSlip As Slip)
      SetSlip(aSlip)     'set slip reference for boat
      aSlip.SetBoat(Me) 'ask slip to set its boat to Me
   End Sub

   'TellAboutSelf method that gets customer info also
   Public Overridable Function TellAboutSelf() As String
      Return stateRegistrationNo & ", " & length & ", " _
      & manufacturer & ", " & year _
      & " customer for boat is " & theCustomer.TellAboutSelf()
   End Function

   (Continue with Get and Set accessor methods)
   . . .
   . . .
End Class
```

Figure 9-20 Boat class definition (partial) that associates with Slip and Customer

The Boat class already is designed to associate with a customer, so this example can also include the Customer class without any modification. Now the power of the association relationships becomes apparent. If you have a Customer reference, you can navigate to find the customer's boat, its slip, and its dock. Similarly, if you have a Dock reference, you can find each slip and navigate to the slip's boat and to the customer who owns it.

The event procedure shown in Figure 9-21 provides a comprehensive test of these associations. The output is shown in Figure 9-22.

```
Private Sub btnAddBoatsAndCustomers_Click(ByVal sender As _
System.Object, ByVal e As System.EventArgs) _
Handles btnAddBoatsAndCustomers.Click

   'declare dock and slip references
   Dim dock1 As Dock
   Dim slip1 As Slip
   Dim slip2 As Slip

   'create the dock
   dock1 = New Dock(1, "Main Cove", True, False)

   'create two slip instances for the dock
   slip1 = New Slip(1, 10, 20, dock1)
   slip2 = New Slip(2, 12, 25, dock1)
```

```
    'create customers
    Dim cust1 As New Customer("Eleanor", "Atlanta", "123-4567")
    Dim cust2 As New Customer("JoAnn", "St Louis", "987-6543")

    'create boats associated with customers
    Dim boat1 As New Boat("GA34567", 28, "Tartan", 2002, cust1)
    Dim boat2 As New Boat("MO98765", 32, "Catalina", 2003, cust2)

    'add boats to slips
    boat1.AssignBoatToSlip(slip1)
    boat2.AssignBoatToSlip(slip2)

    'get dock information from a slip navigating directly (1 to 1)
    Console.WriteLine("The Dock for Slip " & slip1.GetSlipId())
    Console.WriteLine("  " & slip1.GetDock().TellAboutSelf())

    'get boat and customer information for slip navigating
    'directly (1 to 1)
    Console.WriteLine("The Boat for Slip " & slip1.GetSlipId())
    Console.WriteLine("  " & slip1.GetBoat().TellAboutSelf())

    'get dock information navigating from customer
    Console.WriteLine("The Dock for Customer " & cust1.GetName())
    Console.WriteLine("  " _
     & cust1.GetBoat().GetSlip().GetDock().TellAboutSelf())

    'navigate from dock to each slip, its boat and customer
    'first get ArrayList of slips from dock
    Dim slips As ArrayList = dock1.GetSlips()
    'get slip information using slip's ArrayList
    Console.WriteLine("Dock " & dock1.GetDockId() & " has " _
     & slips.Count() & " slips")
    Console.WriteLine("Slips and details for Dock " _
     & dock1.GetDockId())
    'iterate through each slip
    Dim i As Integer
    For i = 0 To slips.Count() - 1
       Console.WriteLine("  " & slips.Item(i).TellAboutSelf())
       Console.WriteLine("  boat " _
        & slips.Item(i).GetBoat().TellAboutSelf())
    Next

End Sub
```

Figure 9-21 Event procedure to test Customer, Boat, Slip, and Dock associations

```
The Dock for Slip 1
  Dock 1 location Main Cove has electricity True has water False
The Boat for Slip 1
  GA34567, 28, Tartan, 2002 customer for boat is Eleanor, Atlanta, 123-4567
The Dock for Customer Eleanor
  Dock 1 location Main Cove has electricity True has water False
Dock 1 has 2 slips
Slips and details for Dock 1
  Slip 1 width 10 length 20 attached to Dock 1 location Main Cove has electricity True has
water False
  boat GA34567, 28, Tartan, 2002 customer for boat is Eleanor, Atlanta, 123-4567
  Slip 2 width 12 length 25 attached to Dock 1 location Main Cove has electricity True has
water False
  boat MO98765, 32, Catalina, 2003 customer for boat is JoAnn, St Louis, 987-6543
```

Figure 9-22 Output for test of Customer, Boat, Slip, and Dock association relationships

Figure 9-23 shows a sequence diagram of the interactions. First, reference variables are declared for a dock and two slips. Next, the dock is instantiated and two slips are instantiated. The association is completed in both directions by the Slip constructor. Next, two customers and two boats are instantiated, and the association between them is completed in both directions by the Boat constructor. Finally, each boat is assigned to a slip using the `AssignBoatToSlip` method, which completes this optional association in both directions.

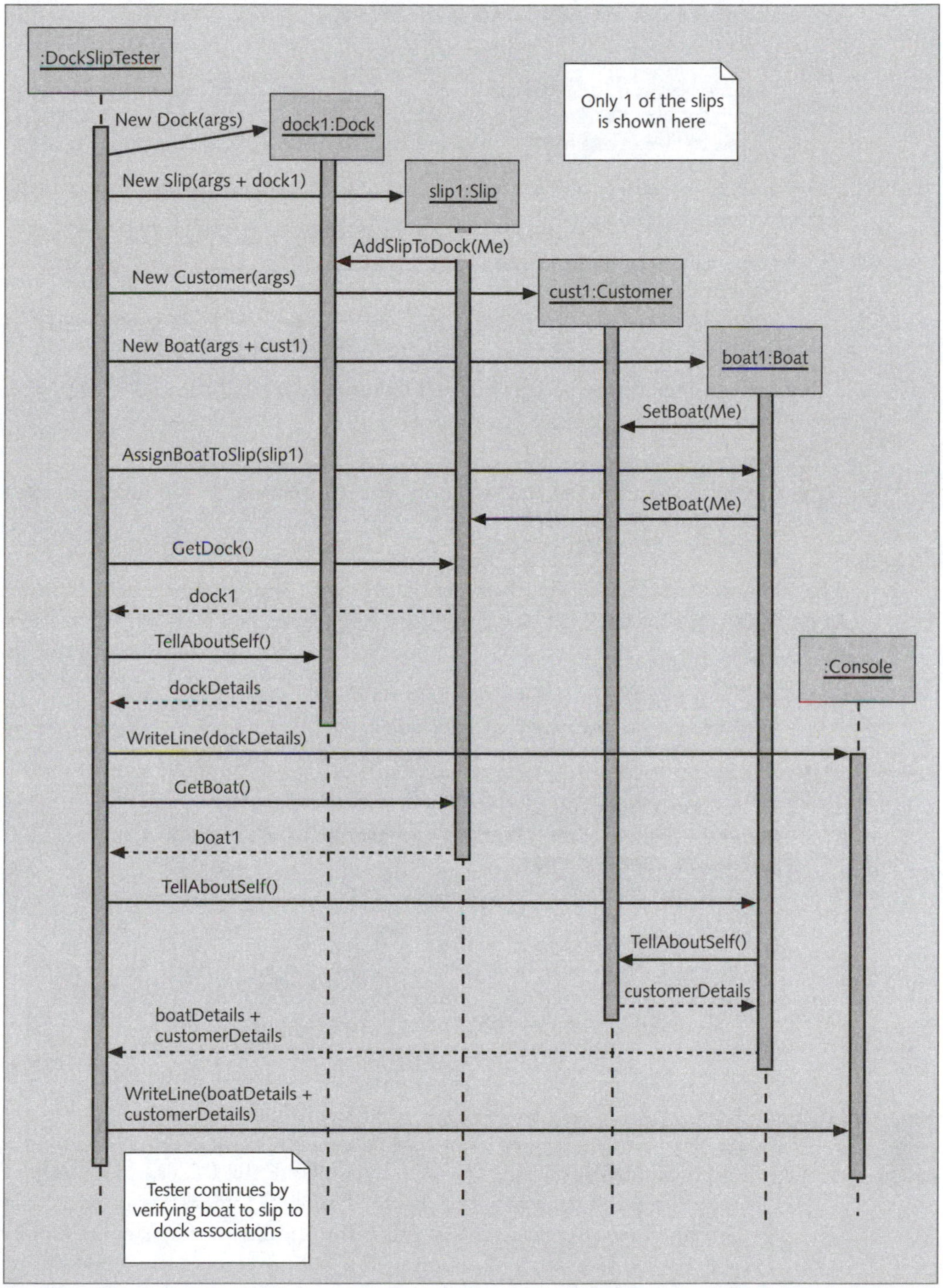

Figure 9-23 Partial sequence diagram for event procedure testing Customer, Boat, Slip, and Dock associations

Once all associations are established, a Slip reference can be used to navigate all the way to the dock instance:

```
'get dock information from a slip navigating directly (1 to 1)
Console.WriteLine("The Dock for Slip " & slip1.GetSlipId())
Console.WriteLine("  " & slip1.GetDock().TellAboutSelf())
```

Next, the Slip reference can be used to navigate to its boat, which also has information about the customer:

```
'get boat and customer information for slip navigating
'directly (1 to 1)
Console.WriteLine("The Boat for Slip " & slip1.GetSlipId())
Console.WriteLine("  " & slip1.GetBoat().TellAboutSelf())
```

Then, a Customer reference can be used to navigate to its boat and its slip, which also has information about the dock:

```
'get dock information navigating from customer
Console.WriteLine("The Dock for Customer " & cust1.GetName())
Console.WriteLine("  " _
 & cust1.GetBoat().GetSlip().GetDock().TellAboutSelf())
```

The one-to-many association between Dock and Slip is also tested. Starting with the `ArrayList` of slips from the dock, each slip is retrieved in a **`For`** loop. The Slip reference is used to get its boat, and the boat's TellAboutSelf method gets information on the boat and the customer:

```
Dim slips As ArrayList = dock1.GetSlips()
'get slip information using slip's ArrayList
Console.WriteLine("Dock " & dock1.GetDockId() & " has " _
 & slips.Count() & " slips")
Console.WriteLine("Slips and details for Dock " _
 & dock1.GetDockId())
'iterate through each slip
Dim i As Integer
For i = 0 To slips.Count() - 1
   Console.WriteLine("  " & slips.Item(i).TellAboutSelf())
   Console.WriteLine("  boat " _
    & slips.Item(i).GetBoat().TellAboutSelf())
Next
```

Hands-on Exercise 4

1. Locate **Example4** in the Chap09\Examples\Ex04 folder in the book's data files. Copy the **Ex04** folder to the Chap09\Exercises folder in your work folder, and then open the project with VB .NET. You should see files such as Dock.vb, Slip.vb, Boat.vb, and Customer.vb, along with a Windows form file. Build the project and run it. Click the **Test Adding Boats and Customers** button and review the output to verify that it matches the output shown in Figure 9-22.

2. Modify the event procedure to add another dock and some slips, as you did in Hands-on Exercise 3. Then add some customers and boats for the slips. Verify that all associations work correctly for the second dock.
3. Modify the TellAboutSelf method to Slip so it gets information about its boat and the boat's owner. If no boat is assigned to the slip, have the string indicate that the slip is available. Write a program to test all associations using the Slip TellAboutSelf method.
4. Close the Example4 project.

CREATING AND USING AN ASSOCIATION CLASS—LEASE

The Lease class, along with subclasses named AnnualLease and DailyLease, was described in Chapter 8. The Lease generalization/specialization hierarchy is an association class in the Bradshaw Marina class diagram, meaning that a Lease is much like an association between a customer and a slip, but with attributes for start date, end date, amount of lease, and so on. The notation in the partial class diagram shown in Figure 9-24 includes a dashed line attaching Lease to the association relationship between Customer and Slip. The association between Customer and Slip is one-to-one, so the dashed line attaching Lease to this relationship means that there is one lease between each customer and slip. Often association classes like Lease result from many-to-many associations, where a customer has many leases and a slip has many leases over a period of time.

9

The example in this section involves five problem domain classes. The Lease superclass is modified to include a Slip reference attribute and a Customer reference attribute. Accessor methods are also included. No other changes have been made to the Lease class introduced in Chapter 8 (see Figure 9-25). The Lease superclass can remain an abstract class. Note also that AnnualLease is a subclass of Lease, and it inherits the association between Lease and Slip and between Lease and Customer. This example includes no changes to the AnnualLease class, even though an AnnualLease instance will now inherit the association with a slip and a customer.

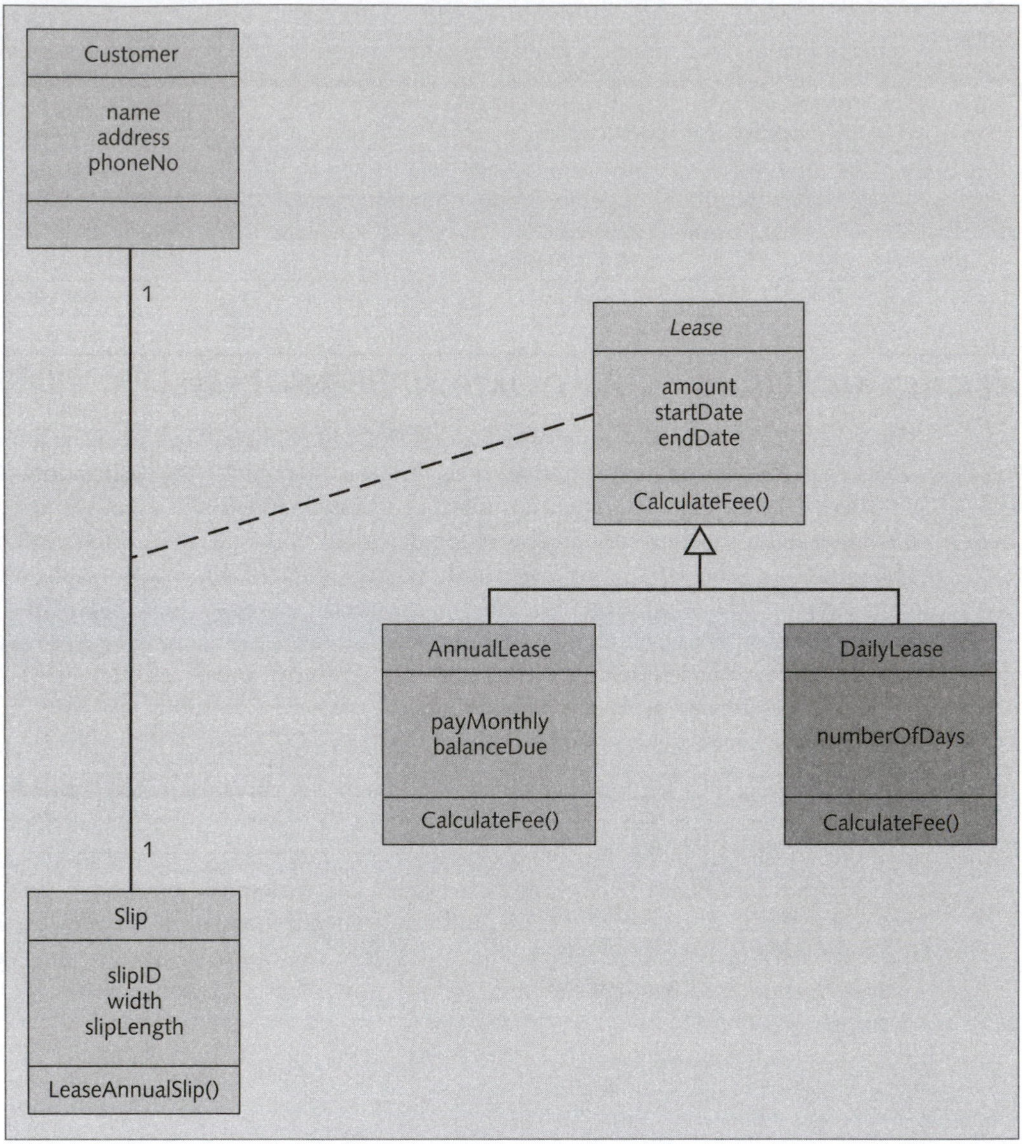

Figure 9-24 Partial class diagram for association class Lease

```
' Lease -- abstract association class
' between Slip and Customer

Public MustInherit Class Lease

   'attributes
   Private amount As Double
   Private startDate As DateTime
   Private endDate As DateTime

   'references to slip and customer
   Private theSlip As Slip
   Private theCustomer As Customer

   'constructor (1 parameter)
   Public Sub New(ByVal aStartDate As DateTime)
      SetStartDate(aStartDate)
      SetEndDate(Nothing)     ' endDate set by subclass
      SetAmount(0)
      'no customer or slip yet. set by subclass.
      SetCustomer(Nothing)
      SetSlip(Nothing)
   End Sub

   'TellAboutSelf method
   Public Overridable Function TellAboutSelf() As String
      Return (startDate & ", " & endDate & ", " & amount)
   End Function

   'custom method CalculateFee based on slip width
   'abstract method all subclasses must implement
   Public MustOverride Function CalculateFee(ByVal aWidth As Integer) _
   As Single

   'Get accessor methods
   Public Function GetStartDate() As DateTime
      Return startDate
   End Function
   Public Function GetEndDate() As DateTime
      Return endDate
   End Function
   Public Function GetAmount() As Double
      Return amount
   End Function
   Public Function GetCustomer() As Customer
      Return theCustomer
   End Function
   Public Function GetSlip() As Slip
      Return theSlip
   End Function

   'Set accessor methods
   Public Sub SetStartDate(ByVal aStartDate As DateTime)
      startDate = aStartDate
   End Sub
   Public Sub SetEndDate(ByVal anEndDate As DateTime)
      endDate = anEndDate
   End Sub
```

9

```
   Public Sub SetAmount(ByVal anAmount As Double)
      amount = anAmount
   End Sub
   Public Sub SetCustomer(ByVal aCustomer As Customer)
      theCustomer = aCustomer
   End Sub
   Public Sub SetSlip(ByVal aSlip As Slip)
      theSlip = aSlip
   End Sub

End Class
```

Figure 9-25 Modified Lease class definition

This example also uses the Boat class from the last section, and associates it with Customer and with Slip. Boat is not directly associated with Lease, so the class definition does not have to change. The Customer class must be changed by adding a Lease reference attribute along with accessor methods.

The Slip class requires more modification because it needs a custom method that creates a Lease instance and associates it with a customer and with a slip. To change the Slip class, you first add a Lease reference attribute along with accessor methods. You also include a method for creating an AnnualLease instance named `LeaseAnnualSlip`. Figure 9-26 shows the completed Slip class definition after modification.

```
' Slip class -
' Modified to associate with Dock and Boat
' Modified to associate with Lease
' with custom method LeaseAnnualSlip

Public Class Slip

   'attributes
   Private slipId As Integer
   Private slipWidth As Integer
   Private slipLength As Integer

   'reference variables point to one dock, one boat, and one lease
   Private theDock As Dock
   Private theBoat As Boat
   Private theLease As Lease

   'constructor (three parameters plus a Dock reference)
   Public Sub New(ByVal aSlipId As Integer, _
    ByVal aSlipWidth As Integer, _
    ByVal aSlipLength As Integer, ByVal aDock As Dock)
      'invoke setter methods to populate attributes
      SetSlipId(aSlipId)
      SetSlipWidth(aSlipWidth)
      SetSlipLength(aSlipLength)
```

```
      'invoke custom method for Dock association
      AddSlipToDock(aDock)
      'set boat and lease to nothing initially
      SetBoat(Nothing)
      SetLease(Nothing)
   End Sub

   'custom method creates an annual lease instance
   'slip takes responsibility for much processing
   Public Sub LeaseAnnualSlip(ByVal aCustomer As Customer, _
    ByVal aStartDate As DateTime, ByVal isPaymonthly As Boolean)
      'create AnnualLease instance and assign it to theLease
      theLease = _
       New AnnualLease(aStartDate, slipWidth, isPaymonthly)
      'tell lease to set its slip to me
      theLease.SetSlip(Me)
      'tell lease to set its customer
      theLease.SetCustomer(aCustomer)
      'tell customer to set its lease
      aCustomer.SetLease(theLease)
   End Sub

   'assign slip to dock (both directions of association)
   Public Sub AddSlipToDock(ByVal aDock As Dock)
      theDock = aDock   ' assign the dock reference to attribute
      aDock.AddSlip(Me) ' ask dock to add Me as slip
   End Sub

   'custom TellAboutSelf gets slip and dock information
   Public Function TellAboutSelf() As String
      Dim slipDetails As String
      slipDetails = "Slip " & slipId _
       & " width " & slipWidth & " length " & slipLength _
       & " attached to " & theDock.TellAboutSelf()
      Return slipDetails
   End Function

   'get accessor methods
   Public Function GetSlipId() As Integer
      Return slipId
   End Function
   Public Function GetSlipWidth() As Integer
      Return slipWidth
   End Function
   Public Function GetSlipLength() As Integer
      Return slipLength
   End Function
   Public Function GetDock() As Dock
      Return theDock
   End Function
   Public Function GetBoat() As Boat
      Return theBoat
   End Function
```

9

```
    Public Function GetLease() As Lease
       Return theLease
    End Function

    'set accessor methods
    Public Sub SetSlipId(ByVal aSlipId As Integer)
       slipId = aSlipId
    End Sub
    Public Sub SetSlipWidth(ByVal aSlipWidth As Integer)
       slipWidth = aSlipWidth
    End Sub
    Public Sub SetSlipLength(ByVal aSlipLength As Integer)
       slipLength = aSlipLength
    End Sub
    Public Sub SetBoat(ByVal aBoat As Boat)
       theBoat = aBoat
    End Sub
    Public Sub SetLease(ByVal aLease As Lease)
       theLease = aLease
    End Sub

End Class
```

Figure 9-26 Modified Slip class definition

The **LeaseAnnualSlip** method first instantiates AnnualLease, assigning the returned reference to a Lease reference. The complete AnnualLease class definition is shown in Chapter 8. Note that you can assign a reference to a subclass to a reference variable of the superclass, as shown in the following code:

```
'custom method creates an annual lease instance
'slip takes responsibility for much processing
Public Sub LeaseAnnualSlip(ByVal aCustomer As Customer, _
 ByVal aStartDate As DateTime, ByVal isPaymonthly As Boolean)
   'create AnnualLease instance and assign it to theLease
   theLease = _
    New AnnualLease(aStartDate, slipWidth, isPaymonthly)
   'tell lease to set its slip to this lease
   theLease.SetSlip(Me)
   'tell lease to set its customer
   theLease.SetCustomer(aCustomer)
   'tell customer to set its lease
   aCustomer.SetLease(theLease)
End Sub
```

The start date and width of the slip are passed to AnnualLease, which invokes the superclass constructor to assign the start date, calculates the lease amount based on slip width, assigns the end date, and sets the balance due if there are to be monthly payments. The next statement asks the lease to set its Slip reference. Then it asks the lease to set its Customer reference. Finally, it asks the customer to set its Lease reference.

Now that Slip, Lease, and Customer are modified, and Boat and AnnualLease are included without modification, code can be written to test the `LeaseAnnualSlip` method, as shown in Figure 9-27. Figure 9-28 shows a sequence diagram that illustrates these interactions between Slip, AnnualLease, and Customer in the test code. Figure 9-29 shows the output.

```
Private Sub btnLeaseSlip_Click(ByVal sender As System.Object, _
ByVal e As System.EventArgs) Handles btnLeaseSlip.Click

   'create the dock
   Dim dock1 = New Dock(1, "Main Cove", True, False)

   'create two slip instances for the dock
   Dim slip1 = New Slip(1, 10, 20, dock1)
   Dim slip2 = New Slip(2, 12, 25, dock1)

   'create customers
   Dim cust1 As New Customer("Eleanor", "Atlanta", "123-4567")
   Dim cust2 As New Customer("JoAnn", "St Louis", "987-6543")

   'create boats associated with customers
   Dim boat1 As New Boat("GA34567", 28, "Tartan", 2002, cust1)
   Dim boat2 As New Boat("MO98765", 32, "Catalina", 2003, cust2)

   'lease slips to customers
   slip1.LeaseAnnualSlip(cust1, New DateTime(2004, 3, 15), True)
   slip2.LeaseAnnualSlip(cust2, New DateTime(2004, 4, 20), False)

   'add boats to slips using lease references
   slip1.GetLease().GetCustomer().GetBoat().AssignBoatToSlip(slip1)
   slip2.GetLease().GetCustomer().GetBoat().AssignBoatToSlip(slip2)

   'get dock information from a slip navigating directly (1 to 1)
   Console.WriteLine("The Dock for Slip " & slip1.GetSlipId())
   Console.WriteLine("   Is " & slip1.GetDock().TellAboutSelf())

   'get boat, customer and lease information for slip
   'navigating directly (1 to 1)
   Console.WriteLine("The Boat details for Slip " _
    & slip1.GetSlipId())
   Console.WriteLine("   Is " & slip1.GetBoat().TellAboutSelf())
   Console.WriteLine("   Lease is " _
    & slip1.GetLease().TellAboutSelf())

   'navigate from dock to each slip, its boat, customer & lease
   'first get ArrayList of slips from dock
   Dim slips As ArrayList = dock1.GetSlips()
   'get slip information using slip's ArrayList
   Console.WriteLine("Dock " & dock1.GetDockId() & " has " _
    & slips.Count() & " slips")
   Console.WriteLine("Slips and details for Dock " _
    & dock1.GetDockId())
```

```
'iterate through each slip
Dim i As Integer
For i = 0 To slips.Count() - 1
   Console.WriteLine("   " & slips.Item(i).TellAboutSelf())
   Console.WriteLine("  boat " _
    & slips.Item(i).GetBoat().TellAboutSelf())
   Console.WriteLine("  lease " _
    & slips.Item(i).GetLease().TellAboutSelf())
Next

'navigate from slip back to slip via lease, customer, and boat
Console.WriteLine("Example navigating from slip1 to slip1: " _
 & vbCrLf _
 & slip1.GetLease().GetCustomer().GetBoat().GetSlip().TellAboutSelf())

      End Sub
```

Figure 9-27 Event procedure that tests the `LeaseAnnualSlip` method involving Slip, Customer, Lease, and Boat

NOTE: The code `& vbCrLf` means carriage return and line feed.

The event procedure first instantiates a dock and two slips. Next, two customers and two boats are instantiated. Recall that Slip automatically creates the association with Dock in both directions, and Boat automatically creates the association with Customer in both directions.

Next, each slip is leased to a customer:

```
'lease slips to customers
slip1.LeaseAnnualSlip(cust1, New DateTime(2004, 3, 15), True)
slip2.LeaseAnnualSlip(cust2, New DateTime(2004, 4, 20), False)
```

Note that the beginning dates are instantiated within the argument lists. The first annual lease will not have monthly payments, and the second annual lease will have monthly payments. Again, the `LeaseAnnualSlip` method of Slip takes responsibility for much of the processing, including instantiating AnnualLease and associating it with the slip and the customer.

The last step is to assign each boat to its slip. Note that a customer might lease a slip while still making arrangements to buy a boat. That is why the `LeaseAnnualSlip` method does not take care of this task. Starting with the slip, the statement navigates to the boat and asks it to assign itself to the slip:

```
'add boats to slips using lease references
slip1.GetLease().GetCustomer().GetBoat().AssignBoatToSlip(slip1)
slip2.GetLease().GetCustomer().GetBoat().AssignBoatToSlip(slip2)
```

All associations can now be verified, including:

- Verifying Slip to Dock
- Verifying Slip to Boat
- Verifying Slip to Lease
- Verifying Dock to Slip to Boat to Customer to Lease

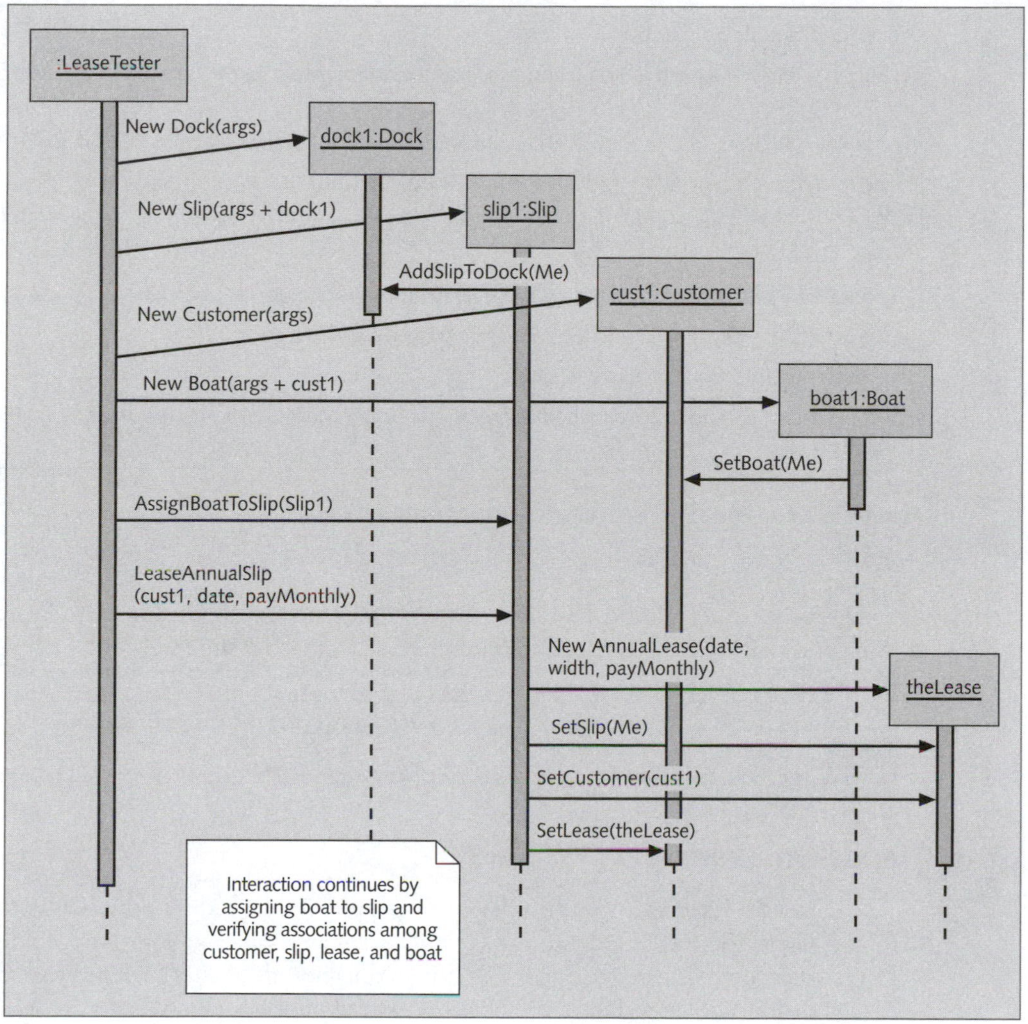

Figure 9-28 Partial sequence diagram for `LeaseAnnualSlip` method

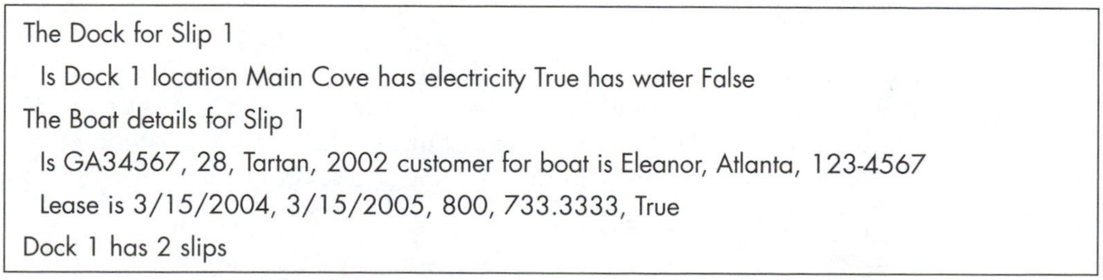

The Dock for Slip 1
Is Dock 1 location Main Cove has electricity True has water False
The Boat details for Slip 1
Is GA34567, 28, Tartan, 2002 customer for boat is Eleanor, Atlanta, 123-4567
Lease is 3/15/2004, 3/15/2005, 800, 733.3333, True
Dock 1 has 2 slips

Figure 9-29 Event procedure output

```
Slips and details for Dock 1
  Slip 1 width 10 length 20 attached to Dock 1 location Main Cove has electricity True has
water False
  boat GA34567, 28, Tartan, 2002 customer for boat is Eleanor, Atlanta, 123-4567
  lease 3/15/2004, 3/15/2005, 800, 733.3333, True
  Slip 2 width 12 length 25 attached to Dock 1 location Main Cove has electricity True has
water False
  boat MO98765, 32, Catalina, 2003 customer for boat is JoAnn, St Louis, 987-6543
  lease 4/20/2004, 4/20/2005, 900, 0, False
Example navigating from slip1 to slip1:
Slip 1 width 10 length 20 attached to Dock 1 location Main Cove has electricity True has
water False
```

Figure 9-29 Event procedure output (continued)

A final test navigates all of the associations from Slip to Boat to Customer to Lease and back to Slip, completing a full circle. This statement accomplishes the final test:

```
'navigate from Slip back to Slip via Lease, Customer, and Boat
Console.WriteLine("Example navigating from slip1 to slip1: " _
 & vbCrLf _
 & slip1.GetLease().GetCustomer().GetBoat().GetSlip().TellAboutSelf())
```

Hands-on Exercise 5

1. Locate **Example5** in the Chap09\Examples\Ex05 folder in the book's data files. Copy the **Ex05** folder to the Chap09\Exercises folder in your work folder, and then open the project with VB .NET. You should see files such as Lease.vb, AnnualLease.vb, Slip.vb, Dock.vb, and Customer.vb, along with a Windows form file. Build the project and run it. Click the **Test Lease Annual Slip** button and review the output to verify that it matches the output shown in Figure 9-29.
2. Add more customers, boats, and slips to the tester program. Lease the slips and test all associations.
3. Add the DailyLease class from Chapter 8 to the example. Note that you do not need to modify DailyLease, but you do need to add a `LeaseDailySlip` method to Slip that is similar to the `LeaseAnnualSlip` method. Modify the tester code so it creates daily leases instead of annual leases.
4. Close the Example5 project.

Chapter Summary

- Association relationships show an important part of the requirements for a business information system and are shown on the class diagram as lines connecting classes. Association relationship examples in the Bradshaw Marina class diagram include: a customer owns a boat, a boat is assigned to a slip, a slip is part of a dock, and so forth.
- Association relationships are implemented in two directions that must be considered separately. For example, one direction indicates that a customer might own a boat, and the other direction indicates that a boat must be owned by one and only one customer. In other words, some association relationships are optional and others are mandatory. Additionally, some have multiplicity of one-to-one, and some have multiplicity of one-to-many. For example, a slip is part of one dock, but a dock contains many slips.
- One-to-one association relationships are implemented in VB .NET by including a reference variable as an attribute in one class that points to an instance of another class. Accessor methods are also included that set or get the reference variable.
- One-to-many association relationships are implemented using an `ArrayList` that contains a collection of reference variables. For example, an `ArrayList` named `slips` is included as an attribute of Dock, and `slips` contains a collection of Slip references. Accessor methods use methods of the `ArrayList` class to add and retrieve reference variables.
- Association relationships can be directly navigated by writing one statement with multiple method calls that are executed from left to right. For example, the statement `aBoat.GetSlip().GetDock().GetLocation()` will get the location of a dock by asking the boat for its Slip reference, which is used to get the Dock reference, which is used to get the dock location.
- An association class on the class diagram is created much like any other class with VB .NET. The association class exists because of a relationship between two classes, such as Lease between Slip and Customer.

Review Questions

1. Describe the two directions of an association relationship between a car and an owner.
2. Give an example of an optional relationship, such as between a person and a pet. Can one direction be optional and one direction be mandatory?
3. Give an example of a mandatory relationship, such as between a mother and a child. Can both directions be mandatory?
4. Give an example of a composition relationship.
5. Give an example of an aggregation relationship.
6. In your own words, describe how an association relationship is implemented using VB .NET.
7. How are one-to-one association relationships implemented differently from one-to-many association relationships?
8. Write a statement that declares an attribute of Pet used to associate with one person.
9. Write the header for a constructor for the Pet class with parameters for name and breed and a Person reference variable with which to associate.
10. Write a statement that declares an `ArrayList` in Person to hold a collection of Pet references.
11. Write a complete accessor method for Pet named `SetPerson` assuming a pet can have only one person.
12. Write a complete method for Pet named `AssignPetToPerson` that establishes the association in both directions.
13. Consider the Mother and Child classes mentioned in Review Question 3. Write the statements to declare a `mother` attribute in Child and a `children ArrayList` in Mother.
14. Write a complete method for Child named `AssignChildToMother` that establishes the association in both directions.
15. Consider a set of classes that are associated together in this sequence: House, Street, City, State, Country, Continent, and Planet. Assume standard accessor methods are used, such as `GetHouse`, `GetStreet`, etc., which return reference variables to associated instances. Write a VB .NET statement that navigates from a house to get the name of the planet where the house is located.

Discussion Questions

1. Why are association relationships so important in business information systems? Can you imagine a business system without association relationships? Discuss.
2. Because association relationships have two directions, a boat might know what slip it is assigned to, but a slip might not know what boat is assigned to it. When would it be desirable to implement one direction of the relationship but not the other? Discuss what might be accomplished by controlling association relationships.
3. This chapter showed one-to-one and one-to-many association relationships in VB .NET. Can you use VB .NET to directly implement many-to-many relationships? If so, explain how you would do so.
4. Relational databases also implement association relationships, but by using foreign keys instead of reference variables. Discuss the key differences between using object references as attributes and using foreign keys in relational databases.

Projects

1. In the Review Questions, you worked with a person and pet example. Implement the example as a VB .NET project. Make sure your tester program tests the associations in both directions.
2. In the Review Questions, you worked with a mother and child example. Implement the example as a VB .NET project. Make sure your tester program tests the associations in both directions.
3. Bradshaw Marina eventually wants to include boat service records in its system. Revise the Bradshaw Marina class diagram to include a BoatServiceRecord class that is associated with Boat. Each boat might have zero or more services, and each service applies to one boat. The attributes of BoatServiceRecord are invoice number, service date, service type, and total charges. Create a project that includes the BoatServiceRecord class plus Boat and Customer. Include a method in Boat named `RecordBoatService` that instantiates BoatServiceRecord. Write a tester program to test the project.

PART 3

Developing Graphical User Interface (GUI) Classes

CHAPTER

10

VB .NET GUI Components Overview

In this chapter you will:

- Learn about the GUI classes in VB .NET
- Understand the code generated by VB .NET
- Handle VB .NET events
- Work with additional GUI controls

Part 2 (Chapters 6–9) of this book dealt with problem domain classes. You learned how to write PD class definitions consisting of attributes and methods, and how to create association and inheritance relationships among PD classes. Here in Part 3 (Chapters 10–12) you will learn how to develop graphical user interface (GUI) classes. You provide a graphical user interface so that users can both enter and display data. This chapter introduces the fundamental GUI components, and Chapter 11 shows you how to develop GUI classes for Bradshaw Marina.

All of the GUI components are instances of the supplied VB .NET GUI classes. As you learned in Chapter 2, if you want to create a GUI form, you use the Windows Form Designer to graphically arrange controls such as labels and buttons onto a window (or form). As you select components from the Toolbox, visually place them on the form, and set their properties in the Properties window, Visual Studio .NET generates the underlying code associated with your design. You complete the user interface by supplying details for the methods that respond to (or handle) user-generated events. An **event** is a signal that the user has taken some action, such as clicking a button or pressing a key on the keyboard. In this chapter you will learn more about events and how to interact with the user by writing code that responds to these events.

Earlier chapters introduced the visual programming techniques you use to develop GUI applications in VB .NET. In Chapter 2 you learned how to create a Windows application, as well as how to use the Toolbox window to select GUI components and position them on a form. You also learned how to manipulate the properties of a form and its components using the Properties window. In Chapter 6 you learned how to use a GUI form as a tester program. After completing this chapter, you will be able to create GUI applications using a variety of controls, including buttons, labels, text boxes, radio buttons, panels, menus, and several others. You will understand the code generated by VB .NET during the visual programming process, and you will know how to write methods to handle user-generated events.

Introducing the GUI Classes in VB .NET

Figure 10-1 shows a window containing many different GUI components. As you learned in Chapter 2, the window is called a form, and is an instance of the Form class. The Form class, like the other GUI classes introduced in this chapter, is a member of the System.Windows.Forms namespace. The form shown in Figure 10-1 consists of several GUI controls, including buttons, labels, text boxes, check boxes, radio buttons, tab pages, and menu items. Table 10-1 describes these and other commonly used GUI controls. Figure 10-2 shows all the controls and components that are available in the Toolbox.

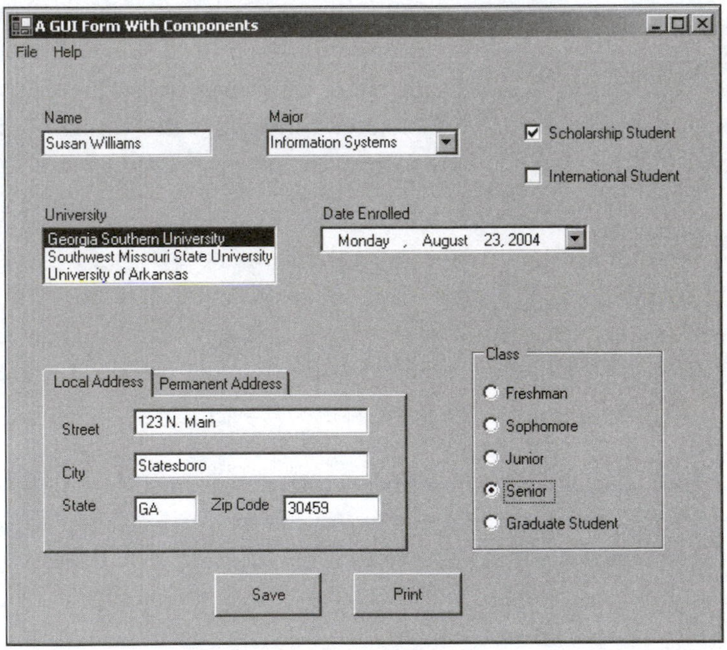

Figure 10-1 Form with GUI components

Table 10-1 Description of Selected GUI Controls

Component	Description
Button	A control that the user clicks to perform an action
CheckBox	A two-state control that enables yes/no (true/false) options. There are no requirements for the number of check boxes that may be checked at a given time.
CheckedListBox	Enables selection of one or more predefined items from a list that includes check boxes. When an item is selected, it appears checked.
ComboBox	Enables selection of one or more predefined items from a list, or entry of a new value
Component	The superclass of all GUI controls
Control	The superclass of all visible GUI controls
DateTimePicker	Enables selection of a date from a calendar
Form	A GUI window with a title bar. Forms usually contain other GUI components.
GroupBox	A container for other GUI components. Usually includes a border and a title, but not scroll bars.
Label	Used to display text (but not to input text)
ListBox	Enables selection of one or more predefined items from a list
MainMenu	Enables the inclusion of drop-down menus on a form
MenuItem	Provides individual menu options for drop-down menus
Panel	A container for other GUI components. Usually includes scroll bars, but not a title or border.
RadioButton	A two-state control that enables yes/no (true/false) options. Enforces mutually exclusive behavior (i.e., only one radio button in a radio button group may be selected at a given time).
TabControl	Enables the inclusion of tab pages on a form
TabPage	Provides individual tab pages for a tab control
TextBox	Used to display and input text
TreeNode	Provides individual nodes within a tree view
TreeView	Displays expandable outlines

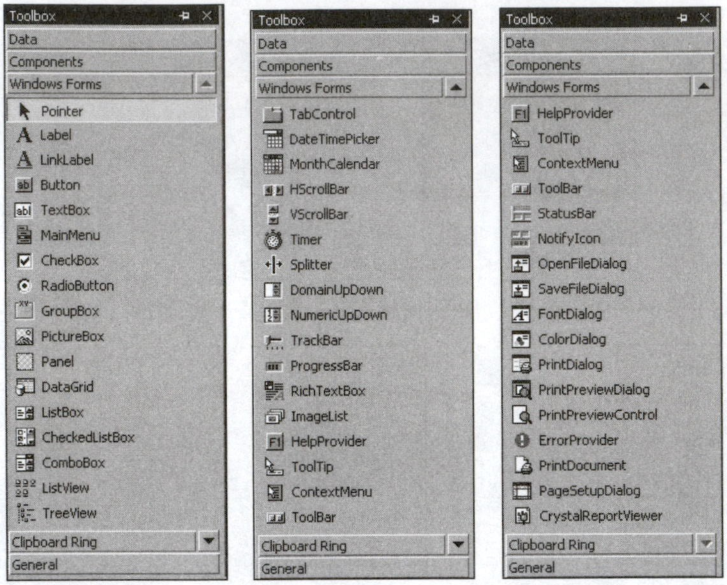

Figure 10-2 Controls and components in the Toolbox

Before you begin developing GUI applications, recognize that the GUI classes take advantage of inheritance. You can see from Figure 10-3 that nearly all of the GUI classes are subclasses of Component (TreeNode is the only GUI class discussed in this chapter that is not a subclass of Component), and that most GUI classes are also subclasses of Control. The difference between a component and a control is that an instance of a **control** has a visible, graphical representation, while an instance of a **component** does not. The Component class is the base class for all GUI components, and the Control class (which is a subclass of Component) provides basic functionality for the visible controls you use on a form. The Component and Control classes contain many important properties and methods that are inherited by their subclasses. As you explore the code generated by VB .NET, you will learn about many of these properties and methods. After you become familiar with the basic concepts and techniques, you can explore the documentation within the VB .NET Help facility to learn more about other GUI classes and their associated properties and methods.

```
Component
   Control
       ButtonBase
              Button
              CheckBox
              RadioButton
       DateTimePicker
       GroupBox
       Label
       ListControl
              ComboBox
              ListBox
                     CheckedListBox
       ScrollableControl
              ContainerControl
                     Form
              Panel
                     TabPage
       TabControl
       TextBoxBase
              TextBox
       TreeView
   Menu
       MainMenu
       ContextMenu
TreeNode
```


Figure 10-3 Hierarchy of selected GUI classes

UNDERSTANDING THE CODE GENERATED BY VB .NET

When you create GUI applications in VB .NET, you use a visual programming process. **Visual programming** generally consists of creating a form, setting its properties, adding controls and components to the form, setting their properties, and then adding the code necessary to handle the events users generate when they interact with your form. As you add controls and modify properties, VB .NET generates the code that handles the details of your form design. The code VB .NET generates for a GUI class definition generally follows the structure you used for problem domain class definitions. However, one conceptual difference between PD classes and GUI classes is that in order for you to see the form instance, you must create an instance of the form and its controls. For this reason, the code generated by VB .NET includes statements to instantiate all of the GUI components (such as buttons, labels, and text boxes) that you want to have on your form, as well as statements to set their properties.

Exploring the FormDemo Program

The first example of a GUI class definition is the FormDemo program you created in Chapter 2. Recall that the form contains a label and a button. When you press the button, a message box appears, as shown in Figure 10-4. The code generated by VB .NET for this application appears in the Code window, as shown in Figure 10-5.

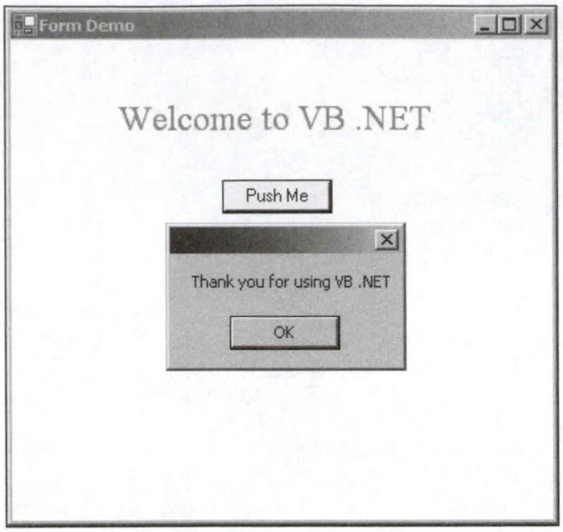

Figure 10-4 FormDemo GUI and its output

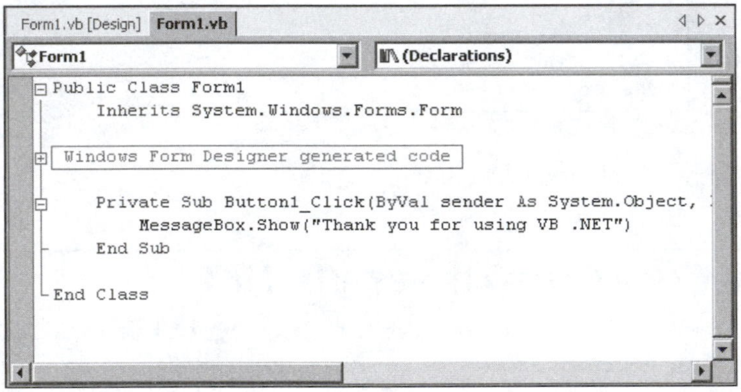

Figure 10-5 Contents of the Code window for the FormDemo program

As you saw in Figure 10-3, the inheritance hierarchy for Form is ContainerControl, ScrollableControl, Control, and Component. This means that the FormDemo class—which is an instance of Form—inherits methods from all four of these superclasses. The first line of code in the class definition reflects this fact by specifying that the FormDemo class inherits (or derives) from the Form class. Notice in Figure 10-5 that the code generated by VB .NET uses fully qualified class names—such as System.Windows.Forms.Form—rather than including a statement to import the Systems.Window.Forms namespace and then using the simple version of the class name in the `Inherits` clause (i.e., `Inherits Form`).

Most of the remaining code generated by VB .NET is collapsed under the heading "Windows Form Designer generated code." You can view this code by clicking the expand node. The code that is revealed is shown in Figure 10-6. (*Note*: Lines that are too long to fit on the page have been broken using the continuation character.)

```
#Region " Windows Form Designer generated code "
    Public Sub New()
        MyBase.New()

        'This call is required by the Windows Form Designer.
        InitializeComponent()

        'Add any initialization after the InitializeComponent() call
    End Sub

    'Form overrides dispose to clean up the component list.
    Protected Overloads Overrides Sub Dispose _
      (ByVal disposing As Boolean)
        If disposing Then
            If Not (components Is Nothing) Then
                components.Dispose()
            End If
        End If
        MyBase.Dispose(disposing)
    End Sub

    'Required by the Windows Form Designer
    Private components As System.ComponentModel.IContainer

    'NOTE: The following procedure is required by the Windows Form
    'Designer
    'It can be modified using the Windows Form Designer.
    'Do not modify it using the code editor.
    Friend WithEvents Label1 As System.Windows.Forms.Label
    Friend WithEvents Button1 As System.Windows.Forms.Button
    <System.Diagnostics.DebuggerStepThrough()> _
      Private Sub InitializeComponent()
            Me.Label1 = New System.Windows.Forms.Label()
            Me.Button1 = New System.Windows.Forms.Button()
            Me.SuspendLayout()
            '
            'Label1
            '
            Me.Label1.Font = New System.Drawing.Font _
                  ("Times New Roman", 18.0!, _
                  System.Drawing.FontStyle.Regular, _
                  System.Drawing.GraphicsUnit.Point, CType(0, Byte))
            Me.Label1.ForeColor = System.Drawing.Color.Red
            Me.Label1.Location = New System.Drawing.Point(48, 32)
            Me.Label1.Name = "Label1"
            Me.Label1.Size = New System.Drawing.Size(272, 48)
            Me.Label1.TabIndex = 0
            Me.Label1.Text = "Welcome to VB .NET"
            Me.Label1.TextAlign = _
                  System.Drawing.ContentAlignment.MiddleCenter
            '
            'Button1
            '
```

10

```
            Me.Button1.BackColor = _
                System.Drawing.Color.FromArgb(CType(255, Byte)' _
                CType(255, Byte), CType(128, Byte))
            Me.Button1.Location = New System.Drawing.Point(144, 96)
            Me.Button1.Name = "Button1"
            Me.Button1.TabIndex = 1
            Me.Button1.Text = "Push Me"
            '
            'Form1
            '
            Me.AutoScaleBaseSize = New System.Drawing.Size(5, 13)
            Me.BackColor = System.Drawing.Color.White
            Me.ClientSize = New System.Drawing.Size(368, 325)
            Me.Controls.AddRange(New System.Windows.Forms.Control() _
                {Me.Button1, Me.Label1})
            Me.Name = "Form1"
            Me.StartPosition = _
                System.Windows.Forms.FormStartPosition.CenterScreen
            Me.Text = "Form Demo"
            Me.ResumeLayout(False)

        End Sub

    #End Region
```

Figure 10-6 Code revealed by clicking the expand node

Notice that the expanded code begins with the **#Region** directive and ends with the **#EndRegion** directive. These directives specify that the code contained within them, by default, collapses into a single line in the Code Editor window. Collapsing this code hides the details associated with the GUI and allows you to concentrate on other portions of the program. Normally, you are not concerned with the code generated by VB .NET and can leave the code in its collapsed format. However, you should be able to read and understand the generated code.

The first block of code defines the constructor of the FormDemo class. The FormDemo constructor first calls its base class constructor. **MyBase** is a keyword that refers to the base class of the current object. In this example, the current object is FormDemo, and its base class is Form. The statement **MyBase.New( )** calls the base class (Form) constructor, which performs necessary initialization activities. The next line of code invokes the InitializeComponent method, which, as you will soon see, initializes property settings for all of the components within the form.

```
Public Sub New()
    MyBase.New()

        'This call is required by the Windows Form Designer.
        InitializeComponent()
        'Add any initialization after the InitializeComponent() call

End Sub
```

The next block of code defines the Dispose method. All subclasses of Component inherit a default implementation of the Dispose method. The Dispose method is a **destructor**—which means it releases system resources when the program ends. As shown in the following code, you often override the default implementation to provide additional functionality, such as disposing of resources used by the components and the form itself. For now, you need not be concerned with the details of this method, but you should understand its purpose.

```
'Form overrides dispose to clean up the component list.
Protected Overloads Overrides Sub Dispose(ByVal disposing As Boolean)
   If disposing Then
       If Not (components Is Nothing) Then
          components.Dispose()
       End If
   End If
   MyBase.Dispose(disposing)
End Sub
```

The next line of code, which is required by the Windows Form Designer, declares an instance of the IContainer class. IContainer is an interface that provides functionality for containers. A **container** is an object that holds other components.

```
'Required by the Windows Form Designer
    Private components As System.ComponentModel.IContainer
```


The next few statements declare the controls you created visually in the Design window—in this case Label1 and Button1. Note once more the use of fully qualified class names (for example, System.Windows.Forms.Label rather than simply Label).

```
'NOTE: The following procedure is required by the
'Windows Form Designer
'It can be modified using the Windows Form Designer.
'Do not modify it using the code editor.
Friend WithEvents Label1 As System.Windows.Forms.Label
Friend WithEvents Button1 As System.Windows.Forms.Button
```

The VB .NET code generator declares each of the controls you created in the Design window using the **`Friend`** access modifier and the **`WithEvents`** keyword. As you learned in Chapter 6, an object declared with the **`Friend`** modifier is accessible only within the assembly where it is declared. The **`WithEvents`** keyword signifies that a control instance may be the source of events, and that such events will be handled by methods that include a `Handles` *`controlName.eventName`* clause in the method declaration. For example, in this program the control that may trigger an event is Button1, and the event of interest is Click. Declaring `Button1` with the **`WithEvents`** keyword means that clicking Button1 will invoke the event handling method that includes the clause `Handles Button1.Click` in the method declaration. Methods that handle events are called **event handlers**.

The remainder of the generated code defines the `InitializeComponent` method. This method first instantiates the label and button instances. It then calls the SuspendLayout method to temporarily suspend layout events while you manipulate the properties (such as size and location) of various controls. The code contained with angle brackets in the method header is a descriptive tag that instructs the debugger not to stop here (i.e., to step through this method) when the program executes in debug mode. Recall that the keyword **Me** refers to the current object, which in this case is FormDemo. (*Note:* Lines that are too long to fit on the page have been broken using the continuation character.)

```
<System.Diagnostics.DebuggerStepThrough()> _
Private Sub InitializeComponent()
   Me.Label1 = New System.Windows.Forms.Label()
   Me.Button1 = New System.Windows.Forms.Button()
   Me.SuspendLayout()
```

The next section of code sets the properties of the label instance in accordance with the values you specified through the Properties window. For example, these statements establish the font, foreground color, location, name, size, tab index, text, and alignment of the label. The tab index (which begins with the value 0) indicates the tab order—the order in which the user moves from one control to the next by pressing the Tab key. By default, the tab order is identical to the order in which you create controls in the Windows Form Designer. You can change the tab order of a control by setting its Tab Index property in the Properties window.

TIP You can also change the tab order of the controls on a form by selecting Tab Order from the View menu, and then clicking the controls in the desired order.

```
'
'Label1
'
Me.Label1.Font = New System.Drawing.Font("Times New Roman", _
    18.0!, System.Drawing.FontStyle.Regular, _
    System.Drawing.GraphicsUnit.Point, CType(0, Byte))
Me.Label1.ForeColor = System.Drawing.Color.Red
Me.Label1.Location = New System.Drawing.Point(48, 32)
Me.Label1.Name = "Label1"
Me.Label1.Size = New System.Drawing.Size(272, 48)
Me.Label1.TabIndex = 0
Me.Label1.Text = "Welcome to VB .NET"
Me.Label1.TextAlign = _
   System.Drawing.ContentAlignment.MiddleCenter
```

Similar statements establish the properties of the button and form instances. Each statement performs an activity that corresponds to an action you completed visually using the Toolbox and the Properties window. The ResumeLayout method applies the pending layout events that were suspended earlier by the SuspendLayout method. The **#EndRegion** statement identifies the end of the code block generated by the Windows Form Designer.

```
'
'Button1
'
Me.Button1.BackColor = System.Drawing.Color.FromArgb _
   (CType(255,Byte), CType(255,Byte), CType(128,Byte))
```

```
        Me.Button1.Location = New System.Drawing.Point(144, 96)
        Me.Button1.Name = "Button1"
        Me.Button1.TabIndex = 1
        Me.Button1.Text = "Push Me"
        '
        'Form1
        '
        Me.AutoScaleBaseSize = New System.Drawing.Size(5, 13)
        Me.BackColor = System.Drawing.Color.White
        Me.ClientSize = New System.Drawing.Size(368, 325)
        Me.Controls.AddRange(New System.Windows.Forms.Control() _
           {Me.Button1, Me.Label1})
        Me.Name = "Form1"
        Me.StartPosition = _
            System.Windows.Forms.FormStartPosition.CenterScreen
        Me.Text = "Form Demo"
        Me.ResumeLayout(False)
    End Sub
#End Region
```

The last few lines of the program define the event handler you created in Chapter 2 to respond to a click event triggered by Button1.


```
Private Sub Button1_Click(ByVal sender As System.Object, _
    ByVal e As System.EventArgs) Handles Button1.Click
    MessageBox.Show("Thank you for using VB .NET")
End Sub
```

Notice once more that the method signature includes the clause `Handles Button1.Click.` Also notice that by convention the method name is `Button1_Click`. This event handler responds to a click event by displaying a message box that includes the statement "Thank you for using VB .NET."

Hands-on Exercise 1 (Part A)

1. Locate the **Chap10\Examples\Ex01\FormDemo** folder in the book's data files.
2. Create a folder named **Chap10\Examples\Ex01** in the work folder on your system, and then copy the **FormDemo** folder to this folder.
3. Using VB .NET, open the **FormDemo** project. You see Form1.vb in the Solution Explorer. Open the form and run the project. Click the **Push Me** button to verify that you see the output shown in Figure 10-4. (*Note*: You will work with this form again in Part B of this exercise.)
4. Close the Form Demo output window, and then press **F7** to view the Code window.
5. Reveal the hidden code generated by the Windows Form Designer by clicking the **expand node** adjacent to the label "Windows Form Designer generated code." Confirm that the code appears as shown in Figure 10-6.

6. Press **Shift+F7** to return to the Design window.
7. Add a label to the form. In the Properties window, change the Text property to **Using VB .NET is fun**.
8. Press **F7** to return to the Code window. Review the code that VB .NET added to your program for this label.
9. Rebuild the project and run it to verify that your modification is working properly, and then close the Form Demo output window.

Handling VB .NET Events

When you develop forms with other types of GUI controls, you supply the details of the event handling procedures associated with those controls. The process of creating these event procedures is virtually identical to the steps you followed when you created the procedure for the Button1.Click event in the FormDemo program. In Chapter 2 you created this event procedure by double-clicking Button1 in the Forms Designer window. VB .NET then placed the code for the Button1_Click method header in the Code window, and you added a statement that handles the event by displaying a message box. In general, when you double-click *any* control in the Forms Designer window, VB .NET automatically inserts the method header for the *most commonly used* event procedure for that control. As with the Button1_Click event procedure, you then supply the details that determine how the procedure responds to the event.

GUI components can be the source of many different events, and at times your programs will need to respond to events other than the most commonly used event for a particular control. For example, you might want the FormDemo program to respond to a MouseEnter event for Button1 by displaying the message "MouseEnter event detected." (A MouseEnter event occurs when the mouse moves into the space occupied by the control.) As shown in Figure 10-7, you can add this event handling method to the FormDemo program by pressing F7 to open the Code window, selecting Button1 from the Class Name drop-down list, selecting MouseEnter from the Method Name drop-down list, and then adding a `MessageBox.Show` statement.

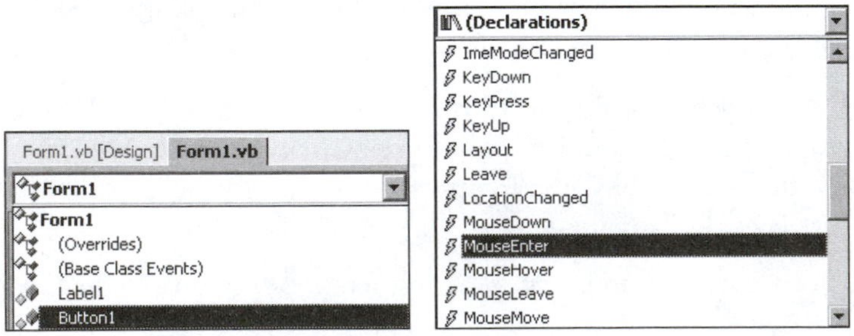

Figure 10-7 Creating an event handling method

Hands-on Exercise 1 (Part B)

1. If necessary, use VB .NET to open the **FormDemo** project that you created in your work folder for Hands-on Exercise 1 (Part A).
2. In the Design window, add a button to the form and set its Text property to **My Button**.
3. Double-click **My Button** to reveal the code editor. You see the Button2_Click procedure. This is the procedure that responds to a click event for this button. Add a statement to the Button2_Click procedure that displays a message box containing your name.
4. Add an event procedure to handle a MouseEnter event for Button1. To do so:
   a. In the Class Name drop-down list, select **Button1**.
   b. In the Method Name drop-down list, select **MouseEnter**. You see the Button1_MouseEnter procedure.
   c. Add a statement to display a message box containing the text **MouseEnter event detected**.
5. Rebuild the project and run it to verify that your modifications are working properly, and then close the Form Demo output window. Then close the project.

WORKING WITH ADDITIONAL GUI CONTROLS

In this section you will learn how to work with additional GUI controls such as radio button, check boxes, list boxes, tab controls, panels, and calendars. Before you begin, it is important to consider some fundamental principles of form design. Most business applications consist of multiple forms. The style and appearance of each form is called its **look and feel**. A key design goal is to provide a consistent look and feel as a user moves among various forms. For example, the size and location of buttons that perform common functions (such as navigating among forms and saving your work) should be consistent from one form to the next. The choice of colors and fonts for various controls should also be consistent throughout the application. Limiting the use of colors and fonts improves their visual impact—when used sparingly, they impart emphasis, but an overabundance of either distracts the user.

Another design goal is ease of use. To the extent possible, the purpose of each control and the layout of the form should be intuitive to the user. Prompts should clearly identify the data to be entered by the user and the actions that will be taken when the user interacts with a control (such as pressing a button). Additionally, the placement and grouping of controls should be logical, and the form should appear uncluttered.

A third design goal is to provide feedback to the user when certain actions (such as adding a record to a file) have been completed, and to inform the user when data entry errors have occurred. Such feedback should be presented to the user in a consistent manner, and with consistent verbiage, tone, and visual elements. Finally, it is good practice to design input forms in a way that minimizes the keystrokes required by the user. Doing so reduces the chance of data entry errors and makes life easier for the user. Achieving these goals requires forethought and planning. It is common for programming teams to develop a set of standards for form design at the outset of a project. Those standards are then enforced rigorously throughout the software development process.

Another standard followed by professional programmers concerns the naming conventions for program variables. Although end users are not aware of the variable names within a program, adhering to a set of naming conventions improves program readability and facilitates program maintenance. VB .NET includes a large number of GUI controls and components. As you observed in the code generated for the FormDemo program, the visual editor (by default) assigns variable names such as Button1, Button2, Label1, and Label2 to the controls you create in the Form Designer window. It is good programming practice to assign more meaningful variable names to these instances. To assign a new variable to a control, you change the Name property for that control in the Properties window. The variable name should reflect both the type of control (button, label, etc.) and its purpose. For example, the TesterFive program in Chapter 6 includes three button instances, named btnCreate, btnDisplay, and btnClose. The "btn" prefix is a naming convention that helps you identify an object as a button. Similar naming conventions are used throughout this text to identify other types of GUI controls. Table 10-2 shows the naming conventions for the controls and components used in this text.

Table 10-2 Naming Conventions for Selected GUI Controls

Component	Prefix
Button	btn
CheckBox	chk
CheckedListBox	chklst
ComboBox	cmb
DateTimePicker	dtp
Form	frm
GroupBox	grp
Label	lbl
ListBox	lst
MainMenu	mnu
MenuItem	mnuitm
Panel	pnl
RadioButton	rad
TabControl	tab
TabPage	tabpg
TextBox	txt
TreeNode	trn
TreeView	trv

Reviewing Forms, Buttons, and Labels

The FormDemo program of Chapter 2 introduced you to some of the commonly used methods and properties of the Button, Form, and Label classes. Recall that all GUI controls are subclasses of the Control class and, therefore, inherit properties, methods, and events from Control. Selected properties, methods, and common events of the Control class are summarized in Table 10-3.

Table 10-3 Selected Properties and Methods of the Control Class

Properties of the Control Class	Description
Anchor	Identifies the manner in which the control is anchored to its parent container (the default is top and left). The distance between the control and the specified edge(s) of the container to which it is anchored remains constant when the container is resized.
BackColor	Indicates the background color of the control
ClientSize	Indicates the size of the client area of the control
Controls	Identifies the collection of controls contained within the control. (The Add and Remove methods of the Control.ControlCollection class add individual controls to the collection. The AddRange and Clear methods of the Control.ControlCollection class add or remove all controls in the collection.)
Dock	Identifies the manner in which the control is docked to its parent container (the default is none). When a control is docked to an edge of its parent container, the specified (and opposite) edges of the control remain attached to the corresponding edges of the parent container when the parent container is resized.
Enabled	Indicates whether the user can interact with the control
Focused	Indicates whether the control has the input focus
Font	Indicates the font associated with the control
ForeColor	Indicates the foreground color of the control
Location	Indicates the coordinates of the upper-left corner of the control, relative to the upper-left corner of its container
Name	Identifies the name assigned to the control
Size	Indicates the size (height and width) of the control
TabIndex	Identifies the tab order of the control within its container
Text	Identifies the text associated with the control
Visible	Indicates whether the control will be visible or hidden from the user

Table 10-3 Selected Properties and Methods of the Control Class (continued)

Methods of the Control Class	
Dispose	Releases the resources used by the control
Focus	Sets the input focus to the control
Hide	Hides the control from the user
ResumeLayout	Applies pending layout events previously suspended by the SuspendLayout method
Show	Displays the control to the user
SuspendLayout	Temporarily suspends layout events while properties of various controls are manipulated

Tables 10-4, 10-5, and 10-6 summarize selected properties, methods, and common events of the Form, Button, and Label classes.

Table 10-4 Selected Methods, Properties, and Events of the Form Class

Properties of the Form Class	Description
	Inherits properties, methods, and events of the Control class
AcceptButton	Identifies the button that is clicked when the user presses the Enter key
AutoScale	Identifies a value indicating whether the form adjusts its size to fit the height of the font used on the form and scales its controls
AutoScaleBaseSize	Indicates the base size used for autoscaling the form
CancelButton	Identifies the button that is clicked when the user presses the Esc key
Menu	Associates a MainMenu instance with the form
Text	Identifies the text that appears in the form's title bar
Methods of the Form Class	
Close	Closes the form and disposes all associated resources
Common Events	
Load	Occurs before a form is displayed. You can use this event to perform various initialization activities.

Table 10-5 Selected Properties and Events of the Button Class

Properties of the Button Class	Description
	Inherits properties, methods, and events from the Control class
Text	Text that appears on the button's label
TextAlign	Sets the alignment of the button's text
Common Events	
Click	Occurs when the user clicks the button

Table 10-6 Selected Methods and Properties of the Label Class

Properties of the Label Class	Description
	Inherits properties, methods, and events from the Control class
Text	Text that appears on the label
TextAlign	Sets the alignment of the label
Common Events	
Click	Occurs when the user clicks the label

All of the VB .NET GUI controls, including those introduced in this chapter, have additional methods and properties that you may want to explore. You can use the Help facility to learn about any GUI class. For example, to view information about all members of the Button class, you can perform the following steps.

To view Help topics about members of the Button class:

1. Click **Help** on the menu bar, and then click **Index**. The Index window appears.
2. In the Index window, click the **Filtered by** list arrow, and then click **Visual Basic and Related**.
3. In the Look for text box, type **Button**.
4. Scroll through the results window until you see the entry "Button class (System.Windows.Forms)."
5. Just below this entry, click **all members**. You see the information shown in Figure 10-8. By clicking the links, you can explore details of the properties, methods, and events of the Button class.
6. Close the Button Members document window.

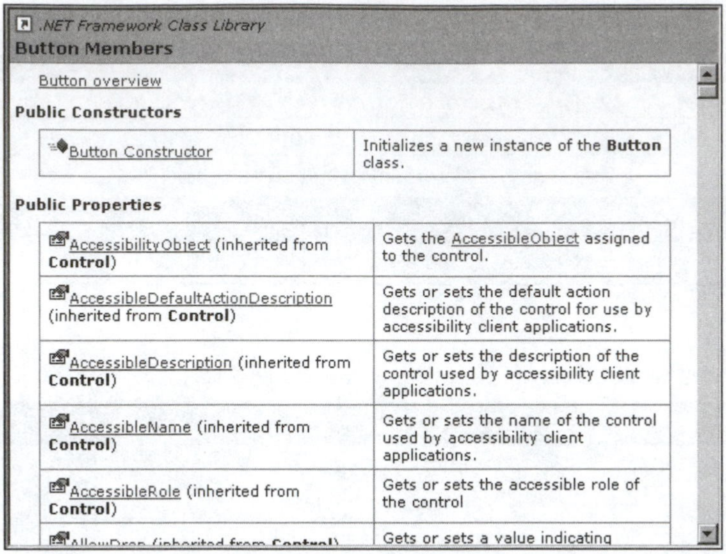

Figure 10-8 Help information for all members of the Button class

You will now learn about other commonly used VB .NET GUI controls, the primary properties and methods of each, and how each control might be used. This chapter will introduce these controls using simple examples. In Chapter 11 you will see how to incorporate these controls into the Bradshaw Marina application.

Using Text Boxes and Combo Boxes

Text boxes are used to display textual information to the user and to enable the inputting of text from the keyboard. When you use a text box to obtain input, the user must type text into the box. A **combo box** extends the functionality of a text box by providing the ability to select an item from a predetermined list of values, in addition to typing a value. Visually, a combo box looks like a text box, but includes a list arrow on its right. When you click the list arrow, a list of values appears and you select an item from that list. In VB .NET, the TextBox and ComboBox classes provide the functionality for these controls.

If you know that the value a user enters into a text box is frequently limited to a set of predefined choices, you should consider using a combo box. The user usually selects from the list, but can enter alternate text when needed. Overall, a combo box reduces the number of keystrokes, which improves the user friendliness of your program and makes it less susceptible to data entry errors. Figure 10-9 shows the result of clicking the list arrow on the combo box control for selecting a student's major in the GUI form presented earlier in this chapter.

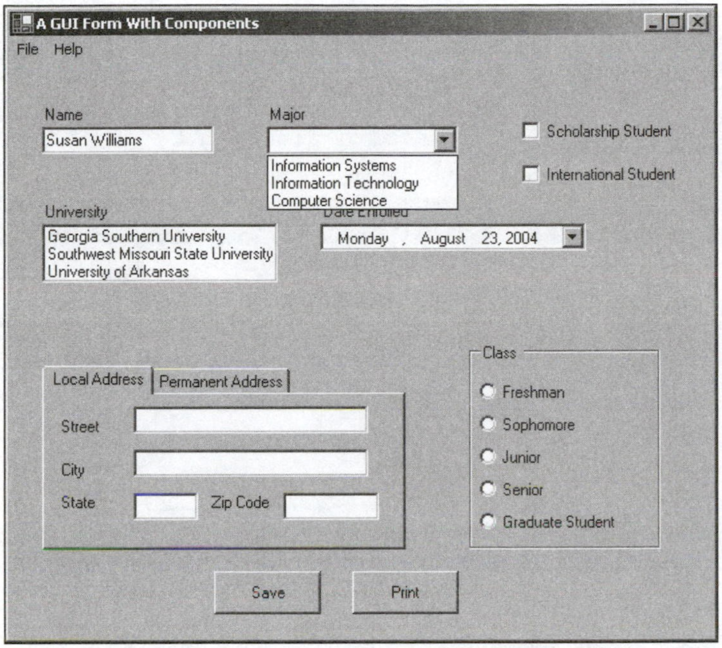

Figure 10-9 Selecting an item from the combo box control

As with buttons and labels, you include a text box or combo box within a form by selecting the appropriate control from the Toolbox, placing it on a form, and then setting its properties through the Properties window. Tables 10-7 and 10-8 summarize frequently used properties, methods, and events for these controls.

Table 10-7 Selected Properties, Methods, and Events of the TextBox Class

Properties of the Textbox Class	Description
	Inherits properties, methods, and events from the Control class
AcceptsReturn	Indicates whether pressing the Enter key creates a new line of text (in a multiline text box) or activates the default button for the form
AcceptsTab	Indicates whether pressing the Tab key types a tab character (in a multiline text box) or moves the input focus to the next control in the tab order
MaxLength	Indicates the maximum number of characters the text box can hold
Multiline	Indicates whether the text box can contain a single line of text (the default) or multiple lines of text
PasswordChar	Indicates the character that is echoed in the text box when a user types a password

Table 10-7 Selected Properties, Methods, and Events of the TextBox Class (continued)

Properties of the Textbox Class	Description
ReadOnly	Indicates whether the text box is read-only or can be edited
Text	Identifies the text contained within the text box
TextAlign	Indicates how text is aligned within the text box
Methods of the TextBox Class	
AppendText	Appends text to the text currently in the text box
Clear	Clears the text currently in the text box
Common Events	
TextChanged	Occurs when the text in the text box changes

Table 10-8 Selected Properties and Events of the ComboBox Class

Properties of the ComboBox Class	Description
	Inherits properties, methods, and events from the Control class
Items	Identifies the items contained within the combo box
MaxDropDownItems	Indicates the maximum number of items that will be shown in the drop-down portion of the combo box
SelectedIndex	Indicates the index of the currently selected item in the combo box
SelectedItem	Identifies the currently selected item in the combo box
Sorted	Indicates whether the items in the combo box are sorted
Text	Identifies the text that is displayed by default in the combo box
Common Events	
SelectedIndexChanged	Occurs when the item selected in the combo box changes

Hands-on Exercise 2

1. Locate the **Chap10\Examples\Ex02\TextBoxAndComboBox** folder in the book's data files. Create a folder named **Chap10\Exercises\Ex02** in the work folder on your system, and then copy the **TextBoxAndComboBox** folder to this folder.
2. Using VB .NET, open the **TextBoxAndComboBox** project. TextBoxAndComboBox_Form.vb appears in the Solution Explorer. Open the form and run the project to verify that it produces the output shown in Figure 10-10.

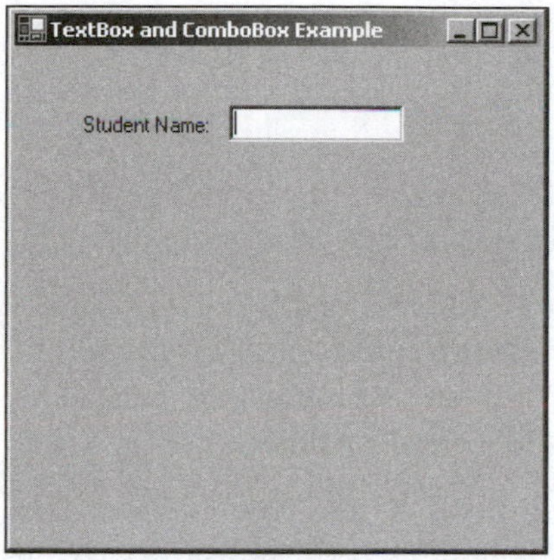

Figure 10-10 Output of the TextBoxAndComboBox project

3. Close the TextBox and ComboBox Example output window. In the Design window, click the **Student Name** text box. (Note that the Name property for this control is txtName.) Set the Text property to your name. Change the ReadOnly property to **True**, and set the TextAlign property to **Center**.

4. In the Design window, add a second label and text box to capture address information.
   a. Use the Properties window to set the Name property for the label to **lblAddress**. Set the Text property to Address:, and set the TextAlign property to **MiddleRight**.
   b. Change the Name property for the text box to **txtAddress**. Delete the value in its Text property so that txtAddress appears blank. Set the Multiline, AcceptsReturn, and AcceptsTab properties to **True**.
5. Add another label and text box to capture a password.
   a. Name the label and text box **lblPassword** and **txtPassword**, respectively.
   b. Set the Text property of lblPassword to **Password:,** and set the TextAlign property to **MiddleRight**.
   c. Change the PasswordChar property for txtPassword to *****.
6. Add a label and combo box to capture zip code information.
   a. Name the label and text box **lblZipCode** and **cmbZipCode**, respectively.
   b. Set the Text property of lblZipCode to **Zip Code**:, and set the TextAlign property to **MiddleRight**.
7. For the cmbZipCode control:
   a. Delete the value in the Text property.
   b. Set the MaxDropDownItems property to **3**.

c. Locate and click the Items property, and then click the **ellipsis** button. The String Collection Editor window appears.

d. In the String Collection Editor window, type the following zip codes (one per line): **30458**, **30459**, **30460**, **30461**.

e. Click **OK** to close the String Collection Editor window.

8. In the Design window, double-click the **Address** text box to add an event handler for txtAddress. In the Code window, notice that the default handler is for the TextChanged event. Add a statement to the txtAddress_TextChanged procedure to display a message box containing the message "txtAddress changed."

9. In the Design window, double-click the **Zip Code** combo box to add an event handler for cmbZipCode. In the Code window, notice that the default handler is for the SelectedIndexChanged event. Add a statement to the cmbZipCode_SelectedIndexChanged procedure to display a message box containing the message "cmbZipCode changed."

10. Build and execute the project to verify that your modifications are working properly, and then close the TextBox and ComboBox Example output window. Then close the project.

Using Check Boxes and Radio Buttons

Check boxes and radio buttons provide the ability to select from options presented within a GUI form. At any given point in time, a check box or radio button is in one of two states: checked (selected) or not checked (not selected). Like Button, the CheckBox and RadioButton classes are both subclasses of ButtonBase, but include additional methods that enable you to determine and set the state of a check box or radio button instance. Checking or unchecking one of these controls creates an event.

A **check box** appears as a small white box and usually includes a label that identifies its purpose. You use the Text property to set the value of the caption (or label) that describes the purpose of the check box. When selected, a check mark appears in the box. It is common to use multiple check boxes on a GUI form to capture combinations of related options that each have a true or false (checked or not checked) state. For example, in the Bradshaw Marina case, you could use two check boxes to indicate whether a dock has electricity and water. Depending on the characteristics of the dock, one, both, or neither check box might be checked. When working with multiple check boxes, there is no requirement that any check box be checked, and conversely, any or all of the check boxes may be checked simultaneously.

Radio buttons are similar to check boxes in many ways, but have important differences. Visually, radio buttons appear as small white circles and have captions (or labels) that identify their purpose. When a radio button is selected, a black dot appears within the circle. Like check boxes, a group of radio buttons represents a set of related options. However, you use radio buttons when you want to enforce business rules that require the options to be mutually exclusive—in other words, when one and only one of the options may be selected at any given time. For example, in the Bradshaw Marina case, a powerboat engine either uses gasoline fuel or diesel fuel (but not both). Tables 10-9 and 10-10 summarize frequently used properties, methods, and events for these controls.

Table 10-9 Selected Properties and Events of the CheckBox Class

Properties of the CheckBox Class	Description
	Inherits properties, methods, and events from the Control class
Checked	Indicates whether the check box is checked (true) or unchecked (false)
CheckState	Indicates the state of a check box: checked (contains a checkmark), unchecked (empty), or indeterminate (checked and shaded)
Text	Identifies the text (label) associated with the check box
Common Events	
CheckedChanged	Occurs when the check property (true or false) changes (i.e., each time the check box is checked or unchecked)

Table 10-10 Selected Properties and Events of the RadioButton Class

Properties of the RadioButton Class	Description
	Inherits properties, methods, and events from the Control class
Checked	Indicates whether the radio button is checked (true) or unchecked (false)
Text	Identifies the text (label) associated with the radio button
Common Events	
CheckedChanged	Occurs when the check property (true or false) changes (i.e., each time the radio button is checked or unchecked)

Hands-on

Hands-on Exercise 3 (Part A)

1. Locate the **Chap10\Examples\Ex03\CheckBoxAndRadioButton** folder in the book's data files. Create a folder named **Chap10\Exercises\Ex03** in the work folder on your system, and then copy the **CheckBoxAndRadioButton** folder to this folder.

2. Using VB .NET, open the **CheckBoxAndRadioButton** project. You see CheckBoxAndRadioButton_Form.vb in the Solution Explorer. Open the form and run the project to verify that it produces the output shown in Figure 10-11. (*Note*: You will work with this form again in Part B of this exercise.)

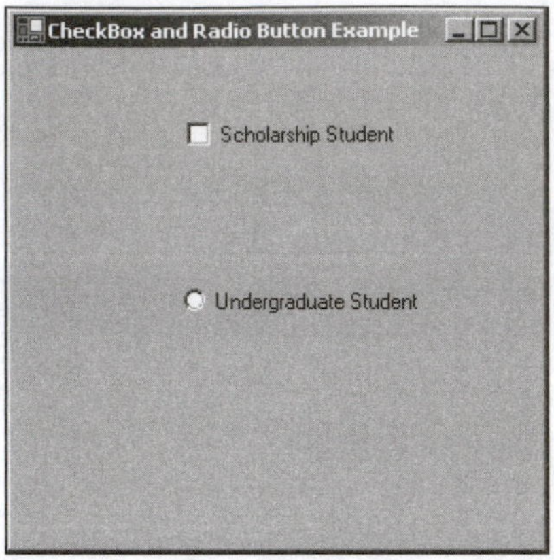

Figure 10-11 Output of the CheckBoxAndRadioButton

3. Close the CheckBox and Radio Button Example output window. In the Design window, add a second check box to capture whether the user is an international student. Place the new check box beneath the Scholarship Student check box.
   a. Use the Properties window to set the Name property to **chkInternational**.
   b. Set the Text property to **International Student**.
4. Add a second radio button and place it beneath the Undergraduate Student radio button.
   a. Use the Properties window to set the Name property to **radGraduate**.
   b. Set the Text property to **Graduate Student**.
5. In the Design window, double-click the **Scholarship Student** check box to add an event handler for chkScholarship. Note that the default handler is for the CheckedChanged event. Add the following statements to the chkScholarship_ CheckedChanged procedure to determine whether the check box is checked and to display an appropriate message:

```
If chkScholarship.Checked Then
        MessageBox.Show("Scholarship check box is checked")
Else
        MessageBox.Show("Scholarship check box is not checked")
End If
```

6. Create a similar event handler for the International Student check box.
7. Double-click the **Undergraduate Student** radio button to add an event handler for radUndergraduate. Note that the default handler is for the CheckedChanged

event. Add the following statements to the radUndergraduate_CheckedChanged procedure to determine whether the radio button is checked and display a message:

```
If radUndergraduate.Checked Then
        MessageBox.Show("Undergraduate radio button is checked")
Else
        MessageBox.Show("Undergraduate radio button is not checked")
End If
```

8. Create a similar event handler for the Graduate Student radio button.
9. Build and execute the project to verify that your modifications are working properly.
10. Close the CheckBox and Radio Button Example output window.

Using Group Boxes and Panels

Group boxes and **panels** are containers that enable you to visually and logically organize groups of related controls. Once you create an instance of the GroupBox or Panel class, you can place other components (such as buttons, labels, and text boxes) inside it. When you move the panel or group box, all the controls within it move together. A group box appears with a border (or frame) around the controls contained within it. A panel does not include a border by default, but you can set the BorderStyle property to change this if desired. Panels may include vertical and horizontal scroll bars, but do not have captions. Group boxes, on the other hand, do not include scroll bars, but usually have a caption. You set the caption using the Text property. Panels and group boxes may be nested—in other words, a group box or panel may contain other group boxes or panels.

Although they may contain any of the GUI controls, a common use of group boxes and panels is to group a set of radio buttons. Several group boxes and panels may be used within a single form to group multiple sets of radio buttons. In this case, mutually exclusive behavior is enforced separately for each group. Group boxes and panels can be the source of several different events, but your programs do not commonly need to respond to these events. Tables 10-11 and 10-12 summarize frequently used methods and properties for these controls.

Table 10-11 Selected Properties of the GroupBox Class

Properties of the GroupBox Class	Description
	Inherits properties, methods, and events from the Control class
Controls	Identifies the collection of controls contained within the group box. (The Add and Remove methods of the Control.ControlCollection class add individual controls to the collection. The AddRange and Clear methods of the Control.ControlCollection class add or remove all controls in the collection.)
Text	Identifies the text (caption) associated with the group box

Table 10-12 Selected Properties of the Panel Class

Properties of the Panel Class	Description
	Inherits properties, methods, and events from the Control class
AutoScroll	Indicates whether the panel will allow the user to use scroll bars to view portions of the panel that would otherwise be out of view
BorderStyle	Indicates the border style for the panel (default is none)
Controls	Identifies the collection of controls contained within the panel. (The Add and Remove methods of the Control.ControlCollection class add individual controls to the collection. The AddRange and Clear methods of the Control.ControlCollection class add or remove all controls in the collection.)

Hands-on Exercise 3 (Part B)

1. If necessary, use VB .NET to open and run the **CheckBoxAndRadioButton** project that you created in your work folder for Hands-on Exercise 3 (Part A). If you completed Part A properly, you see the output shown in Figure 10-12.

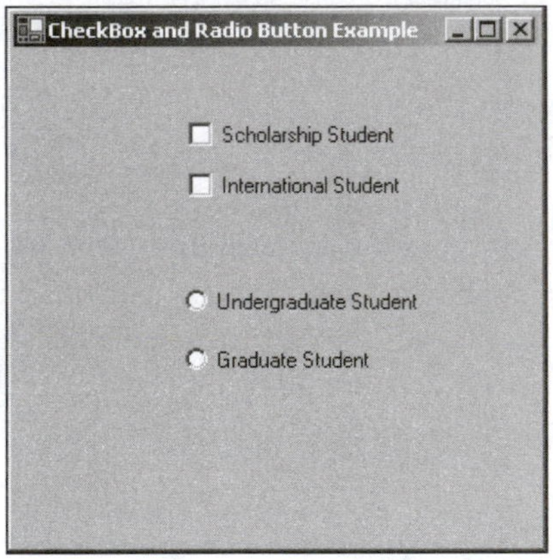

Figure 10-12 Output of the CheckBoxAndRadioButton project after completing Part A

2. Close the CheckBox and Radio Button Example output window. In the Design window, create a group box control. Place the group box in an empty portion of the form. For the group box control:

   a. Use the Properties window to set the Name property to **grpStudentType**.

   b. Set the Text property to **Student Type**.

3. Drag the Undergraduate Student radio button and the Graduate Student radio button into the group box.
4. In the Design window, create a panel. Place the panel in an empty portion of the form. For the panel control:
   a. Use the Properties window to set the Name property to **pnlStudentStatus**.
   b. Set the AutoScroll property to **True**.
   c. Set the BorderStyle property to **FixedSingle**.
5. Drag the Scholarship Student and International Student check boxes into the panel.
6. Press **F7** to view the code editor. Examine the code added by the Windows Form Designer. Note the use of the Controls.AddRange method for both the group box and panel instances.
7. Build and execute the project to verify that your modifications are working properly. Your output should resemble Figure 10-13.

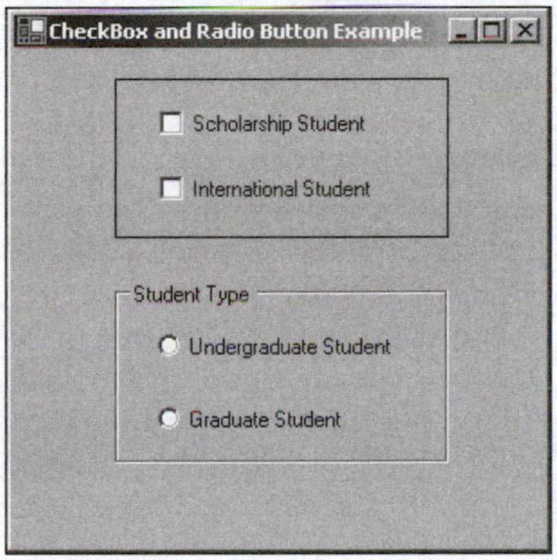

Figure 10-13 Output of the CheckBoxAndRadioButton project with group box and panel controls added

8. Close the CheckBox and Radio Button Example output window. Then close the project.

Using List Boxes and Checked List Boxes

List boxes and checked list boxes provide the ability to select one or more items from a predetermined list of values. **List boxes**, which are instances of the ListBox class, enable you (by default) to select one item from the list, but you can enable the selection of multiple list items by setting the SelectionMode property. **Checked list boxes** extend the functionality of a list box by including a check box to the left of each item in the list. By default, instances of the CheckedListBox class allow the selection of multiple items in the list. When you select an item in the list, a check mark appears in the corresponding check box.

Use a list box or checked list box when you want to force the user to select one or more items from a predetermined list of values without an option to enter alternate values. For example, in the Bradshaw Marina case, you could use a list box to enable the user to select from a list of available slips. Tables 10-13 and 10-14 summarize frequently used properties, methods, and events for these controls.

Table 10-13 Selected Properties, Methods, and Events of the ListBox Class

Properties of the ListBox Class	Description
	Inherits properties, methods, and events from the Control class
Items	Gets the items of the list box
Multicolumn	Indicates whether the list box supports multiple columns
SelectedIndex	Indicates the index of the currently selected item in the list box
SelectedIndices	Indicates the indices of all the currently selected items in the list box
SelectedItem	Identifies the currently selected item in the list box
SelectedItems	Identifies all the currently selected items in the list box
SelectionMode	Indicates whether the user can select a single item or multiple items from the list box
Sorted	Indicates whether the items in the list box are sorted
Methods of the ListBox Class	
ClearSelected	Deselects all items in the list box
GetSelected	Indicates whether the specified item is selected in the list box
SetSelected	Selects (or deselects) the specified item in the list box
Common Events	
SelectedIndexChanged	Occurs when the item selected in the list box changes

Table 10-14 Selected Properties, Methods, and Events of the CheckedListBox Class

Properties of the CheckedListBox Class	Description
	Inherits properties, methods, and events from the Control and ListBox classes
CheckedIndices	Identifies the checked indexes in the checked list box
CheckedItems	Identifies the checked items in the checked list box
Methods of the CheckedListBox Class	
GetItemChecked	Indicates whether the specified item is checked
GetItemCheckState	Indicates the check state of the specified item
SetItemChecked	Sets (checks) the item at the specified index
SetItemCheckState	Sets the check state of the item at the specified index

Table 10-14 Selected Properties, Methods, and Events of the CheckedListBox Class (continued)

Common Events	
ItemCheck	Occurs when the checked state of an item changes
SelectedIndexChanged	Occurs when the item selected in the checked list box changes

Hands-on Exercise 4

1. Locate the **Chap10\Examples\Ex04\ListBoxAndCheckedListBox** folder in the book's data files. Create a folder named **Chap10\Exercises\Ex04** in the work folder on your system, and then copy the **ListBoxAndCheckedListBox** folder to this folder.

2. Using VB .NET, open the **ListBoxAndCheckedListBox** project. You see ListBoxAndCheckedListBox_Form.vb in the Solution Explorer. Open the form and run the project to verify that it produces the output shown in Figure 10-14.

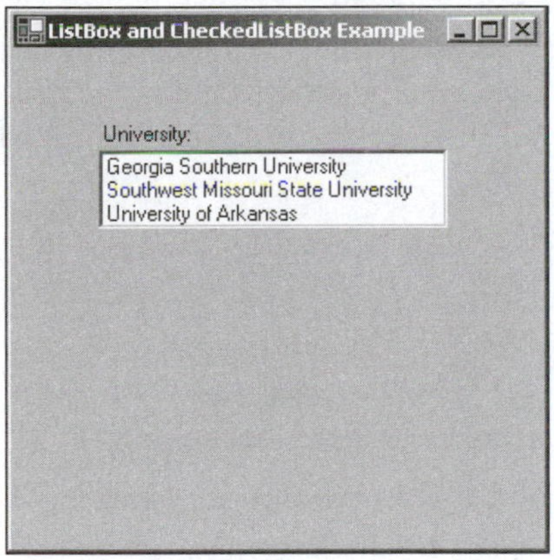

Figure 10-14 Output of the ListBoxAndCheckedListBox project

3. Close the ListBox and CheckedListBox Example output window. Press **F7** to open the Code window, and then review the hidden code created by the Windows Form Designer. In the Properties window, note that the Selection Mode property for the University list box is set to One by default, indicating that only one item may be selected from this list.

4. In the Design window, add a checked list box control to capture information regarding a student's major(s). Place the checked list box beneath the University list box.
   a. Use the Properties window to set the Name property to **chklstMajor**.
   b. Click the **Items** property, and then click the **ellipsis** button. The String Collection Editor window appears.
   c. In the String Collection Editor window, type the following majors (one per line): **Information Technology**, **Computer Science**, **Information Systems**.
   d. Click **OK** to close the String Collection Editor window.
   e. Set the Sorted property to **True**.
   f. Set the CheckOnClick property to **True**.
5. In the Design window, double-click the **University** list box to add an event handler for lstUniversity. Note that the default handler is for the SelectedIndexChanged event. Add the following statement to the lstUniversity_SelectedIndexChanged procedure to determine which item in the list has been selected and display an appropriate message.

```
MessageBox.Show("University selected is: " & lstUniversity.SelectedItem)
```

6. Double-click the **Major** checked list box to add an event handler for chklstMajor. Note that the default handler is for the SelectedIndexChanged event. Add the following statements to the chklstMajor_SelectedIndexChanged procedure to determine which major(s) have been selected and display an appropriate message.

```
'Declare variables as type String
Dim output, checkString As String

'Clear the output string
output = ""

'For each item that is checked in chklstMajor
For Each checkString In chklstMajor.CheckedItems

   'Append the checked item onto the output string
   output = output & checkString & "   "

Next     'End For Loop

'If no items checked, set output string accordingly
If output = "" Then
   output = "No items checked"
End If

'Display the output
MessageBox.Show(output)
```

7. Build and execute the project to verify that your modifications are working properly.
8. Close the ListBox and CheckedListBox Example output window. Then close the project.

Using Tree Views and Tree Nodes

A **tree view**, which is supported by the TreeView class, displays a group of hierarchically related items, where each item (or **tree node**) is represented as an instance of the TreeNode class. As shown in Figure 10-15, a tree view and its associated tree nodes appear as an expandable outline. In the Bradshaw Marina case, you could use the tree view control to display dock and slip information.

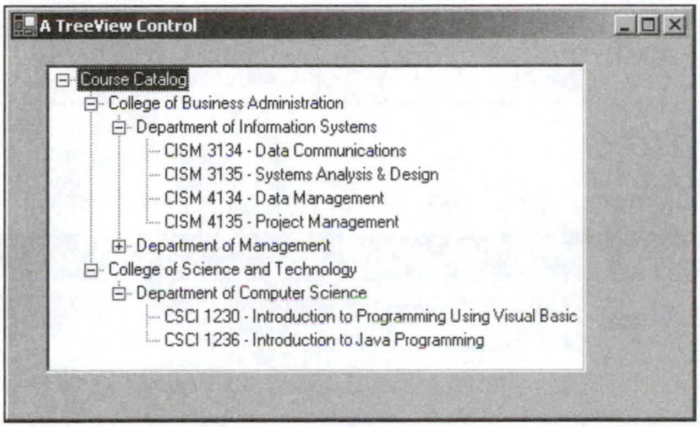

Figure 10-15 TreeView control

Tables 10-15 and 10-16 summarize frequently used properties, methods, and events for these controls.

Table 10-15 Selected Properties, Methods, and Events of the TreeView Class

Properties of the TreeView Class	Description
CheckBoxes	Indicates whether check boxes are displayed next to the nodes in the tree
Indent	Indicates the distance to indent each level in the tree
Nodes	Identifies the collection of tree nodes assigned to the tree
Scrollable	Indicates whether the tree view control displays scroll bars when needed
SelectedNode	Identifies the currently selected node in the tree
ShowLines	Indicates whether lines are drawn between nodes in the tree
ShowPlusMinus	Indicates whether plus (+) and minus (–) signs are displayed next to nodes that contain subnodes. Plus and minus signs indicate that a node can be expanded or collapsed, respectively.
ShowRootLines	Indicates whether lines are drawn between nodes that are at the root of the tree
Sorted	Indicates whether the nodes in the tree are sorted

Table 10-15 Selected Properties, Methods, and Events of the TreeView Class (continued)

Methods of the TreeView Class	
CollapseAll	Collapses all the nodes in the tree
ExpandAll	Expands all the nodes in the tree
GetNodeAt	Retrieves the node at the specified location in the tree
GetNodeCount	Retrieves the number of nodes in the tree, optionally including the nodes in all subtrees
Common Events	
AfterSelect	Occurs after a tree node is selected

Table 10-16 Selected Properties and Methods of the TreeNode Class

Properties of the TreeNode Class	Description
Checked	Indicates whether a tree node is checked or unchecked
FirstNode	Gets the first child node in the tree
FullPath	Gets the path from the root to the current node
Index	Identifies the position of the specified node in the tree
LastNode	Gets the last child node in the tree
NextNode	Gets the next sibling node in the tree
Nodes	Identifies the collection of tree nodes assigned to the current node
Parent	Gets the parent node of the current node in the tree
SelectedNode	Identifies the currently selected node
Text	Identifies the text that appears in the label of the tree node
Methods of the TreeNode Class	
Collapse	Collapses the tree node
Expand	Expands the tree node
ExpandAll	Expands all nodes in the tree
GetNodeCount	Identifies the number of child nodes
Remove	Removes the current node from the tree

Hands-on Exercise 5

1. Locate the **Chap10\Examples\Ex05\TreeViewAndTreeNode** folder in the book's data files. Create a folder named **Chap10\Exercises\Ex05** in the work folder on your system, and then copy the **TreeViewAndTreeNode** folder to this folder.

2. Using VB .NET, open the **TreeViewAndTreeNode** project. You see TreeViewAndTreeNode_Form.vb in the Solution Explorer. Open the form and run the project. Expand the Course Catalog, College of Business Administration, and Department of Information Systems nodes to verify that you see the output shown in Figure 10-16.

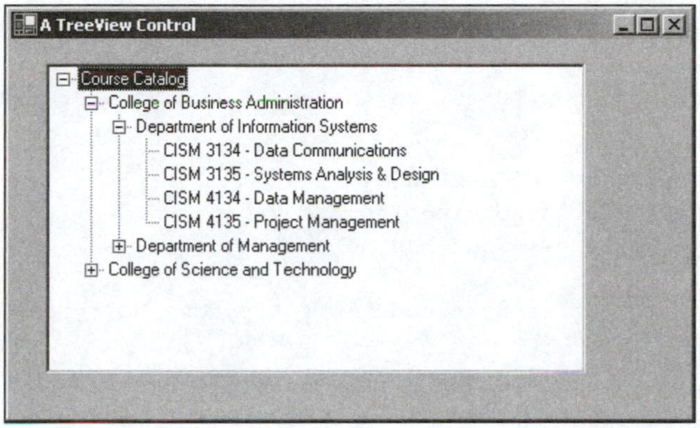

Figure 10-16 Output of the TreeViewAndTreeNode project

3. Close the A TreeView Control output window, and then press **F7** to open the Code window and review the code created by the Windows Form Designer.

4. Press **Shift+F7** to return to the Design window, and then click **Course Catalog** to select the tree view control. In the Properties window, click the **Nodes** property, and then click the **ellipsis** button. The TreeNode Editor window appears.

5. In the TreeNode Editor window, expand the existing nodes and add a child node to a node of your choosing. Click **OK** to close the TreeNode Editor window.

6. In the Design window, double-click the tree view control to add an event handler for trvExample. Note that the default handler is for the AfterSelect event. Add the following statements to the trvExample_AfterSelect procedure to determine which node in the tree has been selected and display a message about this node and other nodes related to it.

```
'Create a variable of type TreeNode
Dim myNode As TreeNode = New TreeNode()

'If a node is selected by the mouse
 If e.Action = TreeViewAction.ByMouse Then

   'Set myNode equal to the node selected
   myNode = trvExample.SelectedNode

   MessageBox.Show("Selected node is " & myNode.Text)
```

```
        'Check for existence of parent node
        If myNode.Parent Is Nothing Then
              MessageBox.Show("Node has no parent")
        Else
              MessageBox.Show("Parent node is " & myNode.Parent.Text)
        End If

        'Check for existence of previous node
        If myNode.PrevNode Is Nothing Then
              MessageBox.Show("Node has no previous node")
        Else
              MessageBox.Show("Previous node is " & myNode.PrevNode.Text)
        End If

        'Check for existence of next node
        If myNode.NextNode Is Nothing Then
              MessageBox.Show("Node has no next node")
        Else
              MessageBox.Show("Next node is " & myNode.NextNode.Text)
        End If

        'Collapse the tree to the root node
        trvExample.CollapseAll()
  End If
```

7. Build and execute the project to verify that your modifications are working properly.
8. Close the A TreeView Control output window. Then close the project.

Using Date/Time Pickers

A **date/time picker** control, which is an instance of the DateTimePicker class, enables you to select a date and time from a calendar and to display the date and time in a number of different formats. Figure 10-17 shows the result of clicking the down arrow on the date/time picker control for selecting a student's enrollment date in the GUI form presented earlier in this chapter. In the Bradshaw Marina case, you could use an instance of this class to enable the user to select the starting date of a lease.

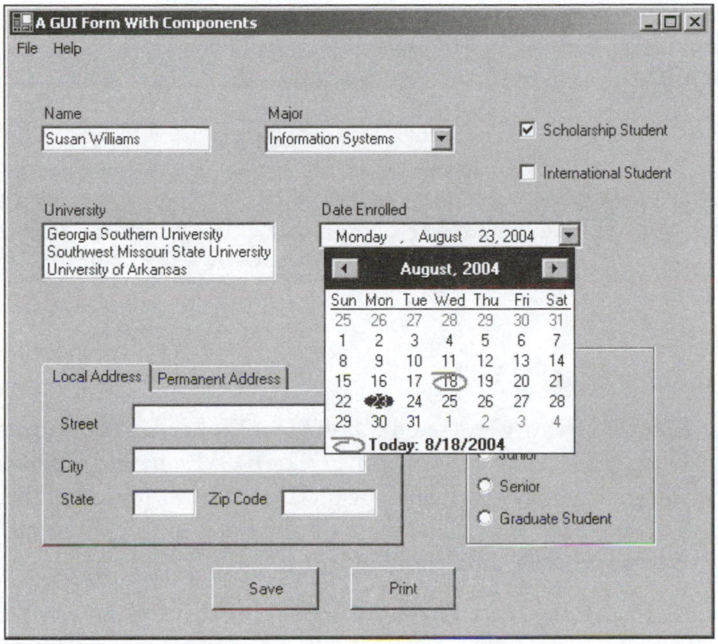

Figure 10-17 Selecting a date from the date/time picker control

Table 10-17 summarizes frequently used properties and events for this control.

Table 10-17 Selected Properties and Events of the DateTimePicker Class

Properties of the DateTimePicker Class	Description
	Inherits properties, methods, and events from the Control class
CalendarFont	Identifies the font used within the calendar
CalendarForeColor	Identifies the foreground color for the calendar
CalendarMonthBackground	Identifies the background color for the calendar month
CalendarTitleBackColor	Identifies the background color for the calendar title
CalendarTitleForeColor	Identifies the foreground color for the calendar title
CustomFormat	Identifies a custom date/time formatting string
Format	Identifies the format for the date/time displayed in the control
MaxDate	Identifies the maximum date and time that can be selected in the control
MinDate	Identifies the minimum date and time that can be selected in the control

Table 10-17 Selected Properties and Events of the DateTimePicker Class (continued)

Properties of the DateTimePicker Class	Description
ShowUpDown	Indicates whether an up-down control can be used to adjust the date/time value displayed in the control
Value	Identifies the date/time value displayed in the control
Common Events	
ValueChanged	Occurs when the date/time value in the control changes

Hands-on Exercise 6 (Part A)

1. Locate the **Chap10\Examples\Ex06\DateTimePickerAndTabControl** folder in the book's data files. Create a folder named **Chap10\Exercises\Ex06** in the work folder on your system, and then copy the **DateTimePickerAndTabControl** folder to this folder. (*Note*: You will work with the date/time picker control in Part A of this exercise, and with the tab control in Part B.)
2. Using VB .NET, open the **DateTimePickerAndTabControl** project. You see DateTimePickerAndTabControl_Form.vb in the Solution Explorer. Open the form and run the project to verify that it produces the output shown in Figure 10-18.

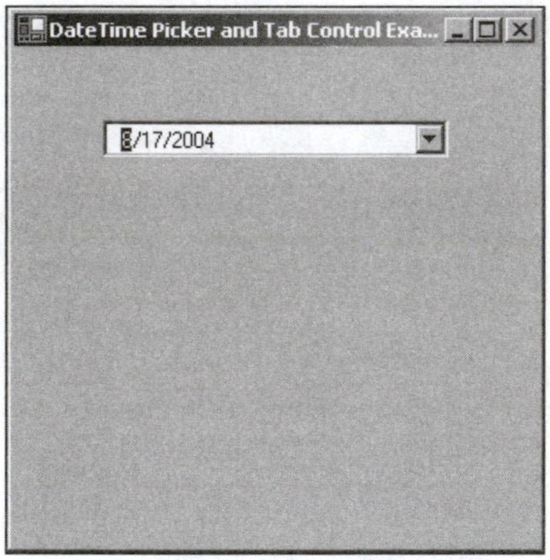

Figure 10-18 Output of the DateTimePickerAndTabControl project

3. Close the DateTime Picker and Tab Control Example output window, and then press **F7** to open the Code window and review the code created by the Windows Form Designer.

4. Press **Shift+F7** to return to the Design window. Use the Properties window to set the following properties of the dtpExample control:
   a. Change the Format property to **Long**. (This will display the date in a longer format.)
   b. Set the MaxDate property to **December 31st** of the current calendar year, and the MinDate property to **January 1st** of the current calendar year.
5. Set the Value property to the date of your birthday this year. (If your birthday is today, set the Value property to the day after your birthday.)
6. Build and execute the project to verify that your modifications are working properly.
7. Close the DateTime Picker and Tab Control Example output window.

Using Tab Controls and Tab Pages

A **tab control** (which is an instance of the TabControl class) provides the functionality for a set of tab pages. Each tab page is an instance of the TabPage class (a subclass of Panel). **Tab pages** are useful when a form requires a large number of controls (too many to fit on a single screen), and those controls can easily be grouped into logical subsets. Each tab page contains one of those subsets and a tab identifying its purpose. The user switches between subsets by clicking the appropriate tab. In the Bradshaw Marina application, you could use a tab control consisting of two tab pages to capture information about boats. One tab page could include controls pertaining to powerboats (number of engines and type of fuel), and the other could include controls pertaining to sailboats (keel depth, number of sails, and motor type). Tables 10-18 and 10-19 summarize frequently used properties and events for these controls.

Table 10-18 Selected Properties and Events of the TabControl Class

Properties of the TabControl Class	Description
	Inherits properties, methods, and events from the Control class
Alignment	Identifies the area of the control in which tabs are aligned (default is top)
Multiline	Indicates whether more than one row of tabs can be displayed
SelectedIndex	Identifies the index of the currently selected tab page
SelectedTab	Identifies the currently selected tab page
ShowToolTips	Indicates whether a tool tip will be displayed when the mouse moves across a tab
TabCount	Identifies the number of tab pages in the tab control
TabIndex	Identifies the tab order of the control within its container
TabPages	Identifies the collection of tab pages within the tab control
Common events	
SelectedIndexChanged	Occurs each time one of the tabs in the tab control is selected

Table 10-19 Selected Properties and Events of the TabPage Class

Properties of the TabPage Class	Description
	Inherits properties, methods, and events from the Control class
Text	Identifies the text that appears on the tab
ToolTipText	Identifies the text that appears in the tab's tool tip
Common Events	
Click	Occurs when the tab page is clicked

Hands-on Exercise 6 (Part B)

1. If necessary, use VB .NET to open the **DateTimePickerAndTabControl** project that you created in your work folder for Hands-on Exercise 6 (Part A).
2. In the Design window, add a tab control. Use the Properties window to:
   a. Set the Name property to **tabExample**.
   b. Set the ShowToolTips property to **True**.
3. In the Properties window, click the **Add Tab** link to add a tab page to the control. Click in the middle of the tab page to display the properties of that page in the Properties window.
   a. Set the Name property of the tab page to **tabButton**.
   b. Use the Toolbox to add a button to the tab page.
   c. Set the Text property of the tab page to **Button Tab**.
   d. Set the ToolTipText property to **This tab contains a button**.
4. Select **tabExample** from the drop-down list in the Properties window to display the properties of the tab control.
5. In the Properties window, click the **Add Tab** link to add another tab page to the tab control.
6. Select the newly added tab from the drop-down list in the Properties window to display the properties of the new tab page.
   a. Set the Name property of the tab page to **tabTextBox**.
   b. Use the Toolbox to add a text box to the tab page.
   c. Set the Text property of the tab page to **TextBox Tab**.
   d. Set the ToolTipText property to **This tab contains a textbox**.

7. Select tabExample from the drop-down list in the Properties window to display the properties of the tab control. Then double-click in the middle of the tab control to add an event handler for tabExample. Note that the default handler is for the SelectedIndexChanged event. Add the following statements to the tabExample_SelectedIndexChanged procedure to determine which tab has been selected and to display a message. (*Note*: When the form loads, it triggers a SelectedIndexChanged event. The If statement prevents the message box from appearing until the user selects a tab.)

```
'If statement prevents message box from displaying until
'the user selects a tab
If Not tabExample.SelectedTab.Text = "" Then
   MessageBox.Show("Selected tab is " & _
         tabExample.SelectedTab.Text)
End If
```

TIP

You could also develop separate event handlers for each individual tab page. By default, the event handler for a tab page responds to the click event.

8. Build and execute the project to verify that your modifications are working properly. The output appears similar to Figure 10-19.

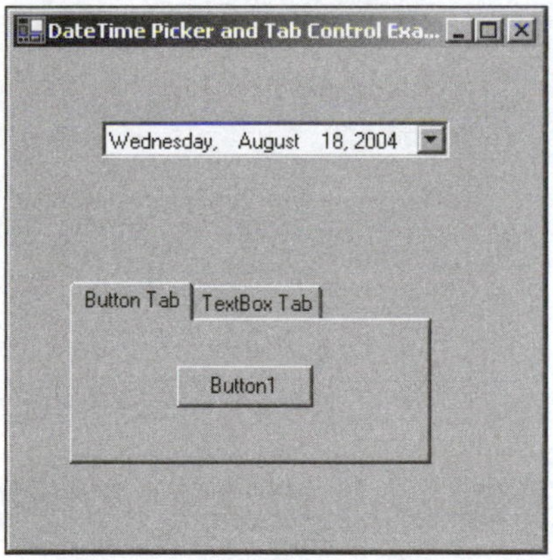

Figure 10-19 Output of the DateTimePickerAndTabControl project after adding a tab control

9. Close the DateTime Picker and Tab Control Example output window. Then close the project.

Using Main Menus and Menu Items

The MainMenu and MenuItem classes allow you to create a set of menus and submenus for a form. The **main menu** control serves as a container for the menu structure. **Menu items** represent individual menu choices within that structure. You associate the menu structure with the form by assigning the MainMenu instance to the Menu property of the form. In the Bradshaw Marina application, you could use menus to enable the user to select commands for performing key tasks, such as adding a new customer, modifying an existing customer, deleting a customer, and so forth. Tables 10-20 and 10-21 summarize frequently used properties and events for these controls.

Table 10-20 Selected Properties of the MainMenu Class

Properties of the MainMenu Class	Description
	Inherits properties, methods, and events from the Control class
MenuItems	Identifies the collection of menu items associated with the menu

Table 10-21 Selected Properties and Events of the MenuItem Class

Properties of the MenuItem Class	Description
	Inherits properties, methods, and events from the Control class
Index	Indicates the position of a menu item within the menu
MenuItems	Identifies the collection of menu items associated with the current menu selection
Shortcut	Identifies the shortcut key or key combination for the menu item
ShowShortcut	Indicates whether the shortcut key associated with the menu item will be displayed
Text	Indicates the text that appears on the menu for this menu item
Common Events	
Click	Occurs when a menu item is clicked

Hands-on Exercise 7

1. Locate the **Chap10\Examples\Ex07\MainMenuAndMenuItem** folder in the book's data files. Create a folder named **Chap10\Exercises\Ex07** in the work folder on your system, and then copy the **MainMenuAndMenuItem** folder to this folder.

2. Using VB .NET, open the **MainMenuAndMenuItem** project. You see MainMenuAndMenuItem_Form.vb in the Solution Explorer. Open the form and run the project to verify that it produces the output shown in Figure 10-20.

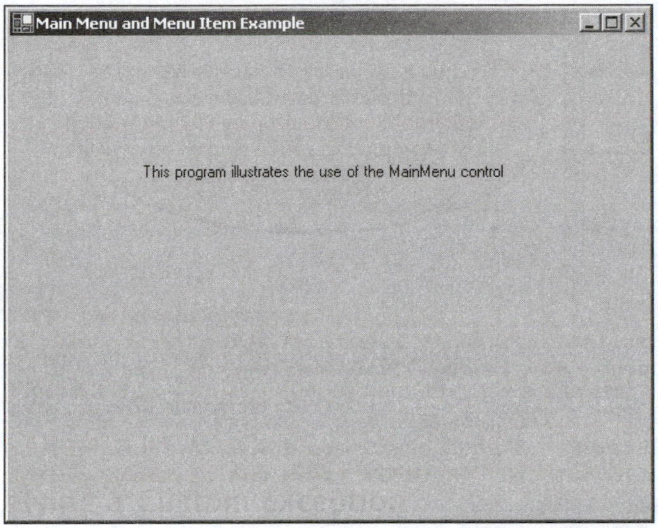

Figure 10-20 Output of the MainMenuAndMenuItem project

3. Close the Main Menu and Menu Item Example output window. Select the MainMenu control from the Toolbox, and then click inside the form to add the menu to the form. You see a Type Here box at the top of the form and a MainMenu1 icon in the lower panel of the Design window, as shown in Figure 10-21.
4. Double-click in the **Type Here** box. Additional Type Here boxes appear immediately below and to the right of the original box. These boxes allow you to create the desired menu structure by adding menus, menu items, and submenu items as needed. Type information into the Type Here boxes to create the menu structure shown in Figure 10-22. Enter this information in the order shown so that the remaining steps in this exercise will be easy to follow.

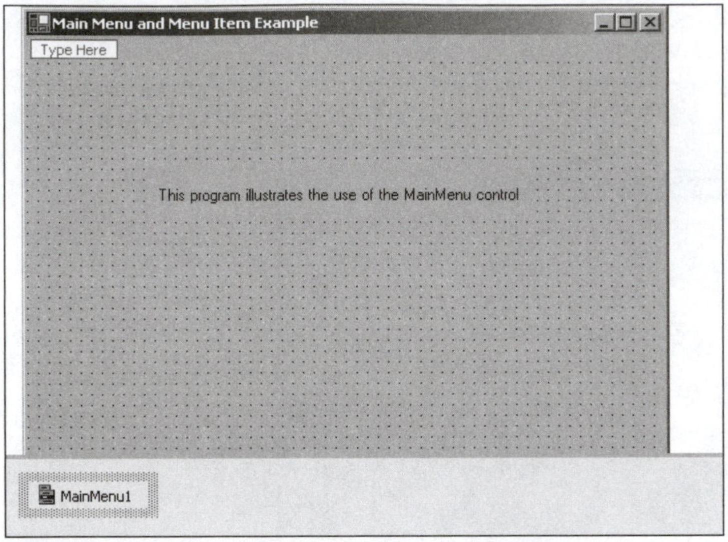

Figure 10-21 Adding a main menu to a form

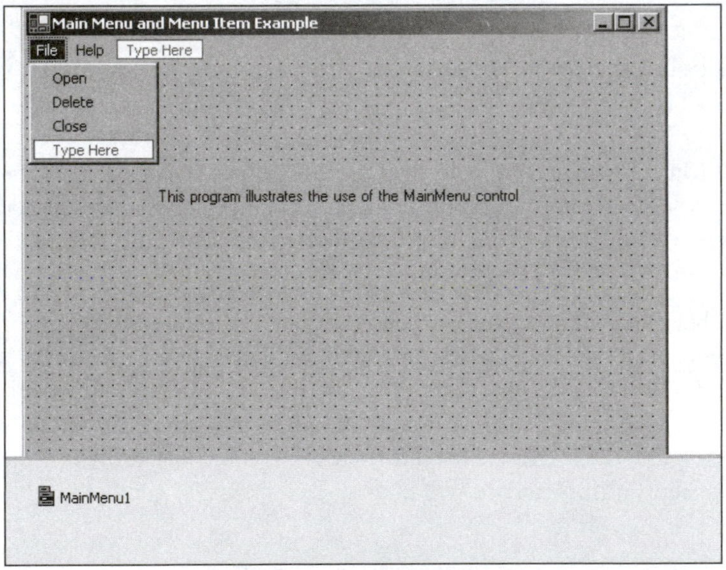

Figure 10-22 Creating a menu structure

5. Click the **MainMenu1** icon in the lower panel of the Design window to select the main menu control. In the Properties window, set its Name property to **mnuMain**.
6. In the Properties window, select **MenuItem1** from the drop-down list to display the properties of the first menu item (File). Change the Name property to **mnuitmFile**.

7. Repeat the previous step for each of the menu items, using appropriate naming conventions for each menu item control (mnuitmHelp, mnuitmOpen, etc.).
8. In the Design window, double-click the **Open** menu item to add an event handler for this control. Notice that the default event handler for this item is the mnuitmOpen_Click procedure. Add the following statement to this procedure to display a message when Open is selected from the File menu:

```
MessageBox.Show("You selected " & mnuitmOpen.Text & " from the menu")
```

9. In the Design window, select the form. In the Properties window, change the Menu property to **mnuMain** to associate this menu with your form.
10. Build and execute the project to verify that your modifications are working properly.
11. Close the Main Menu and Menu Item Example output window. Then close the project.

Chapter Summary

- All of the graphical components you see on VB .NET GUI windows are instances of classes in the System.Windows.Forms namespace. Component is a superclass of all GUI classes. Control is a superclass of all visible components.
- The visual programming process consists of creating a form, setting its properties, adding controls and components to the form, setting their properties, and then adding the code necessary to handle the events users generate when they interact with your form.
- Users interact with GUI screens by entering data and clicking on controls such as buttons and menus. An event is a signal that the user has taken some action, such as clicking a button. The control experiencing the event is called the event source. An event handler is a method or procedure that responds to an event.
- When you define a control using the **`With Events`** modifier, event handlers for that control are named *`controlName_eventName`* and include a `Handles` *`controlName_eventName`* clause in the method signature. An event procedure is invoked whenever the event specified by *`eventName`* occurs for the control specified by *`controlName`*.
- A form instance becomes a visible window. Forms are containers for other components. Other GUI components that can serve as containers include panels and group boxes.
- Labels display data but cannot be used for input. Text boxes can be used to display and input data, and can contain either a single line of text (by default) or multiple lines of text. Combo boxes can also be used to display and input a single line of text, but additionally enable the user to select from a predefined list of values.

- Check boxes and radio buttons enable users to select (deselect) from a list of options. Any number of check boxes in a group of check boxes can be selected at a given time. Radio buttons enforce mutually exclusive behavior, meaning that only one radio button in a group of radio buttons may be selected at a given time. List boxes and checked list boxes enable users to select one or more items from a predefined list of values.
- Tree views and tree nodes display a group of hierarchically related data. Date/time pickers enable users to select a date from a calendar. The date and time can be formatted in many different ways. Tab controls and tab pages are useful when a form requires a large number of controls (too many to fit on a single screen), and those controls can easily be grouped into logical subsets. Each tab page contains one of those subsets. Main menus and menu items allow you to create a set of menus and submenus for a GUI form.
- When designing GUI applications, it is important to adhere to standards that lead to a consistent look and feel, improve ease of use, and reduce the likelihood of data entry errors. It is also important to provide feedback to inform the user when errors have occurred.

Key Terms

check box
checked list box
combo box
component
container
control
date/time picker
destructor
event
event handler
group box
list box
look and feel
main menu
menu item
panel
radio button
tab control
tab page
text box
tree node
tree view
visual programming

Review Questions

1. The VB .NET GUI classes reside in the ________________ namespace.
   a. System.Data
   b. System.IO
   c. System.Web
   d. System.Windows.Forms
2. An instance of the Form class is also a ________________.
   a. component
   b. container
   c. control
   d. all of the above
3. Label is a subclass of ________________.
   a. Component
   b. Container
   c. Control
   d. all of the above
4. The style and appearance of a GUI form and its components is called its ________________.
   a. charisma
   b. public persona
   c. look and feel
   d. style and look
5. When you create an instance of the Button class in the Forms Designer window, VB .NET automatically inserts code that ________________.
   a. declares the button instance
   b. invokes the constructor method of the Button class
   c. sets default properties for the button instance
   d. all of the above
6. The keyword `Me` refers to ________________.
   a. a new button instance
   b. a new form instance
   c. a new component instance
   d. the current object

7. A VB .NET event for a particular control is usually ________________.
   a. the result of the user interacting with that control
   b. identified by the name `eventName.controlName`
   c. difficult to detect
   d. all of the above
8. The event handler that responds to a click event for a button named Button1 is named ________________.
   a. ButtonClickEvent
   b. Button1_Click
   c. Click_Button1
   d. ButtonEvent
9. A ________________ control allows you to select multiple options in a given list or group at once.
   a. radio button
   b. group box
   c. list box
   d. text box
10. A group box would be best used to ________________.
    a. display expandable outlines
    b. enable the selection of one or more items
    c. display and input text
    d. logically group (or contain) other GUI components
11. What property would be used to change the color of text in a label?
    a. ForeColor
    b. BackColor
    c. Font
    d. Color
12. Which method is used to release system resources when a program ends?
    a. Event Handler
    b. Control
    c. Dispose
    d. Exit

13. Anchor is **not** a member of what class?
    a. ContainerControl
    b. Form
    c. Button
    d. MainMenu
14. PasswordChar is a specific property of what control?
    a. Label
    b. TreeNode
    c. Panel
    d. TextBox
15. SelectedIndexChanged is a common event of the ________________ and ________________ control.
    a. combo box, checked list box
    b. combo box, check box
    c. check box, radio button
    d. checked list box, radio button
16. Which method is **not** included in the TreeNode class?
    a. Collapse
    b. Expand
    c. Remove
    d. Text
17. TabPage is a subclass of ________________.
    a. TabControl
    b. Panel
    c. TreeNode
    d. ListControl
18. What naming convention would be best suited to a menu item named File?
    a. mnuFile
    b. lstFile
    c. mnuitmFile
    d. tabFile

19. When designing GUI applications, it is important to adhere to standards that ______________.

a. lead to a consistent look and feel

b. improve ease of use

c. reduce the likelihood of data entry errors

d. all of the above

20. A ______________ control enforces mutually exclusive behavior.

a. combo box

b. list box

c. label

d. radio button

Discussion Questions

1. Use the VB .NET documentation to investigate the context menu control.

a. What is a context menu?

b. What is a context menu used for?

c. What is the inheritance hierarchy for the ContextMenu class?

d. Which public properties of the ContextMenu class are not inherited from superclasses? What do these properties tell you?

e. What are the public events of the ContextMenu class and under what circumstances do they occur?

2. Use the VB .NET documentation to investigate common keyboard and mouse events.

a. In this chapter you were introduced to the MouseEnter event. Identify five other common mouse events and the circumstances under which each occurs.

b. What are the common keyboard events? Under what circumstances do they occur?

3. What is a destructor method? What is the name of the default destructor that is inherited by all subclasses of the Component class? Why is this method often overridden in GUI applications?

4. In this chapter, you learned some fundamental principles for designing GUI forms. What are these principles? Why are they important? Based on your experience thus far, suggest at least one other design principle that you believe should be followed.

5. Why is it important to adhere to conventions for naming variables that represent GUI components, events, and event handlers?

Projects

1. The formula for computing the monthly payment for a loan is: paymentAmount = (amountOfLoan * (rate/12)) / (1 – 1/(1 + rate/12) ^ months) where rate is the annual interest rate (represented as a number between 0 and 1), ^ means raise to the power, and months is the number of months of the loan. Design a GUI application to accept amountOfLoan, rate, and months, and then compute and display the monthly payment amount.

2. Create a form with two buttons: Push Me and Exit. When the Push Me button is clicked, display a "Hello World" message. When the Exit button is clicked, close the form. Make the Exit button the "default" button—i.e., the button that is clicked when the user presses the Enter key. (*Hint*: Use the AcceptButton property of the Form class.)

   a. Modify the program so that when the Enter key (or Exit button) is pressed, a message box containing the message "Are you sure you want to exit this program?" and two buttons (Yes, No) appears. When the Yes button is clicked, close the form. When the No button is clicked, close the message box and return to the form.

   b. Add a combo box to your form. Add at least three values to the drop-down list. Use the SelectedIndex property of ComboBox to determine which item is selected from the drop-down list, and display an appropriate message.

3. Use VB .NET to create the GUI form shown in Figure 10-1. Populate the combo box and list box with the values shown in Figure 10-9.

   a. Add event handlers to the form for each of the following controls: Scholarship Student check box, University list box, Freshman radio button, and Save button. Each event handler should respond by displaying a message identifying the name of the event source (e.g., "Scholarship status changed" or "The Save button clicked").

   b. Add a context menu to the form. The menu should contain two menu items: Clear and Close. Display the context menu when the user right-clicks on the Name text box. When Clear is selected from the pop-up menu, clear the text within the text box. When Close is selected from the pop-up menu, exit the program.

   c. Modify the form so that the context menu also appears when the user right-clicks the Major combo box. When the user selects Clear or Close, clear the text in the Major combo box (or exit the program) in the same manner as you did for the Name text box in Project 3b. (*Hint*: The SourceControl property of the ContextMenu class determines the control that is displaying the context menu. Use VB .NET to research the use of the SourceControl property.)

4. Use VB .NET to create a tree view corresponding to the hierarchy of GUI classes shown in Figure 10-3. Add an AfterSelect event handler that identifies which node in the tree has been selected and displays a message about this node and other nodes related to it.

CHAPTER

11

Using Multiple Forms with Problem Domain Classes

In this chapter you will:

- Develop a GUI class that interacts with a PD class
- Simulate interaction with a database
- Develop a GUI class that interacts with multiple PD classes
- Navigate multiple forms in an integrated system
- Develop a GUI class that navigates a PD association relationship

In Chapter 10 you learned how to write a GUI class to display a form containing various GUI components, such as labels, text boxes, and buttons, as well as how to write methods to handle events. This chapter continues working with these classes, and shows you how to write GUI classes that interact with the Customer and Boat PD classes that you developed in Part 2.

In this chapter you will create a GUI to add a new Bradshaw Marina customer, write a GUI class to find a specific customer, and develop a GUI named AddBoat to add a new boat to the system. The AddBoat GUI shows how to use radio buttons and panels to dynamically change the layout of the form when needed.

The last two examples in this chapter deal with the use of multiple forms. You will see how to create a main menu form that facilitates navigation among multiple forms. Rather than using stand-alone classes, you will use the main menu form to launch these classes as part of an integrated system. You will also see how to navigate a PD association relationship by designing a GUI class to add a customer and the customer's boat together.

Several examples in this chapter use array lists to simulate customer and boat databases. Although data access classes and database processing are described in detail later in this text, this chapter introduces you to some common data access methods using a simulated database approach.

Developing a GUI Class That Interacts with a PD Class

In this section you will see how to develop a GUI class named AddCustomer to input customer attribute values and then create instances of Customer, the PD class you developed in Chapter 6. The GUI form for adding a new customer is shown in Figure 11-1. The form contains a label for the Bradshaw Marina logo. It also contains three labels and three text boxes for inputting customer information, and three buttons.

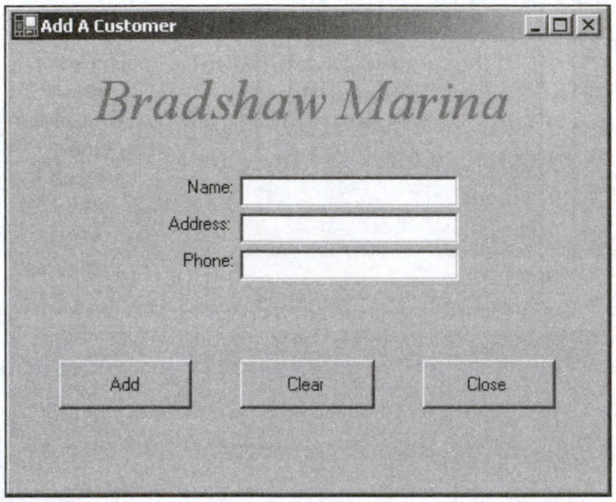

Figure 11-1 Form to add a new customer

As you learned in Chapter 10, to create a form you first create a Windows application, then use the Toolbox and Properties window to add components to the form and set their properties. As you do, VB .NET generates the underlying code. The code generated by VB .NET throughout the visual programming process was explained in detail in Chapter 10. This chapter only explains the code that handles events or illustrates new concepts.

The form in Figure 11-1 uses three text boxes (txtName, txtAddress, and txtPhone) to input the customer name, address, and phone number. Three labels identify these text boxes. Three buttons (btnAdd, btnClear, and btnClose) are used to add a new customer after the data has been entered, to clear the text boxes, and to close the form and terminate processing. The code associated with these controls is generated by the Windows Form Designer.

Adding Variables to the Generated Code

The visual programming process generates the variables necessary to create the GUI, but does not generate all the variables needed to respond to events that result from interaction with the GUI. These variables must be added to the source code through the Code Editor window. Because these variables may be needed in several event handling methods, they are often declared with class scope. For this example, a Customer reference variable is needed to create a new Customer instance from the data entered by the user. Three String variables are used to contain the customer data that is retrieved from the text boxes.

```
Public Class AddCustomer
Inherits System.Windows.Forms.Form

'Declare customer reference variable
Private aCustomer As Customer
'Declare string variables for name, address, and phone
Private customerName, customerAddress, customerPhone As String
```

Handling Events

This example uses three push buttons that correspond to three events: add a customer, clear the form, or close the form. As you learned in the previous chapter, separate methods handle each event. These methods are named btnAdd_Click, btnClear_Click, and btnClose_Click. The events handled by these methods are btnAdd.Click, btnClear.Click, and btnClose.Click, respectively.

The btnClear_Click method calls the ClearForm method. The ClearForm method stores an empty string in each of the text boxes, then invokes the Focus method for the txtName control. The Focus method positions the cursor within the Name text box and sets the input focus to this control. (Note that lines in the following block of code that are too long to fit on the page have been broken using the continuation character.)


```
Private Sub btnClear_Click(ByVal sender As System.Object, _
ByVal e As System.EventArgs) Handles btnClear.Click
      ClearForm()
End Sub

Private Sub ClearForm()
      txtName.Text = ""
      txtAddress.Text = ""
      txtPhone.Text = ""
      txtName.Focus()
End Sub
```

The btnClose_Click method simply closes the form.

```
Private Sub btnClose_Click(ByVal sender As System.Object, _
ByVal e As System.EventArgs) Handles btnClose.Click
      Me.Close()
End Sub
```

The btnAdd_Click method retrieves the data from the text boxes, then validates that the user has entered values for name, address, and phone. If any of the values are missing, a message box prompts the user to enter all of the required data. The technique used here to detect missing data is to evaluate the length of the String instance containing the data. If the length of the String instance is zero, there is no data. If all three data items are entered, a Customer instance is created, a "Customer Added" message box is displayed, and the form is cleared.

```
Private Sub btnAdd_Click(ByVal sender As System.Object, _
ByVal e As System.EventArgs) Handles btnAdd.Click
      'Get values from the text boxes
      customerName = txtName.Text
      customerAddress = txtAddress.Text
      customerPhone = txtPhone.Text
      'Validate that the user has entered values for name,
      'address, and phone
      If customerName.Length = 0 Or _
       customerAddress.Length = 0 Or _
       customerPhone.Length = 0 Then
            MessageBox.Show("Please Enter All Data")
      Else
            'Data is valid -- create a Customer instance
            aCustomer = New Customer(customerName, _
                        customerAddress, customerPhone)
            MessageBox.Show("Customer Added")
            'Clear the form
            ClearForm()
      End If
End Sub
```

Hands-on Exercise 1

1. Locate the **Chap11\Examples\Ex01\Example1** folder in the student data files.
2. Create a folder named **Chap11\Exercises\Ex01** in the work folder on your system, and then copy the **Example1** folder to this folder.
3. Using VB .NET, open the **Example1** project. You should see AddCustomer.vb in the Solution Explorer. Run the project to verify that it produces the output shown in Figure 11-1.
4. Enter several sets of values to confirm that the program adds a customer, clears the form, closes the form, and responds to missing data appropriately.
5. Using the examples from the previous chapter as a guide, replace the push buttons with a drop-down menu containing Add, Clear, and Close options.
6. Close the project.

SIMULATING INTERACTION WITH A DATABASE

You will sometimes need to search for a specific Bradshaw Marina customer and then display the information for that customer, including address and phone number. This section explains how to develop a class named FindCustomer, which lets you find a customer and then display related information using a technique that simulates interaction with a database.

The form to find a customer is shown in Figure 11-2. The form includes a customer list box (lstCustomer), two text boxes (txtCustomerAddress and txtCustomerPhone), three buttons (btnFind, btnUpdate, and btnClose), and a label for the Bradshaw Marina logo (lblLogo).

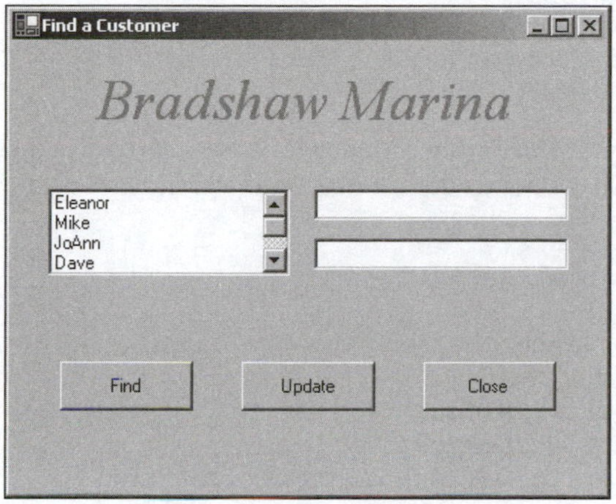

Figure 11-2 Form to find a customer

Creating an Array List of Customers

At this point in the development of the Bradshaw system, you do not yet have a database of customer information. After you create a database in Chapter 14, you can use FindCustomer to retrieve customer records from the database. For now, however, FindCustomer will simulate interaction with a database.

FindCustomer simulates this interaction by creating six Customer instances and then populating an array list with the Customer references. The `ArrayList` class is a member of the System.Collections namespace; thus, FindCustomer begins by importing this namespace and then declaring an instance of the `ArrayList` class to hold the Customer references. It also declares a Customer reference variable to store the Customer instance that is found.

```
Imports System.Collections
Public Class FindCustomer
      Inherits System.Windows.Forms.Form

      'Declare customer reference variable
      Private aCustomer As Customer
      'Declare array to simulate customer database
      Private customers As New ArrayList()
```

An array list works like an array but is dynamic rather than fixed in size. The Add method of the `ArrayList` class appends an element to the end of an array list. A method named CreateCustomers adds Customer instances to the array list.

```
Private Sub CreateCustomers()
      'Create customer instances - simulate database
      customers.Add(New Customer("Eleanor", "Atlanta", "123-4567"))
      customers.Add(New Customer("Mike", "Boston", "467-1122"))
      customers.Add(New Customer("JoAnn", "St. Louis", "765-4321"))
      customers.Add(New Customer("Dave", "Atlanta", "321-4567"))
      customers.Add(New Customer("Brian", "Boston", "467-1234"))
      customers.Add(New Customer("Dan", "St. Louis", "587-4321"))
End Sub
```

The CreateCustomers method is invoked by the PopulateListBox method, which uses the Customer instances to add customer names to the list box on the form.

```
Private Sub PopulateListBox()
      'Create the customer instances
      CreateCustomers()
      'Add the name of each customer to the list
      Dim i As Integer
      For i = 0 To customers.Count - 1
            aCustomer = customers(i)
            lstCustomer.Items.Add(aCustomer.GetName())
      Next
End Sub
```

The PopulateListBox method is invoked from within the constructor of the FindCustomer class as part of the initialization process. Note that the constructor of the FindCustomer class appears in the section of code that is normally hidden in the Code Editor window, and you must expand the code generated by the Windows Form Designer to view or modify the constructor.

```
Public Sub New()
      MyBase.New()

      'This call is required by the Windows Form Designer.
      InitializeComponent()

      'Add any initialization after the InitializeComponent() call

      'Populate the customer list box
      PopulateListBox()
End Sub
```

Handling Events

When the user clicks the Find, Update, or Close button, the associated event handling method is invoked. Similar to previous examples, these methods are named btnFind_Click, btnUpdate_Click, and btnClose_Click, respectively.

Finding a Customer

The purpose of the btnFind_Click method is to determine which customer name is selected on the list box, and then retrieve and display that customer's address and phone number. Recall from Chapter 10 that the **ListBox** class includes a property named SelectedIndex, which returns the index of the item selected on the list. Here, you can take advantage of the fact that the customer names in the list box are in the same sequence as the Customer reference variables stored in the array list. In other words, the first customer name belongs to the customer referenced by the first element in the array list, the second name matches the second customer, and so forth. This means that after you obtain the index of the selected name, you can then use that same index to retrieve the Customer reference stored in the array list. Once you have the Customer reference, you can then invoke the GetAddress and GetPhoneNo methods for the Customer instance to retrieve the values and display them in the text boxes.

```
Private Sub btnFind_Click(ByVal sender As System.Object, _
ByVal e As System.EventArgs) Handles btnFind.Click
      Dim i As Integer
      'Identify the selected index in the list box
      i = lstCustomer.SelectedIndex
      'Find this customer in the ArrayList
      aCustomer = customers(i)
      'Retrieve and display this customer's address and phone
      txtCustomerAddress.Text = aCustomer.GetAddress()
      txtCustomerPhone.Text = aCustomer.GetPhoneNo()
End Sub
```


Updating a Customer

FindCustomer also lets you change a customer's address and phone number. First, you select the customer's name from the list, and then click the Find button to display the customer's values. You can enter the new address and phone number values in the text boxes, and then click the Update button.

The btnUpdate_Click method takes the same approach as btnFind_Click by using the SelectedIndex property to determine the index of the name and retrieve the Customer reference. In this method, however, the values in the text boxes are retrieved and then passed to the SetAddress and SetPhoneNo methods to store the new values for this customer. A "Customer Updated" message box is then displayed, and the address and phone number text boxes are cleared.

```
Private Sub btnUpdate_Click(ByVal sender As System.Object, _
ByVal e As System.EventArgs) Handles btnUpdate.Click
      Dim i As Integer
      'Identify the selected index in the list box
      i = lstCustomer.SelectedIndex
      'Find this customer in the ArrayList
      aCustomer = customers(i)
      'Set this customer's address and phone to the values
```

```
        'entered by the user
        aCustomer.SetAddress(txtCustomerAddress.Text)
        aCustomer.SetPhoneNo(txtCustomerPhone.Text)
        MessageBox.Show("Customer Updated")
        'Clear address and phone text fields
        txtCustomerAddress.Text = ""
        txtCustomerPhone.Text = ""
    End Sub
```

The btnClose_Click method is identical to what you used in AddCustomer.

Hands-on Exercise 2

1. Locate the **Chap11\Examples\Ex02\Example2** folder in the student data files.
2. Create a folder named **Chap11\Exercises\Ex02** in the work folder on your system, and then copy the **Example2** folder to this folder.
3. Using VB .NET, open the **Example2** project. You should see FindCustomer.vb in the Solution Explorer. Run the project to verify that it produces the output shown in Figure 11-2.
4. Find and update several customers to confirm that the program finds and updates customers properly.
5. Notice that if you click the Find button or the Update button before an item is selected on the list, an error occurs. Notice also that the program currently allows you to update the information in the customer address and phone text boxes with empty values. Modify **FindCustomer.vb** so that these errors do not occur.
6. Close the project.

Developing a GUI Class That Interacts with Multiple PD Classes

In this section you will develop a new GUI class named AddBoat that you can use to add a new boat to the Bradshaw system. AddBoat will interact with the Boat, Sailboat, and Powerboat classes you developed in Part 2 to create instances of each type of boat.

You will recall from Part 2 that Boat is the superclass for Sailboat and Powerboat. The class diagram is repeated in Figure 11-3. The attributes of Boat (stateRegistrationNo, length, manufacturer, and year) are common to both subclasses, while the subclasses contain attributes that are unique to them. For example, Sailboat has keelDepth, numberSails, and motorType, and Powerboat has numberEngines and fuelType.

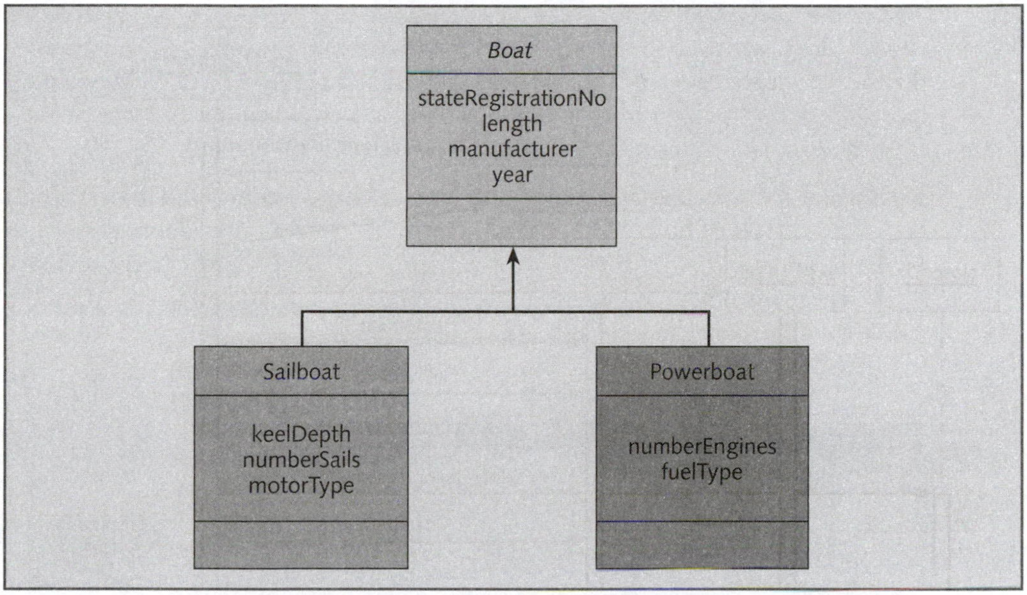

Figure 11-3 Class diagram for Boat, Sailboat, and Powerboat

The AddBoat GUI form is shown in Figure 11-4. Note that the Sailboat radio button is selected, and text boxes appear accordingly to capture sailboat data.

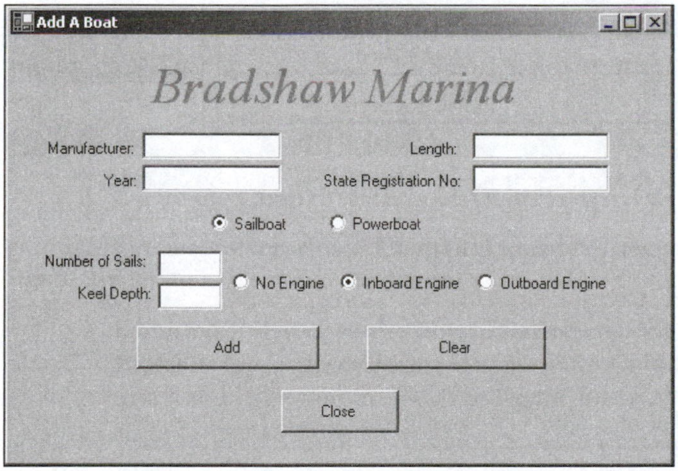

Figure 11-4 Form to add a boat (when the Sailboat radio button is selected)

The upper portion of the form contains labels and text boxes to input the four attribute values for Boat, which are required for both sailboats and powerboats. The middle portion of the form contains two radio buttons (radSailboat and radPowerboat), and two panel instances (pnlSailboat and pnlPowerboat). The user must select either the Sailboat or the Powerboat radio button. The Sailboat button is initially selected as the default.

Each panel contains text boxes and radio buttons that pertain to the information needed for the selected type of boat. If the Sailboat button is selected, pnlSailboat displays, as shown in Figure 11-4. However, if the Powerboat button is selected, pnlPowerboat displays and the form appears, as shown in Figure 11-5. This approach enables you to dynamically change the contents of the panel and the appearance of the form.

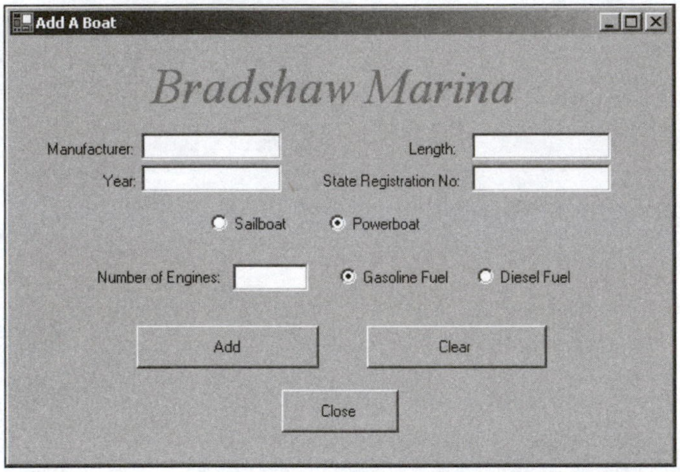

Figure 11-5 Form to add a boat (when the Powerboat radio button is selected)

As shown in Figure 11-4, the sailboat panel contains two text boxes (one for the number of sails and one for the keel depth) and radio buttons for the three sailboat engine options (No Engine, Inboard Engine, or Outboard Engine). The Inboard Engine radio button is selected as the default.

The powerboat panel contains a text box for the number of engines, and two radio buttons for fuel type (Gasoline Fuel or Diesel Fuel). The Gasoline Fuel radio button is selected as the default. See Figure 11-5.

As shown in both figures, the lower portion of the form contains three buttons, just like you saw in the AddCustomer form.

Handling Events

In addition to responding to events generated by clicking the Add, Clear, or Close buttons, this example must also respond to events generated by checking (or unchecking) the Sailboat or Powerboat radio buttons.

Recall from Chapter 10 that checking or unchecking a radio button generates a Checked-Changed event. The radSailboat_CheckedChanged event handling method uses the Checked property of the RadioButton class to determine whether the radSailboat button is checked. If so, the powerboat panel is hidden and the sailboat panel is displayed. Similarly, the radPowerboat_CheckedChanged method determines whether the radPowerboat button is checked; if so, the sailboat panel is hidden and the powerboat panel is displayed.

```
Private Sub radSailboat_CheckedChanged _
(ByVal sender As System.Object, ByVal e As System.EventArgs) _
Handles radSailboat.CheckedChanged
      'If sailboat radio button is checked display the sailboat panel
      If radSailboat.Checked = True Then
            pnlPowerboat.Visible = False
            pnlSailboat.Visible = True
      End If
End Sub

Private Sub radPowerBoat_CheckedChanged _
(ByVal sender As System.Object, ByVal e As System.EventArgs) _
Handles radPowerboat.CheckedChanged
      'If powerboat radio button is checked display the powerboat panel
      If radPowerboat.Checked = True Then
            pnlSailboat.Visible = False
            pnlPowerboat.Visible = True
      End If
End Sub
```

11

Writing the ClearForm Method

The btnClear_Click and ClearForm methods here are similar to the ones in AddCustomer. The btnClear_Click event handling method invokes the ClearForm method, which blanks out all of the text boxes by storing the empty string in them. In addition, ClearForm sets the checked status of radio buttons used within the form back to their default values, and sets the focus to the Manufacturer text box.

```
Private Sub btnClear_Click(ByVal sender As System.Object, _
ByVal e As System.EventArgs) Handles btnClear.Click
    ClearForm()
End Sub
```

```
Private Sub ClearForm()
      txtManufacturer.Text = ""
      txtLength.Text = ""
      txtYear.Text = ""
      txtStateRegNo.Text = ""
      txtNumberOfSails.Text = ""
      txtKeelDepth.Text = ""
      txtNumberOfEngines.Text = ""
      'Set default values of radio buttons
      radSailboat.Checked = True
      radInboardEngine.Checked = True
      radGasoline.Checked = True
      'Set the input focus
      txtManufacturer.Focus()
End Sub
```

Writing the btnAdd_Click Method

The btnAdd_Click method retrieves the manufacturer, length, year, and registration information from their respective text boxes, performs simple data validation of the information, and then invokes either AddSailboat or AddPowerboat, depending on which radio button is selected, to complete the process of adding a boat.

The manufacturer and state registration number are retrieved and validated in the same way the customer name, address, and phone were validated in the AddCustomer example. If the length of either of these strings is zero, then no data has been entered, and an error message is shown. If the manufacturer and state registration information is valid, then btnAdd_Click checks the validity of the data in the Length and Year text boxes. The IsNumeric method is used to determine whether the string data in the Length and Year text boxes can be converted to numeric data. If not, then an error message box is displayed. If the data passes these data validation checks, then either AddSailboat or AddPowerboat is invoked, depending on which radio button is selected. Note that the data items common to both kinds of boats—registration, length, manufacturer, and year—are passed as arguments to these methods.

```
Private Sub btnAdd_Click(ByVal sender As System.Object, _
ByVal e As System.EventArgs) Handles btnAdd.Click
      'Declare variables for boat attributes
      Dim boatLength As Double
      Dim year As Integer
      Dim manufacturer, stateRegistration As String
      'Get reg. no. and manufacturer from text boxes
      stateRegistration = txtStateRegNo.Text
      manufacturer = txtManufacturer.Text
      'Validate that the user has entered reg. no. and manufacturer
      If manufacturer.Length = 0 Or _
       stateRegistration.Length = 0 Then
            MessageBox.Show("Please Enter All Data")
```

```
            Else
                  'Ensure that the value for boat length is numeric
                  If Not IsNumeric(txtLength.Text) Then
                        MessageBox.Show("Boat Length must be numeric")
                  Else
                        boatLength = txtLength.Text
                        'Ensure that the value for year is numeric
                        If Not IsNumeric(txtYear.Text) Then
                              MessageBox.Show("Year must be numeric")
                        Else
                              year = txtYear.Text
                              'Invoke appropriate add method
                              If radSailboat.Checked = True Then
                                    AddSailboat(stateRegistration, _
                                      boatLength, manufacturer, year)
                              Else
                                    AddPowerboat(stateRegistration, _
                                      boatLength, manufacturer, year)
                              End If
                        End If
                  End If
            End If
      End Sub
```

Writing the AddSailboat Method

The AddSailboat method receives the registration, length, manufacturer, and year into parameter variables, and then retrieves the number of sails and keel depth from the text boxes. The IsNumeric method is once again used to determine whether the string data can be converted to numeric values. An error message box is displayed if the data is not valid.

After the number of sails and keel depth are retrieved and converted to numeric data, three If statements determine which of the three motor type radio buttons is selected, and the appropriate value is placed into motorType. Finally, a new Sailboat instance is created and a "Sailboat Added" message is displayed in a message box.

```
      'Method to add a sailboat
      Private Sub AddSailboat(ByVal aStateRegNo As String, _
      ByVal aBoatLength As Double, ByVal aManufacturer As String, _
      ByVal aYear As Integer)
            'Declare variables for sailboat attributes
            Dim numberOfSails As Integer
            Dim keelDepth As Double
            Dim motorType As String
            'Declare a sailboat reference variable
            Dim aSailboat As Sailboat

            'Ensure that the number of sails is numeric
            If Not IsNumeric(txtNumberOfSails.Text) Then
                  MessageBox.Show("Number of sails must be numeric")
```

```
        Else
              numberOfSails = txtNumberOfSails.Text
              'Ensure that the keel depth is numeric
              If Not IsNumeric(txtKeelDepth.Text) Then
                    MessageBox.Show("Keel depth must be numeric")
              Else
                    keelDepth = txtKeelDepth.Text
                    'Determine type of engine
                    If radNoEngine.Checked = True Then
                          motorType = "None"
                    Else
                          If radInboardEngine.Checked = True Then
                                motorType = "Inboard"
                          Else
                                If radOutboardEngine.Checked = True Then
                                      motorType = "Outboard"
                                End If
                          End If
                    End If
                    'Create a sailboat instance
                    aSailboat = New Sailboat(aStateRegNo, aBoatLength, _
                                aManufacturer, aYear, keelDepth, _
                                numberOfSails, motorType)
                    MessageBox.Show("Sailboat Added")
                    ClearForm()
              End If
        End If
  End Sub
```

Writing the AddPowerboat Method

The AddPowerboat method is similar to AddSailboat except that the number of engines is retrieved and there are only two radio buttons to test: radGasoline and radDiesel.

```
'Method to add a powerboat
Private Sub AddPowerboat(ByVal aStateRegNo As String, _
ByVal aBoatLength As Double, ByVal aManufacturer As String, _
ByVal aYear As Integer)
      'Declare variables for powerboat attributes
      Dim numberOfEngines As Integer
      Dim fuelType As String
      'Declare a powerboat reference variable
      Dim aPowerboat As Powerboat

      'Ensure that the number of engines is numeric
      If Not IsNumeric(txtNumberOfEngines.Text) Then
            MessageBox.Show("Number of engines must be numeric")
```

```
        Else
            numberOfEngines = txtNumberOfEngines.Text
            'Determine type of fuel
            If radGasoline.Checked = True Then
                fuelType = "Gasoline"
            Else
                If radDiesel.Checked = True Then
                    fuelType = "Diesel"
                End If
            End If
            'Create a Powerboat instance
            aPowerboat = New Powerboat(aStateRegNo, aBoatLength, _
                    aManufacturer, aYear, numberOfEngines, _
                    fuelType)
            MessageBox.Show("Powerboat Added")
            ClearForm()
        End If
    End Sub
```

Hands-on Exercise 3

1. Locate the **Chap11\Examples\Ex03\Example3** folder in the student data files.
2. Create a folder named **Chap11\Exercises\Ex03** in the work folder on your system, and then copy the **Example3** folder to this folder.
3. Using VB .NET, open the **Example3** project. You should see AddBoat.vb in the Solution Explorer. Run the project to verify that it produces the output shown in Figure 11-4.
4. Enter several sets of values to confirm that the program adds sailboats and powerboats properly.
5. Using the examples in the previous chapter as a guide, modify the AddBoat GUI so that it uses a tab control with two tab pages (rather than panels) to enable the entry of sailboat or powerboat information.
6. Close the project.

NAVIGATING MULTIPLE FORMS IN AN INTEGRATED SYSTEM

Although you can design the Bradshaw Marina system with separate, stand-alone GUI classes for each task, such as AddCustomer, FindCustomer, AddBoat, and so forth, a better approach is to link them through a main menu GUI. Linking these GUIs makes it easier for you to go from one task (such as FindCustomer) to a second (such as AddCustomer). The main menu GUI displays buttons for the available tasks, such as adding a customer and finding a customer. You click one of these buttons to instantiate and display the appropriate GUI. After completing that task, you click a Close button to return to the main menu. In this section you will see how to design a main menu GUI and integrate multiple forms into a single system. First, however, you will learn how to develop a class that provides simulated data access (DA) methods. Each of the GUI forms that comprise the integrated system will use the methods of this class to simulate interaction with a database.

Simulating a Data Access Class

In Part 4 you will learn how to design DA classes that use a relational database and then see how to use the Structured Query Language (SQL) to store and retrieve data for Bradshaw Marina. The focus in this chapter, however, is multiple GUI forms; therefore, here you will simulate the interaction with a database by using an array list of customers and boats. This section describes the simulation of a customer database. The boat database simulation is described in a later section.

You will recall from Part 1 that OO systems employ a three-tier design consisting of GUI classes, PD classes, and DA classes. As their names suggest, the GUI classes provide a graphical interface for the input and display of data, PD classes model the business entities and processes, and DA classes provide data storage and retrieval services. A major advantage of three-tier design is that classes in each tier can be independent of those in another. For example, neither the GUI nor PD classes need to know how the DA classes store data. They only need to be able to invoke methods to store and retrieve data. Similarly, the DA classes are completely unaware of the GUI classes. This independence can dramatically simplify future maintenance chores because modifications to classes in one tier do not require changes to classes in another tier. For example, because the PD and GUI classes are unaware of how the DA classes store and retrieve data, a change from one type of database to another will not affect the GUI and PD classes.

Four of the DA methods—Initialize, GetAll, AddNew, and Update—are introduced here in a new class named CustomerData. The GUI classes invoke these methods but are unaware of their implementation. This means that later you can convert to a real database management system and achieve data persistence (rather than storing data in an array list) without changing the GUI classes. The following list identifies the purpose of the four DA methods:

1. *Initialize*—This method performs initialization tasks in preparation for database access.

2. *GetAll*—This method retrieves references to all instances of the Customer class that are stored in the database.

3. *AddNew*—This method stores a reference to a new Customer instance into the database.

4. *Update*—This method replaces a reference to a particular Customer instance that is stored in the database with a reference to a new Customer instance.

Understanding the CustomerData Class

For this example, the DA methods are defined in a separate class named CustomerData. Because the CustomerData class uses an array list to simulate the database, it begins by importing the System.Collections namespace. An array list named customers and a Customer reference variable named aCustomer are then declared, each with class scope and shared access. Shared access means that these variables are shared with other programming modules in the system.

```
'CustomerData class definition
Imports System.Collections
Public Class CustomerData

      'Declare array to simulate customer database
      Private Shared customers As New ArrayList()

      'Declare Customer reference variable
      Private Shared aCustomer As Customer
```

In the simulated database, the Initialize method creates six Customer instances and stores their references in an array list. As you will recall from the FindCustomer example program, the Add method of the `ArrayList` class appends a new instance to the end of an array list. Declaring the Initialize method with shared access means that it is not associated with a specific instance and can be invoked from other modules by qualifying it with the CustomerData class name.


```
Public Shared Sub Initialize()
      'Create customer instances - simulate database
      customers.Add(New Customer("Eleanor", "Atlanta", "123-4567"))
      customers.Add(New Customer("Mike", "Boston", "467-1122"))
      customers.Add(New Customer("JoAnn", "St. Louis", "765-4321"))
      customers.Add(New Customer("Dave", "Atlanta", "321-4567"))
      customers.Add(New Customer("Brian", "Boston", "467-1234"))
      customers.Add(New Customer("Dan", "St. Louis", "587-4321"))
End Sub
```

The GetAll method returns the `ArrayList` reference containing references to all instances of the Customer class.

```
Public Shared Function GetAll() As ArrayList
      Return customers
End Function
```

When a Customer instance is created, you want to add it to the array list of customers. You accomplish this in the simulated database by passing the new Customer reference variable to the AddNew method through the parameter list, then invoking the Add method of the `ArrayList` class.

```
Public Shared Function AddNew(ByRef newCustomer As Customer)
      customers.Add(newCustomer)
End Function
```

When information for a particular customer changes (such as the customer's address), you want to update it. You accomplish this in the simulated database by passing two arguments to the Update method. The first argument identifies the location of the customer in the array list, and the second is a reference to a Customer instance containing the updated data. The Update method stores the reference to the updated Customer instance at the specified location in the array list.

```
Public Shared Function Update(ByVal index As Integer, _
ByRef thisCustomer As Customer)
      customers(index) = thisCustomer
End Function
```

Integrating Multiple Forms

In this example, you will integrate multiple forms into a single system. The forms in this example include a main menu plus the AddCustomer and FindCustomer GUI forms presented earlier in this chapter. When the system starts, the main menu shown in Figure 11-6 appears. The user navigates to other forms by clicking the buttons on the main menu.

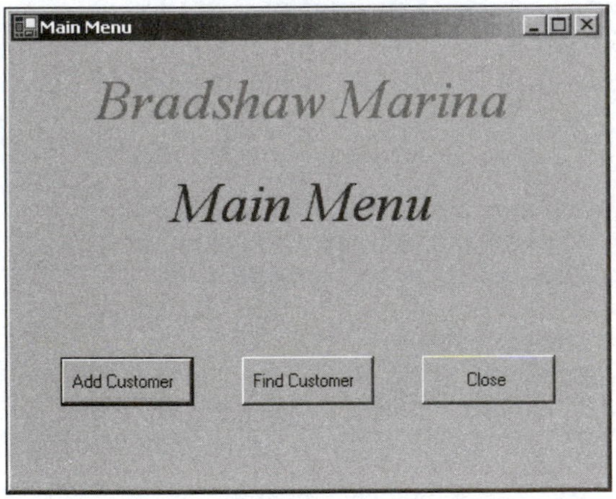

Figure 11-6 Main menu for Bradshaw Marina

The sequence of GUI forms to find and add a customer is shown in Figure 11-7. If you click the Find Customer button on the main menu, the FindCustomer form appears. When you select a customer from the list and click the Find button, the customer's address and phone number are displayed. If you click the Close button, then the FindCustomer form disappears and the main menu reappears.

If you click the Add Customer button on the main menu, the AddCustomer form appears and the main menu closes. You then enter the customer's name, address, and phone number, and click the Add button. A message box appears, showing a "Customer Added" message. You click OK on the message box, and then click the Close button on the AddCustomer form to return to the main menu.

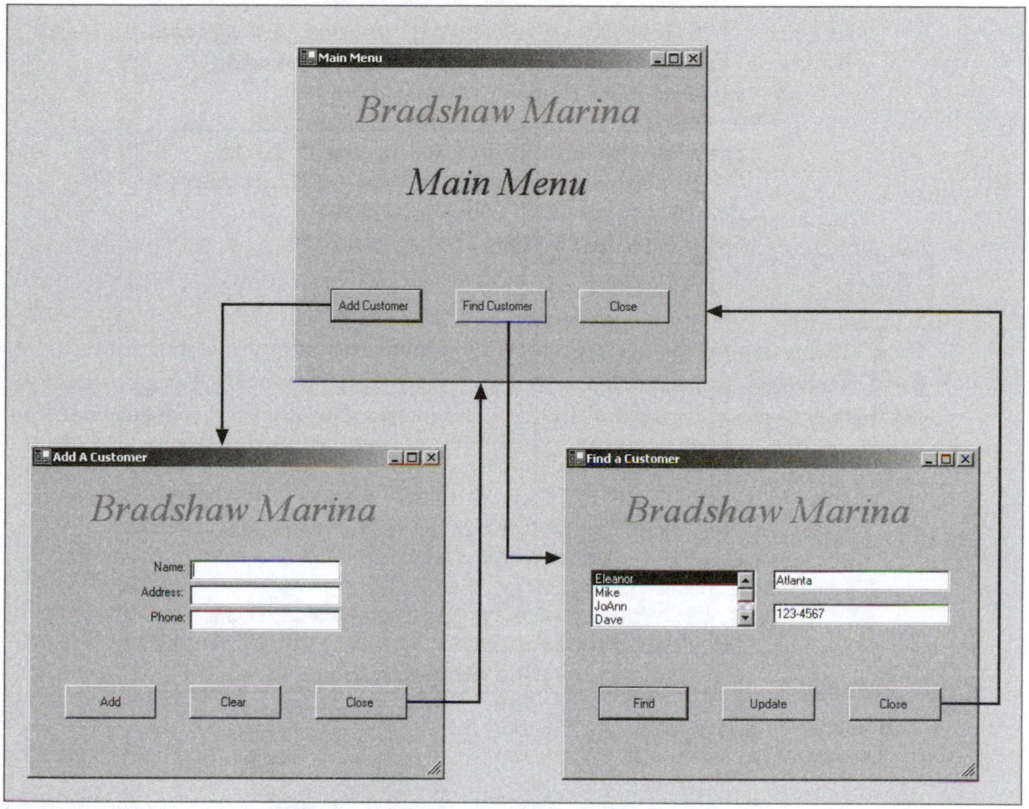

Figure 11-7 GUI sequence to find and add a customer

Designing the Main Menu

The main menu integrates the forms and serves as the startup object for the entire project. The main menu form contains three buttons (btnAdd, btnFind, and btnClose). The btnClose_Click method is identical to the previous examples.

The btnAdd_Click event handling method makes the main menu form disappear by invoking the Hide method. It then instantiates the AddCustomer GUI form and displays it by invoking the ShowDialog method.

The ShowDialog method shows a form as a modal dialog box. When shown as a modal dialog box, a form must be hidden or closed before the next statement in the procedure will be executed. This means that once the AddCustomer GUI is shown, it must later be hidden or closed before other forms in the system can be made visible. After the AddCustomer GUI closes, you redisplay the hidden main menu again by invoking the Show method. You use the Show method (rather than ShowDialog) to redisplay the hidden main menu because it is already displayed modally.

```
Private Sub btnAdd_Click(ByVal sender As System.Object, _
ByVal e As System.EventArgs) Handles btnAdd.Click
      'Hide the main menu form
      Me.Hide()
      'Create and display AddCustomer form
      Dim frmAddCustomerGUI = New AddCustomer()
      frmAddCustomerGUI.ShowDialog()
      'Make the main menu form visible
      Me.Show()
End Sub
```

In a similar manner, when you click the Find Customer button, the FindCustomer GUI form is created and displayed, and the main menu disappears. Because the FindCustomer GUI is displayed as a modal dialog box, the main menu does not reappear until the FindCustomer GUI is hidden or closed.

```
Private Sub btnFind_Click(ByVal sender As System.Object, _
ByVal e As System.EventArgs) Handles btnFind.Click
      'Hide the main menu form
      Me.Hide()
      'Create and display FindCustomer form
      Dim frmFindCustomerGUI = New FindCustomer()
      frmFindCustomerGUI.ShowDialog()
      'Make the main menu form visible
      Me.Show()
End Sub
```

The main menu performs one other important task: it invokes the Initialize method of the DA class. The Initialize method is invoked from within the constructor of the MainMenu class as part of the initialization sequence. Recall that the constructor of the MainMenu class appears in the section of code that is normally hidden in the Code Editor window, and you must expand the code generated by the Windows Form Designer to view or modify the constructor.

```
Public Sub New()
      MyBase.New()

      'This call is required by the Windows Form Designer.
      InitializeComponent()

      'Add any initialization after the InitializeComponent() call
      'Initialize the simulated database
      CustomerData.Initialize()
End Sub
```

Note that because the Initialize method was declared with shared access in the CustomerData class, it is not associated with a specific instance and can be invoked by qualifying it with the class name—in other words, by specifying CustomerData.Initialize().

Finding a Customer

The FindCustomer GUI form in this example is nearly identical to the second example in this chapter. You will, however, notice two important differences in the behavior of the FindCustomer form. First, clicking the Close button causes the main menu to reappear. Second, FindCustomer can display the new customers you add with AddCustomer. This is because the CustomerData class shares the array list of customers with the other program modules, which means that each customer you add to the simulated database is available for display on the FindCustomer form.

The FindCustomer class from the earlier example requires only one change. In the earlier example, FindCustomer had a method named CreateCustomers, which was invoked by the PopulateListBox method. The purpose of this method was to create six Customer instances and store their references in an array list. The new version of FindCustomer invokes the DA class method GetAll to obtain the populated array list. The listing for the new version of FindCustomer (not including the code generated by the Windows Form Designer) is shown in Figure 11-8.


```
Imports System.Collections
Public Class FindCustomer
      Inherits System.Windows.Forms.Form

      'Declare customer reference variable
      Private aCustomer As Customer
      'Declare array to simulate customer database
      Private customers As New ArrayList()
      'Add a statement to the generated code to invoke the
      'PopulateListBox method
      'NOTE: Windows Form Designer generated code goes here

      Private Sub btnFind_Click(ByVal sender As System.Object, _
      ByVal e As System.EventArgs) Handles btnFind.Click
            Dim i As Integer
            'Identify the selected index in the list box
            i = lstCustomer.SelectedIndex
            'Find this customer in the simulated database
            aCustomer = customers(i)
            'Retrieve and display this customer's address and phone
            txtCustomerAddress.Text = aCustomer.GetAddress()
            txtCustomerPhone.Text = aCustomer.GetPhoneNo()
      End Sub
```

```
    Private Sub btnUpdate_Click(ByVal sender As System.Object, _
    ByVal e As System.EventArgs) Handles btnUpdate.Click
          Dim i As Integer
          'Identify the selected index in the list box
          i = lstCustomer.SelectedIndex
          'Find this customer in the simulated database
          aCustomer = customers(i)
          'Set this customer's address and phone to the values
          'entered by the user
          aCustomer.SetAddress(txtCustomerAddress.Text)
          aCustomer.SetPhoneNo(txtCustomerPhone.Text)
          'Update this customer in the simulated database
          CustomerData.Update(i, aCustomer)
          MessageBox.Show("Customer Updated")
          'Clear address and phone text fields
          txtCustomerAddress.Text = ""
          txtCustomerPhone.Text = ""
    End Sub

    Private Sub btnClose_Click(ByVal sender As System.Object, _
    ByVal e As System.EventArgs) Handles btnClose.Click
          Me.Close()
    End Sub

    Private Sub PopulateListBox()
          'Retrieve all customer data from simulated database
          customers = CustomerData.GetAll()
          'Add the name of each customer retrieved to the list
          Dim i As Integer
          For i = 0 To customers.Count - 1
                aCustomer = customers(i)
                lstCustomer.Items.Add(aCustomer.GetName())
          Next
    End Sub
End Class
```

Figure 11-8 FindCustomer.vb listing

Adding a Customer

The AddCustomer GUI class from the first example in this chapter also requires a simple modification. A statement to invoke the AddNew method of the DA class is included in the btnAdd_Click event handling method.

```
    Private Sub btnAdd_Click(ByVal sender As System.Object, _
    ByVal e As System.EventArgs) Handles btnAdd.Click
          'Get values from the text boxes
          customerName = txtName.Text
          customerAddress = txtAddress.Text
          customerPhone = txtPhone.Text
          'Validate that the user has entered values for name,
```

```
        'address, and phone
        If customerName.Length = 0 Or _
         customerAddress.Length = 0 Or _
         customerPhone.Length = 0 Then
              MessageBox.Show("Please Enter All Data")
        Else
              'Data is valid -- create Customer instance
              aCustomer = New Customer(customerName, _
                          customerAddress, customerPhone)
              'Add customer to simulated database
              CustomerData.AddNew(aCustomer)
              MessageBox.Show("Customer Added ")
              'Clear the form
              ClearForm()
        End If
End Sub
```

Hands-on Exercise 4

1. Locate the **Chap11\Examples\Ex04\Example4** folder in the student data files.
2. Create a folder named **Chap11\Exercises\Ex04** in the work folder on your system, and then copy the **Example4** folder to this folder.
3. Using VB .NET, open the **Example4** project. You should see MainMenu.vb in the Solution Explorer. Run the project to verify that it produces the main menu shown in Figure 11-6.
4. Add a new customer and then find this new customer to make sure the classes are working properly. Update this customer's address. Then add another new customer. After adding the second new customer, find the first new customer and confirm that the change you made to the customer's address is still reflected.
5. Close the project.

11

Developing a GUI Class That Navigates a PD Association Relationship

In Part 2 you learned about inheritance and association relationships among PD classes. In Chapter 8 you saw that Boat has two subclasses—Sailboat and Powerboat—and in Chapter 9 you saw that Customer and Boat had a one-to-one association. Figure 11-9 shows a partial class diagram indicating these relationships. This diagram shows that Customer has a reference attribute for Boat and that Boat has a reference attribute for Customer. The Boat instance method AssignBoatToCustomer populates both of these attributes, which link the Customer and Boat instances.

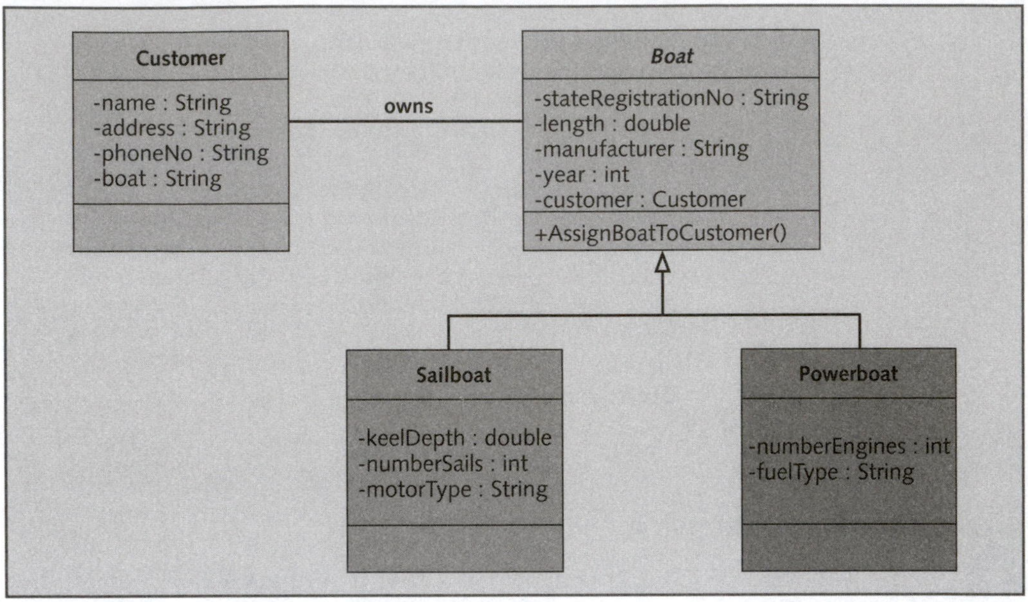

Figure 11-9 Customer and Boat class diagram

In this section you will see how to use these PD relationships with GUI classes. You will make slight modifications to AddCustomer, FindCustomer, and AddBoat from previous examples to develop a multiform system that adds a new customer along with the customer's boat. Then, you will learn how to use the Customer-Boat association to search for a customer and display the customer's address and phone number, plus information about the customer's boat.

Understanding the CustomerAndBoatData Class

In the previous section, you saw how to simulate a customer database using an array list. You will use the same technique here with two array lists—one for customers and one for boats. Previously, you simulated a customer database by using a DA class with four methods: Initialize (to create the Customer instances and add them to the array list); GetAll (to return a reference to an array list containing the Customer references); AddNew (to add a new Customer reference to the array list); and Update (to modify the attributes of a particular customer in the array list).

A similar approach is used to simulate a database that contains both customer and boat information. The Initialize method now invokes two procedures: InitializeCustomer and InitializeBoat.

```
Imports System.Collections
Public Class CustomerAndBoatData

     'Declare array lists to simulate customer and boat database
     Private Shared customers As New ArrayList()
     Private Shared boats As New ArrayList()

     'Declare customer and boat reference variables
     Private Shared aCustomer As Customer
     Private Shared aBoat As Boat

     Public Shared Sub Initialize()
          InitializeCustomer()
          InitializeBoat()
     End Sub
```

The InitializeCustomer procedure creates six Customer instances.

```
Private Shared Sub InitializeCustomer()
     'Create customer instances - simulate database
     customers.Add(New Customer _
               ("Eleanor", "Atlanta", "123-4567"))
     customers.Add(New Customer _
               ("Mike", "Boston", "467-1122"))
     customers.Add(New Customer _
               ("JoAnn", "St. Louis", "765-4321"))
     customers.Add(New Customer_
               ("Dave", "Atlanta", "321-4567"))
     customers.Add(New Customer _
               ("Brian", "Boston", "467-1234"))
     customers.Add(New Customer _
               ("Dan", "St. Louis", "587-4321"))
End Sub
```

The InitializeBoat method creates six Boat instances: three sailboats and three powerboats. The InitializeBoat method, however, also invokes the AssignBoatToCustomer method of the Boat class to link each boat to a customer. Recall from Part 2 that this linkage is accomplished by populating the boat attribute in the Customer instance, and also populating the customer attribute in the Boat instance. To keep this example simple, we assign the first boat to the first customer, the second to the second, and so forth.

```
Private Shared Sub InitializeBoat()
     'Create boat instances
     boats.Add(New Sailboat _
          ("MO34561", 28, "Tartan", 1998, 2, 4.11, "Inboard"))
     boats.Add(New Sailboat _
          ("MO98765", 28, "J-Boat", 1986, 4, 5.0, "None"))
     boats.Add(New Sailboat _
          ("MO12345", 26, "Ranger", 1976, 7, 4.5, "Outboard"))
```

11

```
        boats.Add(New Powerboat _
            ("MO445566", 20, "Bayliner", 2001, 2, "Gasoline"))
        boats.Add(New Powerboat _
            ("MO223344", 24, "Tracker", 1996, 1, "Diesel"))
        boats.Add(New Powerboat _
            ("MO457812", 19, "Ranger", 2001, 1, "Gasoline"))

        'Assign boats to customers
        Dim i As Integer
        For i = 0 To customers.Count - 1
            aCustomer = customers(i)
            aBoat = boats(i)
            aBoat.AssignBoatToCustomer(aCustomer)
        Next
    End Sub
```

After Initialize completes execution, you have two array lists: customers (containing six Customer references) and boats (containing six Boat references). Each Customer instance now contains a boat attribute that references a boat. Similarly, each Boat instance has a customer attribute that references a customer.

The GetAll and Update methods are identical to those used in the previous example. The AddNew method, which added a Customer reference to the customer array list, is replaced by the AddNewBoat method. In addition to adding a Customer reference to the customer array list, AddNewBoat also adds a reference to the customer's boat to the boat array list. To accomplish this, AddNewBoat receives two parameters: a reference to a Customer instance and a reference to a Boat instance. It adds the Boat reference to the boat array list and the Customer reference to the customer array list.

```
Public Shared Function AddNewBoat(ByRef newBoat As Boat, _
ByRef newCustomer As Customer)
    'Add the boat
    boats.Add(newBoat)
    'Add the customer
    customers.Add(newCustomer)
End Function
```

Designing the GUI Sequence

The GUI sequence to add a new customer and boat is shown in Figure 11-10. From the main menu, you click the Add Customer and Boat button, which displays the AddCustomer form. You then enter the customer's name, address, and phone number, and click the Add Boat button, which displays the AddBoat form. Next, you enter the boat information, just as you did in the previous chapter, and click the Add Customer and Boat button. The dialog box then appears with the message "Customer and Boat Added."

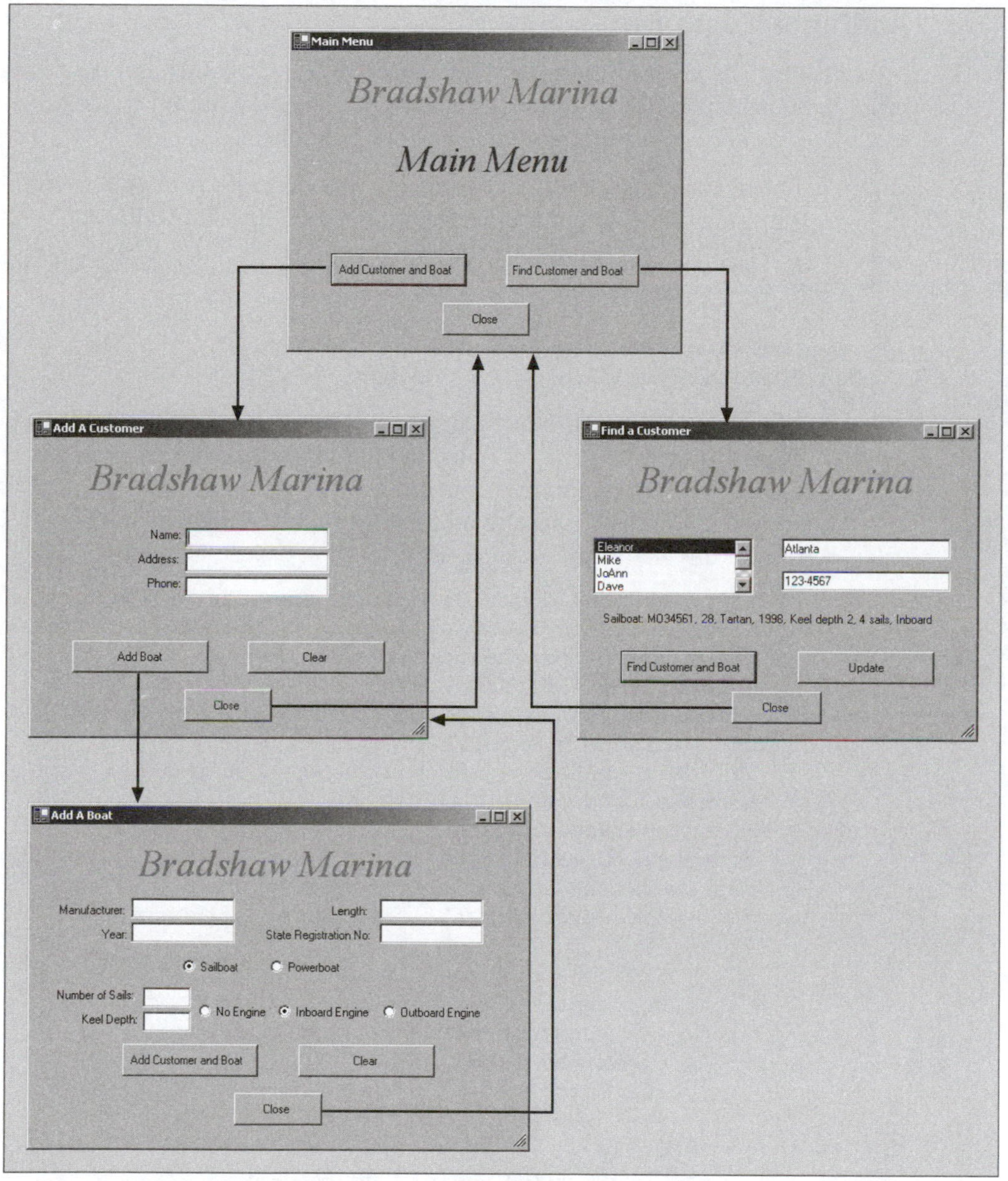

Figure 11-10 GUI sequence to add a customer and boat

The MainMenu class from the previous example is used here with no modification other than the text that appears on the buttons. Only a few, simple modifications to AddCustomer and AddBoat are required.

Adding a Customer

To add a new customer to the system, you click the Add Customer and Boat button on the main menu, which displays the AddCustomer form. The AddCustomer class has three minor modifications from what you saw in the previous example:

1. The text that appears on the button has been changed from Add to Add Boat, and the name of the button has changed from btnAdd to btnAddBoat.
2. A reference variable for the AddBoat form is declared. This variable is declared with class scope.

```
'Declare reference for AddBoat form
Private frmAddBoatGUI As AddBoat
```

3. The btnAddBoat_Click method, which is invoked when the Add Boat button is clicked, now has statements added to instantiate the AddBoat form and make it visible. When AddCustomer instantiates AddBoat, it passes a reference of the newly created Customer instance to the AddBoat constructor, which is modified to receive this argument.

```
Private Sub btnAddBoat_Click(ByVal sender As System.Object, _
ByVal e As System.EventArgs) Handles btnAddBoat.Click
  'Get values from the text boxes
  customerName = txtName.Text
  customerAddress = txtAddress.Text
  customerPhone = txtPhone.Text
  'Validate that the user has entered values for name,
  'address, and phone
  If customerName.Length = 0 Or _
   customerAddress.Length = 0 Or _
   customerPhone.Length = 0 Then
        MessageBox.Show("Please Enter All Data")
  Else
        'Create a customer instance
        aCustomer = New Customer(customerName, _
              customerAddress, customerPhone)
        'Clear the form
        ClearForm()
        'Hide the AddCustomer form
        Me.Hide()
        'Create and display the AddBoat form
        frmAddBoatGUI = New AddBoat(aCustomer)
        frmAddBoatGUI.ShowDialog()
        'Make the AddCustomer form visible
        Me.Show()
    End If
End Sub
```

Adding a Boat

After you enter the customer name, address, and phone number, you click the Add Boat button, which creates a Customer instance and displays the AddBoat form. The AddBoat class requires three simple modifications:

1. Recall that when AddCustomer instantiates AddBoat, it passes a reference of the newly created Customer instance to the AddBoat constructor. You must modify the header of the constructor method to receive this argument.
2. Because the Customer reference passed to the constructor will be needed later by the AssignBoatToCustomer method to link the Customer instance to the Boat instance, you add a statement to the constructor that stores this Customer reference in a variable that has class scope.

```
Public Class AddBoat
        Inherits System.Windows.Forms.Form
        Private aCustomer As Customer

        Public Sub New(ByRef thisCustomer As Customer)
                MyBase.New()

                'This call is required by the Windows Form Designer.
                InitializeComponent()

                'Add any initialization after the InitializeComponent()
                'call

                'Store customer reference in the private class variable
                aCustomer = thisCustomer

        End Sub
```


3. After creating a Sailboat (or Powerboat) instance, the AssignBoatToCustomer method establishes the association between the Customer instance and the Boat instance. The AddSailboat (or AddPowerboat) method then invokes the AddNewBoat method of the DA class, passing two arguments: a reference to the Sailboat (or Powerboat) instance and a reference to the Customer instance. The AddNewBoat method of the DA class adds the Customer and Boat instances to the appropriate array list.

```
'Method to add a sailboat to simulated database
Private Sub AddSailboat(ByVal aStateRegNo As String, _
ByVal aBoatLength As Double, ByVal aManufacturer As String, _
ByVal aYear As Integer)
        'Declare variables for sailboat attributes
        Dim numberOfSails As Integer
```

```
Dim keelDepth As Double
Dim motorType As String
'Declare a sailboat reference variable
Dim aSailboat As Sailboat

'Ensure that the number of sails is numeric
If Not IsNumeric(txtNumberOfSails.Text) Then
    MessageBox.Show("Number of sails must be numeric")
Else
    numberOfSails = txtNumberOfSails.Text
    'Ensure that the keel depth is numeric
    If Not IsNumeric(txtKeelDepth.Text) Then
        MessageBox.Show("Keel depth must be numeric")
    Else
        keelDepth = txtKeelDepth.Text
        'Determine type of engine
        If radNoEngine.Checked = True Then
            motorType = "None"
        Else
            If radInboardEngine.Checked = True Then
                motorType = "Inboard"
            Else
                If radOutboardEngine.Checked = True Then
                    motorType = "Outboard"
                End If
            End If
        End If
        'Create a Sailboat instance
        aSailboat = New Sailboat(aStateRegNo, aBoatLength, _
            aManufacturer, aYear, keelDepth, _
            numberOfSails, motorType)
            'Establish the relationship in both directions

            aSailboat.AssignBoatToCustomer(aCustomer)
            'Add sailboat and customer to simulated database
            CustomerAndBoatData.AddBoat(aSailboat, aCustomer)
            MessageBox.Show("Customer and Sailboat Added")
            'Clear the form
            ClearForm()
        End If
    End If
End Sub
```

Finding a Customer and Boat

Earlier in this chapter you saw how FindCustomer was used to locate and display a customer's address and phone number. FindCustomer displays a list of customer names, and when you click on a specific name, that customer's address and phone number are displayed. Because customers and their boats are linked with an association relationship, you can display the customer's address and phone number plus information about the customer's boat on the same form. In this section you will see how to modify the FindCustomer class to display the customer and boat information together.

For this example, the layout of the FindCustomer GUI requires one slight change. A label is placed below the list box. You use this label to display information about the customer's boat.

As before, the btnFind_Click method uses the SelectedIndex property to identify the index of the customer name selected on the list and retrieve the corresponding Customer reference from the array list. Then, the address and phone number accessor methods for the Customer instance are invoked.

```
Private Sub btnFind_Click(ByVal sender As System.Object, _
ByVal e As System.EventArgs) Handles btnFind.Click
      Dim i As Integer
      'Identify the selected index in the list box
      i = lstCustomer.SelectedIndex
      'Find this customer in the ArrayList
      aCustomer = customers(i)
      'Retrieve and display this customer's address and phone
      txtCustomerAddress.Text = aCustomer.GetAddress()
      txtCustomerPhone.Text = aCustomer.GetPhoneNo()
```


Next, invoking the GetBoat accessor method for the Customer instance retrieves the reference for this customer's boat.

```
'Retrieve this customer's boat reference
aBoat = aCustomer.GetBoat()
```

The TellAboutSelf method is invoked for the Boat instance and the string value returned is used to populate the label.

```
'Display the boat information
lblBoatInfo.Text = aBoat.TellAboutSelf()
```

The TellAboutSelf method used here is an excellent example of polymorphism. Both the Sailboat and Powerboat classes have this method, but when you invoke it here, you don't know whether you are invoking for a sailboat or a powerboat. Although TellAboutSelf in Sailboat is similar to the one in Powerboat, they are completely different methods that return different values. The method in Sailboat returns the sailboat attribute values and the one in Powerboat returns the powerboat attribute values.

Note that when you obtain the Boat reference used to invoke TellAboutSelf, the reference variable has data type Boat, because at that point, you do not know whether the boat is a sailboat or a powerboat.

Boat, Sailboat, and Powerboat all have the TellAboutSelf method. The methods in Sailboat and Powerboat first invoke TellAboutSelf in the Boat class to obtain the common boat attribute values, and then concatenate the string returned with the subclass attribute values.

The TellAboutSelf method of the Sailboat class is shown in the following code. The method invokes the Boat TellAboutSelf method by specifying `MyBase.TellAboutSelf()`. The string value returned is then concatenated with the literal "Sailboat:" and the Sailboat subclass attributes.

```
   'TellAboutSelf overrides and invokes superclass method
   Public Overrides Function TellAboutSelf() As String
          Return ("Sailboat: " & _
          MyBase.TellAboutSelf() & ", Keel depth " _
          & keelDepth & ", " & numberSails & " sails, " _
          & motorType)
End Function
```

The TellAboutSelf method in the Boat superclass is also shown below. It concatenates the string values of the superclass attributes and then returns the result.

```
'TellAboutSelf method
Public Overridable Function TellAboutSelf() As String
      Return (stateRegistrationNo & ", " & length & ", " & _
        manufacturer & ", " & year)
End Function
```

Hands-on Exercise 5

1. Locate the **Chap11\Examples\Ex05\Example5** folder in the student data files.
2. Create a folder named **Chap11\Exercises\Ex05** in the work folder on your system, and then copy the **Example5** folder to this folder.
3. Using VB .NET, open the **Example5** project. You should see MainMenu.vb in the Solution Explorer. Run the project to verify that it produces the main menu and other forms shown in Figure 11-10.
4. Add a new customer and the customer's boat, and then find this new customer to make sure the classes are working properly.
5. Update this customer's address, and then add another new customer and boat. After adding the second new customer and boat, find the first new customer and confirm that the change you made to the customer's address is still reflected.
6. Close the project.

Chapter Summary

- You can write a GUI class that interacts with any number of PD classes. The visual programming process generates the variables needed to produce the GUI, but cannot generate all the variables you may need to respond to user interaction with the GUI. Thus, you often add variables to the GUI class to perform tasks such as validating the data entered by the user and creating instances of PD classes.
- You can test for missing data in a text box by checking the length of the string data for zero.
- The `ArrayList` class is similar to an array but is dynamic rather than fixed in size. The `ArrayList` class includes useful methods and properties such as Add, which appends an element to the end of the array, and Count, which returns the number of elements stored in the array.
- You can simulate interaction with a database by using one or more array lists, such as an array list of customers and an array list of boats.
- You can use panels and radio buttons to dynamically change the appearance of a form in response to user-generated events.
- Instead of having stand-alone classes to accomplish individual tasks such as adding a customer, finding a customer, and adding a boat, you can develop an integrated system using a main menu. A main menu has push buttons that launch other GUIs to accomplish various tasks. This facilitates navigation among multiple forms.
- The ShowDialog method displays a form modally. This ensures that other forms cannot be made visible until the currently displayed form is hidden or closed. This enables you to control the sequence in which forms in a multiform system are displayed.
- You can design a GUI class to add customers and their boats together by linking the AddCustomer GUI to the AddBoat GUI. To launch the AddBoat GUI, you click the Add Boat button on the AddCustomer GUI.
- You can design a GUI to find a customer, display customer data, and display the customer's boat information with a single GUI class by using the association relationship between the Customer and Boat classes. You first retrieve the Customer instance, and then use the Boat reference in that instance to retrieve the boat attribute values.

Review Questions

1. A String instance with zero length means ________________.
   a. the string is unusable, because you cannot have a string with no length
   b. there is no data in the string
   c. you will get an exception
   d. you need to instantiate the string
2. An array list is like an array except ________________.
   a. an array list must be used with the ListBox control
   b. an array list is dynamic rather than fixed in size
   c. you can sort an array list
   d. they are the same
3. To go from one form to another in a multiform system, displaying only one form at a time, you ________________.
   a. use the ShowDialog method to display the first form, then at the appropriate time, hide this form, and instantiate and make the other form visible
   b. use the Show method to show any form at any time
   c. invoke a method in the other form
   d. none of the above
4. The ShowDialog method ________________.
   a. shows a message box
   b. cannot be used when multiple forms are involved in a single application
   c. ensures that the form it displays is hidden or closed before the next statement executes
   d. does not exist
5. The DA method Initialize presented in this chapter ________________.
   a. simulates interaction with a database
   b. is responsible for creating instances in a simulated database
   c. can be invoked by qualifying it with its class name
   d. all of the above

6. The three tiers in a three-tier design are ________________.
   a. AWT, GUI, and DA
   b. GUI, PD, and OS
   c. GUI, PD, and DA
   d. none of the above
7. PD classes ________________.
   a. model the business entities and processes
   b. simulate a database
   c. are instantiated by the main menu
   d. none of the above
8. DA classes ________________.
   a. model the business entities and processes
   b. perform data storage and retrieval tasks
   c. are instantiated by the main menu
   d. none of the above
9. You can pass an instance reference to ________________.
   a. a constructor method
   b. a class method
   c. an instance method
   d. all of the above
10. The GetAll method illustrated in this chapter ________________.
    a. returns a String instance
    b. returns a Customer instance
    c. returns a Boat instance
    d. none of the above
11. The data type of the boat attribute in the Customer class is ________________.
    a. either Sailboat or Powerboat
    b. Object
    c. Boat
    d. none of the above

12. The TellAboutSelf method resides in ________________.
    a. Boat
    b. Sailboat
    c. Powerboat
    d. all of the above
13. The SelectedIndex property is used for ________________.
    a. a text box
    b. a list box
    c. a label
    d. none of the above
14. The GetBoat method resides in ________________.
    a. Customer
    b. Boat
    c. MainMenu
    d. none of the above
15. The IsNumeric method is used to ________________.
    a. convert a string to a numeric value
    b. convert a numeric value to a string
    c. test whether a string can be converted to a numeric value
    d. all of the above
16. To dynamically change the appearance of a form, you can use ________________.
    a. radio buttons and panels
    b. tab controls and tab pages
    c. both of the above
    d. none of the above
17. When you use an array list to simulate interaction with a customer database, the array list stores ________________.
    a. a reference to the actual customer database
    b. a copy of the actual customer database
    c. references to Customer instances, not actual Customer instances
    d. actual Customer instances

18. What is the *major* advantage of the three-tier design, consisting of GUI classes, problem domain (PD) classes, and data access (DA) classes?
    a. Classes in each tier can be independent of those in another.
    b. A program that does not consist of all tiers cannot be used to solve a problem.
    c. The classes in each tier have a direct relationship to classes in other tiers.
    d. The classes can interact on a common public interface.
19. In the statement `Private Shared customers As New ArrayList()`, the key word **`Shared`** means that the `customers` variable is ______________.
    a. only accessible with public methods in that class
    b. shared with other programming modules in the system
    c. accessible until the program terminates
    d. shared with other programs running at the same time
20. When a form is shown as a ______________, it must be hidden or closed before the next statement in the procedure will be executed.
    a. main menu
    b. main dialog box
    c. modal dialog box
    d. private instance

Discussion Questions

1. In the last two chapters, you composed GUI forms using a drag-and-drop technique with an IDE tool. List reasons why you should be able to write VB .NET code (equivalent to that generated by the Windows Forms Designer) to create GUIs without the use of such a tool.
2. The AddBoat design could be altered to use two completely different GUIs: one for sailboats and a second for powerboats. Sketch the GUI design for the AddSailboat and AddPowerboat classes. Describe advantages for choosing this design over the one presented in the chapter.
3. If you were assured by Bradshaw Marina that the only possible values for the number of engines was 1, 2, or 3, you could use radio buttons for these values instead of a text box. Do you think replacing the text box with radio buttons is a better design? Why or why not? Are there additional text boxes that could possibly be replaced with radio buttons or other controls?

4. Assume that you do not have a Boat class; you must use either Sailboat or Powerboat. Describe the changes you would make to the example presented in Hands-on Exercise 3 earlier in this chapter if you had to use only Sailboat and Powerboat and could not use Boat.
5. The designs you used in this chapter required that the Close button return you to the main menu. Visualize a design that includes buttons to bypass the main menu and go directly to another GUI. For example, how would you implement a design that called for direct navigation from the AddBoat GUI to the FindCustomer GUI?
6. The examples in this chapter, including Hands-on Exercise 4, display a single form at a time. Under what conditions would you want to have two or more forms visible at the same time? How could you modify the programs in Hands-on Exercise 4 to have the MainMenu, FindCustomer, and AddCustomer GUIs all visible at the same time?

Projects

1. Locate the Chap11\Projects\Proj01\Project1 folder in the student data files. Create a folder named **Chap11\Projects\Proj01** in the work folder on your system and copy the Project1 folder to this folder. Write a new subclass of Boat named Rowboat with attributes named width and maximumNumberOfPassengers. Include a TellAboutSelf method. The AddRowboat GUI should capture the superclass attributes of Boat and the subclass attributes of Rowboat. Write a tester class named RowboatTester to create two rowboats, and then retrieve and display their attributes to ensure that your new Rowboat class is working properly.
2. Locate the Chap11\Projects\Proj02\Project2 folder in the student data files. Create a folder named **Chap11\Projects\Proj02** in the work folder on your system and copy the Project2 folder to this folder. When you open and run the project, you will see that it is identical to the one presented earlier in Hands-on Exercise 2. Add your Rowboat class to the project, and then modify the AddBoat GUI to accommodate your new Rowboat class by completing the following steps:
   a. Add a third panel named pnlRowboat and a third radio button named radRowboat to the middle portion of the form.
   b. Add text boxes and labels to pnlRowboat to capture rowboat information.
   c. Add a method named AddRowboat to instantiate Rowboat if radRowboat is selected when the Add button is clicked.

d. Modify the event handling methods to ensure that the proper panel is displayed at the appropriate time.

e. Test your modifications to see that they are working properly.

3. Locate the Chap11\Projects\Proj03\Project3 folder in the student data files. Create a folder named **Chap11\Projects\Proj03** in the work folder on your system and copy the Project3 folder to this folder. When you open and run the project, you will see that it is identical to the one presented earlier in Hands-on Exercise 5. Incorporate your Rowboat class and the AddBoat GUI class you created in Project 2 into this project.

4. Locate the Chap11\Projects\Proj04\Project4 folder in the student data files. Create a folder named **Chap11\Projects\Proj04** in the work folder on your system and copy the Project4 folder to this folder. Note that this project currently contains only one file — the Customer problem domain class. Develop a version of FindCustomer that uses the SelectedIndexChanged event of the ListBox class whenever a specific customer is selected from the list. Ensure that the first customer on the list box is selected by default, and that the user cannot update customer information with empty values. Which approach do you think is a better design: using a push button click event or a list box event? Why?

5. Locate the Chap11\Projects\Proj05\Project5 folder in the student data files. Create a folder named **Chap11\Projects\Proj05** in the work folder on your system and copy the Project5 folder to this folder. When you open and run the project, you will see that it is identical to the one presented earlier in Hands-on Exercise 5. Although the designs you have seen so far have not accounted for the possibility, Bradshaw Marina needs to allow for the fact that a customer may own more than one boat. Modify the project to accommodate this possibility. That is, assume that while a customer must own at least one boat, he or she may own any number of boats as an upper limit. As before, assume that each boat is owned by one and only one customer. Use a multiline, read-only text box (rather than a label) to display information about a customer's boats. When a customer owns more than one boat, display information about each boat on a separate line in the text box. The following hints will be helpful in formatting the information you display in the text box:

a. Investigate the AcceptsReturn property and AppendText method of the TextBox class.

b. Use the Chr( ) function to output the ASCII codes that correspond to pressing the Enter key (carriage return and line feed). Chr(13) returns a carriage return, and Chr(10) returns a linefeed.

CHAPTER

12

Web Forms, HTML, and ASP.NET

In this chapter you will:

- Review Internet and Web fundamentals
- Review HTML basics
- Use HTML forms
- Use ASP.NET to develop Web pages
- Create an ASP.NET Web application
- Create an ASP.NET survey application

The **Internet**, an interconnected system of networks that links computers worldwide via the Transmission Control Protocol/Internet Protocol (TCP/IP), currently has an estimated worldwide population of 500 million users and more than 100 million sites. Because of its graphics and animation capabilities, the **World Wide Web**, or simply the Web, represents the largest and perhaps most important segment of the Internet. The Web has changed the development of information systems because target platforms are not important. Instead of writing to a particular platform, the Web uses a standard protocol, **Hypertext Transmission Protocol (HTTP)**, to process information, and a standard markup language, **Hypertext Markup Language (HTML)**, to present information on a computer monitor. A user only needs a **Web browser**, which uses HTML to render the information for a particular display device—whether using Windows, Macintosh, or other computing platform.

This chapter introduces Web development using the Microsoft .NET Framework. After completing this chapter, you will understand the basic concepts of Web development and be able to create static and dynamic Web pages using ASP.NET, the Web development component in Visual Studio .NET. ASP.NET provides Windows-like controls that you can include on a Web page, such as text boxes and buttons. Creating an ASP.NET application using Visual Basic .NET is similar to creating a Windows application—you open the New Projects window, select Visual Basic Projects as the project type, and then select ASP.NET Web Application. The examples and the programs that you create in this chapter are written in VB .NET.

The chapter starts by introducing the Internet, HTML, and ASP. If you are knowledgeable in these topics, you can quickly review or skip these sections.

Understanding Internet and Web Fundamentals

The Web is based on a **client-server** architecture—a form of distributed computing in which software is split between **server** tasks and **client** tasks. For example, when a user requests a Web page, the server finds the page on its hard disk, and returns HTML to the client computer, where a browser translates the HTML and presents it as a Web page. Web servers are identified and accessed via a **Uniform Resource Locator (URL)**, generally called a Web address. To visit a Web site, you type a URL into the Address text box on your Web browser. A Web page is a file with an .htm or .html extension and contains HTML; the file might contain other code as well. The Web page is stored on a server, and the server provides it to the client when the page is requested—when someone enters or selects its address in a browser.

Static and Dynamic Web Pages

Static Web pages have HTML tags only and are designed to simply display information. For example, an organization might display its policies and procedures on a static Web page. When the user requests a static Web page, its content does not change; the server simply sends the Web page to the browser to be displayed. Static Web page processing is shown in Figure 12-1.

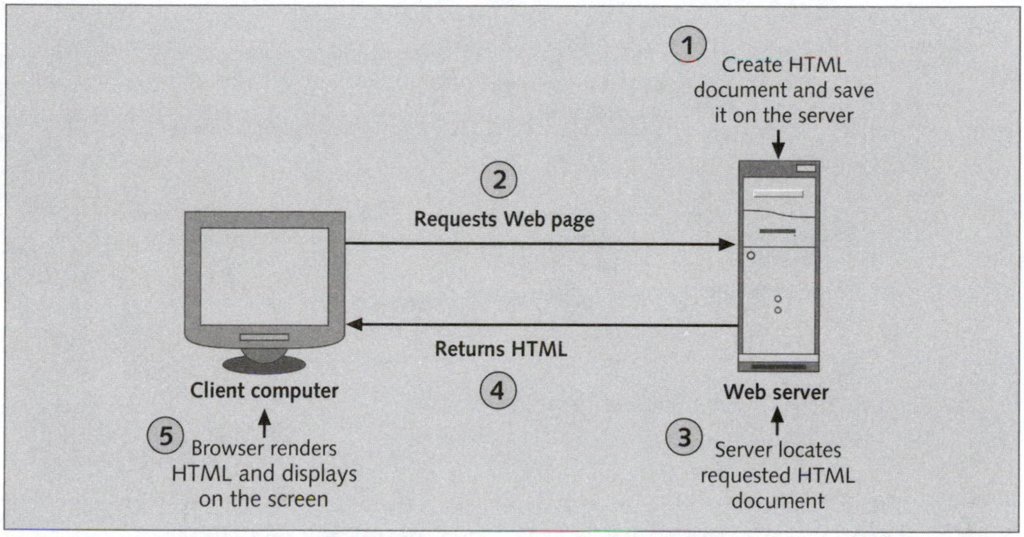

Figure 12-1 Static Web page processing

This figure shows the five steps of processing a static Web page. First, someone creates and saves the HTML pages on the Web server for a Web site. Second, the user requests a Web page. In step three, the server retrieves the requested Web page, and in step four returns the HTML to the client that requested the Web page. In step five, the browser translates the HTML to present the page on the client's display device.

As a markup language, HTML has no features for creating **dynamic Web pages**, which contain content that changes depending on the user's request or preferences. For example, an online shopping Web site such as *Amazon.com* uses dynamic Web pages. When a user searches for a particular item, the Web site finds the item in a database, and updates the Web page with details about the item. Updating content based on user actions makes a Web page dynamic.

To create dynamic Web pages, you can use either client-side code or server-side code. Microsoft developed a server-side Web development technology based on Active Server Pages (ASP), a technology now being supplanted by ASP.NET. ASP is called **Classic ASP** and allows you to embed program scripts in HTML, which can make Web pages dynamic. To create the scripts, you use a scripting language such as VBScript or JavaScript. Server-side technologies for providing dynamic content include ASP, ASP.NET, Common Gateway Interface (CGI), Java Server Pages (JSP), ColdFusion, and Personal Hypertext Preprocessor (PHP).

Most dynamic Web applications access a database or data stored in another format. Figure 12-2 summarizes the steps for requesting a Web page in typical database-driven Web applications.

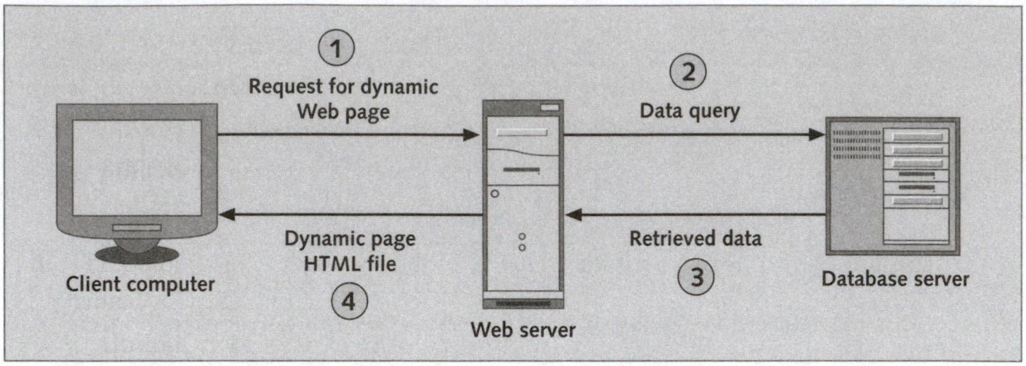

Figure 12-2 Dynamic Web page processing

In step one, a user requests a dynamic Web page, as with a static Web page. However, the dynamic Web page includes HTML form controls where the user can enter data, which is part of the request sent to the server. As the Web server processes the Web page, it requests data from the database in step two. The database server retrieves the requested data and returns it to the Web server in step three. In step four, the Web server processes the data and then creates an HTML page to send back to the client computer. The client browser then renders the HTML to display the page on the client's display device.

Setting Up an IIS Server

When you use Microsoft's Web development technology, you must use their server software, **Internet Information Services (IIS)**. Applications usually run on one computer, and IIS is installed on a different computer that is used only as a server. However, during development, you can have IIS installed on the same computer, allowing it to work as both a Web server and a Web client. All the Web development you do in this book uses this scenario. If the Web server you are using is a Web server other than your computer, see your instructor or network administrator for instructions on accessing the server.

IIS ships with Windows 2000 and Windows XP Professional, but it might not have been installed on your computer. The following steps guide you through installing IIS so you can use your computer as a Web server. Because the installation steps are almost identical in Windows 2000 Professional and Windows XP, the steps for both versions of Windows are covered together. Start by checking to see whether IIS is already installed on your computer.

To install IIS in Windows 2000 and Windows XP Professional:

1. Open the Control Panel. (In Windows 2000, click **Start**, point to **Settings**, and then click **Control Panel**. In Windows XP, click **Start**, and then click **Control Panel**.)
2. Double-click the **Add/Remove Programs** icon. The Add or Remove Programs dialog box opens, as shown in Figure 12-3, listing the programs currently installed on your computer.

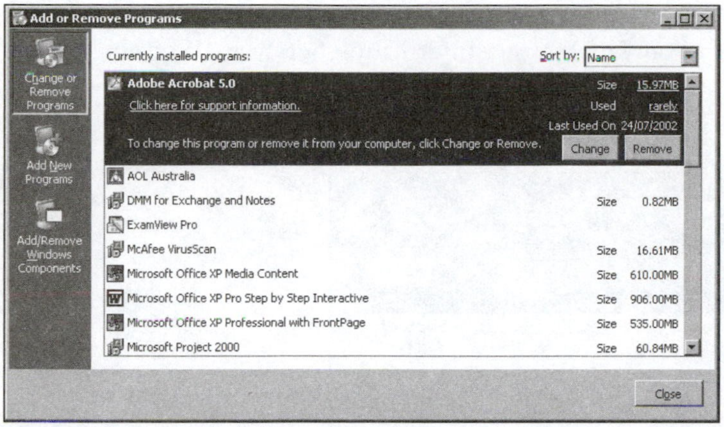

Figure 12-3 Add or Remove Programs dialog box

3. In the left panel of the dialog box, click the **Add/Remove Windows Components** icon. The Windows Components Wizard dialog box opens, listing the components that are available for installation, as shown in Figure 12-4. Locate the Internet Information Services (IIS) component. If it has already been checked, then IIS is already installed on your computer; select **Internet Information Services (IIS)** (the text, not the check box), and then skip to step 4. If the Internet Information Services (IIS) box is not checked, click to check the box, and then click the **Next** button. You may be asked to insert your Windows 2000 or Windows XP Professional installation disk into your computer's CD drive.

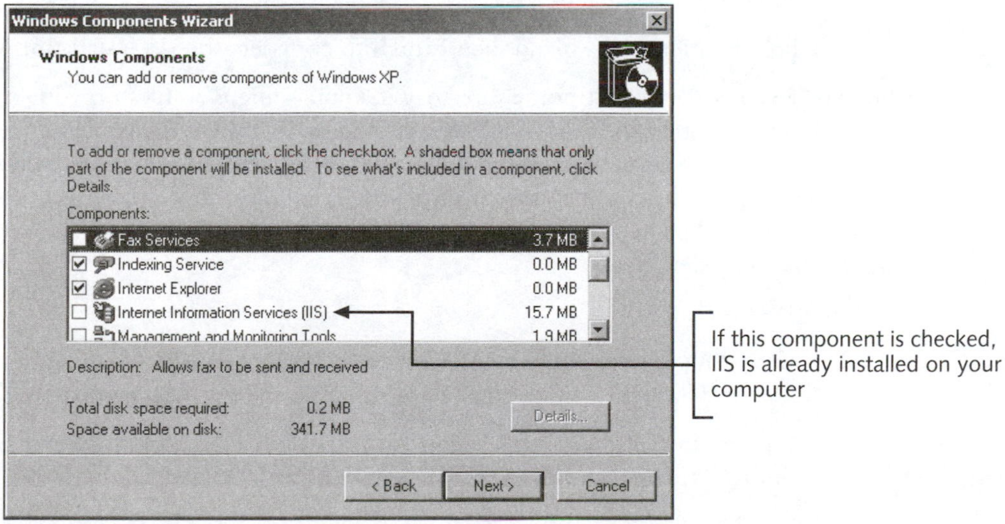

Figure 12-4 Windows Components Wizard dialog box

4. With IIS selected in the Windows Components Wizard dialog box, click the **Details** button. The Internet Information Services (IIS) dialog box opens, listing subcomponents for IIS, as shown in Figure 12-5.

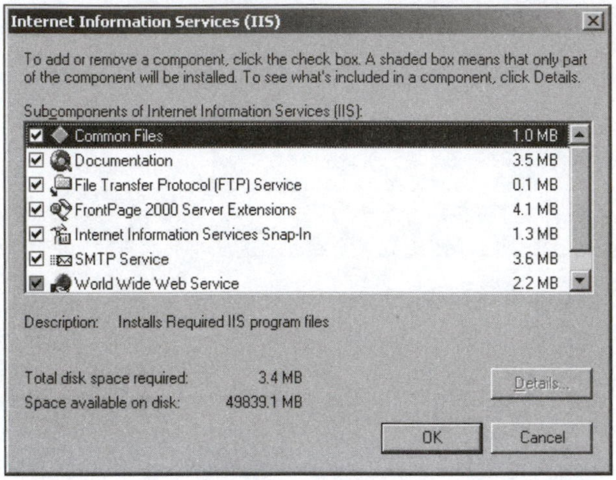

Figure 12-5 Internet Information Services (IIS) dialog box

5. If necessary, select the check boxes for the following options: **World Wide Web Service**, **FrontPage 2000 Server Extensions**, and **Internet Information Services Snap-In**. If you are using IIS 5.0 distributed with Windows 2000, also scroll the list and then select the **Script Debugger** check box. Click the **OK** button.

6. Click the **Next** button and then **Finish** to complete the IIS installation.

When you use IIS, the default home directory for publishing Web files on your computer is c:\inetpub\wwwroot. In the following steps, you verify that these folders have been created, and then test the installation to ensure that IIS is serving Web pages as expected. IIS creates the name of your Web server based on the name of your computer; however, you can change your computer's name. Because you will use "localhost" for your examples, you do not need to change your computer's name.

To test the IIS installation:

1. Open Windows Explorer or My Computer, navigate to the c:\inetpub\wwwroot folder, and locate the localstart.asp file, which is the test Web page.

2. To determine your computer's name in Windows 2000, click the **Start** button, point to **Settings**, and then click **Control Panel**. Double-click the **Network**

and **Dial-up Connections** entry in the Control Panel. Click **Advanced** on the menu bar, and then click **Network Identification**. Click the **Properties** button to view the name of your computer. (You can also use the Properties button to change the computer name.) You use this computer name in the following step. Close all open windows.

To determine your computer's name in Windows XP, click the **Start** button, and then click **Control Panel**. Double-click the **System** icon to open the System Properties dialog box, and then click the **Computer Name** tab. Click the **Change** button to view the name of your computer. (You can also use the Change button to change the computer name.) You use this computer name in the following step. Close all open windows.

3. To browse Web pages on this server, start Internet Explorer. (You might be able to double-click an **Internet Explorer** icon on the desktop to start Internet Explorer, or click the **Start** button and then click **Internet Explorer**.)
4. In the Address text box, type **http://*your_computer_name*/localstart.asp** where *your_computer_name* is the name you found in step 2. Then press **Enter**. Two Web pages open, one a test page similar to the one shown in Figure 12-6.

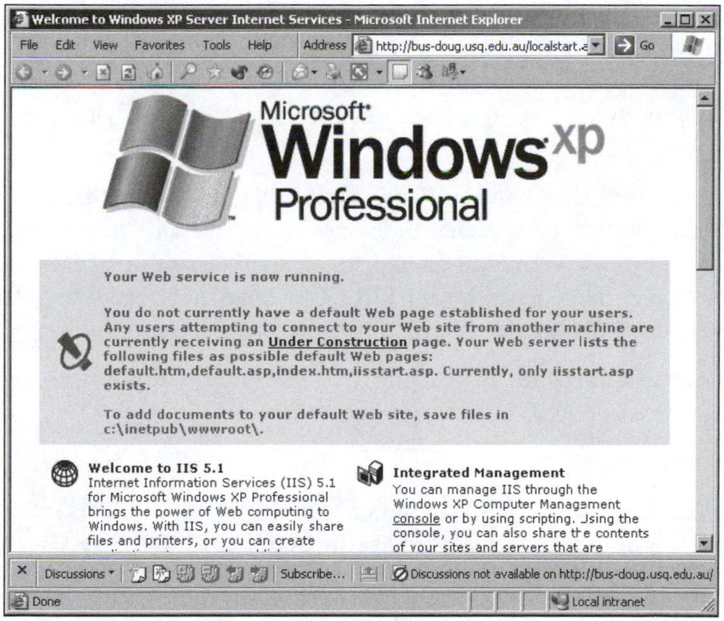

Figure 12-6 IIS installation test Web page

12

5. Because you are using the same computer for the server and the client, you can also use "localhost" as the name of your computer. (This text uses "localhost" for its examples.) In the Address text box, type **http://localhost/localstart.asp** and press **Enter**. The same Web page shown in Figure 12-6 appears again, but the URL will have *localhost* instead of your computer name in the URL.

NOTE: If your browser does not display a Web page similar to the one shown in Figure 12-6, see the "Moving Web Applications and Solving Web Problems" section at the end of this chapter for a possible solution.

Working with Web Directories

To have a user successfully request Web pages stored on a server, you need to understand where to store files on the server so they can be appropriately accessed. Because Web pages are transported using HTTP, the http://www that appears at the beginning of Web addresses indicates that the server will process the files as Web pages. (Many Web sites can be accessed without including the http or http://www at the beginning of their Web address.) When a request for a Web page reaches the server, the server must be able to locate that Web page on its storage system based on the information provided in the URL. When specifying folders on the server, you can specify either a **physical directory** or **virtual directory**.

Physical directories are like those you use to store data files, such as reports and contact information. When you create a folder using Windows Explorer, you are creating a physical directory, such as C:\Chap12\Exercises\Ex01. Chap12 is a folder that resides on the hard disk that is labeled C on your computer; Exercises is a folder within Chap12, and Ex01 is a folder within Exercises.

Virtual directories, on the other hand, are directories that do not physically have to be located in the Web site's root directory. Virtual directories are like alias names that the server refers to and maps to appropriate physical directories of the Web site. Virtual directories benefit Web sites in two ways: They have shorter URLs, making them easier to reference, and they hide the physical directory structure, which helps to avoid security risks.

Because you use virtual directories for storing the assignments for this chapter and for Chapter 16, you can create a virtual directory now.

To create a virtual directory:

1. Use Windows Explorer or My Computer to create physical folders on the hard disk of your computer, such as drive C, as in C:\Chap12\Exercises\Ex01.

2. Right-click the **Ex01** folder, and then click **Sharing** on the shortcut menu. (In Windows XP, you click **Sharing and Security** on the shortcut menu.) The Ex01 Properties dialog box opens.

3. Click the **Web Sharing** tab, and then click the **Share this folder** option button. The Edit Alias dialog box opens, shown in Figure 12-7. You use this dialog box to

create an alias (virtual) name for this directory. By default, the name of the physical folder is provided as the virtual directory name, such as Ex01.

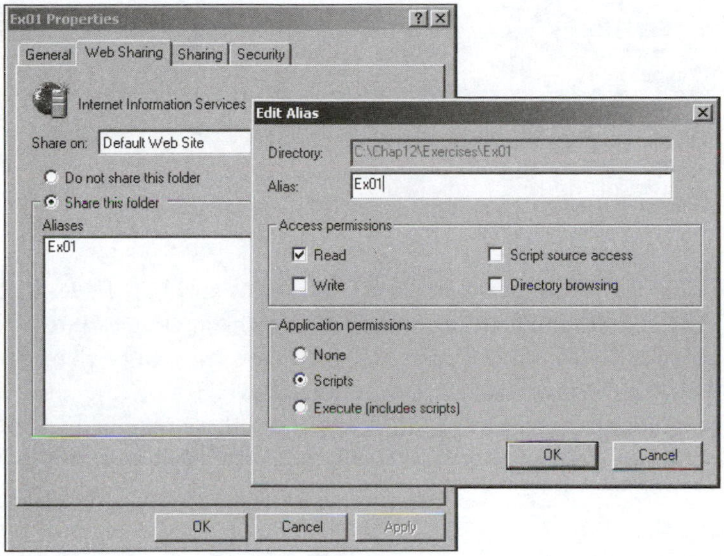

Figure 12-7 Creating a virtual directory

4. Click the **OK** button twice to accept Ex01 as the alias of the virtual directory.
5. Close all open windows.

After setting Ex01 as a virtual directory, you can copy Web files to the physical directory and reference them using the virtual folder in the Address bar of your browser. For example, use the Web address http://localhost/Ex01/*WebFileName*, where *WebFileName* is the name of the file. This address is shorter than the longer physical directory path and doesn't expose the physical path name.

REVIEWING HTML BASICS

HTML provides tags that define the format of a Web page. For example, tags are used to indicate text that should appear bold or italic, or as a heading or as part of a paragraph. HTML tags are predefined and have no relationship to the text they are marking. Tags consist of a left angle bracket (<), a tag name, and a right angle bracket (>). Many tags come in pairs: a start tag and an end tag. The end tag uses a slash (/) to differentiate it from a start tag, and tags may have attributes. For example, Figure 12-8 shows a tag pair that sets text to be a heading.

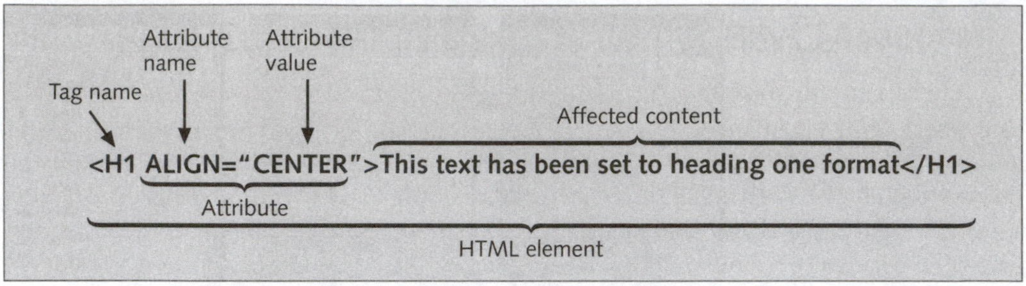

Figure 12-8 HTML tags setting text format

The complete line, start tag through end tag, is referred to as an HTML element. The part between the tags is the content. The attribute, ALIGN, and the attribute value, "CENTER" would center this text in the HTML document. HTML also has empty elements, or single tags, such as the <BR> tag, which forces a line break. HTML is not case sensitive, though uppercase letters are used in the first part of this chapter to differentiate HTML entries from user content and values. ASP.NET generates HTML in lowercase text, as you will see later in the chapter.

Exploring HTML Documents

HTML documents are text or ASCII files that you can create using any text editor, such as Notepad. Although many word processors and other software products can save files as HTML documents, the resulting HTML can be difficult to read. Visual Web development tools such as Microsoft FrontPage and Macromedia Dreamweaver let you create HTML documents using WYSIWYG (what you see is what you get) editing. ASP.NET in Visual Studio .NET also provides these features.

Figure 12-9 shows an HTML document template. The first line is a comment line and only provides program documentation. The tag pairs for HTML headline, title, and body complete a minimal HTML document template.

```
<--! This is a comment line in an HTML file-->
<HTML>
<HEAD>
<TITLE>This appears on the browser title bar</TITLE>
</HEAD>
         ...other relevant header information goes here...
<BODY>
         ...the main part of the Web page goes here...
</BODY>
</HTML>
```

Figure 12-9 HTML document template

The HTML tag pair, <HTML></HTML>, designates the beginning and the end of the HTML document. The HEAD element provides a section for documentation. The content between the TITLE tags will be displayed on the browser's title bar. Although optional, the Web page usually needs the BODY element. There can only be one BODY element in an HTML document. Table 12-1 provides a list of common HTML tags and their usage. Because HTML structure tags have already been covered and form controls will be presented later, they are not included in Table 12-1.

Table 12-1 Common HTML Tags

Tag	Meaning	Useful Attributes
Character level		
<I> </I>	Italic	
<B> </B>	Bold	
<BIG> </BIG>	Font size one size larger than the current font	
<CITE> </CITE>	Citation from published material (italic)	
<CODE> </CODE>	Programming code	
<EM> </EM>	Emphasis, usually bold	
<S> </S>	Alternate for strikethrough	
<SMALL> </SMALL>	Font size one size smaller than the current font	
Block level		
<A> </A>	Anchor tag used for links	HREF, SRC
<BLOCKQUOTE> </BLOCKQUOTE>	Indents and encloses a block of text in quotes; requires 	
 	Line break (carriage return)	ALIGN, FONT
<DIV> </DIV>	Section or division	ALIGN, FONT
<H1> </H1>... <H6> </H6>	Six headline font sizes, H1 being the largest	ALIGN, FONT
<HR>	Horizontal rule	ALIGN, NOSHADE, WIDTH, COLOR, SIZE
<OL> </OL>	Ordered list	TYPE, VALUE
<P> </P>	Logical paragraph	ALIGN
<PRE> </PRE>	Prevents browser formatting	
<STRIKE></STRIKE>	Strikethrough content	
<SUB>	Subscript	
<SUP>	Superscript	
<UL> </UL>	Unordered list	TYPE

12

Table 12-1 Common HTML Tags (continued)

Tag	Meaning	Useful Attributes
Tables		
<TABLE> </TABLE>	Table	ALIGN, BGCOLOR, BORDER, CELLSPACING, CELLPADDING, WIDTH
<TH> </TH>	Table head	ALIGN, ROWSPAN, COLSPAN
<TR> </TR>	Table row	ALIGN, ROWSPAN, COLSPAN, VALIGN
<TD> </TD>	Table data	ALIGN, ROWSPAN, COLSPAN, VALIGN

Browsers ignore blank spaces (white space) and line breaks created with a text editor, and the text is also left-justified. You use HTML tags and codes to control text line spacing (
 for line breaks), horizontal spacing (for a space), and ALIGN=... for aligning to the left, center, or right margin.

NOTE: In order for a Web application to work correctly using IIS, it must be explicitly set as an IIS application. Moving a Web application to a new location also requires resetting the application in its new location as an IIS application. See the last section in this chapter, "Moving Web Applications and Solving Web Problems," for detailed instructions on moving a Web application before you perform any steps or exercises in this chapter.

The first Web page you create in this chapter is a small static Web page.

To create a static Web page:

1. Open a text editor such as Notepad.
2. Type the following text:

```
<HTML>
<HEAD>
<TITLE>  Bradshaw Marina Home Page</TITLE>
</HEAD>
<BODY>
<H1 ALIGN=CENTER>Bradshaw Marina</H1>
<P ALIGN=CENTER><B>Springfield, Missouri</B>
<SMALL><I>Phone: 1-800-555-2222    :
         Fax 1-800-555-1111</I></SMALL><BR>
<H2>Boat and Slip Guide</H2>
<H2>   Contact us for all your marina needs</H2>
</P>
</BODY>
</HTML>
```

3. Save the file as **homepage1.htm** in the Ex01 directory you created earlier.
4. To test the Web page, start your browser, such as Internet Explorer. In the Address text box, type **http://localhost/Ex01/homepage1.htm** and then press **Enter**.

   Your Web page should resemble Figure 12-10; note the spacing and justification. The city, state abbreviation, phone number, and fax number all appear on the same line even though they are on different lines in the HTML code. Also, the HTML code has several spaces between the phone number and the colon and between the colon and the fax number that are removed when rendering to a Web page. You'll fix these problems in the next set of steps.

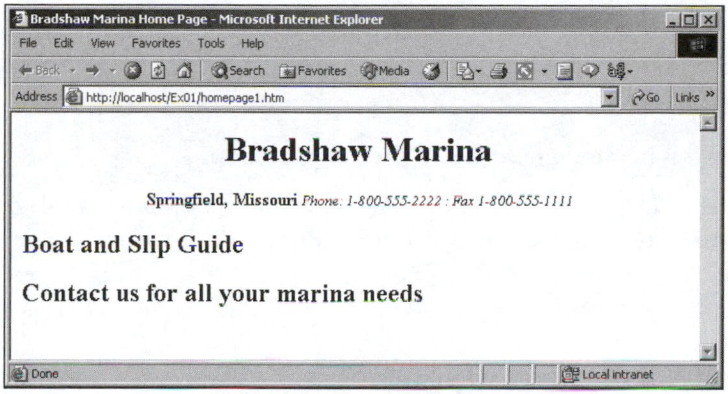

Figure 12-10 Web page with incorrect spacing

TIP: When developing Web pages with a text editor, keep both the browser and text editor open. As you make changes to the HTML page and save the file, you can click the Refresh button on the browser to see the effect of the changes. If the Web page doesn't display any changes, you probably forgot to save the changes you made in the text editor or click the browser's Refresh button. You can also view the source code of a Web page in a browser by clicking View on the browser's menu bar and then clicking Source. HTML will be visible, but program code may not be visible.

Now you can modify the homepage1.htm file you created to fix the line and horizontal spacing.

To modify the homepage1.htm file:

1. Return to homepage1.htm in your text editor.

2. Add the HTML code that appears in bold in the following text. Note that the <BR> tag forces a line break and the escape character   creates a space.

```
<HTML>
<HEAD>
<TITLE>  Bradshaw Marina Home Page</TITLE>
</HEAD>
<BODY>
<H1 ALIGN=CENTER>Bradshaw Marina</H1>
<P ALIGN=CENTER><B>Springfield, Missouri</B>
<BR>
<SMALL><I>Phone: 1-800-555-2222     :   
         Fax 1-800-555-1111</I></SMALL><BR>
<H2>Boat and Slip Guide</H2>
<H2>   Contact us for all your marina needs</H2>
</P>
</BODY>
</HTML>
```

3. Save the file as **homepage2.htm** in the same location.

4. In the Address text box of your browser, type **http://localhost/Ex01/homepage2.htm** and then press **Enter**. Figure 12-11 shows the Web page that opens.

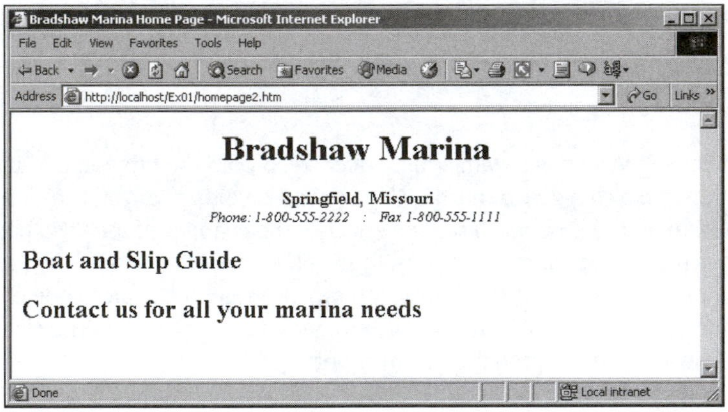

Figure 12-11 Web page with correct spacing

Working with Images and Hyperlinks

You can add images to Web pages using the image tag, <IMG>, with the source attribute, SRC. The <IMG> tag references a graphic image, and the SRC attribute contains the location of the graphic image. The most common Internet graphic images are those with .bmp (bitmap), .gif (graphical interchange format), .jpg or .jpeg (Joint Photographic Experts

Group), .png (portable network graphics), and .tif or .tiff (tagged image file format) file extensions. Note that .bmp files are usually larger than the other file types and thus not often used for Web pages.

To illustrate the use of graphic images on a Web page, suppose you have a file named sabtart_40.jpg that contains a picture of slips. The SRC attribute can use absolute or relative path referencing to allow the browser to locate the graphic image. A relative path specifies a location in relation to the current working directory. If the file containing your graphic is located in the Ex01 virtual directory you created earlier, the following line of HTML would correctly locate it and, in this case, center it on the Web page:

```
<IMG SRC="sabtart_40.jpg" ALIGN="CENTER">
```

However, if you place all your graphic image files in a folder named Images in your virtual directory, then the SRC attribute should be set as follows to correctly locate the file:

```
<IMG SRC="Images/sabtart_40.jpg" ALIGN="CENTER">
```

Hyperlinks, the shortened name for hypertext links, provide the capability to branch to a specified location in the current HTML document, to other HTML documents in your Web site, to other Web pages at another Web site, or to e-mail addresses. The physical link can be a single word, several words, or an image. From using the Web, you know that text links on a Web page are generally underlined and appear in color to signal that they are links.

Suppose your HTML document includes a major section named "All About Slips," and the section does not appear when users open your Web page. Users can click a hypertext link near the top of the HTML document that branches to the "All About Slips" section. At the hypertext link location, you need to create a reference to an anchor at the "All About Slips" section. The following HTML code illustrates how to create the hypertext link and the anchor:


```
<A HREF="#Slips">For more slip information</A>
...
...
<A NAME="Slips">All About Slips</A>
```

The anchor tag with the HREF attribute allows the Web designer to assign a value to the HREF attribute that is used as a reference to another location within the HTML document. The # symbol indicates that the reference is within the current HTML document. The anchor tag with the NAME attribute allows you to create anchors, similar to a bookmark, in an HTML document, and hyperlinks can link to these anchors. For example, when you click the "For more slip information" hypertext link, the "All About Slips" heading and section appear.

Hyperlinks to other Web pages within your Web site or other Web sites let users navigate around your Web site. To link to another Web page in your Web site, you use the HREF attribute of anchor tags without the # symbol. The browser then searches the Web site for the Web page. The following anchor tag associates the "Bradshaw Marina Boats" link with the Sailboats.htm Web page:

```
<A HREF="Sailboats.htm">Bradshaw Marina Boats</A>
```

Rules for relative addressing are the same for the HREF attribute as for the SRC attribute and provide a way to access Web pages in a directory different from the current directory of your Web site.

You can also use images for hyperlinks by including an image tag that references the graphic image within the anchor tags. For example, you can use an image tag to replace the "For more slip information" text link, as in the following HTML code:

```
<A HREF="#Slips"><IMG SRC="Images/sabtart_40.jpg"></A>
```

Now you can include links on the home page Web page you created. You must copy the Images folder with all the graphic images in the C:\Chap12\Examples folder of the text's data files to the C:\Chap12\Exercises\Ex01 directory. You will need the graphic images for Web pages you develop in this chapter.

To add links to the home page Web page:

1. Locate **Ex01** in the Chap12\Examples folder in the book's student data files. Copy the contents of the **Ex01** folder to the Chap12\Exercises\Ex01 directory. Overwrite any existing files, if necessary.

2. With homepage2.htm still open in your text editor, change the HTML code by adding the following bold text:

```
<HTML>
<HEAD>
<TITLE>  Bradshaw Marina Home Page</TITLE>
</HEAD>
<BODY>
<H1 ALIGN=CENTER>Bradshaw Marina</H1>
<P ALIGN=CENTER><B>Springfield, Missouri</B><BR>
<SMALL><I>Phone: 1-800-555-2222     :   
        Fax 1-800-555-1111</I></SMALL><BR>
<H2>Boat and Slip Guide</H2>
<BR>
<A HREF="#Slips"><B>For more slip information</B></A><BR><BR>

<A HREF="#Slips"><IMG SRC="images/sabtart_40.jpg" ALT="Slip Info"></A><BR>

<H2>   Contact us for all your marina needs</H2>
<A HREF="Sailboats.htm">Sailboats</A><BR>
<A HREF="http://www.microsoft.com">Microsoft</A>
</P>
<BR>
<BR>
<BR>
<BR>
<H2><B><A NAME="Slips">All About Slips</A></B></H2>
</BODY>
</HTML>
```

3. Save the file as **homepage3.htm** in the same location. Select **Yes** to overwrite the file, if necessary.

4. In the Address text box of your browser, type **http://localhost/Ex01/homepage3.htm** and then press **Enter**. Figure 12-12 shows the Web page that opens.

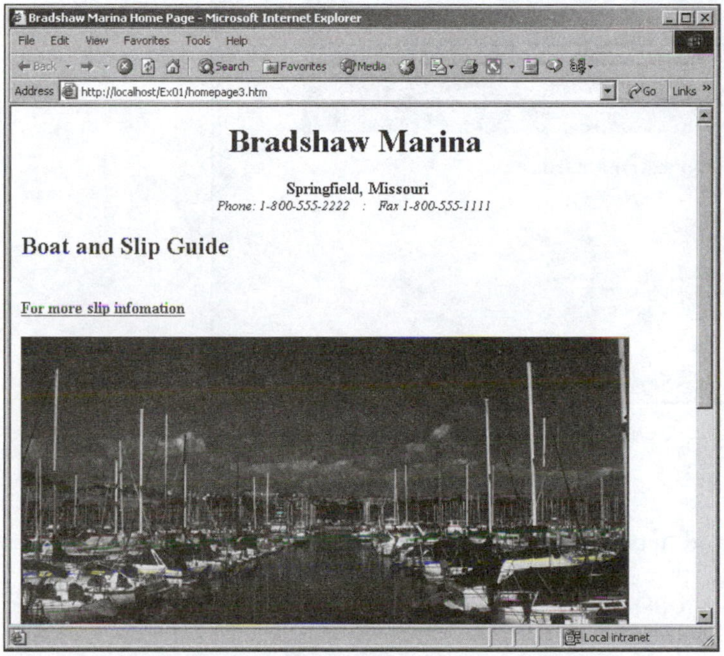

Figure 12-12 Top of Web page with links

5. The first hypertext link references the "All About Slips" section later in the document. Click the hypertext link **For more slip information**. The Web page scrolls down to the "All About Slips" heading, as shown in Figure 12-13.

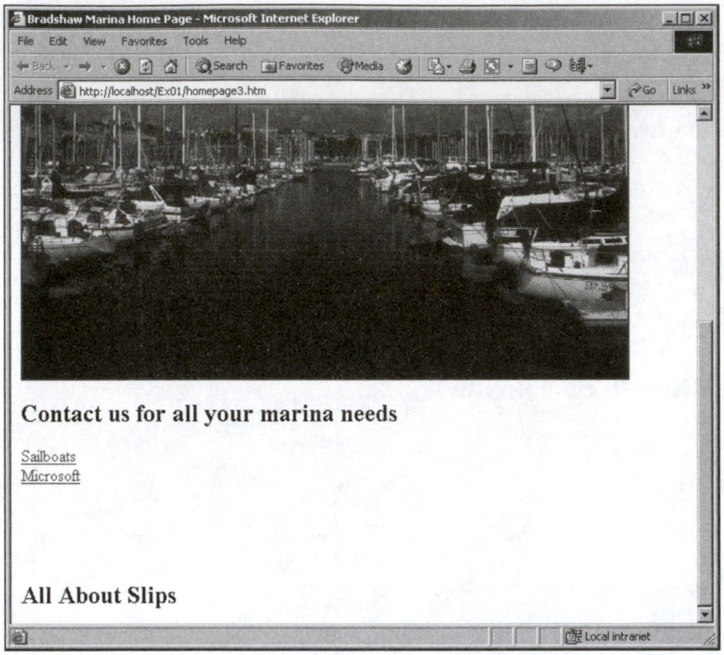

Figure 12-13 Bottom of Web page with links

6. The second hypertext link uses an image of a slip as the link to the same location as the first hypertext link—the "All About Slips" section. The ALT attribute has been included with this image—its behavior is similar to a ToolTip or ScreenTip.

7. Scroll to the top of the Web page, and then point to the image to display the text of the ALT attribute. Click the image. The Web page scrolls down to the "All About Slips" heading as it did earlier.

   The third hypertext link references another Web page named Sailboats.htm. The HTML code for the Sailboats.htm Web page is shown in Figure 12-14. This file must be created and saved for the link to work. Note that this Web page includes a number of sailboat images.

```
<HTML>
<HEAD>
<TITLE>Sailboats</TITLE>
</HEAD>
<BODY>
<H1>Selected Sailboats at Bradshaw Marina</H1><BR>
<BR>
<IMG SRC="images/sabtart_01.gif">   
<IMG SRC="images/sabtart_04.gif">   
<IMG SRC="images/sabtart_06.gif">   
```

```
<IMG SRC="images/sabtart_07.gif">   
<IMG SRC="images/sabtart_19.gif">   
<IMG SRC="images/sabtart_22.gif">   
<IMG SRC="images/sabtart_32.gif">
</BODY>
</HTML>
```

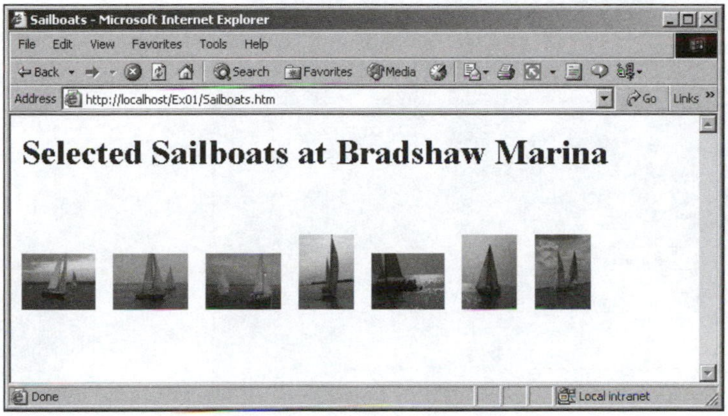

Figure 12-14 Sailboats.htm Web page

8. To test this hypertext link, click the **Sailboats** link to redirect the browser to this Web page. Then click the **Back** button on the browser toolbar to return to the home page.
9. The last hyperlink redirects the browser to Microsoft's home page. Click the **Microsoft** hypertext link to open their home page.

So far, you have opened Web pages by typing their addresses in the Address text box of your browser. For example, entering http://localhost/Ex01/homepage.htm is a request to the server to load the homepage.htm file. You can have a page open automatically without specifying its name in the URL by using default.htm or index.htm as the filename. Although IIS allows you to change the type of file to be used as a default for a Web site, either default.htm or index.htm is usually the first page loaded when the browser goes to your Web site address. For example, if you rename your homepage.htm to default.htm, then this file should load without having to be included as part of the Web address—the address would be http://localhost/Ex01.

A major Web design task deals with the layout of the information on the Web page, which can make it easy or difficult to access and use. HTML tables provide a way to precisely control spacing that results in clear, concise, and creative Web pages. HTML tables are similar to tables in word-processing documents with headers, columns, and rows, and can also merge rows or columns. You can also use images and hypertext links in tables. If you don't want a

Web page to include borders typical of a table, you can insert TABLE codes with the BORDER attribute set to zero. The table will not have a border and lets you place text and objects in a clear design without appearing to use a table. To understand HTML tables, consider the Web page shown in Figure 12-15 and the code for the Web page shown in Figure 12-16. The line breaks on your page might be different. The HTML file is saved as homepage4.htm.

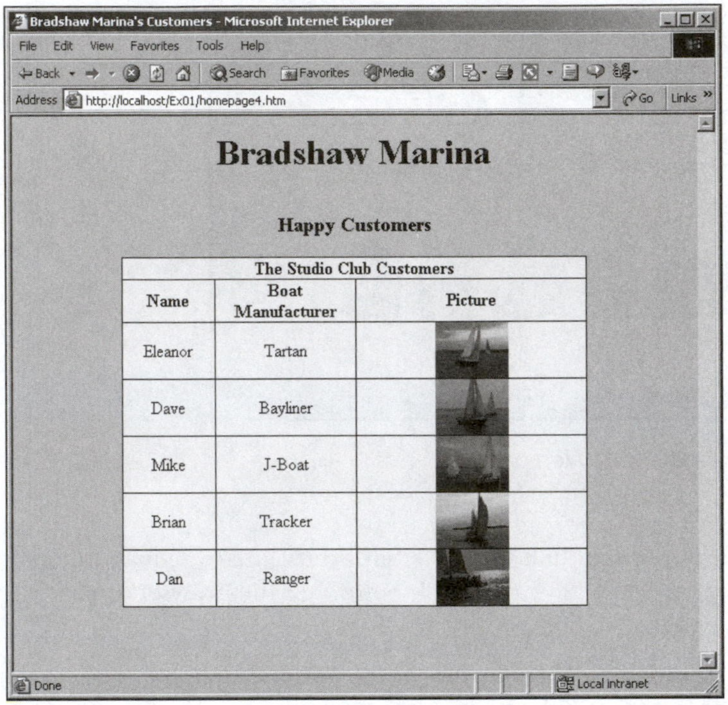

Figure 12-15 Web page using a table

```
<HTML>

<HEAD>
<TITLE>Bradshaw Marina's Customers</TITLE>
</HEAD>

<BODY BGCOLOR="#00FFFF">
<H1 ALIGN=CENTER>Bradshaw Marina</H1>
<BR>
<TABLE BGCOLOR="yellow" BORDER="1" CELLPADDING="0" CELLSPACING="0"
      STYLE="border-collapse: collapse" BORDERCOLOR="#111111"
      WIDTH ="70%" ALIGN=CENTER ID="BradshawMarina1"
      ALIGN=CENTER>
```

```
  <CAPTION ALIGN=TOP><H3>Happy Customers</H3></CAPTION>
  <TH COLSPAN=3>The Studio Club Customers</TH>
  <TR ALIGN=CENTER>
   <TH>Name</TH>
   <TH>Boat Manufacturer</TH>
   <TH>Picture</TH>
  </TR>
  <TR ALIGN=CENTER>
   <TD WIDTH="20%">Eleanor</TD>
   <TD WIDTH="30%">Tartan</TD>
   <TD WIDTH="50%" VALIGN=TOP>
      <IMG SRC="Images/sabtart_01.GIF" WIDTH="68" HEIGHT="51"></TD>
  </TR>
  <TR ALIGN=CENTER>
   <TD WIDTH="20%">Dave</TD>
   <TD WIDTH="30%">Bayliner</TD>
   <TD WIDTH="50%" VALIGN=TOP>
         <IMG SRC="Images/sabtart_04.GIF" WIDTH="68" HEIGHT="51"></TD>
   </TR>
  <TR ALIGN=CENTER>
   <TD WIDTH="20%">Mike</TD>
   <TD WIDTH="30%">J-Boat</TD>
   <TD WIDTH="50%" VALIGN=TOP>
         <IMG SRC="Images/sabtart_06.GIF" WIDTH="68" HEIGHT="51"></TD>
  </TR>
  <TR ALIGN=CENTER>
   <TD WIDTH="20%">Brian</TD>
   <TD WIDTH="30%">Tracker</TD>
   <TD WIDTH="50%" VALIGN=TOP>
         <IMG SRC="Images/sabtart_07.GIF" WIDTH="68" HEIGHT="51"></TD>
  </TR>
  <TR ALIGN=CENTER>
   <TD WIDTH="20%">Dan</TD>
   <TD WIDTH="30%">Ranger</TD>
   <TD WIDTH="50%" VALIGN=TOP>
         <IMG SRC="Images/sabtart_19.GIF" WIDTH="68" HEIGHT="51"></TD>
  </TR>
</TABLE>

</BODY>

</HTML>
```

Figure 12-16 Code for Web page with table

Notice the background color for the Web page has been set in the start body tag. The format for setting the color uses a hexadecimal value or a color constant, whereas the start table tag determines the background color for the table by setting the following attributes:

```
<TABLE BGCOLOR="yellow" BORDER="1" CELLPADDING="0" CELLSPACING="0"
      STYLE="border-collapse: collapse" BORDERCOLOR="#111111"
      WIDTH ="70%" ALIGN=CENTER ID="BradshawMarina1"
      ALIGN=CENTER>
```

The BORDER attribute sets the thickness of the border for the table—a value of zero (0) removes the border from the table. The CELLSPACING attribute sets the amount of space between the inside border lines of adjacent cells in the table. The CELLPADDING attribute sets the amount of space between the inside cell border and the text or object in the cell. The BORDERCOLOR attribute sets the color of the outside border for the table. The WIDTH attribute sets the horizontal size of the table as a percentage of the Web page—an absolute size can also be used. Note the table is centered and has an ID attribute that can be used to reference the table if needed.

Following the start table tag, the next two HTML lines of code create a caption for the table and the column heading within the table.

```
<CAPTION ALIGN=TOP><H3>Happy Customers</H3></CAPTION>
<TH COLSPAN=3>The Studio Club Customers</TH>
<TR ALIGN=CENTER>
   <TH>Name</TH>
   <TH>Boat Manufacturer</TH>
   <TH>Picture</TH>
  </TR>
```

The caption for the table can be placed under the table by setting the ALIGN attribute to BOTTOM. The <TH> </TH> tag pair are for table headings; three columns have been spanned (merged) for this table heading. The <TR> </TR> tag pair designates a row in the table, and the first row contains the table column headings, which are centered by using the ALIGN attribute. Within a table row, the<TD> </TD> tag pair is where the actual data in the table is entered.

After the column headings, each of the next five rows in the table contains information for the different customers. The HTML table code for the first customer row is shown below.

```
<TR ALIGN=CENTER>
   <TD WIDTH="20%">Eleanor</TD>
   <TD WIDTH="30%">Tartan</TD>
   <TD WIDTH="50%" VALIGN=TOP>
      <IMG SRC="Images/sabtart_01.GIF" WIDTH="68" HEIGHT="51"></TD>
  </TR>
```

The WIDTH attribute lets you establish widths for each column. The VALIGN attribute aligns the image vertically, and the image in the table also has WIDTH and HEIGHT attributes to set the size of the image.

As you view the Web page in Figure 12-15, notice that the rows for the images have automatically expanded to the size of the image. Increasing the cell spacing would put some space between the images and the top and bottom of the cells in which the images are located. You can experiment with this Web page by changing attributes such as the table border, the background colors, the cell spacing, and the cell padding.

This chapter covers most basic HTML topics, but does not discuss frames because ASP.NET provides a recommended alternative to framesets (user controls), which will be illustrated in

Chapter 16. Server-side includes (SSIs) are not covered because code-behind (covered later in the chapter) eliminates the need for them. Cascading style sheets (CSSs) provide a powerful way to bring uniformity to Web sites. A CSS is an external file that provides formatting for HTML elements. You can change one file containing the CSS and the changes are reflected in all the Web pages. ASP.NET supports CSSs, but using CSSs is not covered in this text. Also, although HTML has many font features, the ASP.NET GUI provides easy font implementation, which is the approach taken in this text.

Hands-on Exercise 1

1. If necessary, make the Ex01 folder a virtual directory. Using Windows Explorer or My Computer, right-click the **Ex01** folder, and click **Sharing** in Windows 2000 or **Sharing and Security** in Windows XP. In the Ex01 Properties dialog box, click the **Web Sharing** tab. Make sure Ex01 appears in the title of the Web Sharing property sheet and then click the **Share this folder** option button. Then click the **OK** button to make the folder a virtual directory.
2. Test homepage1.htm through homepage4.htm to ensure they work properly. For example, in the Address text box of your browser, type **http://localhost/Ex01/homepage1.htm** and press **Enter**.

Using HTML Forms

Recall that HTML forms let users enter data to customize their requests. Business-to-consumer applications in particular require this capability. HTML forms collect user data and send the input values to the server with the user's request. The server program accesses the user data and responds accordingly—dynamically creating an appropriate Web page and returning HTML to the client browser. You can place one or more form tag pairs, <form> </form>, anywhere within an HTML document.

The start form tag has three attributes that you should usually set—the NAME, ACTION, and METHOD. The NAME attribute should be set because an HTML document can have multiple forms with controls, and the form name lets you reference the control values on a particular form. The METHOD attribute can be set to **POST** or **GET**. When the METHOD attribute is set to POST, the data that the user enters is placed in the form collection of the request object to be passed to the server and is not visible to the user. When the METHOD attribute is set to GET, the data is passed to the server by adding it to the end of the URL address and is visible to the user. The input values are included in the QueryString collection of the request object. Using either the POST or GET method, the user input (consisting of name-value pairs) is placed in one of the request object's collections and can be extracted by server programs. An example name-value pair could be fName=Eleanor. The ACTION attribute specifies to what file program control is transferred when the Web page is submitted. It is usually set to another Web page but can be set to the current Web page.

Using Form Controls

The controls that you can use with HTML forms are similar to many of the controls you have already used in the Windows environment. HTML form controls are also called form elements. Table 12-2 summarizes the form controls.

Table 12-2 HTML Form Controls

INPUT Type or Tag and Typical Attributes	VB .NET Equivalent
<INPUT TYPE= "Text" NAME= "txtName" SIZE = "15" >	Text box
<INPUT TYPE= "Password" NAME ="txtPass" SIZE = "12" >	Password
<INPUT TYPE= "Radio" NAME = "rdbPay" VALUE="MONTHLY"> <INPUT TYPE= "Radio" NAME = "rdbPay" VALUE= "SEMI" > <INPUT TYPE= "Radio" NAME = "rdbPay" VALUE= "ANNUALLY" CHECKED>	Radio buttons
<INPUT TYPE = "Checkbox" NAME="chkSBE" VALUE="sb" CHECKED > <INPUT TYPE = "Checkbox" NAME="chkSKBE" VALUE="skb"> <INPUT TYPE = "Checkbox" NAME="chkCCE" VALUE="cc">	Check boxes
<INPUT TYPE = "Button" NAME ="btnCheck" ONCLICK="btnCheck" VALUE="OK">	Button
<INPUT TYPE = "Submit">	None
<INPUT TYPE = "Reset">	None
<INPUT TYPE= "Hidden" NAME= "txtMessage" VALUE= "True" >	None
<TEXTAREA ROWS="2" NAME="txtWant" > ... ... </TEXTAREA>	Multiline text box
<SELECT NAME="cboColor" <OPTION>"Red"</OPTION> <OPTION>"Blue"</OPTION> <OPTION>"Green"</OPTION> </SELECT>	Combo box

Most of the controls have ASP.NET equivalents that are similar to VB .NET controls for Windows applications. The button control has an ONCLICK event that is triggered when the user clicks the button. In Table 12-2, for example, the ONCLICK event invokes the btnCheck method. You can write code for the event within the tag or you can call a method.

The SUBMIT and RESET buttons have no ASP.NET equivalents. However, in HTML, they are rendered as buttons and include the labels Submit and Reset. When clicked, the Submit button sends the user input from the form controls to the server. The Reset button clears all the form controls. Lastly, the HIDDEN type input control is usually used for communicating some value to another program.

Table 12-3 lists common HTML events in addition to the ONCLICK event.

Table 12-3 HTML Events

HTML Event	Description
OnBlur	Control loses focus
OnChange	Control loses focus and the value has changed
OnClick	Control has been clicked
OndbClick	Control has been double-clicked
OnFocus	Control receives focus
OnKeyDown	Key has been pressed with the control having focus
OnKeyPress	Key has been pressed and released with the control having focus
OnKeyUp	Key has been released with the control having focus
OnMouseDown	Left mouse key pressed while over the control
OnMouseMove	Mouse moves while over the control
OnMouseOut	Mouse moves away from the control
OnMouseOver	Mouse moves over the control
OnMouseUp	Left mouse key released while the control has focus
OnReset	Resets the form removing all user inputs (Reset button)
OnSubmit	Submits the form (Submit button)

Classic ASP Web Development

For many years, ASP has been a very popular technology for building Web applications. After the introduction of the .NET platform with ASP.NET as part of VS .NET, ASP has been dubbed "Classic ASP." Although ASP.NET represents a radically changed Web development technology, it is still based upon and uses parts of ASP. Reviewing ASP will help you understand the new .NET Web technologies, ASP.NET in particular. The .NET platform also maintains backward compatibility with ASP, and VS .NET can be used to maintain ASP or create new ASP applications where warranted.

In a nutshell, ASP is a technology that allows you to mix scripts with HTML code. An HTML document can contain a client-side script. You can change the file extension of any HTML document from .htm to .asp. If you do, the file is processed with the ASP script engine on the *server*. However, if you add a server-side script to an HTML document, then you must change the file extension to .asp for the script to be processed.

ASP allows both client-side and server-side processing in a variety of script languages. Usually, client-side scripting validates data before sending it to the server. You can also use client-side scripting for Web page presentation effects such as animation. Server-side scripting generally accepts user inputs and obtains data from a database if required before processing, rendering, and returning a Web page. Figure 12-17 shows this basic Request/Response model.

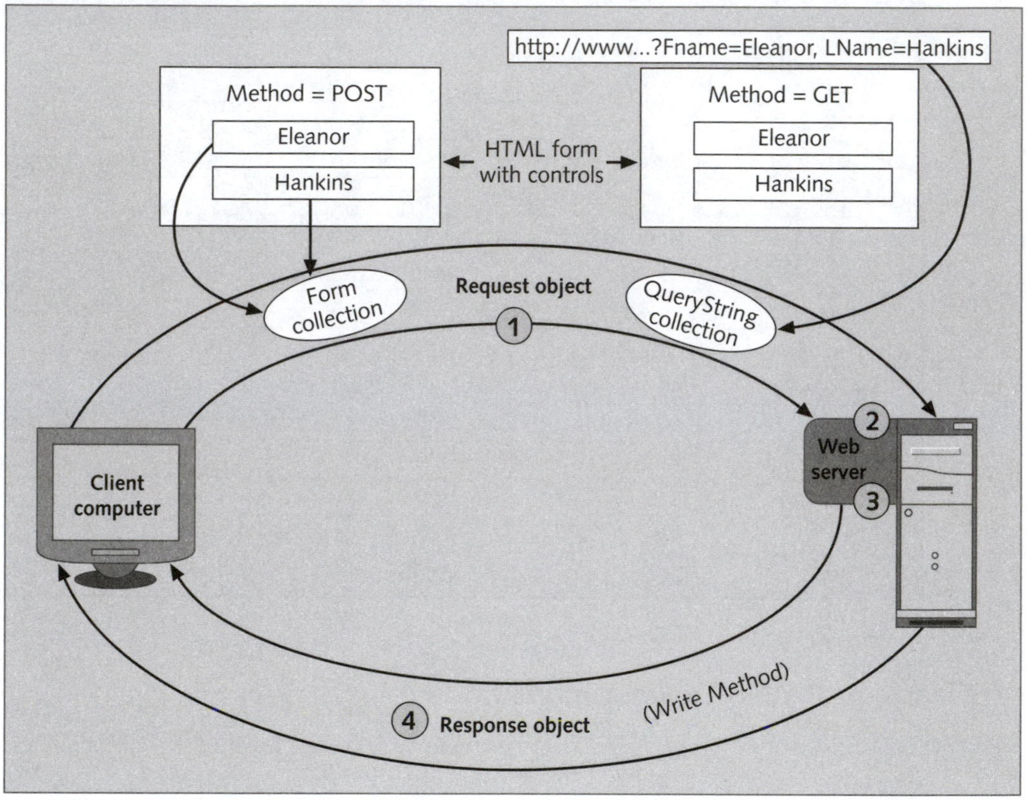

Figure 12-17 Request/Response model

The user inputs from the form's controls are contained in the request object that is sent to the server. The server also has other objects that are needed for Web processing. As discussed later in Chapter 16, the application object and the session object are used for state control since HTTP is a stateless protocol. These objects allow a Web page to keep up with user sessions. For now, you will concentrate on the request and response objects.

Suppose the management of Bradshaw Marina wanted to conduct a Web-based survey of existing and current customers. The survey Web page is shown in Figure 12-18. When this page is submitted, it sends the input data to another Web page on the server for processing.

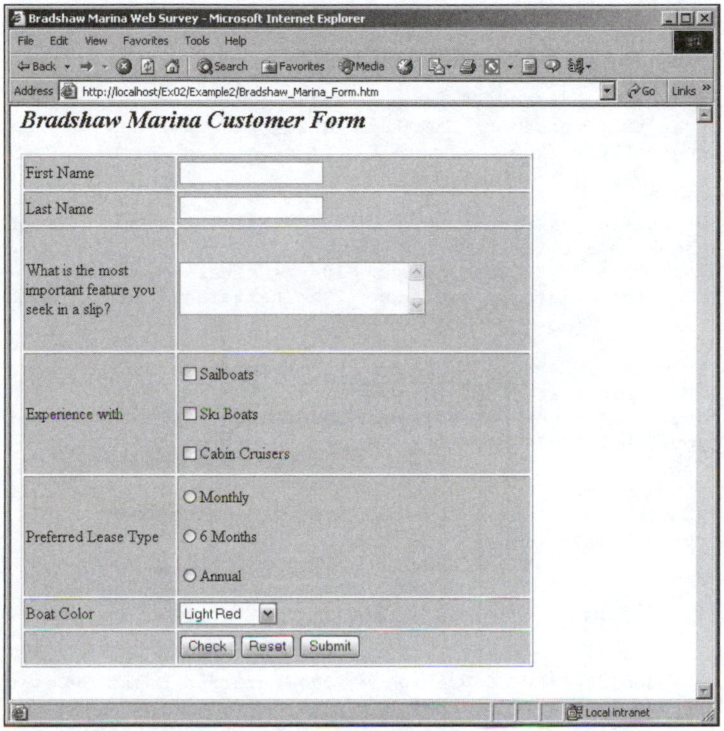

Figure 12-18 Bradshaw Marina Web survey form

Because the survey Web page is an HTML document, it can contain a client-side script. Recall that a form can appear anywhere in the HTML document; in this case, it will appear at the bottom of the HTML document and can be recognized because it is within the body tags. Figure 12-19 shows the code to create the form. The form start tag includes the NAME, ACTION, and METHOD attributes. The ACTION attribute specifies that the file (Web page) Bradshaw_Marina_form.asp on the server will be executed when the Web page is submitted. The METHOD attribute specifies the method, POST in this case, to be used for sending the data to the server Web page. Lastly, the form's name is frmTest. The rest of the form contains the user input controls with layout design via a table.

```
<form name=frmTest action=Bradshaw_Marina_response.asp method=post>
<table border="1" width="72%" height="505">
  <tr>
    <td width="25%" bgcolor="#FFCC66" height="23">First Name</td>
    <td width="70%" bgcolor="#FFCC66" height="23">
         <input type="text" name="txtFirstName" size="20" tabindex="0"
             maxlength="20"></td>
  </tr>
  <tr>
    <td width="25%" bgcolor="#FFCC66" height="23">Last Name</td>
    <td width="70%" bgcolor="#FFCC66" height="23">
         <input type="text" name="txtLastName" size="20" tabindex="1"
             maxlength="20"></td>
  </tr>
  <tr>
    <td width="25%" bgcolor="#FFCC66" height="104">What is the most important
      feature you seek in a slip?</td>
    <td width="70%" bgcolor="#FFCC66" height="104"><textarea rows="3"
         name="txtDesire" cols="28" tabindex="2"></textarea></td>
  </tr>
  <tr>
    <td width="25%" bgcolor="#FFCC66" height="95">Experience with </td>
    <td width="70%" bgcolor="#FFCC66" height="95">
    <input type="checkbox" name="chkSailBoat" value="sb" tabindex="3">Sailboats
      <p><input type="checkbox" name="chkSkiBoat" value="skb" tabindex="4">Ski
          Boats
      </p>
      <p><input type="checkbox" name="chkCabinCruiser" value="cc"
          tabindex="5">Cabin
      Cruisers
      </p>
    </td>
  </tr>
  <tr>
    <td width="25%" bgcolor="#FFCC66" height="95">Preferred Lease Type</td>
    <td width="70%" bgcolor="#FFCC66" height="95">
         <input type="radio" name="rdbType" id=radio1 value="monthly"
          tabindex="6">Monthly
     <p><input type="radio" name="rdbType" id=radio2 value="semi"
         tabindex="7">6 Months </p>
     <p><input type="radio" name="rdbType" id=radio3 value="annually"
         tabindex="8">Annual</p>
    </td>
  </tr>
  <tr>
    <td width="30%" bgcolor="#FFCC66" height="23">Boat Color</td>
    <td width="70%" bgcolor="#FFCC66" height="23">
    <select size="1" name="cboCheckColor" tabindex="9">
        <option value="Red">Light Red</option>
        <option value="Blue">Light Blue</option>
        <option value="Green">Light Green</option>
        <option value="Yellow">Light Yellow</option>
      </select></td>
  </tr>
  <tr>
    <td width="25%" bgcolor="#FFCC66" height="25"> </td>
    <td width="70%" bgcolor="#FFCC66" height="25">
    <input type="button" value="Check" name="btnCheck" tabindex="10" >
    <input type="reset" value="Reset" name="btnReset" tabindex="11">
    <input type="submit" value="Submit" name="btnSubmit" tabindex="12"></td>
  </tr>
```

```
</table>
<input type="Hidden" name="Message" value = "True">
</form>
</body>
</html>
```

Figure 12-19 HTML for survey Web form

For clarity, the user controls have been stripped out of the HTML table rows and are presented in Figure 12-20. All the controls have the NAME and TABINDEX attribute, and they have been assigned values using appropriate coding conventions, such as "txt" as the prefix for a text box. As shown below, the first two input controls are text boxes used to capture the first and last names of the person filling out the survey. Each text box is limited to 20 characters. The TEXTAREA control is similar to a VB .NET multiline text box. However, it has a ROWS attribute to limit the number of rows. The check box controls appear next, and each of their VALUE attributes has been assigned a unique value. Recall that check boxes should be used where the user can check zero, one, or more of the options presented.

```
<input type="text" name="txtFirstName" size="20" tabindex="0" maxlength="20">
<input type="text" name="txtLastName" size="20" tabindex="1"
maxlength="20">
<textarea rows="3" name="txtDesire" cols="28" tabindex="2">
<input type="checkbox" name="chkSailBoat" value="sb" tabindex="3">Sailboats
<input type="checkbox" name="chkSkiBoat" value="skb" tabindex="4">Ski
      Boats
<input type="checkbox" name="chkCabinCruiser" value="cc" tabindex="5">Cabin
Cruisers
<input type="radio" name="rdbType" id=radio1 value="monthly" tabindex="6">Monthly
     <p><input type="radio" name="rdbType" id=radio2 value="semi"
         tabindex="7">6 Months </p>
     <p><input type="radio" name="rdbType" id=radio3 value="annually"
         tabindex="8">Annual
<select size="1" name="cboCheckColor" tabindex="9">
        <option value="Red">Light Red</option>
        <option value="Blue">Light Blue</option>
        <option value="Green">Light Green</option>
        <option value="Yellow">Light Yellow</option>
</select>
<input type="button" value="Check" name="btnCheck" tabindex="10" >
<input type="reset" value="Reset" name="btnReset" tabindex="11">
<input type="submit" value="Submit" name="btnSubmit" tabindex="12">
<input type="Hidden" name="Message" value = "True">
```

Figure 12-20 HTML survey input controls

Radio buttons used with Windows forms are usually placed on a panel or another group control so that only one of a set of options can be selected. HTML radio buttons work differently. The NAME attribute should be assigned the same value for all the radio buttons in a group. Then the ID or VALUE attributes can be used to determine which of the group of radio buttons has been clicked.

Note that the HTML code in Figure 12-20 contains only HTML controls; ASP.NET server controls are covered in detail later in the chapter. The SELECT tag pair provides the functionality of an ASP.NET combo box (sometimes called a drop-down list box). Its SIZE attribute limits the number of items in the drop-down box that can be selected. OPTION tag pairs provide the means for entering the list of entries. This example includes a VALUE attribute for each of the items in the list, although this attribute is optional.

The last four input controls are three buttons and a HIDDEN VALUE control. The RESET button control clears the controls of all the input values except for the combo box where the values are hard coded. The SUBMIT button control sends the form data to the Web page identified by the ACTION attribute. Lastly, the HIDDEN VALUE control has been set to the value of True—if the client-side script is executed before clicking the Submit button, the code changes the hidden value to False.

The script in Figure 12-21 illustrates using VBScript, a subset of Visual Basic, for client-side processing. The script documents how to reference the form's controls and their corresponding values input by the user. The script is separated from the HTML by enclosing it in script blocks. The script attribute LANGUAGE has been set to VBScript, which you should be able to follow. When the form is completed, the OnMouseOver event invokes the btnCheck_OnMouseOver procedure. This procedure presents a message box and then calls the btnCheck_onClick() procedure to echo via message boxes the values of the form's input controls. The DIM statement declares variables to hold the values from the text boxes and the text area controls. VBScript is a subset of VB, and does not allow you to declare variable types. If needed, you can use conversion functions to obtain the appropriate data type. Also, note that the last statement sets the value of the hidden control to False.

```
<html>
<head>
<title>Bradshaw Marina Web Survey</title>
</head>
<script language=vbscript>
   ' The following code is for the onclick event
   ' for the Check button
   sub btnCheck_onclick()
      ' Shows how to reference form controls
      dim fn, ln, txArea
      fn=frmTest.txtFirstName.value     'save first name
      ln=frmTest.txtLastName.value      'save last name
      txArea=frmTest.txtDesire.value      'save text area

      ' Display these text and text area values
      msgbox "First Name is:  " & fn
      msgbox "Last Name is:  " & ln
      msgbox "Desirable features test is:  " & txArea

      ' Display the check boxes if checked
      if frmTest.chkSailBoat.checked then msgbox "Sailboat Experience"
      if frmTest.chkSkiBoat.checked then msgbox "Ski Boat Experience"
      if frmTest.chkCabinCruiser.checked then msgbox "Cabin Cruiser Experience"
```

```
      ' Display which radio button checked
      'if frmtest.radio1.checked then msgbox "Monthly"
      select case true
         case frmtest.radio1.checked : msgbox "Prefer monthly payment"
         case frmtest.radio2.checked : msgbox "Prefer semi-annual payment"
         case frmtest.radio3.checked : msgbox "Prefer annual payment"
         case else :msgbox "none"
      end select

      ' Display the check color from the Selection box
      msgbox frmTest.cboCheckColor.value
      if frmTest.cboCheckColor.value = "Blue" then msgbox "This really means
         light blue"
      end if
      '  Example of referencing a hidden value
      frmTest.Message.value = false

   end sub
   ' Example of events for other form controls
   Sub radio1_onclick()
      msgbox "You selected the Monthly option"
   end sub
   sub chkSailBoat_onclick()
      msgbox "You checked Sailboat"
   end sub
   sub btnCheck_OnMouseOver
      msgbox "Mouse over Check Button"
      call btnCheck_onClick()
   end sub
   sub Submit
      Call frmTest.submit
   end sub
</script>
```

Figure 12-21 Client-side script for the Web survey

12

Three other procedures appear toward the bottom of the script. The radio1_onclick procedure invokes code based on the click event for a radio button and references its value. The chkSailboat_onclick procedure can be used for check boxes. The last procedure simply uses the Call method to submit the form's control values to the Web page (Bradshaw_Marina_response.asp, in this case) identified by the ACTION attribute value of the form's start tag. Clicking the Submit button invokes this procedure and submits the form.

Figure 12-22 contains the server-side code for the Bradshaw_Marina_response.asp Web page. Recall that ASP technology allows you to mix program script with HTML. The tag pair, <% %>, encloses the script so that the ASP script engine can identify the text as ASP code instead of HTML code. ASP files have a page directive that identifies the scripting language, which is VBScript in this case. The next two lines are scripting options. Option Explicit forces the script to declare all variables before their use. Setting the response buffer to True results in the complete page being processed and the results sent back to the client all at once, as opposed to being sent back as each item is processed.

```
<%@ Language=VBScript %>
<% option explicit %>
<% Response.Buffer=true %>
<HTML>
<Head><Title>Response Page</Title></Head>
<BODY>
         <P><h3> This is the response </h3></P>
<%
dim fn, ln, txArea
'  get posted values from submitted form
'  uses the request object
'  uses request.form because Method=Post on submitted form
'  one would use request.querystring if Method=Get
fn=request.form("txtFirstName")
ln=request.form("txtLastName")
txArea=request.form("txtDesire")

'        write these values using the response object
response.write "<BR>" & "The first name is: " & fn & "<BR>"
response.write "<BR>" & "The last name is: " & ln & "<BR>"
response.write "<BR>" & "Desirable features for the dock:  " & txArea & "<BR>"

' see what check boxes have been checked
if request.form("chkSailBoat")= "sb" then  'note can also use ="on"
         response.write "<BR>" & "You have Sailboat experience" & "<BR>"
end if
if request.form("chkSkiBoat")= "skb" then
         response.write "<BR>" & "You have Ski Boat experience" & "<BR>"
end if
if request.form("chkCabinCruiser")="cc" then
         response.write "<BR>" & "You have Cabin Cruiser experience" & "<BR>"
end if

' see which radio button has been selected
select case ucase(Request.Form("rdbType"))
    case "MONTHLY"
       response.write "<BR>" & "You prefer to pay monthly" & "<BR>"
    case "SEMI"
       response.write "<BR>" & "You prefer to pay semi-annually" & "<BR>"
    case "ANNUALLY"
       response.write "<BR>" & "You prefer to pay annually" & "<BR>"
    case else
    response.write "<BR>" & "You didn't select a preferred payment method" &
"<BR>"
end select

'  see which value in the combo box has been selected
response.write "<BR>" & " Boat color is " & request.form("cboCheckColor")

response.write "<BR>" & "The hidden value is: " & request.form("Message")

%>

</BODY>
</HTML>
```

Page directive—sets scripting language to VBScript

Requires declaring variables

Sends back responses all at once

Form collection of the request object that holds the name-value pairs of data from the input form

Figure 12-22 Bradshaw_Marina_response.asp code

HTML code that creates a title and a paragraph response follows the page directive and the options for the Web page. The <% indicates that script will follow, and three variables that will be used to store input data from the request form Web page are declared. On the request Web page form, the METHOD attribute is set to POST, which means that the input form data is stored in the form collection of the request object. The format for retrieving the input values from the request object's form collection is shown below and simply references the values of the text boxes via the NAME attribute specified in the INPUT tags of the form.

```
<HTML>
<Head><Title>Response Page</Title></Head>
<BODY>
        <P><h3> This is the response </h3></P>
<%
dim fn, ln, txArea
'  get posted values from submitted form
'  uses the request object
'  uses request.form because Method=Post on submitted form
'  one would use request.querystring if Method=Get
fn=request.form("txtFirstName")
ln=request.form("txtLastName")
txArea=request.form("txtDesire")
```

This example uses the response object's write method to respond to the client's request. Note that you can mix HTML tags with the script, as shown in the following code. To do this, the HTML tags must be enclosed within double-quote characters to allow the script engine to differentiate the HTML from the script. This code simply echoes back the input form's values of the HTML text boxes and text area. The <BR> tag is used to force line breaks in the output.


```
'         write these values using the response object
response.write "<BR>" & "The first name is: " & fn & "<BR>"
response.write "<BR>" & "The last name is: " & ln & "<BR>"
response.write "<BR>" & "Desirable features for the dock:  " & txArea & "<BR>"
```

After executing the first part of the script, the code checks to see which check boxes on the input form have been checked. Users can check any number of the check boxes. The value of the check box is compared to the VALUE attribute defined in the input form. If the check box is checked, the testing for this VALUE returns a True condition; otherwise, it returns False. You can also check for the lowercase value of ="on". A message containing the boat experience is displayed for each checked box.

```
' see what check boxes have been checked
   if request.form("chkSailBoat")= "sb" then  'note can also use ="on"
      response.write "<BR>" & "You have Sailboat experience" & "<BR>"
   end if
   if request.form("chkSkiBoat")= "skb" then
      response.write "<BR>" & "You have Ski Boat experience" & "<BR>"
   end if
   if request.form("chkCabinCruiser")="cc" then
      response.write "<BR>" & "You have Cabin Cruiser experience" & "<BR>"
   end if
```

The next segment of the code checks to see which radio button has been clicked. The script uses the case structure to compare the VALUE attribute associated with each radio button. All the radio buttons belong to the same group, so users can select only one button. Recall that you assign the NAME attribute the same value for all the radio buttons to have them as part of the same group.

```
'see which value in the combo box has been selected
select case ucase(Request.Form("rdbType"))
   case "MONTHLY"
      response.write "<BR>" & "You prefer to pay monthly" & "<BR>"
   case "SEMI"
      response.write "<BR>" & "You prefer to pay semi-annually" & "<BR>"
   case "ANNUALLY"
      response.write "<BR>" & "You prefer to pay annually" & "<BR>"
   case else
   response.write "<BR>" & "You didn't select a preferred payment method" & "<BR>"
end select
```

The final part of the code determines and displays the color the user selected from the SELECT control on the input form and also displays the value of the hidden value. The ending script tag, %>, determines the end of the script. The final two statements are the normal end to an HTML document.

```
'  see which value in the combo box has been selected
response.write "<BR>" & " Boat color is " & request.form("cboCheckColor")
response.write "<BR>"
response.write "<BR>" & "The hidden value is " & request.form("Message")

%>
</BODY>
</HTML>
```

In summary, ASP is a technology that allows you to mix scripting with HTML code. Script and HTML code in a file with the file extension .asp are processed by the ASP script engine. The ASP script engine can process pure HTML files but does so on the server. Mixing server-side script with HTML provides a strong technology for producing dynamic Web pages. As you will see in the next section, Microsoft's new .NET technology maintains backward compatibility with ASP technology, so you can use ASP.NET to develop these applications. The example's completed survey form is shown in Figure 12-23, and the corresponding output after clicking the Submit button is shown as Figure 12-24.

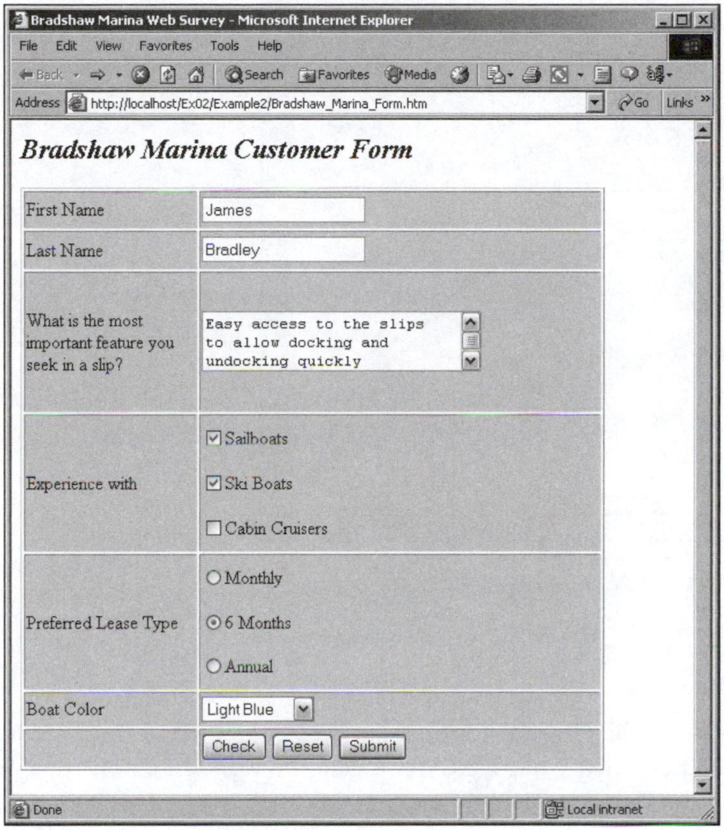

Figure 12-23 Bradshaw Marina completed Web survey form

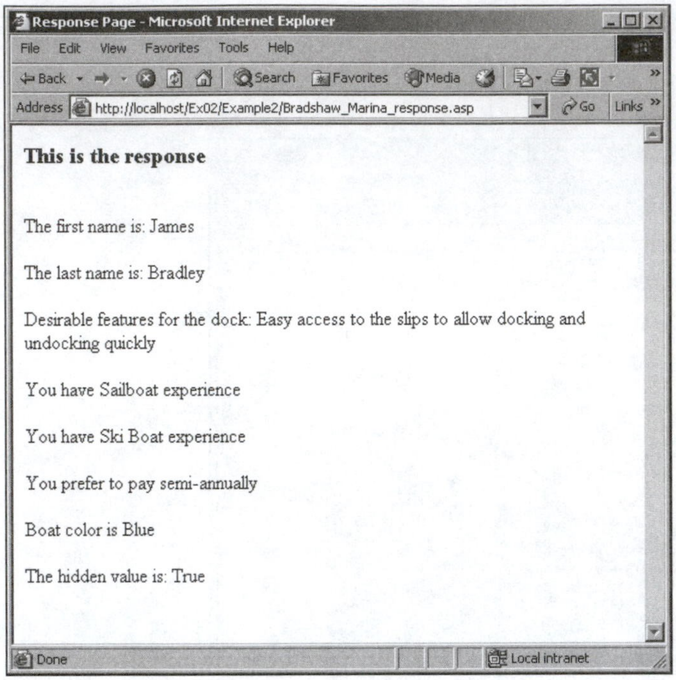

Figure 12-24 Bradshaw Marina response page

Hands-on Exercise 2

1. Locate **Ex02** in the Chap12\Examples in the book's student data files. If necessary, create a folder named **Chap12\Exercises** in the work folder on your system, and then copy the **Ex02** folder to this folder.
2. You now need to make this folder a virtual directory. (See Step 1 of Hands-on Exercise 1 for instructions on creating a virtual directory.)
3. In the Address text box of your browser, type **http://localhost/Ex02/Example2/Bradshaw_Marina_form.htm** and press **Enter**.
4. On the Bradshaw Marina Customer Form Web page, enter appropriate information and then move the mouse over the **Check** button. This invokes the client-side script and opens message boxes that summarize the information you entered. Some controls have been coded to immediately respond to the click event, which is also indicated in a message box.

5. Click the **Submit** button to invoke Bradshaw_Marina_response.asp. This is the Web page invoked via the ACTION attribute on the form tag of the Bradshaw Marina Customer Form Web page. The response Web page echoes the form's input data.
6. Click the **Back** button on the browser toolbar to enter different data. The response Web page should be similar to Figure 12-24.

USING ASP.NET TO DEVELOP WEB PAGES

Microsoft's goal in developing the .NET framework and VS .NET was to provide an integrated development environment (IDE) to support the development of both Windows and Web applications. In Chapter 10, you used VS .NET to develop VB .NET GUI applications using Windows forms. The first part of this chapter provided the basic fundamentals of Web development. In the remaining part of this chapter, you will use ASP.NET to build Web applications—however, recognize that the code for the Web applications will be VB .NET. Because ASP.NET for Web development is similar to developing Windows applications, you will be familiar with many features. However, you now need to learn the Web-related features of ASP.NET, which is an upgrade to ASP. Some of the new features in ASP.NET include drag-and-drop development, dynamic compilation for faster execution, separation of code from content, and **validation controls**. These features will be briefly discussed before you create an ASP.NET application.

Separating Code from Content

ASP.NET separates Web page code from content and presentation (the GUI). Recall that the typical ASP page includes programming script mixed with HTML tags. In ASP, it is difficult to cleanly separate the code from presentation and content. ASP.NET, however, uses a technique called **code-behind** that mimics the event-driven code-behind concept for Windows applications. In ASP.NET, the Web form file containing presentation and content has an .aspx extension and the code-behind file containing the code has an .aspx.vb extension. Double-clicking a control opens the code window with a default event handler for the control and allows you to write code that responds to events. ASP.NET keeps this code in the code-behind file, which is separate from the presentation and content file stored in a file with the .aspx extension.

Figure 12-25 illustrates what happens when a user requests a Web page. The .aspx file is parsed by the ASPX engine, which generates a page class file that is compiled by the CLR before creating the output. The compiled code-behind files are included in the generated page class. The compilation persists—is saved on disk—so the next time the user requests this page, no compilation is required unless the code has changed.

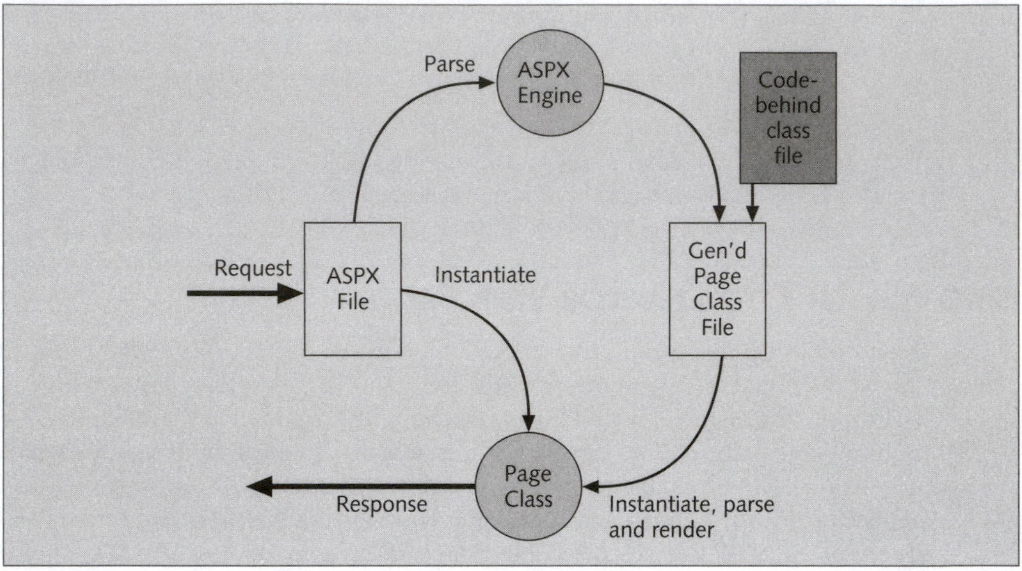

Figure 12-25 ASP.NET dynamic page compilation

Using HTML, HTML Server Controls, and ASP.NET Server Controls

You can use ASP.NET to develop Web applications using HTML, HTML server controls, and ASP.NET Web server controls. You worked with HTML form controls earlier in this chapter. Additionally, ASP.NET can work with HTML server controls. **HTML server controls** are similar to **ASP.NET server controls** but use the HTML form control properties that are different from the ASP.NET server control properties. For example, referencing an HTML text box control uses the VALUE property, but the ASP.NET server control references the TEXT property, as it does in Windows applications. ASP.NET also includes rich controls, such as AdRotator and Calendar, that are not available with HTML server controls.

ASP.NET server controls have properties and methods, and respond to events as Windows controls do. Most ASP.NET server controls support data binding to link the form to data. DataGrid, DataList, and Repeater are examples of data rendering controls that only work if they are bound to an underlying data source. An advantage of using ASP.NET server controls is that they are browser neutral because they detect the browser and render a page based on the browser.

Finally, validation server controls represent a unique group of controls. They are placed on the form just like other ASP.NET server controls and perform validation checks on input data before the form is submitted and processed. A summary validation control displays any errors in one location.

Understanding the ASP.NET Page Event Life Cycle

The ASP.NET Page class has its own properties, methods, and events. The page event life cycle, shown in Figure 12-26, starts by firing the Page_Init event when a page is requested. This occurs before the controls are loaded onto the Web form.

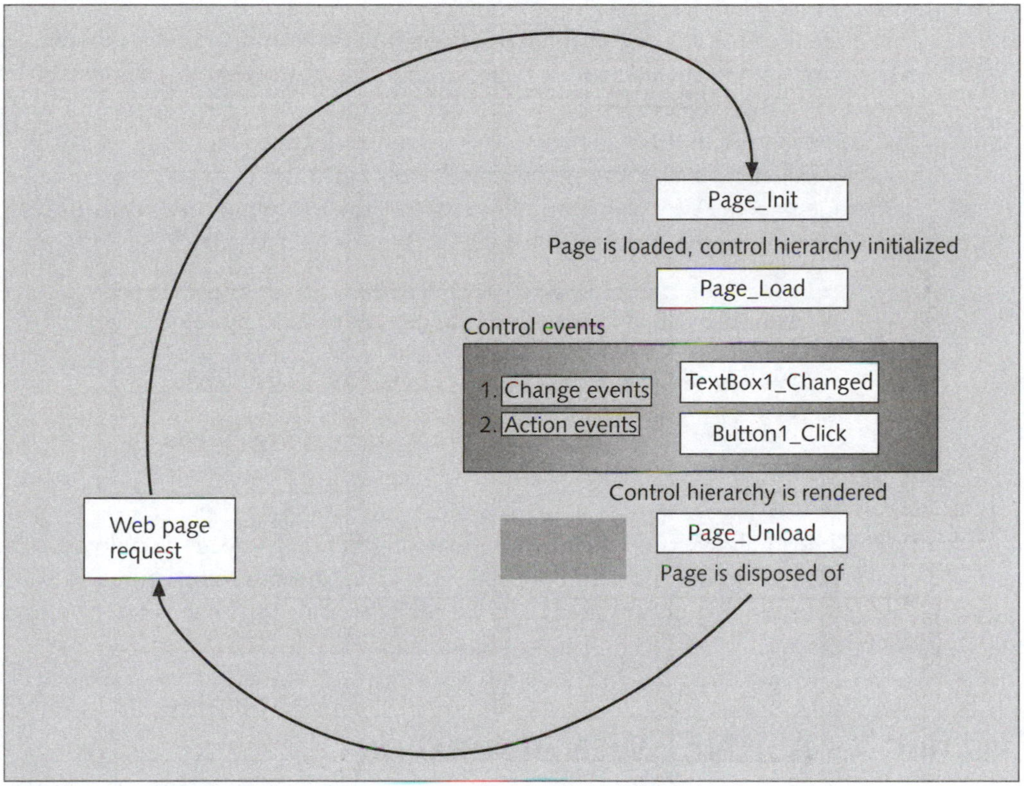

Figure 12-26 ASP.NET Web page life cycle

You may want to do some data connection and initialization when the Page_Init event occurs. The Page_Init method is located in the "Web Form Designer Generated Code" region of the code—you may need to expand the region to locate it. The following example shows the expanded code. Code you add should be placed after the InitializeComponent() method.

```
#Region " Web Form Designer Generated Code "

    'This call is required by the Web Form Designer.
    <System.Diagnostics.DebuggerStepThrough()> Private Sub InitializeComponent()

    End Sub
```

```
    Private Sub Page_Init(ByVal sender As System.Object, ByVal e As
       System.EventArgs) Handles MyBase.Init
        'CODEGEN: This method call is required by the Web Form Designer
        'Do not modify it using the code editor.
        InitializeComponent()

    End Sub

#End Region
```

The Page_Load event occurs after the Page_Init event and typically provides the location where you want to include code to check for postback. **Postback** is a new Web concept and involves the Page_Load method, which can determine the first request of a Web page from any following requests for the page. The second and subsequent requests for the Web form page are called postbacks. Using a postback, you can write code to be executed only on the first request for the Web page form. For example, the following code segment tests for a postback. You may see this written as Page.IsPostBack or me.IsPostBack.

```
Private Sub Page_Load(ByVal sender As System.Object, _
   ByVal e As System.EventArgs) Handles MyBase.Load

   'Put user code to initialize the page here
   If Not IsPostBack Then
      'Put code here for first time page loads
   End If
End Sub
```

Page_Unload allows you to clean up processing before the page is unloaded. This cleanup could include closing files and connections to data, and disposing of unneeded objects. The Page_Unload event occurs after the page has been unloaded but before the page is sent to the browser.

Creating an ASP.NET Web Application

To create your first ASP.NET Web application, you'll start by creating a virtual directory, and then open VS .NET to create an ASP.NET Web application.

To start an ASP.NET Web application:

1. Locate **Ex03** in the Chap12\Examples folder in the book's student files. Copy the **Ex03** folder to the Chap12\Exercises folder on your system. (Create this directory, if necessary.)
2. Create a virtual directory for the Ex03 folder. (See the "To create a virtual directory" in the "Working with Web Directories" section earlier in this chapter for detailed steps on creating a virtual directory.)

3. Start VS .NET by clicking the **Start** button, pointing to **Programs** (**All Programs** in Windows XP), pointing to **Microsoft Visual Studio .NET**, and then clicking **Microsoft Visual Studio .NET**. VS .NET opens to the Start Page.

4. On the Start Page, click the **New Project** button to open the New Project dialog box. Click **Visual Basic Projects** in the Project Types list, if necessary, and click the **ASP.NET Web Application** icon in the Templates list. See Figure 12-27.

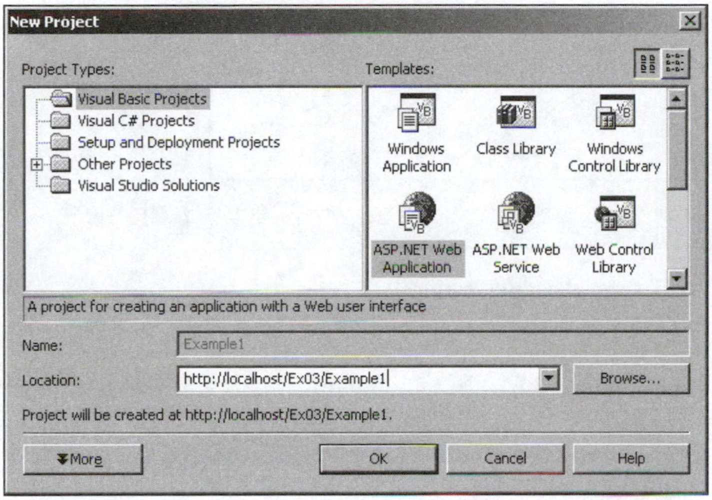

Figure 12-27 New Project dialog box for an ASP.NET Web application

12

5. If this is the first time you have opened an ASP.NET Web Application, the default name path in the Location text box starts with http://localhost and the default Web application name is WebApplication1. Change the location to **http://localhost/Ex03** and then click the **OK** button. The form designer window opens, similar to the one shown in Figure 12-28.

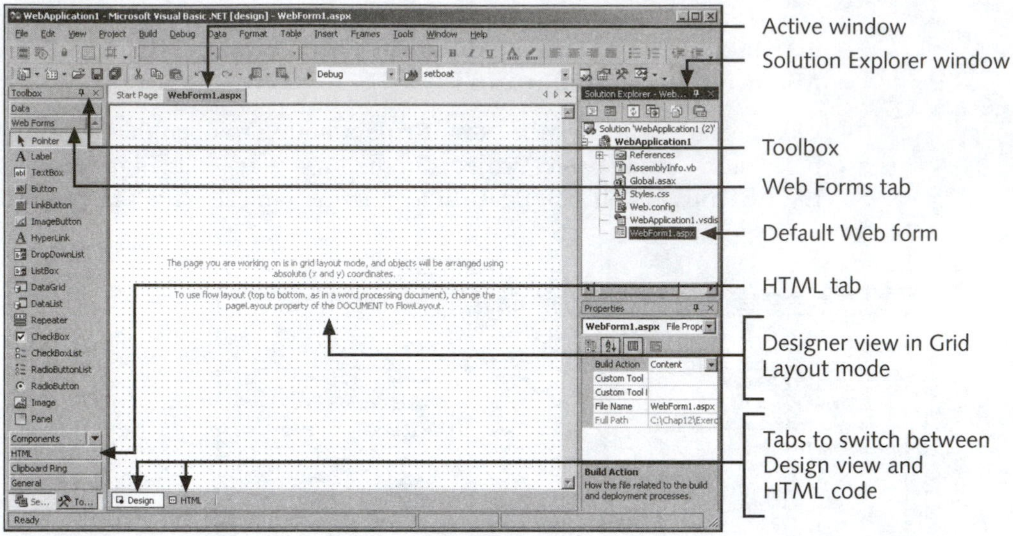

Figure 12-28 ASP.NET form designer window

The Solution Explorer window shows that the form name is WebForm1.aspx. The middle of the form describes the two types of available layout modes. The default for the Web form is Grid Layout mode, but you can use the a Page Layout property in the Properties window to change the layout. The Design and HTML tabs at the lower-left corner of the Web form indicate the current view. When the form designer opens, the Design tab should be selected.

The default tab for the Toolbox is the Web Forms tab, which contains ASP.NET server controls. Note also that the Toolbox also has an HTML tab. As discussed earlier, you can also use the form designer for HTML controls and HTML server controls. An HTML server control is processed on the server, but an HTML control is processed on the client.

Putting controls on the Web form can be done by double-clicking the control on the Toolbox or selecting and dragging the control onto the Web form. To create an HTML server control, double-click the HTML control from the Toolbox's HTML tab, right-click the control, and then click Run As Server Control. You can place the control where you want it on the Web form by dragging it. Figure 12-29 shows a Web form with five server controls and an HTML control. ASP.NET places a symbol at the upper-left corner of the server controls so you can identify which controls on the Web form are server controls. You click the Run button on the toolbar to run the application.

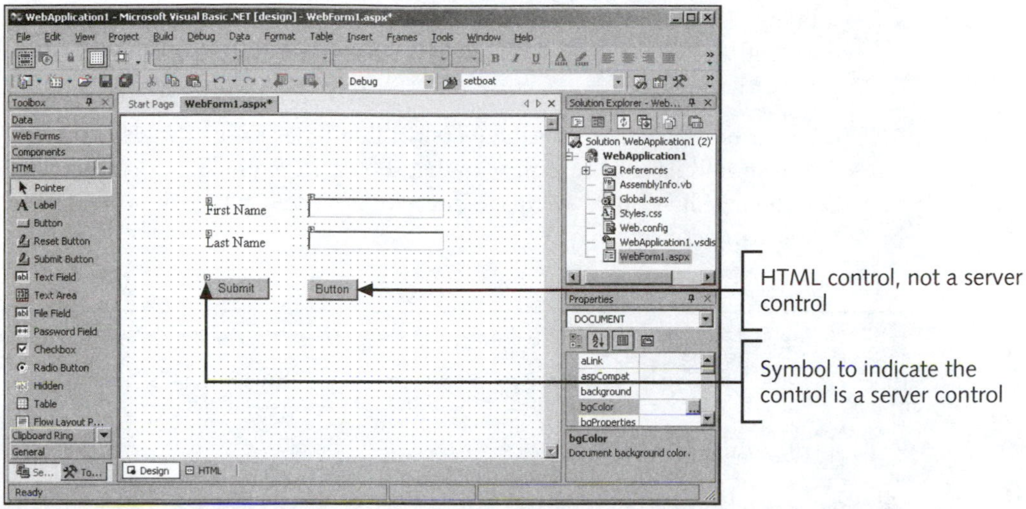

Figure 12-29 Web form with Web server controls and an HTML control

Each ASP.NET server control has a unique tag. Presentation and content code of a Web form are stored in HTML and include ASP.NET server controls with their tags. You'll add controls to the form and then view the code in the next set of steps. You will place five ASP.NET server controls and one HTML control on a Web form as shown in Figure 12-29.

To add controls to the form and view the code-behind:

1. Click the **Toolbox** tab to display the Toolbox, if necessary. Click the **Web Forms** tab on the Toolbox, if necessary, to display the Web Form form controls.
2. Double-click the **Label** control in the Toolbox, drag the label to the middle of the work area, as shown in Figure 12-29, and then type **First Name** in the Text property in the Properties window. Refer to Figure 12-29 to place a label for Last Name on the Web form.
3. Add two text boxes to the Web form by double-clicking the **TextBox** control on the Toolbox and then placing it as shown in Figure 12-29. Repeat for the second text box.
4. Double-click the **Button** control on the Toolbox and place the control under the Last Name text box. Also, change the text on the button by setting its Text property to **Submit** in the Properties window.
5. Click the **HTML** tab on the Toolbox and then double-click the **Button** control. Drag the control to the right of the Submit button. The text on the button will be Button.

Figure 12-29 shows that ASP.NET uses a symbol in the upper-left corner to identify server controls. The HTML button just placed on the Web form is not a server control.

6. Click the **HTML** tab on the Web form designer to see the results in HTML view. You should have code similar to that shown in Figure 12-30. Note that ASP.NET automatically displays the page directive in yellow, which appears shaded in the following code:

```
<%@ Page Language="vb" AutoEventWireup="false" Codebehind="WebForm1.aspx.vb"
Inherits="Ex03.WebForm3"%>
<!DOCTYPE HTML PUBLIC "-//W3C//DTD HTML 4.0 Transitional//EN">
<HTML>
   <HEAD>
      <title>WebForm1</title>
      <meta content="Microsoft Visual Studio.NET 7.0" name="GENERATOR">
      <meta content="Visual Basic 7.0" name="CODE_LANGUAGE">
      <meta content="JavaScript" name="vs_defaultClientScript">
      <meta content=http://schemas.microsoft.com/intellisense/ie5
         name="vs_targetSchema">
   </HEAD>
   <body MS_POSITIONING="GridLayout">
      <form id="Form1" method="post" runat="server">
         <asp:Label id="Label1" style="Z-INDEX: 101; LEFT: 46px; POSITION:
            absolute; TOP: 139px" runat="server" Width="68px">First Name
         </asp:Label>
         <INPUT id="Button2" style="Z-INDEX: 106; LEFT: 148px; POSITION:
            absolute; TOP: 218px" type="button" value="Button" name="Button2">
         <asp:Button id="Button1" style="Z-INDEX: 105; LEFT: 58px; POSITION:
            absolute; TOP: 219px" runat="server" Text="Submit">
         </asp:Button>
         <asp:TextBox id="TextBox2" style="Z-INDEX: 104; LEFT: 148px;
            POSITION: absolute; TOP: 167px" runat="server">
         </asp:TextBox>
         <asp:Label id="Label2" style="Z-INDEX: 103; LEFT: 46px; POSITION:
            absolute; TOP: 171px" runat="server" Width="68px">Last Name
         </asp:Label>
         <asp:TextBox id="TextBox1" style="Z-INDEX: 102; LEFT: 147px;
            POSITION: absolute; TOP: 137px" runat="server"></asp:TextBox>
      </form>
   </body>
</HTML>
```

ASP.NET server controls

Figure 12-30 HTML view of Web page

Note that ASP.NET does its own formatting in terms of line length, etc., in HTML view. The code in Figure 12-30 has been formatted to provide a clearer explanation of its purpose. If you run this program, the code reverts to its original formatting.

The first line of code is a page directive and is enclosed within the <% %> tag pair. The language attribute has been set to Visual Basic .NET, vb, and the code-behind file has the extension .aspx.vb. The code on this page inherits the Web form, in this case WebForm3. An HTML comment follows the page directive, and then after the HTML head and title tags comes the generated documentation. These four lines use meta-tags and represent the self-documenting meta-data relating to this particular Web page.

Locate the first Web server control in the form. It is a label and uses the Web server <asp:Label ... > ..</asp:Label> tag pair. The Web server controls look very much like HTML tag pairs, but each of the Web server controls has its own unique tags. The start tag for these Web server controls has attributes, as does the HTML start tags. An ASP.NET control uses the ID attribute instead of the NAME attribute used in HTML. These attributes are in the Properties window of the Design view and can be more easily set there than typing them in HTML view. The attribute, runat="server", exists for all the ASP.NET controls. Controls with this attribute will be processed on the server. Locate the lone HTML control, the INPUT button control—there is no attribute indicating that it should be processed at the server. However, if you right-click this button in Design view and select Run As Server Control, the runat="server" attribute will be added and it will become an HTML server control.

The question then becomes how to know when to use HTML, HTML server controls, or ASP.NET server controls. For most applications, you use HTML controls and ASP.NET server controls, though you occasionally use all three types of controls. Server controls require a round trip from client to server for processing. Labels containing text that needs no processing are good candidates for using HTML controls. However, choosing between HTML server controls and ASP.NET Web server controls is not as clear. Because ASP.NET Web controls include a richer set of controls, such as data grids, calendars, and validation, it makes sense to concentrate on using them.

You have a choice of how to work in this ASP.NET environment. You can work in Design view by adding controls to the form, or you can enter code in HTML view. Most Web developers use Design view to work with controls, and then switch to HTML view to fine-tune the code.

Creating an ASP.NET Survey Application

Now that you are familiar with building a Web form in ASP.NET, you can create an application for Bradshaw Marina that consists of a form to collect information about boat customers. The information will be collected using a form in one Web page. Then the information is posted on another Web page. In a realistic data collection application, the collected data would be saved in a database. However, your example application will display only the collected information for now. (Database and objective persistence topics are covered later in the book.) Other than saving the data, the example presents the essential concepts of using ASP.NET for Web development. Figure 12-31 shows the first ASP.NET Web page.

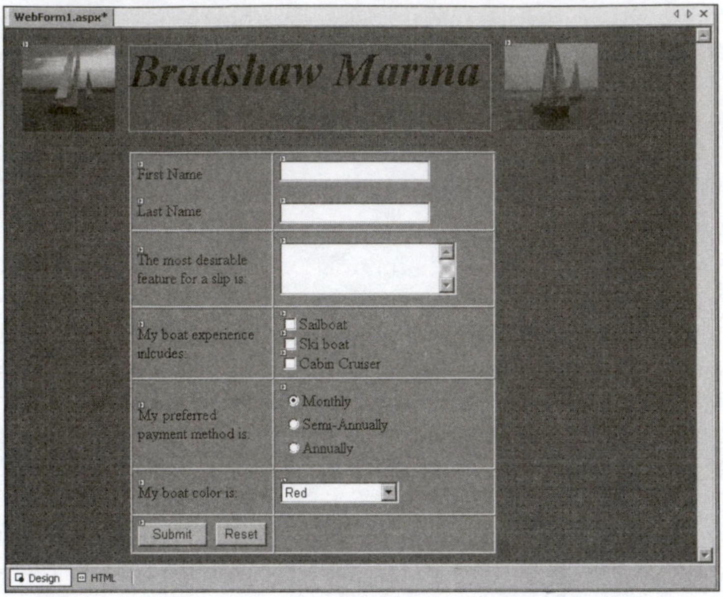

Figure 12-31 Survey Web page using ASP.NET

The top of the Web page includes two ASP.NET image Web server controls that hold pictures of sailboats. An HTML label displays the Bradshaw Marina text located between the two images. For more precise control of the layout, the data collection controls are placed in a table. The table was created by inserting a table, setting the rows and columns, and then sizing it on the Web form. All remaining controls in the table are Web server controls except the Reset button, which is an HTML control. The table's CELLPADDING attribute is set to 5. When placing these controls in the table, you may have to use HTML view and remove some tags, such as paragraph tags, <p></p>, for proper spacing.

The first five rows of the left column are all Web server label controls. The sixth row of the left column contains two buttons. The Submit button is a Web server control, and the Reset button is an HTML control. Code for the Submit button will be discussed after the data collection controls.

The right column of the table consists of the most common data collection controls. All the controls have had their ID properties properly set. The first three of these controls are ASP text box controls with the TextMode property of the third text box set to Multiline. These three text boxes collect the user's first name, last name, and the features he or she wants in a slip. Following the text boxes are three check boxes that record the user's boat experience. Users can check any number of these check boxes. A group of radio buttons collects the preferred method of payment for a slip. Using the radio button list prevents users from selecting more than one radio button. A DropDownList control provides a list of potential boat colors. You add choices to the drop-down list the same way you do in a Windows drop-down list control (also called a combo box control). At design time, this means entering the values into the item property collection.

When you run this example in Hands-on Exercise 3, use HTML view to examine the code for the HTML and ASP.NET controls.

Using the Code-Behind Window

This section discusses writing the code for the survey Web page, creating the second Web page, and passing the collected data from the first Web page to the second Web page for processing. You double-click a control to open the code window for entering code for the most common, default event for that control. Double-clicking the Submit button opens the code-behind window with the insertion point placed so that you can enter code for the click event handler. Figure 12-32 illustrates the code for this code-behind file.

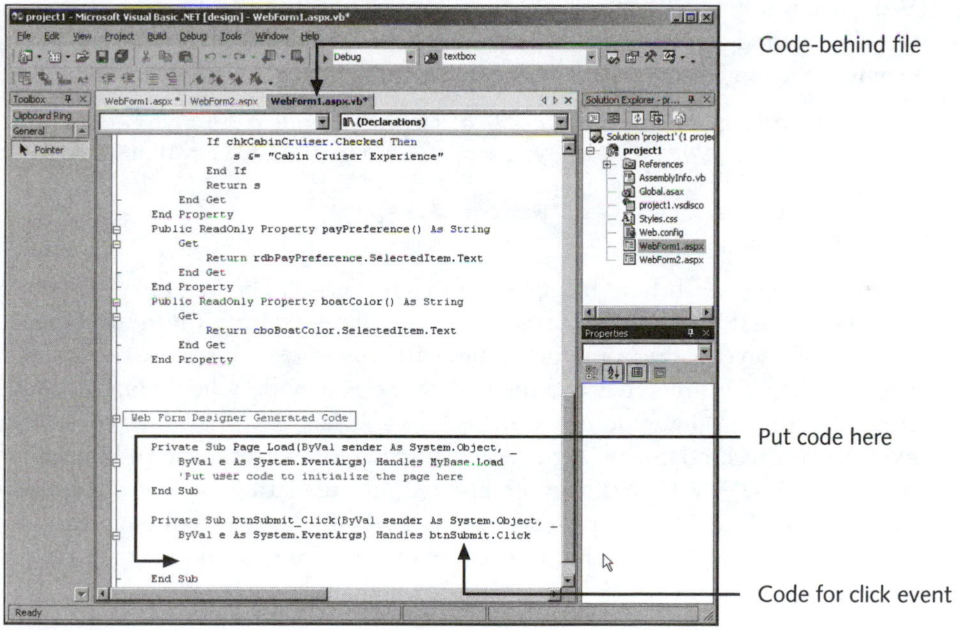

Figure 12-32 The code-behind window

This application requires navigation from one Web page to another and passing the collected data from the source Web page to the target Web page. Recall that the Request/Response model provides one way to do this. The values from the form controls are available in either the form collection or the QueryString collection of the Request object, depending on which method you specified—POST or GET. A different approach is taken here that uses custom page properties and then redirects program control from the source Web page to another Web page so you can still read values from the source Web page. This works because Web form pages are classes, meaning that you can create properties for them as you can for any other class.

The first step to accomplishing this task requires creating read-only properties for each value that will be passed from the source Web page to the target Web page. Each property would return a value you want to pass to the target Web page. For example, the code for the read-only property designed to return text of the First Name text box is as follows:

```
Public ReadOnly Property firstName() As String
   Get
      Return txtFirstName.Text
   End Get
End Property
```

The property firstName allows the target Web page to access the value of the text box on the source page. After all the properties have been coded, the only remaining task for the source Web page is to transfer control to the target Web page. To accomplish this, you use the server transfer method as shown in the code for the click event of the Submit button. For this example, the target Web page is Webform2.aspx.

```
Private Sub btnSubmit_Click(ByVal sender As System.Object, _
        ByVal e As System.EventArgs) Handles btnSubmit.Click

   Server.Transfer("Webform2.aspx")
End Sub
```

The complete code-behind file appears in Figure 12-33. The first lines of code are the generated Protected WithEvents instances for each of the controls on the Web page. Following these entries are the read-only properties—the first three are text boxes. References to the controls and their properties and methods work as they do when you use Windows forms. Instead of passing the value of each check box, If statements are used to determine which experience check boxes the user checked. A string is built to include all the boat experience options, and
 HTML tags are inserted into the string to control for line breaks and horizontal spacing. The completed string is returned. The SelectedItem.Text property of the radio button list holds the value selected by the user for the color of their boat; this value is returned in the property.

```
Public Class WebForm1
    Inherits System.Web.UI.Page
    Protected WithEvents Image1 As System.Web.UI.WebControls.Image
    Protected WithEvents txtFirstName As System.Web.UI.WebControls.TextBox
    Protected WithEvents txtLastName As System.Web.UI.WebControls.TextBox
    Protected WithEvents Label3 As System.Web.UI.WebControls.Label
    Protected WithEvents txtDesire As System.Web.UI.WebControls.TextBox
    Protected WithEvents Label4 As System.Web.UI.WebControls.Label
    Protected WithEvents chkSailboat As System.Web.UI.WebControls.CheckBox
    Protected WithEvents chkSkiBoat As System.Web.UI.WebControls.CheckBox
```

```
    Protected WithEvents Label5 As System.Web.UI.WebControls.Label
    Protected WithEvents Label6 As System.Web.UI.WebControls.Label
    Protected WithEvents btnSubmit As System.Web.UI.WebControls.Button
    Protected WithEvents chkCabinCruiser As System.Web.UI.WebControls.CheckBox
    Protected WithEvents rdbPayPreference As
      System.Web.UI.WebControls.Radio ButtonList
    Protected WithEvents cboBoatColor As System.Web.UI.WebControls.DropDownList
    Protected WithEvents Label2 As System.Web.UI.WebControls.Label
    Protected WithEvents Label1 As System.Web.UI.WebControls.Label
    Protected WithEvents Image2 As System.Web.UI.WebControls.Image

    Public ReadOnly Property firstName() As String
        Get
            Return txtFirstName.Text
        End Get
    End Property
    Public ReadOnly Property lastName() As String
        Get
            Return txtLastName.Text
        End Get
    End Property
    Public ReadOnly Property slipDesire() As String
        Get
            Return txtDesire.Text
        End Get
    End Property
    Public ReadOnly Property boatExperience() As String
        Get
            Dim s As String
            If chkSailboat.Checked Then
                s &= "Sailboat Experience" & vbCrLf
            End If
            If chkSkiBoat.Checked Then
                s &= "Ski Boat Experience" & vbCrLf
            End If
            If chkCabinCruiser.Checked Then
                s &= "Cabin Cruiser Experience"
            End If
            Return s
        End Get
    End Property
    Public ReadOnly Property payPreference() As String
        Get
            Return rdbPayPreference.SelectedItem.Text
        End Get
    End Property
    Public ReadOnly Property boatColor() As String
        Get
            Return cboBoatColor.SelectedItem.Text
        End Get
    End Property

#Region " Web Form Designer Generated Code "

    <System.Diagnostics.DebuggerStepThrough()> Private Sub InitializeComponent()

    End Sub
```

```
    Private Sub Page_Init(ByVal sender As System.Object, ByVal e As
    System.EventArgs) Handles MyBase.Init
        'CODEGEN: This method call is required by the Web Form Designer
        'Do not modify it using the code editor.
        InitializeComponent()
    End Sub

#End Region

    Private Sub Page_Load(ByVal sender As System.Object, _
        ByVal e As System.EventArgs) Handles MyBase.Load
        'Put user code to initialize the page here
    End Sub

    Private Sub btnSubmit_Click(ByVal sender As System.Object, _
        ByVal e As System.EventArgs) Handles btnSubmit.Click

        Server.Transfer("Webform2.aspx")
    End Sub
End Class
```

Figure 12-33 Code for the code-behind file

After the code for all the properties comes the code generated when the Web page is created. As in Windows, you can collapse this region. However, the InitializeComponent() method of the Page_Init event is required, and any code you want to include in this event should follow this statement. For this example, no code was needed for the Page_Init or the Page_Load event.

As stated earlier, the only line of code needed for the Submit button is the Transfer method to pass control to the target Web page. No code is required for the Reset button since it is an HTML control and clears the values of all the controls when clicked. Assume that the target Web page existed. Clicking the Submit button after completing the survey form transfers control to this target Web page. Figure 12-34 displays an example Web page containing results of the survey.

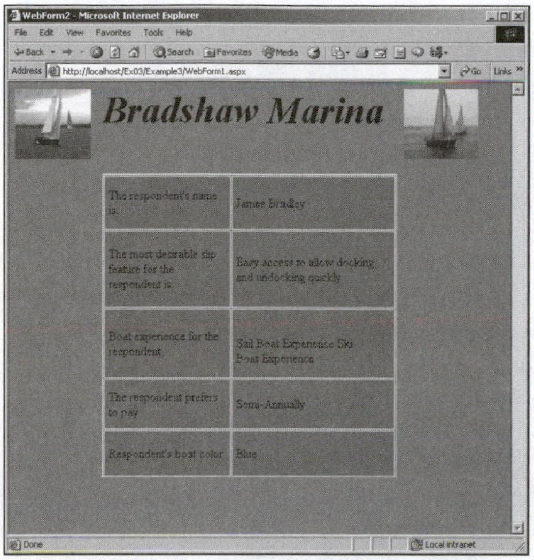

Figure 12-34 Web page with respondent results

Creating the Results Web Page

To complete the Web survey application, a new Web form needs to be added to the project. This can be accomplished by right-clicking the project in the Solutions Explorer window, pointing to Add, and then selecting Add Web Form on the shortcut menu. (You can also click Project on the menu bar, point to Add, and then click Add Web Form.) The default name will be WebForm2.aspx. After adding the form, you need to create a design for displaying the survey results.

As shown in Figure 12-35, a table controls the layout on the Web page. The top part of the Web page is identical to the survey Web page. The left column of the table identifies the output and consists of HTML text only, not Web server controls. However, the right column displays the respondent's results and contains Web server controls as indicated by their symbol near the upper-left corner of the control. The HTML table has also been made a Web server control, noticeable again by its server control symbol.

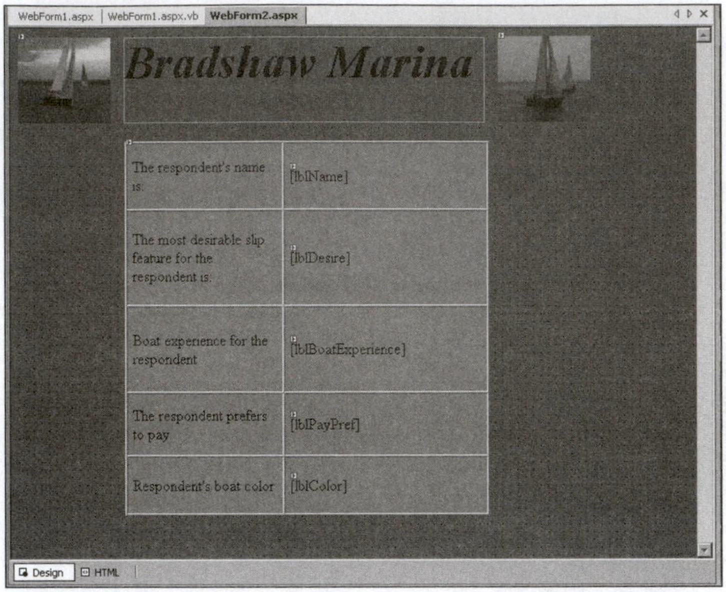

Figure 12-35 Results Web page design

As with all Web pages, instances of visual controls are generated with the Protected WithEvents attribute. For brevity, only the first of these instances is shown in describing the code for this Web page. First, you declare an instance variable that is the same type as the class of the source page, such as WebForm1. The remaining code is for the Page_Load event.

```
Public Class WebForm2
    Inherits System.Web.UI.Page

   'Protected WithEvents Image2 As System.Web.UI.WebControls.Image
   ' Remaining generated code for each control has been deleted
    Dim surveyPage As WebForm1
----Web Form Designer Generated Code goes here---

Private Sub Page_Load(ByVal sender As System.Object, _
   ByVal e As System.EventArgs) Handles MyBase.Load
        'Put user code to initialize the page here

        If Not IsPostBack Then
            surveyPage = CType(context.Handler, WebForm1)

            lblName.Text = surveyPage.firstName & " " & _
                surveyPage.lastName
            lblDesire.Text = surveyPage.slipDesire
            lblBoatExperience.Text = surveyPage.boatExperience
```

```
                lblPayPref.Text = surveyPage.payPreference
                lblColor.Text = surveyPage.boatColor
                Table1.BgColor = surveyPage.boatColor

            End If
        End Sub
```

Recall that postback allows you to determine whether a request for a Web page is the first request for the page. An If statement determines whether this is a first or subsequent Web page request. All the code for this page load event executes only on the first Web page request, as you would not want to run the code for each request unless a change has occurred.

The first line of code within the If statement gets the source page from the context handler object and assigns it to the variable you created, surveyPage in this example. The context handler object must be cast to the type of the source Web page.

The next block of code assigns the property values created in the source Web page to the Text property of ASP.NET label controls on the Web page. For example, the label used to display the respondent's pay preference has an ID of lblPayPref, as shown in Figure 12-36. Its Text property is set to the property value from the source Web page.

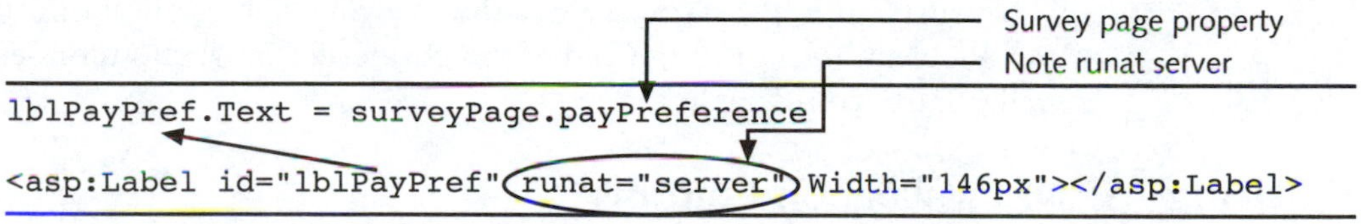

Figure 12-36 Assigning property values to the Text property

The last line of code sets the table background color to the boat color selected in the drop-down list box on the survey page. This shows how easy it is to write code for an HTML server control. Recall from the design in Figure 12-35 that this HTML table was a server control. In HTML view, the table tag contains the runat="server" attribute, which allows the table's properties (attributes) to be easily referenced in the code.

Because ASP.NET includes Web server controls and lets you use the same form designer for HTML, HTML server controls, and Web server controls, it provides both a powerful and flexible development environment. Yet, perhaps the greatest gain is the clean division of code from content and presentation, and making it event driven. This is implemented using code-behind to code for events.

Hands-on Exercise 3

Changes such as adding new Web forms, modifying the Web form names, or moving the application may mean that you must set a start-up Web form. The IDE will prompt you when you need to do this. To set a start-up Web form, right-click the Web form you want as the start-up form, and then click Set as Start Page on the shortcut menu.

Images are used in all the ASP.NET applications in this chapter. The Image control has an ImageURL property that allows you to browse to the location of the image file. If you are using a drive other than C or the image location has moved, then you must set this ImageURL property to the appropriate image location so that they appear on the Web page. If necessary, change the ImageURL property for the following exercise.

1. Use Windows Explorer to navigate to the **Chap12\Exercises\Ex03\Example3** folder in your work folder, and then double-click the **project1.sln** file. The ASP.NET survey application with its two Web forms opens.
2. Run the project. Complete the Web survey and then click the **Submit** button. The results should be similar to Figure 12-34.

   You may need to set the Example3 folder as an IIS application and designate WebForm1.aspx as the start page. See the "Moving Web Applications and Solving Web Problems" section at the end of this chapter for instructions on setting an application as an IIS application.

Using ASP.NET Validation Controls

Data validation represents an important part of any application that accepts user input. Table 12-4 shows the ASP.NET validation controls and describes how to use them.

Table 12-4 Validation Controls

Validation Control	Description
RequiredFieldValidator	Prevents a field from having an entry
CompareValidation	Compares data to a specified value or the value of another control
RangeFieldValidator	Checks to see whether a value is between a lower and upper boundary
RegularExpressionValidator	Checks that the entry matches a pattern defined by a regular expression
CustomValidator	Creates custom code for validation
ValidationSummary	Displays a summary of all the validation controls on the page

These controls can be placed on the Web page just as any other controls and their properties can be in the Properties window. To use the RequiredFieldValidator control, for example, place the control on the form. In the Properties window, set its ControlToValidate property to the control you want to check for a value, and then set its ErrorMessage property to the text you want to display if the validation is triggered. A common use is to ensure that text boxes are not left blank. However, it can also be used with controls such as radio button lists if you require the user to make a selection.

The CompareValidation control compares the input value of a control such as a text box to the value of another control or a constant value. For example, if the user must enter or select two dates, and the second date has to be larger than the first date, use the CompareValidation control. Specify the input control to validate with the ControlToValidate property and set either the ControlToCompare or ValueToCompare depending on whether you want to compare input to the value of a control or a constant value. You can use pattern matching characters for constants to validate input patterns such as e-mail addresses and phone numbers. Be sure to set the ErrorMessage property.

The RangeFieldValidator control provides MinimumValue and MaximumValue properties to check that a control's input is within a range. It also has a Type property to specify the data type of the data to be compared. As in the previous validation controls, you need to specify the ControlToValidate and ErrorMessage properties.

Custom validation controls let you provide your own data validation logic. To create the validation logic, provide a handler for the ServerValidate event. Set the control's ClientValidationFunction to the name of the function that contains the code logic. Depending on the particular validation, you may or may not need to set the ControlToValidate property.

To summarize all the errors trapped by the validation controls, use the ValidationSummary control. Place the ValidationSummary control on the Web form where you want to display the summary.

You can use multiple validation controls for the same Web control. For example, you can check to see that the user enters data and that the values fall within a range. Use the RequiredFieldValidator and the CompareValidator and assign the ControlToValidate properties of both validation controls to the control you are checking.

Adding Validation Controls to the Survey Web Page

This example illustrates the basics of using validation controls. Figure 12-37 shows four RequiredFieldValidator controls and a ValidationSummary control on the Web form. The ValidationSummary control is held in the Web Panel control and placed in the upper-right part of the Web form.

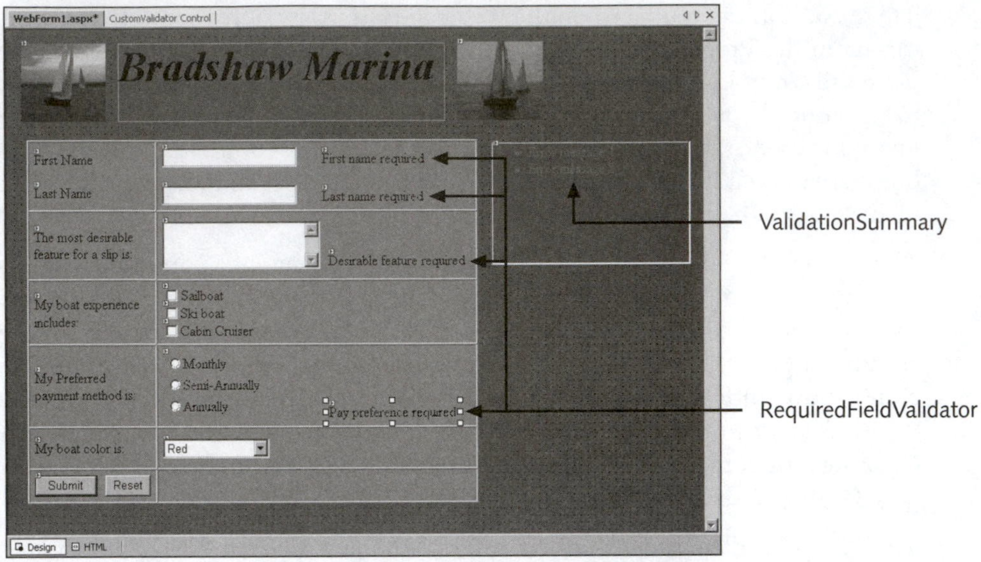

Figure 12-37 Validation controls on the survey Web form

The RequiredFieldValidator controls are placed to the right of the three text box controls for inputting the first name, last name, and desired slip features. The other RequiredFieldValidator control, also placed to the right of the control, checks to ensure that a radio button from the radio button list has been selected.

A Panel control is used to position the summary control. When placing a Panel control on the Web page, it retains the text "Panel," though it is not associated with a Text property. Therefore, you need to click the panel control on the Web form, delete the word Panel, and set the BorderStyle property to None.

All the RequiredFieldValidator controls have their ControlToValidate properties set to the appropriate control, such as txtFirstName. After adding all the validation controls, you click the Start button to open the survey Web form. If you click the Submit button without entering any data, the Web page shown in Figure 12-38 appears.

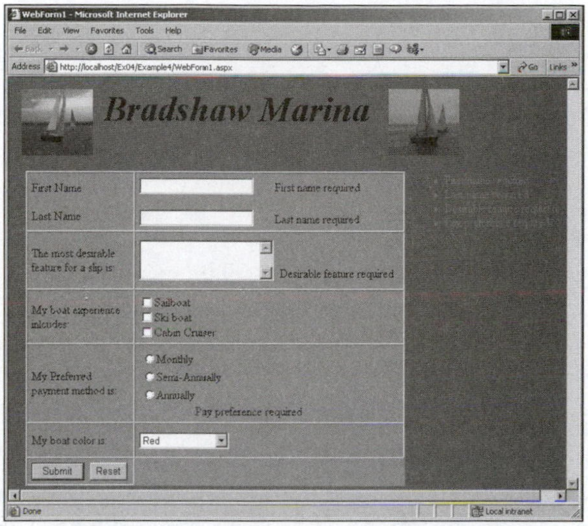

Figure 12-38 Validation error messages for the survey Web form

Recall that the previous example had only one line of code for the Submit button's click event—`Server.Transfer("Webform2.aspx")`. When validation is added to the Web page, you can check to see whether the page has errors by using the isValid method. Control is not transferred to the target Web page unless the page is valid—that is, no validation errors occur. The following code provides an example of using the isValid method:


```
Private Sub btnSubmit_Click(ByVal sender As System.Object, _
   ByVal e As System.EventArgs) Handles btnSubmit.Click

   If Page.IsValid Then
      Server.Transfer("Webform2.aspx")
   End If

End Sub
```

Hands-on Exercise 4

1. Locate **Ex04** in the Chap12\Examples folder in the book's student data files. Copy the **Ex04** folder to the **Chap12\Exercises** folder on your system.
2. Create a virtual directory for the **Ex04** folder. (See Step 1 of Hands-on Exercise 1 for instructions on creating a virtual directory.)

3. In the Chap12\Exercises\Ex04\Example4 folder, double-click the **Project01.sln** file. The survey application opens containing two Web forms. Set **Webform1.aspx** as the startup page, and change **Example4** to an IIS application. Click the **Start** button, complete the survey form, and then click the **Submit** button. The results should be similar to Figure 12-34.

Using ASP.NET with a PD Class

The last example in the chapter uses the PD Customer class. The example uses a data entry Web form to create a number of Customer instances. The values for each Customer instance are passed to another Web form for display and for adding the Customer instance to an `ArrayList`. A Return button allows you to return to the first Web form to enter values for another Customer instance.

The second Web form has two additonal capabilities. It contains a button that displays all the Customer instances in a text box when you click the button. The form also lets you enter a phone number to locate a customer in the `ArrayList` of customers. This is accomplished by providing a text box to enter the phone number of the customer to be found and a Find button to be clicked after the phone number has been entered. Figure 12-39 shows the data entry Web form, and Figure 12-40 shows the results Web form after several Customer instances have been entered.

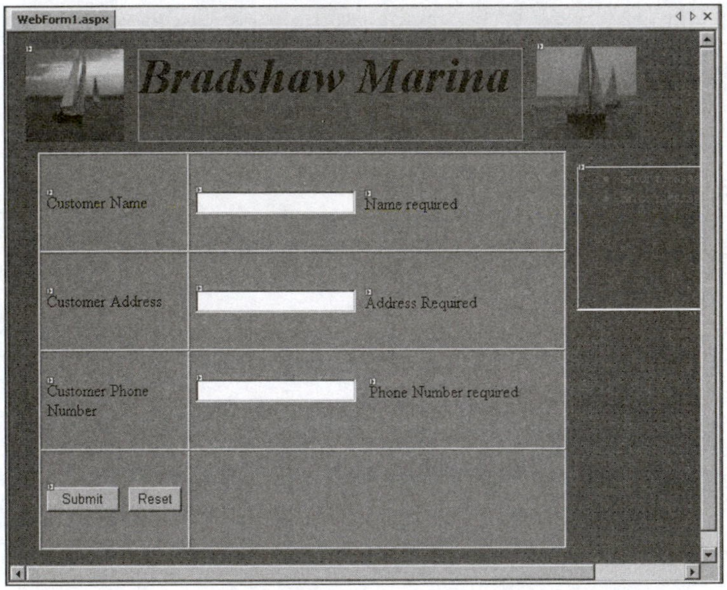

Figure 12-39 Customer data entry Web form

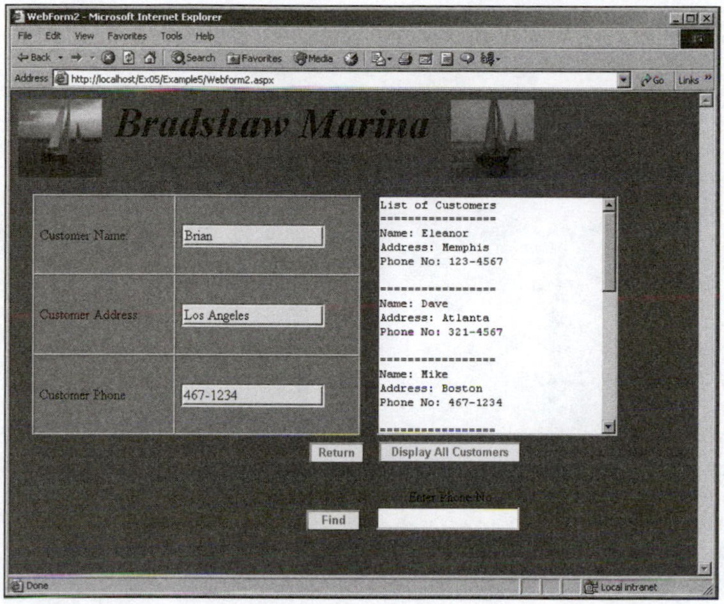

Figure 12-40 Results Web form

The data entry Web form contains the same features used in the previous two examples. The only new feature on the results Web form is the multiline text box, which means it can contain more than one line of text. A text box can be made multiline by changing its TextMode property in the Properties window to Multiline. This results Web form appears when the Submit button on the data entry Web form is clicked, and it displays the input data on labels in the table. The Display All Customers button had been clicked before capturing the Web form shown in Figure 12-40.

To locate a particular customer, enter his or her phone number in the text box and then click the Find button. If the customer is found, his or her attributes are displayed in the multiline text box; otherwise, a not found message appears in the multiline text box indicating that the customer could not be found. Figure 12-41 shows the Web form for successfully finding a customer.

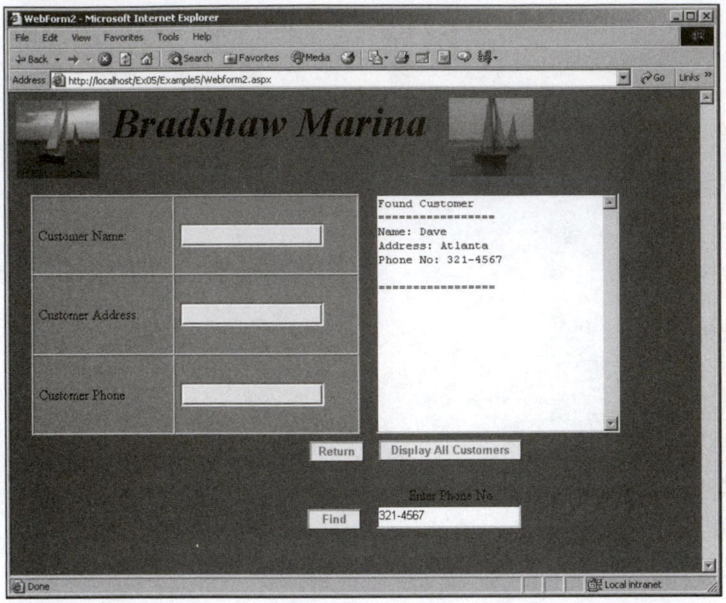

Figure 12-41 Web form when a customer is found

The data entry Web form code includes **`Public`** ReadOnly properties for the text box values to be sent to the results Web form. Its only other code is to tranfer control to the results Web form.

The class-level declarations for the results Web form are shown below. The first declaration defines a reference to the data entry Web form. Then an **`ArrayList`** to hold the Customer instances is declared, followed by declaring two Customer reference variables. The second Customer reference variable is used with the For-Each loop that iterates through the **`ArrayList`** of Customer instances. Three variables to hold Customer attribute values are also declared.

```
Dim surveyPage As WebForm1

Shared customers As New ArrayList()

Dim aCustomer As Customer
Dim cust As Customer

Dim name, address, phone As String
```

The code for the Page_Load event sets the handler to allow getting the values from the data entry Web form and then assigns the values from the text boxes to labels. Next, a Customer instance is created and added to an `ArrayList`, as shown in the following code.

```
Private Sub Page_Load(ByVal sender As System.Object, _
     ByVal e As System.EventArgs) Handles MyBase.Load
     'Put user code to initialize the page here

     If Not IsPostBack Then
          surveyPage = CType(context.Handler, WebForm1)

          lblName.Text = surveyPage.Name
          lblAddress.Text = surveyPage.Address
          lblPhone.Text = surveyPage.PhoneNo

          aCustomer = New Customer(lblName.Text, _
              lblAddress.Text, lblPhone.Text)

          customers.Add(aCustomer)

     End If
 End Sub
```

The code for the Return button uses the server's Transfer method to return to the data entry Web form. The code for the click event of the Display All Customers button is shown below. The code concatenates information to the Text property of the multiline text box. The For-Each code loops through the collection of Customer instances stored in an `ArrayList` and uses the Get accessor methods to get the attribute values. These values are added to the Text property of the multiline text box and appear as in Figure 12-40.

12

```
Private Sub btnDisplay_Click(ByVal sender As System.Object, _
     ByVal e As System.EventArgs) Handles btnDisplay.Click

     txtDisplay.Text = "List of Customers" + vbCrLf
     txtDisplay.Text += "=================" + vbCrLf
     For Each cust In customers
          aCustomer = cust
          ' Could use TellAboutSelf method but couldn't format
          name = aCustomer.GetName
          address = aCustomer.GetAddress
          phone = aCustomer.GetPhoneNo

          txtDisplay.Text += "Name: " & name & vbCrLf
          txtDisplay.Text += "Address: " & address & vbCrLf
          txtDisplay.Text += "Phone No: " & phone & vbCrLf
          txtDisplay.Text += vbCrLf & "=================" & vbCrLf
     Next
 End Sub
```

The code for the click event of the Find button is shown in the following code. The code loops through the Customer instance collection, checking each instance's phone number for a match with the phone number entered in the text box. If the phone number is found, the Customer instance attribute values are displayed in the multiline text box, as shown in Figure 12-41. If no match is found, a message that the customer was not found is displayed in the multiline text box.

```
Private Sub btnFind_Click(ByVal sender As System.Object, _
  ByVal e As System.EventArgs) Handles btnFind.Click

  ' Clear names from labels
  lblName.Text = ""
  lblAddress.Text = ""
  lblPhone.Text = ""

  ' Put values into the text box
  txtDisplay.Text = "Found Customer" + vbCrLf
  txtDisplay.Text += "=================" + vbCrLf

  Dim foundsw As Boolean = False
  txtDisplay.Text = vbNullString

  ' Loop over customers in the ArrayList
  For Each cust In customers
      aCustomer = cust
      phone = cust.GetPhoneNo
      If phone = txtPhone.Text Then
          ' Found customer to display in the textbox
          txtDisplay.Text = "Found Customer" + vbCrLf
          txtDisplay.Text += "=================" + vbCrLf

          name = aCustomer.GetName
          address = aCustomer.GetAddress
          phone = aCustomer.GetPhoneNo

          txtDisplay.Text += "Name: " & name & vbCrLf
          txtDisplay.Text += "Address: " & address & vbCrLf
          txtDisplay.Text += "Phone No: " & phone & vbCrLf
          txtDisplay.Text += vbCrLf & "=================" & vbCrLf
          foundsw = True
      End If
      ' If customer not found display message
      If foundsw = False Then
          txtDisplay.Text = "Customer Not Found"
      End If
  Next
End Sub
```

Hands-on Exercise 5

1. Locate **Ex05** in the Chap12\Examples folder in the book's student data files. Copy the **Ex05** folder to the Chap12\Exercises folder on your system.
2. Create a virtual directory for the **Ex05** folder on your system. (See Step 1 of Hands-on Exercise 1 for instructions on creating a virtual directory.)
3. Move to the **Chap12\Exercises\Ex05\Example5** directory and double-click the **Project01.sln** file. This should open the application that contains two Web forms and uses the Customer PD class. Make **Webform1.aspx** the startup page. Change **Example5** to an IIS application. Click the **Start** button, enter some customer instances, display them all, and then use the **Find** button to find one of the customers.

Moving Web Applications and Solving Web Problems

Moving a Web application usually results in making adjustments before the application will run. This is true whether you are moving static Web pages or an ASP.NET application. This section explains how to solve most problems that involve running a Web application after it has been moved. This section also assumes that the location of the new Web application is a virtual directory or a subfolder of a virtual directory.

ASP.NET stores URL path information for an application in XML format in a file with a .vbproj.webinfo file extension. (This file is located in the folder with the other application files.) If you double-click the file, it opens as shown in Figure 12-42. Use the directional arrow keys to move and change the path to the current location. For example, part of the URL path in the file shown in Figure 12-42 includes Ex05. Assume no other parts of the path change and you moved the Web application to Ex04 from Ex05. You would need to change the Ex05 to Ex04 and then save the file.

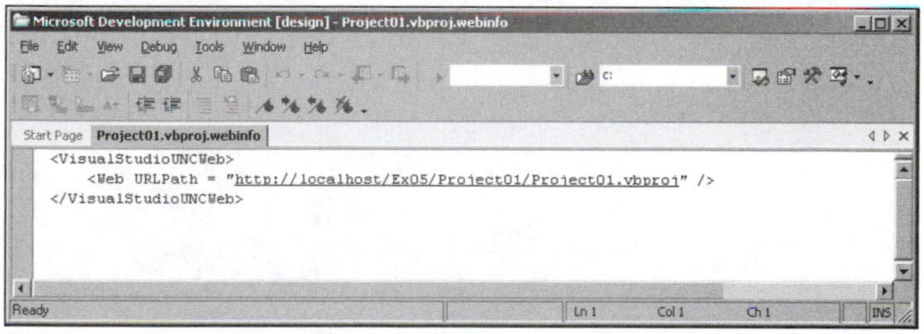

Figure 12-42 ASP.NET URL path file

After making the changes to the URL path, you need to double-click the .vbproj file to open the application. Then click the Start button. When you are prompted to save the .sln file, you should save the file, replacing the old one, and then click the Start button again. Most likely, you will have to set a Start Up Page, and then when you try to run the application again, you may see an error message indicating that the application has not been set as an IIS application. Figure 12-43 shows an example of this error.

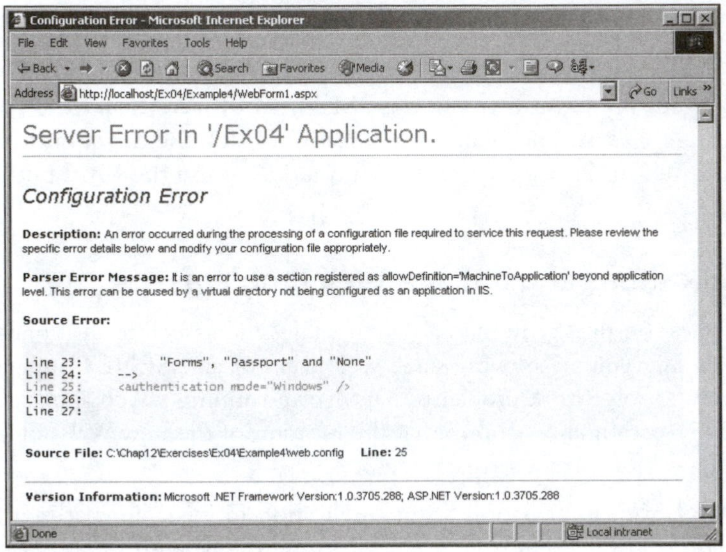

Figure 12-43 Error indicating that an application is not set as an IIS application

Setting the application as an IIS application requires using the Internet Information Services. (You open this window by opening the Control Panel, double-clicking Administrative Tools, and then double-clicking Internet Services Manager for Windows 2000 or Internet Information Services for Windows XP.) In the left pane of the Internet Information Services window, expand your local computer, Web Sites, and Default Web Site icons. See Figure 12-44.

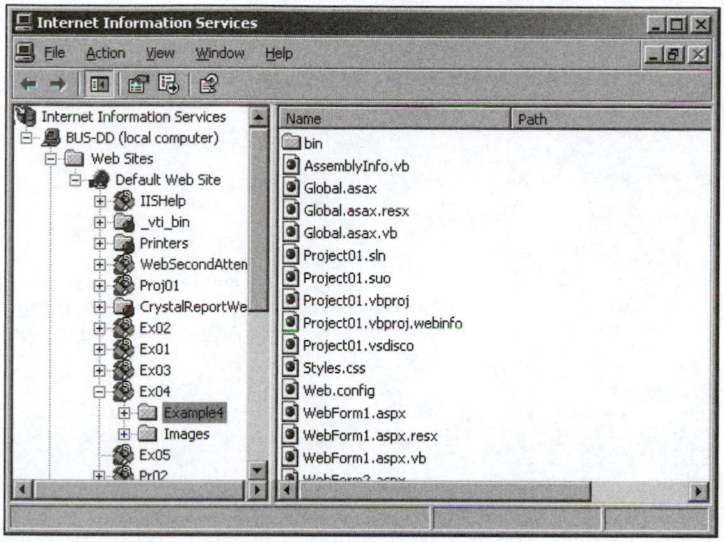

Figure 12-44 Internet Information Services window

To set the Example4 folder as an IIS application:

1. Locate the **Ex04** virtual directory. (See the "To create a virtual directory" section earlier in this chapter for detailed steps on creating a virtual directory.) Expand **Ex04** to show its subfolders.
2. Right-click the **Example4** folder and then click **Properties** on the shortcut menu to open the folder's Properties dialog box.
3. Click the **Directory** tab, if necessary. See Figure 12-45.

12

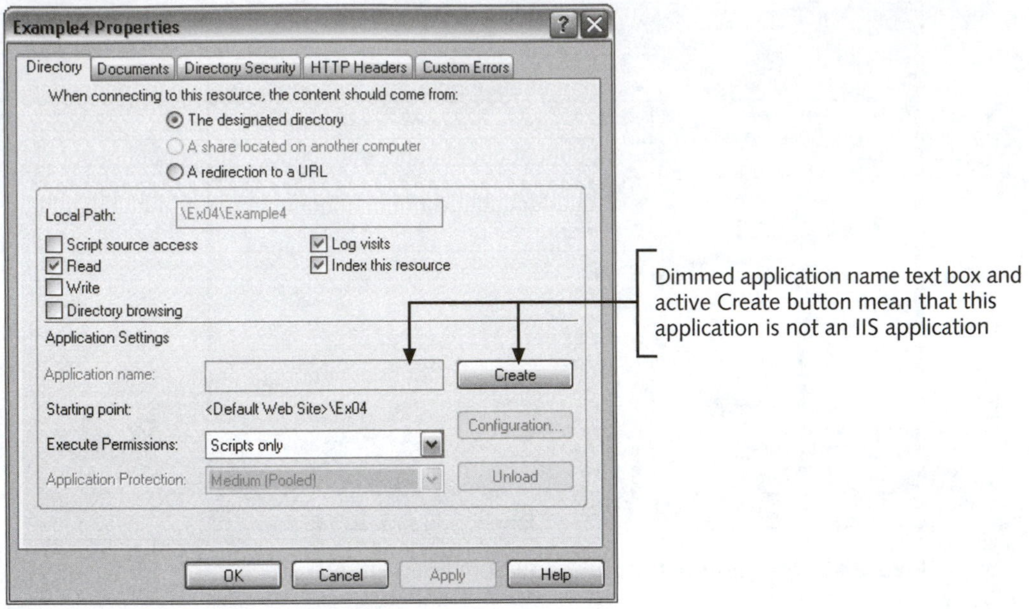

Figure 12-45 Example4 Properties dialog box

4. In the Application Settings area, find the Application name text box and the button to its right. If the application has not been set to be an IIS application, the text box is empty and the button is a Create button. If there is an entry in the text box, the application in the text box has already been set as an IIS application and the button to its right is a Remove button. If the text box is empty, click the **Create** button. Your folder has now been made an IIS application, as shown in Figure 12-46.

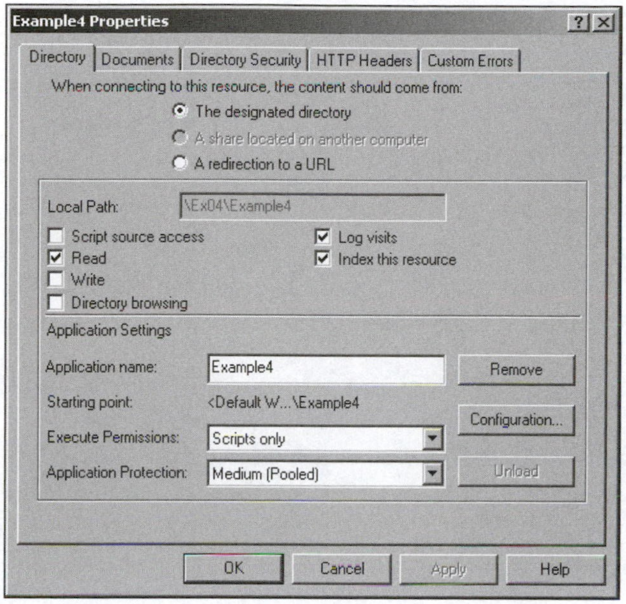

Figure 12-46 Application set as an IIS application

5. Click the **OK** button and close all the open windows related to this task. Your ASP.NET application should now run properly.

When you need to move any Web application, you might need to set the new location as an IIS application, as you have learned when moving ASP.NET applications.

Chapter Summary

- The Web uses the HTTP protocol and the HTML markup language. Web applications can be static or dynamic. HTML tags are used by browsers to render Web pages for display on display devices.
- Web applications use a client-server computing architecture, and Web processing is based on the Request/Response model.
- HTML forms have controls that allow for user input on a Web page to be sent to the server for processing. HTML documents can have client-side scripts to check data before being sent to the server for processing.

- Classic ASP provides a relatively easy technology for creating dynamic Web applications by allowing you to mix programming script with HTML code. The most common scripting languages for Classic ASP are VBScript and JavaScript. ASP code runs on the server and uses the Request/Response model.
- ASP.NET provides new features and concepts for Web development. Although compatible with ASP, ASP.NET provides new and powerful Web server controls. Additionally, ASP.NET provides an event-driven Web development approach that is similar to VB .NET for Windows applications.
- ASP.NET clearly separates code from a Web page's presentation and content. This is accomplished via code-behind.
- ASP.NET has easy-to-use validation controls to help ensure that valid data is entered into Web pages. It also provides a visual drag-and-drop approach to Web development.
- ASP.NET provides a variety of ways to link to Web forms and transfer data from one Web form to another.

Key Terms

ASP.NET server control
Classic ASP
client
client-server
code-behind
dynamic Web pages
GET
HTML server control
hypertext link
Hypertext Transmission Protocol (HTTP)
Hypertext Markup Language (HTML)
Internet
Internet Information Services (IIS)
physical directory
POST
postback
server
static Web pages
Uniform Resource Locator (URL)
Web browser
World Wide Web
validation controls
virtual directory

Review Questions

1. HTML is a ________________.
   a. protocol
   b. Web site
   c. markup language
   d. Web server
2. HTML tags ________________.
   a. are used for the presentation of content
   b. have tag pairs
   c. have single-sided tags
   d. all of the above
3. A Web browser usually ________________.
   a. properly handles white space
   b. properly handles the vertical line spacing of white space
   c. properly handles the horizontal spacing contained in white space
   d. ignores white space
4. The HTML tag pair within which the user could input data would be ________________.
   a. <HEAD></HEAD>
   b. <BODY></BODY>
   c. <FORM></FORM>
   d. <TITLE></TITLE>
5. Two common values for the METHOD attribute of a form are ________________.
   a. SEND, GET
   b. GET, POST
   c. SEND, POST
   d. SUBMIT, RESET
6. The ACTION attribute of the form start tag is used to ________________.
   a. specify the file to invoke when the Web page is submitted
   b. specify to the server the appropriate way to return the requested results
   c. tell the user the status of the Web page on which he or she is working
   d. tell the user what action he or she should take with the data

7. The purpose of an HTML form control's SUBMIT button is ________________.
   a. to refresh the browser for the user
   b. to submit the Web page to the Web server
   c. to retrieve data back from the Web server
   d. to have the browser run an animation on the user's computer
8. When using the Request/Response Web procession model, what two request collections can be used to hold data that the Web server can extract? ________________.
   a. Form, myCollection
   b. QueryString, myCollection
   c. POST, GET
   d. Form, QueryString
9. Classic ASP is a Microsoft technology for dynamic Web processing that ________________.
   a. does not allow script to be intermixed with HTML
   b. can use only VBScript
   c. is processed on the client-side
   d. allows intermixing of script and HTML for server-side processing
10. ASP.NET Web development has the following features: ________________.
    a. uses a drag-and-drop GUI development environment
    b. provides for a clean separation of code and HTML
    c. contains validation controls
    d. all of the above
11. ASP.NET can use the following for Web development: ________________.
    a. HTML
    b. HTML server controls
    c. ASP.NET server controls
    d. all of the above
12. The file extension for an ASP.NET code-behind is: ________________.
    a. .aspx
    b. .aspx.vb
    c. .config
    d. .css

13. The file extension for an ASP.NET Web page that holds the presentation and content is: ________________.

a. .aspx

b. .aspx.vb

c. .config

d. .css

14. One way to pass values from a source ASP.NET Web page to a target ASP.NET Web page is ________________.

a. to use the response object's write method

b. to create properties on the target page and send the page these property values

c. to create read read-only properties on the source page and have the target page access these properties

d. to use the HTML RESET Reset button

15. ASP.NET has validation controls to allow for which of the following types of data checking?

a. a user not entering data

b. a user checking the status of the server

c. a range of values entered by the user input

d. a and c

Discussion Questions

1. What are the advantages of using ASP.NET compared to Classic ASP?
2. How would you design an ASP.NET application that could collect information for the Customer class and save it in an `ArrayList` with each entry into the `ArrayList` serving as an instance of the Customer class?
3. Is it important to be conversant with HTML when you have an event-driven GUI development environment such as ASP.NET? Explain.
4. Describe scenarios where you would use both HTML and ASP.NET Web server controls.
5. Compare and contrast Web application development versus Windows applications. What type of Windows applications would best serve Bradshaw Marina? What type of Web-based applications would best serve Bradshaw Marina?

Projects

1. Using a text editor, design a Web page for Bradshaw Marina that lets users navigate the structure shown in Figure 12-47. This assignment provides a chance for creativity, so include a number of images, such as buttons for navigation. Create four files—homepage.htm, boats.htm, ListSlips.htm, and PresMessage.htm—and save them in the Chap12\Projects\Proj01 folder in the work folder on your system. (Create the folders, if necessary.)

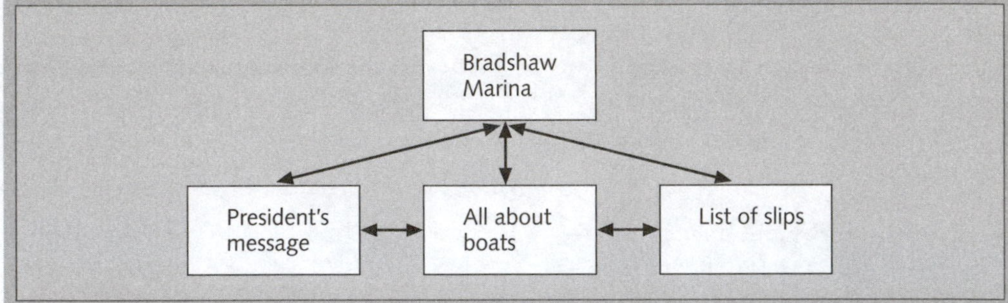

Figure 12-47 Structure of the Bradshaw Marina Web site

2. Complete the following steps:
   - In Windows Explorer or My Computer, copy the Bradshaw_Marina_form.htm file from your Chap12\Exercises\Ex02\Example2 folder to the Chap12\Projects\Proj01 folder and rename it test.htm.
   - Copy the Bradshaw_Marina_response.asp file from your Chap12\Exercises\Ex02\Example2 folder to the Chap12\Projects\Project01 folder and rename it queryString.asp.
   - In the test.htm file, change the form start tag METHOD attribute to GET.
   - In the queryString.asp file, change all the non-comment *request.form* pieces of code to *request.querystring*.
   - Test the page in your browser by typing http://localhost/*workpath*/test.htm in the Address text box (where *workpath* is the path to the project files on your system) and then pressing Enter. Enter appropriate data and click the Submit button. Look at the URL of the Web page and notice that the name-value pairs are added to the end of the URL you entered. There should be a ? (question mark) followed by name-value pairs in a string. All the name-value pairs are concatenated into one string using the concatenation character (&).

3. The Boat class covered in Chapter 9 had four attributes. You will need to add the Boat class to your application and delete from it any references to other PD classes. Using ASP.NET, create a Web application called Project03 that provides the following features: You will need to add the boat class to your application and delete from it any references to other PD classes.
   - Contains the user interface necessary to collect the four attributes for each instance of a boat and includes reset capability
   - Validates that the user has input each of the values for a boat instance
   - Passes the values from the source Web page to a target page for processing
   - Displays the attributes for the boat instance on the target
   - Test your application.
4. Add the following capabilities to Project 3:
   - The application should add the Boat instances to an `ArrayList`.
   - The application should have a button that can display all the Boat instances.
   - The application should be able to locate a particular Boat instance via the StateRegistrationNo attribute.
5. In Chapter 9, you worked with the PD classes of Docks and Slips. You will need to add these to your application and delete from them references to any other PD classes. Create several instances of Dock and corresponding slips. Then have a button that displays each dock, its details, and the slips that belong to it.

PART 4

Developing Data Access Classes

CHAPTER

13

Introduction to Data Access Classes and Persistence

In this chapter you will:

- Examine VB .NET input and output (I/O)
- Make objects persistent
- Design a data access class
- Communicate with a data access class
- Use a relational database with VB .NET

In Part 2 you learned how to design and write problem domain (PD) classes. In Part 3 you learned how to design and write GUI classes that interact with PD classes. In Part 4 you learn to design and write data access (DA) classes that provide data and object storage and retrieval services for both Windows and Web applications. Part 5 shows you how to connect all three tiers of an OO system: GUI, PD, and DA.

Most organizations store their structured data in relational databases, but you should also be familiar with working with files. File input and output (I/O) represents a large part of any programming language because realistic applications require storing and retrieving data, including objects. This is also true for VB .NET; because complete coverage of its I/O constructs could consume a complete text, this chapter only covers basic I/O concepts and presents examples of VB .NET's most useful I/O aspects, particularly those for object persistence.

After completing this chapter, you will be able to use VB .NET's I/O capability to store and retrieve data, including object attributes, in sequential files as well as store and retrieve objects using object serialization. You will be able to design a DA class that can store and retrieve objects using two approaches—storing the object's attributes and storing the objects themselves. You will also be able to design a relational database and use the database to store and retrieve object attributes of the DA class.

EXAMINING VB .NET INPUT AND OUTPUT

Although VB .NET supports traditional, record-oriented I/O via random access capabilities of the File class, the new I/O features of VB .NET implement its input and output around the concept of a **stream**. This simply means that input and output are collections of bytes that transfer data to and from files. The first few examples in this chapter use the **sequential file** capabilities of the two stream classes, **`StreamWriter`** and **`StreamReader`**, which are derived from the **`TextWriter`** and **`TextReader`** classes, respectively. The `StreamWriter` and `StreamReader` classes are located in the **System.IO** namespace; sequential file-handling applications need to import this namespace using the **`Imports`** statement.

The terms "file," "record," and "field" are ways to refer to file-based systems such as a file containing boat attributes.

- A file represents the collection of all the data. A file consists of records.
- A record can be viewed as a row in the file and represents a single entity, such as a boat record for a particular item.
- A record consists of fields. A field, such as stRegNo or length, is an attribute that will be included for each record in the file.

A sequential file consisting of boat attributes is shown in Table 13-1.

Table 13-1 Boat Attribute Sequential File

State Reg No	Boat Length	Manufacturer	Model Year	Cust Phone No
MO12345	26	Ranger	1976	765-4321
MO223344	24	Tracker	1996	467-1234
MO34561	35	Tartan	1998	123-4567
...	...	...	...	...

In this table, the rows represent records and the columns represent fields.

When using streams for sequential files, the concept of records as shown in the boat attributes file is not directly supported. Rather, only streams of bytes are read or written to files. Each I/O access writes or reads one item (stream) to the file.

The first example in this chapter illustrates sequential file processing using `StreamWriter` and `StreamReader`. The example covers basic VB .NET stream concepts and incorporates them with appropriate GUI controls such as toolbars and dialog boxes.

Sequential File Processing

The example in this section uses text boxes on a form that allows users to enter values for each record to be saved to a sequential file. The five text boxes are named txtStRegNo, txtLength, txtManufacturer, txtYear, and txtCustPhoneNo. By clicking a button named Save To File, the user saves the text box values to a sequential file. By clicking the List Records button, the user extracts the data from the file and displays the results in a multiline text box with a vertical scroll bar. A third button, Exit, closes the program. The GUI for the completed and working example is shown in Figure 13-1.

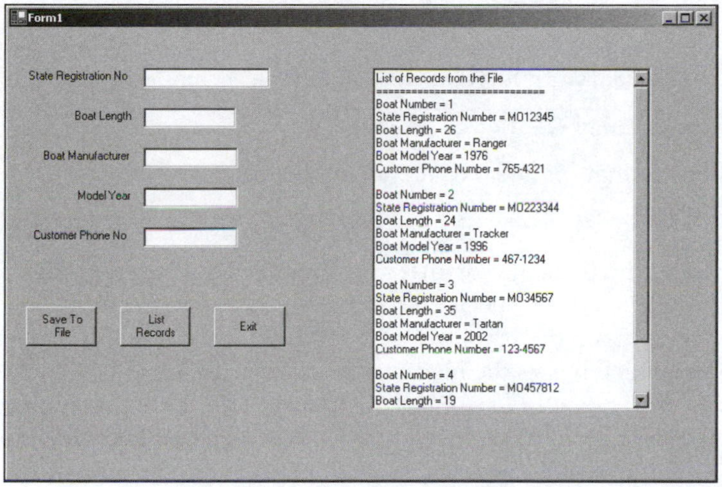

Figure 13-1 Form design for the StreamWriter/StreamReader example

13

General Format for StreamWriter and StreamReader

Only a few methods of the `StreamWriter` class (`Write`, `WriteLine`, `Close`) and `StreamReader` class (`Read`, `ReadLine`, `ReadToEnd`, `Peek`, `Close`) will be discussed in the boat attribute file example. The general formats for instantiating a StreamWriter object and a StreamReader object are shown in Figure 13-2. Examples of instantiations are also included.

StreamWriter

<u>Format</u>

```
Dim objectName as New StreamWriter("Filename")
Dim objectName as New StreamWriter("Filename", BooleanAppend)
```

<u>Examples</u>

```
Dim swInventory as New StreamWriter("a:\boats.txt")
Dim swInventory as New StreamWriter("a:\boats.txt", True)
```

StreamReader

<u>Format</u>

```
Dim objectName as New StreamReader("Filename")
```

<u>Examples</u>

```
Dim srInventory as New StreamReader("a:\boats.txt")
```

Figure 13-2 General format for StreamWriter and StreamReader

The default location of the filename parameter in Figure 13-2 is the Bin directory of the current project. However, you can specify the complete path for the file if you want. For example, you may want to set the complete path reference for the file in this example to C:\Chap13\boats.txt which means the file is on the C drive in the Chap13 folder and the name of the file is boats.txt. The BooleanAppend option in the second version of the constructor allows data to be appended to the end of the existing file if the value is set to True. Declaring the new StreamWriter opens the file if it exists. If the file does not exist, then a new file is created. The file must be open to be used; it does not throw an exception, regardless of whether the file exists or not. Thus, you can declare a StreamWriter in the declaration section of your program or in a procedure.

The code for the sequential file example is shown in Figure 13-3.

```
'SeqFile1--Boat Attributes

'Chapter 13 -- Example 1
Imports System.IO
Public Class Form1
    Inherits System.Windows.Forms.Form
Private Sub btnSave_Click(ByVal sender As System.Object, _
   ByVal e As System.EventArgs) Handles btnSave.Click

   ' Declare StreamWriter
   Dim swBoats As New StreamWriter("a:\Boats.txt", True)

   ' Save a boat record in the file
   swBoats.WriteLine(txtStRegNo.Text)
   swBoats.WriteLine(txtLength.Text)
   swBoats.WriteLine(txtManufacturer.Text)
   swBoats.WriteLine(txtYear.Text)
   swBoats.WriteLine(txtCustPhoneNo.Text)
```

```
    ' Clear text boxes and set focus to state registration no text box
    txtStRegNo.Clear()
    txtLength.Clear()
    txtManufacturer.Clear()
    txtYear.Clear()
    txtCustPhoneNo.Clear()
    txtStRegNo.Focus()

    ' Close the StreamWriter
    swBoats.Close()
End Sub
Private Sub btnListRecords_Click(ByVal sender As System.Object, _
    ByVal e As System.EventArgs) Handles btnListRecords.Click

    Dim boatRecord As New System.Text.StringBuilder()
    Dim stRegNo, manuf, custPhoneNo As String
    Dim length As Single
    Dim year, recNbr As Int32
    Dim myFile As String = "a:\Boats.txt"
    Try
        recNbr = 0
        boatRecord.Append("List of Records from the File" & vbCrLf)
        boatRecord.Append("=============================" & vbCrLf)
        ' Check to see if file exists
        If File.Exists(myFile) And myFile.Length > 0 Then
            ' Declare the StreamReader and set record counter to 0
            Dim srBoats As StreamReader = New StreamReader(myFile)

            ' Loop over records until end of the file is reached
            Do Until srBoats.Peek = -1
                ' Read a record
                stRegNo = srBoats.ReadLine
                length = srBoats.ReadLine
                manuf = srBoats.ReadLine
                year = srBoats.ReadLine
                custPhoneNo = srBoats.ReadLine
                recNbr += 1

                ' Build line for display in multiline text box
                boatRecord.Append("Boat Number = " & _
                    recNbr & vbCrLf)
                boatRecord.Append("State Registration Number = " & _
                    stRegNo & vbCrLf)
                boatRecord.Append("Boat Length = " & _
                    length & vbCrLf)
                boatRecord.Append("Boat Manufacturer = " & _
                    manuf & vbCrLf)
                boatRecord.Append("Boat Model Year = " & _
                    year & vbCrLf)
                boatRecord.Append("Customer Phone Number = " & _
                    custPhoneNo & vbCrLf & vbCrLf)

            Loop
            srBoats.Close()
            boatRecord.Append("End of File")
            txtDisplay.Text = boatRecord.ToString
```

13

```
            txtStRegNo.Focus()
            Else
               MessageBox.Show("File does not exist, enter records")
         End If
      Catch ee As Exception
         MessageBox.Show(ee.ToString)
      End Try
   End Sub

   Private Sub btnExit_Click(ByVal sender As System.Object, _
      ByVal e As System.EventArgs) Handles btnExit.Click

      Me.Close()
   End Sub
```

Figure 13-3 Code for sequential file example

Notice the required **`Imports`** statement at the top of the program for using VB .NET's file I/O.

```
Imports System.IO
Public Class Form1
        Inherits System.Windows.Forms.Form
```

The straightforward code for the Save button begins by declaring a StreamWriter object that references a file, a:\boats.txt, and setting the Append property to True. You can view a file with a .txt file extension in a text editor such as Notepad, which is helpful and recommended. The next five statements use the StreamWriter, swBoats, to write the values from the text boxes to the file. Note that the `WriteLine` method is used instead of the `Write` method. Recall that the values are written in the file one value per line, and the `WriteLine` method places a line terminator at the end of the line it writes.

After writing the record, the code simply clears all the text boxes so they will be available for entering the next record, places the cursor in the State Registration No text box, and closes the StreamWriter. After saving a few records in the file, you should use Notepad to view the records. The `Close` method finishes writing all data from the stream's buffer to the file and releases the system resources. Some records in the file are shown in Figure 13-4.

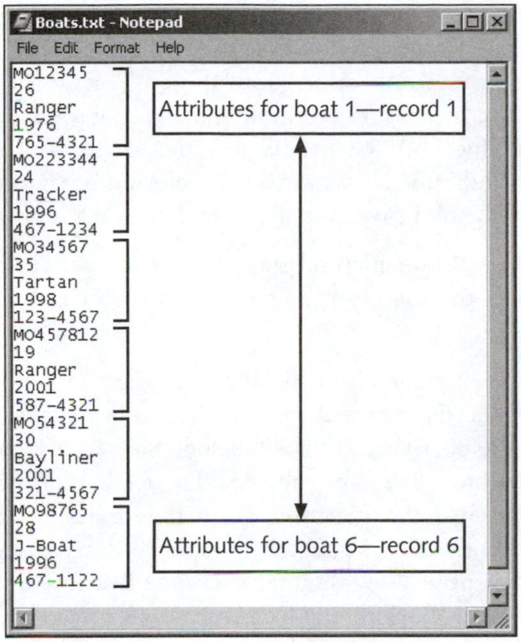

Figure 13-4 Boat attributes file

The btnListRecords code loops over all lines in the file (reading values from the file one value per line), saving the values in corresponding variables plus concatenating the values to a string that will be assigned to the Text property of a multiline text box for displaying all the records in the file. Five of the variables—stRegNo, length, manuf, year, and custPhoneNo—hold the values returned from the file.


```
Dim boatRecord As New System.Text.StringBuilder()
Dim stRegNo, manuf, custPhoneNo As String
Dim length As Single
Dim year, recNbr As Integer
Dim myFile As String = "a:\Boats.txt"
```

Using the StringBuilder class, the variable boatRecord builds a string that will ultimately contain all the boat attributes from the file. Then the string is assigned to the Text property of the multiline text box, txtDisplay, which also has a vertical scroll bar.

Header values are first assigned to the boatRecord string before entering the code that loops over all of the lines in the file, and ending values are assigned after file processing is complete. The string variable, myFile, is assigned the path and filename of the boat file created with the execution of the code in the Save button. The variable myFile is used in declaring the StreamReader, srBoats, and then used later to see if the file exists. Note the format of declaring srBoats.

Errors can occur when trying to access a file that does not exist. You can check to see if a file exists using the `Exists` method of the File object. If the file exists, then the program should loop through the file, extracting and processing values until the end of the file has been reached. Recognize that there must be a means for determining the end of the file. When the end of the file is reached, the .NET file I/O system sets an indicator to -1. The StreamReader's `Peek` method retrieves this indicator, allowing you to determine when the end of the file has been reached. The `Close` method closes the file after all the data is processed.

Within the loop, each of the five `ReadLine` method statements reads one line from the file—one value in this case—and saves the values in the corresponding variables: stRegNo, length, manuf, year, and custPhoneNo.

After reading five lines from the file, the next line of code adds 1 to the record counter, recNbr, used to display the record number. Each record value is then concatenated, using the StringBuilder's `Append` method, to the boatRecord string; included are field identifiers and vbCrLf, an intrinsic constant equivalent to a carriage return and line feed. After the loop, terminated when the end of the file is reached, the StreamReader is closed, and the string "End of File" is concatenated to the boatRecord string. Finally, the boatRecord string is assigned to the Text property of the text box, txtDisplay. When the user clicks the List Records button, a result similar to Figure 13-1 should appear. Clicking the Exit button will close the program.

Hands-on Exercise 1

1. Locate **Ex01** in the Chap13\Examples folder in the student data files. Create a folder named **Chap13\Exercises** in the work folder on your system, and then copy the **Ex01** folder to this folder. Double-click the **SeqFile1.sln** file in the Example1 folder to open the project with VB .NET. Insert a formatted disk into drive A. Run the program, enter a few records using the Save to File button, and then click the **List Records** button. Add a few more records and list them again. Note that the records have been appended because the Append parameter was set to True when declaring the StreamWriter, swBoats.

Adding Toolbars and Dialog Controls

Dialog boxes and toolbars are widely used controls for building professional user interfaces. VB .NET provides a number of dialog controls to enrich the quality of the user interface for front-end applications. In the next project, you will extend the first program of this chapter to include a toolbar and some dialog controls. First, you will add the toolbar; Figure 13-5 presents the form of the application after the toolbar is added.

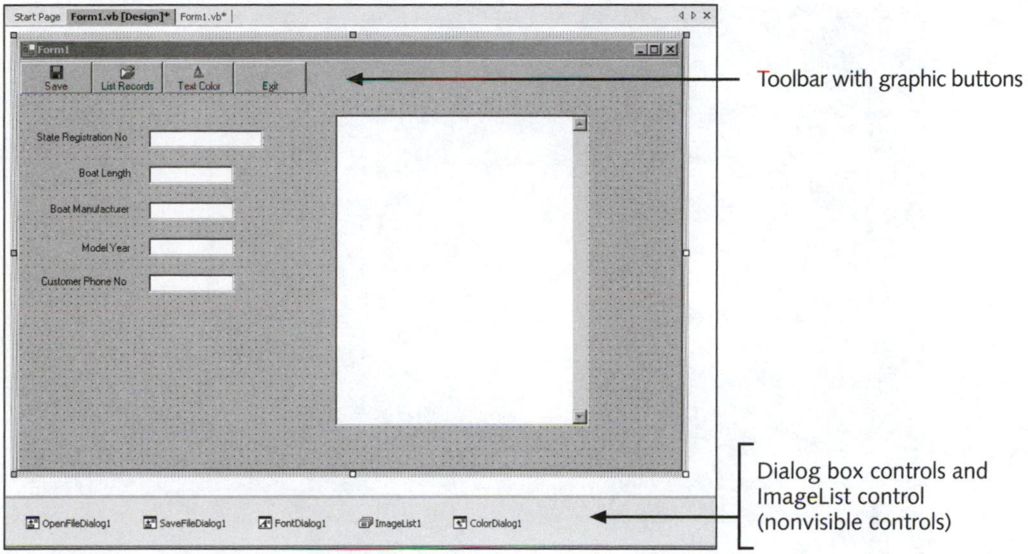

Figure 13-5 Adding a toolbar

This section illustrates how to add the toolbar and ImageList controls to the application. (The next section discusses the dialog controls.) The user interface has been changed from the previous example; in addition to the new toolbar, the three buttons on the previous form have been eliminated. Several of the controls—all the dialog buttons plus the ImageList—are displayed in a window below the form. Unlike previous versions of VB, controls that do not have a user interface are placed in a separate window below the form instead of on the form itself. These controls are not visible when the project is run.

13

Notice that when you add a toolbar control from the Toolbox to a form, it does not have any sizing handles; also, the control docks to the top of the form and spans the width of the form.

The ImageList and Toolbar Controls

Incorporating a toolbar with graphic buttons on a form first requires placing the graphic images into the ImageList control. When you double-click ImageList on the Toolbox, the control is added to the separate window below the form. Select the ImageList control and find the Images property in the Properties window, as shown in Figure 13-6.

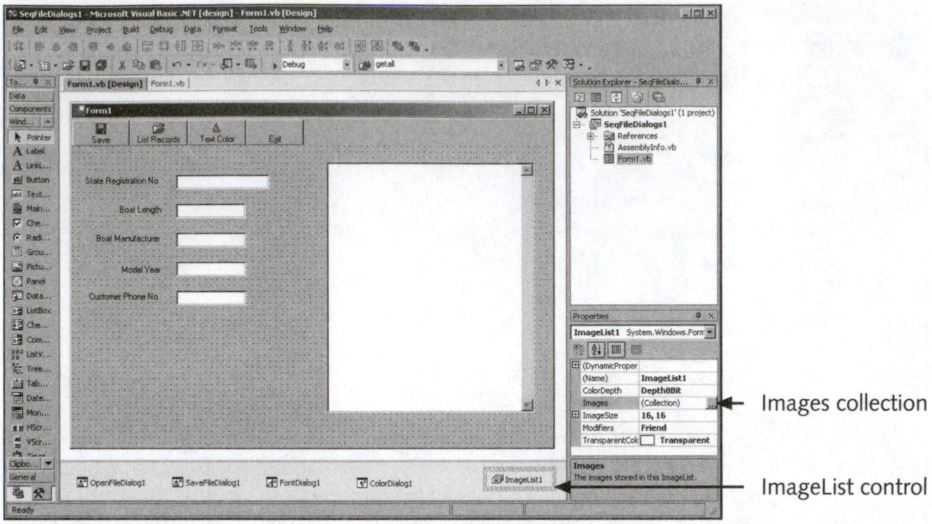

Figure 13-6 Images property collection for an ImageList control

The Images property is a collection of images with an ellipsis button that allows you to add more images. Clicking the ellipsis button opens the Image Collection Editor, as shown in Figure 13-7. Click the Add button to add an image to the collection. Notice the image's index value in the upper-left portion of the Members window. The order in which images are added to the collection is not important because the arrows between the two windows allow you to move images to any position you want. To move an image up or down in the list, select the image and then click the up or down arrow. You can delete images by selecting the image and clicking the Remove button.

Most of Microsoft's images are bitmaps with the .bmp file extension. Thus, you can search your computer or the Web to locate images you may want to use on the toolbar buttons. You can also use other image formats such as .tif, .gif, or .jpg for the toolbar buttons. Note that some images found on the Web may be copyrighted and you may need to obtain permission to use them.

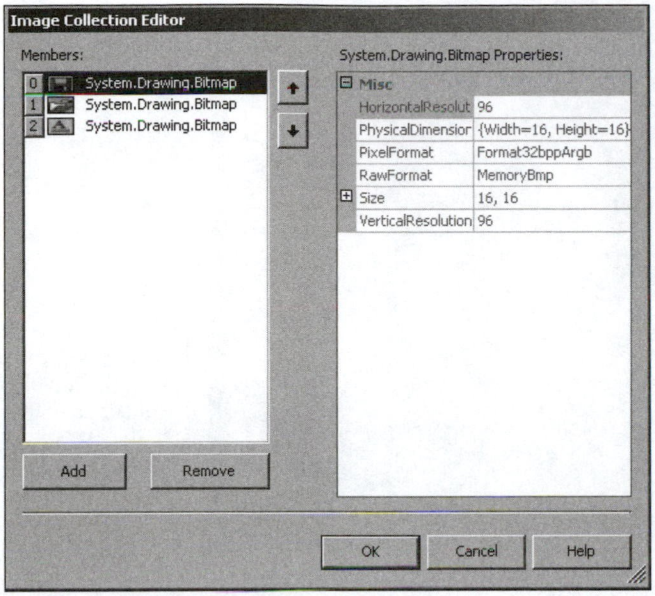

Figure 13-7 Image Collection Editor

The Toolbar Control

After adding the desired images to the ImageList control, you need to add the toolbar control to the form. Then you need to link the toolbar's ImageList property to the ImageList that holds the images you will add to the toolbar buttons. To do this, select the toolbar, locate its ImageList property, and then use the drop-down list box to select the desired ImageList for use on the toolbar buttons, as shown in Figure 13-8. In this case, it should be the ImageList's default name, ImageList1.

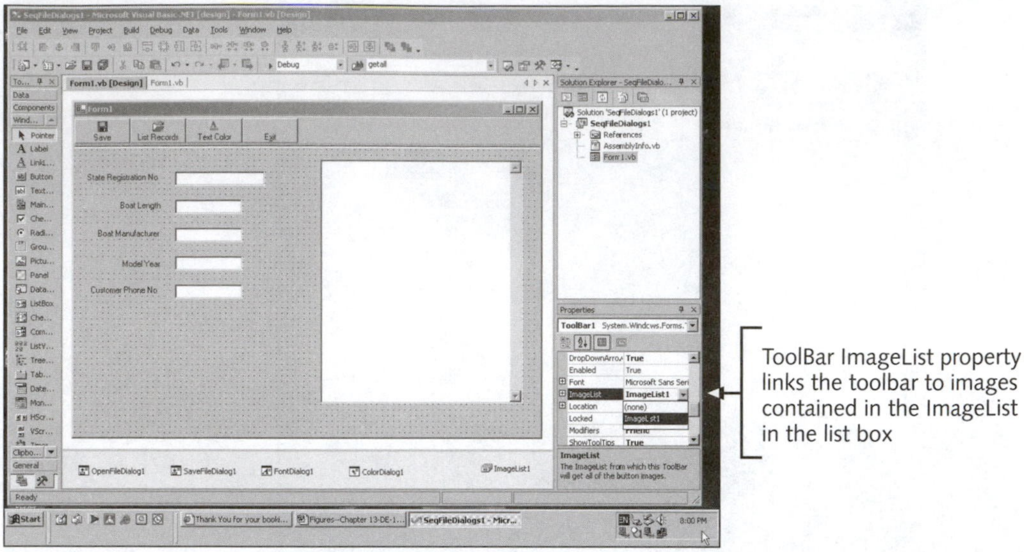

Figure 13-8 ToolBar ImageList property

The toolbar's Buttons property is similar to the ImageList's image collection. If you click its ellipsis button, the ToolBarButton Collection Editor opens. It allows you to add buttons with corresponding images available in the image collection of the ImageList, linked via the toolbar's ImageList property. As shown in the left window of Figure 13-9, four buttons have been added to the toolbar, with indexes of 0, 1, 2, and 3. As shown in the right window, the Tag, ImageIndex, Text, and ToolTipText properties are set to the desired values.

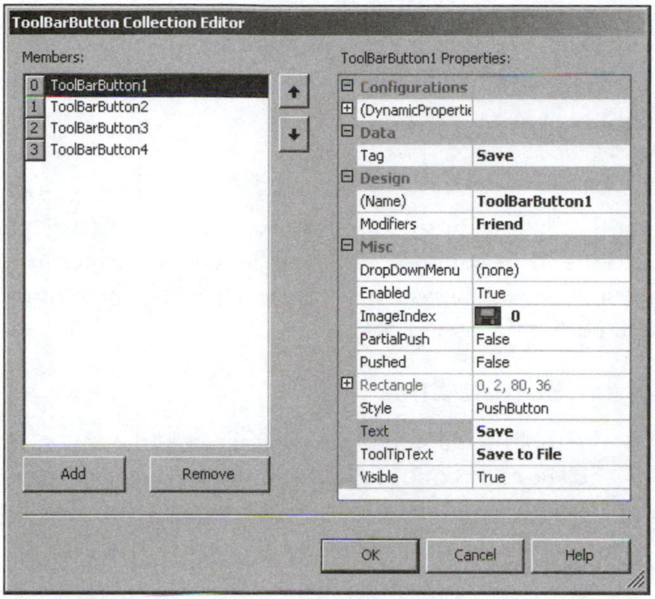

Figure 13-9 ToolBarButton Collection Editor

In Figure 13-9, ToolBarButton1 is selected. The Tag property is set to Save, the ImageIndex property is set to 0 (zero) via the list box—it is the first image in the Image collection—the Text property is set to Save, and the ToolTipText property is set to Save to File. The Tag, Text, and ImageIndex properties all provide a means to determine which button the user clicked. As you will see later, the Tag property in this example is used to determine the flow of program control.

13

Appropriate settings are set for the other three buttons. Clicking OK closes the window and displays a toolbar like the one shown earlier in Figure 13-5. However, note that the width of a button may vary depending on the required width of the text and image on the button. To make all the buttons the same width, expand the toolbar's ButtonSize property and set the width property; in this example, the width is set to 80.

Basically, the toolbar buttons for saving records, listing records, and exiting the program are just replacements for the form buttons used in the first example. Thus, only minor changes are needed to convert the first example to use the toolbar buttons instead of the regular form buttons. You just need to place the code contained in the original buttons into corresponding user-defined Sub procedures. These procedures can then be called based on which button the user clicks.

To accomplish these tasks, first add three skeleton Sub procedures without further code, as follows:

```
Private Sub SaveToFile()
    ' save code goes here
End Sub
```

```
Private Sub ListRecordsFromFile()
   ' code to extract and list records goes here
End Sub

Private Sub StopProgram()
   ' code to exit goes here
End Sub
```

Next, copy the code from the buttons in the previous example to the corresponding Sub procedures and then delete the form buttons. Note that the control names for the toolbar and ImageList have been left at the default values. Code now needs to be written to call the procedures based on which button the user clicks.

Determining a Toolbar Button Click

Double-click anywhere on the toolbar and notice the parameters in the `ByVal e` parameter of the Sub header. It holds `ToolBarButtonClickEventArgs`, which allows you to determine which button the user has clicked. One way to make this determination is shown in Figure 13-10.

```
Private Sub ToolBar1_ButtonClick(ByVal sender As System.Object, _
   ByVal e As System.Windows.Forms.ToolBarButtonClickEventArgs) _
   Handles ToolBar1.ButtonClick

   Select Case e.Button.Tag
      Case "Save" : SaveToFile()
      Case "Open" : ListRecordsFromFile()
      Case "Color" : SetDisplayText()
      Case "Exit" : StopProgram()
      Case Else
   End Select
End Sub
```

Figure 13-10 Code for toolbar

You have two other options for determining which button on the toolbar the user clicked. Recall that in the ToolBarButton Collection Editor, the Text and ImageIndex properties were set to specific values. Thus, replacing the `e.Button.Tag` in the previous code with `e.Button.Text` and using corresponding code statements such as `Case "Save" : SaveToFile()` will accomplish the same task. Likewise, replacing `e.Button.Tag` with `e.Button.ImageIndex` and using corresponding code statements such as `Case 0 : SaveToFile` will accomplish the same tasks as the code in Figure 13-10. With the exception of the Text Color button, the program now should operate correctly because the code has just been moved to procedures invoked by the toolbar buttons instead of the regular form buttons used in the first example.

Adding Dialogs to the Application

Dialog boxes provide richness and standardization for common user interface operations. For example, functions such as opening and saving files, changing colors, or changing fonts should have a common look and feel, regardless of the application. VB .NET includes dialog boxes for this purpose. This section explains how to add the Open File, Save File, Color, and Font dialog boxes to the application. Although the FontDialog control will be discussed, the final application in this section will not include a Font dialog box—you will add it in a later exercise.

The dialog controls are near the bottom of the Toolbox; double-clicking them adds dialog boxes to the separate window just below the form. Figure 13-5, shown earlier, illustrates the application with the Open File, Save File, Color, and Font dialog boxes added to the project.

The Save File Dialog Box

Recall that in the previous section, the code for saving data to a file was moved to a user-defined Sub procedure named SaveToFile. Next, this procedure needs to be modified to take advantage of the Save File dialog box. Figure 13-11 contains the altered code.

```
Private Sub SaveToFile()
   ' SaveFileDialog to get filename and save boat record
   With SaveFileDialog1
      .Filter = "TextFiles (*.txt)|*.txt|All Files (*.*)|*.*"
      .DefaultExt = "txt"
      .InitialDirectory = "c:\VBFiles"
      If .ShowDialog() = DialogResult.OK Then
         Dim swBoats As New StreamWriter(.FileName, True)

         swBoats.WriteLine(txtStRegNo.Text)
         swBoats.WriteLine(txtLength.Text)
         swBoats.WriteLine(txtManufacturer.Text)
         swBoats.WriteLine(txtYear.Text)
         swBoats.WriteLine(txtCustPhoneNo.Text)
         ' Close the StreamWriter
         swBoats.Close()
      End If
   End With
   ' Clear text boxes and set focus to state registration no TextBox
   txtStRegNo.Clear()
   txtLength.Clear()
   txtManufacturer.Clear()
   txtYear.Clear()
   txtCustPhoneNo.Clear()
   txtStRegNo.Focus()
End Sub
```

Figure 13-11 Code for the Save File dialog box

Note that the code uses the default name, SaveFileDialog1. Being a rather long name, the With...End clause makes the coding effort considerably easier. The With clause begins the code for the SaveToFile procedure and sets the Filter, DefaultExt, and InitialDirectory properties. The format for the Filter property requires the complete string to be enclosed in double quotes (") and the major pairs of entries to be separated by the vertical piping character, which is above the Backslash key on most keyboards. Each pair consists of a text segment that will be displayed in a list box and a file type search pattern. For example, "Text Files (*.txt)" is the displayed text segment and "*.txt" is the file type search pattern. The DefaultExt property has been set to the search pattern of .txt, so all files of this type will initially appear when the dialog box opens. Although the InitialDirectory property has been set in this example, it is not required; the user can change this property.

The `ShowDialog` method opens any dialog box; in this case it opens the SaveFile dialog box. Note that the SaveFile dialog opens as a Save As dialog box with "save as" functionality. Figure 13-12 illustrates the dialog box.

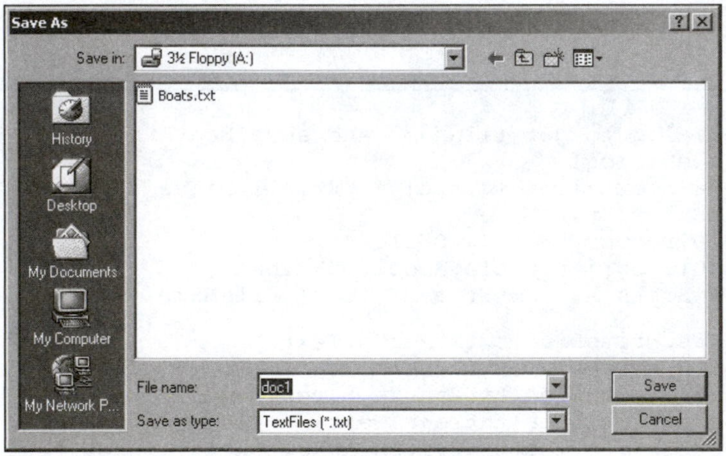

Figure 13-12 Save As dialog box

Note that the window is similar to most dialog boxes for saving files. At the top, the Save in list box allows the user to change drives and directories. The File name text box allows the user to enter a filename; if the user instead selects an existing file from the list of files, the selected name appears in the File name text box. The Save as type text box specifies the file format to which files are saved; in this case, the default file type is .txt.

Referring back to the code in Figure 13-11, an If statement is used to see if the user has clicked the OK button. If the user has clicked the Cancel button, then no code is executed. Following the If statement, the StreamWriter is defined using the Save File dialog box Filename property. It holds the name of the file that the user either selected or entered in the File name text box. The remaining code and logic are identical to that in the first application in this chapter (refer back to Figure 13-3).

OpenFile Dialog Box

The OpenFile dialog box works like the SaveFile dialog box, but in the reverse direction, opening a file for reading instead of opening a file for saving. The code is shown in Figure 13-13. The **With OpenFileDialog1** statement and the next several statements should be easy to follow if you have already reviewed the code for the SaveFile dialog box. The Filter, DefaultExt, and InitialDirectory properties are identical to those in the SaveFileDialog procedure discussed previously. The **ShowDialog** method opens the OpenFile dialog box, as shown in Figure 13-14.

```
Private Sub ListRecordsFromFile()
   Dim stRegNo, manuf, custPhoneNo, myFile As String
   Dim length As Single
   Dim year, recNbr As Int32

   ' OpenFileDialog1 gets filename
   With OpenFileDialog1
      .Filter = "TextFiles (*.txt)|*.txt|All Files (*.*)|*.*"
      .DefaultExt = "txt"
      .InitialDirectory = "c:\VBFiles"
      If .ShowDialog() = DialogResult.OK Then
         myfile = .FileName
         ' Declare Stringbuilder, StreamReader
         Dim boatRecord As New System.Text.StringBuilder()
         recNbr = 0
         boatRecord.Append("List of Records from the File" & vbCrLf)
         boatRecord.Append("==============================" & vbCrLf)
         ' Check to see if file exists
         If File.Exists(myfile) And myfile.Length > 0 Then
            Dim srBoats As StreamReader = _
               New StreamReader(.FileName)
            ' Loop over records until end of the file is reached
            ' -1 denotes end of file
            Do Until srBoats.Peek = -1
               ' Read a record
               stRegNo = srBoats.ReadLine
               length = srBoats.ReadLine
               manuf = srBoats.ReadLine
               year = srBoats.ReadLine
               custPhoneNo = srBoats.ReadLine
               recNbr += 1

               ' Build line for display in multiline text box
                boatRecord.Append("Boat Number = " & _
                recNbr & vbCrLf)
                boatRecord.Append("State Registration Number = " & _
                     stRegNo & vbCrLf)
                boatRecord.Append("Boat Length = " & _
                     length & vbCrLf)
```

13

```
                boatRecord.Append("Boat Manufacturer = " & _
                     manuf & vbCrLf)
                boatRecord.Append("Boat Model Year = " & _
                     year & vbCrLf)
                boatRecord.Append("Customer Phone Number = " & _
                     custPhoneNo & vbCrLf & vbCrLf)
            Loop
            srBoats.Close()
            boatRecord.Append("End of File")
            txtDisplay.Text = boatRecord.ToString
            txtStRegNo.Focus()
         End If
      End If
   End With
End Sub
```

Figure 13-13 Code for the OpenFile dialog box

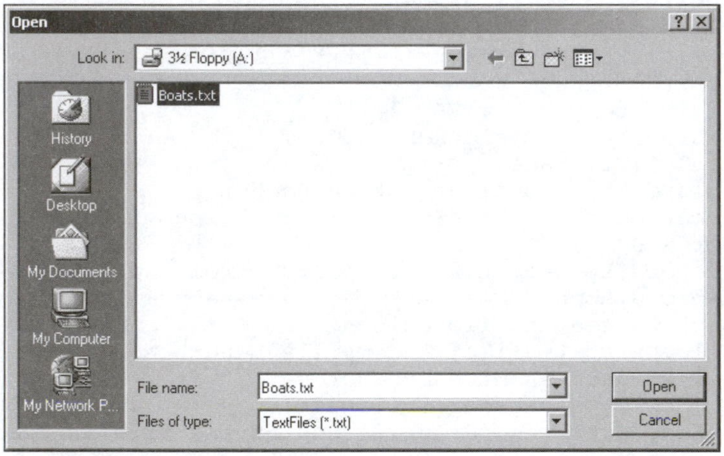

Figure 13-14 Open dialog box

The If statement that follows the Filter, DefaultExt, and InitialDirectory properties is identical to the one in the SaveFileDialog procedure; it simply checks to make sure the user has clicked the OK button. If the user did click the OK button, then the StreamReader is instantiated. The rest of the code is essentially the same as that in the first example.

Adding the Color Dialog Box

The Color dialog box is exceptionally easy to implement. Figure 13-15 contains the minimal code needed to change the text color for the txtDisplay multiline text box. Use the `ShowDialog` method and set the txtDisplay's ForeColor property to the ColorDialog's Color property. The Color dialog box appears in Figure 13-16.

```
Private Sub SetDisplayText()
   With ColorDialog1
      .ShowDialog()
      txtDisplay.ForeColor = .Color
   End With
End Sub
```

Figure 13-15 Code for the Color dialog box

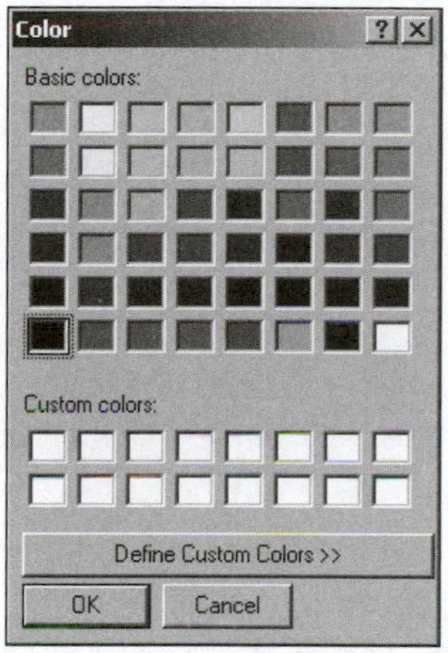

Figure 13-16 Color dialog box

With the previous changes, the program should execute properly using the three new dialog boxes: SaveFile, OpenFile, and Color. The complete program code is shown in Figure 13-17.

```
' Chapter 13--Example2

' Sequential file processing with a toolbar and dialogs
Imports System.IO
Imports System.Text.StringBuilder
Public Class Form1
    Inherits System.Windows.Forms.Form

    Private Sub StopProgram()
        Me.close()
    End Sub

Private Sub SaveToFile()
   ' SaveFileDialog to get filename and save boat record
   With SaveFileDialog1
      .Filter = "TextFiles (*.txt)|*.txt|All Files (*.*)|*.*"
      .DefaultExt = "txt"
      .InitialDirectory = "c:\VBFiles"
```

```
            If .ShowDialog() = DialogResult.OK Then
               Dim swBoats As New StreamWriter(.FileName, True)

               swBoats.WriteLine(txtStRegNo.Text)
               swBoats.WriteLine(txtLength.Text)
               swBoats.WriteLine(txtManufacturer.Text)
               swBoats.WriteLine(txtYear.Text)
               swBoats.WriteLine(txtCustPhoneNo.Text)
               ' Close the StreamWriter
               swBoats.Close()
            End If
         End With
         ' Clear text boxes and set focus to state registration no TextBox
         txtStRegNo.Clear()
         txtLength.Clear()
         txtManufacturer.Clear()
         txtYear.Clear()
         txtCustPhoneNo.Clear()
         txtStRegNo.Focus()
      End Sub

      Private Sub ListRecordsFromFile()
         Dim stRegNo, manuf, custPhoneNo, myFile As String
         Dim length As Single
         Dim year, recNbr As Int32

         ' OpenFileDialog1 gets filename
         With OpenFileDialog1
            .Filter = "TextFiles (*.txt)|*.txt|All Files (*.*)|*.*"
            .DefaultExt = "txt"
            .InitialDirectory = "c:\VBFiles"
            If .ShowDialog() = DialogResult.OK Then
               myfile = .FileName
               ' Declare Stringbuilder, StreamReader
               Dim boatRecord As New System.Text.StringBuilder()
               recNbr = 0
               boatRecord.Append("List of Records from the File" & vbCrLf)
               boatRecord.Append("=============================" & vbCrLf)
               ' Check to see if file exists
               If File.Exists(myfile) And myfile.Length > 0 Then
                  Dim srBoats As StreamReader = _
                     New StreamReader(.FileName)
                  ' Loop over records until end of the file is reached
                  ' -1 denotes end of file
                  Do Until srBoats.Peek = -1
                     ' Read a record
                     stRegNo = srBoats.ReadLine
                     length = srBoats.ReadLine
                     manuf = srBoats.ReadLine
                     year = srBoats.ReadLine
                     custPhoneNo = srBoats.ReadLine
                     recNbr += 1
```

```
                ' Build line for display in multiline text box
                boatRecord.Append("Boat Number = " & _
                recNbr & vbCrLf)
                boatRecord.Append("State Registration Number = " & _
                     stRegNo & vbCrLf)
                boatRecord.Append("Boat Length = " & _
                     length & vbCrLf)
                boatRecord.Append("Boat Manufacturer = " & _
                     manuf & vbCrLf)
                boatRecord.Append("Boat Model Year = " & _
                     year & vbCrLf)
                boatRecord.Append("Customer Phone Number = " & _
                     custPhoneNo & vbCrLf & vbCrLf)

            Loop
            srBoats.Close()
            boatRecord.Append("End of File")
            txtDisplay.Text = boatRecord.ToString
            txtStRegNo.Focus()
         End If
      End If
   End With
End Sub
Private Sub SetDisplayText()
   With ColorDialog1
      .ShowDialog()
       txtDisplay.ForeColor = .Color
   End With
End Sub

'Region " Windows Form Designer generated code "

Private Sub ToolBar1_ButtonClick(ByVal sender As System.Object, _
   ByVal e As System.Windows.Forms.ToolBarButtonClickEventArgs) _
   Handles ToolBar1.ButtonClick

   Select Case e.Button.Tag
      Case "Save" : Call SaveToFile()
      Case "Open" : Call ListRecordsFromFile()
      Case "Color" : Call SetDisplayText()
      Case "Exit" : Call StopProgram()
      Case Else
   End Select

 End Sub
End Class
```

Figure 13-17 Complete code for the dialog example

The FontDialog Control

The FontDialog control lets you change fonts and font colors in applications by setting the Font property for controls such as a label or text box. The following code illustrates how to change the font and the font color. You will be asked to add the FontDialog capability as an extension of the previous example in one of the following exercises.

```
' Set FontDialog control to include color
FontDialog1.ShowColor() = True

' Open the FontDialog window & check if user clicked OK
If FontDialog1.ShowDialog() = DialogResult.OK Then
   txtDisplay.Font = FontDialog1.Font
   txtDisplay.ForeColor = FontDialog1.Color
End If
```

Hands-on Exercise 2

1. Locate **Ex02** in the Chap13\Examples folder in the student data files. Create a folder named **Chap13\Exercises** in the work folder on your system, and then copy the **Ex02** folder to this folder. Double-click the **SeqFileDialogs1.sln** file in the Example2 folder to open the project.
2. Insert a formatted disk into drive A. Run the program, enter a few records using the Save button on the toolbar, and then click the **List Records** button on the toolbar. Experiment with the other toolbar buttons.

Making Objects Persistent

The previous examples in this chapter helped you understand how to store and retrieve information from files, and will be used to achieve **object persistence**. Up until this chapter, any instances of an object were lost when the program stopped running. Of course, any realistic application will require the capability to store and retrieve objects. There are two approaches to achieving persistence: **attribute storage** and **object storage**. Attribute storage involves retrieving the attribute values from the instance to be made persistent, and then writing these values to a file. Figure 13-18 illustrates the attribute storage technique to make a customer instance persistent.

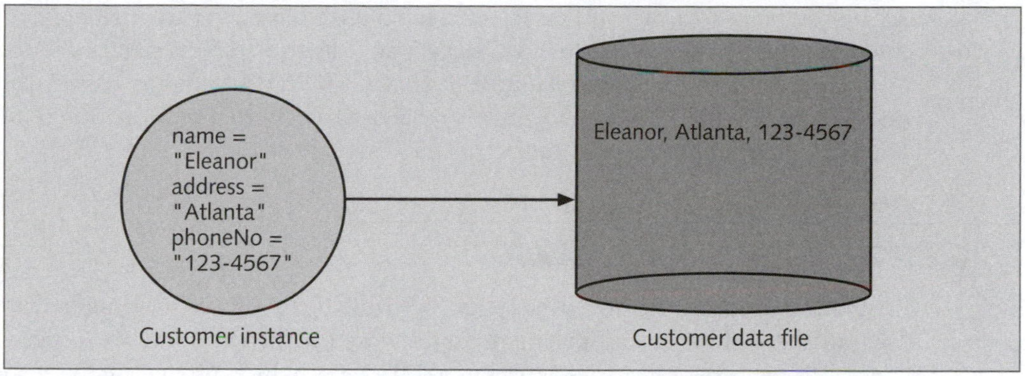

Figure 13-18 Making a customer instance persistent using attribute storage

You will learn how to store and retrieve objects in several different ways:

- Attribute storage and retrieval using the StreamWriter and StreamReader
- Object serialization
- Attribute storage and retrieval using databases

The first object-persistent method saves the object's attributes using sequential files with the `StreamWriter` and `StreamReader` classes. These concepts were previously covered in this chapter, but now will be applied to data access (DA) classes. For example, to make a customer instance persistent, you first invoke the accessor methods to obtain the customer's name, address, and phone number. Then you write these values (attributes) to a customer data file. You can re-create the customer instance later by reversing the process: First, you read the data from the customer data file, and then instantiate Customer using the data values from the file to populate the attributes.

13

However, storing attributes using `StreamReader` and `StreamWriter` may not be the best approach for object persistence. Because of the importance and complexity of object storage and retrieval, the .NET framework provides an easy way to store and retrieve objects—namely **object serialization**. The serialization process transforms an object into a stream that can be saved to a sequential file; deserialization transforms the stream from the file back to the object state before the object was stored. The obvious advantage of serialization is that the object can be retrieved intact; it is not necessary to re-create the object, as you do with attribute storage.

Serialization requires the streams to be formatted. The .NET framework provides two formatters for serialization and deserialization—one is a binary formatter and the other is a SOAP (Simple Object Application Protocol) formatter. The SOAP formatter supports XML and is widely used for Web services applications. SOAP, XML, and Web services will be discussed in Chapter 16.

Finally, databases can be used to make objects persistent. A **database** is one or more files organized to help make queries. The data in a **relational database** is organized into tables that can be related to each other. Each table column represents an attribute and each row represents a record. The **Structured Query Language** (**SQL**) is a standard set of keywords and statements used to access relational databases. VB .NET contains classes with methods you will invoke while working with a relational database. Further explanation of SQL will be included as needed for the next four chapters.

Designing a Data Access Class

The fundamental purpose of a DA class is to provide methods that store and retrieve data and make instances of a PD class persistent. As you saw in Chapter 5, the three-tier OO design model calls for three categories of classes: GUI classes, which provide the user interface for data input and display; PD classes, which model the essential business entities; and DA classes, which provide for data storage and retrieval. This model implements a client-server architecture that is significantly easier to deploy and maintain.

Data storage and retrieval tasks are placed in a DA class for two reasons. First, data input and output code are isolated from other classes, which can dramatically reduce maintenance. Changes in data storage should have no impact on GUI and PD classes. Similarly, GUI and PD modifications generally will not affect DA classes. Second, three-tier architecture supports the client-server model where GUI, PD, and DA functions may reside on multiple machines at various sites. Separate classes for each tier make deployment easier in a client-server environment. For details, see the Deployment chapters (15 and 16) in Part 5. You further isolate the DA class by requiring that DA methods are invoked only by the PD class. This means that only the PD class is aware of the DA class. The services provided by the DA class appear to be provided by the PD class, thus effectively hiding the DA class from all other classes.

Data Access Methods

Generally you will write a separate DA class for each PD class. In this chapter, for example, you will write a DA class named CustomerDA, which provides data storage and retrieval services for customers. Remember, however, that only the PD class will invoke methods in the DA class. Classes that require data storage and retrieval services must invoke the DA methods in Customer, which in turn invoke the CustomerDA methods. This idea is illustrated later in this chapter in the section "Communicating with a Data Access Class."

Recall from Chapter 6 that VB .NET has two types of methods: shared and nonshared. Shared methods, sometimes called "class methods" and implemented with the keyword `Static` in some other languages, are not tied to a specific instance. You invoke shared methods using the class name. Because you will not have instances of the DA class, all of its methods are shared.

Four basic tasks are provided by CustomerDA and thus by Customer: retrieve a customer, store a customer, change a customer's data, and remove a customer. These functions are implemented in the DA class using methods named Find, AddNew, Update, and Delete. Although the statements within these DA methods depend on the specific storage implementation, their signatures remain the same. In other words, clients that invoke these methods are unaware of the specific implementations and need only know the method signature.

These methods and their headers are described in the following sections. Two exception handler classes, NotFoundException and DuplicateException, are created and thrown when needed in the methods. The statements within these methods are described in the implementation sections later in this chapter.

Finding a Customer

The Find method searches for a specific customer; if the customer is found, the method returns a reference to the instance. The examples in this section use the customer's phone number as the key, which means that each customer is uniquely identified by telephone number. The Find method accepts an argument that contains the phone number of the customer to be retrieved. If the customer is found, then a reference to the customer instance is returned. If the customer is not located, the method creates and throws an instance of the custom exception class NotFoundException. The header for the Find method appears as:

```
Public Shared Function Find(ByVal PhoneNo As String) As Customer
```

Adding a Customer

The AddNew method adds a customer to the system. This method receives a reference to the new customer instance as an argument and returns no data. Because you do not want to have duplicate customers stored, this method first determines if there is an existing customer with the same phone number as the customer being added. If an existing customer with the same phone number is detected, the AddNew method will create and throw an instance of the custom exception class DuplicateException. The header appears as:

```
Public Shared Sub AddNew(ByVal aCustomer As Customer)
```

Updating a Customer

In this system, customers may change their address and phone number. The purpose of the Update method is to store these changed values. The Update method receives the customer reference as an argument, locates the existing customer, and replaces the address and phone number values. If the customer cannot be located, then the method throws a NotFoundException. This method does not return a value.

```
Public Shared Sub Update(ByVal aCustomer As Customer)
```

Deleting a Customer

The Delete method removes a customer from the system. Like the Update method, the Delete method first locates the customer whose reference was received as an argument, and then removes it from data storage. Also like the Update method, if the customer cannot be located, the Delete method throws a NotFoundException. This method does not return a value.

```
Public Shared Sub Delete(ByVal aCustomer As Customer)
```

Additional Data Access Methods

The DA classes illustrated in this section have three additional methods: Initialize, Terminate, and GetAll. As their names suggest, the Initialize method performs initialization chores, the Terminate method performs termination tasks, and the GetAll method retrieves all members of a class. The Initialize and Terminate methods receive no arguments and return no data. The actual statements in these methods depend on the specific implementation of the DA class. This chapter illustrates four different implementations; the details for these methods are described in later sections. The Initialize and Terminate method headers are:

```
Public Shared Sub Initialize()
Public Shared Sub Terminate()
```

The GetAll method retrieves all customers that are stored in the system and returns their references in an ArrayList instance. This method takes no arguments.

```
Public Shared Function GetAll() As ArrayList
```

The following code recaps the seven DA method headers:

```
Public Shared Function Find(ByVal PhoneNo As String) As Customer

Public Shared Sub AddNew(ByVal aCustomer As Customer)

Public Shared Sub Update(ByVal aCustomer As Customer)

Public Shared Sub Delete(ByVal aCustomer As Customer)

Public Shared Sub Initialize()

Public Shared Sub Terminate()

Public Shared Function GetAll() As ArrayList
```

Communicating with a Data Access Class

In the previous section you saw that the DA methods are invoked only by the corresponding PD class. In this section, the Customer class invokes methods in CustomerDA. Clients must invoke methods in Customer, which in turn invokes the DA methods. This restriction is imposed to isolate the DA class from all but its matching PD class. To the other classes, it appears that the PD class, Customer, is providing data storage and retrieval for its instances.

To enable Customer to invoke the seven DA methods, you must provide seven corresponding methods in Customer, which are then invoked by clients. The sole purpose of these methods is to act as a buffer between other classes and the DA class. In keeping with the spirit of minimum maintenance, you should design these methods so they will not be sensitive to the data storage method you use. For example, whether you store data using a relational database or a sequential file, you want the seven method headers to remain the same. This feature is demonstrated in the implementation sections later in the chapter.

Finding a Customer

The purpose of the PD Find method is to invoke the DA Find method. It is a shared method because it is not tied to a specific customer instance. Because the DA method returns a customer reference, you want the PD Find method to also return the reference. Similarly, because the DA Find method may throw a NotFoundException, you want the PD Find method to throw an exception if the customer is not found.

The single statement in the PD Find method simply invokes the CustomerDA Find method, passes it the phone number that was received, and then returns the customer reference value that is returned by the DA Find method. The PD Find method appears as:

```
Public Shared Function Find(ByVal PhoneNo As String) As Customer
   Return CustomerDA.Find(PhoneNo)
End Function
```

Adding a Customer

The AddNew method in the PD class invokes the AddNew method in the DA class to store a new customer instance. It is a nonshared method because it is invoked for the new customer instance being added. The method receives no argument and returns no data. Note that the DA AddNew method may throw a DuplicateException. The single statement in the method invokes the AddNew method in CustomerDA, passing it a reference to the new customer instance. The method appears as:

```
Public Sub AddNew()
   CustomerDA.AddNew(Me)
End Sub
```


Changing a Customer

The PD Update method invokes the Update method in the DA class. It is a nonshared method because it is invoked for a specific customer instance. The DA Update method may throw a NotFoundException. The method invokes the Update method in CustomerDA, passing a reference to the new customer instance. The method appears as:

```
Public Sub Update()
   CustomerDA.Update(Me)
End Sub
```

Deleting a Customer

The Delete method in the PD class invokes the Delete method in the DA class. Like the Update method, the Delete method is a nonshared method, may throw an exception, and passes a reference of the customer instance being deleted. The method code is:

```
Public Sub Delete()
   CustomerDA.Delete(Me)
End Sub
```

Additional Problem Domain Methods

Because the DA classes in the previous section have the additional methods Initialize, Terminate, and GetAll, you must also include them in the PD class. All of these are shared methods that simply invoke the corresponding method in the DA class. The GetAll method returns an ArrayList.

```
Public Shared Sub Initialize()
   CustomerDA.Initialize()
End Sub
Public Shared Sub Terminate()
   CustomerDA.Terminate()
End Sub
Public Shared Function GetAll() As ArrayList
   Return CustomerDA.GetAll
End Function
```

Implementing Persistence with a Sequential File

Attribute storage, which calls for the storage of attribute values, is used in the following example for sequential access files. The Initialize method reads the customer records containing the attribute values for customers, creates a customer instance for each record, and then places the references for these customer instances into an ArrayList instance. This technique permits the ready access of a particular customer without additional file input and output. Similarly, the Terminate method iterates the ArrayList and writes the attribute values for each customer instance to the file.

The CustomerDA class for the sequential files class begins with **`Imports`** statements for ArrayList and VB .NET I/O namespaces. The VB .NET I/O namespace package contains all the classes this example needs for file input and output. The Collections namespace contains the **`ArrayList`** class.

```
Imports System.IO
Imports System.Collections
```

One variable is declared at the beginning of the CustomerDA class. It is an ArrayList reference variable named customers, which will contain references to all the customer instances. A second variable that is used in the Initialize and Terminate methods is assigned to a sequential file to be used in this example. As you can see, the name of the sequential file is customerFile.txt; the file is on the A drive.

```
' Declare a Shared ArrayList called customers
Shared customers As New ArrayList()
' Declare a string and set to file
Shared cFile As String = "a:\customerFile.txt"
```

The Initialize Method

The purpose of the Initialize method is to read all the customer's attribute values from the sequential file, create customer instances, and store references for these instances in an ArrayList.

The first statement in the Initialize method creates the ArrayList instance named customers, which will be populated with references to customer instances.

```
customers = New ArrayList()
```

The remainder of the method is executed only if a customer data file exists. The If statement invokes the `Exists` method and the length property for the file instance named customerFile. The file must exist and not have a length of zero before the method will attempt to read data. The test for zero length is necessary because it is possible that there are no records in the file.

```
If File.Exists(cFile) And cFile.Length > 0 Then
```

Following the If statement is a statement that declares string variables to contain the customer attribute values. The statements that create a StreamReader instance and invoke its ReadLine method to read the customer's name, address, and phone number are placed in a Try block, because if an I/O error occurs, an exception will be thrown. The argument passed to the StreamReader constructor is a reference to the file.

```
Dim name, address, phoneNo As String
   Try
       ' Declare a StreamReader and point to file
       Dim CustomerFile As New StreamReader(cFile)
```

Next comes a Do loop that invokes the ReadLine method to read the customer's name, address, and phone number, create an instance of Customer, and add the customer reference to the ArrayList customers. This loop continues until the Peek method returns -1, signaling the end of the file. The StreamReader is then closed.

```
' Loop over file until end of file-- Peek = -1
Do Until CustomerFile.Peek = -1
   name = CustomerFile.ReadLine
   address = CustomerFile.ReadLine
   phoneNo = CustomerFile.ReadLine
   ' If name returned, then add to customers
   If name <> Nothing Then
      customers.Add(New Customer(name, address, phoneNo))
   End If
Loop
```

The last part of the Initialize method is a Catch block that executes if an exception is thrown by any of the statements in the Try block.

```
Catch e As Exception
   Console.WriteLine(e.ToString)
End Try
```

The complete Initialize method is shown in Figure 13-19.

13

```
' Initialize Method
   Public Shared Sub Initialize()

         ' Check for file existence that includes data
         If File.Exists(cFile) And cFile.Length > 0 Then
            ' Declare temporary values to hold values returned from file
            Dim name, address, phoneNo As String
            Try
               ' Declare a StreamReader and point to file
               Dim CustomerFile As New StreamReader(cFile)
               ' Loop over file until end of file-- Peek = -1
               Do Until CustomerFile.Peek = -1
                  name = CustomerFile.ReadLine
                  address = CustomerFile.ReadLine
                  phoneNo = CustomerFile.ReadLine
                  ' If name returned, then add to customers
                  If name <> Nothing Then
                     customers.Add(New Customer(name, address, _
                        phoneNo))
                  End If
               Loop
               CustomerFile.Close()
            Catch e As Exception
                Console.WriteLine(e.ToString)
            End Try
         End If
   End Sub
```

Figure 13-19 CustomerDA Initialize method for sequential file storage

The Terminate Method

The Terminate method is responsible for creating a file that contains attribute values for all the customer instances referenced by the ArrayList customers. First, the method assigns a string variable to the file path location. This string variable will be used for creating a StreamWriter instance. Next, the StreamWriter instance is created within a Try block and an instance of Customer, cust, is created. Cust will be used to iterate, using the For Each structure, over the customers ArrayList, which holds customer instances. The For Each structure works with all collections. Note that an alternative approach for this looping structure would be to use a traditional For Next loop with an index because the Count property of the ArrayList returns the number of customers it holds. Three string variables representing name, address, and phone number are declared. Next, for each customer reference in the customers ArrayList, attribute values are obtained by invoking accessor methods; these values are then written to the sequential file by invoking the `WriteLine` method. All of this code is placed within a Try block because an I/O error can occur, which would cause an exception to be thrown. The Terminate method is shown in Figure 13-20.

```
' Terminate Method
Public Shared Sub Terminate()

   Try
      ' Instantiate a StreamWriter
      Dim customerFile As New StreamWriter(cFile, True)
      Dim cust As Customer
      ' Define String variables to hold object attributes
      Dim name, address, phoneno As String
      ' Loop over customers ArrayList -- getting and saving attributes
      For Each cust In customers
         name = cust.GetName
         address = cust.GetAddress
         phoneno = cust.GetPhoneNo

         customerFile.WriteLine(name)
         customerFile.WriteLine(address)
         customerFile.WriteLine(phoneno)
      Next
         customerFile.Close()
   Catch e As Exception
         Console.WriteLine(e.ToString)
   End Try
End Sub
```

Figure 13-20 CustomerDA Terminate method for sequential file storage

The Find Method

All of the existing customer instances are referenced by the ArrayList instance named customers. Therefore, the Find method simply iterates the customers ArrayList, seeking a customer instance with a phone number that matches the value received by the method. If the customer is found, its reference is returned. If none is found, a NotFoundException is thrown. The Find method is shown in Figure 13-21.


```
' Find Function--Throws NotFoundException if Not Found
Public Shared Function Find(ByVal PhoneNo As String) As Customer
   ' Define two object variables and boolean variable--set to False
   Dim cust As New Customer()
   Dim acustomer As New Customer()
   acustomer = Nothing
   Dim foundIt As Boolean = False
   ' Loop ArrayList customers for each customer
   For Each cust In customers
      acustomer = cust
      ' If found, set foundit to true
      If cust.GetPhoneNo = PhoneNo Then
         foundIt = True
            Exit For
      End If
```

```
    Next
    If foundIt = True Then
        Return acustomer
    Else
        Throw New NotFoundException(" Not Found ")
    End If
End Function
```

Figure 13-21 CustomerDA Find method for sequential file storage

At the top of the method, two customer reference variables named aCustomer and cust are declared. Again, cust will be used with the For Each structure to iterate through the customers ArrayList and aCustomer is set to Nothing. The next statement declares a Boolean variable named `foundIt` and initializes its value to False.

A For Each loop iterates over the ArrayList customers. The first statement in the loop retrieves a reference to the customer instance and assigns it to aCustomer. Then, an If statement determines whether a matching phone number exists. If there is a match, then `foundIt` is set to True, and the loop is terminated. Note that the loop will also end after it has iterated through all the customer instances in the customers ArrayList. The For Each structure controls looping through collections.

At the end of the Find method, an If statement checks the value of `foundIt`. If the value is true, then a reference to the customer instance is returned. If false, then an instance of NotFoundException is created and thrown to the invoking method.

The AddNew Method

Invoke this method to add a customer to the system. Because all customer references in this example are stored in an ArrayList, the AddNew method adds the new reference to the ArrayList after checking for a duplicate phone number, which in this example is assumed to be a duplicate customer. The method is shown in Figure 13-22.

```
' AddNew Method--Throws DuplicateException if exists
Public Shared Sub AddNew(ByVal aCustomer As Customer)
    ' Set Boolean variable to False, String variable for phoneno
    Dim exists As Boolean = False
    Dim cust As Customer
    Dim existPhoneNo As String
    ' Loop ArrayList customers for each customer
    For Each cust In customers
        existPhoneNo = cust.GetPhoneNo
        ' If already exists, do not add
        If existPhoneNo = aCustomer.GetPhoneNo Then
            exists = True
            Exit For
        End If
    Next
```

```
    If exists = True Then
       Throw New DuplicateException("Customer Already Exists")
    Else
       customers.Add(aCustomer)
    End If
End Sub
```

Figure 13-22 CustomerDA AddNew method for sequential file storage

The method begins by declaring a Boolean variable named `exists` and initializing it to `False`. The variable, cust, again is declared as a customer to be used with the For Each structure. A string variable, existPhoneNo, is declared to hold the phone number values. Next, a For Each loop searches the customers ArrayList to determine if this customer already exists; if so, a DuplicateException is thrown. The loop ends whenever a duplicate customer is detected or the end of the customers ArrayList is reached.

The first statement within the loop retrieves the customer reference. The second statement determines if there is a match between the new customer's phone number and the existing customer's number. If a match is found, the variable `exists` is set to `True` and the loop ends.

The If statement following the loop tests the contents of the `exists` variable. If it is `True`, then an instance of DuplicateException is created and thrown. If, however, the `exists` variable contains `False`, then a reference for the new customer is added to the ArrayList.

The Update Method

The Update method for sequential file storage contains no code because nothing needs to be done. Updates are made to the customer instance by invoking accessor methods (setName, setAddress, setPhoneNo), which change the attribute values for the specified instance. When processing concludes, the Terminate method writes the attribute values for all of the instances to a sequential file. See Figure 13-23.

13

```
Public Shared Sub Update(ByVal aCustomer As Customer)
    ' Nothing required--Changes via setter methods
    Return
End Sub
```

Figure 13-23 CustomerDA Update method for sequential file storage

The Delete Method

The Delete method removes a customer from the system. It accomplishes this task by removing the customer from the ArrayList customers. Then the Terminate method saves all the customers in the ArrayList customers to the sequential file. Thus, in this sequential file example, you delete a customer by removing the reference for the customer instance from the customers ArrayList. See Figure 13-24.

```
'Delete Method--Throws NotFoundException if not found
Public Shared Sub Delete(ByVal aCustomer As Customer)
   Dim foundIt As Boolean = False
   Dim phoneNo As String = aCustomer.GetPhoneNo
   Dim i As Integer = 0
   Dim cust As Customer
   ' Loop ArrayList customers for each customer
   For Each cust In customers
      ' If found, set foundit to True and remove from customers
      If cust.GetPhoneNo = phoneNo Then
         foundIt = True
         customers.RemoveAt(i)
         Exit For
      End If
      i = i + 1
   Next
   If Not foundIt Then
      Throw New NotFoundException(" Not Found ")
   End If
End Sub
```

Figure 13-24 CustomerDA Delete method for sequential file storage

The method begins by declaring a Boolean variable named **`foundIt`** and initializing it to **`False`**. Then a string variable is assigned a value by invoking the GetPhoneNo accessor method to obtain the customer's telephone number. An integer variable is defined to be used as the index value within the customers ArrayList because the index value will be necessary for removing it from the collection. A For Each loop iterates the customers ArrayList, seeking a reference for the customer with a matching telephone number. If the desired customer is found, its reference is removed from the ArrayList by invoking the RemoveAt method, passing the index of the reference. If no matching customer is found, then the method throws a NotFoundException.

The GetAll Method

The ArrayList instance named customers contains references to all existing customer instances. The GetAll method simply returns a reference to this ArrayList. The invoking method can then retrieve the desired customer reference from the ArrayList. This method is shown in Figure 13-25.

```
Public Shared Function GetAll() As ArrayList
        Return customers
End Function
```

Figure 13-25 CustomerDA GetAll method for sequential file storage

The DuplicateException and NotFoundException Classes

The DA classes DuplicateException and NotFoundException inform the invoking client of a problem. Figure 13-26 shows these two classes.

```
Public Class DuplicateException
    Inherits Exception
    Public Sub New(ByVal message As String)
        MyBase.New(message)
    End Sub
End Class

Public Class NotFoundException
    Inherits Exception
    Public Sub New(ByVal message As String)
        MyBase.New(message)
    End Sub
End Class
```

Figure 13-26 DuplicateException and NotFoundException classes

Testing CustomerDA for Sequential File Implementation

In this section you will create an application to test the DA you developed in the previous sections. To do so, you would open a new application, place a button on the form, and set the Text property to "Tester for Data Access Class." The code for this button simply invokes a user-defined Sub procedure with the testing code. This is done to allow the traditional usage of `e` for catching exceptions; `e` is an argument in all controls and thus cannot be used without modification. The code for testing the DA class methods will be described in some detail here, because it is used without modification in object serialization and relational database examples later in this chapter. This tester code will:

- Create two customer instances
- Invoke the Initialize method
- Invoke the AddNew method to add the two new customers to storage
- Retrieve a reference to the first customer by invoking the Find method
- Invoke the GetAll method to retrieve references to both customers
- Invoke the Delete method for the second customer and verify the deletion
- Change the first customer's address and verify the change using the Update method
- Invoke the Terminate method

These tasks are shown graphically in the sequence diagram in Figure 13-27; the tester code is shown in Figure 13-28. Note that to reduce clutter, the sequence diagram omits the invocation of accessor and display methods.

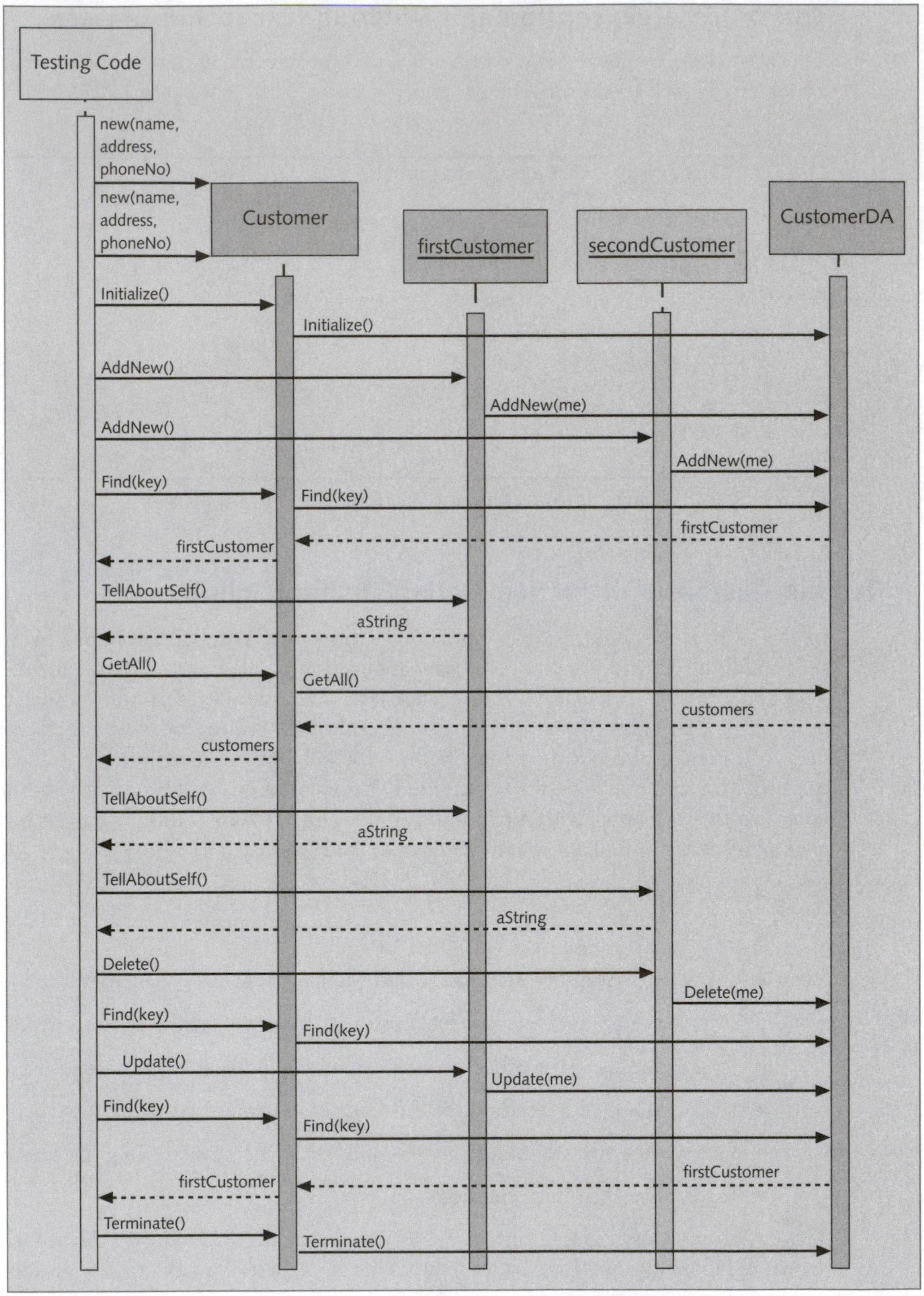

Figure 13-27 Sequence diagram for testing the DA classes

The testing program first creates two customer instances and stores their references into firstCustomer and secondCustomer. Next, it invokes the Initialize method to prepare for subsequent processing. Note that the program is aware of the Customer class, but is not aware of CustomerDA. The program must invoke methods in Customer, which in turn invokes the appropriate methods in CustomerDA. This relationship is clearly shown in the sequence diagram.

Next, the testing program invokes AddNew twice, once for firstCustomer and once for secondCustomer, to add these two customers to storage. In this example, the customer references are stored in an ArrayList instance, customers, which is not written to the sequential file until the Terminate method is invoked. However, the testing program is completely unaware of the specific storage implementation. The statements that invoke the AddNew method are placed within a Try block because it can throw a DuplicateException if you attempt to add a customer who already exists. Customers are identified by their telephone number.

After the two customers are added, the Find method is invoked using the first customer's telephone number as an argument. This statement is also placed in a Try block because Find can throw a NotFoundException. When the reference for the first customer is returned, its TellAboutSelf method is invoked.

Next, the GetAll method is invoked to obtain an ArrayList instance containing references for all customers stored. In this example, there are only two customers: Eleanor and Mike. Following the statement that invokes the GetAll method is a loop that iterates the ArrayList instance, which was returned to retrieve each customer reference and invoke TellAboutSelf for each of them. The string returned from TellAboutSelf is then displayed.

The Delete method is then invoked to remove the second customer, Mike, from storage. Remember that the testing program is unaware of how the customer is removed, but that after invoking the Delete method, the customer is simply gone. After deleting Mike, the Find method is invoked to see if Mike can be found—indeed, he is not there. Again, the statement that invokes the Delete method is placed within a Try block because a NotFoundException could be thrown.

13

Next, the address for the first customer is changed by invoking the SetAddress accessor method, and then invoking the Update method. The SetAddress method changes the attribute value in the instance, and the Update method makes the change to the customers ArrayList. This change becomes persistent because the Terminate method writes all the customers from the customers ArrayList to a sequential file. The change is verified by invoking Find for the first customer.

The testing program then invokes the Terminate method, which writes the customers' attributes to the sequential file, making them persistent. The last statement displays a message box telling you the program has completed and asks you to look at the output. You should also look at the CustomerFile on disk. If it did not exist before this testing program was run, it should only contain the one record for Eleanor. This is because the program created two customers, Eleanor and Mike, but deleted Mike. Unless you change the customers you add to the testing program, you should erase the CustomerFile from disk between runs because the file will already have Eleanor. Figure 13-28 shows the complete testing code, and the output from the testing program is shown in Figure 13-29. In the output, notice that "Not Found" appears in boldface to make it easier to see, and the trace is indented to make it easier to follow. The NotFoundException occurs because Mike was deleted and the Find method could not locate him.

```
' Chapter 13--Example 3
' Object persistence using a sequential file
Imports System.IO
Imports System.Collections
Public Class Form1
   Inherits System.Windows.Forms.Form
Private Sub testDAClasses()
   ' Instantiate two customers and Initialize
   Dim firstCustomer As New Customer("Eleanor", "Atlanta", "123-4567")
   Dim secondCustomer As New Customer("Mike", "Boston", "467-1234")

      Customer.Initialize()
      ' Test AddNew
      Try
         firstCustomer.AddNew()
         secondCustomer.AddNew()
         Console.WriteLine("Added Two customers")
      Catch e As DuplicateException
         Console.WriteLine(e.message.ToString)
      End Try

      ' Test Find Method
      Try
         firstCustomer = Customer.Find("123-4567")
         Console.WriteLine("Find: " & firstCustomer.TellAboutSelf)
      Catch e As NotFoundException
         Console.WriteLine(e.message.ToString)
      End Try

      ' Test GetAll
      Dim allcustomers As ArrayList = Customer.GetAll
      Dim cust As Customer
      For Each cust In allcustomers
         firstCustomer = cust
         Console.WriteLine("Get all: " & firstCustomer.TellAboutSelf)
      Next

      ' Test Delete method
      Try
         secondCustomer.Delete()
         Console.WriteLine("Delete: " & secondCustomer.TellAboutSelf)
         ' Try to find customer just deleted
         secondCustomer = Customer.Find("467-1234")
         Console.WriteLine("Delete: " & secondCustomer.TellAboutSelf)
      Catch e As NotFoundException
         Console.WriteLine(e.message.ToString)
      End Try
```

```
    ' Test Update by changing address of Eleanor
    Try
       firstCustomer = Customer.Find("123-4567")
       firstCustomer.SetAddress("Clayton")
       firstCustomer.Update()
       ' Display address after change
       firstCustomer = Customer.Find("123-4567")
       Console.WriteLine("Update: " & firstCustomer.TellAboutSelf)
    Catch e As NotFoundException
       Console.WriteLine(e.message.ToString)
    End Try

    'Test Terminate Method--can view results in file
    Customer.Terminate()
    MessageBox.Show("Test Script Completed--See results")
    Me.Close()
  End Sub

  Private Sub btnTester1_Click(ByVal sender As System.Object, _
     ByVal e As System.EventArgs) Handles btnTester1.Click

     TestDAClasses()
  End Sub
End Class
```

Figure 13-28 DA testing program listing

```
Added Two customers
Find: Name = Eleanor, Address = Atlanta, Phone No = 123-4567
Get all: Name = Eleanor, Address = Atlanta, Phone No = 123-4567
Get all: Name = Mike, Address = Boston, Phone No = 467-1234
Delete: Name = Mike, Address = Boston, Phone No = 467-1234
Not Found
Update: Name = Eleanor, Address = Clayton, Phone No = 123-4567
```

Figure 13-29 Output of the testing program

Hands-on Exercise 3

1. Locate **Ex03** in the Chap13\Examples folder in the student data files. Create a folder named **Chap13\Exercises** in the work folder on your system, and then copy the **Ex03** folder to this folder. Open the project with VB .NET by double-clicking the **DAclasses.sln** file in the Example3 folder. The DAclasses project includes the Customer, CustomerDA, DuplicateException, and NotFoundException classes as well as the form containing one button that executes the testing program.

2. Note that CustomerDA will use drive A for the customerFile.txt file, unless you alter the file location at the beginning of CustomerDA. Insert a formatted disk in drive A and delete customerFile.txt on the disk if it exists.
3. Run the project and click the button to execute the testing program. Verify that the program output is as shown in Figure 13-29.

Implementing Persistence with Object Serialization

When you implement persistence using object serialization, you employ object storage that stores entire instances. This approach contrasts with the attribute storage techniques you saw in the previous section. With object serialization, you write and read complete object instances to a file. Instances are retrieved intact, so you do not need to re-create them.

Changing from sequential access file processing to object serialization involves adding the attribute `<Serializable()>` to the Customer definition header and changing the Initialize and Terminate methods in CustomerDA. No other classes are affected, and you use the same testing program as you did in the previous examples. The `<Serializable()>` attribute would also need to be added to any classes derived from it. Note that serialization uses the **`FileStream`** class instead of the `StreamReader` and `StreamWriter` classes that were derived from the `Text` class.

The CustomerDA Initialize method for sequential file access instantiated a StreamWriter and a StreamReader using the `WriteLine` and `ReadLine` methods to store and retrieve attribute values. With object serialization, you instantiate FileStream and invoke its Serialize and Deserialize methods to store and retrieve objects, respectively.

VB .NET allows you to select one of two formatters for serialization and deserialization: binary and SOAP. The SOAP formatter stores the serialized object in XML. Because XML is in text format, any text editor can view the serialized objects that are stored using the SOAP formatter. Two namespaces must be imported to allow instantiating a binary formatter. The namespaces are shown in the following code:

```
Imports System.Runtime.Serialization
Imports System.Runtime.Serialization.Formatters.Binary
```

If you want to use a SOAP formatter, then that namespace also needs to be imported. However, you will need to add a reference (via the Add References option in the Project menu) to the `System.Runtime.Serialization.Format.Soap` assembly. After you add the reference, the **`Imports`** statement would be the same except for replacing the word Binary with SOAP.

Only the few changes in the Initialize method from the previous example are discussed in this section, because the basic logic has not changed. Other than the previous **`Imports`** statements, the other new statements are the instantiation of the FileStream and the formatter. These two statements are shown in the following code:

```
Dim CustomerFile As New FileStream(cFile, _
   FileMode.OpenOrCreate, FileAccess.Read)
Dim bfCustomer As BinaryFormatter = New BinaryFormatter()
```

Within the Do loop, the Deserialize method reads each customer instance from the file and adds a reference to the cust ArrayList. Note that the object read from the file must be cast to the type `Customer`. This statement is shown in the following code:

```
cust = CType(bfCustomer.Deserialize(CustomerFile), Customer)
```

The loop terminates when the end of the file is reached—when the current file position is the same value as the length of the file. If an error occurs while retrieving the objects, the exception is displayed using Console.WriteLine. The CustomerDA Initialize method with modifications for object serialization is shown in Figure 13-30.

```
' Initialize Method
Public Shared Sub Initialize()

   Dim name, address, phoneNo As String
   ' Check for file existence that includes data
   If File.Exists(cFile) And cFile.Length > 0 Then
      Try
         ' Declare a FileStream and point to file
         Dim CustomerFile As New FileStream(cFile, _
         FileMode.OpenOrCreate, FileAccess.Read)
         Dim bfCustomer As BinaryFormatter = New BinaryFormatter()
         Dim cust As Customer
         CustomerFile.Seek(0, SeekOrigin.Begin)
         ' Loop over file until eof
         Do Until CustomerFile.Position = CustomerFile.Length
            ' Must convert type to customer
            cust = CType(bfCustomer.Deserialize(CustomerFile), _
                        Customer)
            name = cust.GetName
            address = cust.GetAddress
            phoneNo = cust.GetPhoneNo
            ' Add customer to ArrayList Customers if Name present
            If name <> Nothing Then
               customers.Add(New Customer(name, address, phoneNo))
            End If
         Loop
         CustomerFile.Close()
      Catch e As Exception
         Console.WriteLine(e.ToString)
      End Try
   End If
End Sub
```

Figure 13-30 CustomerDA Initialize method for object serialization

13

The CustomerDA Terminate method for sequential access file storage instantiated StreamWriter and invoked its `WriteLine` method to output the attribute values. When using a serialized file, you instantiate FileStream and then invoke its Serialize method to output each instance. The logic is to retrieve each customer reference from the ArrayList, as in the previous Terminate method example (refer back to Figure 13-20). Here, however, the Serialize method is invoked to write the instance (the whole object) to the file instead of writing the individual attribute values. As in the Deserialize method in the previous Initialize method, the Serialize method also requires a formatter; you must import the appropriate namespaces. The remaining logic has not changed from the Terminate method in the previous example. The instantiation of FileStream and the formatter are the same as shown in Figure 13-30, except that the filemode is now Append. Figure 13-31 shows the Terminate method with modifications for using object serialization. Notice that after all instances have been written to the file, the FileStream Close method is invoked. This is necessary to complete the output process.

```
' Terminate Method
Public Shared Sub Terminate()

   Try
      ' Instantiate a FileStream--Append (Note True)
      Dim customerFile As New FileStream(cFile, FileMode.Append)
      Dim bfCustomer As BinaryFormatter = New BinaryFormatter()
      Dim cust As Customer
      ' Define string variables to hold object attributes
      Dim name, address, phoneno As String
      ' Loop over customers ArrayList -- getting and saving attributes
      For Each cust In customers
         '-----------------------------
         name = cust.GetName
         address = cust.GetAddress
         phoneno = cust.GetPhoneNo
         '-----------------------------
         ' Write (serialize) the object to the file
         bfCustomer.Serialize(customerFile, cust)

         Next
         customerFile.Close()
   Catch e As Exception
      Console.WriteLine(e.ToString)
   End Try
End Sub
```

Figure 13-31 CustomerDA Terminate method for object serialization

Like the previous example, the modifications required for object serialization were made to CustomerDA. Don't forget that you also had to add the serialization attribute to the Public Customer class. This clause implements the Serializable interface, which then permits instances of Customer to be stored in a file. You will continue to use the same testing program as in the previous section and the output is identical.

Hands-on Exercise 4

1. Locate **Ex04** in the Chap13\Examples folder on the book's CD. Create a folder named **Chap13\Exercises** in the work folder on your system, and then copy the **Ex04** folder to this folder. Double-click **DAclasses2.sln** in the Example4 folder to open the project with VB .NET. The project includes all the classes necessary for the project to run.
2. Note that CustomerDA will use drive A for the customerFile.txt file, unless you alter the file location at the beginning of CustomerDA. Insert a formatted disk in drive A and delete customerFile.txt on the disk if it exists.
3. Run the project and click the button to execute the testing program. Verify that the program output is similar to the output from Example3.
4. Delete **customerfile.txt**. Change the formatter to SOAP and rerun the testing software. Open **customerFile.txt** to view the results.

Using Relational Databases with VB .NET

This book assumes that you have had some exposure to Microsoft Access and that you can perform basic database operations. This section provides a quick overview of relational databases and the requisite VB .NET features for accessing and processing them. Relational databases are usually referred to as database management systems (DBMSs) because of all their query and management features.

A relational database provides tools for you to organize data into tables. In a DBMS, each column represents a field and each row represents a record. Figure 13-32 shows the table used in this example for customers. Customers are identified by their telephone number. A field used to uniquely identify a record is called a **primary key**. Primary keys are described and illustrated more thoroughly in Chapter 14.

In the following sections you will learn how to use SQL and how to access a relational database. First, you will develop a project to learn VB .NET concepts, and then you will use these concepts to design a CustomerDA class with methods that implement persistence with a database.

CustomerTable : Table

Name	Address	PhoneNo
Eleanor	Atlanta	123-4567
Mike	Boston	467-1234

Figure 13-32 Customer table

Structured Query Language

Structured Query Language (SQL) is a popular, standardized language used to manage and query relational databases. This section introduces SQL basics and illustrates four SQL statements. More complex database applications are discussed in Chapter 14. For the remainder of this chapter, only a few SQL statements will be used.

You previously learned that a DA class performs four basic tasks: retrieve a customer, store a customer, change a customer's data, and delete a customer. You also saw that these functions are implemented in the DA class using methods named Find, AddNew, Update, and Delete. When you use a relational database, these four methods invoke methods to execute SQL statements.

The Find method uses the SQL SELECT statement to retrieve a specific customer's record from the database. For all SQL statements in this text, SQL keywords appear in all capital letters to differentiate them from user-defined entries in the SQL statement. This is only a convention of the book, because SQL is not case sensitive. The SQL statement to retrieve Eleanor's record is:

```
SELECT Name, Address, PhoneNo
    FROM CustomerTable
    WHERE PhoneNo = '123-4567'
```

Following the SELECT keyword are the columns of the database tables the user wants to extract. Note that a database can have many tables and you can select columns from more than one table. In this case, the column names are Name, Address, and PhoneNo. Following the SQL keyword FROM are the database table names from which selected columns are to be extracted. In this case, there is only one table, CustomerTable, as you can verify by viewing the database. The WHERE clause provides a means of restricting the rows in a search based on the stated condition or conditions. In this case, the condition that follows the WHERE clause restricts the search to rows where the phone number equals 123-4567. Recall that phone number is a primary key and thus must be unique for a column in a table. In other words, this SELECT statement essentially searches for a particular individual. Notice that string values are enclosed by single quotes (`'`).

The AddNew method uses the SQL INSERT INTO statement to add a new customer's record to the database. For example, the following SQL statement will add a customer's record to CustomerTable in the database. A list of column names from CustomerTable follows the table name and must be enclosed in parentheses. If you have values to be inserted for every column in the table, the list and parentheses can be omitted, as shown in the second INSERT statement in the following code. The variables following the VALUES keyword contain the attribute values of the customer to be inserted into a row of CustomerTable. Literals are used for data values in this example; realistically, however, you will need to use variables in SQL statements instead of literals. In the next example, you will review the syntax for having variables in SQL statements.

```
INSERT INTO CustomerTable (Name, Address, PhoneNo)
    VALUES  ('William', 'Houston', '444-3333')
                          Or
```

```
INSERT INTO CustomerTable
    VALUES  ('William', 'Houston', '444-3333')
```

The Update method employs the SQL UPDATE statement to change the contents of one or more fields in a customer's record. The following SQL statement replaces the customer's name and address with the values contained in the variables:

```
UPDATE CustomerTable SET Name = name, Address = address
WHERE PhoneNo = '123-4567'
```

The Delete method executes the SQL DELETE statement, which specifies the key value of the customer to be deleted.

```
DELETE FROM CustomerTable WHERE PhoneNo = '756-4321'
```

Accessing a DBMS with VB .NET

Microsoft has a long history of technologies for accessing data. With VB .NET, you basically have the option of using ADO (Active-X Data Objects) or **ADO .NET**. ADO adheres to a more traditional client-server model that processes data from a data store on the server, all the while maintaining a constant connection to the server. By contrast, ADO .NET works in a disconnected mode, only connecting to the server when data is needed from the data store or updates back to the data store are required. The ADO approach results in data being kept and processed in a **recordset**, while ADO .NET relies on the concept of **datasets** as the basis for processing data. Actually, a dataset is just cached data, and again, VB .NET only connects to the data store when it requires data or needs to update data in the original data store. VB .NET also has a specialized class, DataReader, that is optimized for reading data from a data source.

VB .NET Database Access Classes

All the examples in this book use the Microsoft Access relational database software. Originally, VB .NET has two **managed providers** (also referred to as .NET providers) for accessing data: the **OleDb data provider**, designed for accessing Microsoft Access databases and other non-SQLServer data sources, and the **SQLServer data provider**, designed for accessing Microsoft SQLServer databases. The SQLServer data provider is optimized for accessing and processing SQLServer databases as it bypasses the OleDb layer and goes directly to the SQLServer. Microsoft has added a managed provider for Oracle, and more managed data providers are expected in the future for DBMS vendors. OleDb stands for "object linking and embedding for database." The emphasis with ADO .NET is to provide access to all data and not just relational data. A large part of ADO .NET is devoted to XML, destined to be a growing storage format type. In addition to these managed data providers, **object database connectivity** (**ODBC**) can be used to access most other databases. Also, the OleDb classes work with Microsoft SQLServer, although they are not as optimized for SQLServer as its managed provider, **SQLClient**. Thus, all the examples in this text will use the OleDb classes; only minimal syntax changes would be required for implementing with Microsoft SQLServer or using ODBC.

The namespaces for the two managed data providers for Microsoft Access and SQLServer are OleDb and SQLClient. The **`Imports`** statements for these namespaces are:

```
Imports System.Data
Imports System.Data.OleDb
Imports System.Data.SqlClient
```

Notice that the Data namespace should be included as well to provide the broadest capability for working with data. SQLClient will not be used in this text, but the **`Imports`** statement is included here to show you how to use it. Figure 13-33 illustrates the overall view of how VB .NET creates and processes datasets. The data source can be of any type, but in this text, it will always be Microsoft's Access database. A data connection links data sources to data adapters. Data adapters are the most complex of the classes. In Figure 13-33, note that the Select, Insert, Update, and Delete command boxes in the diagram correspond to the SELECT, INSERT, UPDATE, and DELETE SQL commands. In fact, they are designed as one-to-one matches to handle this functionality. These four data adapter commands are instance properties of the data adapter.

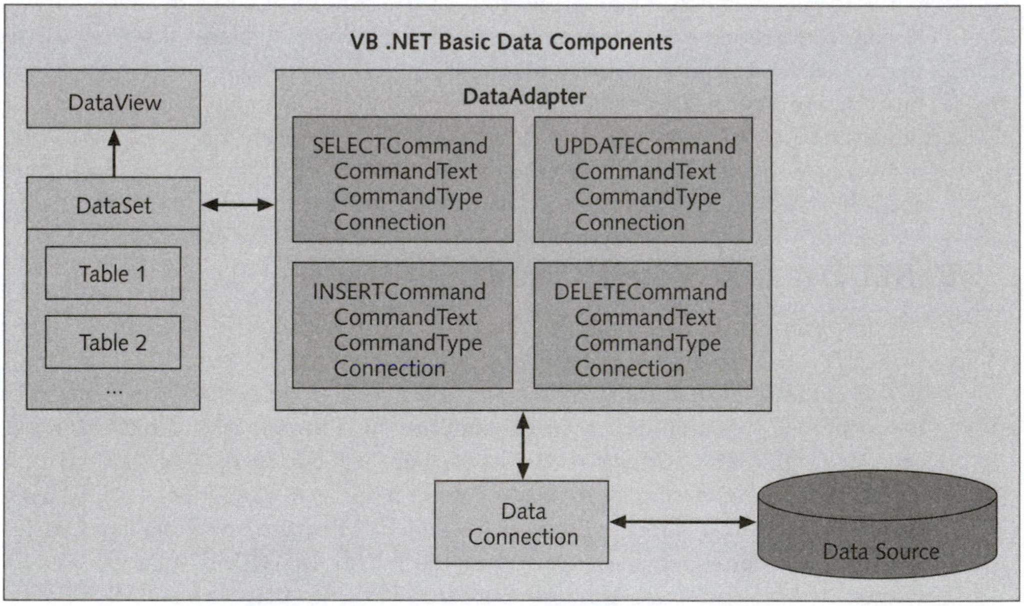

Figure 13-33 VB. NET basic data components

Each of the four commands of a data adapter—Select, Insert, Update, and Delete—requires a CommandText, CommandType, and Connection property to be set to appropriate values. You may not need all four of the commands in a given application. For example, a large percentage of applications extract, filter, enhance, and format information for the best possible presentation. In such a case, only the Select command would be needed because no maintenance of the original data source would be required.

At the left of the diagram, the DataSet and DataView are shown. A DataView can be created from any DataSet and have many useful capabilities, but it will not be extensively covered in this text. Notice that the DataSet is composed of tables. VB .NET creates the DataSet tables, consisting of rows and columns that can be processed like relational databases, regardless of the format of the data source. For example, data from an XML data source placed in a DataSet table would be transformed to a relational-type structure of rows and columns. Recall that DataSets are not continuously connected to their original data sources; rather, a connection is established when there is a need to get data from the data sources or when updates need to be written back to the data sources.

VB .NET and DBMS Example

The following project provides you with the basic concepts and code structures necessary to work with data from a relational database, including selecting, adding, updating, and deleting rows from a table. The GUI includes a data grid and four buttons: Add Record, Update Record, Delete Record, and Find.

Figures 13-34 through 13-39 show the GUI when the project is started and when the buttons are clicked in sequence from left to right. Figure 13-34 shows the project at startup. Figure 13-35 shows the result of clicking the Add Record button. Figure 13-36 shows the result of clicking the Update Record button—the address is changed from Houston to Chicago. Clicking the Delete button deletes the record containing William, as shown in Figure 13-37. An input box is used when the Find button is clicked to have users enter the phone number of the person they want to locate in the database. A message box displays the results of the search. Figures 13-38 and 13-39 verify that the Find function works correctly.

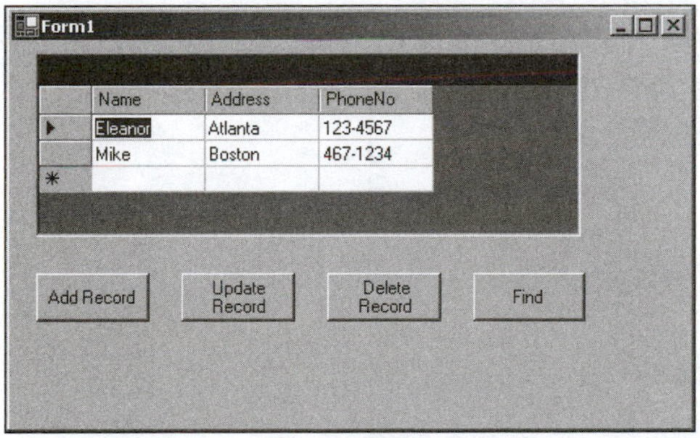

Figure 13-34 DataGrid form at startup

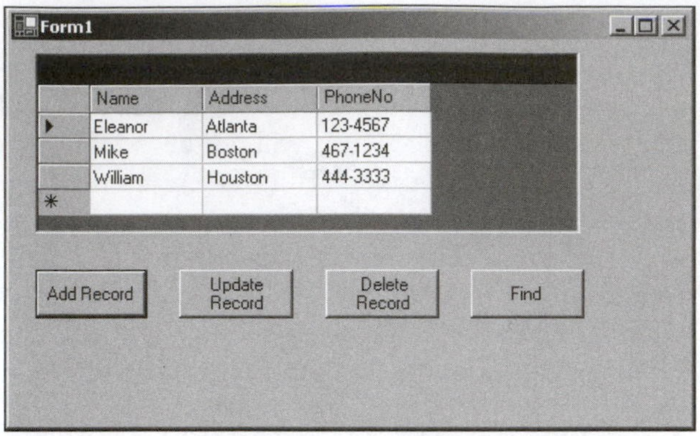

Figure 13-35 DataGrid form after adding a record to CustomerTable

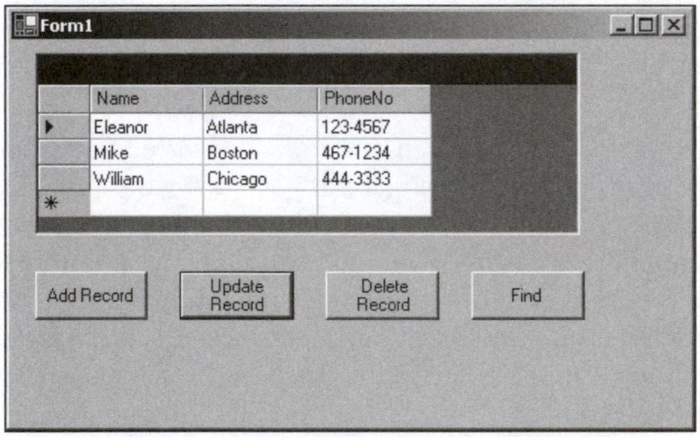

Figure 13-36 DataGrid form after updating a record in CustomerTable

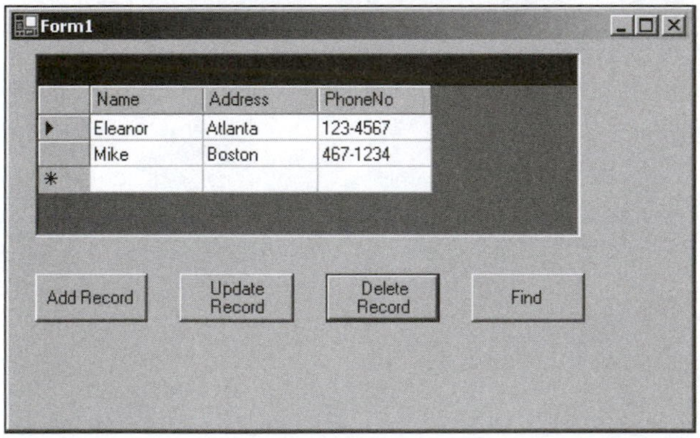

Figure 13-37 DataGrid form after deleting a record in CustomerTable

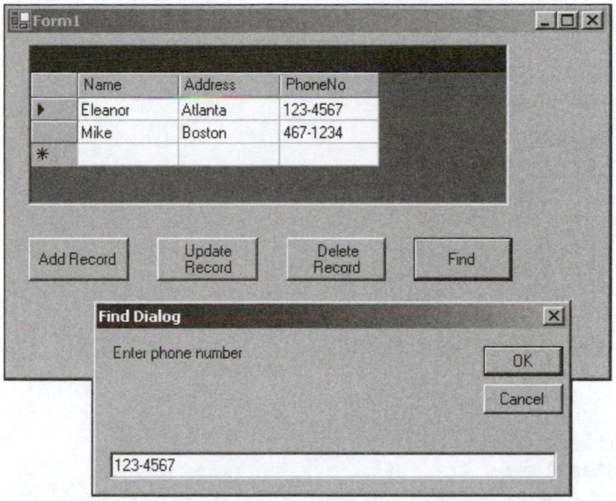

Figure 13-38 Finding a record in CustomerTable

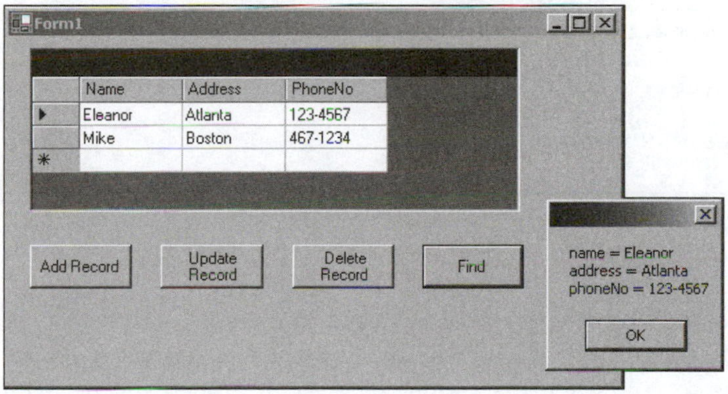

Figure 13-39 Display of the record found in CustomerTable

This database, named Customers.mdb, is in the bin folder of the application by default. A physical path can also be used. The database contains two records in CustomerTable. The code makes a connection to the database in only one place in the program, where it can be used by all the routines. As shown in Figure 13-40, it is placed directly under the Form header. Following this statement is a procedure that essentially returns all the rows and columns of the customer database and binds the dataset to a databound grid.

```
' Chapter 13--Example 5
' Introduces the basic database processing
Imports System.Data
```

```
Imports System.Data.OleDb
Imports System.Runtime.Serialization.Formatters.Soap
Public Class Form1
    Inherits System.Windows.Forms.Form

   Shared cnnCustomer As New _
        OleDbConnection("Provider=Microsoft.Jet.OLEDB.4.0; " & _
        "Data Source=customers.mdb")

   Private Sub ListRecords()
      ' Declare a new instance of a dataset
      Dim dsCustomer As New DataSet()

      ' Declare a string SQL statement
      Dim sql As String = "SELECT * FROM customerTable"

      ' Declare a new instance of an adapter
      ' Select command and connection command
      Dim adpCustomer As New _
         OleDbDataAdapter(sql, cnnCustomer)

      'Fill ds and bind to datagrid
      Try
         adpCustomer.Fill(dsCustomer, "custTable")
         DataGrid1.DataSource = _
         dsCustomer.Tables("custTable").DefaultView
      Catch ee As Exception
         MsgBox(ee.ToString)
      End Try
      dsCustomer = Nothing
   End Sub
```

Figure 13-40 Namespaces, connection, and list records code

The **`Imports`** statements provide the classes needed to connect to and process data from Customers.mdb. OleDb is used because the data source is a Microsoft Access database. There are two ways to connect to data sources—a connection string or a **data source name (DSN)**. You will use the connection string approach here for two reasons. First, you can see what provider is being used and where the data source exists. Second, connection via DSN requires using an ODBC driver to walk through a number of steps to define the data provider and the data source location. If the data source is on a server separate from your computer, you probably would not have the necessary data access privileges to connect the DSN, and would need to request the creation of the DSN from your computer center staff. However, using a DSN certainly makes the connection statement shorter, as only the DSN name needs to be assigned to the connection.

The first segment of the connection, `Provider=Microsoft.Jet.OLEDB.4.0`, is the provider—in this case, the provider for Access 2000 or later. The second segment of the connection specifies the location of the database, `Data Source=C:\Chap13\Exercises\customers.mdb`.

The ListRecords Sub procedure begins by creating an instance of a dataset followed by a string variable assigned to a SQL statement. The * wildcard in the SQL statement tells the code to select all columns from the table.

Recall from Figure 13-33 that a data adapter can have four different command type properties—Select, Insert, Update, and Delete. Further, each of the commands includes CommandText, CommandType, and Connection properties. The instance of a data adapter that is created and used in this example is an alternate format that eliminates the need to explicitly include the CommandText and CommandType properties. Furthermore, the Fill method handles the functions to open and close a connection, as described later in this section. Thus, the format shown in the following fragment reduced the number of lines of code:

```
Dim adpCustomer As New OleDbDataAdapter(sql, cnnCustomer)
```

For this format of the data adapter, the SQL string directly corresponds to the CommandText property, with the assumption that its CommandType is CommandType.Text. Note that if you wanted to use a stored procedure here, you only need to set the CommandType to CommandType.StoredProcedure and assign the name of the stored procedure to the CommandText property.

After the data adapter has been created, any tables in the dataset need to be populated. The adapter's Fill method accomplishes this task. Note also that the data connection was not explicitly opened anywhere in the code. The Fill method takes care of this task, opening and closing the connection if it has not been explicitly opened. The statements for filling the dataset and binding it to a data grid are placed in a Try Catch block in case of an error.

```
Try
   adpCustomer.Fill(dsCustomer, "custTable")
   DataGrid1.DataSource = dsCustomer.Tables("custTable").DefaultView
Catch e As Exception
   MsgBox(e.ToString)
End Try
```

13

The format of the Fill method requires the first parameter to be a dataset name, dsCustomer in this case. The second parameter is the name of the table in the dataset; in this case, the name is custTable. The name of the table is important, because the table is composed of collections of rows and columns that you may need to directly access. The statement following the Fill method binds a data grid with its default name, DataGrid1, to custTable of the dataset and assigns it to a default DataView. Actually, the default view is essentially equal to the DataSet table but provides the functionality available to a DataView.

When the program starts, one line of code in the Form_Load event is executed. It calls the ListRecords procedure, which selects all the records from CustomerTable and binds them to DataGrid1. The screen shown in Figure 13-35 appears when the program starts; the code is below.

```
Private Sub Form1_Load(ByVal sender As System.Object, _
         ByVal e As System.EventArgs) Handles MyBase.Load
```

```
        cnnConnection.Open()
        ListRecords()
    End Sub
```

The buttons that provide the functionality to add, update, and delete records could use code similar to that in the ListRecords procedure. However, this approach would result in a dataset, meaning that the query returns values for the dataset. Actions like insert, update, and delete do not return values; therefore, you should use the data adapter's InsertCommand, UpdateCommand, and DeleteCommand properties because they are designed to be used for action queries.

The code for the Add Record, Update Record, and Delete Record buttons is shown in Figure 13-41. The code for the Find button, which also returns a record if it finds one, is also included. Each of the Add, Update, and Delete procedures calls the ListRecords procedure to list the results of the changes.

```
Private Sub btnAdd_Click(ByVal sender As System.Object, _
    ByVal e As System.EventArgs) Handles btnAdd.Click

    ' Declare a string SQL statement
    Dim name As String = "William"
    Dim address As String = "Houston"
    Dim phoneno As String = "444-3333"
    Dim sql As String = "INSERT INTO customerTable " & _
        "VALUES ('" & name & "', '" & address & "'," & _
        "'" & phoneno & " ')"

    Dim adpCustomer As New OleDbDataAdapter()
    '   Assign Insert Commands and Execute
    Try
        adpCustomer.InsertCommand = New OleDbCommand(sql)
        adpCustomer.InsertCommand.Connection = cnnCustomer
        adpCustomer.InsertCommand.ExecuteNonQuery()

        ListRecords()  ' Invoke ListRecords method
    Catch ee As Exception
        MsgBox(ee.ToString)
    End Try
End Sub

Private Sub btnUpdate_Click(ByVal sender As System.Object, _
    ByVal e As System.EventArgs) Handles btnUpdate.Click

    ' Declare a string SQL statement
    Dim sql As String = "UPDATE customerTable SET Address =" & _
        "'Chicago' WHERE PhoneNo = '444-3333'"

    Dim adpCustomer As New OleDbDataAdapter()
    '   Assign Update Commands and Execute
    Try
        adpCustomer.UpdateCommand = New OleDbCommand(sql)
        adpCustomer.UpdateCommand.Connection = cnnCustomer
        adpCustomer.UpdateCommand.ExecuteNonQuery()
```

```
            ListRecords()  ' Invoke ListRecords method
        Catch ee As Exception
            MsgBox(ee.ToString)
        End Try
    End Sub

    Private Sub btnDelete_Click(ByVal sender As System.Object, _
        ByVal e As System.EventArgs) Handles btnDelete.Click

        ' Declare a string SQL statement
        Dim sql As String = "DELETE FROM customerTable WHERE " & _
            "PhoneNo = '444-3333'"
        Dim adpCustomer As New OleDbDataAdapter()
        '   Assign Delete Command and Execute
        Try
            adpCustomer.DeleteCommand = New OleDbCommand(sql)
            adpCustomer.DeleteCommand.Connection = cnnCustomer
            adpCustomer.DeleteCommand.ExecuteNonQuery()

            ListRecords()  ' Invoke ListRecords method
        Catch ee As Exception
            MsgBox(ee.ToString)
        End Try

    End Sub

    Private Sub btnFind_Click(ByVal sender As System.Object, _
        ByVal e As System.EventArgs) Handles btnFind.Click
        Dim sqlQuery As String
        Dim custRow As DataRow
        Dim dsCustomer As New DataSet()
        dsCustomer.Clear()
        Dim key As String
        key = InputBox("Enter phone number", "Find Dialog", "")
        Try

            sqlQuery = "SELECT Name, Address, PhoneNo " & _
                "FROM CustomerTable " & _
                "WHERE phoneNo = '" & key & "'"
            Dim adpCustomer As New _
               OleDbDataAdapter(sqlQuery, cnnCustomer)
            adpCustomer.Fill(dsCustomer, "CustTable")

            If dsCustomer.Tables("CustTable").Rows.Count > 0 Then
                ' Found Customer
               Dim name, address, phoneNo, display As String
               name = _
                 dsCustomer.Tables("CustTable").Rows(0).Item("Name")
               address = _
                 (dsCustomer.Tables("CustTable").Rows(0).Item("address"))
               phoneNo = _
                 dsCustomer.Tables("CustTable").Rows(0).Item("phoneNo")
                display = "name = " & name & vbCrLf & _
                      "address = " & address & vbCrLf & _
                      "phoneNo = " & phoneNo
                MessageBox.Show(display)
            Else
```

13

```
                ' Did not find customer
                MsgBox("Didn't Find Customer")
            End If
        Catch ee As OleDb.OleDbException
            MessageBox.Show(ee.ToString)
        End Try
        dsCustomer = Nothing
    End Sub

    Private Sub Form1_Load(ByVal sender As System.Object, _
        ByVal e As System.EventArgs) Handles MyBase.Load

        cnnCustomer.Open()
        ListRecords()   ' Invoke ListRecords method
    End Sub

    Private Sub Form1_Closing(ByVal sender As Object, _
        ByVal e As System.ComponentModel.CancelEventArgs) _
            Handles MyBase.Closing

        If cnnCustomer.State.Open Then
            cnnCustomer.Close()
            cnnCustomer = Nothing
        End If
    End Sub
```

Figure 13-41 Code for the remaining buttons in the database

The code for adding, deleting, and updating are very similar. Basically, an SQL statement is created to accomplish the desired function. Then, an instance of a data adapter is created, and an instance of one of its command properties—InsertCommand, UpdateCommand, or DeleteCommand, depending on the function—is created using an SQL statement. Next, the command's Connection property is set to a connection. Finally, the adapter's ExecuteNonQuery method is invoked to execute the query. The three statements in the following code are from the Delete procedure, and should illustrate these concepts. The Insert and Update procedures contain the same statements, except the data adapter's command properties are set to InsertCommand and UpdateCommand, respectively.

```
adpCustomer.DeleteCommand = New OleDbCommand(sql)
adpCustomer.DeleteCommand.Connection = cnnCustomer
adpCustomer.DeleteCommand.ExecuteNonQuery()
```

Note that the data in the procedures for adding, updating, and deleting records are hard-coded. However, the Add procedure and the Find procedure include some code that needs further explanation. In the Add procedure, an SQL statement uses variables instead of hard-coded entries in the WHERE clause. SQL requires the final result of columns and fields of type text or character to be enclosed by single quotes. This accounts for the strange syntax of the WHERE clause of the SQL statement in the following code:

```
Dim sql As String = "INSERT INTO customerTable " & _
   "VALUES ('" & name & "', '" & address & "'," & _
   "'" & phoneno & " ')"
```

The general syntax `'" & var1 & "'`, where `var1` is a variable, uses the single-double quote format because the column data type is text and the text value must be enclosed in single quotes. The syntax `"& var1 &"` is used for numeric variables. VB .NET adds the space between the double quotes and the ampersand (&).

The Find procedure uses an input box to request a phone number from the user to see if there is a match in the dataset. If the record is found in the dataset, then the data adapter's Fill method saves it in a dataset table. An If statement is used to determine whether any rows (records) exist in the dataset, as shown in the following code. The remaining lines retrieve the name, address, and phone number from the current row that has been found. Finally, the customer information, if found, is displayed in a message box.

```
If dsCustomer.Tables("CustTable").Rows.Count > 0 Then
    ' Found Customer
    Dim name, address, phoneNo, display As String
    name = _
      dsCustomer.Tables("CustTable").Rows(0).Item("Name")
    address = _
      (dsCustomer.Tables("CustTable").Rows(0).Item("address"))
    phoneNo = _
      dsCustomer.Tables("CustTable").Rows(0).Item("phoneNo")
    display = "name = " & name & vbCrLf & _
                "address = " & address & vbCrLf & _
                "phoneNo = " & phoneNo
    MessageBox.Show(display)
Else
    ' Did not find customer
    MsgBox("Didn't Find Customer")
End If
```


Hands-on Exercise 5

1. Locate **Ex05** in the Chap13\Examples folder in the student data files. Create a folder named **Chap13\Exercises** in the work folder on your system, and then copy the **Ex05** folder to this folder. Copy the **Customers.mdb** database from the Chap13\Examples folder on the CD to the Chap13\Exercises folder on your computer. This should match the connection object's data source location.

2. Double-click the **DBbasics.sln** file in the Example5 folder to open the application. Run the application and, in order, click the **Add Record**, **Update Record**, **Delete Record**, and **Find** buttons. After clicking the Find button, enter **123-4567** for the phone number. You should find the first customer in the table.

Implementing Object Persistence with a Database

The previous examples of persistence—sequential files and object serialization—had the Initialize method read all the customers and store their references into an ArrayList. Then the various methods manipulated the customer instances using the ArrayList. When processing was complete, the Terminate method wrote the customers back to a file.

Using a relational database calls for a different approach. The Initialize method establishes a connection to the database, the processing methods Find, AddNew, Update, Delete, and GetAll access the database directly, and the Terminate method closes the database connection to release system resources.

In addition to importing the collections namespace for ArrayList, the CustomerDA class for a relational database imports the Data and OleDb namespaces.

```
Imports System.Data
Imports System.Data.OleDb
Imports System.Collections
```

Like the previous CustomerDA classes you saw, this one also has variables declared with class scope. The first variable declares a connection and the second variable is an ArrayList reference variable named customers, which contains references to all the customer instances. Then comes the declaration of a reference variable, aCustomer, to reference Customer. The last statement declares three variables to be used for customer attribute values.

```
Public Class CustomerDA
    ' Declare a connection
    Shared cnnCustomer As New _
        OleDbConnection("Provider=Microsoft.Jet.OLEDB.4.0; " & _
        "Data Source=C:customers.mdb")
    ' Declare a new ArrayList instance
    Shared customers As New ArrayList()
    ' Declare an instance of Customer
    Shared aCustomer As Customer
    ' Declare variables for Customer attribute value
    Shared name, address, phoneno As String
```

The Initialize Method

The purpose of the Initialize method in this example is to create a connection instance that links to the database. The connection's Open method can throw an exception; therefore, the statements that invoke this method are placed in a Try block. The appropriate Catch blocks follow. The complete Initialize method is shown in Figure 13-42.

```
' Initialize Method
Public Shared Sub Initialize()
```

```
   Try
      ' Try to open the connection
      cnnCustomer.Open()
   Catch e As Exception
      Console.WriteLine(e.ToString)
   End Try
End Sub
```

Figure 13-42 CustomerDA Initialize method for a relational database

The Terminate Method

The Terminate method for a relational database is considerably simpler and shorter than in the previous implementations. Here, the Terminate method simply invokes the Close method for the connection instance. This code is placed within a Try block because an exception will be thrown if an error is detected. The Terminate method is shown in Figure 13-43.

```
' Terminate Method
Public Shared Sub Terminate()

   Try
      cnnCustomer.Close()
      cnnCustomer = Nothing
   Catch e As Exception
      Console.WriteLine(e.Message.ToString)
   End Try
End Sub
```

Figure 13-43 CustomerDA Terminate method for a relational database

The Find Method

The logic of the Find method is straightforward. The data adapter uses its SELECT command and connection to retrieve a specific customer's attribute values from the database. These values are returned within an instance of a dataset that is populated via the data adapter. If the desired customer is found, attribute values are saved to variables from which a customer instance is then created and returned to the invoking method. If the desired customer is not found, the method throws a NotFoundException. The Find method is shown in Figure 13-44.

```
' Find Method--Throws NotFoundException if Not Found
Public Shared Function Find(ByVal key As String) As Customer
   aCustomer = Nothing
   Dim dsCustomer As New DataSet()
      Try
```

```
            ' Define the SQL statement using the phoneno key
            Dim sqlQuery As String = "SELECT Name, Address, PhoneNo " & _
               "FROM CustomerTable WHERE phoneNo = '" & key & "'"
            Dim adpCustomer As New _
               OleDbDataAdapter(sqlQuery, cnnCustomer)
            adpCustomer.Fill(dsCustomer, "CustTable")
            If dsCustomer.Tables("CustTable").Rows.Count > 0 Then
               Dim custRow As DataRow
               custRow = dsCustomer.Tables("custTable").Rows(0)
               name = custRow.Item("Name")
               address = custRow.Item("address")
               phoneno = custRow.Item("phoneno")
               aCustomer = New Customer(name, address, phoneno)
            Else
               Throw New NotFoundException("Not Found")
            End If
            dsCustomer = Nothing
         Catch e As OleDb.OleDbException
            Console.WriteLine(e.Message.ToString)
         End Try
         Return aCustomer
End Function
```

Figure 13-44 CustomerDA Find method for a relational database

The first statement initializes a customer reference variable named aCustomer to a null value. Next, an instance of a dataset is created, followed by an SQL SELECT statement being assigned to a string variable. The form of the data adapter used here requires two parameters: The first is an SQL statement or the name of a stored procedure, and the second is the connection object. The data adapter then takes care of linking to the database and executing the SQL statement. The data adapter's Fill method populates an instance of a dataset named dsCustomer. Recall that a DataSet is a disconnected data cache that consists of tables, and the Fill method allows you to assign a table name for the data it is about to receive.

An If statement is used to see if the dataset's table contains any rows of data; if so, then the customer was found. If the customer was found, then the row values are assigned to variables holding the customer's name, address, and phone number. These variables are then used to create a customer instance. However, if the customer is not found, a NotFoundException is created and thrown. The last line of the method returns the customer reference.

The AddNew Method

Invoke this method to add a customer to the system by executing an SQL INSERT statement. The method is shown in Figure 13-45. The method first invokes the Customer accessor methods to obtain the attribute values, then invokes the Find method to see if this customer already exists. If it does, a DuplicateException is thrown. The statement that invokes the Find method is placed in a Try block, and if the potentially new customer is not currently in the database, a

NotFoundException is thrown. The Catch block for the NotFoundException contains the statements to add the customer to the database because the customer does not currently exist in the database. In the case of adding, updating, or deleting in a database, no data is returned from the query; thus, no dataset is needed. Therefore, the AddNew, Update, and Delete methods will use the data adapter's InsertCommand, UpdateCommand, and DeleteCommand properties, respectively. For the AddNew method, the data adapter's InsertCommand property is set to an SQL INSERT string, assigned as a connection, and then the ExecuteNonQuery method takes care of executing the SQL statement.

```
' AddNew Method--Throws DuplicateException if exists
Public Shared Sub AddNew(ByVal aCustomer As Customer)
   ' Get customer information
   name = aCustomer.GetName
   address = aCustomer.GetAddress
   phoneno = aCustomer.GetPhoneNo
   ' Declare a string SQL statement
   Dim sqlInsert As String = "INSERT INTO customerTable " & _
      "VALUES ('" & name & "', '" & address & "'," & _
      "'" & phoneno & " ')"

   Try
      Dim c As Customer = Customer.Find(phoneno)
      Throw New DuplicateException(" Customer Exists ")
   Catch e As NotFoundException
      Try
         Dim adpcustomer As New OleDbDataAdapter()
         adpcustomer.InsertCommand = New OleDbCommand(sqlInsert)
         adpcustomer.InsertCommand.Connection = cnnCustomer
         adpcustomer.InsertCommand.ExecuteNonQuery()
      Catch sqle As OleDb.OleDbException
         Console.WriteLine(sqle.ToString)
      End Try
   End Try
End Sub
```

Figure 13-45 CustomerDA AddNew method for a relational database

13

The Update Method

The Update method for a relational database first invokes accessor methods to retrieve a customer's attribute values and then invokes the Find method to ensure that the customer record exists. If the customer is not found, the Find method throws a NotFoundException and the Update method rethrows it to the invoking client method. If the customer's record is found, then the data adapter's ExecuteNonQuery method uses its UPDATE command to update the rows of the table. The code is shown in Figure 13-46.

```
' Update Method
Public Shared Sub Update(ByVal aCustomer As Customer)
' Get Customer information
   name = aCustomer.GetName
   address = aCustomer.GetAddress
   phoneno = aCustomer.GetPhoneNo
   Dim sqlUpdate As String = "Update CustomerTable" & _
      " SET Name = '" & name & "', Address = '" & address & "'," & _
      " WHERE PhoneNo = '" & phoneno & "'"
   Try
      Dim c As Customer = Customer.Find(phoneno)
      Dim adpcustomer As New OleDbDataAdapter()
      adpcustomer.UpdateCommand = New OleDbCommand(sqlUpdate)
      adpcustomer.UpdateCommand.Connection = cnnCustomer
      adpcustomer.UpdateCommand.ExecuteNonQuery()
   Catch e As Exception
      Console.WriteLine(e.ToString)
   End Try
End Sub
```

Figure 13-46 CustomerDA Update method for a relational database

The Delete Method

The Delete method for a relational database is similar to the Update method. First, the Customer accessor method, GetPhoneNo, is invoked to get the customer's phone number. Then the Find method is invoked to see if the customer record for this phone number exists. If not, a NotFoundException is thrown. If the customer record is found, then the data adapter's ExecuteNonQuery method uses its DELETE command and its Fill method to delete the record from the database. The Delete method code is shown in Figure 13-47.

```
'Delete Method--Throws NotFoundException if not found
Public Shared Sub Delete(ByVal aCustomer As Customer)
   Dim phoneno, sqlDelete As String
   phoneno = aCustomer.GetPhoneNo
   sqlDelete = "DELETE FROM CustomerTable " & _
      "WHERE PhoneNo = '" & phoneno & "'"
   Try
      Dim c As Customer = Customer.Find(phoneno)
      Dim adpCustomer As New OleDbDataAdapter()
      adpCustomer.DeleteCommand = New OleDbCommand(sqlDelete)
      adpCustomer.DeleteCommand.Connection = cnnCustomer
      adpCustomer.DeleteCommand.ExecuteNonQuery()
   Catch e As Exception
      Console.WriteLine(e.ToString)
   End Try
End Sub
```

Figure 13-47 CustomerDA Delete method for a relational database

The GetAll Method

The GetAll method for a relational database illustrates how to work with a result set instance that contains multiple rows of data. The GetAll method is shown in Figure 13-48. Like the Find method, GetAll uses a data adapter's SELECT command and Fill method to execute a SQL SELECT statement. The SQL statement for GetAll retrieves the attributes for all the customers in CustomerTable of the dsCustomer dataset. If there are any rows in the dataset, then the code loops over the collection one row at a time. Each iteration retrieves a customer's name, address, and phone number, creates a customer instance, and adds the customer's reference to an ArrayList. After retrieving all rows of the result set, the ArrayList reference named customers is returned to the invoking method.

```
' GetAll Method
Public Shared Function GetAll() As ArrayList
   Dim dsCustomer As New DataSet()
   Dim sqlQuery As String = "SELECT Name, Address, PhoneNo " & _
      "FROM CustomerTable"
   Try
      Dim adpCustomer As New _
         OleDbDataAdapter(sqlQuery, cnnCustomer)
      adpCustomer.Fill(dsCustomer, "CustTable")
      If dsCustomer.Tables("CustTable").Rows.Count > 0 Then
         Dim dsRow As DataRow
         'Clear the array list customers.clear()
         For Each dsRow In dsCustomer.Tables("CustTable").Rows
            name = dsRow("Name")
            address = dsRow("Address")
            phoneno = dsRow("PhoneNo")
            Dim aCustomer As New _
               Customer(name, address, phoneno)
            customers.Add(aCustomer)
         Next
      Else
      ' No records in database
      End If
      dsCustomer = Nothing
   Catch e As Exception
      Console.WriteLine(e.ToString)
   End Try
   Return customers
End Function
```

Figure 13-48 CustomerDA GetAll method for a relational database

13

Testing CustomerDA for a Database Implementation

You can test the CustomerDA class for the relational database using the same customer and testing programs you used in the previous examples. However, CustomerTable already includes Eleanor and Mike as customers, so you may want to use different customers for firstCustomer and secondCustomer—perhaps as follows:

```
Dim firstCustomer As New Customer("Heather", "Miami", "321-7654")
Dim secondCustomer As New Customer("George", "Oakland", "444-3333")
```

The testing program alters the address for the first customer (Heather, in this case) and deletes the second customer (George, in this case). Only the second customer in the database is deleted by the testing program. Thus, to return the database to its original state, you need to delete the added record. The output should be similar to the previous object persistence examples; verify that everything works correctly.

Hands-on Exercise 6

1. Locate **Ex06** in the Chap13\Examples folder in the student data files. Create a folder named **Chap13\Exercises** in the work folder on your system, and then copy the **Ex06** folder to this folder.
2. Double-click **dbDAclasses1.sln** in the Example6 folder to open the application. Run the testing code to verify that it works correctly.

Chapter Summary

- Object persistence means that you store instance data for future retrieval. You can achieve persistence by storing either attribute values or entire instances.
- You design a data access (DA) class to provide methods that store and retrieve data to make instances of PD classes persistent.
- You generally write a separate DA class for each PD class. You communicate with the DA class by invoking its methods from the corresponding PD class. Classes that require data storage and retrieval services must invoke PD methods, which in turn invoke DA methods. This restriction is imposed to isolate the DA class from all but its matching PD class.
- A DA class performs four basic tasks: retrieve, store, change, and delete. These tasks are implemented in the DA class using methods named Find, AddNew, Update, and Delete. The DA class also has a GetAll method that returns an ArrayList referencing all PD instances, plus Initialize and Terminate methods.

- VB .NET's stream approach to I/O views data input and output as simply a flow of bytes, or datastream. This abstraction permits you to focus on data without dealing with physical I/O devices. VB .NET contains classes with methods to input and output data to the various types of files.
- You achieved persistence in this chapter using sequential files, object serialization, and relational databases. In each case, however, only the DA class was aware of the specific storage technique being used. The same PD and testing program classes were used for each implementation.
- A relational database permits you to organize your data into tables. Each column represents a field and each row represents a record. Structured Query Language (SQL) is a popular, standard language used to access relational databases. VB .NET contains classes with methods to invoke when working with relational databases.

Key Terms

ADO .NET
attribute storage
data source name (DSN)
database
dataset
`FileStream`
managed provider
object database connectivity (ODBC)
object persistence
object serialization
object storage
OleDb data provider
primary key
recordset
relational database
sequential file
SQLClient
SQLServer data provider
stream
`StreamReader`
`StreamWriter`
Structured Query Language (SQL)
System.IO
`TextReader`
`TextWriter`

13

Review Questions

1. SQL is a ________________.
   a. DBMS
   b. keyword
   c. class
   d. language

2. OleDb is a provider for ________________.
   a. IBM DB2
   b. Microsoft Access
   c. Microsoft SQLServer
   d. b and c
3. SQLClient is a provider for ________________.
   a. IBM DB2
   b. Microsoft Access
   c. Microsoft SQLServer
   d. b and c
4. The namespace that contains the classes needed for database access is ________________.
   a. System.Data.OleDb
   b. System.Runtime.Serialization
   c. System.Data.SQL
   d. System.Runtime.Formatters
5. The OleDbDataAdapter class contains which command that matches with a corresponding SQL statement?
   a. SELECT
   b. UPDATE
   c. DELETE
   d. INSERT
   e. all of the above
6. A relational database table always has ________________.
   a. subtables
   b. rows and columns
   c. a key field
   d. a relationship with other tables
7. The SQL keyword ________________ is used to retrieve data from a relational database.
   a. DELETE
   b. INSERT
   c. FIND
   d. SELECT

8. The DA classes are hidden from ________________.
   a. GUI classes
   b. PD classes
   c. GUI and PD classes
   d. all but PD classes
9. When data needs to be obtained from a data source, the data adapter's ________________ method selects the data and places it in a ________________.
   a. Select, Place
   b. Get, recordset
   c. Fetch, Dataset
   d. Fill, Dataset
10. VB .NET treats stream I/O ________________.
    a. just like other languages do
    b. as a stream of bytes
    c. as structured records
    d. dependent upon the physical device
11. Object serialization is a(n) ________________.
    a. RDBMS tool for storing attributes
    b. VB .NET tool for storing object instances
    c. class
    d. language
12. ODBC is a ________________.
    a. DBMS
    b. keyword
    c. protocol
    d. language
13. A primary key is ________________.
    a. used to identify a record
    b. a special field to sequence data
    c. an attribute of a DBMS instance
    d. part of SQL

14. The Customer class in this chapter ______________.

a. has DA methods

b. is the only class permitted to invoke CustomerDA methods

c. is a PD class

d. all of the above

15. Which of the following statements is true about a dataset?

a. It is populated with an adapter's Fill method.

b. It consists of one or more relational-type tables.

c. You can reference the rows and columns of a table in a dataset.

d. All of the above are true.

16. A NotFoundException is ______________.

a. a supplied Exception class

b. a member of the VB .NET exception namespace

c. seldom used

d. none of the above

17. OleDb.OleDbException is ______________.

a. a supplied Exception class

b. a member of the VB .NET exception namespace

c. seldom used

d. none of the above

Discussion Questions

1. What are the advantages and disadvantages of removing the DA methods from the CustomerPD class and permitting the GUI applications to invoke them directly?
2. Do you think you can apply the Customer class from the object serialization example in Hands-on Exercise 4 to the other exercises? Why or why not?
3. Why do you think the GetAll method is not used as a surrogate for Find? In other words, why can you not remove the Find method and instead invoke the GetAll method, then search the ArrayList for the customer you want? Under what conditions might you want to take this approach?

4. This chapter did not address the use of object databases. But based on what you know about databases, describe how you think using an object database could differ from using a relational database.
5. Which of the implementations described in this chapter would be the best for Bradshaw Marina? Why?

Projects

The Customer class used in the examples in this chapter contained three attributes: name, address, and phone number. Assume that Bradshaw Marina has decided to track each customer's e-mail address. Use the database approach for this project.

1. Use Microsoft Access to add this new attribute to the database table. You may want to create another database file.
2. Make the necessary modifications to the Customer and CustomerDA classes and testing script used in the relational database example to accommodate this new attribute.
   a. In the Customer class, add the e-mail attribute, write getter and setter methods, and update the constructor and TellAboutSelf methods.
   b. In the testing program, modify the statements that instantiate Customer to include e-mail as an argument to the constructor.
   c. In the CustomerDA class, modify the AddNew, Find, and Update methods to accommodate the new attribute.
3. Test your modifications.

CHAPTER

14

Creating More Complex Database Applications

In this chapter you will:

- Implement a one-to-one association in a database application
- Implement a one-to-many association in a database application
- Apply parent-child (hierarchical) dataset relationships
- Implement an association class in a database application

In the previous chapter you learned several techniques for implementing object persistence. You were introduced to data access (DA) classes and their methods, and used these to create applications to read and write object attributes to sequential files using the VB .NET `StreamReader` and `StreamWriter` classes. You learned about object serialization and how to use it to read and write entire objects via VB .NET's Stream class and its binary and XML formatters. You also learned how to develop applications that access information in a relational database using DA methods and SQL statements to select, insert, update, and delete rows within a relational table. The select, insert, update, and delete capabilities were implemented using the VB .NET SelectCommand, InsertCommand, UpdateCommand, and DeleteCommand properties of OleDbDataAdapter.

The concepts you learned in the previous chapter provide a good foundation for the development of more complex database applications. However, you worked with a relational database that contained only a single table, which is unusual. In fact, relational databases often include many, even thousands of tables. One advantage of a relational database over other forms of persistence is that it can easily combine information from different tables to answer business questions. For example, while it is helpful to produce a list of all customers in a database or to retrieve the name and address of a customer with a particular phone number, it is more helpful to produce lists of all customers and the state registration numbers of the boats they own.

In this chapter you will learn to develop database applications that involve multiple tables. First, you will learn how to implement the one-to-one relationship between Customer and Boat on the Bradshaw Marina class diagram. Next, you will see how to implement the one-to-many relationships between Dock and Slip. Finally, you will learn to implement the more complex Lease application.

This chapter includes both Hands-on Exercises at the end of each section to test the concepts you've learned and steps within sections to open database tables in Microsoft Access and examine their data and relationships.

IMPLEMENTING A ONE-TO-ONE ASSOCIATION IN A DATABASE APPLICATION

In Chapter 9 you reviewed the Bradshaw Marina class diagram, which is reproduced in Figure 14-1 and shows the problem domain classes the Bradshaw system needs. Recall that the relationships between Customer and Boat are mandatory one-to-one relationships in both directions. That is, a customer always owns exactly one boat and a boat is always owned by exactly one customer.

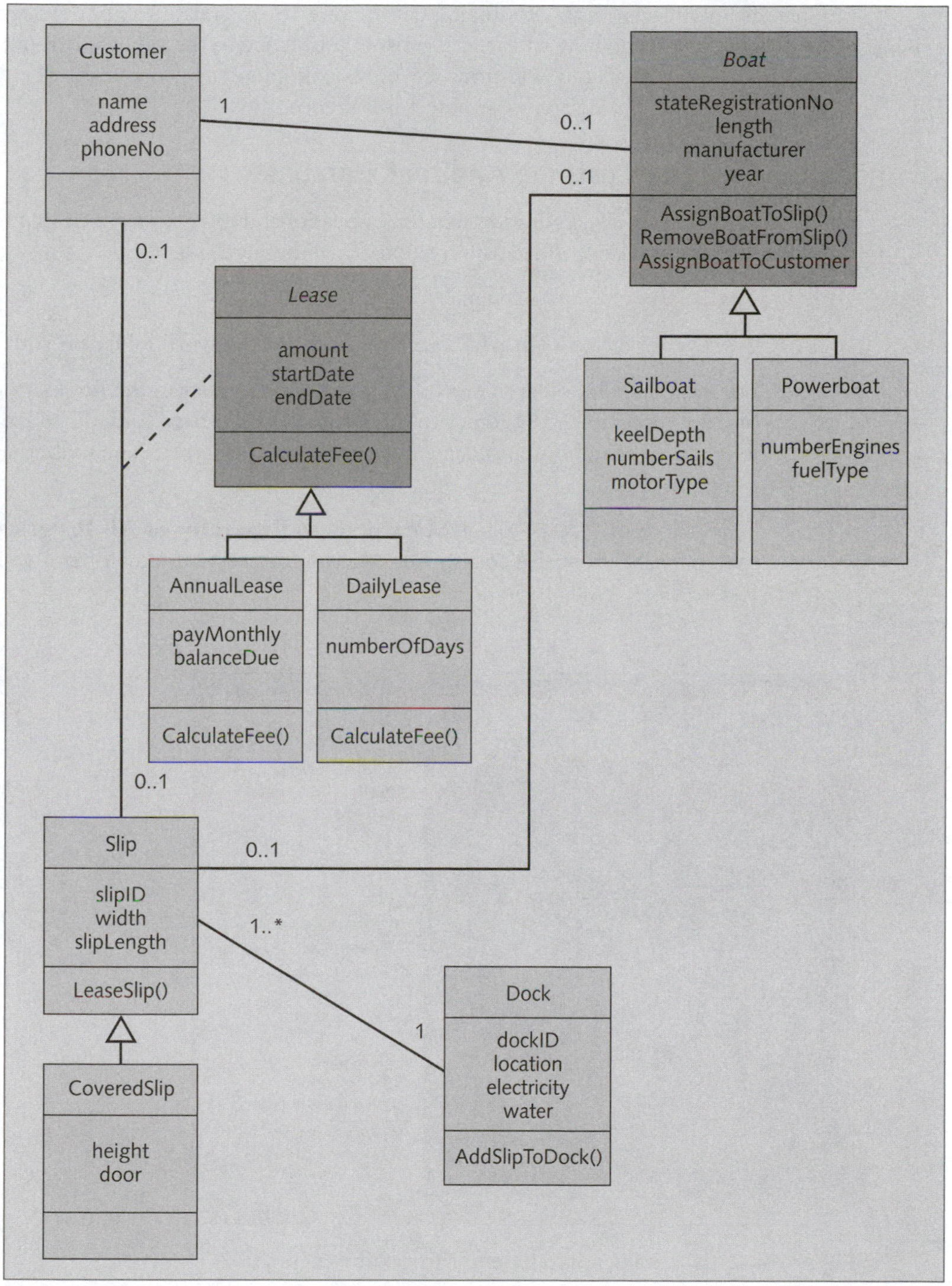

Figure 14-1 The Bradshaw Marina class diagram

In Chapter 9 you learned how to implement the one-to-one relationships between instances of these two classes, and how to navigate from one instance to the other when object persistence was not required. You will now see how to implement this one-to-one association using a relational database to achieve object persistence.

Understanding the CustomerAndBoat Database

To develop the VB .NET application that uses a relational database, you must first understand the structure of the relational database tables that will be involved.

To examine the structures of these tables:

1. If necessary, create a Chap14\Exercises folder in the work folder on your system.
2. Locate the **Ex01** folder in the Chap14\Examples folder in the book's student data files and copy the **Ex01** folder to the **Chap14\Exercises** folder. The Example1 folder contains a bin subfolder, and CustomerAndBoatDatabase.mdb is contained in the bin folder.
3. Start Microsoft Access. (Click **Start**, point to **Programs** or **All Programs**, and then click **Microsoft Access**.) The Microsoft Access window opens, as shown in Figure 14-2.

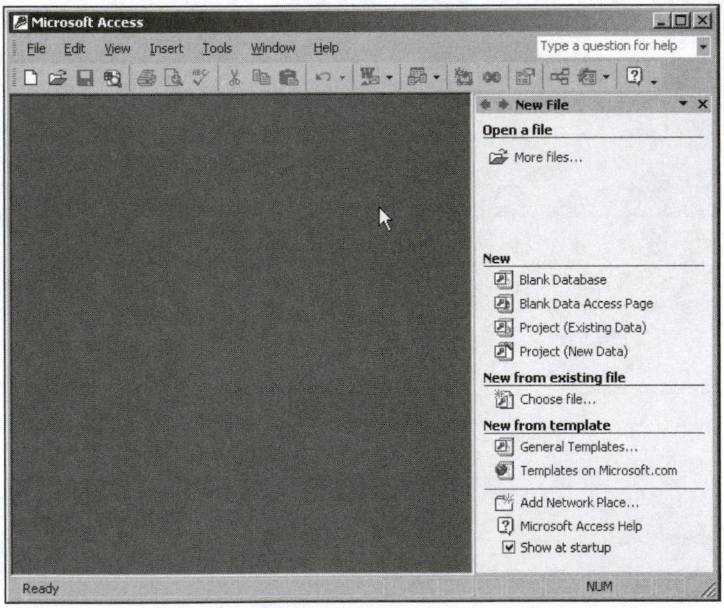

Figure 14-2 Opening a database in Microsoft Access 2002

4. Click **More files** in the Open a file section of the New File task pane. In the Open dialog box, navigate to the **Chap14\Exercises\Ex01\Example1\bin** folder in your work folder, and then double-click **CustomerAndBoatDatabase.mdb**. The CustomerAndBoatDatabase window opens. This window lists the tables in the database—BoatTable and CustomerTable—as shown in Figure 14-3.

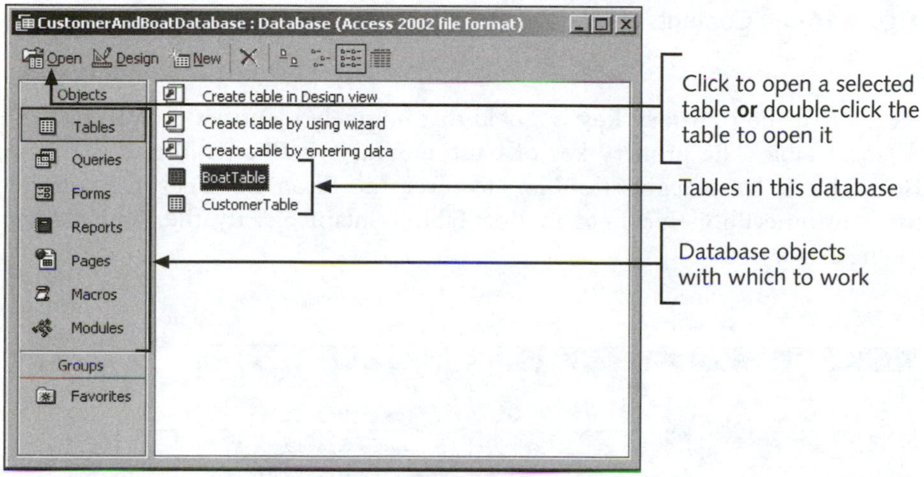

Figure 14-3 The CustomerAndBoatDatabase window

5. Double-click **BoatTable** to view its contents. Notice that this table contains five fields (or columns)—StateRegistrationNo, BoatLength, Manufacturer, Year, and CustomerPhoneNo—as shown in Figure 14-4.

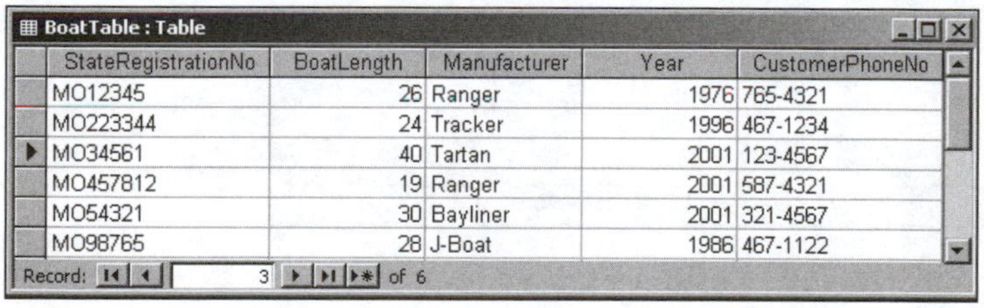

BoatTable : Table

StateRegistrationNo	BoatLength	Manufacturer	Year	CustomerPhoneNo
MO12345	26	Ranger	1976	765-4321
MO223344	24	Tracker	1996	467-1234
MO34561	40	Tartan	2001	123-4567
MO457812	19	Ranger	2001	587-4321
MO54321	30	Bayliner	2001	321-4567
MO98765	28	J-Boat	1986	467-1122

Record: 3 of 6

Figure 14-4 Contents of BoatTable

6. Close the BoatTable : Table window. In the database window, double-click **CustomerTable** to view its contents. Notice that this table includes three fields—Name, Address, PhoneNo—as shown in Figure 14-5.

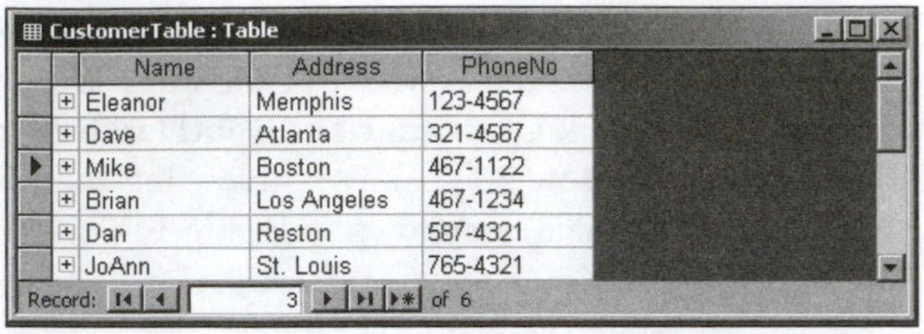

Name	Address	PhoneNo
Eleanor	Memphis	123-4567
Dave	Atlanta	321-4567
Mike	Boston	467-1122
Brian	Los Angeles	467-1234
Dan	Reston	587-4321
JoAnn	St. Louis	765-4321

Figure 14-5 Contents of CustomerTable

Recall that the **primary key** is a field that uniquely identifies each record in a relational database table. The primary key of CustomerTable is PhoneNo, and the primary key of BoatTable is StateRegistrationNo. However, the PhoneNo field in CustomerTable and the CustomerPhoneNo field in BoatTable contain exactly the same information. See Figure 14-6.

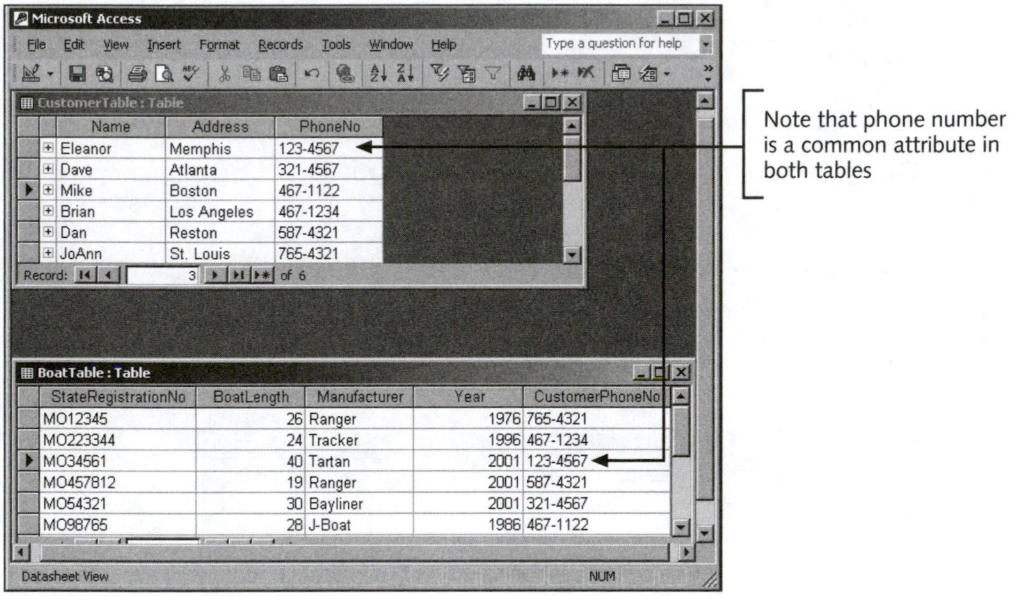

Name	Address	PhoneNo
Eleanor	Memphis	123-4567
Dave	Atlanta	321-4567
Mike	Boston	467-1122
Brian	Los Angeles	467-1234
Dan	Reston	587-4321
JoAnn	St. Louis	765-4321

StateRegistrationNo	BoatLength	Manufacturer	Year	CustomerPhoneNo
MO12345	26	Ranger	1976	765-4321
MO223344	24	Tracker	1996	467-1234
MO34561	40	Tartan	2001	123-4567
MO457812	19	Ranger	2001	587-4321
MO54321	30	Bayliner	2001	321-4567
MO98765	28	J-Boat	1986	467-1122

Figure 14-6 Common field in CustomerTable and BoatTable

Tables in a relational database often share a common field that links information in one table to information in the other table. For example, if you know that the boat with state registration number MO34561 in BoatTable has the value 123-4567 for CustomerPhoneNo, you can find the customer in CustomerTable whose primary key (PhoneNo) is 123-4567 and retrieve that customer's name and address. The CustomerPhoneNo field in BoatTable is called a **foreign key**, which is a field in one table (in this case, BoatTable) that serves as a primary key in a related table (CustomerTable). Foreign keys establish common attributes that allow you to link information in different tables. In Microsoft Access, common attributes are shown in the Relationships window, as in Figure 14-7. To open this window, click the Relationships button on the toolbar or click Tools on the menu bar, then click Relationships.

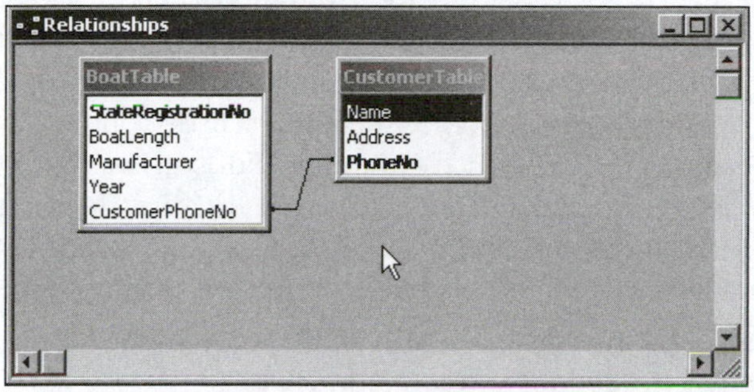

Figure 14-7 Relationships diagram for CustomerTable and BoatTable

The line that connects the CustomerPhoneNo field in BoatTable to the PhoneNo field in CustomerTable indicates that these fields (or columns) link information in the two tables.

Using SQL to Join Tables in the Database

In Chapter 13 you learned how to specify SQL statements to insert, delete, update, and select information from a single table. When two tables are involved, SQL uses foreign and primary keys to link information in one table to information in another table. In SQL terms, this is referred to as **joining** the tables. For example, the following SQL statements find and display the state registration number and manufacturer of all boats in BoatTable together with the name, address, and phone number of each boat's owner.

14

```
SELECT StateRegistrationNo, Manufacturer, Name, Address, PhoneNo
FROM  BoatTable, CustomerTable
WHERE CustomerPhoneNo = PhoneNo
```

Recall that the SELECT clause identifies the fields (or columns) from the database that you want to retrieve. Because these columns come from two different tables, the FROM clause specifies the names of both tables involved in the query. The WHERE clause specifies the join condition; in this case, it matches CustomerPhoneNo in BoatTable to PhoneNo in CustomerTable. Similarly, the following SQL statements display the name and address of the owner of the boat with state registration number MO98765.

```
SELECT StateRegistrationNo, Name, Address
FROM BoatTable, CustomerTable
WHERE CustomerPhoneNo = PhoneNo
AND StateRegistrationNo = 'MO98765'
```

In this case, the WHERE clause specifies both the join condition and the primary key value for an item. In general, WHERE clauses can specify any number of conditions that must be satisfied. You will use SQL statements of this type when you work with multiple tables in a relational database.

Establishing a Common Connection to the Database

In Chapter 13 you learned how to create and use a CustomerDA class to access a single table (CustomerTable) in a relational database. Recall that the CustomerDA class established a connection to CustomerDatabase and that the CustomerDA class was the only class to use that connection. Now two DA classes—one for Customer and one for Boat—should work together through a common connection to CustomerAndBoatDatabaseConnect. To establish a common connection, you need a new class, named CustomerAndBoatDatabaseConnect. The sole responsibility of this class is to manage the connection to the database. Before defining the class, you must import the namespace, System.Data.OleDb. After the **`Imports`** statement comes the class definition statement and declaring a reference variable for the connection.

```
Imports System.Data.OleDb
Public Class CustomerAndBoatDatabaseConnect
    Shared aConnection As OleDbConnection
```

Next, the Initialize method establishes the connection to the database. This method is similar to the Initialize method used in Chapter 13. Now, however, the connection instance is returned to the calling program so that the connection can be shared with all the classes that need it. See Figure 14-8. When no physical path to the database is provided for the Data Source parameter, the database is assumed to be in the bin folder of the application. In this chapter, the databases for all the applications will be in the bin folder. You may be required to set the Data Source to a physical path. For example, the physical path for this exercise is: `"Data Source=C:\Chap14\Exercises\Ex01\Example1\bin\CustomerAndBoatDatabase.mdb"`.

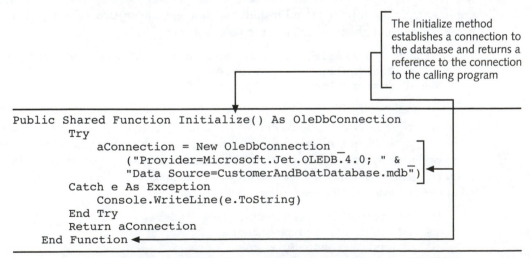

The Initialize method establishes a connection to the database and returns a reference to the connection to the calling program

```
Public Shared Function Initialize() As OleDbConnection
       Try
           aConnection = New OleDbConnection _
               ("Provider=Microsoft.Jet.OLEDB.4.0; " & _
               "Data Source=CustomerAndBoatDatabase.mdb")
       Catch e As Exception
           Console.WriteLine(e.ToString)
       End Try
       Return aConnection
   End Function
```

Figure 14-8 Initialize method of the CustomerAndBoatDatabaseConnect class

The only other method needed in this class is one to terminate the connection.

```
Public Shared Sub Terminate()
        Try
            aConnection.Close()
        Catch e As Exception
            Console.WriteLine(e.ToString)
        End Try
    End Sub
```

Modifying the Customer Class

To create a database application that uses CustomerTable and BoatTable, you modify the Customer class from Chapter 13 to reflect the link between the two tables. First, you include a boat reference attribute. This enables a customer instance to know about its associated boat instance. In the constructor, you initialize the boat reference to nothing. Then you include setter and getter methods to set and retrieve this value. For this application, you use the common database connection established by the CustomerAndBoatDatabaseConnect class. See Figure 14-9 for a partial listing of the revised Customer class with the changes noted.

```
' Customer Class with added methods for DA Class
' Chapter 14
Imports System.Data.OleDb
Public Class Customer
    ' Attributes
    Private name As String
    Private address As String
    Private phoneNo As String
    ' Reference variable for Boat instances
    Private theBoat As Boat

    ' Constructor (3 parameters)
    Public Sub New(ByVal aName As String, ByVal anAddress As String, _
        ByVal aPhoneNo As String)

        name = aName
        address = anAddress
        phoneNo = aPhoneNo
        SetBoat(Nothing)
    End Sub

    '-----------Begin Data Access Shared Methods-----
    Public Shared Sub Initialize(ByVal c As OleDbConnection)
        CustomerDA.Initialize(c)
    End Sub
      ...
    Public Shared Sub Terminate()
        CustomerDA.Terminate()
    End Sub
    '------------End Data Access Shared Methods--------
```

Include a boat reference variable (→ Private theBoat As Boat)

Initialize the boat reference to Nothing (→ SetBoat(Nothing))

Use the shared database connection (→ Public Shared Sub Initialize(ByVal c As OleDbConnection))

```
    ...
    ' Get accessor methods
    Public Function GetBoat() As Boat      ← Include a get accessor method to get
        Return theBoat                        the value of the boat reference
    End Function

    ' Set accessor methods
    Public Sub SetBoat(ByVal aBoat As Boat) ← Include a set accessor method to set
        theBoat = aBoat                        the value of the boat reference
    End Sub

    ...

End Class
```

Figure 14-9 The Customer class

Introducing the BoatDA Class

The CustomerAndBoatDatabase application must find, add, delete, and update records in BoatTable. For this reason, it needs a BoatDA class. Patterned after the CustomerDA class, BoatDA imports the System.Data.OleDb (to support a database connection) and System.Collections (to support an ArrayList) namespaces and declares a boat reference variable and an ArrayList of boat references. (The GetAll method will use the ArrayList.) Variables are then defined for the database connection and the boat attribute values.

```
Imports System.Data.OleDb
Imports System.Collections
Public Class BoatDA
    Shared boats As New ArrayList()
    Shared aBoat As Boat

    ' Declare variable for connection to database
    Shared aConnection As OleDbConnection

    ' Declare variables for Boat attribute values
    Shared stateRegistrationNo, manufacturer As String
    Shared length As Single
    Shared year As Integer
    Shared phoneno As String
```

Understanding the Initialize and Terminate Methods of the BoatDA Class

The Initialize and Terminate methods of the BoatDA class use the database connection established by the CustomerAndBoatDatabaseConnect class to open a connection. The Terminate method closes the connection. See Figure 14-10.

```
' Initialize class--Open connection
    Public Shared Sub Initialize(ByVal c As OleDbConnection)
        Try
            aConnection = c
            If aConnection.State.closed Then
                aConnection.Open()
            End If
        Catch e As Exception
            Console.WriteLine(e.Message.ToString)
        End Try
    End Sub

    ' Terminate class--Close the connection
    Public Shared Sub Terminate()
        Try
            aConnection.Close()
            aConnection = Nothing
        Catch e As Exception
            Console.WriteLine(e.Message.ToString)
        End Try
    End Sub
```

Use the shared database connection

Figure 14-10 Initialize and Terminate methods of the BoatDA class

Understanding the Find and GetAll Methods of the BoatDA Class

The Find method of the BoatDA class defines an SQL SELECT statement that retrieves a particular record from BoatTable. The argument list specifies the primary key of the record to be retrieved.

```
' Find method
Public Shared Function Find(ByVal key As String) As Boat
    aBoat = Nothing
    Dim dsBoat As New DataSet()
    ' Declare the SQL statement to find boat
    Dim sqlQuery As String = "Select StateRegistrationNo, BoatLength, " & _
        "Manufacturer, Year From BoatTable " & _
        "WHERE StateRegistrationNO = '" & key & "'"
```

A data adapter is created to execute the SQL query and fill the dataset table, BoatTable, of the dataset, dsBoat, with the results of the query. To determine whether any records were found, check the count of the number of rows of dsBoat's BoatTable. If a record was found, then a DataRow (dr) is created and set to the first row in BoatTable. The data from this row is extracted and used to create an instance of Boat called aBoat that is then returned to the calling program. If the desired record cannot be found in the table, a NotFoundException is thrown.

```
' Execute the SQL query
Try ' Declare data adapter and fill the dataset table
    Dim adptBoat As New OleDbDataAdapter(sqlQuery, aConnection)
    adptBoat.Fill(dsBoat, "BoatTable")
```

14

```
            ' Check if dataset table contains any rows
            If dsBoat.Tables("BoatTable").Rows.Count > 0 Then
                  ' Declare data row variable set to first row in the table
                  Dim dr As DataRow = dsBoat.Tables("BoatTable").Rows(0)
                  stateRegistrationNo = dr("StateRegistrationNo")
                  length = dr("BoatLength")
                  manufacturer = dr("Manufacturer")
                  year = dr("Year")
                  ' Create the boat instance
                  aBoat = New Boat(stateRegistrationNo, length, manufacturer, year)
            Else
                  Throw New NotFoundException("Not Found")
            End If
                  dsBoat = Nothing
        Catch e As OleDb.OleDbException
                  Console.WriteLine(e.Message.ToString)
        End Try
          Return aBoat
      End Function
```

The GetAll method of the BoatDA class is similar to the Find method, but returns an ArrayList of boat references rather than a single instance. See Figure 14-11.

```
' GetAll method
Public Shared Function GetAll() As ArrayList
      Dim dsBoat As New DataSet()
      ' Define the SQL query statement for the GetAll method
      Dim sqlQuery As String = "SELECT StateRegistrationNo, BoatLength, " & _
            "Manufacturer, Year FROM BoatTable"

      ' Execute the SQL statement
      Try ' Declare data adapter and fill the dataset table
            Dim adptBoat As New OleDbDataAdapter(sqlQuery, aConnection)
            adptBoat.Fill(dsBoat, "BoatTable")
            ' Check dataset table to see if it contains any rows
            If dsBoat.Tables("BoatTable").Rows.Count > 0 Then
                Dim dr As DataRow
                ' Clear array list
                boats.Clear()
                ' Loop over each row of dataset table
                ' Extract the boat attributes
                For Each dr In dsBoat.Tables("BoatTable").Rows
                    stateRegistrationNo = dr("StateRegistrationNo")
                    length = dr("BoatLength")
                    manufacturer = dr("manufacturer")
                    year = dr("Year")
                    ' Create boat instance
                    Dim aBoat As New Boat(stateRegistrationNo, length, _
                        manufacturer, year)
                    boats.Add(aBoat)
```

```
            Next
        End If
    Catch e As Exception
        Console.WriteLine(e.Message.ToString)
    End Try
    Return boats
End Function
```

Figure 14-11 GetAll method of the BoatDA class

Understanding the AddNew Method of the BoatDA Class

The AddNew method of the BoatDA class is similar to the AddNew method of the CustomerDA class of Chapter 13; it focuses on boat attributes rather than customer attributes. The AddNew method begins by extracting boat attributes from the boat instance received in the argument list.

```
' AddNew-retrieve the boat attribute values
Public Shared Sub AddNew(ByVal aboat As Boat)
  ' Get boat attribute values
  stateRegistrationNo = aboat.GetStateRegistrationNo
  length = aboat.GetLength
  manufacturer = aboat.GetManufacturer
  year = aboat.GetYear
  phoneno = aboat.GetCustomer.GetPhoneNo
```

Assume for a moment that the retrieved attribute values are MO33333, 25, Tartan, 1999, and 764-7414. You could use the following SQL statement to insert this information into BoatTable:

```
INSERT INTO BoatTable
VALUES ('MO33333', 25, 'Tartan', '1999', '764-7414')
```

14

Recall that the INSERT INTO clause identifies the table and columns into which data will be inserted. If you are inserting a value for each column in the table, then the column names can be omitted, as has been done in this case. The VALUES clause identifies, in order, the values to be inserted into the BoatTable columns. The entries in the VALUE clause are also specified in parentheses and separated by commas. Remember that each of the values representing a table column of type text is enclosed in single quotes. When you define a SQL INSERT statement within a VB .NET program, the parentheses, single quotes, and commas must be included so that when all values are substituted for variable names, the resulting SQL statement is syntactically correct. In the following code, notice how the sqlInsert string concatenates string literals with variables to achieve the desired effect:

```
' Declare a string SQL statement
Dim sqlInsert As String = "INSERT INTO BoatTable " & _
      "VALUES ('" & stateRegistrationNo & "', " & length & ", " & _
      " '" & manufacturer & " ', " & year & ", '" & phoneno & "')"
Console.WriteLine("The sql Statement is: " & sqlInsert)
```

Defining a SQL statement like the previous one can be confusing, and errors in the definition of the SQL statement can cause unexpected problems at runtime. Including a `Console.WriteLine` statement enables you to view the SQL statement, which is helpful while debugging. Once you have the program working properly, you can delete (or comment out) the `Console.WriteLine` statement. As an alternative to writing the sqlInsert string, you can set a breakpoint at the first statement following the sqlInsert declaration and when the program breaks, move the cursor over the sqlInsert string to display its value.

Before executing the SQL INSERT statement, the code checks to confirm that the database does not already contain the boat. Recall that the definition of a relation forbids two records with the same primary key. You invoke the Find method to find a record with the primary key value of the boat to be added. If it finds the boat record, a DuplicateException is thrown. If it does not, the SQL statement is executed.

```
        Dim adptBoat As New OleDbDataAdapter()
        Try ' Use Find method to see if boat exists
            Dim c As Boat = Find(phoneno)
            Throw New DuplicateException(" Boat Exists ")
        Catch e As NotFoundException
            Try ' Execute INSERT SQL statement if not found
                adptBoat.InsertCommand = New OleDbCommand(sqlInsert)
                adptBoat.InsertCommand.Connection = aConnection
                adptBoat.InsertCommand.ExecuteNonQuery()
            Catch sqle As Exception
                Console.WriteLine(sqle.ToString)
            End Try
        End Try
    End Sub
```

Understanding the Update and Delete Methods of the BoatDA Class

The Update and Delete methods extract attributes from the boat instance received in the argument list, then define appropriate SQL statements. Recall that the syntax for an UPDATE statement identifies the name of the table to be updated, followed by a SET clause where you specify the columns that will be updated and new values that will be assigned. You do not have to specify a value for each column in the table, but only for those columns containing a value that should be changed, as in the following example:

```
UPDATE BoatTable SET BoatLength = 30, Manufacturer = 'Tartan', Year = 2002
WHERE StateRegistrationNo = 'MO123345';
```

Notice that in the SET clause, values for columns that are of the numeric type are not enclosed in single quotes, but values for columns that are of the string (or text) type are. Also, note that variable-value pairs are separated by commas. In Microsoft Access 2002, Year is a keyword within a SQL statement, and it must be enclosed in brackets when referenced as a column name, as has been done in the SQL UPDATE statement for this method. The Update method for the BoatDA class is shown in Figure 14-12.

```
' Update method
Public Shared Sub Update(ByVal aBoat As Boat)
        ' Retrieve the Boat attributes
        stateRegistrationNo = aBoat.GetStateRegistrationNo
        length = aBoat.GetLength
        manufacturer = aBoat.GetManufacturer
        year = aBoat.GetYear

        ' Define SQL statement using boat reg key
        Dim sqlUpdate As String = "UPDATE BoatTable " & _
            "SET BoatLength = " & length & ", " & _
                "Manufacturer = '" & manufacturer & "', " & _
                "[Year] = " & year & " " & _
            "WHERE StateRegistrationNo = '" & stateRegistrationNo & "'"
                                                        Year must be in brackets
        Dim adptBoat As New OleDbDataAdapter()
        ' See if this boat already exists
        ' NotFoundException is thrown by Find method
        Try
            Dim b As Boat = Boat.Find(stateRegistrationNo)
            ' If found execute the SQL statement
            adptBoat.UpdateCommand = New OleDbCommand(sqlUpdate)
            adptBoat.UpdateCommand.Connection = aConnection
            adptBoat.UpdateCommand.ExecuteNonQuery()
        Catch e As NotFoundException
            Console.WriteLine(e.Message.ToString)
        End Try
End Sub
```

Figure 14-12 Update method of the BoatDA class

Similarly, recall that the syntax for an SQL DELETE statement specifies the table name and the primary key value of the record to be deleted. An example of an SQL statement to delete a record from BoatTable follows:


```
DELETE FROM BoatTable WHERE StateRegistrationNo = 'MO12345';
```

The Delete method for the BoatDA class is shown in Figure 14-13.

```
' Delete method
Public Shared Sub Delete(ByVal aBoat As Boat)
        ' Retrieve the state registration no (key)
        stateRegistrationNo = aBoat.GetStateRegistrationNo

        ' Create the SQL statement
        Dim sqlDelete As String = "DELETE FROM BoatTable " & _
            "WHERE StateRegistrationNo = '" & stateRegistrationNo & "'"
        Dim adptBoat As New OleDbDataAdapter()
        ' See if this boat already exists in the database
        ' NotFoundException is thrown by Find method
```

```
        Try
            Dim b As Boat = Boat.Find(stateRegistrationNo)
            ' If found, execute the SQL statement
            adptBoat.UpdateCommand = New OleDbCommand(sqlDelete)
            adptBoat.UpdateCommand.Connection = aConnection
            adptBoat.UpdateCommand.ExecuteNonQuery()
        Catch e As NotFoundException
            Console.WriteLine(e.Message.ToString)
        End Try
End Sub
```

Figure 14-13 Delete method of the BoatDA class

Both the Update and Delete methods invoke the Find method to determine whether the database has a boat with the state registration number specified in the SQL statement. If so, the SQL statement to update (or delete) that record is executed. Otherwise, the Find method throws a NotFoundException and exits the method.

Modifying the Boat Class to Work With BoatDA

You can now extend the functionality of the Boat problem domain class to take advantage of the capabilities in BoatDA. The Boat class needs four shared methods to invoke the Initialize, Find, GetAll, and Terminate methods in the BoatDA class, and three instance methods to invoke the BoatDA AddNew, Update, and Delete methods. The only other change in the Boat class is a revision of the TellAboutSelf method. This method is changed slightly to improve readability of the information returned to the calling program. The code for the revised Boat class is shown in Figure 14-14.

```
Imports System.Data
Imports System.Data.OleDb
Public Class Boat
    ' Attributes
    Private stateRegistrationNo As String
    Private length As Single
    Private manufacturer As String
    Private year As Integer
    ' Reference variable for Customer instance
    Private theCustomer As Customer

    ' Constructor (four parameters)
    Public Sub New(ByVal aStateRegistrationNo As String, _
        ByVal aLength As Single, _
        ByVal aManufacturer As String, ByVal aYear As Integer)

        stateRegistrationNo = aStateRegistrationNo
        length = aLength
        manufacturer = aManufacturer
        year = aYear
    End Sub
```

```
' Constructor (four parameters plus customer reference)
Public Sub New(ByVal aStateRegistrationNo As String, _
 ByVal aLength As Single, _
 ByVal aManufacturer As String, ByVal aYear As Integer, _
 ByVal aCustomer As Customer)
    ' Set values of attributes using accessor methods
    SetStateRegistrationNo(aStateRegistrationNo)
    SetLength(aLength)
    SetManufacturer(aManufacturer)
    SetYear(aYear)
    ' Since boat must have a customer, assign it in constructor
    AssignBoatToCustomer(aCustomer)
End Sub

' Custom method to assign a Boat to a Customer
Public Sub AssignBoatToCustomer(ByVal aCustomer As Customer)
    SetCustomer(aCustomer)  ' Set customer reference for boat
    aCustomer.SetBoat(Me)   ' Ask the customer to set its boat
End Sub

' Boat DA Shared Methods
Public Shared Sub Initialize(ByVal c As OleDbConnection)
    BoatDA.Initialize(c)
End Sub
Public Shared Function Find(ByVal key As String) As Boat
    BoatDA.Find(key)
End Function
Public Shared Function GetAll() As ArrayList
    BoatDA.GetAll()
End Function
Public Shared Sub Terminate()
    BoatDA.Terminate()
End Sub

' Boat DA Instance Methods
Public Sub AddNew()
    BoatDA.AddNew(Me)
End Sub
Public Sub Delete()
    BoatDA.Delete(Me)
End Sub
Public Sub Update()
    BoatDA.Update(Me)
End Sub

' TellAboutSelf method
Public Overridable Function TellAboutSelf() As String
    Return ("State Reg Nbr = " & stateRegistrationNo & _
            ", Boat Length = " & length & _
            ", Manufacturer = " & manufacturer & _
            ", Year = " & year)
End Function
```

14

```
    ' Get Accessor Methods
    Public Function GetStateRegistrationNo() As String
        Return stateRegistrationNo
    End Function
    Public Function GetLength() As Single
        Return length
    End Function
    Public Function GetManufacturer() As String
        Return manufacturer
    End Function
    Public Function GetYear() As Integer
        Return year
    End Function
    Public Function GetCustomer() As Customer
        Return theCustomer
    End Function

    'Set accessor methods
    Public Sub SetStateRegistrationNo(ByVal aStateRegNo As String)
        stateRegistrationNo = aStateRegNo
    End Sub
    Public Sub SetLength(ByVal aLength As Double)
        length = aLength
    End Sub
    Public Sub SetManufacturer(ByVal aManufacturer As String)
        manufacturer = aManufacturer
    End Sub
    Public Sub SetYear(ByVal aYear As Integer)
        year = aYear
    End Sub
    Public Sub SetCustomer(ByVal aCustomer As Customer)
        theCustomer = aCustomer
    End Sub

End Class
```

Figure 14-14 Boat class

Modifying the CustomerDA Class

You can now change the CustomerDA class to support joining the information from BoatTable and CustomerTable. The CustomerDA class begins much as it did before, but now includes a boat reference variable and variables to represent boat attributes.

```
Imports System.Data.OleDb
Imports System.Collections
Public Class CustomerDA
    Shared customers As New ArrayList()  ' Customer references
    Shared aCustomer As Customer
    Shared aBoat As Boat
    Shared aConnection As OleDbConnection
```

```
' Declare variables for Customer attribute values
Shared name, address, phoneno As String

' Declare variables for the Boat attribute values
Shared stateRegistrationNo, manufacturer As String
Shared length As Single
Shared year As Integer
```

The Initialize and Terminate methods of the CustomerDA class are identical to their counterparts in the BoatDA class and are not repeated here.

Understanding the Find and GetAll Methods of the CustomerDA Class

The capability of the Find method of the CustomerDA class can be extended to retrieve data from both tables. To do so, you first change the SQL statement. In the WHERE clause, specify both the join condition *and* the primary key value for the customer of interest. You use the values in the result set to create a boat instance and a customer instance. The boat instance invokes the AssignBoatToCustomer method to establish the two-way relationship with its customer instance. The customer instance, which now includes a pointer to the boat instance, is then returned to the calling program. The Find method of the CustomerDA class is shown in Figure 14-15.

```
' Find method--Throws NotFoundException if Not Found
Public Shared Function Find(ByVal key As String) As Customer
      aCustomer = Nothing
      ' Define the SQL statement using the phoneno key
      Dim sqlQuery As String = "SELECT Name, Address, PhoneNo, " & _
            "StateRegistrationNo, BoatLength, Manufacturer, Year " & _
            "FROM CustomerTable, BoatTable " & _
            "WHERE phoneNo = CustomerPhoneNo AND phoneNo = '" & key & "'"
      ' Declare dataset
      Dim dsCustBoat As New DataSet()
      Try      ' Execute query & fill dataset
            Dim adptCustomer As New OleDbDataAdapter(sqlQuery, aConnection)
            adptCustomer.Fill(dsCustBoat, "CustBoatTable")

            ' If record in row, found it; extract data
            If dsCustBoat.Tables("CustBoatTable").Rows.Count > 0 Then
                Dim dr As DataRow
                dr = dsCustBoat.Tables("CustBoatTable").Rows(0)

                name = dr("Name")
                address = dr("address")
                phoneno = dr("phoneno")
                stateRegistrationNo = dr("StateRegistrationNo")
                length = dr("BoatLength")
                manufacturer = dr("Manufacturer")
                year = dr("Year")
```

14

```
            ' Create customer & boat instance; assign to customer
            aCustomer = New Customer(name, address, phoneno)
            aBoat = New Boat(stateRegistrationNo, length, _
                    manufacturer, year)
            aBoat.AssignBoatToCustomer(aCustomer)

        Else    ' Nothing retrieved, throw error
            Throw New NotFoundException("Not Found")
        End If
        dsCustBoat = Nothing
    Catch e As OleDb.OleDbException
        Console.WriteLine(e.ToString)
    End Try
    Return aCustomer
End Function
```

Figure 14-15 Find method of the CustomerDA class

Note that as before, the Find method still returns a single customer instance, but with one important difference. As shown in Figure 14-16, the instance now contains a reference to the customer's boat instance.

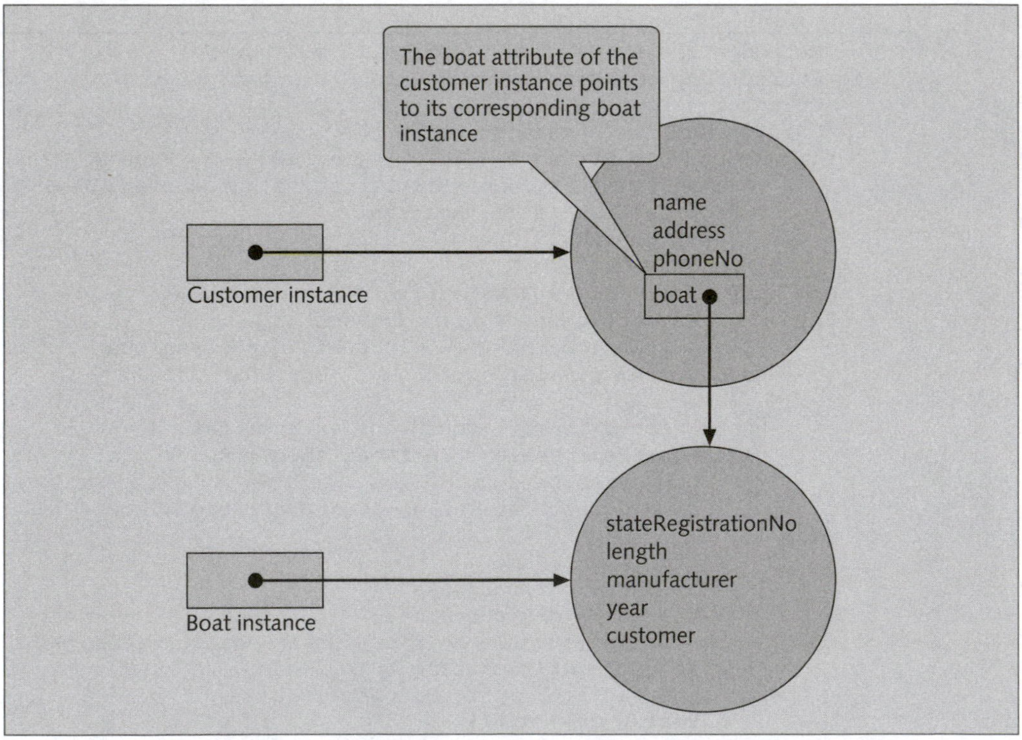

Figure 14-16 Customer instance with a reference to its boat instance

This means that it is not necessary to execute a separate SQL statement to find the boat in BoatTable. The values of the attributes, by design, are already available. Including a boat attribute in the Customer class definition makes this possible. Including the boat attribute establishes the aggregation (or composition) relationship "customer has boat." The AssignBoatToCustomer method in the Boat class establishes which boat belongs to the customer. The ability to return a single customer instance, yet have related information available, is one of the strengths of the object-oriented approach.

The GetAll method is similar to the Find method but returns an ArrayList of customer references rather than a single customer reference. Note that both the Find method and the GetAll method now return information about a customer and that customer's boat.

Understanding the AddNew Method of the CustomerDA Class

Recall that there is a mandatory one-to-one relationship between Customer and Boat. This means that there must be a customer record for every boat record, and conversely, there must be a boat record for every customer record. The AddNew method in the CustomerDA class must enforce this requirement.

After inserting a customer record into CustomerTable, the AddNew method of the CustomerDA class invokes the AddNew method of the BoatDA class to insert the associated boat record into BoatTable. This modification preserves the integrity of the database. See Figure 14-17.

```
' AddNew method --Throws DuplicateException if exists
Public Shared Sub AddNew(ByVal aCustomer As Customer)

        ' Get customer information
        name = aCustomer.GetName
        address = aCustomer.GetAddress
        phoneno = aCustomer.GetPhoneNo
        ' Get boat instance via customer
        aBoat = aCustomer.GetBoat

        ' Declare a string to hold SQL statement
        Dim sqlInsert As String = "INSERT INTO customerTable " & _
            "VALUES ('" & name & "', '" & address & "', '" & phoneno & " ')"
        Dim adptCustomer As New OleDbDataAdapter()

        Try
            Dim c As Customer = Find(phoneno)
            Throw New DuplicateException(" Customer Exists ")
    Catch e As NotFoundException
        Try
            ' See if boat exists
            Dim b As Boat = Boat.Find(aBoat.GetStateRegistrationNo)
            Throw New DuplicateException("Boat Exists")
```

```
        Catch ee As NotFoundException
            Try ' Assign Insert Commands and Execute
                adptCustomer.InsertCommand = New OleDbCommand(sqlInsert)
                adptCustomer.InsertCommand.Connection = aConnection
                adptCustomer.InsertCommand.ExecuteNonQuery()
                ' Add boat
                Try
                    aBoat.AddNew()
                Catch de As DuplicateException
                    Console.WriteLine(de.Message.ToString)
                End Try
            Catch sqle As OleDb.OleDbException
                Console.WriteLine(sqle.ToString)
            End Try
        End Try
    End Try
End Sub
```

When the AddNew method inserts a record into CustomerTable, a record is also added to BoatTable

Figure 14-17 AddNew method of the CustomerDA class

Understanding the Delete and Update Methods of the CustomerDA Class

The Delete method of the CustomerDA class also must preserve the integrity of the database by enforcing the mandatory one-to-one relationship between Customer and Boat. When a customer record is deleted from the database, the corresponding boat record also must be deleted. See Figure 14-18.

```
' Delete method--Throws NotFoundException if not found
Public Shared Sub Delete(ByVal aCustomer As Customer)
        phoneno = aCustomer.GetPhoneNo
        Dim sqlDelete As String = "DELETE FROM CustomerTable " & _
            "WHERE PhoneNo = '" & phoneno & "'"
        Dim adptCustomer As New OleDbDataAdapter()
        ' Delete the record
        Try
            Dim c As Customer = Customer.Find(phoneno)
            adptCustomer.DeleteCommand = New OleDbCommand(sqlDelete)
            adptCustomer.DeleteCommand.Connection = aConnection
            adptCustomer.DeleteCommand.ExecuteNonQuery()
            '  Delete Customer's Boat
            Try
                aCustomer.GetBoat.Delete()
            Catch e As NotFoundException
                Console.WriteLine(e.Message.ToString)
            End Try
        Catch e As Exception
            Console.WriteLine(e.ToString)
        End Try
End Sub
```

When the Delete method deletes a record from CustomerTable, a record is also deleted from BoatTable

Figure 14-18 Delete method of the CustomerDA class

The Update method of the CustomerDA class remains unchanged from Chapter 13, as the purpose of this method is to update information in CustomerTable only.

Testing the New CustomerAndBoatDatabase Application

The testing script verifies the classes in the CustomerAndBoatDatabase application. First, the script declares necessary reference variables. Next, the testing script invokes the Initialize method of the CustomerAndBoatDatabase class to establish the connection to the database. The testing script passes this connection to the Customer and Boat Initialize methods.

```
Imports System.Data.OleDb
Imports System.Collections
Public Class Form1
       Inherits System.Windows.Forms.Form

Shared aCustomer As Customer
    Shared aBoat As Boat
    Shared customers As ArrayList
    Shared boats As ArrayList
    Shared c As OleDbConnection = CustomerAndBoatDatabaseConnect.Initialize

Private Sub testDAClasses()
' Initialize the databases
        Boat.Initialize(c)
        Customer.Initialize(c)
```

This is shown graphically in the sequence diagram in Figure 14-19.

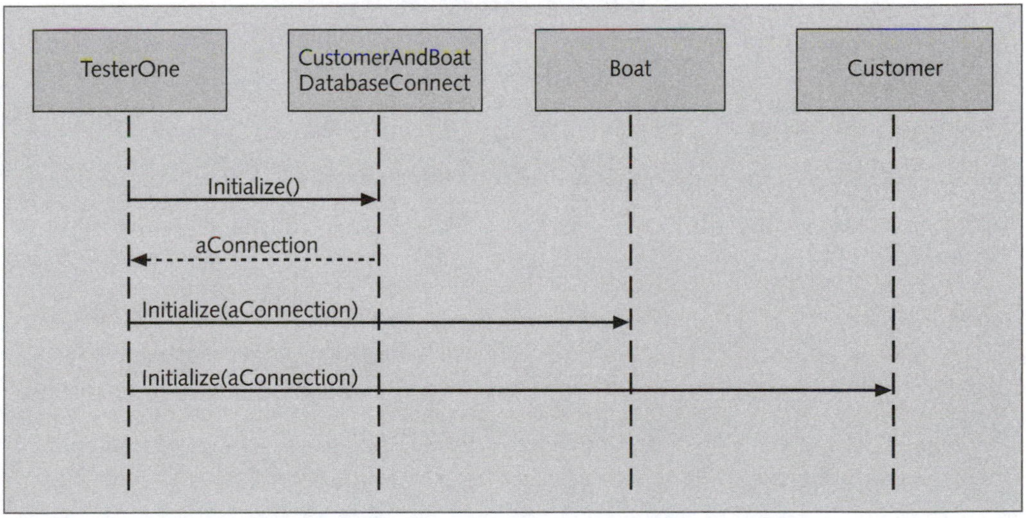

Figure 14-19 Sequence diagram to connect to the database

The testing script then attempts to retrieve the customer and boat information from the database for the customer whose phone number is 123-4567. The testing script invokes the Find method of the Customer class, which invokes the Find method of the CustomerDA class. Recall that the Find method in the CustomerDA class executes a SELECT statement that joins the two tables and retrieves information about both the desired customer and the customer's boat. The Customer and Boat classes use this information to create corresponding customer and boat instances. The testing script then calls its own printDetails procedure to display the customer and boat details.

```
Try     ' Get a customer and their boat
      acustomer = Customer.Find("123-4567")
      Call printDetails()
Catch e As NotFoundException
      Console.WriteLine(e.Message.ToString)
End Try
```

The sequence diagram in Figure 14-20 illustrates this process. In the printDetails procedure, the customer instance invokes its TellAboutSelf method to report customer details, then navigates to the associated boat instance to invoke the Boat TellAboutSelf method.

```
Private Sub printDetails()
        Try
            Console.WriteLine(vbCrLf)
            Console.WriteLine("Found " + acustomer.GetName + _
                " and associated boat")
            Console.WriteLine("    " + acustomer.TellAboutSelf)
            Console.WriteLine("    " + acustomer.GetBoat.TellAboutSelf)
        Catch e As NotFoundException
            Console.WriteLine("Customer Not Found")
        Catch e As Exception
            Console.WriteLine(e.ToString)
        End Try
End Sub
```

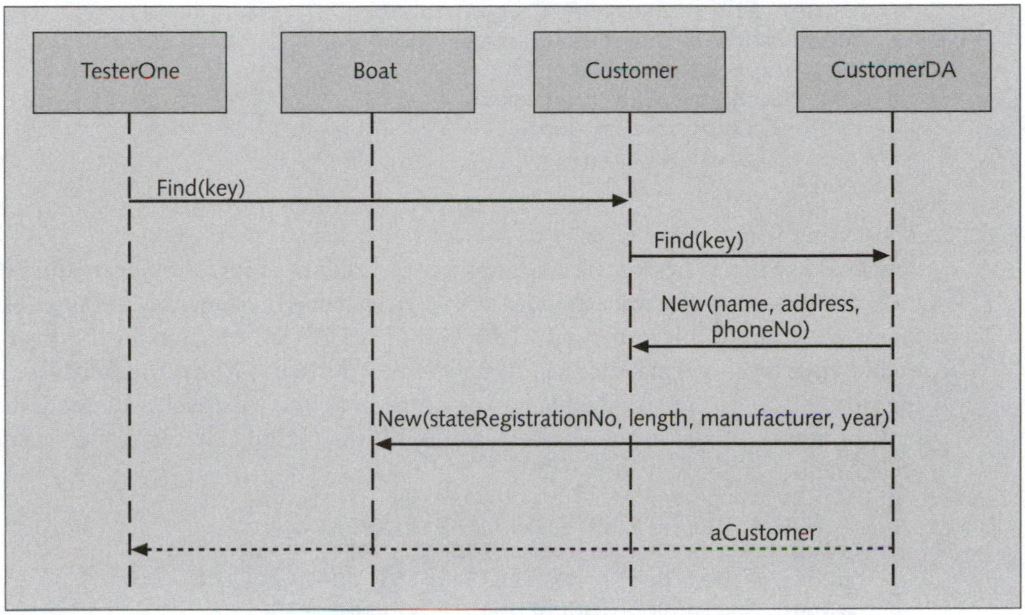

Figure 14-20 Sequence diagram to find a customer and that customer's boat

To test the possibility that an attempt to find a record in the database might be unsuccessful, the testing script tries to retrieve information from the database for the customer with phone number 000-0000. In this case, no such customer exists in the database. The SQL query produces a result set with no data, and the CustomerDA class throws a NotFoundException error. The testing script catches the exception and displays the message, "Did not find 000-0000."

```
'  Try to get a non-existent customer and their boat
Try
      aCustomer = Customer.Find("000-0000")
      printDetails()
Catch e As NotFoundException
      Console.WriteLine(vbCrLf & "Did not find 000-0000")
End Try
```

Next, the testing script verifies the CustomerDA GetAll method, which executes a query that joins information in the two tables and returns information about all customers and boats in the database via an ArrayList of customer reference variables. A For Each loop iterates over all the customers in the ArrayList to report the results of the GetAll method.

```
' Get all customers & their boats
customers = Customer.GetAll
Dim cust As Customer
For Each cust In customers
        aCustomer = cust
        printDetails()
Next
```

The testing script then creates a new customer instance (with PhoneNo 339-4990) and a new boat instance. The boat instance invokes its AssignBoatToCustomer method to associate itself with its customer instance. The customer instance then invokes its AddNew method. Recall that the AddNew method of the CustomerDA class executes an INSERT statement to add customer information to CustomerTable, and then invokes the AddNew method of the BoatDA class to insert information about the boat into BoatTable. If a duplicate customer or boat already exists in the database, the AddNew method throws a DuplicateException error, and the entire operation ends.

```
' Add a new customer and their boat
aCustomer = New Customer("Ed", "KC", "339-4990")
aBoat = New Boat("MO112233", 25, "S-2", 1984)
aBoat.AssignBoatToCustomer(aCustomer)
Try
    aCustomer.AddNew()
    Console.WriteLine(vbCrLf & "Ed and his boat added")
Catch e As DuplicateException
    Console.WriteLine(e.Message.ToString)
End Try
```

To verify that the new customer (with phone number 339-4990) and the corresponding boat have been added to the database, the testing script then invokes the Find method to find the newly added customer.

```
' Try to find new customer and their boat
Try
    aCustomer = Customer.Find("339-4990")
    printDetails()
Catch e As NotFoundException
    Console.WriteLine("Did not Find 339-4990")
End Try
```

To test the Delete method, the testing script calls the Delete method of the CustomerDA class to delete the newly added customer from the database. The Delete method executes an SQL DELETE statement to delete the customer record from CustomerTable, then invokes the Delete method of the BoatDA class to delete the associated record in BoatTable. The testing script then calls the Find method of the CustomerDA class to verify that the customer record has been deleted from the database.

```
' Try to delete the new customer and their boat
Try
    aCustomer.delete()
```

```
        Console.WriteLine(vbCrLf & "Ed deleted" & vbCrLf)
    Catch e As NotFoundException
        Console.WriteLine(e.Message.ToString)
    End Try

    Try
        aCustomer = Customer.Find("339-4990")
        printDetails()
    Catch e As NotFoundException
        Console.WriteLine("Did Not Find 339-4990")
    End Try
```

The testing script for the Update method first issues a command to find the record in the database for the customer with phone number 123-4567. The Find method returns the desired customer instance, which includes a pointer to the associated boat instance. The testing script invokes a setter method to change the address of the customer instance, and then invokes the Update method to change this record in the database. Next, the testing script invokes a setter method to change the length of the boat instance, then calls the Update method for the boat instance to update the boat record in the database. If the customer or boat cannot be found in the database, a NotFoundException error is thrown, and exits the method. The testing script confirms that the database has been updated by calling the Find method to locate the revised customer record.

```
    ' Change Eleanor's address to Miami and her boat length to 40
    Try
        aCustomer = Customer.Find("123-4567")
        printDetails()
        ' Change customer address
        aCustomer.SetAddress("Miami")
        aCustomer.update()
        ' Change boat length
        aCustomer.GetBoat.SetLength(40)
        aCustomer.GetBoat.Update()
        Console.WriteLine(vbCrLf & "Eleanor updated")
    Catch e As NotFoundException
        Console.WriteLine(e.Message.ToString)
    End Try

    ' Get Eleanor and her boat
    Try
        aCustomer = Customer.Find("123-4567")
        printDetails()
    Catch e As NotFoundException
        Console.WriteLine(e.Message.ToString)
    End Try
```

Finally, the testing script displays a message that the script has finished and calls the Terminate methods of the Customer and Boat classes to close their respective connections, then calls the Terminate method of the CustomerAndBoatDatabaseConnect class. Then the form is closed and the program stops. Figure 14-21 shows the testing script output.

```
Found Eleanor and associated boat
  Name = Eleanor, Address = Memphis, Phone No = 123-4567
  State Reg No = MO34561, Boat Length = 35, Manufacturer = Tartan, Year = 1998

Did not find 000-0000

Found Brian and associated boat
  Name = Brian, Address = Los Angeles, Phone No = 467-1234
  State Reg No = MO223344, Boat Length = 24, Manufacturer = Tracker, Year = 1996

Found Dan and associated boat
  Name = Dan, Address = Reston, Phone No = 587-4321
  State Reg No = MO457812, Boat Length = 19, Manufacturer = Ranger, Year = 2001

Found Eleanor and associated boat
  Name = Eleanor, Address = Memphis, Phone No = 123-4567
  State Reg No = MO34561, Boat Length = 35, Manufacturer = Tartan, Year = 1998

Found Mike and associated boat
  Name = Mike, Address = Boston, Phone No = 467-1122
  State Reg No = MO98765, Boat Length = 28, Manufacturer = J-Boat, Year = 1986

Found JoAnn and associated boat
  Name = JoAnn, Address = St. Louis, Phone No = 765-4321
  State Reg No = MO12345, Boat Length = 26, Manufacturer = Ranger, Year = 1976

Found Dave and associated boat
  Name = Dave, Address = Atlanta, Phone No = 321-4567
  State Reg No = MO54321, Boat Length = 30, Manufacturer = Bayliner, Year = 2001

Ed and his boat added

Found Ed and associated boat
  Name = Ed, Address = KC, Phone No = 339-4990
  State Reg No = MO112233, Boat Length = 25, Manufacturer = S-2, Year = 1984
```

Figure 14-21 Output of the test script program

```
Ed deleted

Did Not Find 339-4990

Found Eleanor and associated boat
  Name = Eleanor, Address = Memphis, Phone No = 123-4567
  State Reg No = MO34561, Boat Length = 35, Manufacturer = Tartan, Year = 1998

Eleanor updated

Found Eleanor and associated boat
  Name = Eleanor, Address = Miami, Phone No = 123-4567
  State Reg No = MO34561, Boat Length = 40, Manufacturer = Tartan, Year = 1998
```

Figure 14-21 Output of the test script program (continued)

Hands-on Exercise 1

1. If necessary, locate the **Ex01** folder in the Chap14\Examples folder in the book's student data files and copy this folder to the **Chap14\Exercises** folder you created earlier. The Example1 folder in the Ex01 folder contains all the VB .NET files for a solution for Example1.
2. To ensure that the CustomerAndBoatDatabase.mdb database file is not write-protected, check the properties of this file:
   a. Start Windows Explorer, and navigate to the **CustomerAndBoatDatabase** file.
   b. Right-click **CustomerAndBoatDatabase**, and then click **Properties**.
   c. If the Read-only attribute is checked, uncheck it, and then click **OK**. Otherwise, click **Cancel**. Close Windows Explorer.
3. Close Access and double-click the **Chap14Example1.sln** file in the Chap14\Exercises\Ex01\Example1 folder to open VB .NET, click the **Start** button, and then click the only button on the Windows form to run the test script.
4. Verify that the output of the testing script matches the output of the text.

Before updating, the database has an address of Memphis for Eleanor and her boat length is 35. The testing script changes her address from Memphis to Miami and her boat's length from 35 to 40. If you want to run this project again, open the database in Microsoft Access, open CustomerTable, and reset the address to Memphis, open BoatTable and reset the BoatLength to 35.

Implementing a One-to-Many Association in a Database Application

In the previous example you learned how to implement the one-to-one association between Customer and Boat in a relational database application. Other one-to-one associations on the Bradshaw Marina class diagram (such as the one between Boat and Slip) would be implemented similarly. Recall, however, that the relationship between Dock and Slip is a one-to-many relationship. That is, a dock contains many slips, and a slip belongs to exactly one dock. You will learn how to implement the one-to-many relationships that exist between Dock and Slip. The application you are about to develop will allow the business owner to get a report that provides all available information about a dock, including details about each of its slips.

Understanding the Tables in DockAndSlipDatabase

Before you work with the VB .NET programs that accomplish a one-to-many relationship, look at the structure of the relational database tables that will be involved in this application.

To examine the structures of DockTable and SlipTable:

1. Locate the **Ex02** folder in the Chap14\Examples folder in the student data files. Copy the **Ex02** folder to the **Chap14\Exercises** folder in your work folder. **DockAndSlipDatabase.mdb** is contained in the bin folder of Example2.
2. Double-click **DockAndSlipDatabase.mdb** to open the database in Microsoft Access. The database contains two tables: DockTable and SlipTable.
3. Open **DockTable** and view its contents. It contains four columns—DockId (the primary key), Location, Electricity, and Water. DockId is an integer value representing the dock number. Location is a string value representing the dock location. The Electricity and Water columns indicate whether the dock has electricity and water. In the VB .NET class definitions, these variables have been treated as true/false (Boolean) values. However, because Access does not directly support Boolean data types, the database uses an integer value of 1 to indicate that the service is available, and a 0 to indicate that it is not. See Figure 14-22.

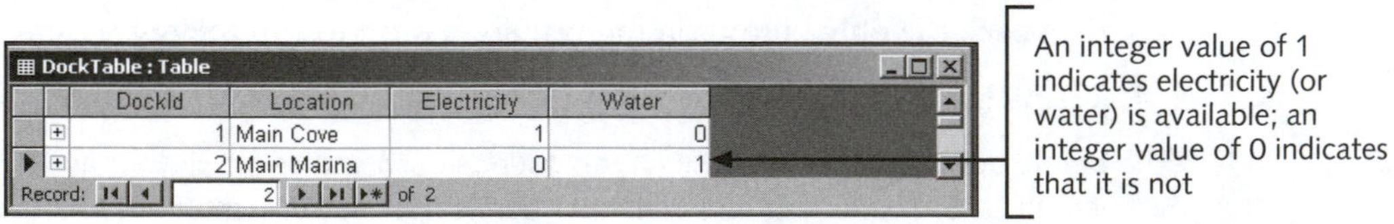

Figure 14-22 Contents of DockTable

4. Open **SlipTable** and view its contents. It contains five columns—SlipNo, DockId, Width, SlipLength, and BoatId. Because slips on each dock are numbered sequentially beginning with 1, both SlipNo and DockId must uniquely identify a slip. Together, SlipNo and DockId form a **concatenated key**, which is a key that contains more than one field (or column) in the database. See Figure 14-23.

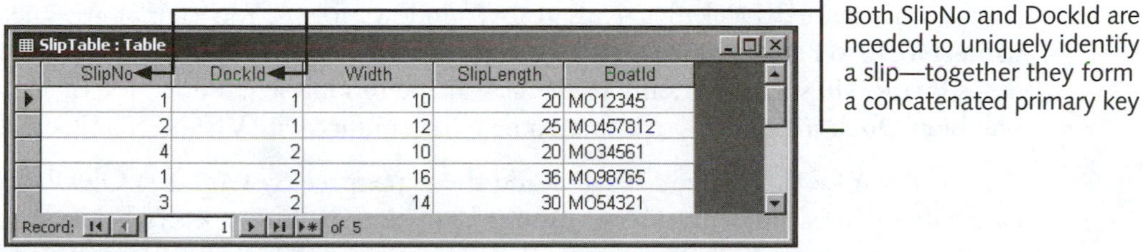
SlipTable : Table

SlipNo	DockId	Width	SlipLength	BoatId
1	1	10	20	MO12345
2	1	12	25	MO457812
4	2	10	20	MO34561
1	2	16	36	MO98765
3	2	14	30	MO54321

Record: 1 of 5

Both SlipNo and DockId are needed to uniquely identify a slip—together they form a concatenated primary key

Figure 14-23 Contents of SlipTable

5. The DockId column in SlipTable is a foreign key to information in DockTable. Similarly, BoatId is a foreign key to information in BoatTable (although this information is not needed in this application). Figure 14-24 shows the relationship between DockTable and SlipTable. SlipNo and DockId in SlipTable are bold to indicate they are the primary key.

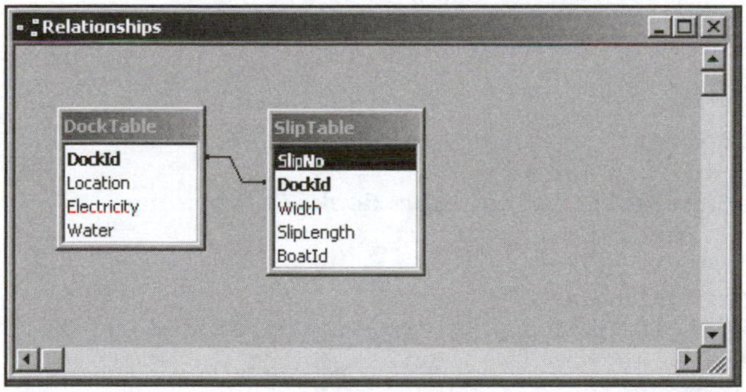

Figure 14-24 Relationships diagram for DockTable and SlipTable

Establishing a Common Connection to DockAndSlipDatabase

As with the CustomerAndBoatDatabase application, you need a separate program to establish a single connection to DockAndSlipDatabase. The PD and DA classes that require access to the database then share this connection. Except for the specified data source name, the

DockAndSlipDatabaseConnect code is identical to the CustomerAndBoatDatabaseConnect code, and therefore is not discussed here. The code for this program is included in the Example2 folder for this chapter in the book's student data files.

Modifying the Dock and Slip Classes

You were first introduced to the Dock and Slip classes in Chapter 9. You will now modify these classes to support object persistence in a relational database application. VB .NET contains a class named Dock that is used for Windows forms. You cannot use the same class name, Dock, to represent a Bradshaw Marina dock if class methods are to be used with Windows forms. Thus, for this example, the class name to represent a dock for Bradshaw Marina will be mDock instead of Dock to eliminate the conflict with VB .NET's Dock class.

Within the mDock class, you need to add the namespace System.Data.OleDb for the database classes for accessing and processing databases. The mDock class does not currently require methods to insert, update, or delete dock records. The fact that docks (and slips) will be added, removed, and updated rarely is something that would have been discovered during analysis. For simplicity, these methods are not included in the following examples. The last modification to the mDock class is to include a TellAboutSelf method. A partial listing (accessor methods omitted) of the revised mDock class appears in Figure 14-25.

```
' Chapter 14 Example2 Dock
' Class mDock
Imports System.Data.OleDb
Imports System.Collections
Public Class mDock
    ' Attributes
    Private dockID As String
    Private location As String
    Private electricity As Boolean
    Private water As Boolean

    ' References to slips associated with dock (1 to many)
    Private slips As ArrayList

    ' Constructor (four parameters)
    Public Sub New(ByVal aDockID As String, ByVal aLocation As String, _
      ByVal anElectricity As Boolean, ByVal aWater As Boolean)
        'invoke setter methods to populate attributes
        SetDockId(aDockID)
        SetLocation(aLocation)
        SetElectricity(AnElectricity)
        SetWater(aWater)
        slips = New ArrayList()
    End Sub

    ' Customer method AddSlipToDock
    Public Sub AddSlipToDock(ByVal aSlip As Slip)
        slips.Add(aSlip)
        aSlip.SetDock(Me)
    End Sub
```

```
' Add the slip reference to the ArrayList instance
Public Sub AddSlip(ByVal aSlip As Slip)
    slips.Add(aSlip)
End Sub

' DA Shared Methods
Public Shared Sub Initialize(ByVal c As OleDbConnection)
    DockDA.Initialize(c)
End Sub
Public Shared Function Find(ByVal key As Integer)
    Return DockDA.Find(key)
End Function
Public Shared Function GetAll() As ArrayList
    Return DockDA.GetAll
End Function
Public Shared Sub Terminate()
    DockDA.Terminate()
End Sub

' Return the ArrayList containing slip references
Public Function GetSlips() As ArrayList
    Return slips
End Function

'TellAboutSelf method
Public Function TellAboutSelf() As String
    Dim dockDetails As String
    dockDetails = "Dock " & dockID _
     & " Location: " & location _
     & ", Has Electricity= " & electricity _
     & ", Has water= " & water
    Return dockDetails
End Function
```

Figure 14-25 mDock class

The Slip class from Chapter 9 already includes the code necessary to associate a slip with its dock. Slips (like docks) are rarely added, removed, or updated; thus, the Slip class does not need Insert, Delete, or Update methods. Furthermore, in the DockAndSlipDatabase application, slip information is needed only when dock information is retrieved. The Find and GetAll methods of the DockDA class will retrieve information about a dock and all of its slips, which means that the Slip class does not need Find and GetAll methods of its own. Accordingly, you do not need to modify the Slip class and you do not need a SlipDA class.

Introducing the DockDA Class

The DockAndSlipDatabase application will need to access information in DockTable. For this reason, you need a DockDA class. The DockDA class is similar to the other DA classes with which you have worked, except that it does not require methods to insert, delete, or update dock information. The class begins by importing the necessary namespaces, then defining dock and slip reference variables, as well as an ArrayList of dock references. Next, it declares variables for the database connection, followed by variables to hold the slip and dock attribute values.

```
' Chapter 14 -- Example2 DockDA
' Dock DA class
Imports System.Data.OleDb
Imports System.Collections

Public Class DockDA
    Shared aSlip As Slip
    Shared aDock As mDock
    Shared docks As New ArrayList()

    Shared aConnection As OleDbConnection

    ' Declare variable for slip attribute values
    Shared slipNo, width, dockId As Integer
    Shared slipLength As Double

    ' Declare variables for dock attribute values
    Shared id As Integer
    Shared location As String
    Shared electricity, water As Boolean
```

Methods to initialize and terminate the connection to the database are identical to those used previously in other DA classes, and are not repeated here. The code for these methods is included in the book's student data files.

Understanding the Find Method of the DockDA Class

The Find method of the DockDA class defines the SQL SELECT statement needed to extract dock and slip information from the database. The WHERE clause, which specifies both the join condition and the primary key value for the dock of interest, is followed by an ORDER BY clause. The ORDER BY clause specifies that the information returned by the query is to be sorted in order by slip number.

```
"SELECT DockTable.DockId, Location, " & _
      "Electricity, Water, SlipNo, Width, SlipLength " & _
      "FROM DockTable, SlipTable " & _
      "WHERE DockTable.DockId = SlipTable.DockId " & _
      "AND DockTable.DockId = " & key & " ORDER BY SlipNo"
```

The query result set contains dock attributes and slip attributes for every slip on the designated dock. You can picture the result set as a temporary table of its own. If you direct the SQL query to find DockId=1, for example, the result set would include the information shown in Table 14-1.

Table 14-1 Result Set of the Find Method When DockId=1

DockId	Location	Electricity	Water	SlipNo	Width	SlipLength
1	Main Cove	1	0	1	10	20
1	Main Cove	1	0	2	12	25

Note that in the result set, information for Dock 1 is repeated for each slip on that dock. The information for Dock 1 is also repeated for each slip. However, as the system retrieves items from the dataset, it should obtain the dock attributes and create a dock instance only once. You can avoid unnecessary handling of the dock attributes by using a Boolean variable named dockCreated. You initially set the value of dockCreated to False, then check its value within the For loop. The first time through the loop, the value of dockCreated is False, so dock attributes are retrieved and used to create a dock instance. You then set the value of dockCreated to True so that subsequent passes through the result dataset will not create a new dock instance. Note that in VB .NET, a zero (0) represents False and any other value represents True. In our system, 0 is used for False and 1 for True in the database.

```
Dim dsDockSlip As New DataSet()
Try     ' Execute Query, fill dataset
    Dim adptDockSlip As New OleDbDataAdapter(sqlQuery, aConnection)
    adptDockSlip.Fill(dsDockSlip, "DockSlip")
    Dim dr As DataRow
    Dim dockCreated As Boolean = False
    ' Check for rows in dataset table
    If dsDockSlip.Tables("DockSlip").Rows.Count > 0 Then
        ' Loop over all the rows in the table
        For Each dr In dsDockSlip.Tables("DockSlip").Rows
            ' Create dock if first time through loop
            If Not dockCreated Then
                dockId = dr("DockId")
                location = dr("Location")
                electricity = dr("Electricity")
                water = dr("Water")

                ' Create a dock instance
                aDock = New mDock(dockId, location, _
                    electricity, water)
                dockCreated = True
            End If
```

Slip attributes are retrieved on each pass through the dataset, and a corresponding slip instance is created each time. Recall that the Slip constructor method establishes the two-way connection between Slip and Dock by invoking the AddSlipToDock method.

```
            slipNo = dr("SlipNo")
            width = dr("width")
            slipLength = dr("slipLength")

            ' Create slip instances--
            ' Note there may be more than one slip per dock
            aSlip = New Slip(slipNo, width, slipLength, aDock)
        Next
        dsDockSlip = Nothing
```

If the specified dock in the SQL statement cannot be found in the database, the code throws a NotFoundException error and exits the method. Otherwise, the dock instance, complete with an ArrayList of its slip instances, is returned to the calling program.

```
            If Not dockCreated Then
                Throw New NotFoundException("Dock Not Found")
            End If
        Catch e As OleDb.OleDbException
            Console.WriteLine(e.Message.ToString)
        End Try
        Return aDock
    End Function
```

Understanding the GetAll Method of the DockDA Class

The GetAll method is similar to the Find method, except that the SQL query returns dock and slip information for all docks and slips in the marina, sorted in order by dock and then by slip.

```
Dim sqlQuery As String = "SELECT DockTable.DockId, Location, " & _
        "Electricity, Water, SlipNo, Width, SlipLength " & _
        "FROM DockTable, SlipTable " & _
        "WHERE slipTable.DockId = DockTable.DockId " & _
        "ORDER BY DockTable.DockId, SlipNo"
```

In this case, the result set includes the information shown in Table 14-2.

Table 14-2 Result Set of the GetAll Method

DockId	Location	Electricity	Water	SlipNo	Width	SlipLength
1	Main Cove	1	0	1	10	20
1	Main Cove	1	0	2	12	25
2	Main Marina	0	1	1	16	35
2	Main Marina	0	1	3	14	30
2	Main Marina	0	1	4	10	20

In the result set, information for *every* dock is repeated for each slip on that dock. Information for Dock 1 is repeated twice. Information for Dock 2 is repeated three times. However, the system should retrieve dock information and create a dock instance only once for each dock. The code takes this into consideration by incorporating what is known as control-break logic. A **control-break** occurs when there is a change in the value of a variable that is used to group a list of sorted items. In this case, slips are sorted in order by slip number and grouped with dock number being the grouping (or control) field. When the dock number changes, information about a different dock needs to be extracted.

As shown in Figure 14-26, the variables thisDockId and prevDockId determine when a control-break (change in dock number) occurs. The program initially sets the value of thisDockId equal to the DockId obtained from the first row of the dataset. Each time through the outer For Next loop, the program stores this value of the control field in prevDockId and then extracts the remaining dock attributes from the dataset and creates a dock instance. A reference to the dock instance is added to the ArrayList that will be returned to the calling program. The inner For Next loop executes until a change in DockId occurs (a control-break) or the end of the dataset is reached.

On each pass through the inner For Next loop, the program extracts slip attributes from the current row of the dataset and creates a slip instance. Recall that when a slip instance is created, the AddSlipToDock method is invoked to associate the slip with its dock. The program then moves to the next row of the dataset and sets the value of this DockId equal to the DockId obtained from the current row of the dataset. When the inner For Next loop detects a change in the dock number, control returns to the outer For Next loop and the entire process is repeated until all rows of the dataset are processed.

```
Try    ' Execute the SQL statement and fill the dataset
    Dim dsDockSlip As New DataSet()
    Dim adptDockSlip As New OleDbDataAdapter(sqlQuery, aConnection)
    adptDockSlip.Fill(dsDockSlip, "DockSlip")

    ' Define working variables
    Dim dr, dra As DataRow
    Dim i, j, thisDockId, prevDockId, nbrInDS As Integer
    ' Get the number of rows in the dataset table
    nbrInDS = dsDockSlip.Tables("DockSlip").Rows.Count - 1
    ' If rows in the table then process
    If nbrInDS > 0 Then
          thisDockId = dsDockSlip.Tables("DockSlip").Rows(0).Item("DockId")
          ' Clear array list
          docks.Clear()
          For i = 0 To nbrInDS
                dr = dsDockSlip.Tables("DockSlip").Rows(i)
                ' Save value of control-break field
                prevDockId = thisDockId
                location = dr("location")
                electricity = dr("Electricity")
                water = dr("Water")
                ' Create a dock instance
                aDock = New mDock(thisDockId, location, electricity, water)
                docks.Add(aDock)
                ' Loop over rows until a change in dock id
                For j = i To nbrInDS
                      dra = dsDockSlip.Tables("DockSlip").Rows(j)
                      thisDockId = dra("DockId")
                      If thisDockId > prevDockId Then Exit For
                      slipNo = dra("slipNo")
                      width = dra("width")
                      slipLength = dra("SlipLength")
                      ' Create slip instances for the dock
                      aSlip = New Slip(slipNo, width, _
                            slipLength, aDock)
                Next
                i = j - 1
          Next
          dsDockSlip = Nothing
    End If
  Catch e As OleDb.OleDbException
    Console.WriteLine(e.Message.ToString)
  End Try
  Return docks
End Function
```

Outer For loop executes until the end of the result set is reached

Dock attributes are extracted on each pass through the outer For loop

Slip attributes are extracted on each pass through the inner For loop

Inner For loop executes until a new dock is encountered (or the end of the result set is reached)

Figure 14-26 Control-break logic in the GetAll method of the DockDA class

The control-break logic should now be clear. The outer loop executes once for each new value of the DockId in the dataset. On each pass, the outer loop extracts a dock attribute and creates a dock instance. The inner loop executes once for each slip of the dock, extracting attributes for the slip and creating a new slip instance. When all the rows in the dataset have been processed, the program returns an ArrayList of dock instances to the calling program. Each dock instance contains an ArrayList of references to its slips.

Testing the DockAndSlipDatabase Application

The test script for the classes in the DockAndSlipDatabase application first declares the necessary variables and the connection to the database is established. Next, it attempts to find Dock 1. If it finds the dock in the dataset, the Find method returns a reference to that dock instance. The dock instance includes references to its slips. The printDetails method displays information about the dock and its slips. Next, the test script attempts to find Dock 2, and if successful, displays information about Dock 2 and its slips. Finally, the test script invokes the GetAll method, which produces a list of all docks and the slips that belong to each of them. The source code for the test script is shown in Figure 14-27, and the output from this program is shown in Figure 14-28.

```
Imports System.Data.OleDb
Imports System.Collections

Public Class Form1
    Inherits System.Windows.Forms.Form
    Shared aSlip As Slip
    Shared aDock As mDock
    Shared docks, slips As ArrayList
    Shared c As OleDbConnection = DockAndSlipDataBaseConnect.Initialize

    Private Sub testDAClasses()

        ' Initialize the database
        mDock.Initialize(c)
        Try
            aDock = mDock.Find(1)
            Console.WriteLine(vbCrLf & "Results of Find dock 1:")
            printDetails()
        Catch e As NotFoundException
            Console.WriteLine(e.Message.ToString)
        End Try

        Try
            Console.WriteLine(vbCrLf & "Results of Find dock 2:")
            aDock = mDock.Find(2)
            printDetails()
        Catch e As NotFoundException
            Console.WriteLine(e.Message.ToString)
        End Try
```

```
        Console.WriteLine(vbCrLf & "Results of GetAll")
        docks = mDock.GetAll
        Dim dcks As mDock
        For Each dcks In docks
            aDock = dcks
            printDetails()
        Next
        MessageBox.Show("Testing Script Complete, See Results")
        mDock.Terminate()
        Me.Close()
    End Sub
    Private Sub printDetails()
        Console.WriteLine(vbCrLf & aDock.TellAboutSelf)
        slips = aDock.GetSlips
        Dim slps As Slip
        For Each slps In slips
            aSlip = slps
            Console.WriteLine("    " + aSlip.TellAboutSelf)
        Next

    End Sub
    Private Sub btnTester1_Click(ByVal sender As System.Object, _
        ByVal e As System.EventArgs) Handles btnTester1.Click

        testDAClasses()
    End Sub
```

Figure 14-27 The test script program

```
Results of Find dock 1:

Dock 1 Location: Main Cove, Has Electricity= True, Has water= False
  Slip 1  Width: 10  Length: 20
  Slip 2  Width: 12  Length: 25

Results of Find dock 2:

Dock 2 Location: Main Marina, Has Electricity= False, Has water= True
  Slip 1  Width: 16  Length: 35
  Slip 3  Width: 14  Length: 30
  Slip 4  Width: 10  Length: 20
```

Figure 14-28 Output of the test script program

```
Results of GetAll:

Dock 1 Location: Main Cove, Has Electricity= True, Has water= False
  Slip 1  Width: 10  Length: 20
  Slip 2  Width: 12  Length: 25

Dock 2 Location: Main Marina, Has Electricity= False, Has water= True
  Slip 1  Width: 16  Length: 35
  Slip 3  Width: 14  Length: 30
  Slip 4  Width: 10  Length: 20
```

Figure 14-28 Output of the test script program (continued)

Hands-on Exercise 2

1. Open the **Example2** folder in the Chap14\Exercises\Ex02 folder in the work folder on your system. The Example2 folder contains all the VB .NET files for a solution for Example2.
2. Recall that the Example2 folder contains a bin subfolder where the DockAndSlipDatabase.mdb file is stored. If necessary, change the properties of the bin folder and the DockAndSlipDatabase.mdb file to remove the Read-only property, as explained in Hands-on Exercise 1.
3. Double-click the **Chap14Example2.sln** file in **Chap14\Exercises\Ex02\Example2** to open the Chap14Example2 VB .NET application, and then click the **Start** button.
4. Click the button on the form to run the testing program. Verify that the results match those in Figure 14-28.

APPLYING PARENT-CHILD (HIERARCHICAL) DATASET RELATIONSHIPS

The control-break logic described in the previous section applies mostly for reporting applications. You will find this logic built into the report capabilities of some programming languages (such as COBOL's report generator) or in separate report generator products such as Crystal Reports. Basically, control-break logic is needed if you work with data stored as a flat file (or joined tables of a database), but the application is best represented by a hierarchical, or parent-child, relationship. For example, you can consider the dock and slip relationship as a parent-child relationship. A dock can have many slips, but each slip must be associated with only one dock. To report the information about docks and slips, the tables DockTable and

SlipTable were joined into a table of rows and columns—essentially a flat file. Recall that the dock data was duplicated. (Refer back to Table 14-2.)

If you could establish a parent-child relationship between DockTable and SlipTable, the processing logic would be much simpler and more intuitive. The logic would be that for each row of DockTable, iterate over SlipTable finding all the slips that belonged to the corresponding dock. Visually, the relationship is shown in Figure 14-29.

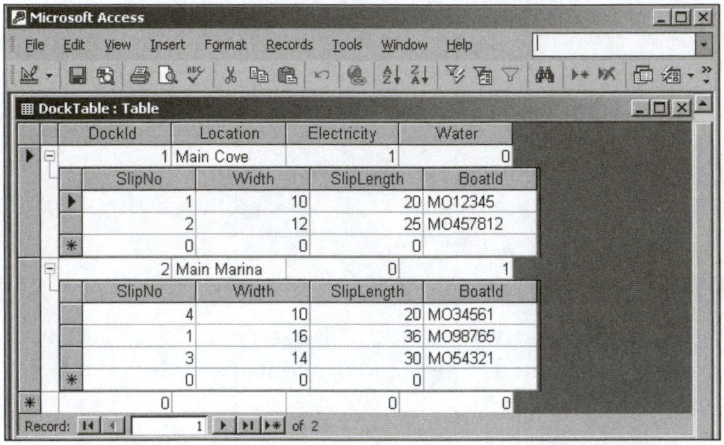

Figure 14-29 Parent-child (hierarchical) relationship of DockTable and SlipTable

VB .NET datasets provide the functionality of establishing parent-child relationships of the tables in a dataset. To illustrate the concepts, the GetAll method of the DockDA class from the previous example will be rewritten using a parent-child relationship of a dataset. The first part of the GetAll method declares an ArrayList to hold the dock and slip references extracted from the dataset. Then two DataTable variables, dtDocks and dtSlips, are declared—dtDocks will serve as the **parent table** and dtSlips will serve as the **child table**. A dataset is also declared.

SQL SELECT statements to extract the data from the two tables are declared, and then the two data adapters execute their corresponding SQL SELECT statements, filling their corresponding tables in the dataset with data extracted from the database tables. Next, dtDocks and dtSlips are set to the appropriate DataTable in the dataset. This segment of the code follows:

```
' GetAll method using parent-child approach
Public Shared Function GetAll() As ArrayList
    ' Declare data tables for the dataset
    Dim dtDocks, dtSlips As DataTable
```

```
' Declare the SQL queries to get each table
Dim sqlDocks As String = "SELECT DockId, Location, " & _
        "Electricity, Water " & _
    " FROM DockTable ORDER BY DockID"
Dim sqlSlips As String = "SELECT SlipNo, DockID, " & _
        "Width, SlipLength " & _
    "FROM SlipTable ORDER BY DockId, SlipNo"
' Declare a new dataset to hold the docks and slips tables
Dim dsDocksSlips As New DataSet("DocksAndSlips")

Try     ' Create adapters
    Dim adptDocks As New OleDbDataAdapter(sqlDocks, aConnection)
    Dim adptSlips As New OleDbDataAdapter(sqlSlips, aConnection)
    ' Fill the dataset with two tables, naming them docks and slips
    adptDocks.Fill(dsDocksSlips, "Docks")
    adptSlips.Fill(dsDocksSlips, "Slips")
    ' Set the tables in the datasets to corresponding data tables
    dtDocks = dsDocksSlips.Tables("Docks")
    dtSlips = dsDocksSlips.Tables("Slips")
```

A VB .NET dataset, in addition to holding table objects, can also have **DataRelation** objects. Creating a DataRelation simply requires declaring the DataRelation, assigning it a user-defined name, and associating the column from each DataTable to serve as the relationship between the parent and child tables. In this case, the relationship column is DockId from each DataTable as shown in the following code. After declaring the relationship, it is then added to the dataset.

```
' Declare a relationship named DocksSlips
' dtDocks is parent table, dtSlips is child table
Dim drDocksSlips As New DataRelation("DocksSlips", _
    dtDocks.Columns("DockId"), _
    dtSlips.Columns("DockId"))

' Add relation to dataset
dsDocksSlips.Relations.Add(drDocksSlips)
```

14

Now that the relationship has been added to the dataset, you can loop over the collection of rows for the parent table, dtDocks in this case, getting all the child rows from the child table for that particular dock and saving the child rows in a DataRows collection, drDockSlip in this case. Note that the GetChildRows method retrieves all the child rows (slips) from the child DataTable for a particular dock. It is then easy to loop over the DataRows collection containing all the child rows for the given dock. As before, instances of docks and slips are created and saved in the ArrayList docks. The remaining code to do this is shown below.

```
' Declare a datarow for the parent and the child
' Declare datarows for all the child rows of the parent
Dim drDock, drSlip, drDockSlip() As DataRow
```

```
        ' Clear array list
        docks.Clear()
        For Each drDock In dtDocks.Rows
            ' Extract the data from the parent table
            id = drDock("DockID")
            location = drDock("Location")
            electricity = drDock("Electricity")
            water = drDock("Water")
            ' Create a new dock and add to the docks ArrayList
            aDock = New mDock(id, location, electricity, water)
            docks.Add(aDock)
            ' Get all the child rows for this parent
            drDockSlip = drDock.GetChildRows("DocksSlips")
            ' Loop over child rows, extract data and create slip
            For Each drSlip In drDockSlip
                slipNo = drSlip("SlipNo")
                width = drSlip("Width")
                slipLength = drSlip("SlipLength")
                aSlip = New Slip(slipNo, width, slipLength, aDock)
            Next
        Next
        dsDocksSlips = Nothing
    Catch e As OleDb.OleDbException
        Console.WriteLine(e.Message.ToString)
    End Try
    ' Return the docks ArrayList
    Return docks
End Function
```

Hands-on Exercise 3

1. Locate **Ex03** in the Chap14\Examples folder in the book's student data files. Create a folder named **Chap14\Exercises\Ex03** on your system, and then copy the **Ex03** folder to this folder. The Example3 folder contains all the VB .NET files for a solution for Example3.

2. The Example3 folder contains a bin subfolder where the DockAndSlipDatabase.mdb file is stored. If necessary, change the properties of the bin folder and the DockAndSlipDatabase.mdb file to remove the Read-only property, as explained in Hands-on Exercise 1.

3. Double-click the **Chap14Example3.sln** file in the Chap14\Exercises\Ex03\Example3 folder to open this VB .NET application, and then click the **Start** button.

4. Click the button on the form to run the testing program. Verify that the results match those in Figure 14-28.

IMPLEMENTING AN ASSOCIATION CLASS IN A DATABASE APPLICATION

You have learned how to implement one-to-one and one-to-many associations in a relational database application. To develop a complete database application for Bradshaw Marina, however, you must also implement the Lease association class. The Lease class, along with its AnnualLease and DailyLease subclasses, was first introduced in Chapter 8. In Chapter 9 you learned how to create and use the Lease class when persistence was not an issue. You will now learn how to implement the Lease association class in a relational database application.

Understanding the Tables in CustomerLeaseSlipDatabase

This application involves three database tables: CustomerTable, LeaseTable, and SlipTable. Before developing the VB .NET programs needed for this application, review these tables.

To review these tables:

1. Locate **Ex04** in the Chap14\Examples folder in the book's student data files, and copy it to the **Chap14\Exercises** folder in the work folder on your system.
2. Double-click **CustomerLeaseSlipDatabase.mdb** in the bin folder of Chap14\Exercises\Ex04\Example4 to open it in Microsoft Access. Notice that the database contains three tables: CustomerTable, LeaseTable, and SlipTable.
3. View the contents of CustomerTable, LeaseTable, and SlipTable. See Figure 14-30.

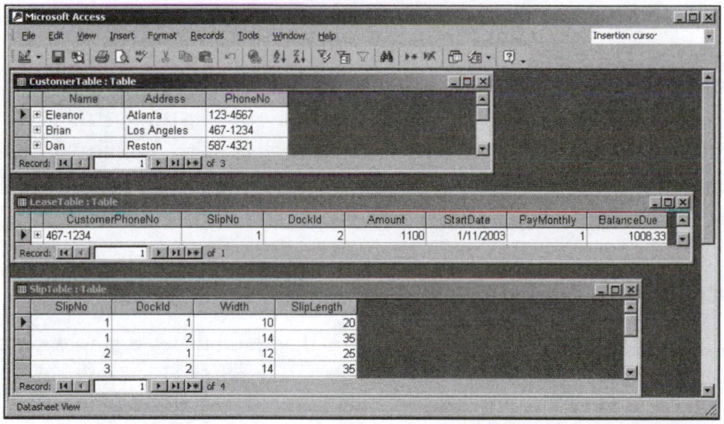

Figure 14-30 Contents of CustomerTable, LeaseTable, and SlipTable

4. Recall from Chapter 9 that there is exactly one lease between each customer and slip. For this reason, you can use a customer's phone number (CustomerPhoneNo) as the

primary key for LeaseTable. A customer's phone number (PhoneNo) is also the primary key for CustomerTable, which means that you can use the customer phone number in LeaseTable as a foreign key to link to the information in CustomerTable.

5. LeaseTable contains columns for slip number and dock ID. These columns serve as a concatenated foreign key to records in SlipTable. Figure 14-31 depicts these relationships.

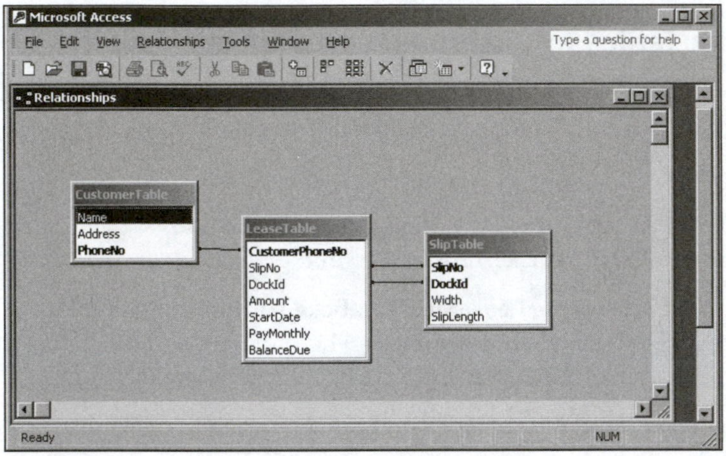

Figure 14-31 Relationships diagram for CustomerTable, LeaseTable, and SlipTable

The CustomerLeaseSlip application involves the use of four problem domain classes—Customer, Slip, Lease, and AnnualLease. It also involves the use of three data access classes—CustomerDA, SlipDA, and LeaseDA—as well as a test and a class to establish a connection to the database. For classes that have been discussed previously, only the modifications needed for the CustomerLeaseSlip application will be discussed here.

Establishing a Connection to CustomerLeaseSlipDatabase

As with DockAndSlipDatabase, you need a program that establishes a single connection to CustomerLeaseSlipDatabase. The PD and DA classes involved in this application will share this connection. The CustomerLeaseSlipConnect program is identical to the other connect programs in this chapter (except, of course, the specified data source name) and is not discussed here. The code for this program is included in the book's student data files.

Modifying the Customer Class

For this application, you need to associate a customer instance with its lease instance. To do this, add a lease reference to the list of attributes defined in the Customer PD class. Recall that the Lease class is an abstract class, which means that you cannot create lease instances.

Instead, you must create instances of one of its subclasses (AnnualLease or DailyLease). In this example, the lease instance is of the AnnualLease type. The constructor initially sets the value of the AnnualLease reference variable to nothing. You include setter and getter methods to set and retrieve the AnnualLease reference variable. A partial listing of the Customer class source code is shown in Figure 14-32. Only the parts relevant to the changes required for this application are included here. The complete Customer class is contained in Example4 in the Chap14\Examples\Ex04 folder for this text.

```
Customer Class with added methods for DA Class
' Chapter 14 -- Example4
Imports System.Data.OleDb
Public Class Customer
    ' Attributes
    Private name As String
    Private address As String
    Private phoneNo As String
    ' Reference variable for lease instance
    Private lease As AnnualLease

    ' Constructor (3 parameters)
    Public Sub New(ByVal aName As String, ByVal anAddress As String, _
        ByVal aPhoneNo As String)

        name = aName
        address = anAddress
        phoneNo = aPhoneNo
        SetLease(Nothing)        'Initially set to nothing
    End Sub
    Public Function GetLease() As AnnualLease
        Return lease
    End Function

    Public Sub SetLease(ByVal aLease As AnnualLease)
        lease = aLease
    End Sub
```

Figure 14-32 Customer class with lease attribute

14

Modifying the Lease and AnnualLease Classes

The Lease problem domain class from Chapter 8 requires similar modification. The Lease class must associate a lease with its customers and slips. Accordingly, you add a slip reference variable and a customer reference variable to the attribute list and initially set them to Nothing in the constructor. Include getter and setter methods to retrieve and set these values. Recall that Lease is an abstract class and you cannot create lease instances. In this application, LeaseTable contains information about instances of the AnnualLease subclass. Accordingly, the Lease class does not require DA methods. Necessary DA methods will instead be added to the concrete AnnualLease subclass. The modified Lease class definition is shown in Figure 14-33.

```
Lease -- abstract association class
' between Slip and Customer

Public MustInherit Class Lease

    ' Attributes
    Private amount As Double
    Private startDate As DateTime
    Private endDate As DateTime

    ' References to slip and customer
    Private theSlip As Slip
    Private theCustomer As Customer

    ' Constructor (1 parameter)
    Public Sub New(ByVal aStartDate As DateTime)
        SetStartDate(aStartDate)
        SetEndDate(Nothing)    ' endDate set by subclass
        SetAmount(0)
        ' No customer or slip yet, set by subclass
        SetCustomer(Nothing)
        SetSlip(Nothing)
    End Sub

    ' TellAboutSelf method
    Public Overridable Function TellAboutSelf() As String
        Return ("Start Date: " & startDate & _
        "   End Date: " & endDate & _
        " Lease Amount=" & amount)
    End Function

    ' Custom method CalculateFee based on slip width
    ' Abstract method all subclasses must implement
    Public MustOverride Function CalculateFee(ByVal aWidth As Integer) _
    As Single

    'Get accessor methods
    Public Function GetStartDate() As DateTime
        Return startDate
    End Function
    Public Function GetEndDate() As DateTime
        Return endDate
    End Function
    Public Function GetAmount() As Double
        Return amount
    End Function
    Public Function GetCustomer() As Customer
        Return theCustomer
    End Function
    Public Function GetSlip() As Slip
        Return theSlip
    End Function
```

```
    ' Set accessor methods
    Public Sub SetStartDate(ByVal aStartDate As DateTime)
        startDate = aStartDate
    End Sub
    Public Sub SetEndDate(ByVal anEndDate As DateTime)
        endDate = anEndDate
    End Sub
    Public Sub SetAmount(ByVal anAmount As Double)
        amount = anAmount
    End Sub
    Public Sub SetCustomer(ByVal aCustomer As Customer)
        theCustomer = aCustomer
    End Sub
    Public Sub SetSlip(ByVal aSlip As Slip)
        theSlip = aSlip
    End Sub

End Class
```

Figure 14-33 Lease class with slip and customer attributes

DA methods need to be added to the AnnualLease subclass from Chapter 8 to support this application. As shown in Figure 14-34, only four DA methods are needed: Initialize, Terminate, Find, and AddNew. For brevity, only the first part of the class and the required DA methods are shown in Figure 14-34; the complete code for the Lease class is contained in Example4 of the book's student data files.

```
' Chapter 14 -- Example4
' AnnualLease -- a subclass of Lease
Imports System.Data.OleDb

Public Class AnnualLease
    Inherits Lease

    ' Attributes in addition to those inherited from Lease
    Private balanceDue As Single
    Private payMonthly As Boolean

    ' Constructor (three values as parameters)
    Public Sub New(ByVal aStartDate As DateTime, _
     ByVal aSlipWidth As Integer, _
     ByVal isPayMonthly As Boolean)
        ' Invoke superclass constructor
        MyBase.New(aStartDate)
        ' Calculate end date
        Dim yearLater As DateTime = aStartDate.AddYears(1)
        ' Invoke superclass method to set end date
        SetEndDate(yearLater)
        ' Invoke superclass SetAmount method after getting
        ' Fee amount from CalculateFee method
```

```
        SetAmount(CalculateFee(aSlipWidth))
        ' Set payMonthly
        SetPayMonthly(isPayMonthly)
        ' Set balance due if applicable
        If payMonthly Then
            SetBalanceDue(GetAmount() - GetAmount() / 12)
        Else
            SetBalanceDue(0)
        End If
    End Sub

    ' DA shared Methods---------------------------------------
    Public Shared Sub Initialize(ByVal c As OleDbConnection)
        AnnualLeaseDA.Initialize(c)
    End Sub
    Public Shared Function Find(ByVal key As String) As AnnualLease
        Return AnnualLeaseDA.Find(key)
    End Function
    Public Shared Sub Terminate()
        AnnualLeaseDA.Terminate()
    End Sub

    ' DA Non-shared method
    Public Sub AddNew()
        AnnualLeaseDA.AddNew(Me)
    End Sub
```

Figure 14-34 AnnualLease class with DA methods included

Modifying the Slip Class

The Slip class must associate a slip with its corresponding lease and customer. To accomplish this, you add an AnnualLease reference to the attribute list and set its value to Nothing in the constructor.

```
' Chapter 14 Example4
' Slip Class
Imports System.Data.OleDb
Imports System.Collections
Public Class Slip
    ' Attributes
    Private slipId As Integer
    Private slipWidth As Integer
    Private slipLength As Integer

    ' Reference variables
    Private DockId As Integer
    Private lease As AnnualLease

    ' Constructor (three parameters plus a Dock reference)
    Public Sub New(ByVal aSlipId As Integer, ByVal aSlipWidth As Integer, _
        ByVal aSlipLength As Integer, ByVal aDockId As Integer)
```

```
        'invoke setter methods to populate attributes
        SetSlipId(aSlipId)
        SetSlipWidth(aSlipWidth)
        SetSlipLength(aSlipLength)
        'invoke custom method for Dock association
        setDock(aDockId)
        setLease(Nothing)
    End Sub
```

Include getter and setter methods to retrieve and set the lease reference.

```
' Get accessor methods
Public Function GetSlipId() As Integer
    Return slipId
End Function
Public Function GetSlipWidth() As Integer
    Return slipWidth
End Function
Public Function GetSlipLength() As Integer
    Return slipLength
End Function
Public Function GetDockID() As Integer
    Return DockId
End Function
Public Function getLease()
    Return lease
End Function

' Set accessor methods
Public Sub SetSlipId(ByVal aSlipId As Integer)
    slipId = aSlipId
End Sub
Public Sub SetSlipWidth(ByVal aSlipWidth As Integer)
    slipWidth = aSlipWidth
End Sub
Public Sub SetSlipLength(ByVal aSlipLength As Integer)
    slipLength = aSlipLength
End Sub
Public Sub SetDock(ByVal aDockId As Integer)
    DockId = aDockId
End Sub
Public Sub SetLease(ByVal aLease As AnnualLease)
    lease = aLease
End Sub
```

Three DA methods—Initialize, Terminate, and Find—are needed as well. These methods are similar to those used in the other domain classes. The only notable exception is that the Find method includes two parameters in its parameter list—one for slip number and one for dock ID. Recall that slip number and dock ID, taken together, form the concatenated primary key for SlipTable, and for that reason you need both items to locate a particular slip in the database.

```
' DA shared methods--------------------------------------
Public Shared Sub Initialize(ByVal c As OleDbConnection)
    SlipDA.Initialize(c)
End Sub
Public Shared Function Find(ByVal aSlipNo As Integer, _
    ByVal aDockId As Integer) As Slip
    Return SlipDA.Find(aSlipNo, aDockId)
End Function
Public Shared Sub Terminate()
    SlipDA.Terminate()
End Sub
```

You also need to define a custom method that associates the slip with its corresponding lease instance. This method, named LeaseAnnualSlip, enables the Slip class to take responsibility for much of the processing involved in the "customer lease slip" application. The LeaseAnnualSlip method requires three arguments—a customer reference variable (including the customer for whom the lease is being made), a date reference variable (indicating the start date for the lease), and a Boolean variable (indicating whether the lease will be paid in monthly installments or in full at the time the lease is made). The start date and payment information, together with the width of the slip, are used to create a new instance of the AnnualLease class.

```
' Custom method LeaseAnnualSlip creates AnnualLease instance
Public Function LeaseAnnualSlip(ByVal aCustomer As Customer, _
    ByVal aStartDate As DateTime, _
    ByVal isPaymonthly As Boolean) As AnnualLease

    ' Create AnnualLease instance and assign it to lease attributes
    ' width is an attribute of this slip
    lease = New AnnualLease(aStartDate, slipWidth, isPaymonthly)
```

The AnnualLease instance invokes its SetSlip and SetCustomer methods to associate itself with the slip and customer instances. Then, the customer instance invokes its SetLease method to associate itself with the newly created annual lease. A reference to the AnnualLease instance, which now contains references to its customer and slip, is then returned to the calling program.

```
    ' Tell lease to set its slip to this slip
    lease.SetSlip(Me)
    ' Tell lease to set its customer
    lease.SetCustomer(aCustomer)
    ' Tell customer to set its lease
    aCustomer.SetLease(lease)
    Return lease
End Function
```

Introducing the SlipDA Class

Recall that the database application illustrating the one-to-many relationship between Dock and Slip did not require a SlipDA class. In that application, the Find and GetAll methods of the dock performed the task of locating all of the slips for a dock. In the CustomerLeaseSlip application, however, you must find a particular slip so that it can be leased to a customer. Thus, you now need a SlipDA class.

The SlipDA class begins by declaring variables for slip attributes and those needed to establish the database connection. This is followed by the Initialize and Terminate methods, which are identical to those in the other DA classes.

```
' Chapter 14 -- Example4
' SlipDA class
Imports System.Data.OleDb
Public Class SlipDA
    Shared aSlip As Slip

    ' Declare variables for the database connection
    Shared aConnection As OleDbConnection

    ' Declare variables for Slip attribute values
    Shared slipNo, slipWidth, dockId As Integer
    Shared slipLength As Double

    ' Establish the database connection
    Public Shared Sub Initialize(ByVal c As OleDbConnection)
        Try
            ' Try to open the connection
            aConnection = c
            If Not aConnection.State.Open Then
                aConnection.Open()
            End If
        Catch e As Exception
            Console.WriteLine(e.Message.ToString)
        End Try
    End Sub

    ' Terminate the connection
    Public Shared Sub Terminate()
        ' Define string and assign to file
        Try
            aConnection.Close()
            aConnection = Nothing
        Catch e As Exception
            Console.WriteLine(e.ToString)
        End Try
    End Sub
```

The only other method the SlipDA class needs is a Find method. The Find method defines a SQL SELECT statement that returns information from SlipTable for a particular slip. Items extracted from the dataset are used to create a new slip instance. This slip instance is returned to the calling program.

```
    ' Find method
Public Shared Function Find(ByVal aSlipNo As Integer, _
    ByVal aDockId As Integer) As Slip

    aSlip = Nothing
    ' Define the SQL statement
    Dim sqlQuery As String = "SELECT SlipNo, DockID," & _
        "Width, SlipLength FROM SlipTable " & _
        "WHERE SlipNo = " & aSlipNo & " AND DockId = " & aDockId & " "

    Dim dockDS As New DataSet()

    Try
        ' Get the Dock
        Dim adptDock As New OleDbDataAdapter(sqlQuery, aConnection)
        adptDock.Fill(dockDS, "Docks")
        Dim dr As DataRow
        ' Check for rows in the dataset table
        If dockDS.Tables("Docks").Rows.Count > 0 Then
            dr = dockDS.Tables("Docks").Rows(0)
            slipNo = dr("SlipNo")
            dockId = dr("DockId")
            slipWidth = dr("Width")
            slipLength = dr("SlipLength")
            ' Create a slip instance
            aSlip = New Slip(slipNo, slipWidth, slipLength, dockId)
        Else     ' Dock was not found
            Throw New NotFoundException("Not Found")

        End If
        dockDS = Nothing

    Catch e As OleDb.OleDbException
        Console.WriteLine(e.Message.ToString)

    End Try
    Return aSlip
End Function
```

Introducing the AnnualLeaseDA Class

In the CustomerLeaseSlip application, you must find and insert information about annual leases in the database. This means that you need an AnnualLeaseDA class. The

AnnualLeaseDA class begins by declaring variables for AnnualLease attributes, then defines standard Initialize and Terminate methods.

```
' Chapter 14 -- Example4
' AnnualLeaseDA class
Imports System.Data.OleDb
Public Class AnnualLeaseDA
    Shared aCustomer As customer
    Shared aSlip As slip
    Shared aLease As AnnualLease
    Shared payMonthly As Boolean

    Shared name, address, phoneNo As String

    Shared slipNo, slipWidth, dockId As Integer
    Shared slipLength As Double

    Shared amount, balanceDue As Double
    Shared startDate As DateTime

    ' References to customer and slip
    Dim customer As customer
    Dim slip As slip

    ' Declare  variables for database connection
    Shared aConnection As OleDbConnection

    Public Shared Sub Initialize(ByVal c As OleDbConnection)
        Try
            ' Try to open the connection
            aConnection = c
            If Not aConnection.State.Open Then
                aConnection.Open()
            End If
        Catch e As Exception
            Console.WriteLine(e.Message.ToString)
        End Try
    End Sub
    Public Shared Sub Terminate()
        ' Define string and assign to file
        Try
            aConnection.Close()
            aConnection = Nothing
        Catch e As Exception
            Console.WriteLine(e.ToString)
        End Try
    End Sub
```

Understanding the Find Method of the AnnualLeaseDA Class

The Find method of the AnnualLeaseDA class requires an SQL query that retrieves data from three different tables: CustomerTable, LeaseTable, and SlipTable. Recall that the primary key of both LeaseTable and CustomerTable is customer phone number. This means that LeaseTable and CustomerTable can be joined on the common phone number attribute. Recall also that the slip number and dock ID attributes in LeaseTable together comprise a concatenated foreign key that can be used to join SlipTable. The WHERE clause uses these relationships for joining the three tables.

```
' Find method
Public Shared Function Find(ByVal key As String) As AnnualLease
    ' Retrieve Lease, Customer and Slip Data
    aCustomer = Nothing
    ' Define the SQL query
    Dim sqlQuery As String = "Select Name, Address, PhoneNo, " & _
        "LeaseTable.SlipNo, Amount, StartDate, " & _
        "PayMonthly, BalanceDue, " & _
        "SlipTable.DockId, Width, SlipLength " & _
        "FROM CustomerTable, LeaseTable, SlipTable " & _
        "WHERE PhoneNo = '" & key & "' " & _
        "AND CustomerPhoneNo = '" & key & "' " & _
        "AND LeaseTable.SlipNo = SlipTable.SlipNo " & _
        "AND LeaseTable.DockId = SlipTable.DockId"
```

The extracted data from the database tables is placed in a dataset. Items from the dataset are processed in a straightforward manner. Because VB .NET uses a zero (0) to represent the condition of False and any other integer to represent the condition of True, no conversion is needed when extracting PayMonthly from the database.

```
Dim ALds As New DataSet()
Dim dr As DataRow
Try
    Dim adptAL As New OleDbDataAdapter(sqlQuery, aConnection)
    adptAL.Fill(ALds, "ALtable")
    If ALds.Tables("altable").Rows.Count > 0 Then
        dr = ALds.Tables("altable").Rows(0)
        ' Get the values from the datarow
        ' Customer info
        name = dr("name")
        address = dr("address")
        phoneNo = dr("phoneno")
        ' Slip info
        slipNo = dr("slipNo")
        amount = dr("amount")
        startDate = dr("startdate")
        payMonthly = dr("paymonthly")
        balanceDue = dr("balanceDue")
        ' Dock info
```

```
            dockId = dr("dockId")
            slipWidth = dr("Width")
            slipLength = dr("slipLength")
```

The information obtained from the dataset is used to create customer, lease, and slip instances. The AnnualLease instance invokes the SetCustomer method to establish a link with the customer instance; the slip instance invokes the SetLease method of the Slip class to establish a link of the slip instance to the AnnualLease instance, and the customer instance invokes the setLease method of the Customer class to establish a link with the AnnualLease instance. Provided that no errors occur, the program returns an AnnualLease instance to the calling program.

```
             ' Create Customer, Lease, & Slip instances
              aCustomer = New Customer(name, address, phoneNo)
              aLease = New AnnualLease(startDate, slipWidth, payMonthly)
              aSlip = New Slip(slipNo, slipWidth, slipLength, dockId)

              aLease.SetCustomer(aCustomer)   ' Link Lease to Customer
              aSlip.SetLease(aLease)          ' Link Slip to Lease
              aCustomer.SetLease(aLease)      ' Link Customer to Lease
              aLease.SetSlip(aSlip)           ' Link Lease to Slip

          Else     ' Nothing was retrieved
              Throw New NotFoundException("Not Found")
              ALds = Nothing
              adptAL = Nothing
          End If
      Catch e As OleDb.OleDbException
          Console.WriteLine(e.Message.ToString)
      End Try
      Return aLease
  End Function
```

Understanding the AddNew Method of the AnnualLeaseDA Class

14

The AddNew method of the AnnualLeaseDA class adds a lease record to the database. The argument list receives a reference to the annual lease that will be added. The lease amount, balance due, payment type, and start date, along with references to the slip instance and customer instance that are associated with this lease, are extracted from the lease instance.

```
Public Shared Sub AddNew(ByVal aLease As AnnualLease)
        ' Declare integer variable for payMonthly
        Dim intPayMonthly As Integer

        ' Retrieve the lease attributes
        amount = aLease.GetAmount
        balanceDue = aLease.GetBalanceDue
        payMonthly = aLease.GetPayMonthly
        If payMonthly = True Then
            intPayMonthly = 1
        Else
            intPayMonthly = 0
```

```
            End If
            startDate = aLease.GetStartDate

            aSlip = aLease.GetSlip
            aCustomer = aLease.GetCustomer
```

The program extracts the customer phone number from the customer instance, then extracts the slip number and dock ID from the slip instance. Next, the Boolean variable payMonthly is converted to the integer values of 0 (False) or 1 (True) to allow storing this field in the database.

```
        ' Retrieve the customer's phoneno
        phoneNo = aCustomer.GetPhoneNo
        ' Retrieve the slipNo and dockId from the slip
        slipNo = aSlip.GetSlipId
        dockId = aSlip.GetDockID
```

Before executing the SQL statement that inserts this information into LeaseTable, you must see if the lease already exists in the database.You do this by checking to see if its primary key already exists in the database. If so, a DuplicateException is thrown. Otherwise, the program adds the lease record to the database.

```
            ' Create the SQL statement
            Dim sqlInsert As String = "INSERT INTO LeaseTable " & _
                "VALUES ('" & phoneNo & "', " & slipNo & ", " & _
                "" & dockId & ", " & amount & ", '" & startDate & "', " & _
                "" & intPayMonthly & ", " & balanceDue & " )"

            Dim adptAL As New OleDbDataAdapter()
            ' Determine if this lease already exists in the database
            Try
                Dim a As AnnualLease = AnnualLease.Find(phoneNo)
                Throw New DuplicateException("Lease Exists")
            Catch e As NotFoundException
                Try ' Assign Insert Commands and Execute
                    adptAL.InsertCommand = New OleDbCommand(sqlInsert)
                    adptAL.InsertCommand.Connection = aConnection
                    adptAL.InsertCommand.ExecuteNonQuery()
                Catch ee As OleDb.OleDbException
                    Console.WriteLine(ee.Message.ToString)
                End Try
            End Try
        End Sub
    End Class
```

Testing the CustomerLeaseSlip Database Application

The testing script begins by importing the classes (namespaces) required for the ArrayList and database processing. Then, the testing script declares an instance of the AnnualLease,

Customer, and Slip classes. Next, it establishes a connection to the CustomerLeaseSlip database and passes the connection to the Initialize methods of the Customer, AnnualLease, and Slip classes.

```
' Chapter 14 -- Example4
' Testing script
Imports System.Data.OleDb
Imports System.Collections

Public Class Form1
    Inherits System.Windows.Forms.Form

    Shared c As OleDbConnection = CustomerLeaseSlipConnect.Initialize
    ' Declare instances of AnnualLease, Customer, and Slip
    Shared aLease As AnnualLease = Nothing
    Shared aCustomer As Customer = Nothing
    Shared aSlip As Slip = Nothing

    Private Sub testDAClasses()
        ' Initialize the database connections

        Customer.Initialize(c)
        AnnualLease.Initialize(c)
        Slip.Initialize(c)
```

The testing script attempts to add a new record to LeaseTable—in this case, to show a customer is leasing the first slip in Dock 1. The Find method of the Customer class locates the record in CustomerTable for the customer with PhoneNo 123-4567, and then the Find method of the Slip class locates the record in SlipTable for Slip 1 on Dock 1. Each Find method returns an instance corresponding to the information in the database tables. The slip instance invokes its LeaseAnnualSlip method, which creates a new AnnualLease instance.

```
Try     'Get a Customer and Slip
    aCustomer = Customer.Find("123-4567")
    Console.WriteLine(vbCrLf & "Customer Information:" & _
        vbCrLf & aCustomer.TellAboutSelf)
    aSlip = Slip.Find(1, 1)
    Console.WriteLine(vbCrLf & "Slip Information:" & _
        vbCrLf & aSlip.TellAboutSelf)

    ' Lease slip to customer
    Dim aStartDate As DateTime = #8/26/2003#
    Dim payMonthly As Boolean = False

    aLease = aSlip.LeaseAnnualSlip(aCustomer, aStartDate, payMonthly)

Catch e As NotFoundException
    Console.WriteLine(e.Message.ToString)
End Try
```

The testing script calls the AddNew method of the Lease class to add the new lease to the database. If a lease for this customer already exists in the database, a DuplicateException is thrown.

```
Try      ' Add a new lease to the database
    aLease.AddNew()
    Console.WriteLine(vbCrLf & "New lease record added")
Catch e As DuplicateException
    Console.WriteLine(vbCrLf & "Lease Already Exists")
End Try
```

Next, the test script attempts to retrieve the newly added record from LeaseTable. The program passes the phone number 123-4567 to the Find method of the AnnualLease class. The Find method locates the lease record in LeaseTable and returns a reference to an AnnualLease instance containing that information. Recall that each AnnualLease instance contains references to its associated customer and slip instances. Their references invoke appropriate TellAboutSelf methods, which display the customer, lease, and slip details. Lastly, the test script closes the database connection and informs the user that the test script has completed.

```
        Try
            aLease = AnnualLease.Find("123-4567")
            aLease.GetCustomer()
            aLease.GetSlip()
            Console.WriteLine(vbCrLf & "Lease Information: " & _
                aLease.TellAboutSelf & vbCrLf & _
                aCustomer.TellAboutSelf & vbCrLf & aSlip.TellAboutSelf)
        Catch ee As NotFoundException
            Console.WriteLine(ee.Message.ToString)
            Customer.Terminate()
            Slip.Terminate()
            AnnualLease.Terminate()
            CustomerLeaseSlipConnect.Initialize()

        End Try

        MessageBox.Show("TestScript Completed--Review Output")
        Customer.Terminate()
        AnnualLease.Terminate()
        Slip.Terminate()

        Me.Close()
    End Sub

    Private Sub btnTester1_Click(ByVal sender As System.Object, _
        ByVal e As System.EventArgs) Handles btnTester1.Click

        testDAClasses()
    End Sub
```

The output of the test script is shown in Figure 14-35.

```
Customer Information:
Name = Eleanor, Address = Atlanta, Phone No = 123-4567

Slip Information:
Slip 1  Width: 10  Length: 20

New lease record added

Lease Information: Start Date: 8/26/2003  End Date: 8/26/2004 Lease Amount=800,
   BalanceDue=0  PayMonthly: False
Name = Eleanor, Address = Atlanta, Phone No = 123-4567
Slip 1  Width: 10  Length: 20
```

Figure 14-35 Output of the test script

Hands-on Exercise 4

1. Double-click the **Chap14Example4.sln** file in the Chap14\Exercises\Ex04\Example4 folder in your work folder to open VB .NET.
2. Click the **Start** button, and then click the only button on the Windows form. The testing script runs and indicates when it has finished.
3. Verify that the output of the testing script matches Figure 14-35.

NOTE: Running this program adds a record to LeaseTable. If you want to run this project again, open the database in Microsoft Access, open LeaseTable, and then delete the new record.

Chapter Summary

- Relational databases often include multiple tables. Information in different tables (such as CustomerTable and BoatTable) can be linked when the tables share a common attribute (such as phone number).
- A primary key is an attribute (or combination of attributes) that uniquely identifies a single record in a relational database table.
- A foreign key is an attribute (or column) in one relational database table that serves as a primary key in a different (or foreign) table. Primary/foreign key columns represent the common attributes used to link information in different tables.

- A concatenated key (primary or foreign) is one that consists of more than one attribute (or column) in the database table.
- Information in multiple relational tables that are linked via primary and foreign keys can be retrieved from the database by specifying a join condition in the WHERE clause of an SQL statement.
- An ORDER BY clause can be included in an SQL statement to sort the information returned by the query in a particular order.
- When multiple tables are required for a database application, the DA methods are modified to accommodate a more elaborate SQL statement. PD classes may also require minor modifications to reflect useful table linkages. For example, to make use of the fact that CustomerTable and BoatTable are related through a common phone number attribute, a customer attribute is added to the Boat PD class, a boat attribute is added to the Customer PD class, and methods to set and get these attributes must be provided.
- When multiple tables are involved, DA Insert and Delete methods must incorporate measures to preserve the integrity of the database. This means, for example, that when a customer record is inserted (or deleted), a corresponding boat record is also inserted (or deleted).
- When using multiple tables, DA Find and GetAll methods return a single instance of the specified type. This instance, however, will normally include one or more references to other instances of other types. Information retrieved from the database tables can be found by navigating these instances.
- A control-break occurs when there is a change in the value of a variable that is used to group a list of sorted items. Control-break logic is very common in business applications.
- VB .NET datasets provide the functionality to visualize and process data hierarchically—referred to as a parent-child relationship. This is accomplished by creating a DataRelation specifying the parent table, the child table, and the columns (fields) of the parent and child tables to serve as the basis for the relationship.

Key Terms

child table	DataRelation	parent table
concatenated key	foreign key	primary key
control-break	join	

Review Questions

1. Consider a relationship between the classes Person and Pet. Assume that every pet has exactly one owner and that a person may own none or many pets. Explain how you would implement these relationships in VB .NET.
2. Assume that the information to be tracked in the Pet and Person application includes pet identification number, pet name, pet type (dog, cat, etc.), person social security number, person name, person address, and person phone number. How would you structure the tables in a relational database for the Pet and Person application? In other words, what columns would you include in the Pet table and what columns would you include in the Person table?
3. Identify the column (or columns) in each table that would serve as a primary key for the Pet and Person application.
4. Identify the column (or columns) in each table that would serve as foreign keys for the Pet and Person application.
5. Which DA methods would you suggest including in the Person class? Which would you include in the Pet class? Why?
6. Suppose that a list of all owners and their pets is needed. Give the SQL statement needed to extract this information from the database.
7. Suppose a person whose social security number is 111-11-1111 acquires a new cat named Molly, and that Molly's identification number is C123. Give the SQL statement needed to insert the new record into the Pet table. Assume that information for this owner is already in the Person table.
8. Explain the steps that you would take to protect the integrity of the database when a new pet is added to the database.
9. Explain the steps that you would take to protect the integrity of the database when an existing owner is removed from the database.
10. Can you think of a time when it would be necessary to add or remove a record from the Pet table and *not* add or remove a record from the Person table? Explain how you would address this situation.

Discussion Questions

1. As you learned in Chapter 9, one-to-one associations have two directions. Consider the association between a boat and a slip: A boat occupies exactly one slip, and a slip is occupied by at most one boat. State how you would structure the tables for a BoatAndSlip relational database application?
2. Recall that to implement the one-to-one association between Customer and Boat in the CustomerAndBoat database application, you included a boat attribute in the Customer class, and a customer attribute in the Boat class. You included an AssignBoatToCustomer method in the Boat class to establish the relationship in both directions—i.e., this method associates a customer with the boat, and associates the boat with its customer. Why not include an AssignCustomerToBoat method in the Customer class to set the customer for this boat? What, if any, is the advantage of AssignBoatToCustomer? Why not have both methods?
3. In the CustomerAndBoat database application, you included a boat attribute in the Customer class, and a customer attribute in the Boat class. The Find method of the CustomerDA class for this application finds both the customer and the customer's boat. Given that a reference to a customer is present, why not use BoatDA instead of CustomerDA to find the boat associated with the customer? What are the pros and cons of doing it each way?
4. Relational databases implement relationships using foreign keys. OO VB .NET applications implement relationships using reference variables. Now that you have had some experience with both, discuss what you see as the major differences between using object references as attributes and using foreign keys in relational databases. What are the similarities?

Projects

Question 1 refers to the program and database used for Hands-on Exercise 2.

1. In Microsoft Access, open DockAndSlipDatabase in the Example2 folder and add several new slips to SlipTable. Leave the BoatID column in SlipTable empty to indicate that these slips are unoccupied. Modify the testing script, Dock, and DockDA program in Hands-on Exercise 2 to retrieve information about all of the unoccupied slips, including the location and availability of water and electricity on the associated

dock. (*Hint*: To select rows in SlipTable that do not have a value in the BoatID column, include the condition *SlipTable.BoatID IS NULL* in the WHERE clause of the SQL statement.

2. Extend the capabilities of the DockAndSlipDatabase application so that when the Find method of the Dock class is invoked, information is available not only about a dock and its slips, but also about the boat that occupies the slip and the customer who owns the boat. To do this, you will need to add BoatTable and CustomerTable to DockAndSlipDatabase. (An easy way to do this for BoatTable, for example, is to open CustomerAndBoatDatabase, select BoatTable, and use "copy and paste" features to copy it to DockAndSlipDatabase.) Modify the testing program to invoke the Find method for Dock 1 and report all dock, slip, boat, and customer details. Then invoke the Find method for Dock 2 and report all corresponding details. You do not need to invoke the GetAll method in this version of the testing program.

3. Refer to the programs and database you used in Hands-on Exercise 4. Suppose that Bradshaw Marina wants to track each lease that a customer makes over time. For example, a customer with phone number 123-4567 could have one lease with a start date of August 26, 2003, and another lease with a start date of August 26, 2004. With this in mind, modify LeaseTable, which you used in Hands-on Exercise 4, to track multiple leases for each customer. Write a new testing program that adds a second lease for the customer with phone number 123-4567 and check the LeaseTable of the database to see if the second lease has been added.

4. For Project 3 at the end of Chapter 9, you developed an application to track boat service records. Recall that each boat might have zero or more services, and each service applies to one boat. The attributes of BoatServiceRecord are invoice number, service date, service type, and total charges. The project you created for Chapter 9 included the BoatServiceRecord class plus Boat and Customer, with the capability to associate the customer with the boat, and a method in the Boat class named RecordBoatService to instantiate BoatServiceRecord. Convert this project to a relational database application. Write a testing program that inserts several service records into ServiceTable, making sure that at least one boat has more than one service record. The testing program should then retrieve records from the boat table (for the boats that have been serviced) and report information about the boat, its owner, and service performed on the boat.

PART 5

Deploying the Three-Tier Application

CHAPTER

15

Assembling a Three-Tier Windows Application

In this chapter you will:

- Review three-tier design
- Combine a problem domain class, a data access class, and a GUI
- Use multiple GUIs and add an instance to a database
- Use GUIs with multiple problem domain classes to interact with a database

In this chapter, the first chapter of Part 5, you will learn how to combine problem domain classes, GUI classes, and data access classes to form a complete information system module that provides a user interface, required system functionality, and the object persistence needed in client-server applications.

In Part 4 you learned how to use data access classes to provide object persistence. You learned that object persistence can be achieved in various ways, although most business applications today require a relational database. A problem domain class is designed to interact with a corresponding data access class that implements object persistence. As you changed from sequential files to indexed files to a relational database, the problem domain class and the tester program did not have to change. The only change required was to the data access class.

In Part 3 you learned how to create GUI classes that can respond to user actions. You created GUI classes by combining built-in VB .NET classes to design forms with controls such as pull-down menus, buttons, lists, and labels. The GUI classes you created interacted with your problem domain classes, but object persistence was only simulated.

The two chapters in Part 5 take the OO development concepts and techniques you have learned about problem domain classes, GUI classes, and data access classes and combine them to form a complete system module. This chapter demonstrates how to implement modules of the Bradshaw Marina application as a stand-alone system. Chapter 16 demonstrates how to implement three-tier application modules on the Web.

Reviewing Three-Tier Design

In Chapter 5 you learned about three-tier design as an architecture for structuring OO applications. The three tiers include GUI classes, problem domain classes, and data access classes. The user interacts with GUI class instances, and the GUI instances interact with problem domain classes and instances. Problem domain classes and instances interact with data access classes that handle storing and retrieving data from files or databases. Figure 15-1 shows how the three tiers interact to find a customer.

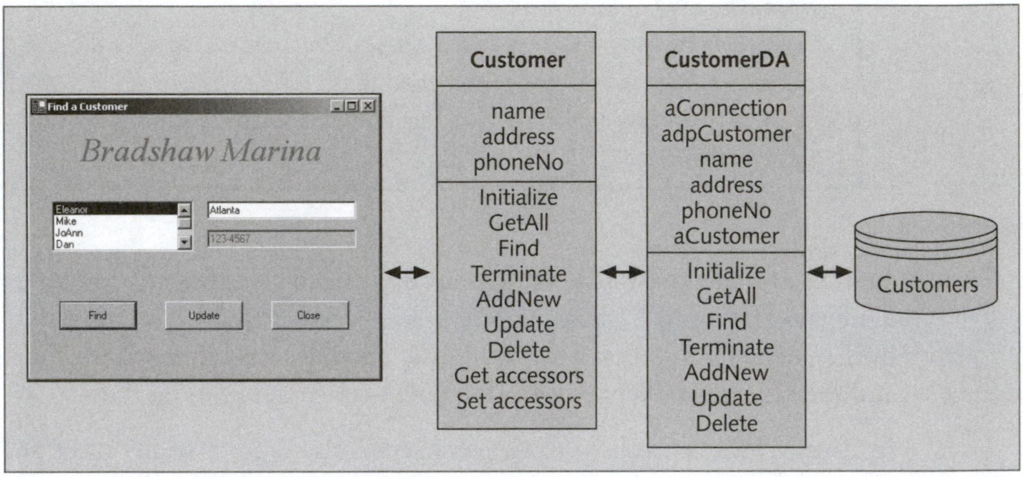

Figure 15-1 Three-tier design to find a customer

Having three tiers separates the functionality required for the user interface, the business application objects, and the database implementation. System maintenance is simplified as many changes made to the GUI do not affect the problem domain classes and data access classes. Similarly, many changes made to the data access classes do not affect the problem domain classes or the GUI. For example, the database management software can be upgraded or changed by modifying data access classes, but the problem domain and GUI classes are not affected. Similarly, the graphical user interface can be upgraded or changed without affecting the other tiers.

Three-tier design also provides benefits for distributing applications across the network. GUI classes can reside on the client machine, problem domain classes and instances can reside on a server, and the database can reside on another server. In this way, three-tier design lends itself to client-server architectures.

Three-Tier Design and the Development Process

Three-tier design provides a framework for organizing the system development process that is emphasized in this book. Recall that OO system development is done *iteratively*, with some analysis, some design, and some implementation occurring before continuing with more analysis, more design, and more implementation. OO system analysis involves defining the requirements for the system—the use cases and problem domain classes required. Each use case is expanded into multiple scenarios that define the functions the system provides to users. The problem domain classes are initially defined in terms of their attributes and a few key methods. Additional details about the problem domain classes are added during each iteration.

OO system design involves adding details that specify how the system will be physically implemented. One detail involves the user interface: How will the user interact with the system to complete each use case? Therefore, GUI classes are designed to allow the user to interact with problem domain instances to complete a task. Another design detail involves object persistence: How will a database be used to store and retrieve data so objects are available over time? Therefore, data access classes are designed. User interface design and the physical design of the database are system design issues. Writing code to define problem domain classes, GUI classes, and data access classes is a system implementation issue (see Figure 15-2).

OO Analysis

Define use cases and scenarios
Define problem domain classes

OO Design

Add design details to problem domain classes
Define GUI classes
Define data access classes

OO Implementation

Write code to implement PD, GUI, and DA classes

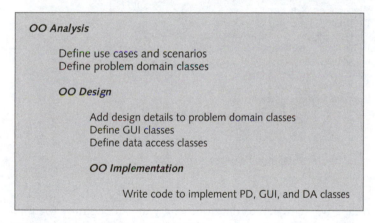

Figure 15-2 OO analysis, design, and implementation phases

The system development process as demonstrated for Bradshaw Marina starts with planning the project and defining the problem. The next step is defining use cases and problem domain classes. Therefore, Chapter 5 described the business system requirements for Bradshaw Marina and introduced the use case diagram and class diagram. Figure 15-3 shows these steps at the beginning of the development process.

Begin project:

Plan the project
Define the problem
Define key system use cases
Define problem domain classes
Complete class diagram

First iteration:

Pick one or more use cases
Define use cases in more detail
Identify and design classes needed for use cases
Write the problem domain class code and test
Design and implement GUI required for use cases
Review GUI and functionality with users and revise
Design and implement data access classes for use cases
Complete system internals and controls
Thoroughly test all use cases

Second iteration:

Pick additional use cases
Define use cases in more detail
Define classes needed for use cases
Write the problem domain class code
Design and implement GUI for use cases
Review GUI and functionality with users and revise
Design and implement data access classes for use cases
Complete system internals and controls
Thoroughly test all use cases

Continue with third iteration:

Pick additional use cases

Figure 15-3 Steps in the iterative development process

Because you use an iterative approach to development, you can begin by focusing on some important use cases in the first iteration. In the Bradshaw case, you identified the problem domain classes involved in the use cases, and you implemented initial versions of them using VB .NET. You added a constructor and accessor methods that all classes need, and you added some of the key custom methods. You tested the problem domain classes each time you added more functionality. You added validation and exception handling. You added subclasses, interfaces, custom exceptions, and association relationships. These techniques were covered in Chapters 5 through 9. You did not worry about the user interface or about object persistence, but you did do some analysis, some design, and some implementation.

In a system development project, you would not try to implement all problem domain classes in detail all at once. Instead, you would identify the key classes needed for one or more of the use cases required in the system. Then you would implement those classes. You might move ahead by designing the user interface for those use cases, creating some GUI classes needed by users to interact with the system. As you saw in Part 3, the GUI classes take the place of the tester programs you initially wrote to test the problem domain classes. In other words, you could simply plug in the GUI class in place of the tester program. Therefore, you did some design and some implementation for the user interface in the iteration.

In Chapter 11 you combined GUI classes with problem domain classes. You did not have to change the problem domain classes at all to add the GUI. You also added a class that simulated object persistence, and modified the GUI classes to interact with the simulated data access class.

Then your attention turned to object persistence and database management. You added data access classes that took the place of simulated object persistence. In the case of a relational database, you designed the database, created the database tables, and included foreign keys to join the tables. You have done some design and implementation for data access in the iteration.

At this point, most of your problem domain tier, GUI tier, and data access tier are complete for the use cases you have considered. When the three tiers are complete, final adjustments are made to combine them into a working system module. That is what you will learn how to do in this chapter.

Iterative development for the project continues, however. One approach is to begin the next iteration focusing on another use case. With Bradshaw Marina, the first iteration might focus on customers and their boats. The second iteration might focus on docks, slips, and leases. The third iteration might focus on reports and queries.

You might divide the project team based on specialties for each iteration. One team member might focus on problem domain classes and continue to refine the use cases and scenarios. Another team member might write the code and test the problem domain classes, while another might specialize on the GUI tier. Another team member might focus on the data access tier. As long as the team coordinates its work based on the use cases and problem domain classes, it is easy to divide the work when using iterative development and three-tier design.

Combining a PD Class, a DA Class, and a GUI

The first example combining a problem domain class, a data access class, and a GUI that you will implement involves the Customer problem domain and data access classes from Chapter 13, and the FindCustomer GUI from Chapter 11. Recall that the FindCustomer GUI retrieves information about a specific customer, as shown in Figure 15-4.

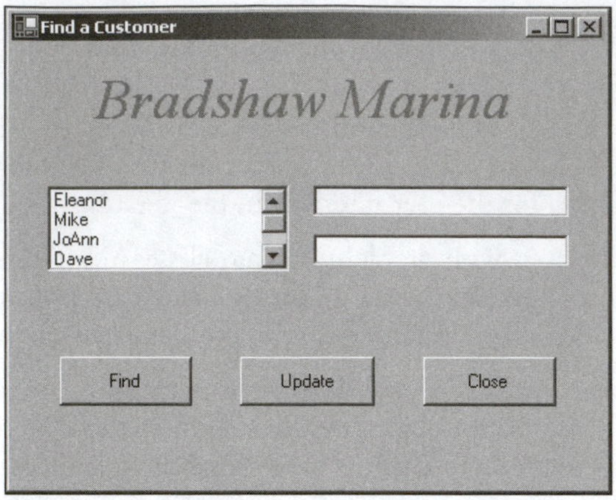

Figure 15-4 The FindCustomer GUI from Chapter 11

Reviewing the Customer Problem Domain Class

The Customer problem domain class was introduced in Chapter 5 and was the first problem domain class implemented for the Bradshaw Marina system development project. Several versions of the Customer class have been used in this book. In Chapter 5 the Customer class included a parameterized constructor and standard accessor methods. In subsequent chapters you included a TellAboutSelf method, multiple constructors, validation and exception handling, and other features. In Chapter 9 you learned how to implement association relationships between Customer and other problem domain classes, such as the one between Customer and Boat. Additional attributes and methods were added to implement the association relationships.

In Chapter 11, GUI examples not requiring object persistence used these versions of the Customer problem domain class *without* further modification. The Customer class did not have to be modified in order for the GUI classes to add or find a customer because the GUI class created customers to be used for testing. The GUI class simply substituted for the tester program.

In Chapters 13 and 14 the Customer class interacted with data access classes that implemented sequential files, indexed files, and a relational database. The GUI tier was set aside, and tester programs were used to test the Customer problem domain class and its interaction with a data access class. Therefore, the Customer class was completed so that it would work with a corresponding data access class named CustomerDA, independent of the underlying data access approach being employed. In other words, because CustomerDA handles the details associated with object persistence, no further modification is required within the Customer PD class when the underlying data access technique changes (such as from sequential files to relational databases). The Customer problem domain class from Chapter 13 is shown in Figure 15-5.

```
'Chapter 15 Example 1
' Customer Class with added methods for DA Class
' From Chapter 13
```

```
Imports System.Data
Imports System.Data.OleDb
Public Class Customer
    'attributes
    Private name As String
    Private address As String
    Private phoneNo As String

    '------------Begin Data Access Shared Methods-----
    Public Shared Sub Initialize()
        CustomerDA.Initialize()
    End Sub
    Public Shared Function Find(ByVal PhoneNo As String) As Customer
        Return CustomerDA.Find(PhoneNo)
    End Function
    Public Shared Function GetAll() As ArrayList
       Return CustomerDA.GetAll
    End Function
    Public Shared Sub Terminate()
        CustomerDA.Terminate()
    End Sub
    '------------End Data Access Shared Methods---------
    '------------Begin Data Access Instance Methods-----
    Public Sub AddNew()
        CustomerDA.AddNew(Me)
    End Sub
    Public Sub Update()
        CustomerDA.Update(Me)
    End Sub
    Public Sub Delete()
        CustomerDA.Delete(Me)
    End Sub
    '------------End Data Access Instance Methods-----
    'get accessor methods
    Public Function GetName() As String
        Return name
    End Function
    Public Function GetAddress() As String
        Return address
    End Function
    Public Function GetPhoneNo() As String
        Return phoneNo
    End Function

    'set accessor methods
    Public Sub SetName(ByVal aName As String)
        name = aName
    End Sub
    Public Sub SetAddress(ByVal anAddress As String)
        address = anAddress
    End Sub
    Public Sub SetPhoneNo(ByVal aPhoneNo As String)
        phoneNo = aPhoneNo
    End Sub
```

```
    Public Function TellAboutSelf() As String
        Dim info As String
        info = "Name = " & GetName() & _
         ", Address = " & GetAddress() & _
         ", Phone No = " & GetPhoneNo()
        Return info
    End Function

    ' property named CustomerName
    Public Property CustomerName() As String
        Get
           Return name
        End Get
        Set(ByVal aName As String)
            name = aName
        End Set
    End Property
    '------------------Begin Constructors---------------
    'default constructor
    Public Sub New()
    End Sub
    'constructor (3 parameters)
    Public Sub New(ByVal aName As String, _
            ByVal anAddress As String, ByVal aPhoneNo As String)
        name = aName
        address = anAddress
        phoneNo = aPhoneNo

    End Sub
    '------------------End Constructors--------------
End Class
```

Figure 15-5 Customer class definition that interacts with CustomerDA

Recall that this version of the Customer problem domain class includes four class methods (Initialize, Terminate, GetAll, and Find) and three instance methods (AddNew, Update, and Delete) that interact with the data access class named CustomerDA. Customer no longer simulates data access using hard-coded customer data; instead, it interacts with an actual data access class. Note that all of the DA methods in the Customer class, when invoked, simply pass the request to the CustomerDA class, which does the actual processing. In this way, the tester program or GUI class always invokes the DA methods of the Customer class, and the Customer class always passes on the request to CustomerDA. The details associated with object persistence are essentially hidden (or encapsulated) within CustomerDA, as was explained in Chapter 13.

Reviewing the Customer Data Access Class

Chapter 13 introduced the CustomerDA class. You created different versions of CustomerDA to implement various approaches to object persistence, including sequential files, indexed files, and a relational database. Chapter 14 continued the discussion about relational database implementation with data access classes, and CustomerDA was modified to allow an association relationship between Customer and Boat and Customer and Lease. Because the three-tier example you are currently assembling involves only the Customer problem domain class, you can use the Chapter 13 version of the CustomerDA class definition, which is shown in Figure 15-6.

```
'Chapter 15 Example 1
' Chapter 13 - Example ------DA classes using dbms
' for single table example with CustomerTable
Imports System.Data.OleDb
Imports System.Collections
Public Class CustomerDA
    Shared customers As New ArrayList() ' Customer references
    Shared aCustomer As Customer

    'Declare a connection. Eliminate the hard-coded path to
    'the database by putting the database file in the
    'project's Bin folder

    Shared cnnCustomer As New
    OleDbConnection("Provider=Microsoft.Jet.OLEDB.4.0; " & _
    "Data Source=CustomerDatabase.mdb")

    'Declare variables for Customer attribute values
    Shared name, address, phoneno As String

    'Initialize Method (chapter 13 example)
    'no connection passed as reference
    Public Shared Sub Initialize()
        Try
           ' Try to open the connection
           cnnCustomer.Open()
        Catch e As Exception
           Console.WriteLine(e.ToString)
        End Try
    End Sub

    ' Terminate Method (chapter 13 example)
    Public Shared Sub Terminate()
        Try
           cnnCustomer.Close()
           cnnCustomer = Nothing
        Catch e As Exception
           Console.WriteLine(e.Message.ToString)
        End Try
    End Sub

    ' AddNew Method --Throws DuplicateException if exists
    Public Shared Sub AddNew(ByVal aCustomer As Customer)

        ' Get customer information
        name = aCustomer.GetName
        address = aCustomer.GetAddress
        phoneno = aCustomer.GetPhoneNo
```

15

```
        ' Declare a string SQL statement
        Dim sqlInsert As String = "INSERT INTO customerTable " & _
        "VALUES ('" & name & "', '" & address & "', '" & phoneno _
                & " ')"
        Dim adpcustomer As New OleDbDataAdapter()
        Try
           Dim c As Customer = Find(phoneno)
           Throw New DuplicateException(" Customer Exists ")
        Catch e As NotFoundException
           Try    ' Assign Insert Commands and Execute
               adpcustomer.InsertCommand = _
                               New OleDbCommand(sqlInsert)
               adpcustomer.InsertCommand.Connection = _
                               cnnCustomer
               adpcustomer.InsertCommand.ExecuteNonQuery()
           Finally
           End Try
       End Try
   End Sub

   ' Find Method--Throws NotFoundException if Not Found
   Public Shared Function Find(ByVal key As String) As Customer

       Dim acustomer As New Customer()
       acustomer = Nothing
       Dim dsCustomer As New DataSet()
       Try
           ' Define the SQL statement using the phoneno key
           Dim sqlQuery As String = _
                "SELECT Name, Address, PhoneNO " & _
           "FROM CustomerTable WHERE phoneNo = '" & key & "'"
           Dim adpCustomer As New _
            OleDbDataAdapter(sqlQuery, cnnCustomer)
           adpCustomer.Fill(dsCustomer, "CustTable")
           If dsCustomer.Tables("CustTable").Rows.Count > 0 Then
              Dim custRow As DataRow
              custRow = _
                          dsCustomer.Tables("custTable").Rows(0)
              name = custRow.Item("Name")
              address = custRow.Item("address")
              phoneno = custRow.Item("phoneno")
              acustomer = _
                          New Customer(name, address, phoneno)
           Else
              Throw New NotFoundException("Not Found")
           End If
           dsCustomer = Nothing
       Catch e As OleDb.OleDbException
           Console.WriteLine(e.Message.ToString)
       End Try
       Return acustomer

   End Function
```

```
' GetAll Method
Public Shared Function GetAll() As ArrayList
    Dim dsCustomer As New DataSet()
    Dim sqlQuery As String = "SELECT Name, Address, PhoneNo " _
            & "FROM CustomerTable"
    Try
        Dim adpCustomer As New _
          OleDbDataAdapter(sqlQuery, cnnCustomer)
        adpCustomer.Fill(dsCustomer, "CustTable")
        If dsCustomer.Tables("CustTable").Rows.Count > 0 Then
            Dim dsRow As DataRow
            ' Clear the array list
            customers.Clear()
            For Each dsRow In dsCustomer.Tables("CustTable").Rows
                name = dsRow("Name")
                address = dsRow("Address")
                phoneno = dsRow("PhoneNo")
                Dim aCustomer As New _
                 Customer(name, address, phoneno)
                customers.Add(aCustomer)
            Next
         Else
            ' No records in database
         End If
         dsCustomer = Nothing
     Catch e As Exception
         Console.WriteLine(e.ToString)
         Throw New NotFoundException("Not Found")
     End Try
     Return customers

 End Function

 ' Update Method
 Public Shared Sub Update(ByVal aCustomer As Customer)

     ' Get Customer information
     name = aCustomer.GetName
     address = aCustomer.GetAddress
     phoneno = aCustomer.GetPhoneNo

     Dim sqlUpdate As String = "Update CustomerTable " & _
      "SET Name = '" & name & "', Address = '" & address & _
               "'," & "PhoneNo = '" & phoneno & "' " & _
      "WHERE PhoneNo = '" & phoneno & "'"
     Try
         Dim c As Customer = Customer.Find(phoneno)
         Dim adpcustomer As New OleDbDataAdapter()
         adpcustomer.UpdateCommand = New _
                  OleDbCommand(sqlUpdate)
         adpcustomer.UpdateCommand.Connection = cnnCustomer
         adpcustomer.UpdateCommand.ExecuteNonQuery()
     Catch e As Exception
         Console.WriteLine(e.ToString)
     End Try
 End Sub
```

15

```
    'Delete Method--Throws NotFoundException if not found
    Public Shared Sub Delete(ByVal aCustomer As Customer)
        Dim phoneno, sqlDelete As String
        phoneno = aCustomer.GetPhoneNo
        sqlDelete = "DELETE FROM CustomerTable " & _
         "WHERE PhoneNo = '" & phoneno & "'"
        Try
            Dim c As Customer = Customer.Find(phoneno)
            Dim adpCustomer As New OleDbDataAdapter()
            adpCustomer.DeleteCommand = New _
                         OleDbCommand(sqlDelete)
            adpCustomer.DeleteCommand.Connection = cnnCustomer
            adpCustomer.DeleteCommand.ExecuteNonQuery()
        Catch e As Exception
            Console.WriteLine(e.ToString)
        End Try
    End Sub
End Class
```

Figure 15-6 CustomerDA class definition for Example 1

The CustomerDA class is explained in detail in Chapter 13. Recall that the data access class implements the details associated with the data access methods defined earlier in the Customer class, throwing exceptions if a new customer already exists or if a customer that is to be deleted or updated cannot be found.

The CustomerDA class from Chapter 13 requires no changes for use in this three-tier example. For convenience, however, the database file (CustomerDatabase.mdb) has been placed within the project's bin folder, enabling the hard-coded path to the data source to be removed from the code. Otherwise, the CustomerDA class from Chapter 13 is used here *without modification*.

Together, the Customer problem domain class, the Customer data access class, and a GUI or tester program provide the structure needed to implement the three-tier approach. The tester program or GUI invokes the DA methods of the Customer class, which passes the request to the CustomerDA class for processing. The CustomerDA class returns the result to Customer, and Customer returns the result to the tester program or GUI class.

The Customer PD and DA classes from Chapter 13 are complete and ready to use. You can now complete a GUI class to implement the first example.

Updating the FindCustomer GUI

The final tier for this example is based on the FindCustomer GUI introduced in Chapter 11, Example 4. This version of FindCustomer was designed to interact with the original Customer class and the simulated data access class, CustomerData. The FindCustomer GUI class is almost ready to work with the Customer and CustomerDA classes from Chapter 13. Only a few minor modifications are required.

FindCustomer begins as before by declaring a Customer reference variable and an array of customer references to hold the information obtained from the database.

```
'Chapter 15 Example 1
Imports System.Collections
Public Class FindCustomer
    Inherits System.Windows.Forms.Form

    'Declare customer reference variable
    Private aCustomer As Customer

    'Declare array of customers (no longer simulated)
    Private customers As New ArrayList()
```

However, unlike the example in Chapter 11, this first three-tier example does not include a MainMenu GUI. Thus, FindCustomer (rather than MainMenu) must initialize the database. The constructor of the FindCustomer class accomplishes this task by invoking the Initialize method of the Customer class. Recall that Customer in turn invokes the Initialize method of the CustomerDA method where the database connection is actually created. As before, you add another statement to the constructor (in the hidden code) to populate the list box once the database connection is established.

```
'Add statements to generated code to:
'initialize the database and populate the list box
Public Sub New()
    MyBase.New()

    'This call is required by the Windows Form Designer.
    InitializeComponent()
    'Add any initialization after the InitializeComponent() call

    'Initialize the database
    Customer.Initialize()
    'Populate the customer list box
    PopulateListBox()
End Sub
```


The PopulateListBox method now uses the GetAll method of the Customer class to retrieve customer instances from the database. Because there is a possibility that no customer instances will be found in the database, the GetAll method is invoked within a try-catch block. Setting the selected index to 0 prohibits a runtime error from occurring if the user presses the Find button before selecting an item on the list.

```
Private Sub PopulateListBox()
    'Get the customers from the database
    'Add try-catch to trap not found exception
    Try
        customers = Customer.GetAll()
        'Add the name of each customer to the list
        Dim i As Integer
```

```
            For i = 0 To customers.Count - 1
                aCustomer = customers(i)
                lstCustomer.Items.Add(aCustomer.GetName())
            Next
            'Set the selected index to 0
            lstCustomer.SelectedIndex = 0
        Catch nfe As NotFoundException
            MessageBox.Show("No records found in database")
        End Try
    End Sub
```

Note that this code does not change from the Chapter 11 version, except for substituting the Customer GetAll method for the hard-coded creation of customer instances and the inclusion of a try-catch block.

The event handling method for the Find button does not require any modification from the Chapter 11 version. The index of the customer selected within the list box is used to retrieve the customer's address and phone number. Notice that in this example, it is not necessary to invoke the Find method of the Customer class to find the requested information because it already exists within the array of customer instances returned by the GetAll method to populate the list box.

```
    Private Sub btnFind_Click _
    (ByVal sender As System.Object, ByVal e As System.EventArgs) _
    Handles btnFind.Click
        Dim i As Integer
        'Identify the selected index in the list box
        i = lstCustomer.SelectedIndex
        'Find this customer in the array list
        aCustomer = customers(i)
        'Retrieve and display this customer's address and phone
        txtCustomerAddress.Text = aCustomer.GetAddress()
        txtCustomerPhone.Text = aCustomer.GetPhoneNo()
    End Sub
```

The event handling method for the Update button now invokes the Update method of the Customer class to update customer information in the database. Because the customer record might not be found in the database, a try-catch block is used.

```
    Private Sub btnUpdate_Click _
    (ByVal sender As System.Object, ByVal e As System.EventArgs) _
    Handles btnUpdate.Click
        Dim i As Integer
        'Identify the selected index in the list box
        i = lstCustomer.SelectedIndex
        'Find this customer in the array list
        aCustomer = customers(i)
        'Set this customer's address to the value entered by
        'the user.
```

```
    aCustomer.SetAddress(txtCustomerAddress.Text)
    'Update this customer in the database
    'Use try-catch to trap possible "not found" error
    Try
        aCustomer.Update()
        MessageBox.Show("Customer Updated")
    Catch ee As NotFoundException
        MessageBox.Show("This customer could not be found")
    End Try

    'Clear address and phone text fields
    txtCustomerAddress.Text = ""
    txtCustomerPhone.Text = ""
  End Sub
```

Also recall that the customer phone number is the primary key for the customer table in the database. Because primary keys cannot be changed, the code to update this attribute is removed. Accordingly, for this example, the Enabled property of the CustomerPhone text box is set to False. The FindCustomer GUI appears as shown in Figure 15-7.

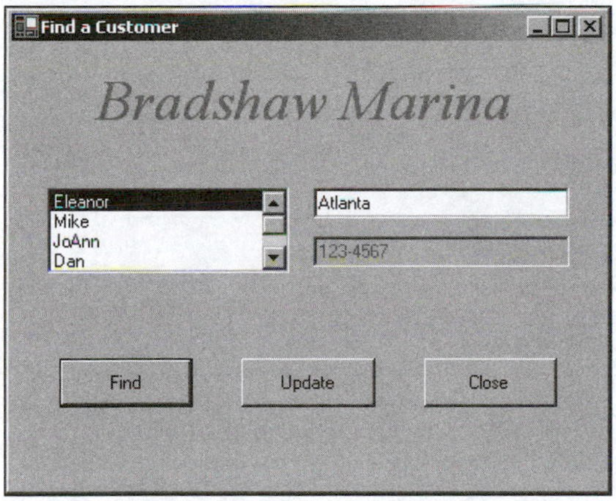

Figure 15-7 The FindCustomer GUI for Example 1

One final change is needed within the event handler for the Close button. Because this example does not include a main menu GUI, the event handler for the Close button is responsible for terminating the connection to the database.

```
Private Sub btnClose_Click(ByVal sender As System.Object, _
ByVal e As System.EventArgs) Handles btnClose.Click
    'Add call to terminate database for Chapter 15
    Customer.Terminate()
    Me.Close()
End Sub
```

The three tiers are now complete. FindCustomer asks for the array of customers from Customer, and Customer passes the request on to CustomerDA. CustomerDA queries the database for each customer record and uses the record to instantiate a Customer instance. A reference to the instance is put in the array list. When all customers are instantiated, CustomerDA returns the array list to Customer, which returns it to the FindCustomer GUI. FindCustomer can now get information from any customer using the array index and standard accessor methods. Figure 15-8 shows a sequence diagram that illustrates the interaction of the three tiers.

Recall that CustomerDA throws the NotFoundException and DuplicateException, so these must be included for the example to run. They are identical to the exceptions used for CustomerDA in Chapter 13.

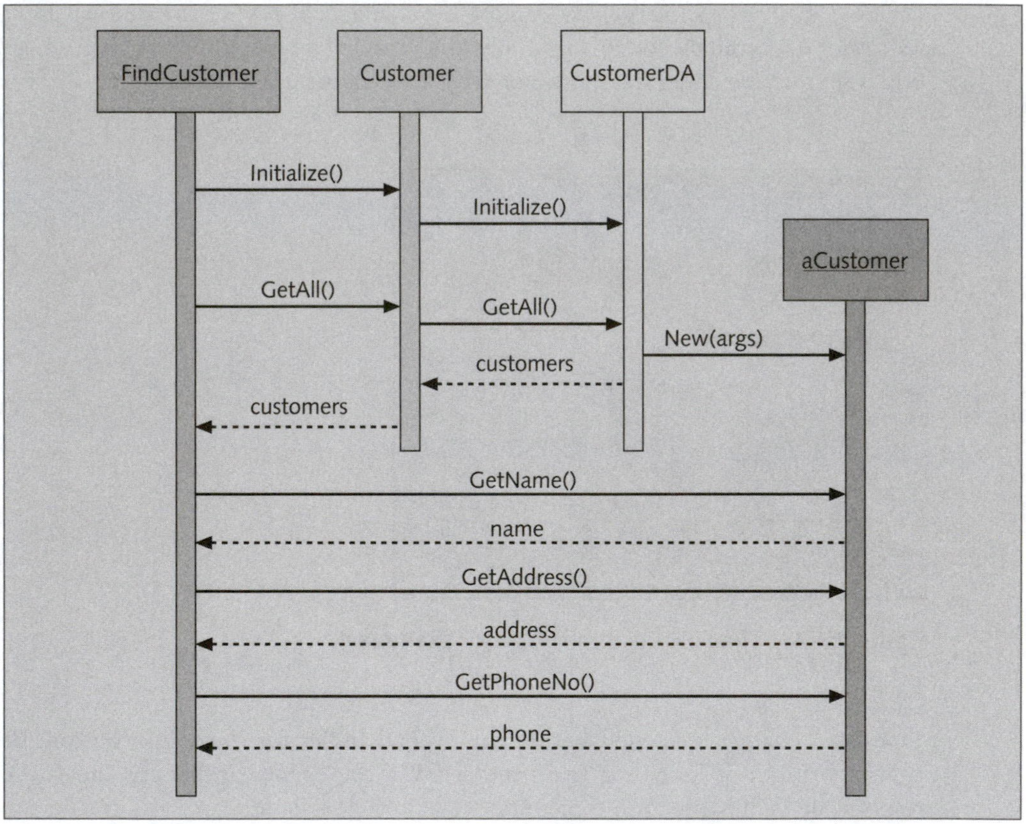

Figure 15-8 FindCustomer sequence diagram showing three-tier design

Hands-on Exercise 1

1. Locate the **Chap15\Examples\Ex01\Example1** folder in the book's student data files.
2. Create a folder named **Chap15\Exercises\Ex01** in the work folder on your system, and then copy the **Example1** folder to this folder.
3. Using VB .NET, open the **Example1** project. You see FindCustomer.vb and related files in the Solution Explorer. Run and test the project to verify that it produces the output shown in Figure 15-7.
4. Create a second version of FindCustomer named FindCustomerByPhone that lists phone numbers in the list box and then finds the customer's name and address. Run and test the example.
5. Add the capability to update the customer's name or address to your FindCustomerByPhone GUI. Include Find, Update, and Close buttons. Run and test the example.
6. The FindCustomer GUI requests the array list of customers from Customer (which gets it from CustomerDA) and then gets the needed customer reference from the array list. This means that the Find method of the CustomerDA is not used. Create a GUI named FindOneCustomer that allows the user to type a phone number in a text box that is used to find a single customer instance in the database. In other words, initialize the database but do not use the GetAll method. Instead, use the Customer Find method when the user clicks the Find button. Run and test the example.

USING MULTIPLE GUIS AND ADDING AN INSTANCE TO THE DATABASE

The second three-tier example uses multiple GUIs and adds an instance to the database using a data access class. This example is based on Example 4 in Chapter 11. A main menu allows the user to either find a customer or add a new customer. The FindCustomer GUI above is modified slightly to work with the main menu, as it did in Chapter 11. The AddCustomer and MainMenu GUIs from Chapter 11 are also modified slightly to work with the data access classes. The same two custom exceptions are required: NotFoundException and DuplicateException. The MainMenu, FindCustomer, and AddCustomer GUIs are shown in Figure 15-9.

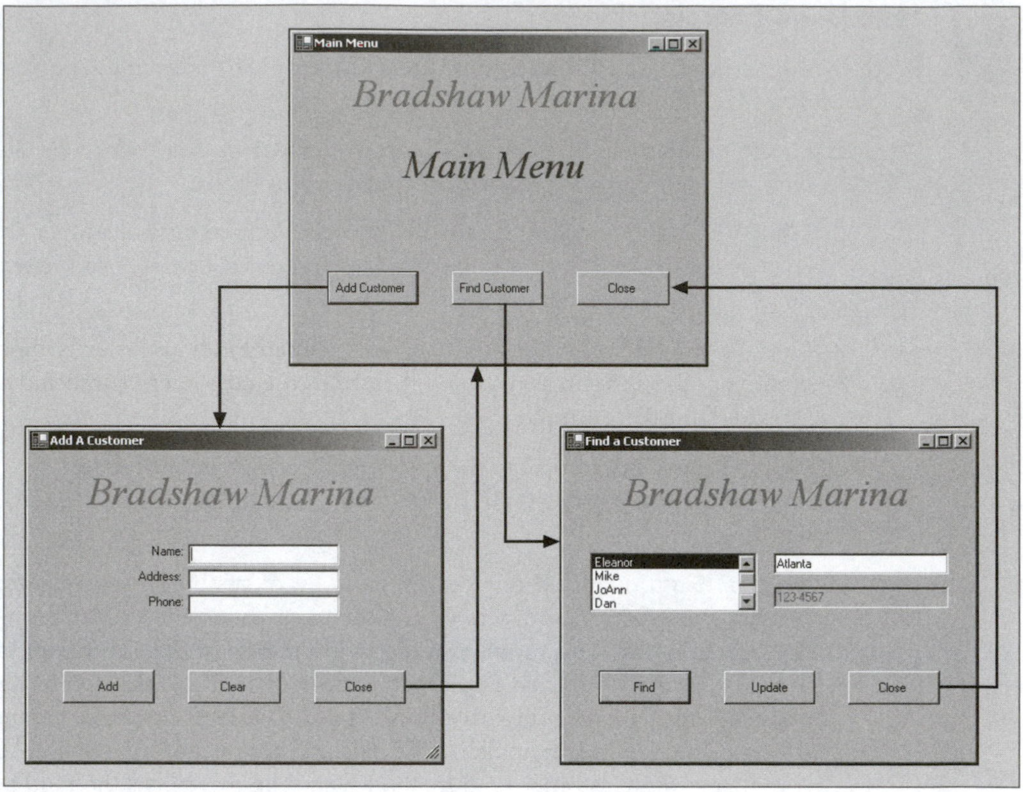

Figure 15-9 MainMenu, FindCustomer, and AddCustomer GUIs for Example 2

Note that Customer and CustomerDA as defined in the previous example above *do not have to be modified* for this second example. Both Customer and CustomerDA already include the capability to add a new customer when asked. You are simply plugging in a new set of GUIs to handle user interaction.

Reviewing the MainMenu GUI

The MainMenu GUI class is virtually identical to the version described in Chapter 11. Only two minor changes are needed. The MainMenu GUI establishes and terminates the connection to the database. Now that you have data access classes, you invoke the Initialize method of the Customer class to initialize the database—rather than invoking the Initialize method of CustomerData. As before, you invoke the Initialize method from within the constructor of the MainMenu GUI class.

```
Public Sub New()
    MyBase.New()
```

```
        'This call is required by the Windows Form Designer.
        InitializeComponent()

        'Initialize the database
        Customer.Initialize()

    End Sub
```

Similarly, you add a statement to the `btnClose_Click` procedure to terminate the connection to the database.

```
    Private Sub btnClose_Click(ByVal sender As System.Object, _
    ByVal e As System.EventArgs) Handles btnClose.Click
        'Terminate connection to database
        Customer.Terminate()
        Me.Close()
    End Sub
```

The `btnAdd_Click` and `btnFind_Click` procedures of the MainMenu GUI remain unchanged from Chapter 11, performing the tasks of instantiating and displaying the appropriate forms.

```
    Private Sub btnAdd_Click(ByVal sender As System.Object, _
    ByVal e As System.EventArgs) Handles btnAdd.Click
        'Hide the main menu form
        Me.Hide()
        'Create and display AddCustomer form
        Dim frmAddCustomerGUI = New AddCustomer()
        frmAddCustomerGUI.ShowDialog()
        'Make the main menu form visible
        Me.Show()
    End Sub

    Private Sub btnFind_Click(ByVal sender As System.Object, _
    ByVal e As System.EventArgs) Handles btnFind.Click
        'Hide the main menu form
        Me.Hide()
        'Create and display FindCustomer form
        Dim frmFindCustomerGUI = New FindCustomer()
        frmFindCustomerGUI.ShowDialog()
        'Make the main menu form visible
        Me.Show()
    End Sub
```


Reviewing the AddCustomer GUI

The AddCustomer GUI was first introduced in Chapter 11 along with FindCustomer. For this example, you change AddCustomer to allow it to work with data access classes. The only change to this class occurs within the `btnAdd_Click` method where a try-catch block is added and the AddNew method of the CustomerDA class (rather than the CustomerData class) is called.

As before, the AddCustomer GUI obtains customer information from the user, validates that the data entered by the user is correct, and creates a corresponding Customer instance. It then asks the new Customer instance to add itself to the database.

```
Private Sub btnAdd_Click(ByVal sender As System.Object, _
ByVal e As System.EventArgs) Handles btnAdd.Click
    'Get values from the text boxes
    customerName = txtName.Text
    customerAddress = txtAddress.Text
    customerPhone = txtPhone.Text
    'Validate that the user has entered values for name,
    'address and phone
    If customerName.Length = 0 Or _
        customerAddress.Length = 0 Or _
        customerPhone.Length = 0 Then
            MessageBox.Show("Please Enter All Data")
    Else
        'Data is valid -- create Customer instance
        aCustomer = New Customer(customerName, _
                    customerAddress, customerPhone)

        'Ask the new customer instance to add itself
        'Use try-catch block in case duplicate exception
        'is thrown by AddNew() method
           Try
               aCustomer.AddNew()
               MessageBox.Show("Customer Added")
               'Clear the form
               ClearForm()
           Catch ee As DuplicateException
              MessageBox.Show _
                  ("That customer already exists in the database")
               'Do not clear the form so user can see and fix the error
               txtName.Focus()
           End Try
       End If
    End Sub
```

Recall that the AddNew method of the Customer class passes on the AddNew request to CustomerDA. CustomerDA uses an SQL INSERT statement to add the new customer record to the database. A try-catch block is required because the AddNew method throws a DuplicateException if the key to the new customer (the phone number) already exists in the database. If the exception is caught by `btnAdd_Click`, a message dialog is displayed.

The remainder of the AddCustomer class definition as presented in Chapter 11 is unchanged.

Updating the FindCustomer GUI

The FindCustomer GUI class used in the previous example in this chapter requires no change other than those that enable it to work with the MainMenu GUI. Recall that in this example, the MainMenu GUI (rather than the FindCustomer GUI) establishes and terminates the connection to the database. Thus, you remove the statements that invoke the Initialize and Terminate methods from the FindCustomer class. No other changes are necessary.

Hands-on Exercise 2

1. Locate the **Chap15\Examples\Ex02\Example2** folder in the book's student data files.
2. Create a folder named **Chap15\Exercises\Ex02** in the work folder on your system, and then copy the **Example2** folder to this folder.
3. Using VB .NET, open the **Example2** project. You see AddCustomer.vb, FindCustomer.vb, MainMenu.vb, and related files in the Solution Explorer. Run and test the example by adding several new customers, including a customer with a duplicate phone number and a customer with a required value left blank. After you have added a few customers, make sure you can find them.
4. Modify your FindCustomerByPhone GUI from Hands-on Exercise 1 so it can be integrated into the example. The changes required are similar to the changes made to FindCustomer in this example. Modify MainMenu so it allows the user to choose to find a customer based on a phone number and then to update the customer. Run and test the example.
5. Review how to add and use a menu bar and pull-down menus with a GUI as explained in Chapter 10. Modify MainMenu so it uses a menu bar as well as the buttons. Run and test the example.

USING GUIS WITH MULTIPLE PROBLEM DOMAIN CLASSES

You will now see how to create an application that combines multiple GUIs with multiple problem domain and data access classes. This example combines the MainMenu, FindCustomer, AddCustomer, and AddBoat GUIs you have seen in this chapter and in Chapter 11, together with the Customer, CustomerDA, Boat, BoatDA, and CustomerAndBoatDatabaseConnect classes from Chapter 14. Except for the labels on the buttons, the MainMenu, FindCustomer, AddCustomer, and AddBoat GUIs are identical in appearance to those you have seen previously. These GUIs are shown in Figure 15-10. Only minor modifications are needed to make them work in a three-tier application.

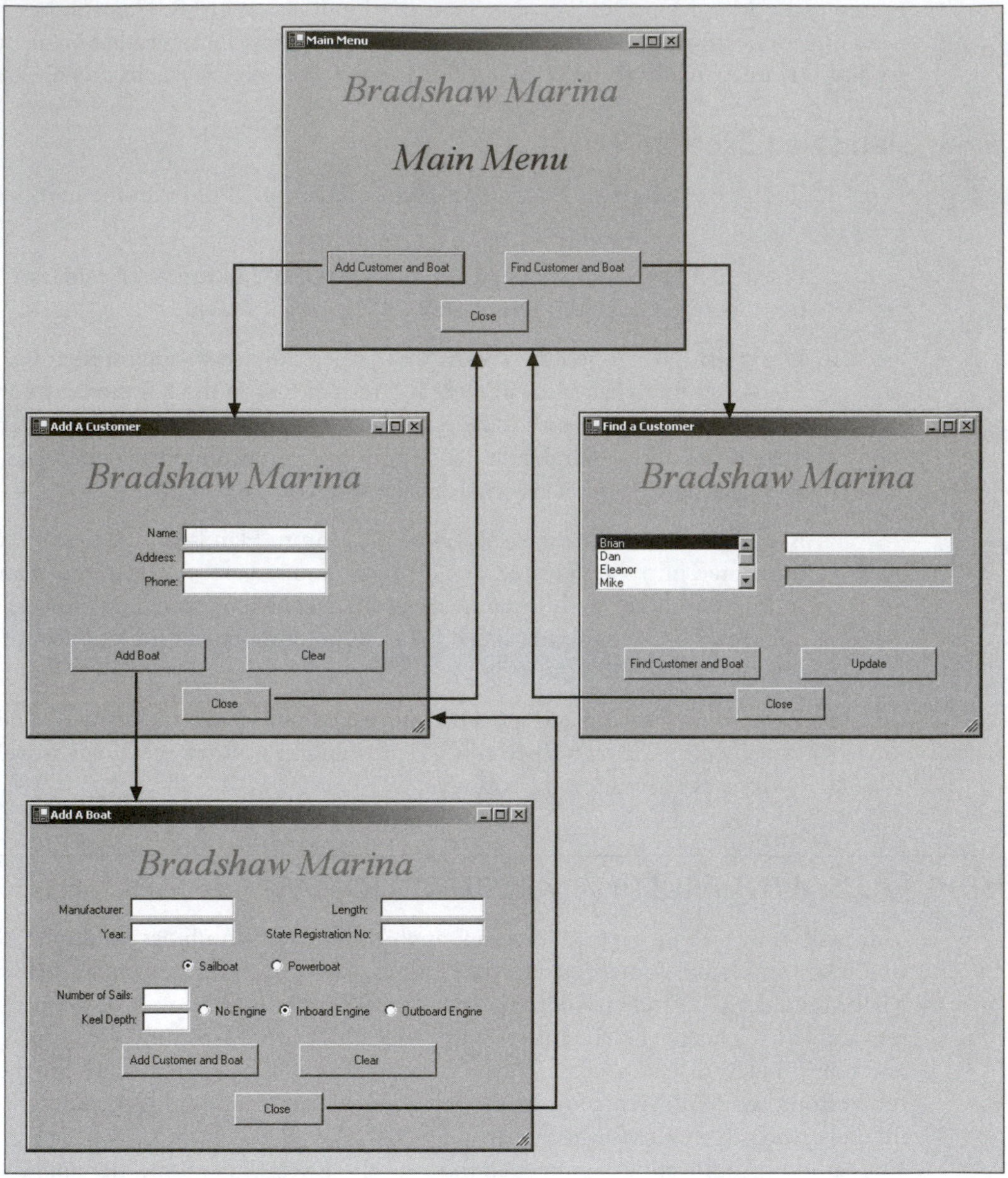

Figure 15-10 MainMenu, FindCustomer, AddCustomer, and AddBoat GUIs for Example 3

Reviewing the Customer and Boat PD and DA Classes From Chapter 14

The Chapter 14 versions of the Customer and Boat problem domain and data access classes, as well as the CustomerAndBoatDatabaseConnect class, are used here *without modification*. The

Customer and Boat problem domain classes include attributes and methods that associate a customer with his or her boat. As you will recall, establishing the association relationship between Customer and Boat requires including a Boat reference variable in Customer and a Customer reference variable in Boat, as well as providing accessor methods for these attributes. The multiplicity between Customer and Boat is one-to-one in both directions, meaning that a customer is always associated with exactly one boat, and a boat is always associated with exactly one customer. This association relationship was introduced in Chapter 9 and implemented in the Customer data access class in Chapter 14. That is, the version of the Customer data access class implemented in Chapter 14 navigates the association relationship between Customer and Boat, ensuring that when customer information is added to (or deleted from) the database, so is the associated information about the customer's boat.

The final three-tier example uses a relational database named CustomerAndBoatDatabase.mdb. This database includes two tables: CustomerTable and BoatTable. BoatTable includes a foreign key named CustomerPhoneNo that allows the tables to be joined. This database is also used without modification from Chapter 14.

Modifying the MainMenu GUI

As in the previous example, the MainMenu GUI opens and closes the connection to the database. In this case, the database consists of two tables: CustomerTable and BoatTable. Recall from Chapter 14 that access to these tables is shared between the Customer and Boat classes through a common connection to the database. Thus, similar to the examples in Chapter 14, the constructor of the MainMenu GUI first invokes the Initialize method of the CustomerAndBoatDatabaseConnect class to establish the common connection, then shares this connection by passing it as an argument to the Initialize methods of the Customer and Boat classes.

```
'Chapter 15 Example 3
Imports System.Data.OleDb
Imports System.Collections

Public Class MainMenu
    Inherits System.Windows.Forms.Form

    'Added for Chapter 15
    'Declare variable for database connection
    Dim aConnection As OleDbConnection

    'Add statements to hidden code to initialize the
    'connection to the database

    Public Sub New()
        MyBase.New()

        'This call is required by the Windows Form Designer.
        InitializeComponent()

        'Add any initialization after the InitializeComponent() call
```

```
        aConnection = CustomerAndBoatDatabaseConnect.Initialize()
        Customer.Initialize(aConnection)
        Boat.Initialize(aConnection)
    End Sub
```

The MainMenu GUI closes the connection to the database in the `btnClose_Click` procedure.

```
Private Sub btnClose_Click(ByVal sender As System.Object, _
ByVal e As System.EventArgs) Handles btnClose.Click
        'Terminate added for Chapter 15
        Customer.Terminate()
        Boat.Terminate()
        Me.Close()
End Sub
```

No further changes are required. As before, the `btnFind_Click` and `btnAdd_Click` methods of the MainMenu GUI instantiate and display the appropriate form.

```
Private Sub btnAdd_Click(ByVal sender As System.Object, _
ByVal e As System.EventArgs) Handles btnAdd.Click
        'Hide the main menu form
        Me.Hide()
        'Create and display the AddCustomer form
        Dim frmAddCustomerGUI = New AddCustomer()
        frmAddCustomerGUI.ShowDialog()
        'Make the main menu form visible
        Me.Show()
End Sub

Private Sub btnFind_Click(ByVal sender As System.Object, _
ByVal e As System.EventArgs) Handles btnFind.Click
        'Hide the main menu form
        Me.Hide()
        'Create and display the FindCustomer form
        Dim frmFindCustomerGUI = New FindCustomer()
        frmFindCustomerGUI.ShowDialog()
        'Make the main menu form visible
        Me.Show()
End Sub
```

Modifying the FindCustomer GUI

The FindCustomer GUI requires very little modification from the previous example. The FindCustomer GUI must now recognize the association between Customer and Boat. Thus, a Boat reference variable is included in the class definition.

```
'Chapter 15 Example 3
Imports System.Collections
Public Class FindCustomer
   Inherits System.Windows.Forms.Form

   'Declare array to hold customer instances from database
   Private customers As New ArrayList()

   'Declare customer and boat reference variables
   Private aCustomer As Customer
   Private aBoat As Boat
```

Similarly, when the user pushes the Find Customer and Boat button, the `btnFind_Click` method retrieves and displays not only the customer's name, address, and phone number, but also the reference to the customer's boat. A label named lblBoatInfo is included to hold information about the customer's boat.

```
Private Sub btnFind_Click(ByVal sender As System.Object, _
ByVal e As System.EventArgs) Handles btnFind.Click
       Dim i As Integer
       'Identify the selected index in the list box
       i = lstCustomer.SelectedIndex
       'Find this customer in the ArrayList
       aCustomer = customers(i)
       'Retrieve and display this customer's address and phone
       txtCustomerAddress.Text = aCustomer.GetAddress
       txtCustomerPhone.Text = aCustomer.GetPhoneNo
       'Retrieve this customer's boat reference
       aBoat = aCustomer.GetBoat()
       'Display the boat information
       lblBoatInfo.Text = "Customer Boat (4 attributes only) " _
        + aBoat.TellAboutSelf()
End Sub
```

The remainder of the FindCustomer GUI is unchanged from the previous example. A sequence diagram illustrating this version of FindCustomer is shown in Figure 15-11.

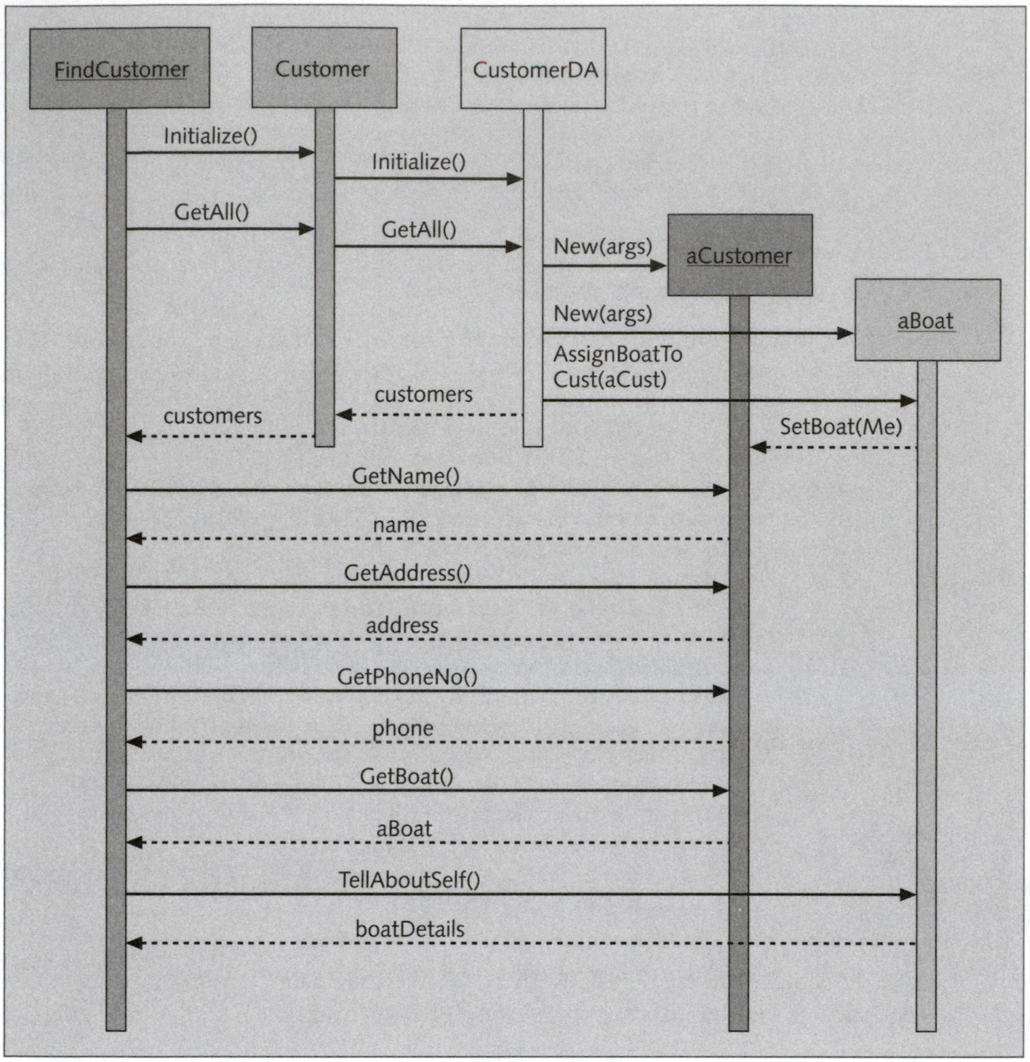

Figure 15-11 FindCustomer sequence diagram for Example 3

Reviewing the AddCustomer GUI from Chapter 11

The AddCustomer GUI in this example is identical to the AddCustomer GUI presented in Chapter 11. As you will recall, AddCustomer validates customer information entered by the user and creates a corresponding instance of Customer. It then calls the AddBoat GUI, passing the newly created Customer instance as an argument. The AddBoat GUI captures information about the customer's boat, then adds the customer information to CustomerTable and the boat information to BoatTable.

Note that in this example the AddCustomer GUI does not interact directly with the database. Instead, the AddCustomer GUI passes customer information to the AddBoat GUI, and the AddBoat GUI inserts records into both tables. This is by design—*a customer must be associated with a boat.* Therefore, you do not want to add a customer to CustomerTable until information about the customer's boat is available to be added to BoatTable.

Because the AddCustomer GUI for this example does not interact with the database, it is identical to the version presented in Chapter 11. This version of AddCustomer is shown in Figure 15-12. (Note that the code generated by the Windows Form Designer requires no modification and is omitted from this listing.)

```
'Chapter 15 Example 3
'Same as Chapter 11
Public Class AddCustomer
    Inherits System.Windows.Forms.Form

    'Declare customer reference variable
    Private aCustomer As Customer
    'Declare string variables for name, address and phone
    Private customerName, customerAddress, customerPhone As String

    'Declare reference for AddBoat form
    Private frmAddBoatGUI As AddBoat

    'Windows Form Designer generated code goes here

    Private Sub btnAddBoat_Click(ByVal sender As System.Object, _
    ByVal e As System.EventArgs) Handles btnAddBoat.Click
        'Get values from the text boxes
        customerName = txtName.Text
        customerAddress = txtAddress.Text
        customerPhone = txtPhone.Text
        'Validate that the user has entered values for name, address _
        and phone
        If customerName.Length = 0 Or _
         customerAddress.Length = 0 Or _
         customerPhone.Length = 0 Then
            MessageBox.Show("Please Enter All Data")
         Else
            'Create a customer instance
            aCustomer = New Customer(customerName, customerAddress, _
                          customerPhone)
            'Clear the form
            ClearForm()
            'Hide the AddCustomer form
            Me.Hide()
            'Create and display the AddBoat form
            frmAddBoatGUI = New AddBoat(aCustomer)
            frmAddBoatGUI.ShowDialog()
            'Make the AddCustomer form visible
            Me.Show()
        End If
    End Sub
```

15

```
    Private Sub ClearForm()
        txtName.Text = ""
        txtAddress.Text = ""
        txtPhone.Text = ""
        txtName.Focus()
    End Sub

    Private Sub btnClear_Click(ByVal sender As System.Object, _
    ByVal e As System.EventArgs) Handles btnClear.Click
        ClearForm()
    End Sub

    Private Sub btnClose_Click(ByVal sender As System.Object, _
    ByVal e As System.EventArgs) Handles btnClose.Click
        Me.Close()
    End Sub
End Class
```

Figure 15-12: The AddCustomer GUI From Chapter 11

Modifying the AddBoat GUI

The AddBoat GUI for this example is also similar to the version presented in Chapter 11. Recall from Chapter 11 that the AddBoat constructor receives a Customer reference variable in the parameter list. AddBoat validates the boat information entered by the user, creates a corresponding instance of Boat, and establishes the two-way association between the customer and boat instances. In this three-tier example, AddBoat must now add the boat record to BoatTable and add the associated customer record to CustomerTable.

Before examining the code responsible for achieving this, it is important to recognize that in its current form BoatTable stores only those attributes that are common to both sailboats and powerboats—it does not store sailboat and powerboat attributes. In other words, although sailboat and powerboat attributes are captured and validated by the AddBoat GUI, the sailboat and powerboat details are not persistent. To make sailboat and powerboat attributes persistent, you would create DA classes for Sailboat and Powerboat, and modify the database design to include sailboat and powerboat attributes. For now, the AddBoat GUI creates instances of the Boat class, rather than instances of Sailboat and Powerboat. Accordingly, the original concrete Boat class is used without its Sailboat and Powerboat subclasses.

The AddBoat GUI begins as before. The parameter list for the constructor method includes a reference to the Customer instance that is passed in by the AddCustomer GUI. This Customer reference is then stored in a variable with class scope so that it is accessible throughout the program.

```
'Chapter 15 Example 3
Public Class AddBoat
    Inherits System.Windows.Forms.Form
```

```
'Declare a Customer reference variable
Private aCustomer As Customer

'Within the generated code:
'  1. Modify the parameter list for the constructor method to
'     accept a customer reference argument.
'  2. Add a statement to the generated code to store the
'     Customer instance that is passed to the constructor.

Public Sub New(ByRef thisCustomer As Customer)

   MyBase.New()

   'This call is required by the Windows Form Designer.
   InitializeComponent()

   'Add any initialization after the InitializeComponent() call

   'Store customer reference in the private class variable
   aCustomer = thisCustomer

End Sub
```

The `radSailboat_CheckChanged`, `radPowerboat_CheckChanged`, and `btnAdd_Click` methods also remain unchanged from Chapter 11.

```
Private Sub radSailboat_CheckedChanged _
(ByVal sender As System.Object, ByVal e As System.EventArgs) _
Handles radSailboat.CheckedChanged
      'If sailboat radio button is checked display the sailboat panel
      If radSailboat.Checked = True Then
         pnlPowerboat.Visible = False
         pnlSailboat.Visible = True
      End If
End Sub

Private Sub radPowerBoat_CheckedChanged _
(ByVal sender As System.Object, ByVal e As System.EventArgs) _
Handles radPowerBoat.CheckedChanged
    'If powerboat radio button is checked display the powerboat panel
    If radPowerBoat.Checked = True Then
       pnlSailboat.Visible = False
       pnlPowerboat.Visible = True
    End If
End Sub

Private Sub btnAdd_Click _
(ByVal sender As System.Object, ByVal e As System.EventArgs) _
Handles btnAdd.Click
    'Declare variables for boat attributes
    Dim boatLength As Double
    Dim year As Integer
    Dim manufacturer, stateRegistration As String
```

```
        'Get reg. no. and manufacturer from text boxes
        stateRegistration = txtStateRegNo.Text
        manufacturer = txtManufacturer.Text
        'Validate that the user has entered reg. no. and manufacturer
        If manufacturer.Length = 0 Or _
         stateRegistration.Length = 0 Then
            MessageBox.Show("Please Enter All Data")
        Else
            'Ensure that the value for boat length is numeric
            If Not IsNumeric(txtLength.Text) Then
               MessageBox.Show("Boat Length must be numeric")
            Else
               boatLength = txtLength.Text
               'Ensure that the value for year is numeric
               If Not IsNumeric(txtYear.Text) Then
                  MessageBox.Show("Year must be numeric")
               Else
                  year = txtYear.Text
                  'Invoke the appropriate add method
                  If radSailboat.Checked = True Then
                     AddSailboat(stateRegistration, boatLength, _
                        manufacturer, year)
                  Else
                     AddPowerboat(stateRegistration, boatLength, _
                        manufacturer, year)
                  End If
               End If
            End If
        End If
    End Sub
```

As before, the AddSailboat and AddPowerboat methods validate the sailboat and powerboat information entered by the user. However, because only the four common boat attributes are actually stored in the database, these methods create an instance of the Boat class, rather than an instance of Sailboat or Powerboat. The association relationship between Customer and Boat is established by invoking the AssignBoatToCustomer method of the Boat class. The AddNew method of the Customer class adds the customer and boat information to the database.

Recall from Chapter 14 that the Customer class passes the request to add a new customer to the database to the AddNew method of the CustomerDA class. The AddNew method of the CustomerDA class extracts information from the customer instance (including a reference to the customer's boat), inserts a record into CustomerTable, and then calls the AddNew method of the Boat class. The Boat class passes the request to add a new boat to the database to the AddNew method of the BoatDA class, which inserts a record into BoatTable. This sequence preserves the integrity of the database, enforcing the requirement that each customer be associated with exactly one boat. The attempt to insert a record into the database is included within a try-catch block to detect the possibility that the customer (or boat) already exists in the database.

```
'Method to add a sailboat and customer
'only the four boat attributes are actually stored in the database
Private Sub AddSailboat(ByVal aStateRegNo As String, _
ByVal aBoatLength As Double, ByVal aManufacturer As String, _
ByVal aYear As Integer)
    'Declare variables for sailboat attributes
    Dim numberOfSails As Integer
    Dim keelDepth As Double
    Dim motorType As String

    'Ensure that the number of sails is numeric
    If Not IsNumeric(txtNumberOfSails.Text) Then
        MessageBox.Show("Number of sails must be numeric")
    Else
        numberOfSails = txtNumberOfSails.Text
        'Ensure that the keel depth is numeric
        If Not IsNumeric(txtKeelDepth.Text) Then
            MessageBox.Show("Keel depth must be numeric")
        Else
            keelDepth = txtKeelDepth.Text
            'Determine type of engine
            If radNoEngine.Checked = True Then
                motorType = "None"
            Else
                If radInboardEngine.Checked = True Then
                    motorType = "Inboard"
                Else
                    If radOutboardEngine.Checked = True Then
                        motorType = "Outboard"
                    End If
                End If
            End If
            'Create a Boat instance - sailboat attributes are not
            'persistent
            Dim aBoat As Boat
            aBoat = New Boat(aStateRegNo, aBoatLength, _
                   aManufacturer, aYear)

            'Establish the association in both directions
            aBoat.AssignBoatToCustomer(aCustomer)

            'Add the customer and the boat to the database
            'The CustomerDA.AddNew invokes Boat.AddNew
            Try
                aCustomer.AddNew()
                MessageBox.Show("Customer and Boat Added")
            Catch de As DuplicateException
                MessageBox.Show("Sorry: " + de.Message.ToString)
            End Try
            'Clear the form
```

15

```
                ClearForm()
            End If
        End If
    End Sub
```

The AddPowerboat method requires similar changes. The `btnClear_Click` and `btnClose_Click` methods do not require any modification.

Hands-on Exercise 3

1. Locate the **Chap15\Examples\Ex03\Example3** folder in the book's student data files.
2. Create a folder named **Chap15\Exercises\Ex03** in the work folder on your system, and then copy the **Example3** folder to this folder.
3. Using VB .NET, open the **Example3** project. You see AddBoat.vb, AddCustomer.vb, FindCustomer.vb, MainMenu.vb, and related files in the Solution Explorer. Run and test the example.
4. In Hands-on Exercise 1 you added a GUI that searched for the customer using the phone number as an alternative to searching by name. Create a similar GUI named FindCustomerAndBoatByPhone. Run and test the example.
5. In Hands-on Exercise 1 you also added a GUI that searched for a customer based on a typed-in phone number. Create a similar GUI for this example, but without the ability to update customer information.
6. Include a MainMenu GUI that works with the three FindCustomer GUIs (find customer by name, find customer by phone, and find one customer) you have implemented for this Hands-on Exercise. Include a menu bar and drop-down menus as well as buttons.

Chapter Summary

- Three-tier design is a strategy for creating OO applications that are easy to maintain because the three tiers communicate using messages while hiding their implementations. One tier can be modified without affecting the other tiers. In previous chapters you learned how to create and test each tier. In this chapter you learned how to combine the three tiers together into a working application module.
- Three-tier design provides a framework that lends itself to iterative development, where some analysis, some design, and some implementation are completed and then the process repeats with more analysis, more design, and more implementation. A good approach to use to complete an iteration is to define and create problem

domain classes, then GUI classes, and then data access classes for one or two use cases at a time. That is the process followed in this book.

- The first example was FindCustomer, which demonstrated one GUI, one problem domain class, one data access class, and a database with one table. The example reads from the database but does not update it.
- The second example demonstrated multiple GUIs, including MainMenu, AddCustomer, and FindCustomer. One problem domain and one data access class are used, but the example involves adding records to the database.
- The third example used multiple GUIs, two problem domain classes with an association relationship, two corresponding data access classes, and a database with two tables. The CustomerDA class looks up customer records and boat records based on a relational join and then instantiates and associates customers and boats.

Review Questions

1. Explain how system maintenance is simplified with three-tier design.
2. Explain how three-tier design provides benefits for distributing an application across a network.
3. Explain how three-tier design can be used to define the tasks done in each iteration of the development process.
4. Review Figure 15-2. In which life cycle phase would you define needed code for a problem domain class that included a constructor and standard accessor methods?
5. Again referencing Figure 15-2, in which life cycle phase would you define needed code for problem domain class static methods such as Initialize, Find, and GetAll?
6. In which life cycle phase would you define the needed GUI classes? The needed data access classes? The needed database schema?
7. Explain how defining, coding, and testing the PD classes, GUI classes, and DA classes involves several analysis, design, and implementation iterations within an iteration that completes a use case.
8. Review the sequence diagram shown in Figure 15-8. Why does it include Customer (not underlined) as well as <u>aCustomer</u> (underlined) on the same diagram?

9. Again consider the sequence diagram shown in Figure 15-8. This interaction instantiates customers from the database so the user can find them. Therefore, Update and AddNew methods are not invoked. If the example did update or add a new customer instance, where would the messages from the GUI point: to Customer, to CustomerDA, or to aCustomer? Why?
10. What is the difference in function between problem domain setter methods and the Update method?
11. What is the difference in function between the problem domain class constructor and the AddNew method?
12. The GUIs from Chapter 11 required little revision in this chapter even though data access classes and a relational database are included. Briefly list the changes that were made to MainMenu, FindCustomer, and AddCustomer compared with the versions used in Chapter 11.
13. The FindCustomer GUI in the last example in this chapter did not use the Sailboat and Powerboat subclasses. A similar example in Chapter 11 did include these subclasses, where object persistence was only simulated. Briefly describe the changes you would have to make to the example in this chapter to include the subclasses and make sailboat and powerboat attributes persistent.

Discussion Questions

1. Discuss the strategy used in one iteration for Bradshaw Marina: to create PD classes, GUI classes, and then DA classes. Why does it make sense to create the GUI classes before the data access classes? Or does it matter? What are a few reasons why different team members might focus on each activity?
2. Consider the design approach used for CustomerDA in Example 3. The GetAll method returned an array list of customers, but only after instantiating both customers and boats, and associating boats and customers. The Find method also instantiated both customers and boats, AddNew instantiated both customers and boats, and so forth. Why does CustomerDA in this example deal with both customers and boats rather than just with customers? In the complete Bradshaw Marina system, what other responsibilities for instantiation might CustomerDA have? What are some additional methods that might be included to handle all of the requirements? (*Hint*: Consider the association relationship between Customer and Lease.)

3. Given the discussion in Question 2, what are some additional methods that might be included in BoatDA? In SlipDA? In DockDA? In LeaseDA? To what extent would well-conceived use cases and scenarios help define the methods needed?
4. Consider the following design strategy: Have each PD class setter method invoke the Update method so any change to an attribute value is updated in the database immediately. What would be a specific problem with this strategy related to the constructor? What would be a specific problem with this strategy related to database management?

Projects

1. Consider an application that contains the Student class. A student has an ID, a name, a phone number, a grade point average, and a major. Draw a class diagram showing the Student class and the StudentDA class, including methods required for data access. Create a three-tier application with a relational database, a MainMenu GUI, a GUI for adding a student, and a GUI for finding and updating a student. You will need a database containing one table with test data, a Student class, and a StudentDA class. Create a tester program to test the classes and the database. Then add the MainMenu, AddStudent, and FindStudent GUI classes.
2. Recall the Person and Pet example from Chapter 9. Implement the database for the example with two tables—a person table and a pet table. The pet table should have a foreign key corresponding to the person ID field to allow the tables to be joined. Create a Person class, a Pet class, a PersonDA class, and a PetDA class. Note that you will need a PersonAndPetDatabaseConnect class similar to the examples with multiple data access classes in Chapter 14. As sample data, add at least four person records and four pet records to the database. Assume initially that a person has zero or one pet and a pet is owned by one and only one person. Write a tester program that tests the GetAll, Find, and Delete methods of these classes.
3. For the Person and Pet example in Project 2, design and implement GUI classes to test the AddNew, Find, and Update methods of these classes. Include a MainMenu GUI, an AddPerson GUI, an AddPet GUI, a FindAPerson GUI, and a FindPersonAndPet GUI. Continue to assume that a person is not required to have a pet, but a pet must be associated with one person. Therefore, FindAPerson will return only person information, and will do so for all persons—even a person who does not have a pet. But because each pet must be associated with a person, the FindPersonAndPet GUI can include person information for each pet.

The FindAPerson and FindPersonAndPet GUIs should include a button that enables the user to update person information. The AddPerson GUI can be similar to AddCustomer, but AddPet should allow the user to select from a list the person who owns the pet.

4. Consider what changes are required to modify the Person and Pet example so the association relationship is zero-to-many: a person can own many pets. Create a FindPersonAndPet GUI that will display more than one pet for a person, and add it to the example created for Project 3. (*Hint*: The database does not need to be changed, but you will need to change the Person and PersonDA classes.)

CHAPTER

16

Assembling a Three-Tier Web Form Application

In this chapter you will:

- Understand the concept of state for Web applications
- Create an ASP.NET user control
- Use data binding technology
- Develop a Web application for Bradshaw Marina
- Learn about XML and Web services

In this last chapter of the text, you will build upon the concepts learned earlier to develop a three-tier Web application for Bradshaw Marina. Chapter 12 presented the introductory concepts of Web development and using ASP.NET to create Web applications. Chapters 13 and 14 provided the details for object persistence, file input and output, and creating problem domain classes to develop three-tier applications. Chapters 15 and 16 round out three-tier development, with Chapter 15 focusing on Windows forms and Chapter 16 discussing Web-based applications.

Although Chapter 12 provided an introduction to ASP.NET, you need to explore more of its features and concepts before attempting the final Bradshaw Marina Web application. In this chapter, you will learn about the concept of **state** as it relates to the Internet. You will learn to use ASP.NET user controls to enhance the Bradshaw Marina Web application. ASP.NET also has powerful data binding capabilities that let you connect the property of a control to an underlying source of data. You will use data binding technology in the Bradshaw Marina Web application.

UNDERSTANDING THE CONCEPT OF STATE FOR WEB APPLICATIONS

The Internet uses Hypertext Transmission Protocol (HTTP), which is a **stateless protocol**. Recall from Chapter 12 that when a user requests a Web page, the message is sent using an HTTP request object to a Web server requesting a particular page. If the Web server finds the requested Web page, it processes the data as appropriate to create and return an HTML stream to the Web browser via an HTTP response object. HTTP is considered a stateless protocol because it doesn't know whether the request is a single request or part of a sequence of requests from the same user.

HTTP was designed to be stateless to provide for maximum scalability, meaning that its capacity grows and shrinks according to demand. Maintaining a continuous connection between the browser and the Web server as a user browses pages would require significant resources that would burden the server. Instead, as a stateless protocol, HTTP can connect the browser and Web server only when necessary. However, working in a stateless environment makes Web development more complex than in other environments, such as Windows, where the client computer maintains a permanent connection to the servers. In the following section, you examine how the Internet traditionally maintains state (using the Application object, the Session object, and cookies), and then explore how ASP.NET maintains state.

Maintaining State

Because HTTP is a stateless protocol, several approaches to maintaining state are available, including the following:

- *Application state*—uses the Application object for information that needs to be available to all users on the site
- *Session state*—uses the Session object to save information only for the duration of the session of a particular client
- *Cookies*—save small amounts of information, less than 4 K, in a file on the client's computer that persists for an assigned length of time
- *Database*—saves large amounts of information that persists beyond the session

Every Web application has one Application object that can be programmed for storing and retrieving information; the information is available to all users of the Web application. Conversely, there is one Session object for each user—it also provides the means for storing and retrieving information but only for one user. Persistence of the information lasts only until the user exits the Web site. ASP.NET can also manage session state without cookies, although it defaults to using its own cookies for the length of a session.

Understanding Application State and the Application Object

The **Application object** provides a mechanism for establishing global information that can be shared among all users of a Web application. In ASP.NET, the application variables are stored centrally and can be conveniently accessed through the Application property of the ASP.NET Page class. ASP.NET includes a Global.asax file within a project that serves as a place to enter the initial application state variable. Figure 16-1 shows this file in the Solution Explorer window in ASP.NET.

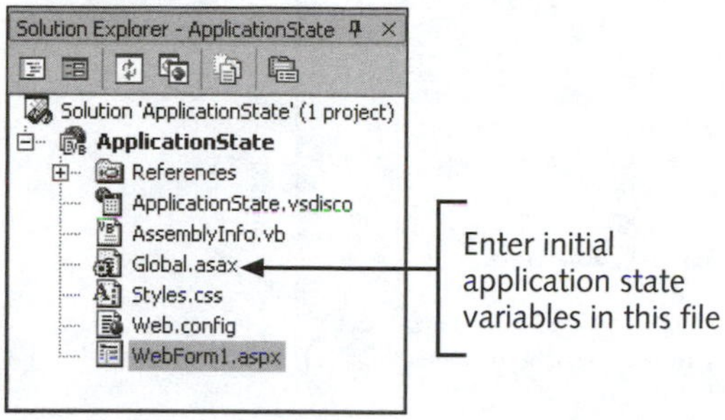

Figure 16-1 Global.asax file

The design of the default Web form is included in the Global.asax file, shown in Figure 16-2.

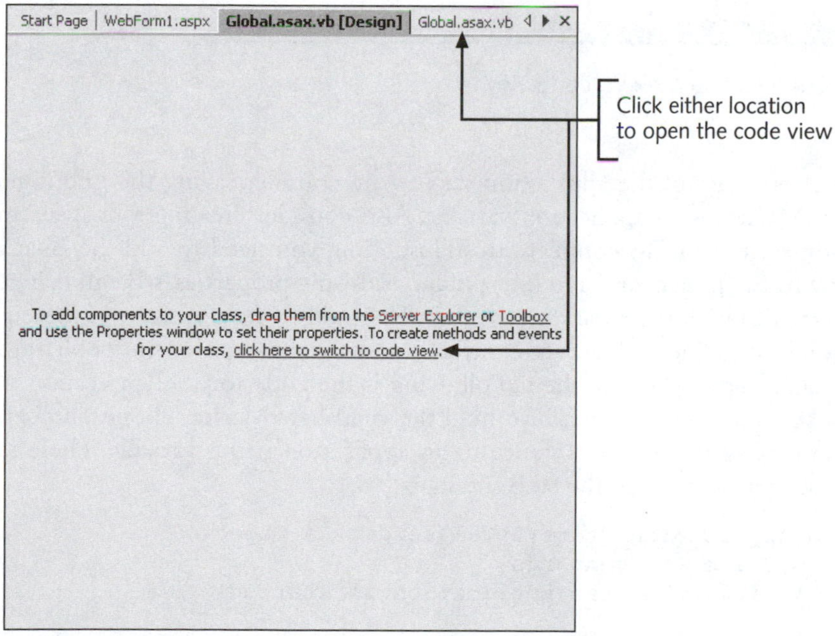

Figure 16-2 Global.asax.vb [Design] view

The code view shown in Figure 16-3 contains the event handlers for several application and session events, including the start and end events.

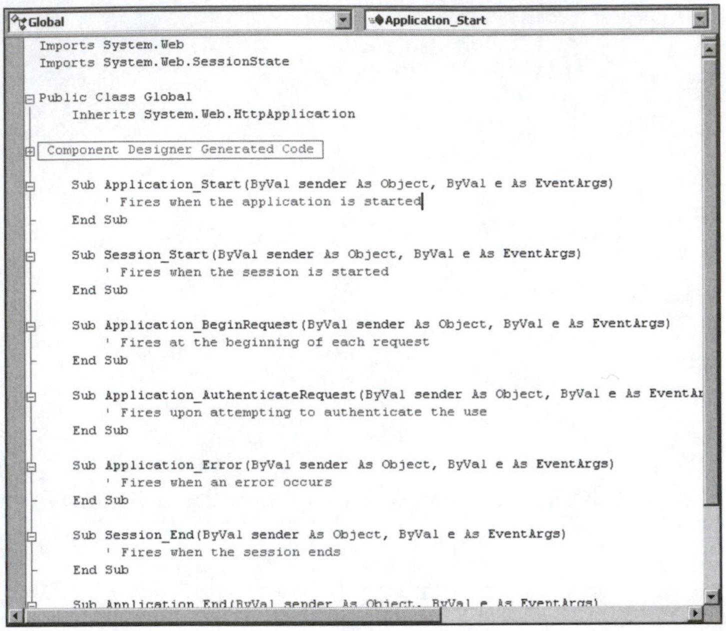

Figure 16-3 Global.asax.vb code view

To illustrate the use of the application start event, consider saving the phone number for Bradshaw Marina as an application variable. Also consider creating a boat instance in the application start event. To complete this illustration, you need to add the Boat class from Chapter 9 to the project and add four public read-only properties: stRegNo, lngth, manuf, and btYear. Although the Boat's getter methods could be used instead of these properties, data binding for some Web server controls automatically exposes the public properties—thus, it makes sense to create them. Following is the code for the application start event. The first statement sets a variable to hold the Bradshaw Marina phone number. The second statement assigns a boat instance to an application string variable. These application variables are set once when the Web site starts.

```
Sub Application_Start(ByVal sender As Object, _
   ByVal e As EventArgs)
   ' Fires when the application is started

   Application("BradshawMarinaPhone") = "840-123-5432"
   Application("boatState") = New _
            Boat("MO1234567", 24, "Ranger", 2002)
End Sub
```

To illustrate how you can use these application variables, consider working with a Web page that has Web server labels to identify and display boat properties. These values are stored as application variables. For example, you could use the following label names for displaying the values: lblPhone, lblStRegNo, lblLength, lblManuf, and lblYear. Two buttons also appear on the form; one with the text "Display" and the other with the text "New Phone No."

Users could then click the Display button first to show the initial application variable values set at the application start event, and then click the New Phone No button to change and display the new phone number. In the following code for the Display button, the first statement extracts the value for the application variable holding the phone number and assigns it the label's Text property. Then a boat instance is created by converting the application string variable, boatState, to a type of boat. The next four lines reference the public read-only properties added to the Boat class to assign these attribute values to the Text property of labels. Clicking the Display button produces a Web form similar to the one shown in Figure 16-4.

```
Private Sub btnShowBoat_Click(ByVal sender As System.Object, _
     ByVal e As System.EventArgs) Handles btnShowBoat.Click

     ' Put Bradshaw Marina phone number on a label
     lblPhone.Text = Application("BradshawMarinaPhone")

     ' Create a boat instance from the application string
     Dim aBoat As Boat = CType(Application("boatState"), Boat)

     ' Put boat information on labels
     lblStReg.Text = aBoat.stateRegNo
     lblLength.Text = aBoat.lngth
     lblManuf.Text = aBoat.manuf
     lblYear.Text = aBoat.btYear

 End Sub

 Private Sub btnNewPhoneNo_Click(ByVal sender As System.Object, _
     ByVal e As System.EventArgs) Handles btnNewPhoneNo.Click
     Application.Lock()
     Application("BradshawMarinaPhone") = "840-123-4567"
     Application.UnLock()
     lblPhone.Text = Application("BradshawMarinaPhone")
 End Sub
```

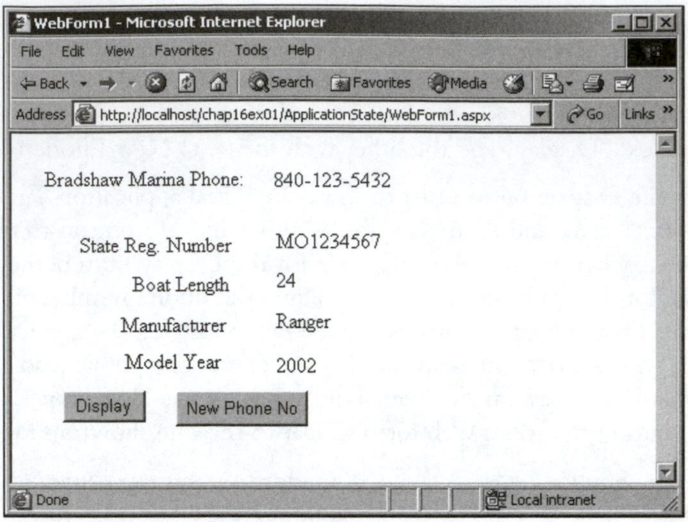

Figure 16-4 Application variable values

Because application variable values are available to all users of the Web site, you could encounter conflicts if multiple users try to change the same variable's value at the same time. Therefore, the application's Lock method should be invoked before changing the value of an application variable, and the application's Unlock method should be invoked after the change has been made. The code for the New Phone No button shows how to change the phone number using the Lock and Unlock methods and then display the new phone number. Figure 16-5 illustrates the changed phone number when clicking the New Phone No button after the Display button has been clicked.

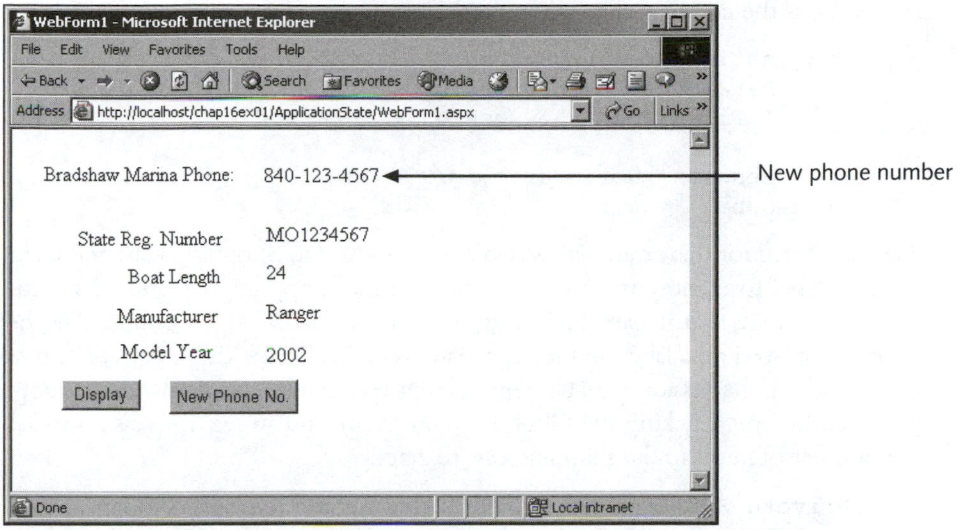

Figure 16-5 New phone number for application variable

Although you can store boat instances using the Application object, doing so makes them available to all users and would degrade the Web performance if all applications stored large amounts of data using the Application object. Recall that there is only one Application object for each Web application. Instead, a database on a different computer would be the preferred storage method of boat instances. However, assigning a boat instance to an application variable does show how the Application object handles objects. The phone number example is also a good candidate to use as an application variable because it changes infrequently.

Understanding Session State and the Session Object

The **Session object** provides a way to keep information about a user throughout multiple requests to a Web application. A session begins when the user enters the Web site and ends when the user leaves the Web application or a timeout occurs. The default timeout is typically 20 minutes. On e-commerce Web sites, many shopping cart or basket Web applications are based on session data. You can also use session data for personalizing Web pages. As shown earlier in Figure 16-3, the Session object in the Global.asax code view has event handlers for the start and end of a session.

For example, suppose you want to create a simple shopping cart on a Web site. The shopping cart application adds 1 to the number of items in the shopping cart when a button is clicked and clears out the shopping cart when another button is clicked. If Bradshaw Marina sold souvenirs, a shopping cart would be needed. This is accomplished by using a session variable to track the number of items in the shopping cart.

Following is the code for the session start event. The session variable is set to zero.

```
Sub Session_Start(ByVal sender As Object, _
     ByVal e As EventArgs)
     ' Fires when the session is started

     Session("NbrInCart") = 0
 End Sub
```

The Web form for this example has two buttons—Add to Shopping Cart and Clear Shopping Cart—a label to identify the displayed count in the shopping cart, and a label to display the number of items in the cart. Following is the code for the three events. The shopping cart value is displayed on a label on the page load event. Each time the Add to Shopping Cart button is clicked, the session variable representing the number of items in the shopping cart is increased by one. Clicking the Clear Shopping Cart button sets the session variable holding the number of items in the shopping cart to zero.

```
Private Sub Page_Load(ByVal sender As System.Object, _
     ByVal e As System.EventArgs) Handles MyBase.Load
     'Put user code to initialize the page here

     lblCount.Text = Session("NbrInCart")
 End Sub

 Private Sub btnAdd_Click(ByVal sender As System.Object, _
     ByVal e As System.EventArgs) Handles btnAdd.Click

     Session("NbrInCart") += 1
     lblCount.Text = Session("NbrInCart")
 End Sub

 Private Sub btnClear_Click(ByVal sender As System.Object, _
     ByVal e As System.EventArgs) Handles btnClear.Click

     Session("NbrInCart") = 0
     lblCount.Text = Session("NbrInCart")
 End Sub
```

The Web form for this shopping cart application appears in Figure 16-6. Note that the user loses the shopping cart count, and any other session variable values, when the session ends. Cookies provide a more permanent way to store information and are discussed next.

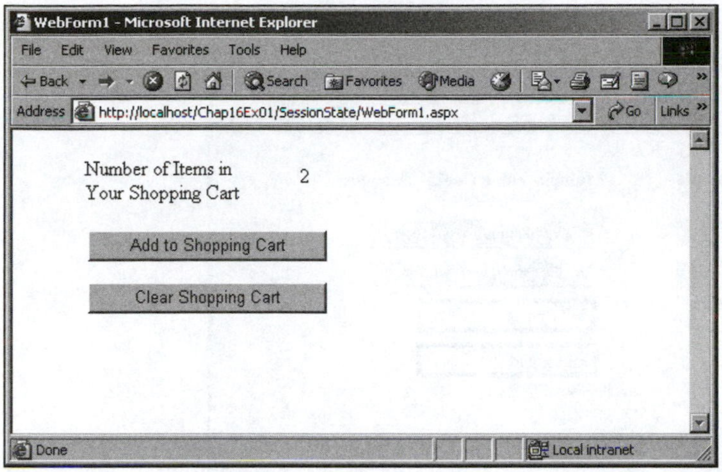

Figure 16-6 Shopping cart Web application

Using Cookies

A **cookie** is a small text file saved on your computer by the Web application to which you are connected. Web sites often use cookies for keeping user preferences and information for logons. In general, cookies provide a way to save state beyond the current visit. Your browser defaults to allow your computer to accept cookies, but you can change the settings to prevent cookies from being written to your computer. Applications can set an expiration date for a cookie; otherwise, it expires when the session ends.

Cookies can be single-value or multiple-value. As Figure 16-7 shows, the left panel of the Web form contains two buttons. Clicking the Create Single Cookie button creates a single-value cookie and assigns it an expiration date. Clicking the Display Single Cookie button retrieves the cookie and displays it on the label below the buttons.

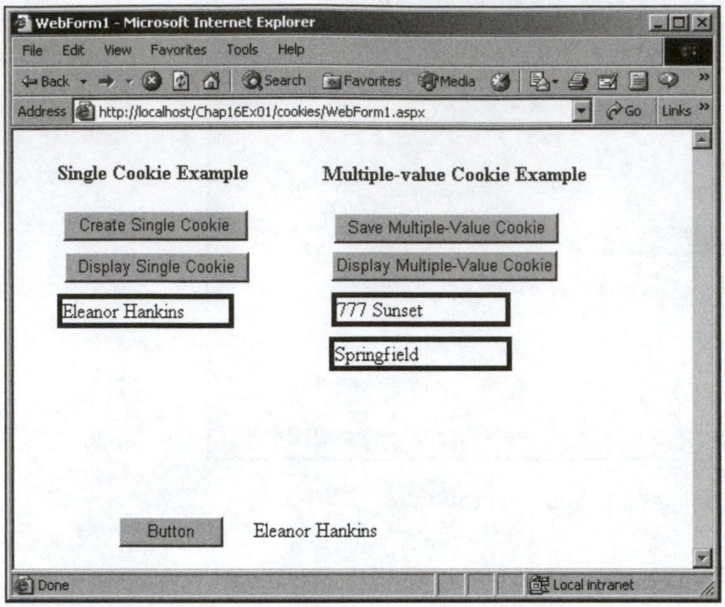

Figure 16-7 Example of single-value and multiple-value cookies

The right panel on the Web form contains two buttons and two labels. Clicking the Save Multiple-Value Cookie button creates a multiple-value cookie and assigns it an expiration date. Clicking the Display Multiple-Value Cookie button retrieves the values for the multiple-value cookie and displays these values on labels below the buttons. The code for the four buttons appears in Figure 16-8. The button descriptions are meaningful enough to reflect the code they contain.

```
Private Sub btnCreateSingleCookie_Click(ByVal sender As System.Object,_
  ByVal e As System.EventArgs) Handles btnCreateSingleCookie.Click

        Response.Cookies("CustomerName").Value = "Eleanor Hankins"
        Response.Cookies("CustomerName").Expires = _
            DateAdd(DateInterval.Month, 3, Today)
End Sub

Private Sub btnDisplayCookie_Click(ByVal sender As System.Object, _
   ByVal e As System.EventArgs) Handles btnDisplayCookie.Click

    lblDisplaySingleCookie.Text = _
            Request.Cookies("CustomerName").Value
End Sub

Private Sub btnSaveMVCookie_Click(ByVal sender As System.Object,_
   ByVal e As System.EventArgs) Handles btnSaveMVCookie.Click
```

```
        Response.Cookies("bmAddress")("StreetAddress") = "777 Sunset"
        Response.Cookies("bmAddress")("CityAddress") = "Springfield"
        Response.Cookies("bmAddress").Expires = _
            DateAdd(DateInterval.Month, 3, Today)
End Sub

Private Sub btnDisplayMVCookie_Click(ByVal sender As System.Object, _
        ByVal e As System.EventArgs) Handles btnDisplayMVCookie.Click

        lblAddressCookie.Text = _
            Request.Cookies("bmAddress")("StreetAddress")
        lblCityCookie.Text = _
            Request.Cookies("bmAddress")("CityAddress")
End Sub
```

Figure 16-8 Code for creating and retrieving cookies

You write cookies using the response object and retrieve them using the request object. In the single-value cookie example, the cookie name is `CustomerName`. Because ASP.NET, like VB .NET, has Intellisense, when you enter a period following the response, a list of properties and methods appears. For single-value cookies, the Intellisense list shows the value property, which is the one being set to a value. The code to set the expiration date uses the DateAdd method and sets the expiration date to three months from the date called Today, which is obtained from the computer.

The button to retrieve the single-value cookie uses the request object to retrieve the cookie's value. This value is then assigned to the Text property of a label that will display its value on the Web form.

The format of multiple-value cookies is different from single-value cookies. The name of the cookie appears first. As shown earlier in Figure 16-8, the cookie name is **`bmAddress`** and has two elements—**`StreetAddress`** and **`CityAddress`**. The Save Multiple-Value Cookie button writes the cookie and sets its expiration date. The Display Multiple-Value Cookie button retrieves the cookie values and assigns them to the Text property of labels for display on the Web form.

This example illustrates writing single-value and multiple-value cookies. When the application is run, clicking the buttons on the Web form to save the single-value and multiple-value cookies results in the cookies being written to your computer. Close the program, run it again, and then click the button on the bottom of the Web form. It will retrieve the cookie from your computer and display the cookie on the label.

Using the ASP.NET Session State Control

By default, ASP.NET uses cookies to track user requests that belong to a particular session. ASP.NET has its own system for these cookies—it does not use the response/request objects—and they only persist for the session. With increasing awareness of security risks, alternatives to cookies for state control are being sought. ASP.NET can be configured to work without cookies using its own session state model. In this model, the ASP.NET server serializes all objects in the session collection to the session state store at the end of each Web request. The default settings for ASP.NET is to keep the session state store in cached memory but can be configured to store the session state to a database.

CREATING AN ASP.NET USER CONTROL

User controls are Web forms that consist of ASP server controls and HTML code without the <HTML>, <HEADER>, and <TITLE> tags. A **user control** file is created within an existing application and has an .ascx extension. It allows you to develop parts of a Web form that can be used across all or many of the Web forms in an application. A user control must be registered before it can be used, as discussed later in this chapter.

For example, you could create a Web application navigation system as a user control. Then you could easily place it in all the Web forms of the Web application. An advantage to this approach is that you can change the user control, which involves changing only one file; these changes affect all the Web pages for which it is registered—a much easier task than changing all the Web forms in the application.

Recall from Chapter 12 that user controls provide a viable alternative to HTML frames. User controls also are familiar to developers accustomed to using server-side includes with Classic ASP.

User controls can be easily created within the ASP.NET form designer. For example, the Bradshaw Marina Web site includes a horizontal navigation bar of buttons that are used on all the Web forms of the application, as shown in Figure 16-9. Because this user control is within an existing application, the solution window shows a number of other files.

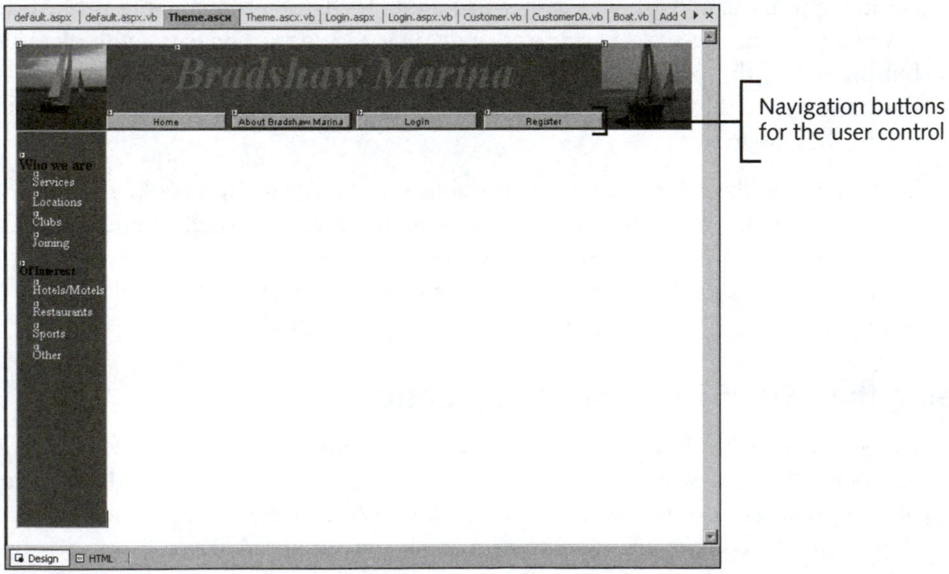

Figure 16-9 Navigation user control

The top navigation area consists of an image control with an image of a sailboat on the left and right, and in between a "Bradshaw Marina" label and four navigation buttons—Home, About Bradshaw Marina, Login, and Register. The left side of the page includes other text controls, some of which are designed for navigation, such as the "Services," "Locations," and "Clubs" labels. To create a user control, right-click the project in the solutions window and select Add New Item to open the Add New Item dialog box. Then click the Web User Control icon in the right pane as shown in Figure 16-10.

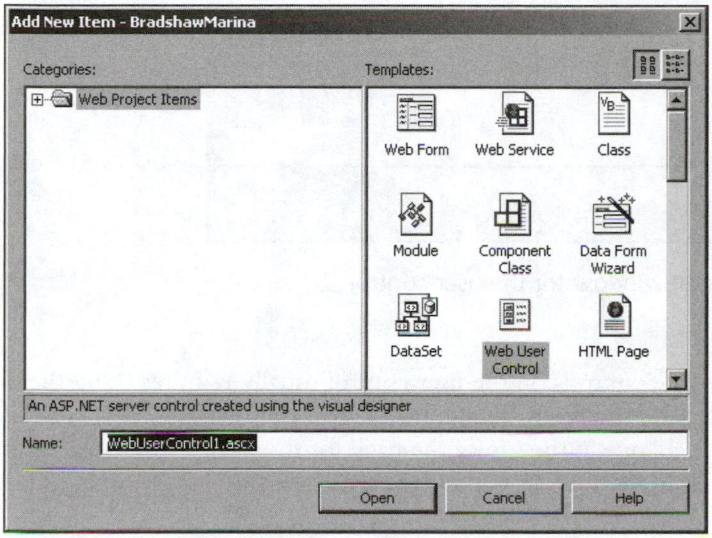

Figure 16-10 Web User Control dialog box

To accept the default name, click the Open button to open the Design window for the user control. This window is shown in Figure 16-11. Your window might contain different files.

16

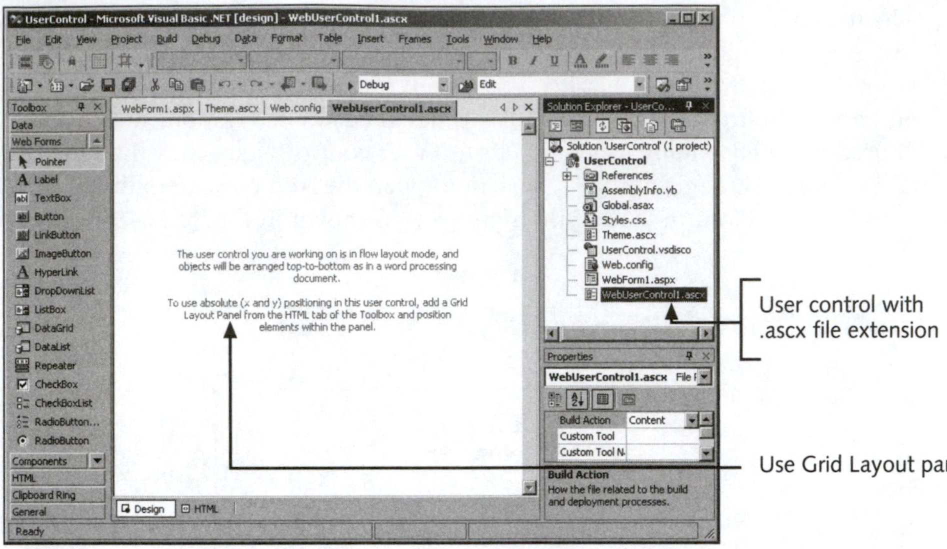

Figure 16-11 Design window for the user control

Precisely laying out the controls on the user control usually requires using the GridLayout panel, similar to the one shown in Figure 16-12. The Bradshaw Marina Web site includes two GridLayout panels: one at the top of the page for the navigation bar, and one that will contain user controls in the middle of the page. Your window might contain different files.

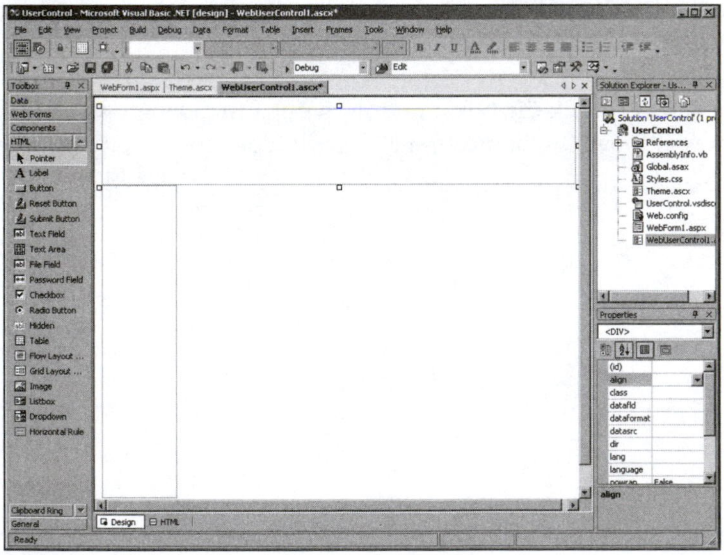

Figure 16-12 User control GridLayout panel

After placing the GridLayout panels that you need on the design form, you place Web controls on the user control. For example, to create the navigation bar in the Bradshaw Marina Web site, you could place an image control in the top horizontal GridLayout panel—one to the left and one to the right to resemble the sailboat images shown earlier in Figure 16-9. The image control has an ImageURL property with a browse button to allow locating the appropriate image. To retrieve the image for the image control, you would click the browse button on the ImageURL property and locate the image to be placed in the image control.

Because the buttons and some text are for navigation, they require action when they are clicked. You can use either Web server controls or HTML controls with anchor tags for your navigation controls. The advantage of using HTML controls is that you can format the controls using events such as OnBlur and OnMouseOver because these operations are executed on the client. On the other hand, Web server controls are processed on the server. The idea with Web server controls is to bundle changes and send them to the server with a major event such as a click event. For example, suppose you want to create the Web server control for the Login button, which users click to navigate to the login Web form. The response object's redirect method is the only line of code needed to handle this task, and is shown in the following code:

```
Private Sub btnLogin_Click(ByVal sender As System.Object, _
   ByVal e As System.EventArgs) Handles btnLogin.Click

   Response.Redirect("Login.aspx")
End Sub
```

After completing the design and code for the navigation buttons on the top panel of the user control, you need to complete two tasks before the user control can be used with a Web form. First, you must use a page directive to register the Web form. The page directive essentially converts a user control to an ASP Web server control with a name and tag prefix. To include a page directive for the Bradshaw Marina form, for example, you would click the HMTL tab to move to HTML view of the Web form. Then place the page directive shown in Figure 16-13 at the top of the HTML code either before or after the existing page directive that was generated. In this case, the tag prefix property has been set to "theme" and the tag name has been set to "Layout."

Part of generated page directive when form was created

```
<%@ Page Language="vb" AutoEventWireup="false" Codebehind="default.aspx.vb"
<%@ Register TagPrefix="theme" TagName="Layout" Src="Theme.ascx" %>

<form id="Form1" method="post" runat="server">
    <theme:layout id="Layout1" runat="server" />
```

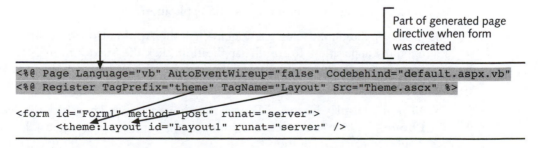

Figure 16-13 Page directive

Notice that the user control works like other ASP tags, except the tag prefix is used instead of the "asp" prefix and it must be inserted within the HTML form tags. For clarity, some generated HTML has been omitted from Figure 16-13. After completing these two tasks, the user control will be included as part of the Web page when it loads. You add the page directive and tags to all of the pages that use this user control.

Hands-on Exercise 1

1. Locate the **Chap16Ex01** folder in the Chap16\Examples student files. Use Windows Explorer to create the folders named **Chap16\Exercises** as necessary in the work folder on your system and copy **Chap16Ex01** to the Exercises folder.

   NOTE: While other chapters in this book provide files in a folder named Ex01, this chapter uses a folder named Chap16Ex01 to avoid conflicts with the virtual directory you created in Chapter 12 for the Ex01 folder.

2. Make the Chap16Ex01 folder a virtual directory. Right-click the **Chap16Ex01** folder and then click **Sharing** on the shortcut menu. (In Windows XP, you click **Sharing and Security** on the shortcut menu.) In the Chap16Ex01 Properties dialog box, click the **Web Sharing** tab, and then click the **Share this folder** option button.
3. In the Edit Alias dialog box, click the **OK** button to accept Chap16Ex01 as the name of the virtual directory. Click **OK** to close the Chap16Ex01 Properties dialog box.
4. The four Web applications (folders) in the **Chap16\Exercises\Chap16Ex01** folder are:
   - ApplicationState
   - SessionState
   - Cookies
   - UserControl

   Note that all Web applications using IIS including Application State and the others in the preceding list, must be set as an IIS application. Please review the "Moving Web Applications and Solving Web Problems" section in Chapter 12 for instructions on setting an application as an IIS application.
5. In the ApplicationState folder, double-click the **ApplicationState.sln** file to open the application. To run the application, click the **Start** button. Note that if you are prompted to set a start-up page, right-click WebForm1.aspx and select Set As Start Page.
6. Click the **Display** button and check the phone number. Then click the **New Phone No.** button and notice that the phone number has changed. Close the ApplicationState application.

7. Repeat Step 5 for the .sln files in the SessionState, Cookies, and UserControl folders to run these applications.
   a. Experiment with the shopping cart in the SessionState application.
   b. When running the Cookies application, note that when you click the buttons to save the single-value and multiple-value cookies, the application is writing cookies (files) on your computer. Click the Display buttons to show the values of the cookies. After running the application and writing the cookies, you need to exit the program to end the session. Then open the application and click the button on the form to display the single-value cookie—Eleanor Hankins.
   c. Notice that the UserControl application has two Web forms: WebForm1.aspx and Theme.ascx. Theme.ascx is the user control—be sure to double-click it to view its design and also notice that the user control has been registered to WebForm1.aspx so that it will display with WebForm1.aspx. Note that the Web forms for the links on the user control have not been added to the application. The focus here is on how to build and register the user control.

Using Data Binding Technology

Data binding technology provides a means to tie the property of a control to an underlying source of data. For example, you can bind the Text property of a text box to a column in a table. The text box value will be the value for the current row of the column. These controls are then called **data bound** or **data aware** controls. Binding controls to the underlying data saves code because you do not have to repopulate the controls as the data changes—this is done automatically. The underlying data source usually comes from data tables but can also be any collection such as an array list.

Binding Data to a Drop-Down List

The Web form shown in Figure 16-14 contains three user controls: a drop-down list box, a label, and a button. You can initially populate the drop-down list box with the names of four boat manufacturers by using values from an array list. The Change Value button serves to change the values in the array list. These changes are reflected in the list box.

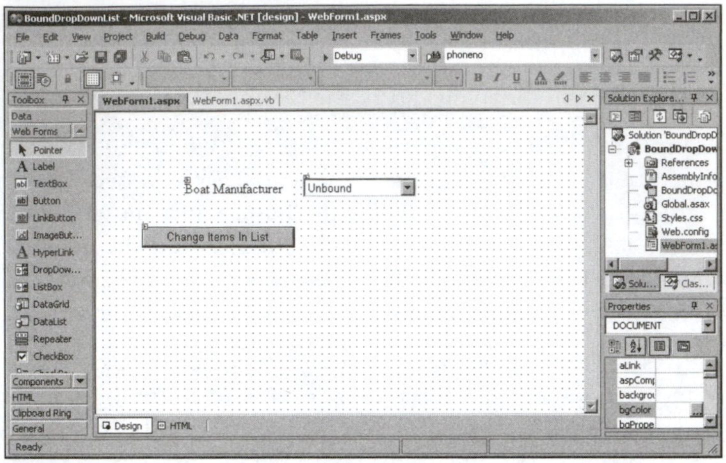

Figure 16-14 Web form design with the three controls

Following is the code to create the array list and bind its values to the drop-down list box:

```
Dim boatManufacturers As New ArrayList()

 Private Sub bindArrayList()
     ddlBoats.DataSource = boatmanufacturers
     ddlBoats.DataBind()
 End Sub

 Private Sub Page_Load(ByVal sender As System.Object, _
  ByVal e As System.EventArgs) Handles MyBase.Load
     'Put user code to initialize the page here

     boatManufacturers.Add("Ranger")
     boatManufacturers.Add("J-Type")
     boatManufacturers.Add("Tartan")
     boatManufacturers.Add("Bayliner")

     boatManufacturers.Sort()

     bindArrayList()

 End Sub
```

You need to declare the array list at the Web form level so that it can be used in more than one method. The code in the page load event adds four boat manufacturers to the array list and then sorts the array list. Next, a method is called to bind the drop-down list to the array list. This method assigns the DataSource property of the list box to the array list, and then invokes its DataBind method to complete the data binding.

The Page class also has a DataBind method that binds all the controls on the form when invoked. The code for the method is **Page.DataBind()**. The code for the button to remove a boat manufacturer, add a boat manufacturer, and then bind the array list to the drop-down list box is as follows.

```
Private Sub btnChangeValue_Click(ByVal sender As System.Object, _
     ByVal e As System.EventArgs) Handles btnChangeValue.Click

     ' Change the values in the ArrayList
     boatManufacturers.Remove("J-Type")
     boatManufacturers.Add("Ventura")

     ' Invoke the method to bind the ArrayList values
     bindArrayList()

 End Sub
```

Figure 16-15 shows the Boat Manufacturers Web page before the values in the list box change in the underlying data source, which is an array list. Figure 16-16 shows the same Web page after the values changed in the array list. Notice that the boat manufacturer J-Type has been removed, the boat manufacturer Ventura has been added to the array list, and the list is sorted.

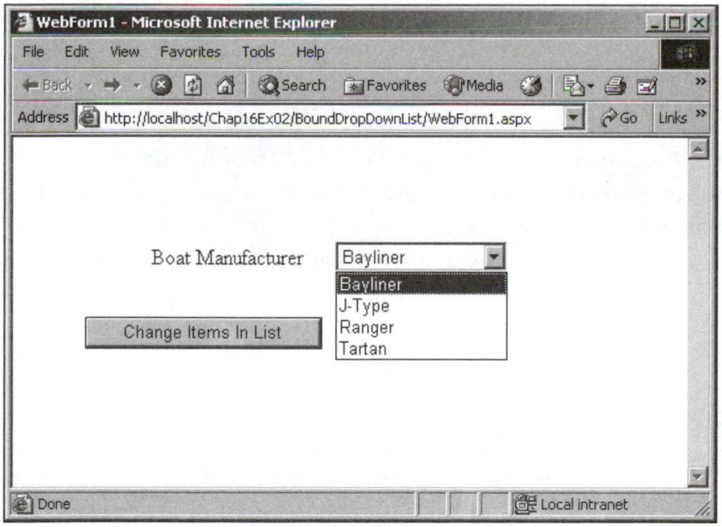

Figure 16-15 Bound drop-down list box with initial array list values

16

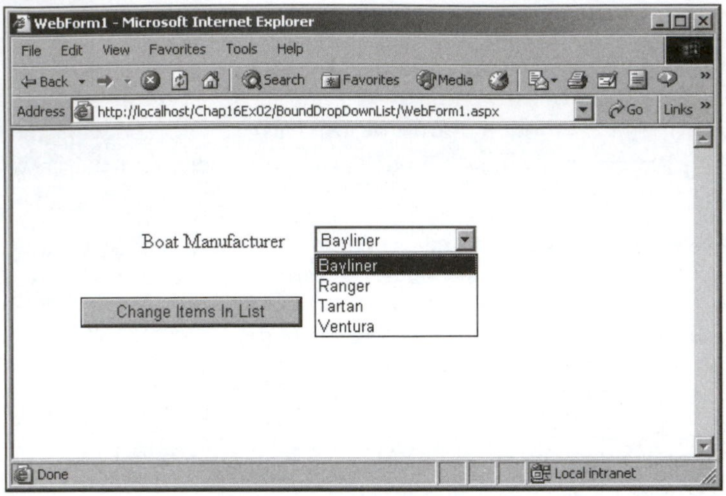

Figure 16-16 Bound drop-down list box after array list values changed

Understanding the DataGrid Control

ASP.NET provides three "data bound only" controls designed for presenting data on Web forms—the Repeater, the DataList, and the DataGrid. The DataGrid control is like an HTML table that provides enhanced features such as column sorting, pagination, in-grid updating, and flexible formatting. Because the DataGrid control provides the richest features of the three, you will focus on it in this chapter.

For the Bradshaw Marina Web site, you could use a data grid for the Boat class. You would therefore need to add the Boat class from Chapter 9 to your Web application. (To add a class, click File on the ASP.NET menu bar, and then click Add Existing Item.) Recall from Chapter 9 that the Bradshaw Marina system associates boats and customers, so the Boat class will reference the Customer class. You would also need to add the Customer class to your Web application. Then you could place and size a DataGrid control similar to the one shown in Figure 16-17.

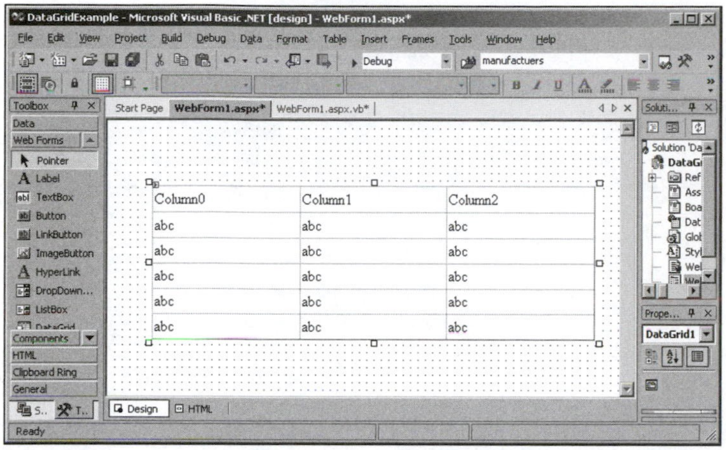

Figure 16-17 DataGrid control on a Web form

You could add boats to an array list, and then use this array list as the data source to which the data grid is bound. To add boats to an array list, you could place the following code in the Page_Init event handler that executes upon the first Web form request. The code assumes that an array list named boats has been declared. Recall that you expand the Web Form Designer Generated Code region to locate the Page_Init event handler, and then insert the code after the Initialize() method.

```
Private Sub Page_Init(ByVal sender As System.Object, _
     ByVal e As System.EventArgs) Handles MyBase.Init
     'CODEGEN: This method call is required by the Web Form Designer
     'Do not modify it using the code editor.
     InitializeComponent()

     boats.Clear()
     boats.Add(New Boat("MO12345", 20, "Ranger", 1996))
     boats.Add(New Boat("MO23456", 24, "Bayliner", 1998))
     boats.Add(New Boat("MO34567", 26, "Ventura", 2003))
     boats.Add(New Boat("MO45678", 22, "Bayliner", 1999))
     boats.Add(New Boat("MO56789", 30, "Bayliner", 2004))
     boats.Add(New Boat("MO11112", 22, "Ventura", 1996))
     boats.Add(New Boat("MO21111", 27, "Ranger", 1997))
     boats.Add(New Boat("MO12121", 24, "Bayliner", 2000))
     boats.Add(New Boat("MO22222", 33, "Ranger", 2001))
     boats.Add(New Boat("MO33123", 20, "Ranger", 2003))
     boats.Sort(0, 0, Nothing)
 End Sub
```

16

In two-tier applications, the data grid is typically bound directly to the data sets of a database. In three-tier applications, the array list intermediates as the middle tier between the data and the presentation. An ASP.NET DataTable control effectively handles the data and binds the grid to it. To create a table, you define the columns and add the rows of data to the column. Figure 16-18 shows the code for a method that creates the table and adds the values of the boat array list to the table. Note the declarations at the Page class level.

```
' Declare an array list for holding boats
 Private boats As New ArrayList()

 ' Declare a data view, variables for page no. and sort key
 Private dv As DataView
 Shared NP As Integer
 Shared SK As String

Private Sub createBoatTable(ByVal boats As ArrayList, _
     Optional ByVal sortkey As String = "StateRegNo", _
     Optional ByVal newpage As Integer = 0)

     ' Define a reference variable of type Boat
     Dim myboat As Boat

     ' Define the columns in the table
     Dim dt As New DataTable()
     Dim dr As DataRow
     dt.Columns.Add(New DataColumn("StateRegNo", GetType(String)))
     dt.Columns.Add(New DataColumn("BoatLength", GetType(Integer)))
     dt.Columns.Add(New DataColumn("Manufacturer", GetType(String)))
     dt.Columns.Add(New DataColumn("Year", GetType(Integer)))

     ' Populate the data table
     For Each myboat In boats
         dr = dt.NewRow  ' create row buffer to hold data

         dr("stateRegNo") = myboat.GetStateRegistrationNo
         dr("BoatLength") = myboat.GetLength
         dr("Manufacturer") = myboat.GetManufacturer
         dr("Year") = myboat.GetYear

         dt.Rows.Add(dr) ' add the data to the data table
     Next

     ' Make sure the sortkey and page number do not create an error
     If sortkey = Nothing Then sortkey = "stateregno"
     If newpage < 0 Or newpage > DataGrid1.PageCount - 1 Then newpage = 0

     ' Assign a dataview to the default view of the data table
     dv = dt.DefaultView

     ' Sort the dataview
     dv.Sort = sortkey
     ' Set the data grid page
     DataGrid1.CurrentPageIndex = newpage
```

Creating the columns

Populating the columns

```
    ' Set datagrid data source and bind the datagrid
    DataGrid1.DataSource = dv
    DataGrid1.DataBind()
End Sub
```

Figure 16-18 Method to create table and populate with boat data

To create a table, you first declare a new data table and a data row, dt and dr in this case. Next, add four columns to the columns collection using appropriate column headings to represent the four attributes of the Boat class. Following is the code to create the columns:

```
Dim dt As New DataTable()
Dim dr As DataRow
dt.Columns.Add(New DataColumn("StateRegNo", GetType(String)))
dt.Columns.Add(New DataColumn("BoatLength", GetType(Integer)))
dt.Columns.Add(New DataColumn("Manufacturer", GetType(String)))
dt.Columns.Add(New DataColumn("Year", GetType(Integer)))
```

After the table has been created, you need to populate the table with the data from the boat array list. A reference variable of type boat is declared and used to loop over all the boats held in the boat array list. With each cycle of the loop, a new row for the table is created to hold values for that row. The Boat methods are used to obtain values for each of the attributes to be stored in the row. After the row has been populated, the add method adds the row to the table with the following code:

```
For Each myboat In boats
    dr = dt.NewRow

    dr("stateRegNo") = myboat.GetStateRegistrationNo
    dr("BoatLength") = myboat.GetLength
    dr("Manufacturer") = myboat.GetManufacturer
    dr("Year") = myboat.GetYear

    dt.Rows.Add(dr)
Next
```

16

The data grid can now be bound to this data table, which is now the data source. To do so, you can assign the default view of the data table to a data view variable, dv. The following code binds the data to the table. The first statement assigns a data view of the table data. The DefaultView method is a copy of the data table but allows sorting and filtering operations. (Sorting and pagination data bound to the data grid will be explained shortly.) The last two statements assign the data grid to the data source and then invoke the DataBind method, respectively.

```
' Assign a data view to the default view of the data table
 dv = dt.DefaultView
```

```
' Sort the data view
dv.Sort = sortkey
' Set the datagrid page
DataGrid1.CurrentPageIndex = newpage

' Set the datagrid data source and bind the data grid
DataGrid1.DataSource = dv
DataGrid1.DataBind()
```

Now that the data grid and table have been created and bound to one another, you can focus on configuring the data grid. You can define the general properties of the grid, including how data is sorted, and set properties of the columns, the paging behavior, the format of the grid, and the border of the grid.

When the data grid is set up for sorting, it captures the data click on the column heading and passes that value as **e.SortExpression** to an event handler. The following event handler extracts the sort key (determined by which column heading is clicked) and invokes the method that creates the table and rebinds it to the grid—after sorting.

```
Private Sub DataGrid1_SortCommand(ByVal source As Object, _
   ByVal e As System.Web.UI.WebControls.DataGridSortCommandEventArgs) _
   Handles DataGrid1.SortCommand

   SK = e.SortExpression
   createBoatTable(boats, SK, 0)

End Sub
```

Pagination also requires an event handler for determining the page index in the data grid. When you click a page number or a Next or Previous button on a data grid, the data grid page index is sent to the event handler as **e.NewPageIndex**. The code within the event handler extracts the page number and invokes the method to rebuild the data grid based on the page index the user selected.

```
Private Sub DataGrid1_PageIndexChanged(ByVal source As Object, _
   ByVal e As System.Web.UI.WebControls.DataGridPageChangedEventArgs) _
   Handles DataGrid1.PageIndexChanged

   NP = e.NewPageIndex
   createBoatTable(boats, SK, NP)

End Sub
```

To configure a data grid in ASP.NET, you click the data grid to select it, and then click the Property Builder button at the bottom of the Property window to open the Properties dialog box for the selected data grid. As shown in Figure 16-19, you use the tabs in the panel on the left of this dialog box to work with categories of properties. By default, this dialog box opens to the General tab. To sort data in a DataGrid control, you must check the Allow sorting box.

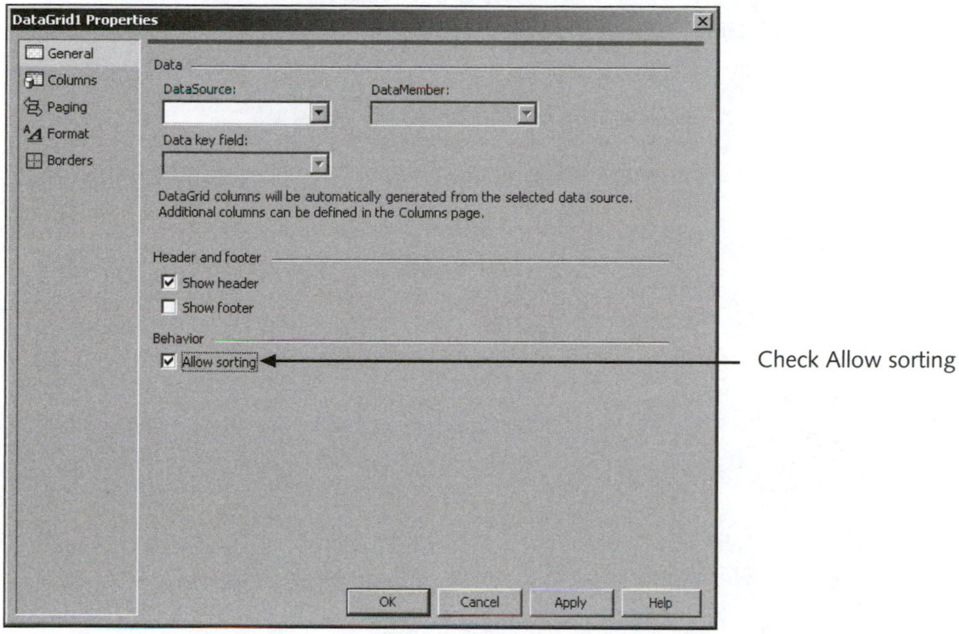

Figure 16-19 General tab in the DataGrid Properties dialog box

To define information about the columns, click the Columns tab. Figure 16-20 shows the Columns properties, including an entry in the Sort expression text box. To sort on a column, you move a column from the Available columns list to the Selected columns list, if necessary, and then click the column in the Selected columns list. Then you enter a sort expression, which is usually the name of the data field you want to sort. Repeat this process for all the columns you want to include in the table. You should also deselect the Create columns automatically at run time check box because, by default, the AutoGenerateColumn property is set to True and ASP.NET will add a data grid column for each column in the table—four in this case. You can change this setting here or in the Properties dialog box. Also note the option of making a column read-only—this will be used later for the Bradshaw Marina Web site.

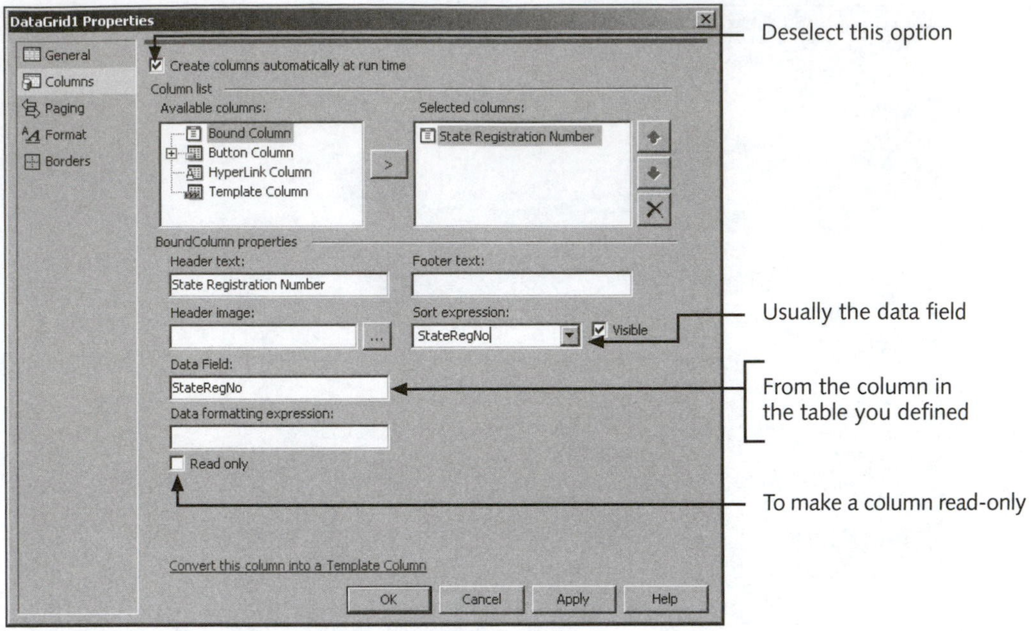

Figure 16-20 Defining a data grid column

Figure 16-21 displays the Paging tab, which defines the options to support pagination. The Allow paging check box is selected so that the data grid uses pages instead of scrolling continuously. The Page size text box lets you set the number of rows in the data grid you want as a page. To test how paging works, you should change this value so that it is less than the number of rows in your table. For example, if your table has 10 rows, change the page size to 5—then your form will have two pages.

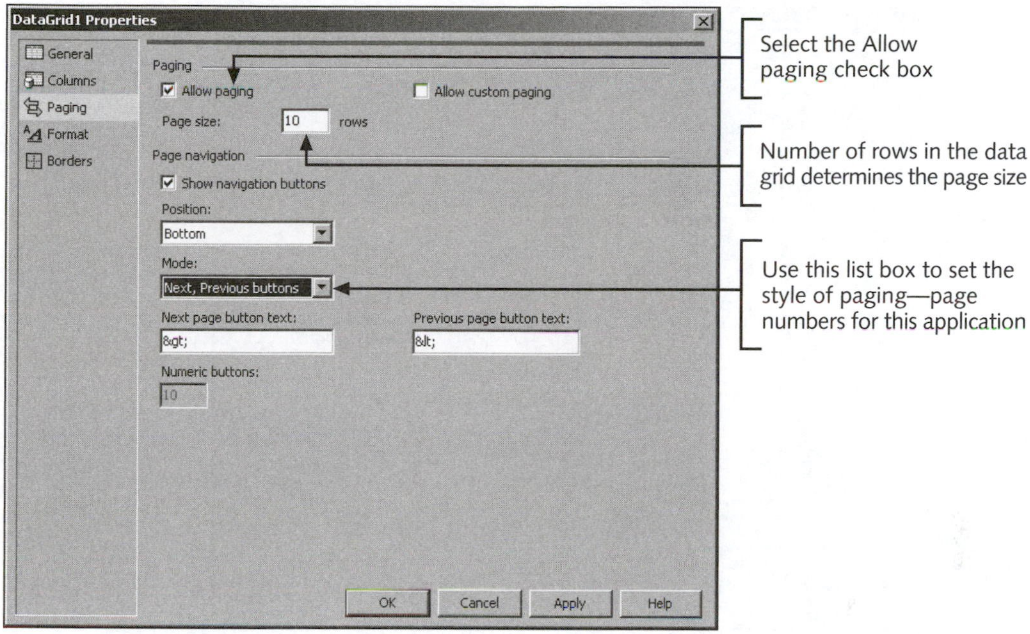

Figure 16-21 Paging tab

You use the Format tab (shown in Figure 16-22) to format column headers, footers, and other items such as alternating columns. Note the tree view structure, which you can use to set display properties for the columns. Also note the zero-based referencing for the columns, which you may need for referencing the columns in code.

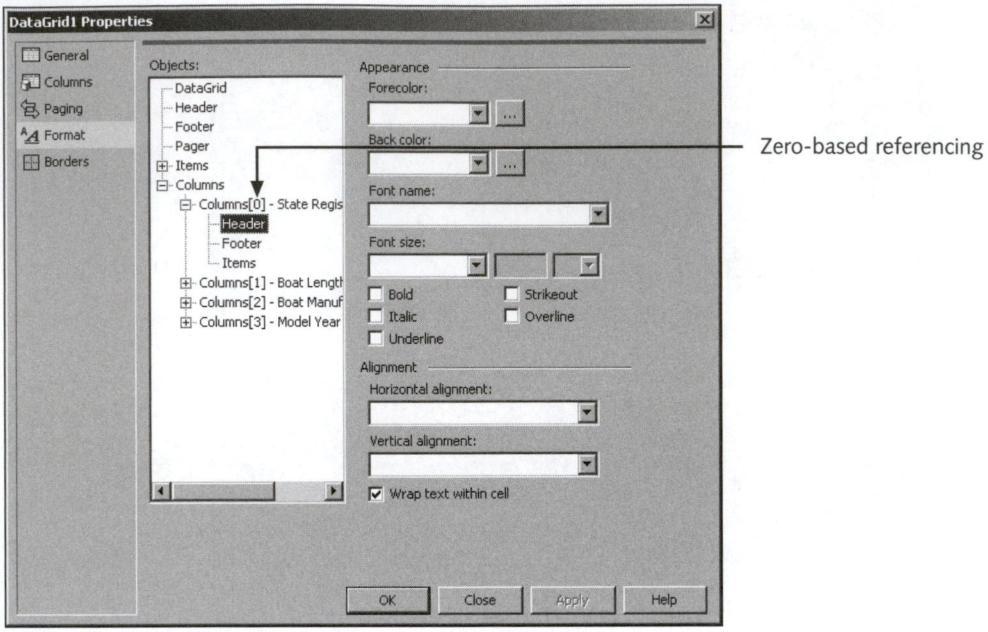

Figure 16-22 Format tab

After setting the properties of your data grid, you would click the OK button and see a data grid on the form designer similar to the one shown in Figure 16-23.

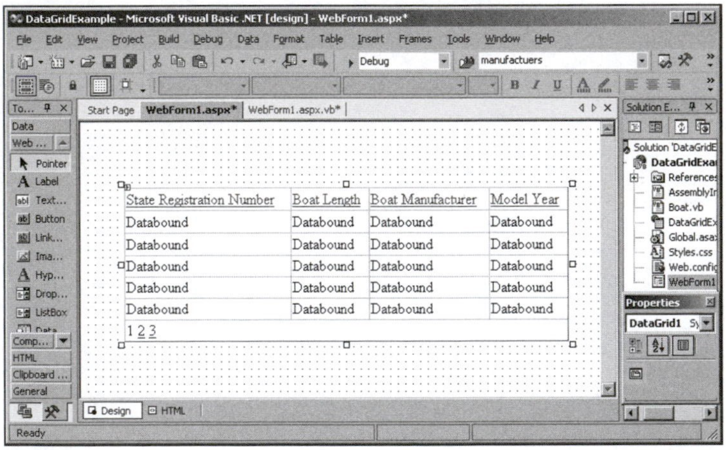

Figure 16-23 Data grid with bound columns in Design view

At startup, the createBoatTable method is invoked to populate the data view and bind the data grid. The following code is placed in the page load event and only executed the first time by checking for a **postback**. Note that the createBoatMethod has two optional parameters, and this call to the method only provides one of the optional parameters (arguments). The comma (,) in the parameter list represents a placeholder for the optional parameter, and the method will then use the default value defined in the parameter list of the method.

```
Private Sub Page_Load(ByVal sender As System.Object, _
   ByVal e As System.EventArgs) Handles MyBase.Load
   'Put user code to initialize the page here

   If Not IsPostBack Then
      'Invoke the method to bind boat attributes
      createBoatTable(boats, "StateRegNo", )

   End If
End Sub
```

Clicking the Start button results in the data grid being displayed with the default settings, as shown in Figure 16-24. The column headings are underlined to represent that they can be clicked. Data bound to the grid is then sorted in that column. All four columns shown in Figure 16-24 can be sorted. The page number appears at the bottom left of the grid. When a page number other than the current page number is clicked, then the data grid is repopulated based on that page number in the grid.

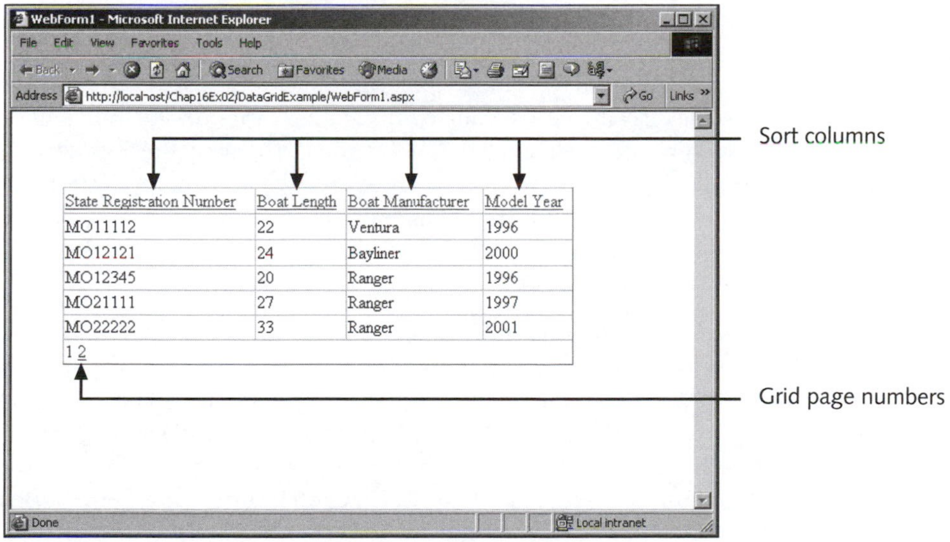

Figure 16-24 Data grid at startup

Hands-on Exercise 2

1. Locate **Chap16Ex02** in the Chap16\Examples folder in the student data files. Copy this folder to the **Chap16\Exercises** folder in the work folder on your system. Make Chap16Ex02 a virtual directory. (See Hands-on Exercise 1 for instructions on creating a virtual directory.) You also need to set BoundDropDownList as an IIS application. See the "Moving Web Applications and Solving Web Problems" section in Chapter 12 for instructions on setting an application as an IIS application.
2. In the BoundDropDownList folder, double-click the **BoundDropDownList.sln** file to open the application. Designate Webform1.aspx as the start page. Then click the **Start** button to run the program. View the boat manufacturers in the drop-down list box, and note that it includes a J-Type manufacturer. Then select a manufacturer or click outside the drop-down list box. Click the **Change Items in List** button and view the list of boat manufacturers—J-Type has been replaced with Ventura. Also note that the list is sorted. Close the application.
3. In the DataGridExample folder, double-click **DataGridExample.sln** to open the application. (You need to set DataGridExample as an IIS application and designate WebForm1.aspx as the start page.) Click the **Start** button to run the program and then experiment with sorting and pagination features of the data grid by clicking page numbers and column headings. (Refer back to Figure 16-24.)
4. Close the DataGridExample application.

Developing a Web Application for Bradshaw Marina

In this section, you examine developing a core Web site for Bradshaw Marina that you can develop into a complete Web site on your own or use as a model for other Web sites. The parts of the Web site that are not complete will be noted. To create the Web site, you will use a three-tier approach. Figure 16-25 shows a three-tier Web-based application architecture. Recall from Chapter 12 and parts of this chapter that the request/response Web model also applies to three-tier architecture, except that the browser requests and responses interface with a middle tier—tier 2 in this case.

You developed three-tier applications in Chapter 15 using Windows forms. In this chapter, you develop a Bradshaw Marina Web site that provides the functionality of the third example in Chapter 15 but in a Web environment. In previous chapters, you worked extensively with all the PD and DA classes. The Bradshaw Marina Web site uses similar PD and DA classes from the third example in Chapter 15—except for data connection references. Thus, those classes will not be repeated here. The Web application also uses the same CustomerAndBoatDatabase application that was used in Chapters 14 and 15.

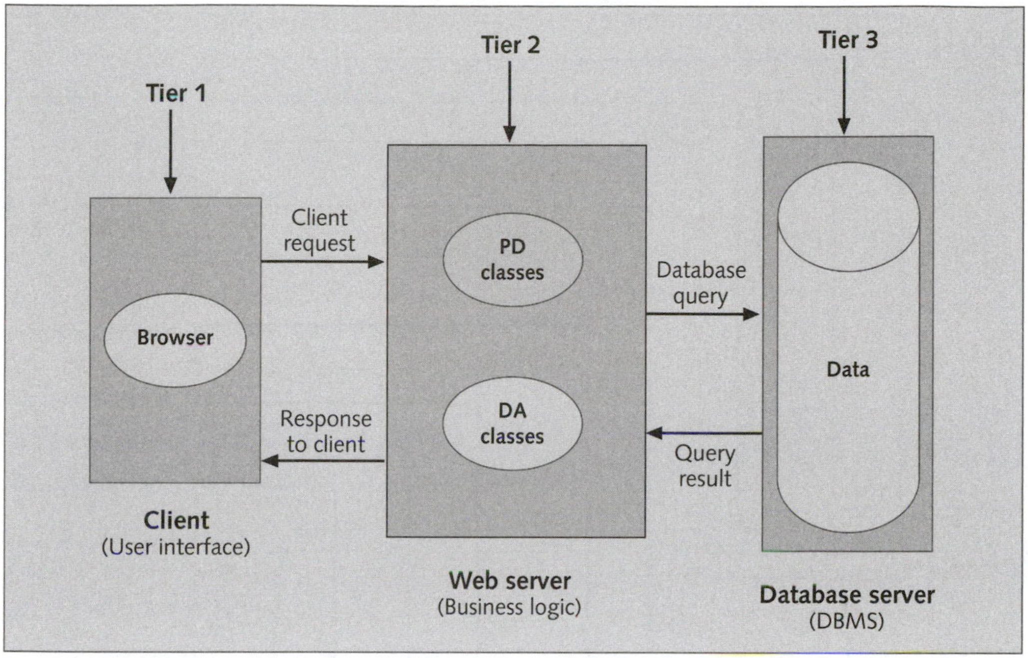

Figure 16-25 Three-tier Web application development environment

Bradshaw Marina Web Site Design

The design of the Bradshaw Marina Web site includes a user control to provide basic navigation between pages using Web server control buttons. The user control will be used on each Web form to provide consistency. This user control is similar to the one you examined earlier in the chapter.

The design of the Bradshaw Marina home page is shown in Figure 16-26, which includes the controls on the home page that perform most of the processing for the Web site. The default.aspx file is used for the home page; theme.ascx and its code-behind file, theme.ascx.vb are the user control files. The Web form also indicates that a user control has been registered to work with the Web form.

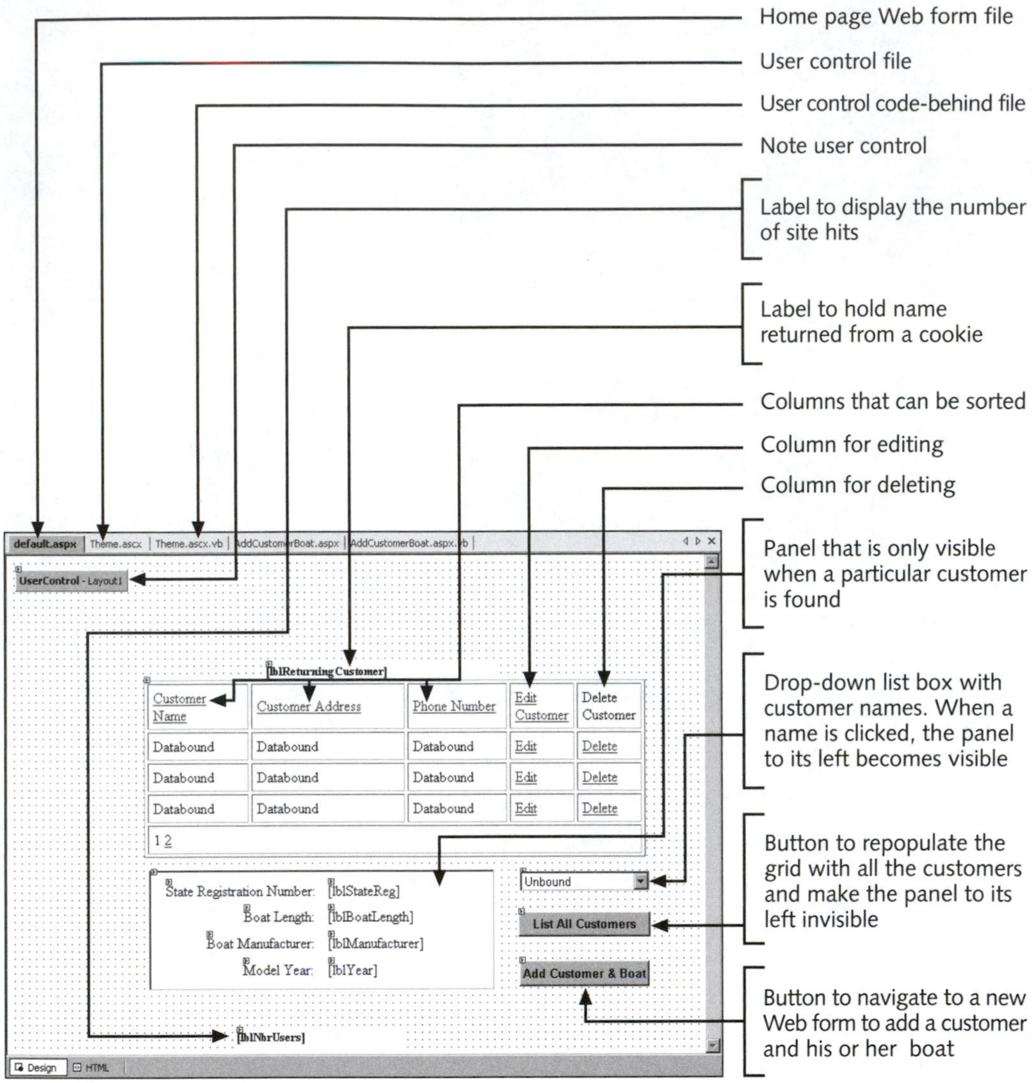

Figure 16-26 Bradshaw Marina home page Web form

Designing the Bradshaw Marina Home Page

The center of the Web form contains a data grid that is bound to the customer attributes of name, address, and phone number using the techniques described in the previous section. Two columns in the grid also allow you to update and delete customer information. The editing and deleting capabilities of the data grid will be explained later.

When a user successfully logs on to the Web site, the Web application writes cookies to save the customer's name and address. The lblReturning Customer control above the data grid is a label that holds the name of the customer if he or she returns to the site before the cookies expire.

The drop-down list box under the grid is bound to the customer name. When the user clicks the name, the following actions occur:

- The customer's boat is retrieved.
- The panel to the left of the drop-down list box appears and is populated with the boat attributes of the customer.
- The grid resizes to show only the selected customer.

Users click the List All Customers button to show all the customers in the data grid and hide the panel showing boat information. They click the Add Customer & Boat button to navigate to a new Web form where they can add a new customer and boat. The lblNbrUsers control displays the number of times the page has been visited.

Figure 16-27 shows the Web form before a customer is selected.

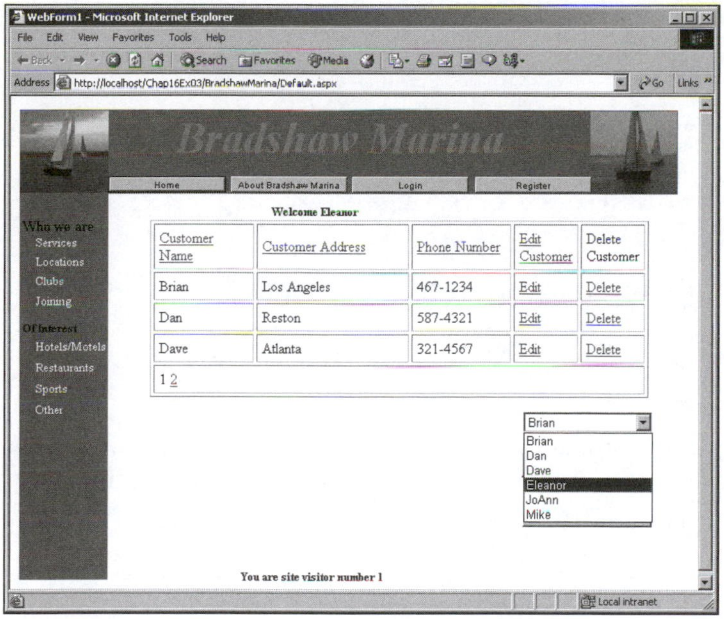

Figure 16-27 Web form before selecting a customer

The navigation bar at the top of the Web page is a user control that includes four horizontal navigation buttons. In this chapter, the first three will be fully implemented. The register Web form exists but has not been completed.

Although the drop-down list covers two buttons when the list arrow is clicked, as it is in Figure 16-27, the list of the customers in the grid shows that the customer names are the same as those used from the database in Chapters 14 and 15.

Figure 16-28 shows the Web form after a customer is selected, specifically how the form changes when Eleanor is clicked in the drop-down list box. The boat attributes for Eleanor are now displayed in the panel under the grid, and the grid is resized to show only information for Eleanor.

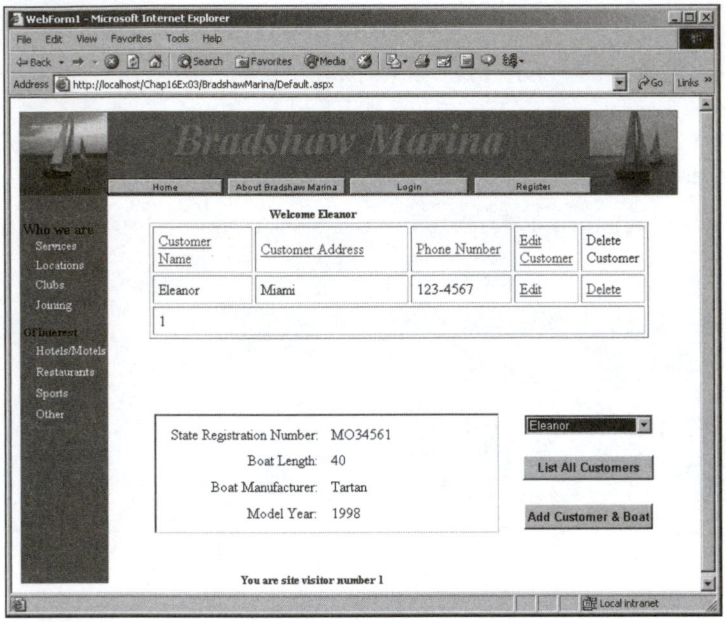

Figure 16-28 Web form after selecting a customer

If you click the List All Customers button to reset the initial settings and show a complete list of customers, clicking the Edit link in a row changes the form as follows:

- The form adds text boxes to the name and address columns.
- On the row where you clicked Edit, the words Update and Cancel replace the word Edit.

Figure 16-29 shows these results. Recall that the phone number serves as the primary key for customer, so the Phone Number column should not be allowed to change. No text box is included in that column. This was accomplished by checking the Read only option on the Columns tab of the data grid's property pages.

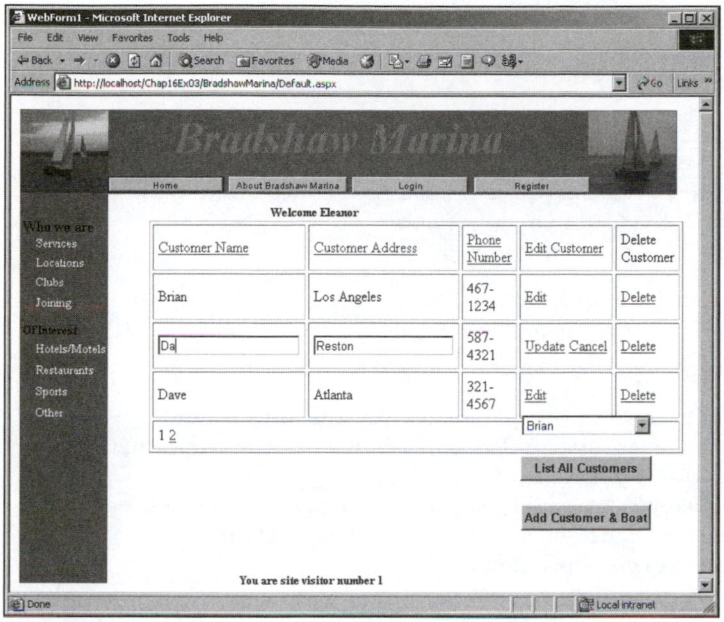

Figure 16-29 Editing a customer in the data grid

If you remove the last character from Dan's name and click the Update button, the name is changed on the form and in the database—it would appear as "Da" in both places. To verify that the change has been made, you could check the Customer table in the database. To delete a record, you click Delete in the row for the customer you want to delete.

Examining the Code for the Default Web Form

To support the database and array list capabilities of ASP.NET, you need to import the appropriate namespaces. You would also need to perform other housekeeping chores such as declaring the database connection, array lists, and variables. The following code shows how to perform these tasks. The data view and the two variables to support sorting and paging of the data grid are also declared here. After the following code, you would include the generated instances of the controls on the form, which are not reproduced here.

16

```
Imports System.Data.OleDb
Imports System.Collections
Public Class WebForm1
   Inherits System.Web.UI.Page

   ' Declare a connection
    Dim aConnection As New OleDbConnection()

    ' Declare a data view
    Dim dv As New DataView()
```

```
' Declare variables for customer and boat instances
Dim aCustomer As Customer
Dim aBoat As Boat

' Declare an array list for the customer instances
Shared customers As ArrayList
' Declare variables for the sort key and page index
Shared SK As String = "Name"
Shared NP As Integer = 0
```

The Page_Init event handler establishes a connection to the database and initializes the connections, as shown in the following code. When you are working in VB .NET, you have to expand the Web Form Designer Generated Code region to find this event handler.

```
Private Sub Page_Init(ByVal sender As System.Object, _
        ByVal e As System.EventArgs) Handles MyBase.Init
        Handles MyBase.Init
        'CODEGEN: This method call is required by the Web Form Designer
        'Do not modify it using the code editor.
        InitializeComponent()

        aConnection = CustomerAndBoatDatabaseConnect.Initialize()
        Customer.Initialize(aConnection)
        Boat.Initialize(aConnection)

    End Sub
```

The page load event follows the page init event in the life cycle of a Web form. It can determine whether a client Web form request is the first or subsequent request. The code for the page load event appears in Figure 16-30. First, all the customers in the database are loaded into an array list using the GetAll method for the Customer class. The BindToGrid method is then called—it creates a table, populates it from the array list of customers, and then binds it to the data grid.

An application-level variable is incremented by one to count this client as one that has visited this Web site. Recall that all clients logged on to this site have access to this application variable. The Lock and Unlock methods are used to avoid contention for the application variable.

```
Private Sub Page_Load(ByVal sender As System.Object, _
    ByVal e As System.EventArgs) Handles MyBase.Load

    If Not IsPostBack Then

        customers = Customer.GetAll
        ' Invoke the bind method
        BindToGrid(customers, Nothing, 0)

        ' Add to number of site visits
        Application.Lock()
        Application("nbrUsers") += 1
```

```
        Application.UnLock()
        lblNbrUsers.Text = "You are site visitor number " & _
            Application("nbrUsers")
        ' Get customer cookie if it exists
        Try
            Dim cName As String = Request.Cookies("Name").Value
            Dim cAddress As String = Request.Cookies("Address").Value
            lblReturningCustomer.Text = "Welcome " & cName
        Catch ce As Exception
            lblReturningCustomer.Text = " "
        End Try
    End If
    ' Make panel and controls invisible------------------------

    pnlBoat.Visible = False

    lblBtReg.Visible = False
    lblBtLength.Visible = False
    lblBtYear.Visible = False
    lblBtManufacturer.Visible = False
    lblStateReg.Visible = False
    lblBoatLength.Visible = False
    lblManufacturer.Visible = False
    lblYear.Visible = False

    ' ------------------------------------------------------------

  End Sub
```

Figure 16-30 Code for the page load event

After incrementing the application-level variable, the program tries to read a name and an address cookie, which would have been written for a customer who has successfully logged on within the cookie duration period. If the program finds the cookies, then the value of the cookie is extracted and displayed on a label above the data grid.

The last segment of code sets the panel control and boat attributes so they are not visible. This is accomplished by setting their visible property to False.

A method that binds the data to the data grid is shown in Figure 16-31. This code logic is identical to the data grid example you already examined. Note that customer attributes are used instead of boat attributes and that the attributes are retrieved from the database.

```
Private Sub BindToGrid(ByVal customers As ArrayList, _
     Optional ByVal sortkey As String = "name", _
     Optional ByVal newpage As Integer = 0)

     Dim myCust As Customer
     Dim dt As New DataTable()
     Dim dr As DataRow
```

```
        dt.Columns.Add(New DataColumn("Name", GetType(String)))
        dt.Columns.Add(New DataColumn("Address", GetType(String)))
        dt.Columns.Add(New DataColumn("PhoneNo", GetType(String)))

        For Each myCust In customers
            dr = dt.NewRow

            dr("Name") = myCust.GetName
            dr("Address") = myCust.GetAddress
            dr("PhoneNo") = myCust.GetPhoneNo

            dt.Rows.Add(dr)
        Next

        dv = dt.DefaultView

        If sortkey = Nothing Then sortkey = "name"
        If newpage = Nothing Or newpage < 0 _
            Or newpage > DataGrid1.PageCount - 1 Then
            newpage = 0
        End If

        dv.Sort = sortkey
        DataGrid1.CurrentPageIndex = newpage

        DataGrid1.DataSource = dv
        DataGrid1.DataBind()

        ddlNames.DataSource = dv
        ddlNames.DataTextField = "Name"
        ddlNames.DataValueField = "PhoneNo"
        ddlNames.DataBind()

End Sub
```

Figure 16-31 Code for the BindToGrid method

When a name in the drop-down list box is clicked, the name selected is used to search for the boat for the selected customer. The code for this event is shown in Figure 16-32.

NOTE: Note that because of the separation of the client and server, all events for Web server controls are not immediately posted back to the server for processing. This is true for the drop-down list box. Thus, you must set its AutoPostBack property to True.

The first part of the code simply sets the panel and the controls that hold the boat attributes so they will be visible.

```
Private Sub ddlNames_SelectedIndexChanged(ByVal sender As System.Object, _
        ByVal e As System.EventArgs) Handles ddlNames.SelectedIndexChanged
```

```
        Dim i As Integer
        ' Make panel and controls visible------------------------------

        pnlBoat.Visible = True
        lblBtReg.Visible = True
        lblBtLength.Visible = True
        lblBtYear.Visible = True
        lblBtManufacturer.Visible = True
        lblStateReg.Visible = True
        lblBoatLength.Visible = True
        lblManufacturer.Visible = True
        lblYear.Visible = True

        ' ------------------------------------------------------------

        i = 0
        Dim nPhoneNo As String = ddlNames.SelectedItem.Value
        Dim cust As Customer
        For Each cust In customers
            If cust.GetPhoneNo = nPhoneNo Then
                ' Do nothing but get index value of ArrayList
                Exit For
            End If
            i = i + 1
        Next

        aCustomer = customers(i)

        aBoat = aCustomer.GetBoat

        lblStateReg.Text = aBoat.GetStateRegistrationNo
        lblBoatLength.Text = aBoat.GetLength
        lblManufacturer.Text = aBoat.GetManufacturer
        lblYear.Text = aBoat.GetYear

        customers.Clear()
        customers.Add(aCustomer)
        BindToGrid(customers, SK, 0)

    End Sub
```

Figure 16-32 Code for the drop-down list box click event

Normally, the index value from clicking the drop-down list box would be used directly to retrieve associated boat values. However, in a data bound control where the customer data can be sorted, the index of the selected customer in the drop-down list box may not match the index of the customer in the array list of customers. Thus, a search logic using a For-Each loop is used to match the selected customer from the drop-down list box to the same customer in the array list of customers. Then, the customer's boat can be determined. The For-Each loop compares the customer phone number of each customer in the array list to the phone number of the customer selected in the drop-down list box until a match is found. A counter is used as an index for the array list of customers. Once the match is made, the customer's boat attributes are obtained using the Boat getter methods and then are displayed on labels.

The last part of the code clears the array list of customers and adds the customer selected from the drop-down list box to the grid. The method to bind the data to the data grid is then invoked, and the result is that only one customer will be displayed in the data grid.

The code for the button to have all the customers appear in the data grid follows. The first part of the code makes the panel and controls that hold boat attributes not visible. Then the GetAll method is invoked to get all the customers, which are then bound to the grid by the code in the BindToGrid method.

```
Private Sub btnAllCust_Click(ByVal sender As System.Object, _
     ByVal e As System.EventArgs) Handles btnAllCust.Click

     ' Make panel and controls invisible-----------------------------

     pnlBoat.Visible = False
     lblBtReg.Visible = False
     lblBtLength.Visible = False
     lblBtYear.Visible = False
     lblBtManufacturer.Visible = False
     lblStateReg.Visible = False
     lblBoatLength.Visible = False
     lblManufacturer.Visible = False
     lblYear.Visible = False

     ' ------------------------------------------------------------

     customers = Customer.GetAll
     ' Invoke the bind method
     BindToGrid(customers, SK, NP)

    End Sub
```

The button to add a customer and a boat only contains one line of code. The response object's Redirect method redirects program control to another Web form, AddCustomerBoat.aspx in this case. This code is as follows:

```
Private Sub btnAddCustBoat_Click(ByVal sender As System.Object, _
        ByVal e As System.EventArgs) Handles btnAddCustBoat.Click

        Response.Redirect("AddCustomerBoat.aspx")
End Sub
```

The Edit and Delete columns of the data grid can be added using the Property Builder, similar to the way the data columns were added. However, the Edit and Delete columns are button columns instead of bound columns, as shown by their icons in the selected columns window in Figure 16-33.

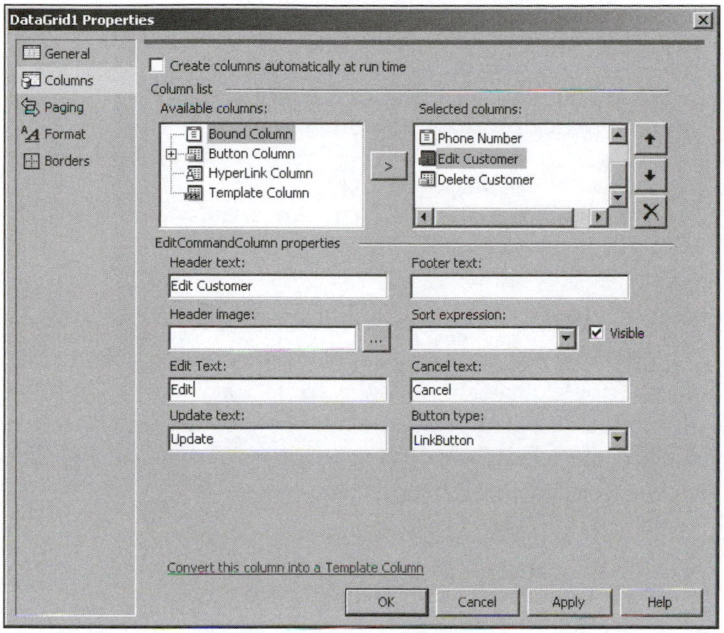

Figure 16-33 Creating the data grid Edit column

Some code must also handle the required processing for updating, canceling, and deleting. To do this, set references to event handlers for edit, update, cancel, and delete events in the HTML view within the opening asp:datagrid tag. In this case, the references are OnEditCommand="DataGrid1_Edit", OnCancelCommand="DataGrid1_Cancel", onDeleteCommand="DataGrid1_Delete" and OnUpdateCommand="DataGrid1_Update". Note that HTML is formatted automatically, so you may have to look for the asp:datagrid code in the HTML window. After finding it, you need to define event handlers as shown in the following code:

```
<asp:datagrid
        OnUpdateCommand="DataGrid1_Update"
        OnDeleteCommand="DataGrid1_Delete"
        OnCancelCommand="DataGrid1_Cancel"
        OnEditCommand="DataGrid1_Edit"
        DataKeyField="phoneNo"
```


Note that the names in lines two through five of the code (those beginning with "DataGrid1") are names defined by the programmer. In the last line of code, "phoneNo" is the data field.

Following is the code for the Edit command. In the Edit column, the row clicked is sent to the event handler where it is set to the data grid's EditItemIndex property. Note that clicking Edit on a row in the data grid replaces "Edit" with "Update" and "Cancel". This indicates that you can now change values in the row, and then click Update to save these values to the database. Then the BindToGrid method binds the data to the data grid.

```
Sub DataGrid1_Edit(ByVal sender As Object, _
     ByVal e As DataGridCommandEventArgs)

     DataGrid1.EditItemIndex = e.Item.ItemIndex
     ' Reference row, do update, invoke bind
     BindToGrid(customers, SK, NP)
    End Sub
```

The following code is for the update event. Recall that for editing, text boxes were placed in the row (refer back to Figure 16-29). Also note that the Phone Number column does not have a text box because it should not be changed—it is the primary key for the CustomerTable and has been set as read-only in the data grid. The first two lines of code declare reference variables as text boxes and then collect the values from the text boxes of the data grid. Because the phone number is not in a text box, you obtain its value as a table cell.

```
Sub DataGrid1_Update(ByVal sender As Object, _
ByVal e As DataGridCommandEventArgs)

Dim nameText As TextBox = CType(e.Item.Cells(0).Controls(0), TextBox)
Dim addressText As TextBox = CType(e.Item.Cells(1).Controls(0), TextBox)
Dim phoneCell As TableCell = e.Item.Cells(2)

Dim name As String = nameText.Text
Dim address As String = addressText.Text
Dim phoneNo As String = phoneCell.Text

aCustomer = New Customer(name, address, phoneNo)
aCustomer.update()
customers = Customer.GetAll()

DataGrid1.EditItemIndex = -1
BindToGrid(customers, SK, NP)

End Sub
```

After obtaining the values from the data grid, a customer instance is created and its Update method makes the changes. Notice that the data grid's EditItemIndex is set to -1, which turns editing off. Turning the edit mode off removes the words Update and Cancel and replaces them with Edit. Then the BindToGrid method binds the data to the data grid.

The following code for canceling only requires turning off the edit mode and rebinding the data:

```
Sub DataGrid1_Cancel(ByVal sender As Object, _
     ByVal e As DataGridCommandEventArgs)
```

```
        DataGrid1.EditItemIndex = -1
        BindToGrid(customers, SK, NP)
    End Sub
```

The code for deleting a record follows. It looks similar to the code for updating but does not specify text boxes. Thus, the values in the data grid are obtained as table cells. After obtaining the values from the data grid, a customer instance is created and its Delete method deletes the customer. The resulting data is then rebound to the data grid. That completes the code for this Web form.

```
Sub DataGrid1_Delete(ByVal sender As Object, _
        ByVal e As DataGridCommandEventArgs)

        Dim nameCell As TableCell = e.Item.Cells(0)
        Dim addressCell As TableCell = e.Item.Cells(1)
        Dim phoneCell As TableCell = e.Item.Cells(2)

        Dim name As String = nameCell.Text
        Dim address As String = addressCell.Text
        Dim phoneNo As String = phoneCell.Text

        aCustomer = New Customer(name, address, phoneNo)
        aCustomer.delete()
        customers = Customer.GetAll()
        BindToGrid(customers, SK, NP)
        End Sub
```

Designing the AddCustomerBoat Web Form

The AddCustomerBoat Web form only needs text boxes to capture data for a customer and a boat. Figure 16-34 shows the design for this Web form. Because the form collects data, it uses the Web validation controls to validate data. (Recall that validation controls were introduced in Chapter 12.) Error messages captured by the validation controls will be displayed to the right of the text boxes so users can easily see them. Under the individual error messages, a summary of all the captured error messages will be displayed. Each text box uses the RequiredFieldValidator control to ensure that a value is entered into the text box.

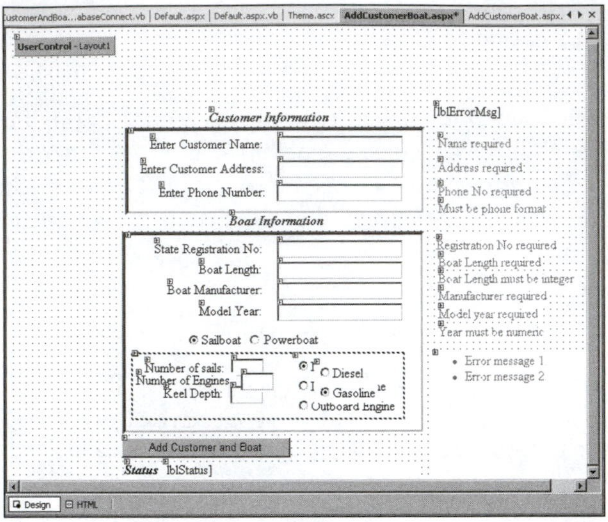

Figure 16-34 The AddCustomerBoat Web form design

Three values, the boat length, model year, and phone number, require further checking. The boat length must be double, the year must be an integer, and the phone number must contain only numbers and also match a correct pattern for phone numbers—three numbers, a dash, three numbers, and a dash followed by four numbers. The CompareValidator control can accomplish the task of making sure that these three entries meet the data validation requirements. Note that these three text boxes have two validation errors—one for the required field validation and the other for the compare validation.

The bottom part of the panel where boat data is to be entered looks as though the design is unfinished. However, that area contains two panels, with one panel layered over the other. For this form, the Boat class must be extended to be of the type sailboat or powerboat. The form uses a radio button list control with Sailboat and Powerboat radio buttons, and sets the default boat type to sailboat. Figure 16-35 shows the Web form as it appears when it opens, and Figure 16-36 shows the Web form when the radio button for a boat type of powerboat has been selected. Note that each of the Web forms includes the user control.

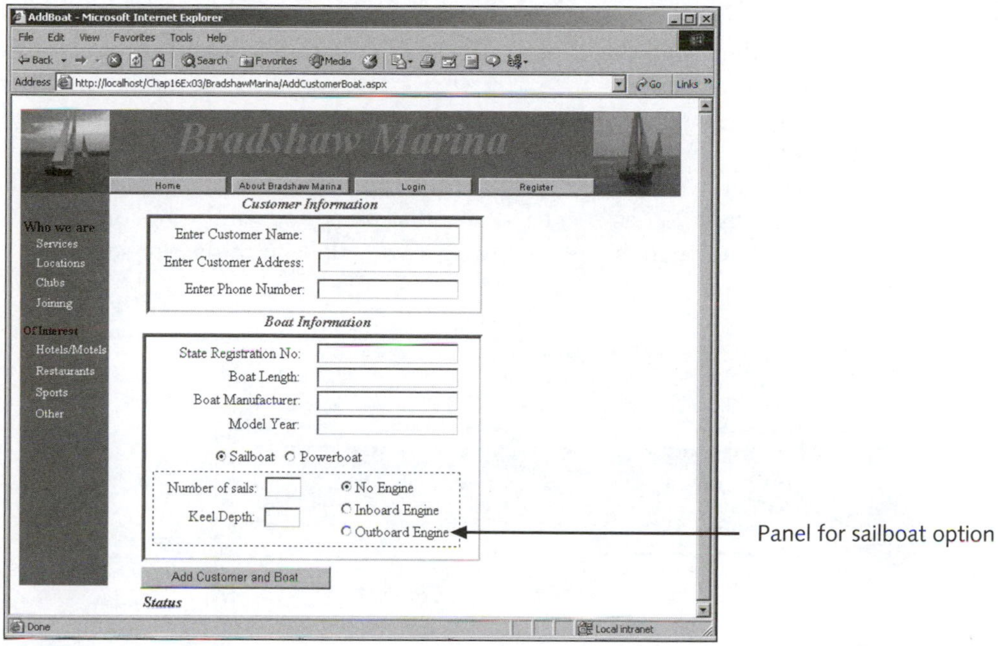

Figure 16-35 The AddCustomerBoat Web form—sailboat

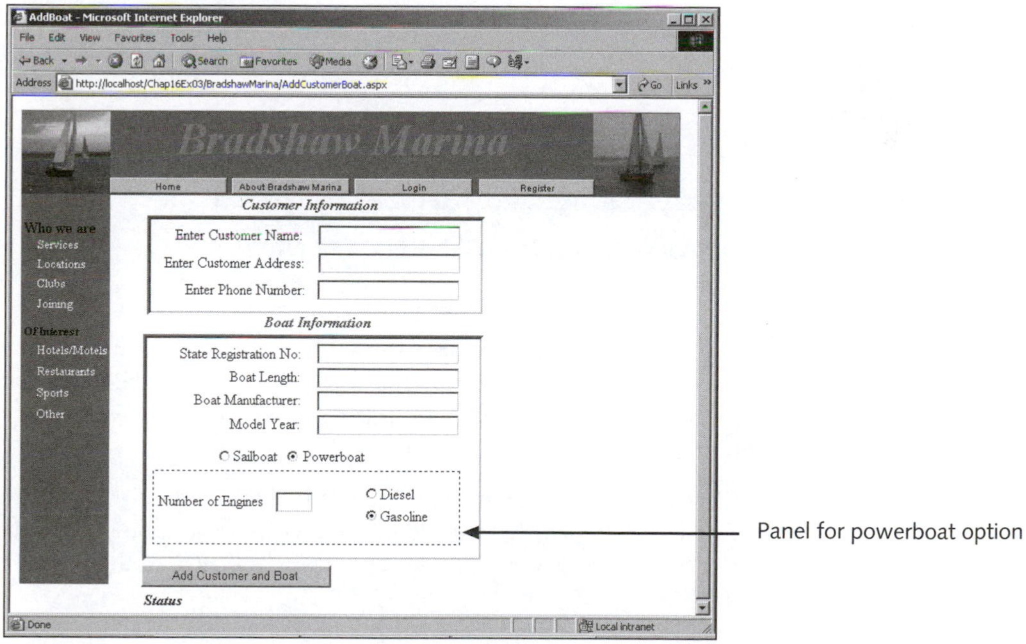

Figure 16-36 The AddCustomerBoat Web form—powerboat

16

Figure 16-37 shows how data validation works. The validation controls are triggered by a click event on the page. Thus, if you click the Add Customer and Boat button before entering any data, the Validate method of the Page class is invoked and all the validation controls perform their checks. All the error messages will be displayed as shown in Figure 16-37. Note that when the Validate method is invoked, the Web form remains open until you have completed the form. For example, if you click the Home navigation button, the home page does not open until you have entered data that passes the validation control checks. However, the Back button on the browser toolbar will take you to the previous page.

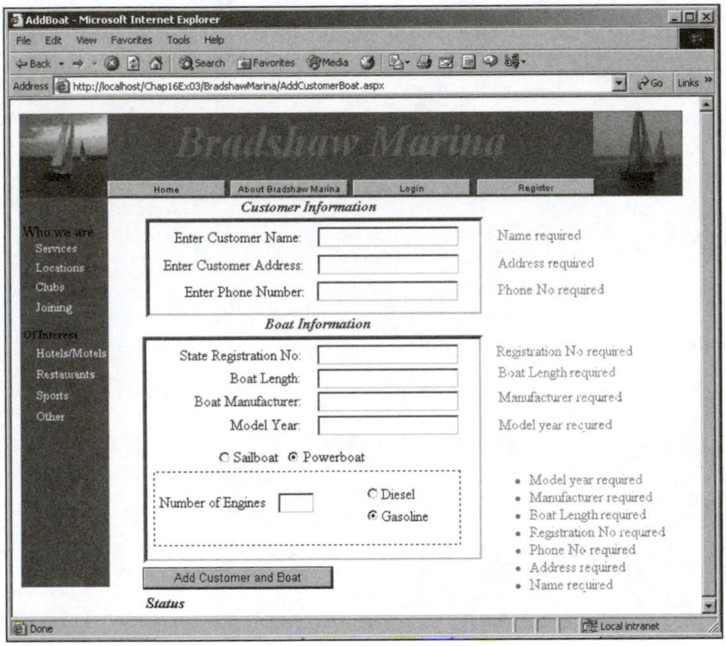

Figure 16-37 The AddCustomerBoat Web form with errors

Both the individual and summary errors are shown to the right of the user controls. The two fields that require further checking only show the validation check. If you enter letters into the Phone Number text box instead of numbers, the compare validator error message appears, indicating that noninteger values were used.

If you add customers and boats and then click the Home button, the data grid on the home page includes those new customers. As you add customers and boats, additional page numbers appear on the data grid as necessary so you can scroll from one page of the grid to the next.

Code for the AddCustomerBoat Web Form

To write the code for the AddCustomerBoat Web form, you need to declare reference variables for a Customer class and define three string variables for customer attributes, as in the following code:

```
Public Class AddBoat
    Inherits System.Web.UI.Page

    ' Declare customer reference variable
    Private aCustomer As Customer
    ' Declare string variables for name, address, and phone
    Private customerName, customerAddress, customerPhone As String
```

Following is the code for the Add Customer and Boat button. Variables are defined to hold the values of customer and boat attributes. The validation controls ensure that the customer and boat information is true. Thus, you only need to check the isValid property of the page; if the page is valid, the form continues processing. If the page is valid, then a new customer is added and a message indicating they were added appears on a label.

Note that the code for the Sailboat and Powerboat classes is not shown here, but it is available with the files that accompany this book.

```
Private Sub btnAdd_Click(ByVal sender As System.Object, _
        ByVal e As System.EventArgs) Handles btnAdd.Click

  Dim customerName, customerAddress, CustomerPhone As String
  Dim stateRegNo, manufacturer As String
  Dim boatLength, modelYear As Integer


  If Page.IsValid Then
      aCustomer = New Customer(customerName, customerAddress, CustomerPhone)
      lblStatus.Text = aCustomer.GetName
      If rblBoatType.Items(0).Selected Then
          addSailboat(stateRegNo, boatLength, manufacturer, modelYear)
      ElseIf rblBoatType.Items(1).Selected Then
          addPowerboat(stateRegNo, boatLength, manufacturer, modelYear)
      End If
  End If
End Sub
```

16

Recall that a radio button list is used to select the boat type. Based on the boat type, one of the two panels must be hidden, as in the following code:

```
Private Sub rblBoatType_SelectedIndexChanged(ByVal sender As
System.Object, _
ByVal e As System.EventArgs) Handles rblBoatType.SelectedIndexChanged

        If rblBoatType.Items(0).Selected Then
            ' Sailboat
```

```
            pnlPowerboat.Visible = False
            lblNumberOfEngines.Visible = False
            txtNumberOfEngines.Visible = False
            rblFuel.Visible = False

            pnlSailBoat.Visible = True
            lblNumberOfSails.Visible = True
            lblKeelDepth.Visible = True
            txtNumberOfSails.Visible = True
            txtKeelDepth.Visible = True
            rblEngine.Visible = True
        Else
            ' Powerboat
            pnlPowerboat.Visible = True
            lblNumberOfEngines.Visible = True
            txtNumberOfEngines.Visible = True
            rblFuel.Visible = True

            pnlSailBoat.Visible = False
            lblNumberOfSails.Visible = False
            lblKeelDepth.Visible = False
            txtNumberOfSails.Visible = False
            txtKeelDepth.Visible = False
            rblEngine.Visible = False

        End If
    End Sub
```

Designing the Startup Web Form

The startup Web form includes a navigation button user control that users click to open the login page. Figure 16-38 shows the login Web form in design mode. Validation controls are again used to ensure that data has been entered into the text boxes. Because the phone number is the primary key, it can be used to check whether the person logging on is a customer. An acknowledgment message is displayed if the person is a customer, and a message indicating that the customer cound not be found appears if the customer is not found in the customer table in the data source.

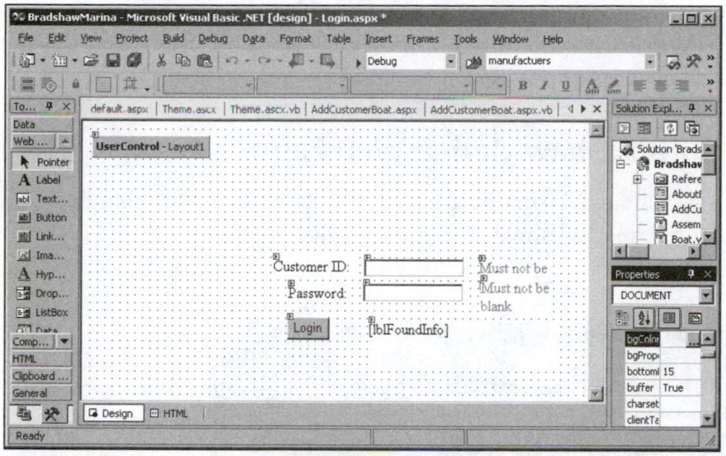

Figure 16-38 Login Web form in design mode

If an existing customer logs on, the Web form shown in Figure 16-39 appears. In this case, Eleanor logged on and the form displayed a welcome message. Although not visible, a name cookie and an address cookie were written with an expiration date three months from today's date. Eleanor's name appears at the top of the data grid because she logged on before and the cookies have not yet expired.

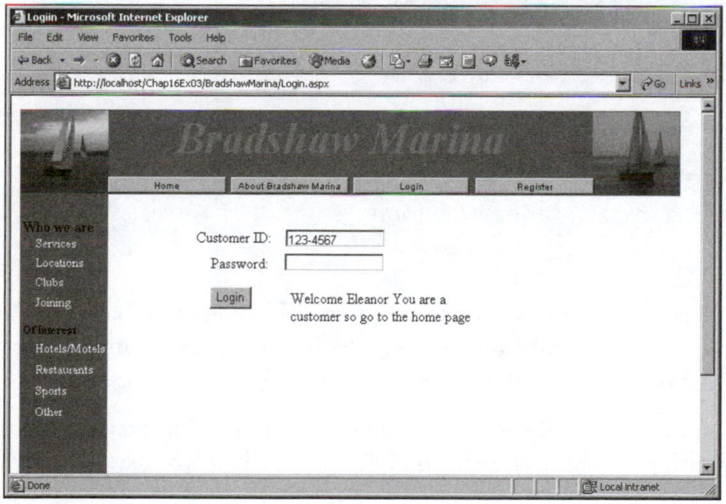

Figure 16-39 Successful logon

Names and passwords are usually kept in a separate table and a Web form would search for both. In this sample Web form, the phone number for the customer serves as the login ID and the password has been ignored.

Designing the AboutBradshawMarina Web Form

Clicking the About Bradshaw Marina button opens a static Web page that provides information about Bradshaw Marina, as shown in Figure 16-40.

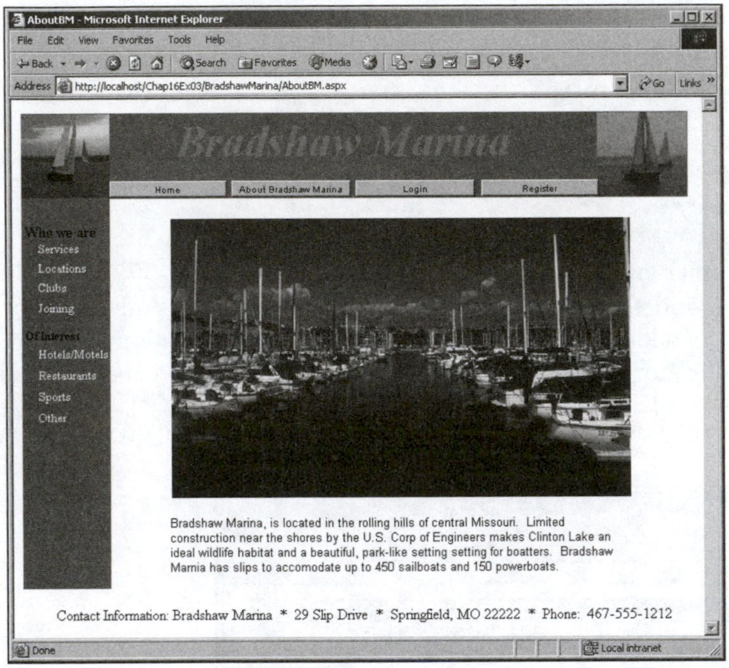

Figure 16-40 AboutBradshawMarina Web form

A Register button is also included on the horizontal navigation bar. The Web site is designed so that clicking this button opens a Web form where users can register by providing personal information. (The registration part of the Web site has not been inplemented.)

While this chapter focuses on Web form development, keep in mind that the Web site works because of the underlying design of the PD and DA classes, which you have already examined.

Hands-on Exercise 3

1. Locate the **Chap16Ex03** folder in the Chap16\Examples folder in the student data files. Copy this folder to the **Chap16\Exercises** folder in the work folder on your system. Make Chap16Ex03 a virtual directory. (See Hands-on Exercise 1 for

instructions on creating a virtual directory.) You also need to set BradshawMarina as an IIS application. See the "Moving Web Applications and Solving Web Problems" section in Chapter 12 for instructions on setting an application as an IIS application.

2. Locate the **CustomerAndBoatDatabase.mdb** in the Chap16\Examples folder and copy it to the Chap16 folder in your work folder. The location of the database is set in the CustomerAndBoatDatabaseConnect.vb code as drive C. If your Chap16 folder is not on drive C, you need to change the database location in the CustomerAndBoatDatabaseConnect.vb file and make sure that the Data Source value matches the position of CustomerAndBoatDatabase.mdb.
3. Locate the **Images** folder in the Chap16\Examples folder and copy it to the Chap16 folder, if necessary.
4. In the BradshawMarina folder, double-click the **BradshawMarina.sln** file to open the application. Designate Default.aspx as the start page. Then click the **Start** button. Note that the URLImage property has been used to link to the images, which are specified as located on drive C. If your images are on a different drive, you may need to change the URLImage property of the images.
5. Test the program. Experiment by adding several new customers and boats. View the tables in the database to ensure that the database is working properly. Test the pagination of the grid after adding a few customers. Finally, edit and delete customer information.
6. Close the BradshawMarina application.

Introduction to XML and Web Services

XML (Extensible Markup Language) has become a much-discussed topic over the past several years. Perhaps the hype exceeds the reality, but nonetheless XML cannot be ignored as it provides a way to integrate disparate data sources within an organization and distribute applications across enterprises via the Internet. Certainly, most structured data are kept in databases, but research indicates that considerably more data (word-processing documents, spreadsheets, e-mails, etc.) exists in formats other than database format. Thus, most of the database vendors are rapidly moving toward supporting XML as a format for data storage. Microsoft has hinted that by 2006, all their systems will store information in a common XML format with SQL Server as the data storage engine. The increasing use of XML validates its importance.

XML was developed as a technology to overcome some of the more serious limitations of HTML. Three of these limitations are:

- HTML cannot handle hierarchical structures.
- HTML tags do not relate to the content.
- Web developers are limited to using the existing fixed HTML tag set.

Hierarchical structures are often implemented in Web sites but with difficulty because HTML has no natural way to handle these structures. For example, HTML tags do not provide a means for having a boat element consisting of attributes. XML utilizes tags similar to HTML but allows you to define such hierarchical structures. Part of a sample XML file describing the boat table values used for the previous example is shown in Figure 16-41.

```
  <?xml version="1.0" standalone="yes" ?>
- <NewDataSet>
-   <Boats>
      <StateRegistrationNo>MO223344</StateRegistrationNo>
      <BoatLength>24</BoatLength>
      <Manufacturer>Tracker</Manufacturer>
      <Year>1996</Year>
      <CustomerPhoneNo>467-1234</CustomerPhoneNo>
  </Boats>
-   <Boats>
      <StateRegistrationNo>MO457812</StateRegistrationNo>
      <BoatLength>19</BoatLength>
      <Manufacturer>Ranger</Manufacturer>
      <Year>2001</Year>
      <CustomerPhoneNo>587-4321</CustomerPhoneNo>
  </Boats>
      .
      .
      .
  </NewDataSet>
```

Figure 16-41 Boats and attributes in an XML file

The first line of the file is the XML prolog, which informs the receiving application that the file is an XML document adhering to the particular version of XML—version 1.0 in this case. There must be only one prolog per XML file. This sample file was generated using the WriteXML dataset method with the standalone=yes attribute added, though this attribute is not always needed. An XML file must also have a unique opening and closing tag pair (<NewDataSet> and </NewDataSet>), similar to an HTML file, which must have the <HTML> and </HTML> tag pair.

Within the <NewDataSet> and </NewDataSet> tags are sets of boat entries and corresponding attributes producing a hierarchical structure that cannot be accomplished with

HTML tags alone. Thus, XML overcomes this weakness of HTML. Although XML uses the angle brackets (< >), similar to HTML, note that the tag names themselves are not fixed. In this case, there are tags for boats as well as all the attributes of a boat. This means that tags can be extensible and not fixed, as in HTML.

The extensibility of XML provides a technology for formatting or representing data. If an industry such as the retail industry could agree on tag representations for data that needed to be exchanged between the retail enterprises, then Internet exchange between applications would become much easier from an application development point of view. Don't overlook the difficulty of accomplishing a common tag specification for data—it is difficult enough within an enterprise and certainly more difficult across enterprises. Legacy systems and other existing applications within each enterprise steer them toward specifications that more resemble the data representation in their own organizations and may need to be changed considerably to comply with a generally agreed-upon standard. However, if accomplished, XML offers many benefits; it has tools for translating data—DTD(document type definition) and XSD (XML schema definition)—resulting in seamless data interchange between applications.

NOTE: Unlike HTML, XML is case sensitive; like HTML, XML code is text and thus can be easily created and written. Because it is text, XML usually can get through firewalls that filter out some other formats.

Finally, the capability of XML to define tags in terms of the data they represent is a distinct advantage over HTML. This is sometimes referred to as "self-describing." Using a tag pair such as <H3> VB .NET Basics </H3> for a text title relays no relationship between the tags and the text. HTML provides no means to do this, whereas XML does, as demonstrated in the previous XML boat example. Cascading style sheets and extensible style sheets are generally used for presentation purposes because XML tags do not provide presentation information.

XML Example Application

This section provides an example of how XML could be used with the Bradshaw Marina Web site. This example retrieves customer and boat information from a database and stores it in a dataset. The dataset's WriteXML method will create an XML file and store the dataset values in XML format. The application will then retrieve the data from the XML file and bind it to a data grid. The XML Web form in Design mode is shown in Figure 16-42.

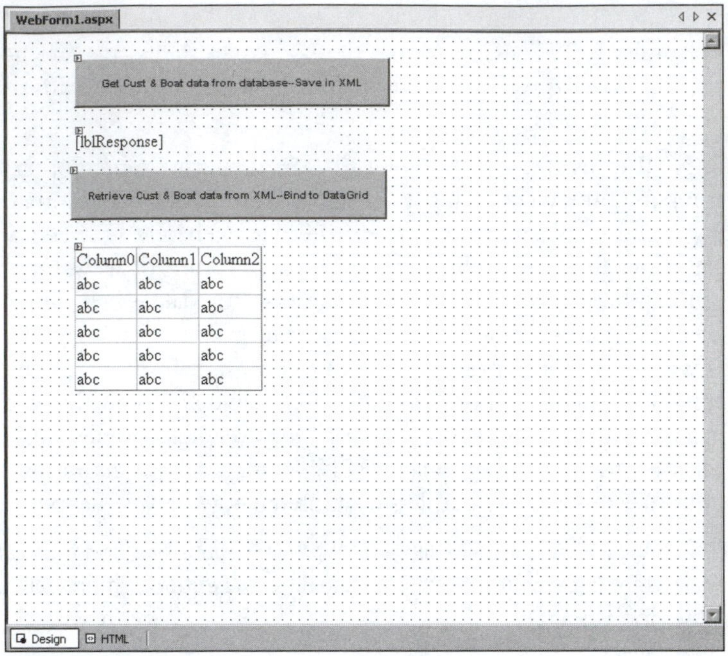

Figure 16-42 XML Web form in Design mode

When clicked, the top button on the Web form obtains the customer and boat attributes from the database and then writes these to an XML file. Below the button, a label indicates that the XML file has been successfully written. Following is the code for this button and the required `Imports` statement. The first part of the code declares the variables and objects needed to retrieve the attributes from the database. After checking to see whether filling the dataset results in any data, the dataset's WriteXML method creates the XML file named CustomerAndBoats.xml and populates it with the information. The file is saved in the same physical location as the Web application. A label is used to show that the XML file has been created.

```
Imports System.Data.OleDb
Private Sub btnSaveXML_Click(ByVal sender As System.Object, _
   ByVal e As System.EventArgs) Handles btnSaveXML.Click

   Dim dsCustBoats As New DataSet()
   Dim cnConnection As New OleDb.OleDbConnection _
      ("Provider=Microsoft.Jet.OLEDB.4.0; " & _
      "Data Source=C:\Chap16\CustomerAndBoatDatabase.mdb")

   Dim strSQL As String = "SELECT Name, Address, PhoneNO, " & _
      "StateRegistrationNo, BoatLength, Manufacturer, Year " & _
```

```
            "FROM CustomerTable, BoatTable " & _
            "WHERE CustomerTable.PhoneNo = BoatTable.CustomerPhoneno"

        Dim adptBoats As New OleDb.OleDbDataAdapter(strSQL, cnConnection)
        adptBoats.Fill(dsCustBoats, "CustomerAndBoats")
        If dsCustBoats Is Nothing Then
            Exit Sub
        Else
            dsCustBoats.WriteXml(Server.MapPath("CustomerAndBoats.xml"))
            lblResponse.Text = "XML File Created"
        End If
    End Sub
```

Part of the generated XML file containing two customers with their attributes and their corresponding boat attributes appears in the following code:

```
<?xml version="1.0" standalone="yes"?>
<NewDataSet>
  <CustomerAndBoats>
    <Name>Eleanor</Name>
    <Address>Memphis</Address>
    <PhoneNO>123-4567</PhoneNO>
    <StateRegistrationNo>MO34561</StateRegistrationNo>
    <BoatLength>40</BoatLength>
    <Manufacturer>Tartan</Manufacturer>
    <Year>1998</Year>
  </CustomerAndBoats>
  <CustomerAndBoats>
    <Name>Mike</Name>
    <Address>Boston</Address>
    <PhoneNO>467-1122</PhoneNO>
    <StateRegistrationNo>MO98765</StateRegistrationNo>
    <BoatLength>28</BoatLength>
    <Manufacturer>J-Boat</Manufacturer>
    <Year>1986</Year>
  </CustomerAndBoats>
```


Following is the code for the lower button on the Web form. After declaring a new dataset, the dataset's ReadXML method retrieves the data from the XML file and populates the dataset. Then the dataset is bound to a data grid. Because these are dataset methods, they are not tied to the form of the original data source.

```
Private Sub btnRetrieveAndBind_Click(ByVal sender As System.Object, _
   ByVal e As System.EventArgs) Handles btnRetrieveAndBind.Click

   Dim dsCustBoats As New DataSet()

   dsCustBoats.ReadXml(Server.MapPath("CustomerAndBoats.xml"))
```

```
        DataGrid1.DataSource = dsCustBoats
        DataGrid1.DataBind()

    End Sub
```

After clicking the first and second button when the application is run, the Web form shown in Figure 16-43 appears. You could also use XML files with other Bradshaw Marina applications. For example, you could convert the databases to XML format. Then DA methods to access the XML files could be written without affecting the overall functionality of the application. All the code using the datasets would be the same.

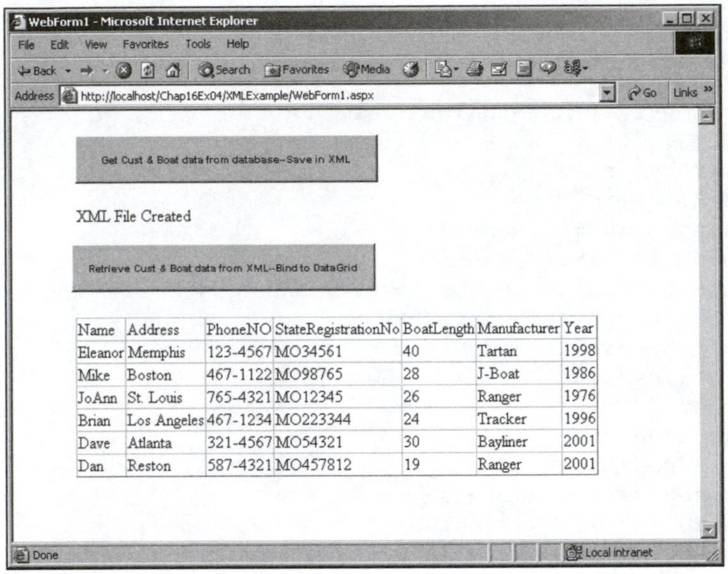

Figure 16-43 XML Web form after buttons are clicked

Understanding Web Services

Technically, a **Web service** is the resulting service for any HTTP request. This could be a request sent to a search engine or a request for price information from a business-to-consumer Web site. However, the more common view of a Web service is that it is based on the Internet and XML (essentially XML Web services) and performs a specific functional requirement. For example, Microsoft's Passport (soon to be renamed) provides a service for organizations that subscribe to Microsoft Passport. Basically, it authenticates a user so a customer who has already provided information does not need to supply it again to any organization that has access to the passport service. Other Web services might convert temperatures from one scale to another, or convert currency to obtain the current conversion rates before performing stock market services.

Microsoft describes an XML Web service as "a component that can be called over a TCP/IP network by other applications and performs a specific function—anything from calculations and credit card validation to complex order processing—and returns values to the calling application. What makes XML Web services unique is that they can be called across the Web. XML Web services are invoked using HTTP or SOAP requests and exchange data with other components using XML. As such, they can form an integral part of ASP.NET Web applications, providing services not only to your applications, but to any application that has Web access, making them ideal for business-to-business transactions."

The .NET framework provides the tools for easily creating Web services. As indicated, a Web service performs some specific task somewhat like a function. ASP.NET has a template for creating a Web service, similar to the templates for creating a Web form or a user control. The following technologies are also involved in creating Web services :

- Simple Object Access Protocol (SOAP)
- Web Services Description Language (WSDL)
- Universal Description, Integration, and Discovery (UDDI)

Simple Object Access Protocol (SOAP) is a messaging protocol that provides a way to wrap information required to be sent with a request to a Web service and also serves as a wrapper for the information returned from the Web service. This wrapper eliminates any of the structural problems associated with using HTTP—HTTP simply moves the wrapper to the Web service and from the Web service back to the client. What is inside the wrapper is not important in HTTP and can even include objects. The wrapper is called a SOAP envelope.

Recall that a Web service can work like a function. To use a function, you would have to know what parameters the function required and the values it would return. A Web service also needs to have a way for the consumer of the Web service to know what to send it and what it will get back. **Web Services Description Language (WSDL)** accomplishes this task. WSDL is a standard that defines all of the interactions of a Web service regardless of the computing platform on which the Web service is running—in other words, it is a cross-platform standard. In a nutshell, WSDL takes care of describing the method names of a Web services and their required parameters and return values.

To use a Web service, a Web services proxy on the client computer acts as a relay between the consumer (client request) and the Web service. The proxy receives the consumers (clients) request for the Web services, wraps it up (including any parameters needed) and forwards it to the Web service—in XML format. The Web service uses the parameters to perform its function, wraps up the results, and sends it back to the proxy—also in XML format. The proxy then unwraps the results and makes it available to the consumer (client) application. SOAP and WSDL do all this, but note that ASP.NET hides all this from the developer. You can use WSDL from a prompt line if you're not using ASP.NET—recall that it is a cross-platform standard.

Universal Description, Integration, and Discovery (UDDI) provides a mechanism for discovering available Web services. The Microsoft UDDI service allows developers of Web services to register their Web services free of charge. The UDDI database can be browsed for available Web services. When using ASP.NET, a discovery file is automatically created for you.

Developing a Web Service for Bradshaw Marina

Suppose that Bradshaw Marina wants to create a Web service that determines the rental charges for its slips. The logic for this service is that the rental charges are based on the length of the boat for a dock. Boats up to 30 feet in length can use a standard dock with a monthly rental fee of three dollars per foot. However, boats longer than 30 feet require a special dock and rent for five dollars per foot, starting at 30 feet. No boats over 50 feet can be docked.

Note that if all marinas had the same logic for rentals, then this Web service could be made available for any marina that wished to use it.

To create the Web service in ASP.NET, you use the New Project dialog box shown in Figure 16-44.

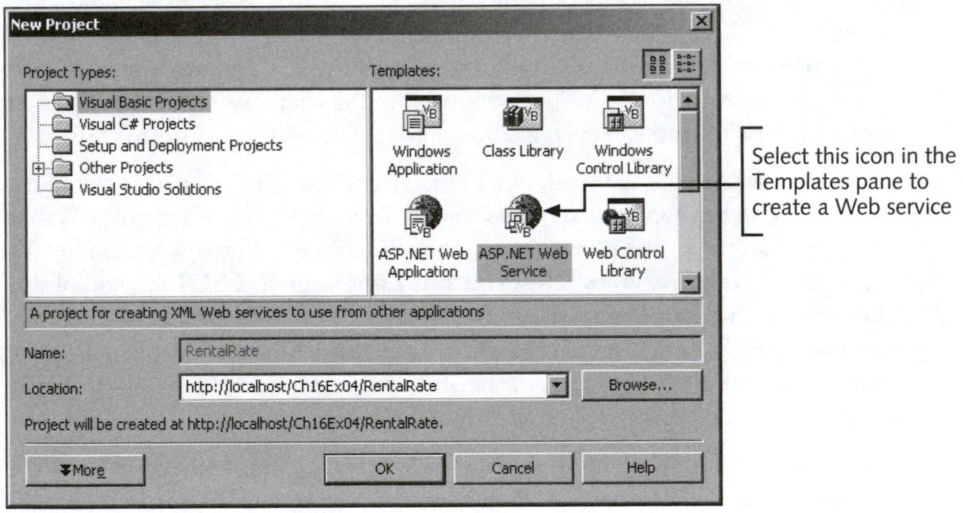

Figure 16-44 Creating an ASP.NET Web service

NOTE: You can examine the RentalRate application in the Chap16\Examples\Chap16Ex04 folder in your student data files.

The start page shown in Figure 16-45 is used for creating a Web service in a project named RentalRate. VS .NET automatically generates all the necessary files and references to support this new Web service. Note that the default name for the .asmx file is Service1 and that it has a corresponding code-behind file with an .asmx.vb file extension. Also note that there is a RentalRate.vsdisco file in the Solution Explorer window. This file will include discovery information that allows the Web service to be located later in the application when a reference to it is made from an application that uses the Web service.

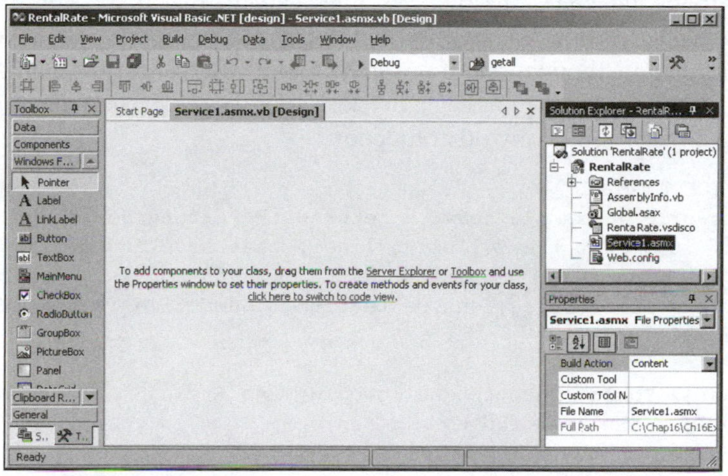

Figure 16-45 Start page for the RentalRate Web service

Following is the code for Service1.asmx, which shows the one line of code as two lines. The language is specified as Visual Basic, and the code-behind file is named Service1.asmx.vb. The class is set as RentalRate.Service1. Note that if you change the name of your class anywhere else, you will need to make sure you change it here as well.

```
<%@ WebService Language="vb" Codebehind="Service1.asmx.vb"
   Class="RentalRate.Service1" %>
```


Following are the first few lines of code in the Web service template that ASP.NET provides. The first line imports the Web services namespace. A namespace declaration follows the `Imports` statement. You should change the URL of the namespace to match your Web services location and add a description for the Web service so that other potential users will know what the Web service accomplishes. Note the `:=` operator for assigning the namespace and description.

```
Imports System.Web.Services

<WebService(Namespace := "http://tempuri.org/")> _
```

```
Public Class Service1
    Inherits System.Web.Services.WebService
```

The code after the changes could resemble the following:

```
<WebService(Namespace := "http://localhost/Chap16/Chap16Ex04/Rental-
Rate/", Description := "Determines Dock Rental Rates")> _
Public Class Service1
    Inherits System.Web.Services.WebService
```

The rest of the default code-behind file illustrates how to create a Web service by providing comments in the following code. The first few lines explain that if the comments were removed, this code would create a Web service that displays "Hello World." The Web service looks like a regular function, though it has a <Web Method()> attribute preceding the function header. The attribute is enclosed in angle brackets and designates the function as a Web service. Everything else works like any other function.

```
' WEB SERVICE EXAMPLE
' The HelloWorld() example service returns the string Hello World.
' To build, uncomment the following lines, then save and build the
project.
' To test this Web service, ensure that the .asmx file is the start page
' and press F5.
'
'<WebMethod()> Public Function HelloWorld() As String
'  HelloWorld = "Hello World"
' End Function
```

The RentalRate Web service logic needs to be coded in place of the template code. Thus, you should eliminate or change the comments and change the code to accomplish the logic for computing the rental rate for Bradshaw Marina's slips. Following is a code solution. The function name has been changed and a variable for the length of the boat has been included in the function's parameter list. The function has been declared as a type of decimal. The code logic uses the Select Case programming construct to see whether the "passed in length" parameter is outside the range of 0 to 50. If so, then a zero is returned. Otherwise, if the length is less than or equal to 30, the function returns the length multiplied by 3; if the length is greater than 30 but less than 50, the function returns the length multiplied by 5.

```
<WebMethod()> Public Function CalcRentalRate(ByVal length As Single) _
        As Decimal

        Select Case length
            Case Is < 0, Is > 50
                Return 0
            Case Is <= 30
                Return length * 3
            Case Else
                Return length * 5
        End Select
    End Function
```

The resulting Web service form resembles the one shown in Figure 16-46.

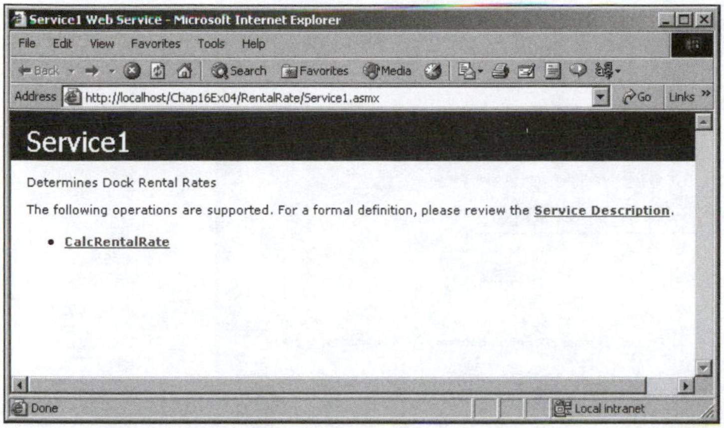

Figure 16-46 RentalRate Web service form

The CalcRentalRate link opens the Web form shown in Figure 16-47. It automatically creates a text box for you to enter the parameter the Web service needs. Also included are instructions on how to use the Web service and a button to click after you have entered the required parameter values. In this case, 25 has been entered for the length of the boat for which the rental rate is to be computed. Before clicking the Invoke button, notice that you can scroll down to view the SOAP XML file.

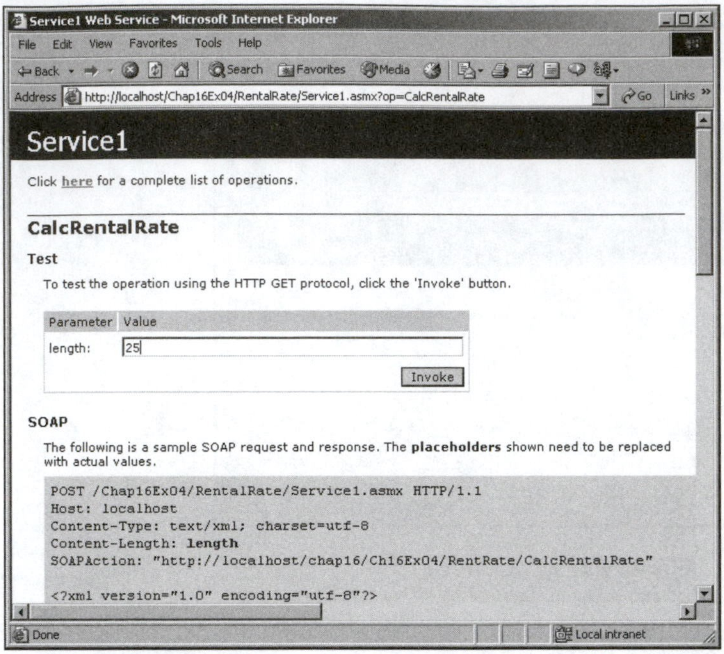

Figure 16-47 Entering test data in the Web service

If you click the Invoke button, you expect a result of 75 because the rental rate for boats 30 feet or less in length is three dollars per foot. See Figure 16-48. Note that you could use an Extensible Style Sheet Language (XSL) to transform the results into a desired format.

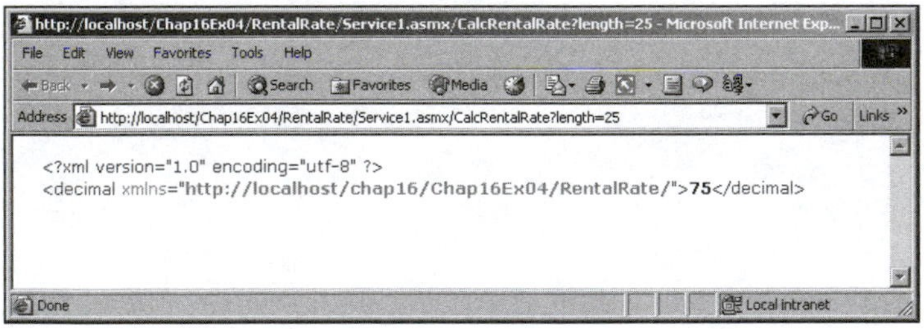

Figure 16-48 Web service result value

If you click the service description link illustrated earlier in Figure 16-46, a file opens that was created by WSDL. Part of this service description file is shown in Figure 16-49.

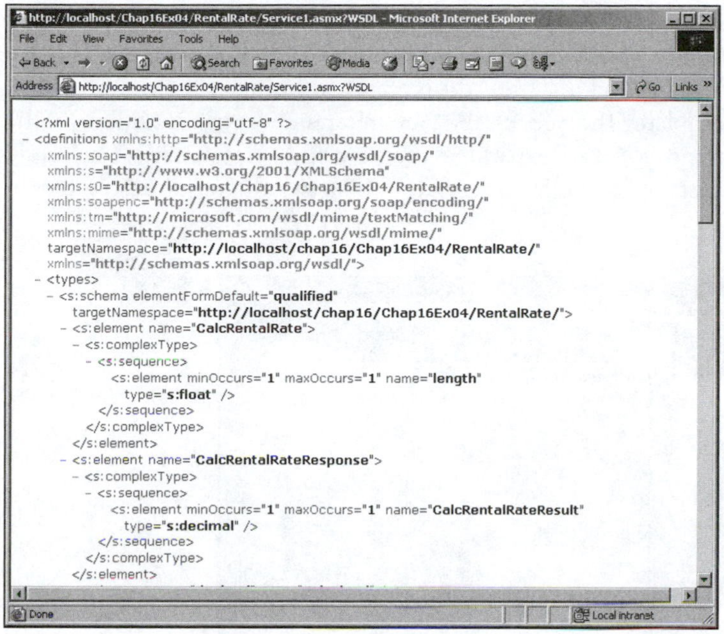

Figure 16-49 WSDL XML file

Next, an ASP.NET application needs to be created that can make use of the RentalRate Web service. The Web form of this application will be rather basic, containing only the following controls:

- A label to inform the user about the Web service
- A text box for the user to enter the boat length and its identifying descriptive label
- A label to display the result value and its identifying descriptive label
- A button to invoke the Web service

NOTE: You can examine the WebService application in the Chap16\Examples\Chap16Ex04 folder in the student data files.

Before the Web service can be used, a connection or reference to it has to be established. To do this, you right-click the project file in the Solution Explorer window and select the Add Web Reference option. An Add Web Reference dialog window opens with links to UDDI locations in case you wish to search for a Web service. It also includes an address box for you to enter the URL for a Web service—assuming you know the URL. The Web service needed here is the one just created, so rather than search UDDI locations, you enter the URL for the Web service just created. The CalcRentalRate service name (recall that this is the name of the Web service function) should appear in the left pane of the dialog box with available references in the right pane of the dialog window. This dialog box is shown as Figure 16-50. Clicking the Add Reference button on the bottom right of the dialog window completes the process. A Web reference entry is added to the Solution Explorer window and you can expand it to view these references. This view can help when creating an instance of the Web service, as it shows the required referencing.

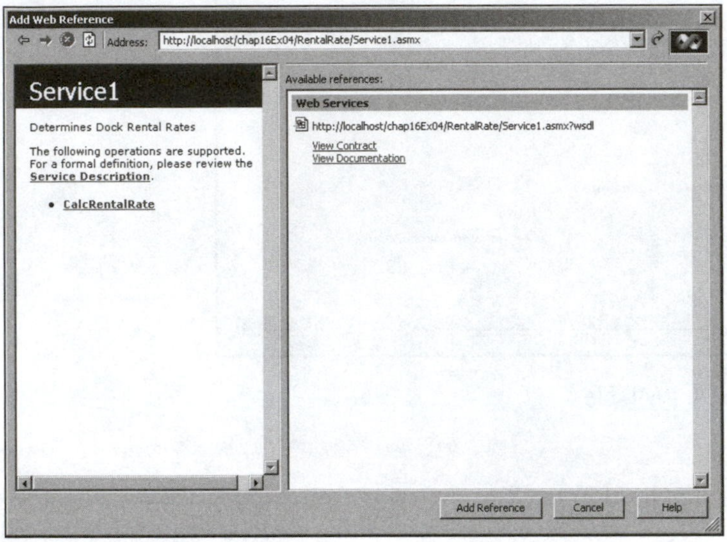

Figure 16-50 Add Web Reference window

After the Web service is made available to the Web form, you would add the following code for the button click event. The first task is to create an instance of the Web service, which is accomplished with the first line of code. The Web reference entry in the Solution Explorer window provides all the information needed for this reference. After establishing a reference to the Web service, a variable is declared to accept a boat length value from a text box. Finally, the Text property of a label is assigned to the resulting value when the CalcRentalRate method of the Web service is invoked. The value is formatted to currency.

```
Private Sub btnCalcRate_Click(ByVal sender As System.Object, _
   ByVal e As System.EventArgs) Handles btnCalcRate.Click

   ' Declare an instance of the RentalRate Web service
   Dim crr As New WebService.localhost.Service1()
   ' Declare a variable to hold the boat length
   Dim boatLength As Single
```

```
        boatLength = CType(txtBoatLength.Text,Double)
        lblRentalRate.Text = Format(crr.CalcRentalRate(boatLength), "Currency")

    End Sub
```

The Web form with its results is shown as Figure 16-51. The purpose of this illustration has been to show how to create and consume a Web service. It should provide sufficient background for you to create any number of Web services.

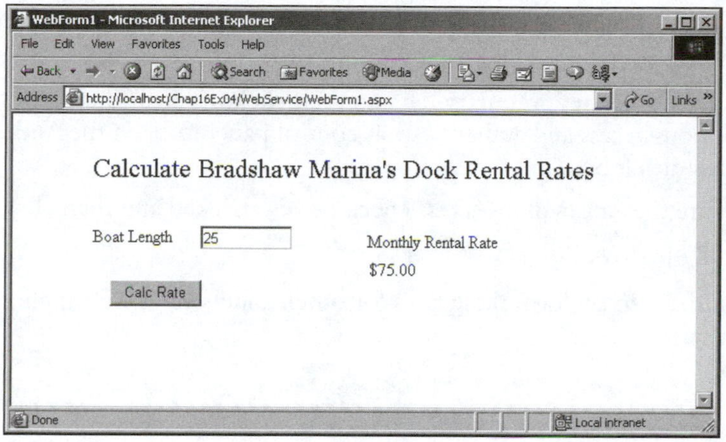

Figure 16-51 Web form using the RentalRate Web service

Hands-on Exercise 4

1. Locate the **Chap16Ex04** folder in the Chap16\Examples folder on the book's CD. Copy this folder to the **Chap16\Exercises** folder in the work folder on your system. Make Chap16Ex04 a virtual directory. (See Hands-on Exercise 1 for instructions on creating a virtual directory.) You also need to set XMLExample as an IIS application. See the "Moving Web Applications and Solving Web Problems" section in Chapter 12 for instructions on setting an application as an IIS application.
2. Locate the **CustomerAndBoatDatabase.mdb** file in the Chap16\Examples folder and copy it to the Chap16Ex04 folder.
3. In the Chap16\Exercises\Chap16Ex04\XMLExample folder, double-click the **XMLExample.sln** file to open the example. Designate WebForm1.aspx as the start page. Then run the application. Click the top button and then the bottom button to obtain the results shown in Figure 16-43. Close the application.
4. Set RentalRate and WebService as IIS applications. See the "Moving Web Applications and Solving Web Problems" section in Chapter 12 for instructions on setting

an application as an IIS application. To test the RentalRate application, you may also need to set Service1.asmx as the start page.

5. To test RentalRate, double-click the **RentalRate.sln** file. Close the application, and then double-click the **WebService.sln** file to open the application. Designate WebForm1.aspx as the start page. Then run the application.

   Due to increased security, your XP installation may need permissions changed to access a Web service when an application is run. To change the permissions, complete the following tasks:

   - Open IIS, right-click the **Chap16\Exercise\Chap16Ex03** folder and select **Properties** to open the pages Properties dialog box.
   - Click the **Directory Security** tab and then click the **Edit** button in the Anonymous access and authentication control panel to open the Authentication Methods dialog box.
   - Make sure the Anonymous access check box is checked and then click **OK**.
   - Close all open windows.

   You might have to preform these tasks for other folders with Web applications.

Chapter Summary

- HTTP is a stateless protocol. Application state, Session state, and cookies are available to assist in maintaining state between the client and the server.
- Application variables are available for all the users of a site. Session variables are good choices for maintaining state for the duration of a session. Shopping carts typically use session variables. Cookies are used to store small amounts of information on a client computer where persistence beyond a session is needed.
- Web processing, whether two tier or three tier, relies on the request/response model.
- ASP.NET user controls provide consistency to Web forms. ASP.NET also provides data binding technology that allows properties of Web server controls to be bound to an underlying data source.
- The DataGrid control provides a powerful and flexible approach for displaying information on a Web form.
- ASP.NET validation controls provide a convenient method for handling input data validation.

- Separation of client and server is a reason for not providing event handlers for all events on Web server controls. For example, a mouse-over event just to change the color of text would require a round trip to the server. Usually, data is collected and held until an event like a click event occurs, at which time all the collected data is sent to the server for processing.
- ASP.NET has the capability to differentiate the first request for a Web form from subsequent requests. This allows processing of startup requirements only once.
- ASP.NET Web forms are compiled for faster execution. The compiler is a just-in-time compiler.
- XML, a self-describing data formatting technology, provides a text-based data storage format that supports hierarchical data structures.
- ASP.NET uses XML, and its datasets have XML methods that provide easy storage, retrieval, and manipulation of XML data.
- Web services distribute logic over the Internet. A Web service accomplishes a specific task much like a function or method. SOAP is a technology that provides wrappers around structures sent to a Web service and returned from a Web service. Its data format is in XML. WSDL is a platform-independent standard for describing data for Web services. UDDI has been established to assist in locating and using Web services.

Key Terms

Application object
cookie
data aware
data bound
data binding
postback
Session object
Simple Object Access Protocol (SOAP)
state
stateless protocol
Universal Description, Integration, and Discovery (UDDI)
user control
Web service
Web Services Description Language (WSDL)
XML

Review Questions

1. Do you think ASP.NET is good for Web application development?
2. Why are some events such as OnBlur not supported by Web server controls?

3. What is a stateless protocol? Can you explain it in everyday terminology?
4. What are the advantages of a code-behind file?
5. If you needed to keep certain information about a client visit to a Web site, what means are available to accomplish this task?
6. What does the term "data bind" mean?
7. What are the advantages of a data grid?
8. If you needed to have consistent Web pages, what approach in ASP.NET would you consider?
9. On a user control, can you use both HTML and Web server control? If so, what guides this decision?
10. What approach would you use if you had to write code for a shopping cart?
11. What does "postback" mean? Where in ASP.NET can you determine if a postback has occurred?
12. What would be some of the controls most often used for data binding?

Discussion Questions

1. Do you think ASP.NET validation controls provide enough capability to be routinely used?
2. Do you think the recent emphasis on security has resulted in more people setting their browsers to not accept cookies?
3. Explain how ASP.NET has improved over Classic ASP. Are there applications in which it makes sense to use Classic ASP even when developing with ASP.NET?
4. The Application object can hold information that all clients can access. Also, it is persistent beyond the duration of a session. What are the advantages and disadvantages of using the Application object for saving data?
5. What other features would you add to the Bradshaw Marina Web site?

Projects

1. The Bradshaw Marina Web site was not fully implemented in this chapter. Use Windows Explorer to create the folders named **Chap16\Project1\Pr01** as necessary in the work folder on your system and copy the Bradshaw Marina Web site to this folder. Make Chap16\Project1\Pr01 a virtual directory, rename the Web site and make it an IIS application. Locate the **DockandSlipDatabasePrj1.mdb** on the Chap16\Examples student files and copy it to the Chap16 folder. Then make the following additions to the Web site:
   a. The user control for the Web site is named Theme.ascx.vb. Change it by adding a red horizontal line across the bottom of the user control. Then add a horizontal navigation bar underneath the red line with buttons like those on the top horizontal navigation bar. Make sure the buttons in the new navigation bar have the same functionality as the buttons in the top navigation bar. On the AddCustomersBoats Web form, move the status and corresponding label up and to the right of the Add Customer and Boat button so the horizontal rule does not pass through the label.
   b. Test the user control to make sure it works correctly.
   c. Recall that when the user selects a customer from the drop-down list on the home page, the customer's boat is displayed. Put a button underneath the panel that displays the boat information and set its Text property to Get Dock and Slip. When this button is clicked, a new Web form should open that displays dock and slip information in a table.
   d. Test the new functionality by selecting a customer name that has a boat in a slip for dock 1. Repeat this for a customer that has a boat in a slip for dock 2.
   e. In part d, a Web form displays the dock and slip information for a particular customer and boat. Add the capability to also have all the slips for the dock displayed on the Web form. The slips for the dock should be displayed in a data grid.
   f. Test the new functionality for both dock 1 and dock 2.
   g. All the links in the Web site were not implemented. Create Web forms for each of the links and test them. The linked-to Web forms need not be complete—they can just be stubs.

2. Create a personal Web site using ASP.NET. Be sure to include a user control. Also, be creative enough to have data that needs to be saved in a database.

16

Glossary

.NET common language runtime (CLR) — a component of the .NET Framework that manages code at execution, provides core services such as memory management, thread execution, code safety verification, data typing, compilation, and other services

.NET framework class library — a component of the .NET Framework that provides reusable classes of objects that work with the common language runtime

abstract class — a class that cannot be instantiated and only serves to allow subclasses to inherit from it

abstract method — a method without any statements that must be overridden by a corresponding method in a subclass

accessibility — specifies which classes can access variables and methods: Public (all classes have access), Private (access only from within this class), Friend (classes within the same application) and Protected (subclasses); default is that classes within the same package have access

accessor method — a method that provides access to attribute values

active object — an object that is executing or controlling part of an interaction

activity diagram — a UML diagram useful for showing the steps followed in a use case or scenario

actor — the person or entity using the system

ADO .NET — ActiveX Data Objects are a set of classes that provide data access services

Application object — provides a mechanism for establishing global information that can be shared across all users of the Web application

argument — a value being passed to a method; the value is received into a parameter variable declared in the method header

arithmetic operators — symbols used for addition, subtraction, multiplication, and division (+, -, *, /, %)

ASP.NET Server Control — a server-side component that includes a user interface and the related functionality

assembly — one or more files deployed as a VB.NET application

assignment compatible — concept that the value of one variable may be assigned to another variable

assignment operator — (=); assigns the value on the right side of the equal sign to the variable named on the left side

association class — a class that exists as a byproduct of an association relationship

association relationships — how objects of different classes are associated with each other

attribute — characteristic of an object that takes on a value

attribute storage — making an instance persistent by storing its attribute values in a file

breakpoint — a flag set by the programmer that instructs the debugger to pause program execution at a particular line of code

browser — a program that displays Web pages. Internet Explorer or Netscape Navigator

C# — one of the new programming languages from Microsoft that are a part of .NET

C++ — a programming language that adds OO features to become a superset of C

cardinality — entity relationship diagram term for multiplicity

Catch block — a block of code beginning with the keyword `Catch` that executes if the specified exception is caught

check box — a two-state control that enables yes/no (true/false) options

checked list box — enables selection of one or more predefined items from a list that includes check boxes

child table —VB .NET datasets provide the functionality to visualize and process data hierarchically—referred to as a parent-child relationship

class — objects are classified as a type of thing

class definition —VB .NET code written to represent a class containing attribute definitions and accessor methods

class diagram — a UML diagram showing classes and their relationships

class header — a line of code that identifies the class and some of its characteristics

class method — a method not associated with a specific instance; a Shared method

class variable — a variable not associated with a specific instance; a Shared variable

Classic ASP — a Microsoft-developed server-side Web development technology based on active server pages (ASP)

client — the computer that issues a request in a client-server model of distributed processing

client object — the object invoking a method

client-server computing — a form of distributed processing in which a client requests an action and the server performs it

code-behind — a technology that allows programming logic to be kept in a separate file (with an extension of .aspx.vb) from the visual parts of Web Forms page, which consists of visual elements (such as HTML, server controls, and static text), while the code-behind file contains the program logic

combo box — enables selection of one or more predefined items from a list, or the entry of a new value

comment — a documentation statement that is not executed, begins with single quote

component — GUI classes such as Button, CheckBox, and so forth

component-based development — refers to the fact that components interact in a system using a well-defined interface but might be built using a variety of technologies

compound expression — consists of two expressions joined using the logical operators And or Or

concatenated key — a key (primary or foreign) that is comprised of more than one field (or column) in the database

concatenation operator — (&); joins values together into a string

concrete class —a class that can be instantiated, as opposed to an abstract class

constant — a variable with a value that does not change; uses the keyword `Const` instead of `Dim`

constructor — a special method that is automatically invoked whenever you create an instance of a class; it has no return type

control — a GUI component

control break — a change in the value of a variable used to group a list of items

cookie — a small text file saved on your computer by the Web application to which you are connected

custom exception — an exception that is written specifically for an application

custom method — a method written to do some processing; in contrast, accessor methods are written to store and retrieve attribute values

data aware — identifies control properties that can be bound to an underlying data source; values from the underlying data source are automatically displayed in the data aware property of a control

data bound — identifies control properties that can be bound to an underlying data source; values from the underlying data source are automatically displayed in the data aware property of a control

data source name — a name used by VB .NET instead of the actual database name

database — one or more files organized into tables to facilitate queries; each table column represents an attribute and a row represents a record (or an instance)

databinding — a technology that connects a field in a data source and a property of a control

DataRelation — used to define a parent-child relationship by specifying the parent table, the child table and the columns (fields) of the parent and child tables to serve as the basis for the relationship

dataset — a supplied class (DataSet) whose instances contain cached data retrieved from a database

date/time picker — a control that enables you to select a date and time from a calendar and to display the date and time in a number of different formats

debugger — a set of tools that enable you to monitor the progress of a program at runtime and help you isolate errors that keep your program from running as intended

default constructor — a constructor method consisting of a header and an empty code block

destructor — a method that destroys an instance

dynamic binding — occurs when the JVM resolves which method to invoke when the system runs

dynamic model — a model such as the sequence diagram that shows objects interacting

dynamic Web page — a Web page that changes based on information retrieved from a database

encapsulation — occurs when an object has attributes and methods combined into one unit

event — a user-generated action, such as clicking a button or pressing a key on the keyboard

event handler — a method that is invoked in response to an event

event procedure — a procedure that you write to respond to an event such as clicking a button

exception — an object instance; more specifically, an instance of the Throwable class or one of its subclasses

Extensible Markup Language (XML) — a rich, tag-based, text-based system to define complex documents and data structures such as invoices, making it useful for Business-to-Business and Web Services applications

external event — something that happens outside the system that results in system processing

file — a collection of related records

`FileStream` — a class that exposes a Stream around a file, supporting both synchronous and asynchronous read and write operations, making it useful for object persistence via serialization

`Finally` block — a block of code beginning with the keyword **`Finally`** that will execute regardless of whether an exception is caught

foreign key — an attribute (or combination of attributes) in one database table that serves as a primary key in a different database table

form definition — code that defines a form

format mask — an argument passed to the DecimalFormat constructor that determines how a number will be displayed

function procedure — a procedure written as a function

generalization/specialization hierarchy — a hierarchy of superclasses and subclasses; sometimes called an inheritance hierarchy

Get — an HTML form method attribute used for exposing data to the server by adding name/value pairs to the URL, which can then be retrieved by the server for processing

getter — get accessor method

group box — a container for visually and logically organizing groups of related controls; a group box usually has a caption and appears with a border (or frame) around the controls contained within it

GUI object — an object that is part of the user interface to the system

handle — a special type of button that allows you to resize a form or window

hidden window — a window that appears as a tab along the side of the screen enabling you to keep frequently needed tools and resources readily available without cluttering the screen

Hypertext Markup Language (HTML) — a language used to format information that is displayed in a Web browser

HTML Server control — an HTML control that has been set to execute at the server by adding the runat="Server" attribute to the HTML control

hyperlink — short notation for hypertext link (*see* hypertext link)

Hypertext Transfer Protocol (HTTP) — the standard communication protocol used by most Web browsers and Web servers

hypertext link — text (underlined in blue by default) that links to another location when clicked by the user

identifier — the name of a class, method, or variable

immutable —values that cannot be changed or mutated

implements — a keyword indicating that a class requires implementing methods in an Interface

incremental development — life cycle approach where some of the system is completed and put into operation before the entire system is finished

information hiding — occurs when encapsulation hides the internal structure of objects, protecting them from corruption

`Inherits` — a keyword indicating a class extends a super class

instance — a specific object that belongs to a class (synonym of object)

instance method — a method associated with a specific instance; a nonstatic method

instance variable — a nonstatic variable; each instance maintains its own copy of the variable

instantiate — to create a new instance of the class

integer division operator — (\) used to produce an integer result

Integrated Development Environment (IDE) — a set of software tools that helps programmers code, test, and document programs

Intellisense — a code completion feature of the Visual Studio IDE that helps you complete lines of code by matching words

`Interface` — a VB .NET component that defines abstract methods and constants; classes that implement the interface must override the abstract methods

Internet — The vast collection of interconnected networks that are linked using the TCP/IP protocols and function as a single network

Internet Information Services (IIS) — The Web server software from Microsoft that processes Web pages when they are requested

join — linking tables in a relational database that share a common attribute

keyword — a word that has special meaning in a programming language and is used in writing statements

lifeline — a dashed line representing a sequence of time that an object exists on a sequence diagram

list box — a control that allows the user to select an item from a list

literal — a value defined within a statement

logical model — model showing what is required in the system independent of the technology used to implement it

logical operators — OR (| |) and AND (&&)

look and feel — the overall appearance of GUI components

loop counter — a variable used to count the number of times a loop is executed

main-menu — a top-level menu in a system

managed providers — classes that allow access to data sources using managed code to retrieve, update, and manipulate data

menu item — a selectable item in a menu

message — a request sent asking an object to invoke, or carry out, one of its methods

method — what an object is capable of doing

method overriding — invoking the method of a subclass in place of the method in the superclass if both have the same signature (name, return type, and parameter list)

method signature — the method name and its parameter list

model-driven approach — a systems development approach where developers create graphical models of the system requirements and the system design

model-driven development — creating logical and physical models during analysis and design to describe system requirements and designs

module definition — code that defines a module

module header — the header of a code module

modulus operator — *see* remainder operator

multiple inheritance — the ability to "inherit" from more than one class

multiplicity — the number of associations possible between objects (*see* cardinality)

`MustInherit` — a keyword indicating that a method must be overridden in any subclass

`MyBase` — a VB .NET keyword that references any constructor in the base class

namespace — a group of related classes, similar to a library

naturalness — a benefit of OO because people more naturally think about their world in terms of objects

nested if — an if statement written inside another if statement

nested loop — a loop within a loop

`Nothing` — keyword indicating null

`NotInheritable` — a keyword indicating a class cannot be extended into a subclass

object — a thing that has attributes and behaviors

object identity — each object has a unique address, meaning you can find it, or refer to it, and send it a message

object persistence — making an object instance exist over time by storing the instance or its data in a file for future retrieval

object serialization — a Java technique to accomplish object storage

object storage — making an instance persistent by storing the instance in a file

object-oriented analysis (OOA) — defining system requirements in terms of problem domain objects and their interactions

object-oriented design (OOD) — designing the system in terms of classes of objects and their interactions, including the user interface and data access classes

object-oriented information system development — analysis, design, and implementation of information systems using object-oriented programming languages, technologies, and techniques

object-oriented programming (OOP) — writing program statements that define or instantiate classes of objects that implement object interactions

OleDb data provider — a .NET data provider that uses the OleDb driver for connecting to a data source, executing commands, and retrieving results when working with Microsoft Access data sources and other data sources that do not have a specific .NET data provider

one-dimensional array — an array consisting of elements arranged in a single row (or column)

Open Database Connectivity (ODBC) — a protocol that provides methods to a Microsoft Access database

Option Explicit — indicates variables must be declared before use

Option Strict — indicates variable data type cannot be automatically converted or cast to another data type

overloaded method — a method within the same class having the same name as another, but with a different parameter list

overridden method — a method with the *same signature* as an *inherited* method

panel — a container for visually and logically organizing groups of related controls; a panel may include a border and scroll bars, but does not have a caption

parameter — a variable declared in a method header that receives an argument value

parameterized constructor — a constructor method that receives arguments, usually used to populate attribute values

parent table — the parent table of a parent-child relationship between two dataset tables. For example, a parent table could consist of docks and the child table would consist of all the slips. There would typically be many slips (child rows) in the slips table for each dock (parent row) of the docks table

persistent objects — objects that are available for use over time

physical directory — the full path of a directory or folder, for example, c:\chap12\Exercises\Ex01\Example1

physical model — model showing how a system component will be implemented using a specific technology

polymorphic method — a method in one class with the same signature as a method *in a second class*

polymorphism — in OO, refers to the way different objects can respond in their own way to the same message

Post — an HTML form method attribute used for sending data to the server. Name/value pairs are placed in the forms collection of the Request object and can be retrieved by the server for processing

post-test loop — a loop that tests the terminating condition at the end of the loop

pre-test loop — a loop that tests the terminating condition at the beginning of the loop

primary key — a field that is used to uniquely identify a record

primitive data type — one of the basic VB .NET data types (Byte, Short, Long, Integer, Double, Boolean, Date, Char, and String) for which certain operations are pre-defined

primitive variable — a variable declared with one of the primitive data types

`Private` — an access modifier (keyword) that signifying that no other object can directly read or modify the value of an attribute

problem domain object — objects that are specific to the business application

procedure — a block of code enclosed by a declaration statement and an End statement which performs a set of actions, such as a frequently used calculation or database operation; Procedures are invoked from elsewhere in a program, and when they finish executing, return control to the calling code

procedure header — a line of code that declares the name of a procedure, its level of accessibility, its parameter list, and the return data type (if any)

project — a mechanism for grouping related programs together so that they are easier to find, manage, and work on

property — similar to a method, but to a client it appears as an attribute. A property begins with a header indicating that you are writing a property definition and ends with **`End Property`**

protected access — signifies that an attribute value can be directly accessed by subclasses

Public — an access modifier signifying that an attribute value can be directly accessed by any object

radio button — a GUI control that enables a user to select one and only one option within a given group of options

recordset — a cache of memory that stores the result of a query

reference variable — a variable that uses a class name as a data type and refers to or points to an instance of that class

relational database — data organized into tables which may be related to each other

remainder operator — (%); one of the arithmetic operators used to produce a remainder resulting from the division of two integers

reuse — a benefit of OO that allows classes to be developed once and used many times

scenario — one of several variations to the steps followed in a use case

scope — the visibility of a variable

sequence diagram — a UML diagram showing object interaction

sequential file — a file with its records stored in sequential order, one after the other

server — the computer in a client-server model of distributed processing that receives client requests and performs the desired actions

server object — the object whose method is being invoked

session object — an object that is used by the server in an http-based, client-server application to maintain state control

setter — set accessor method

Simula — the first programming language using OO concepts

SmallTalk — the first general-purpose OO programming language

solution — a container for one or more projects

spiral model — life cycle approach that emphasizes the iterative nature of development by showing the project as a spiral starting in the middle and working out

SQLClient — the namespace that holds the data access classes for use with database applications that use Microsoft SQLServe

SQLServer data provider — a .NET data provider specifically designed for accessing Microsoft SQLServer

standard method — *see* accessor method

startup object — the module within the startup project where execution begins when VB .NET runs your application

startup project — the project that will execute first when you run your application

state — data or variables that are maintained over a sequence of Web requests or with multiple Web users of an application

state event — something that happens when the state of an object in the system changes that results in system processing

statechart — a UML diagram showing the transitions that objects make from state to state

stateless protocol — a protocol that inherently provides no means to maintain state (data or variables) over a series of Web requests; HTTP is a stateless protocol

static model — a model such as the class diagram that shows system constructs but no interactions

static Web pages — Web pages that contain HTML tags only; they are designed to display information, not to change it

stored procedure — a query that can be referenced by the query name

Stream — a concept whereby data transfers from and to files are represented as streams of bytes

`StreamReader` — a class that supports inputting data from sequential files

`StreamWriter` — a class that supports outputting data to sequential files

structure — used to represent primitive data types; a structure is similar to a class in that it has methods, but data are primitive rather than objects

Structured Query Language (SQL) — a standard set of keywords and statements used to access relational databases

Sub procedure — a procedure that does not return a value

subclass — a class that inherits from a superclass

superclass — a general class that a subclass can inherit from

system analysis — to study, understand, and define the requirements for a system

system design — process of creating physical models showing how the various system components will be implemented using specific technology

system requirements — define what the system needs to accomplish for users in business terms

tab control — a GUI control that manages a related set of tab pages

tab page — a GUI control that represents a single tab page within a tab control; a tab page can contain many other GUI controls, such as text boxes, radio buttons, panels, etc.

template — a pattern for creating a specific type of application

temporal event — an event that occurs at a specific point in time that results in system processing

text box — a GUI control that enables the user to input information; a text box can also be used to display information to the user

`TextReader` — a class that supports the inputting of character data

`TextWriter` — a class that supports the outputting of character data

three-dimensional array — an array that conceptually has rows, columns, and pages

three-tier design — a method of system design that requires that the collection of objects that interact in an OO system are separated into three categories of classes (problem domain classes, GUI classes, and data access classes)

Tree node — a GUI control that represents a single node within a TreeView

Tree view — a GUI control that displays a hierarchically related set of labeled items (or tree nodes)

`try` block — a block of code beginning with the keyword `try`; code that invokes a method that may throw an exception is placed in a `try` block

two-dimensional array — an array that conceptually has both rows and columns

Unified Modeling Language (UML) — an accepted standard for OO analysis and design diagramming notation and constructs

Uniform Resource Locator (URL) — specifies the location of a document to be loaded by the Web browser; most often take the form of *protocol://hostname.port.file*

use case — a system function that allows the user to complete a task

use case diagram — a UML diagram showing use cases and actors

user control — a file with an .ascx file extension that can contain HTML markup as well as controls and code-behind program logic, and enhance reuse as they can be used by any Web page

validation controls — GUI controls that perform validation checks on input data before a form is submitted and processed

VB .NET — the latest version of Visual Basic, created specifically for the .NET framework; VB .NET is a pure, object-oriented programming language

virtual directory — a directory (folder) where a Web application can run like it is in its root directory but is not physically located on the client

visual programming — the process of visually creating a form, setting its properties, adding controls and components to the form, setting their properties, and then adding the code necessary to handle the events users generate when they interact with your form

Visual Studio. NET — the integrated development environment which contains VB .NET and other .NET programming languages

waterfall method — life cycle approach where all of analysis is completed before design can start, and all of design is completed before programming can start

Web — a nickname for the World Wide Web

Web browser — a program that interprets HTML and presents information on computer monitors

Web services — typically refers to XML Web services and is a program that can be accessed from another program over the Internet using SOAP (Simple Object Access Protocol)

Windows application — an application that runs in the Windows environment

World Wide Web — a segment of the Internet that supports graphics and animation capabilities

Index

Note:

- A page number followed by *tbl* references a table
- A page number followed by *fig* references a figure

A

B

G

H

L

M

N

O

P

R

S

W